. . . Increasingly, we are coming to recognize that both the questions and the answers in . . . matters of "fact" depend largely on one's choice (considered or unconsidered) of some overall narrative as best describing what happened or how the world works. We now understand that stories are not just recipes for stringing together a set of "hard facts"; that, in some profound, often puzzling way, stories construct the facts that comprise them. For this reason, much of human reality and its "facts" are not merely recounted by narrative but constituted by it. To the extent that law is fact-contingent, it is inescapably rooted in narrative.

—Anthony Amsterdam and Jerome Bruner
Minding the Law

Facts Still Can't Speak for Themselves

Reveal the Stories that Give Facts Their Meaning

Second Edition

Facts Still Can't Speak for Themselves

Reveal the Stories that Give Facts Their Meaning

Second Edition

Eric Oliver

NITA
National Institute for Trial Advocacy

Address inquiries to:

Reprint Permission
National Institute for Trial Advocacy
1685 38th Street, Suite 200
Boulder, CO 80301-2735
Phone: (800) 225-6482
Fax: (720) 890-7069
Email: permissions@nita.org

ISBN 978-1-60156-439-9 (print)
eISBN 978-1-63281-407-4 (eBook)

FBA 1439

Library of Congress Cataloging-in-Publication Data
Oliver, Eric G., 1954- author.

Facts still can't speak for themselves : reveal the stories that give facts their meaning / Eric Oliver, Metasystems, Ltd. -- Second edition.

pages cm
Includes bibliographical references and index.
ISBN 978-1-60156-439-9

1. Forensic oratory. 2. Trial practice. I. Title.
K181.O43 2015
347'.075--dc23

2015005672

Printed in the United States.

Wolters Kluwer

Official co-publisher of NITA.
WKLegaledu.com/NITA

CONTENTS

Chapter Two: Lives of Their Own

Chapter Three: In the Beginning

Chapter Eight: Start, Look, and Listen: Visual and Verbal Aids and Evidence

Chapter Nine: Sowing Premium Seeds: Story Delivery

Foreword, 2015

Even after working with Eric Oliver for years in preparing and trying challenging cases to verdict, it is sometimes still surprising how effectively the tools he equips you with can blast through the biggest obstacles. Looking back at the instances, time after time, when the most difficult facts were transformed into mere sidelights, or even case strengths, there is no doubt that "the juice is worth the squeeze" in learning what Eric has to share.

Perfect cases live in a perfect world, and if we lived in a perfect world we would not need trial lawyers, much less teachers like Eric. If you can imagine your jurors not just understanding, but also feeling deeply in their hearts the justice of your client's cause, warts and all, you can imagine how these lessons will resonate in your trial practice.

It has always been easy to recognize that what Eric imparts points the way to powerful methods to present your case—and especially to the less accessible but more important parts of decision making that they never teach you about in law school. This book, and especially the insights that the 2015 update adds from the Eric's years of hard work since the First Edition, provide the key to unlock these methods for immediate use for the folks who need your help.

For me, this hit home most clearly during the final preparations for the opening and trial plan of a case for military veterans poisoned by toxins during the reconstruction of a contaminated Iraqi facility by a government contractor. There was no shortage of obstacles and landmines in bringing the case story to life, starting with the passage of years since the exposures and the distance between the experiences of our soldiers serving overseas and our jurors. Our veterans also faced the reality that no government contractor ever been held liable in our justice system for wrongs committed in Iraq or Afghanistan, no matter how egregious the misconduct.

Sitting, standing, and pacing for days in a Detroit hotel room to piece together the story's point of view, sequence, visual imagery, characters, and theme, backed up by meaningful focus group research, brought home to me how far I had traveled from what I had ingested about how to present a case in law school and in my first years of practice. Following the tried and true habits of trial lore, simply spilling the cleverly phrased pile of factual nuggets before the "lottery winners" who happened to show up for jury duty on the first day of trial, would almost certainly have ended in little or no chance, or maybe just a chance, of justice.

Envisioning instead how the story was best packaged, and how it might be unpackaged in the minds of each of our twelve jurors, while paying careful attention to both the verbal and non-verbal presentation tools available to any human being (even recovering law school attendees), opened a whole new world of possibilities.

And treating with respect the whole brain of the jurors led to the jury delivering an outstanding verdict that loudly rejected the carefully crafted verbal pyrotechnics of the previously untouchable contractor.

No book, class, or teacher can promise you the magic formula to guarantee, without fail, the best possible outcome for your case. But spending your time and effort in understanding, and then using what Eric Oliver has to share, is the best bet out there.

Mike Doyle

Mike Doyle's trial practice at Doyle LLP Trial Lawyers in Houston, Texas, includes the representation of plaintiffs in maritime personal injury; international and transnational personal injury, including work and holiday injury claims; and insurance bad faith. Mike has obtained many multi-million dollar verdicts, judgments, and settlements.

Foreword, 2005

My wonderful friend Eric Oliver possesses an uncommon blend of brilliance and common sense. Whenever you read what he has to say you are brought to new understandings, yet you feel as though you've always known it. But you have not. It just feels that way because it is so right. That's why reading his work—especially and including this book—often feels like running into a bunch of dear old friends you had forgotten. But on reflection you realize that what he's said is new and important—and you wonder why someone hasn't told us this before.

So what is *Eric Oliver up to this time?*

In one way, it's damned disturbing.

Eric posits—without quite admitting it—a kind of anarchy. He tells us, ". . . Each decision maker builds a private version of the case story . . . ." OK, that doesn't sound so bad. But then he finishes the sentence: (and you always need to listen to how Eric finishes his sentences) ". . . and [each listener] draws a subjective decision based on [his] subjective retelling of the case."

That means each listener tells himself essentially a different story, different from what you thought you presented and imposingly different from every other listener's story. It is *that* story that will rule *that* listener's decisions about the case.

Think about the implications!

It's a sink-or-swim situation, and Eric will teach you how to travel these anarchic waters.

You'll come to see that *Facts Can't Speak for Themselves* goes farther, wider, and deeper than just your cases. As you digest what Eric is saying, you'll start thinking about how it applies not solely to judges or juries, but to the other "fact finders" in our lives: our mates, children, parents, neighbors, partners, friends, enemies—everyone. This book will even help you understand how and why you are really responding to what people try to persuade you of or just tell you. Eric just explains how human beings respond to presentations of any kind, not just legal ones. And we are all human beings, so this applies to all of us, not just jurors or judges. Any human being listening to a presentation tells himself a story that differs from the stories of every other human being listening to that same presentation.

Before you start reading, a word of caution: this is not easy stuff. Whatever word in the dictionary means the opposite of "glib," that is where you will find Eric's picture. If it were easy, all the rest of us would have it all figured out by now.

You need to read Eric Oliver carefully, thoughtfully, and reflectively. When you do, it's always worth it. Once you've digested this book, it's safe to say you will neither try cases nor approach other interactions in the same ways you did.

It is easy to think that an individual fact finder's response is founded simply on the interplay between the case and the fact finder's background and attitudes. But with each listener telling a different story, there is no absolute "case." No matter how assertively and confidently you insist "This is my case!" there is no case which doesn't shift from listener to listener. The uncertain mix of each fact finder's private memories, stories, and attitudes leaves no two people responding in the same way, regardless how thorough and probing the voir dire may be.

So what do you do?

Read this book. Carefully.

For example, pay close attention to what Eric says about your fact finders' presumptions. Theirs are not always yours. If you build and present your case with presumptions different than theirs, you cannot persuade. You won't even communicate. All you'll be able to do is hope your opponent does a worse job than you. That's no way to build a case or a career. Instead, this book shows you how to find out what those presumptions are and what to do about them.

A number of years ago, Eric provided me with one of his distillations of his decades of experience, study, and research, a single sentence that helps define how we should all be doing our work. He said, "You can't tell where a fact finder is going until you know where she is coming from." This book helps you find out where they are coming from, including the parts the jurors themselves can neither articulate nor even really grasp. As Eric points out, those are the parts that most control juror decision making. And, they are a lot more involved than influences traceable to zip codes, jobs, or lifestyles.

This book explains how your case story will remind people of the private specifics of where they are "coming from." Out of the infinite number of possibilities in each fact finder's unique warehouse and unconscious imaginings spring perceptions of your case. With them, the fact finder builds a story with which to imagine and judge your case facts. This book shows how their private stories are the most influential factor in decision making.

The core of our decision making, Eric teaches, is the part we do *without thinking*. So in focus groups we need to see how jurors get where they go without thinking, because that is what will decide your case. It's not what the focus jurors tell you they think. It's identifying what they do with your case story without thinking. On this basis, he shows you how to shape and present your case in ways that will encourage fact finders to imagine winning versions of your story, rather than versions that undermine it.

The path to understanding this is not as easy as picking up the quick advice of most trial advocacy books. Eric takes us through the long, dark tunnel of the functioning mind. This book is substantial, thought provoking, and demanding. The results are lucid, as is the lucidity at the end of every tunnel. So, is the unpredictable, anarchistic mind of each decision maker to be feared? You bet. So, we need Eric's book.

And if you are lucky, opposing counsel will either just have skimmed it or not read it at all.

David Ball

David Ball, of Malekpour Oliver Ball Consulting, is the nation's most influential trial consultant. In addition to being a pioneer in adapting the methods of film and theater presentation for use in trials, Dr. Ball wrote two of the bestselling trial strategy books ever published: David Ball on Damages *and—with Reptile cofounder Don Keenan—*Reptile: The 2009 Manual of the Plaintiff's Revolution.

Preface, 2015

Every solution should be made as simple as possible, but no simpler.
—*Albert Einstein*

In the ten years since I published *Facts Can't Speak for Themselves*, the approach I devised for developing case stories with focus groups and the techniques for delivering those stories in any decision-making venue (jury, bench, mediation, negotiation, etc.) have continued to prove as effective as ever in case after case. However—and as I often say, "You never want to take just one answer for the whole story"—experience truly is the best teacher, and there are lessons I have learned along the way since 2005—so, I was pleased when the folks at NITA approached me about updating the book for a new edition.

My experience during the intervening years has taught me that there are a number of revisions (and, OK, a few corrections) I can offer to improve the way trial lawyers can get answers to the fundamental questions this book still asks about their clients' cases:

- What is the case story?
- How does one deliver that story in the most persuasive way to a—or any—decision maker?

Perhaps the most significant realization I've made in the interim is that delivering a case *as a story* is pretty easy to do in *theory*; but to actually deliver a case as a story in practice? That still can prove to be a challenge.

Some new material I've picked up along the way since 2005 concerns what the researchers have been calling "embodied narrative," and how attorneys can better equip themselves in *practice*—to see, from the decision maker's perspective, the absolute importance of *having a story* and *delivering* that story, fleshed out with a "human face." Additionally, something that validates the need to not just talk, but to *act* in ways that respect the "whole brain" of each of each decision maker, is reflected by the expanded attention *mirroring to achieve rapport* has been getting.

The research on human judgment, communication, and influence, as well as how perceptions of "a stack of facts" and the legal rules applied to them, actually produce legal decisions, has revealed a great deal since the first edition of this book. The research also reveals a stronger, more comprehensive direction to approaching a legal decision maker—one which respects the mental processes of each individual—no matter who they are, professional or layperson, or both, as they go about doing the job.

At the beginning of the 2005 Preface, I wrote the following about the "story model" for legal decision making:

> [T]his model replaced the old ideal of decision makers as empty vessels, objectively waiting to be filled with the facts and law attendant on a legal matter, and only starting to render a judgment after the last fact and last legal rule had been dispensed. Professionals in the field now know that that view is more ideal than it is real. But, they also have realized that the notion of any decision maker basing their judgment solely on pre-existing biases, beliefs, and/or attitudes—regardless what the facts and law show—is not a wholly accurate model either. The community has now settled on the idea that each decision maker builds her own private version of the case story, drawing a final decision based on that subjective (re)telling of the case.
>
> But just because the best thinkers in the field have agreed that the story model is the best way we have to explain how anyone—professional or layperson—arrives at judgments in legal matters, doesn't mean all working legal professionals out there have caught up to this conclusion.

I would like to be able to report that all trial professionals have "caught up" to the realities of decision-maker perceptions and how they each build their own stories to "embody" the case stories they are asked to assess and judge. Yet, although all legal decision makers do the job the same way, most attorneys and trial professionals continue to act as if "the decision maker as empty vessel" model is still in effect, that the only variable that counts is what an attorney has to say about the facts and law to those waiting "empty vessels." This is certainly made clear by the number of focus groups that continue to be run to find out *"If* we'll win, *"* instead of to find out *"How* to win — *if possible."*

The primary dynamic behind effective legal persuasion certainly hasn't changed—it is still the dynamic between what is available consciously to decision makers (reflecting the *minority* of what the "whole brain" processes) and what simply isn't available, or within conscious reach or direction (reflecting the *majority* of what the "whole brain" processes, i.e., other-than-consciously). However, since it is the efforts directed toward the other-than-conscious processing that certainly pay off, it is all the more disheartening that so many focus groups still are run strictly by inquiry and examination of the *conscious* brain. Unfortunately, this presumes that whatever is in a decision maker's mind is easily available and " just for the asking."

Since *Facts Can't Speak for Themselves* first came out, I have had numerous opportunities to challenge my prescriptions for case story development and delivery. Some factors, like mirroring to establish and maintain rapport, have had their profile rise in importance, while some other factors have proven to be less essential to the outcomes all trial attorneys seek for their clients' case stories.

The new bottom line? The answer to the natural follow-up question to the book's title, "If facts don't decide cases, then what does?" Managing decision makers' perceptions:

- *Perceptions* of the facts (and law) decide cases;
- Those perceptions are not objective, but subjective and unique to each decision maker;
- To influence legal decisions, you must work to *manage* decision makers' perceptions.

And, managing legal decision makers' perceptions is done in three ways:

- Establishing and maintaining rapport;
- Engaging decision makers in an compelling story;
- Inviting decision makers to adopt and use certain mental images.

The most efficient path to updating the book seemed to be step by step, chapter by chapter. What the reader can make use of is the supplement I've added after each of the nine chapters. Some of them simply suggest adjustments, some reveal evolved content, and some provide entirely new thinking. (And there will be a few corrections, too.)

Even so, the following is just as true now as it was in 2005:

> Few attorneys have trouble with the idea of investing time and resources in discovering the facts in a case. They have few qualms about fighting for the best application of the law to their presentation of that case for judgment, in or out of court. Investing similar effort to discover the best way to deliver the most effective version of the story those facts and law represent is just the next logical step.

My goal, as always, is to continue providing trial professionals with the process and means to reveal the strongest version of their clients' case stories, and to plan and deliver those stories in the most persuasive way possible to any decision maker, in any forum.

Eric Oliver

Preface, 2005

For more than twenty years, the best minds at work on the nature of legal decision making have been aiming at what is now commonly called the "story model" to explain the mental process producing legal judgments. This model replaced the old ideal of decision makers as empty vessels, objectively waiting to be filled with the facts and law attendant on a legal matter, and only starting to render a judgment after the last fact and last legal rule had been dispensed. Professionals in the field now know that view is more ideal than real. But they also know that the notion of decision makers basing their judgments solely on preexisting biases, beliefs, and attitudes—regardless of what the facts and law show—is not a wholly accurate model either. The community has now settled on the idea that each decision maker builds a private version of the case story before her and draws a final decision based on that subjective retelling of the case.

But just because the best thinkers in the field have agreed that the story model is the best way we have to explain how anyone—professional or layperson—arrives at judgments in legal matters, that doesn't mean that all the working legal professionals out there have caught up with this conclusion. Many professionals are well aware of what we now know about how people make their decisions, whether those people are judges, jurors, or members of panels or boards. But the way they practice preparing for and presenting the best possible case for their clients hasn't really kept pace with what is known about those waiting to sit in judgment of those cases—and the potentially unlimited versions of case stories they embody.

This book proposes some straightforward steps to help legal professionals incorporate much that we do know about the story-building process that decision makers apply to legal matters—in court, in bench trials, in arbitration, in facilitated mediation, or other structured approaches to conflict resolution. Five major points are covered:

1) How legal decision makers construct their own case stories and use them to judge cases. The most significant aspect is that all decision makers, professional or layperson, re-author their own version of the case story presented to them and go through several versions—not just one—before they arrive at the one they will use for deciding. Though this process takes place mostly outside conscious control or direction, it can be influenced if it is well explored and appreciated beforehand.

2) How legal professionals (attorneys and trial consultants) have yet to make all the adjustments needed to deal with the reality of this story model in their preparation and presentation of case stories in settlement talks, negotiation, and at trial.

3) How the crafting and communicating of a case as a story can be the most direct and influential way of addressing decision makers' private versions before they finish constructing them.

4) How discovering which forms a case story will likely take and how best to present that story later on are best done in structured focus groups, not mock trials or unstructured "kitchen table" focus groups.

5) How to construct the best case presentation possible from what the groups provide, using communication techniques designed to influence the process both consciously and outside of conscious reach.

The most accepted, yet under-appreciated dynamic involved in the whole complex of persuasion and story-constructing factors is the interplay between the consciously available facilities of decision makers and the majority of their processing, which happens outside of and prior to conscious knowledge or direction. If we truly want to have insight into the way people rebuild the case stories they are offered, in and out of court, we need to demonstrate some respect for the very different rules that those two parts of every decision maker's mind employ. This approach opens up hitherto untouched areas of possibility when seeking out the most persuasive version of the facts and law to bring to decision makers in any venue.

Developing a working appreciation for the influence conveyed by *how* something is portrayed, as well as what is specifically said, can help twice over: first, by gleaning the very most from every focus group convened on any matter, and second, by turning around to present what the group has provided about the case story in the way most likely to be accepted by the eventual receivers. Approaching decision makers in ways that demonstrate appreciation for their process, not our methods, can help a lot. In contrast, asking questions of group participants in hindsight ("Would you be more or less likely to accept the plaintiff's position if you knew X, Y, or Z were true?") has been shown to be a very *ineffective* way to discover how each person is arranging his private version of any case story. This type of question presupposes that each person listening has conscious access to what is demonstrably an other-than-conscious process. They can and will answer such questions. But their answers will contain large doses of guessing and fiction.

Focus groups, approached well, can answer two very important questions that cannot be answered in any other way:

- What is this case story?
- How can that story best be presented?

That some trial professionals may have so far assumed that these two answers were self-evident just reveals some of the rich ground to be covered. We can end up with a plan for the presentation of a case that represents the best possible packaging of a legal case story for *whatever* set of decision makers end up hearing it. And that very same plan can be contracted or expanded to meet the needs of the particular venue in which it will be decided: from a twenty-minute presentation through a facilitation panel or formal negotiation, to a full-scale trial. Given a fair chance, and approached with some respect for how both parts of their minds work on a case story, focus group participants will happily provide the interested legal professional with all that and more from their own story building talents and abilities.

Few attorneys have trouble with the idea of investing time and resources in discovering the facts in a case. They have few qualms about fighting for the best application of the law to their presentation of that case for judgment, in or out of court. Investing similar effort in discovering the best way to deliver the most effective version of the story that those facts and law represent is just the next logical step.

Eric Oliver

Acknowledgements

First and foremost, the host of people who have contributed to the evolution of my work throughout the last decade—I am deeply grateful to each and every one of you for so many opportunities to keep moving forward.

The people at NITA for inviting me to update *Facts Can't Speak for Themselves* for a new edition, especially managing editor Marsi Buckmelter: first, for her tremendous patience regarding my schedule, and second, for having to deal with the technical challenge of linking revisions to a ten-year-old "very unstable and buggy" original Word document.

The dedicated folks at the American Association of Justice who have included me in their CLE faculty for over twenty years, introducing me to the majority of the plaintiff attorneys I know. Working with these attorneys along the way provided me with the opportunity to challenge and focus my evolving ideas firsthand.

The hundreds of focus group participants I have worked with, who have responded with unalloyed sincerity, brutal honesty, and stalwart good humor over the last decade as I navigated my glacial learning curve.

The attorneys who have embraced my life's work by not only incorporating it into their own practices, but also by passing it along to other attorneys—hopefully to the benefit of all their clients: Mike Doyle, Michael Carter, Keith Hebeisen, Charlie Moore, Greg Curtner, Ken Suggs, Al Stewart, Steve Jensen, John Griffin, Roger Pardieck, Bradley Cosgrove, John Eddie Williams, and Peter Krause.

My fellow trial cconsultants, who prize case story delivery over dissection: David Ball, Josh Karton, Amy Pardieck, Katherine James, and Alan Blumenfeld.

Caroline Orser, who reminds me every day that the *stories* are everything, and these stories are "the closest to Shakespeare you can get in real life."

Last, but absolutely not least, *our clients*, whose worst circumstances can often provoke truly inspired performances on their behalf.

Eric Oliver

CHAPTER ONE

MAKING UP YOUR MIND

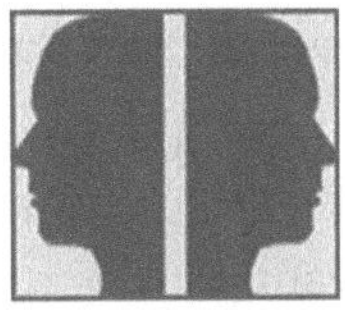

We don't see things as they are, we see things as we are.
—*Anaïs Nin*

1.1 Seeds of Judgment

Trial attorneys assess the merits of their cases in many ways. Judges and mediators use different criteria, and the parties in conflict will understandably have their own views of the relative value of their causes. But it is the impartial, peer-based judgments of regular citizens that America wisely chose to trust, in most cases, to make the final determination over professionals or the parties in conflict. However, at any level of the justice system, when it comes to the actual human beings involved, not just the roles they may play, it turns out that we all make decisions about these conflicts in much the same way. No matter how we may think we do it, *we each make up a story.*

If our stories are the source of the decisions producing judgments (both formal research and simple observation are pretty well settled on that point), then it is important that all professionals in the trial world adjust to that reality. From the start of a case's life, the attorneys and other professionals developing it will need to present a story wherever that case will be heard and seen. They still have to adhere to the system of rules, procedures, and laws, and they are still obliged to work with and through the facts in evidence. Yet, that is just part of the process, not the end. An equally important part is the development and delivery of the case *as a story* to meet the human decision makers where everyone will be starting the judgment process in their official roles as judge, mediator, or juror.

We need not abandon our ideal of jurors or judges who attempt to receive the case stories presented by both sides as objectively as they can. The traditional paradigm of weighing every fact after all have been submitted and the law has been imposed on the process has given way in scientific and legal communities to a different model of how it's done. This model for legal decision making accepts that the human experiences of the decision maker and the intellectual goals of impartiality need to coexist. In a conflict, the former often prevail over the latter.

This appreciation of the process from the decision maker's viewpoint was well articulated in 1960 by Judge E. Barrett Prettyman:

> What manner of mind can go back over a stream of conflicting statements of alleged facts, recall the intonations, the demeanor, or even the existence of the witnesses and retrospectively fit all these recollections into a pattern of evaluation and judgment given him for the first time after the events? The human mind cannot do so.

Probably most professionals working in the trial field have yet to fully adjust their practices to the human truth cited by Judge Prettyman. Not only will the judge or juror of the presentation be formulating his own story to make sense of each party's story, much of the process will be happening in the moment delivery takes place. It often has as much or more to do with *how* the story is presented as with the discrete facts, *and* with the fact that both the conscious and other-than-conscious faculties of the judge or juror will be engaged all the time. Those processes operating in and out of conscious control do not include only the intellect. Perceptions, emotional reactions, memory, beliefs, and imagination are all working to produce each decision maker's version of the case story. In the end, it is how those who have received the case presentation build their own versions that determines the meanings on which they will base their decisions, rather than the meanings the lawyers or parties may have drawn for themselves and tried to communicate. The fact that decision makers build their own case stories from which to derive fair judgments has yet to be fully accounted for by most professionals preparing and presenting cases in mediation or negotiation, or in court where the decision makers' stories will be built and applied. Yet, that fact is widely acknowledged today.

Researchers of juror decisions have been proposing models centered on story formation for more than twenty years. For far longer, students of language and culture have held that the drive toward *narrative* is the path we take to learn and pass on both. Yet, few lawyers and not all trial consultants have considered the adjustments needed to the accepted way of crafting and communicating a client's case in order to catch up to what we now know. While good attorneys always find time to learn and develop the facts in a case, few put comparable effort into learning and developing the case story. Still, it is the story and not the facts that determines verdicts and settlements for decision makers.

1.2 Terrain of the Story Context

The ground where the seeds of a decision will be planted lies behind the eyes and between the ears of each decision maker. It is the life experiences and the stories generated and valued from those experiences of each person that will decide the case. Although the same observations apply to judges, mediators, and negotiators who may or may not be attorneys, let's consider the subjective context of these case stories from the perspective of the juror.

Once selected and seated, each juror begins struggling to make sense of the case stories in a way that is personally meaningful—both as an individual and a member of a functioning jury. Influence as a group member begins from the outset as well, although jurors are instructed not to discuss case facts aloud within the group until deliberations begin.

These days, there is little doubt within the community researching or simply observing juror situations that many jurors do not trust the system they have joined, and jurors are increasingly getting the message that the system does not trust them either. Jurors are frequently not clear on their job description, nor are they always competently aided by the instructions they receive for doing the job. They are not always clear on the procedures directly and indirectly affecting the way they do it, and they are often forced into responding quite anxiously by the whole environment.

However, research over time has shown some remarkable consistencies in this "behind-the-eyes-and-between-the-ears" territory in which all case stories will be redeveloped and then decided. It has demonstrated that jurors take their jobs very seriously, despite feeling overburdened and ill-helped by the system that bestows these jobs. Some research indicates that their group status and the desire to do their job well may tend to moderate some otherwise strong personal biases they bring to the courthouse.

Ultimately, according to the research, most jurors have a very strong desire to "get it right" and not be fooled in the process.

Researchers agree that as people do their jobs as jurors, they will each be formulating subjective versions of any story before them *during* the presentation, not afterwards. It is through the themes of these stories they construct that they will deliberate toward their verdict. What is not always understood is that about half the deliberation time will be spent alluding to their own life experiences and the lessons drawn from them so as to provide a meaningful context for the story themes and content at issue. Of course, these themes emerge through each person "referencing" his or her own life experiences and lessons to develop a personal version of the case story, and coming up with a theme after most of the initial referencing has been done unconsciously. But that part of the process is not as obvious as others. The structures of their own inner worlds tend to shape the final arrangement of the case stories they hear, regardless of the intentions, backgrounds, or experience of the advocates working before them. A seemingly trivial but actually serious reminder of this separate story context, always at work in every juror's mind, is this frequently retold exchange between a lawyer and witness:

> **Attorney:** Is your appearance here today pursuant to a subpoena you received?
>
> **Witness:** No. This is how I always dress.

It is important for the trial professional reading this exchange to recognize that it speaks to more than just a superficial misunderstanding of legalese. It is a working example of what the jury system actually seeks. The witness knows what "appearance" is and responds based on that knowledge. In that context, can the answer be seen as wrong? More importantly, if the goal is to pass on the most effective story to a person operating out of that context, *should* that answer be considered wrong? Shouldn't the question become more responsive to the answer in its own context?

Each juror builds her own story from her own unique perspective on the stories being presented. Thus, no two will be exactly alike, although often consensus conclusions will be reached from widely different paths. The path each person travels is not composed of the extremes imagined by courts in the past, nor of the presumed bias many lawyers and other professionals have contemplated in more recent years. The process is not a passive one of collecting all facts without considering them until so instructed. But neither is it a preemptive act of imposing preexisting biases or prejudgments from a predictable set of life characteristics sorted into demographic, sociographic, or psychographic piles. People are usually neither totally objective nor totally subjective. The lessons learned from their individual lives cannot be wholly disengaged from their brains as they receive a case story, but neither are they the first and last word most jurors hear, turning deaf ears to any differences in the case story from their own life stories.

1.3 Story Elements

There are certain, basic elements common to any story that lawyers bring to decision makers, as well as to the stories decision makers simultaneously construct to understand the lawyers' offerings. Whether or not these basic story elements are purposely provided in the presentation, when the story forms in the listener's head, these are the elements that will appear, which are common to almost all stories people tell themselves and each other. Because they are so basic, people will usually fill them in even when no real effort has been made to include them when developing and presenting the case. This gap-filling feature[1] of story formation among jurors and judges is quite well known, but again, it is not yet something that

---

1. Filling in gaps in the immediate story and the distortion of our memories of that story after the fact, with and without the help of someone questioning us about it, are both well-known phenomena. Different aspects are referred to as schemas (or schemata), mental models, and various other terms. In essence, we all construct a good deal of the case stories we believe we simply receive. The construction process is affected by our memories, our interaction with our environment (e.g., surroundings, speaker, story context), and our perceptual apparatus, as well as by the purely verbal content of the message and the connections it may prompt for each listener. In fact, this constructive activity continues each time we recall the message or experience, singly or in conversation, filling in perceived gaps and changing the story yet again. *See* Dan Schacter, *Searching for Memory: The Brain, the Mind and the Past* (New York: Basic Books, 1996): 63–71, 104–133; Elizabeth F. Loftus and J. C. Palmer, "Reconstruction of Automobile Destruction: An Example of the Interaction between Language and Memory," *Journal of Verbal Learning and Verbal Behavior* 13 (1974): 585; and Elizabeth F. Loftus, D. G. Miller and H. J. Burns, "Semantic Integration of Verbal Information into a Visual Memory," *Journal of Experimental Psychology* 4 (1978): 19.

many professionals regularly take into account when they work up a case. Wherever someone perceives that these elements are missing or only partly provided by the case story *teller*, they will be fully filled in by the story's *judges*. The question for legal professionals trying to bring the best story forward on a client's behalf is not whether to craft and communicate a story, but how to find the best one for each case and how to put its elements across.

It is not the facts, but the stories the decision makers build from and around those facts, that create the personal meanings that lead to judgments for and against those listener-created stories. The concern for trial professionals is not whether stories are going to be constructed from their written or spoken case presentations. They will. The concern is how to create the story presentation that most effectively influences the whole subjective process in the best interests of the client. Since a straight line is still the shortest distance between points, using a story to influence the decision makers' stories seems wise. When you accept the fact that they will be filling in any missing elements, then it seems foolish not to make the effort to use your story to influence theirs.

THE MOST BASIC CASE STORY ELEMENTS

Theme	➲ What is this story really all about?	➲ The theme of a story provides the means to determine what is important, what is a priority and what is not. The theme a decision maker creates for a case story provides a bridge to the personal meaning that will be derived.
Scope	➲ How far does this story reach?	➲ The story's scope covers the full reach of time, actions, and individuals involved. The scope a decision maker creates for a case story provides the personal frame of reference to be applied, the context in which the story plays itself out.
Point of View	➲ Who's in the center of this story? ➲ Who or *what* provides the primary point of reference?	➲ In both criminal and civil cases, motive is a factor. And in order to determine cause, people need what trial consultants call a "locus (center) of control of the significant actions," that is, who or what portrays the active party or ingredient in the story constructed by each decision maker. The point of view that a decision maker creates for a case story provides a direction in which to look for responsibility.
Sequence	➲ What happens in this story?	➲ The story sequence is a potent and frequently under-utilized lever that focuses attention and helps establish significance of one fact over another. The sequence a decision maker adopts for a case story's events sorts the facts and the rules governing them, into their meaningful relationships for that person.

The law in a criminal case expects jurors to vote in favor of either the prosecution's case story or the defendant's story of alternative events/interpretations or problems in the prosecutor's presentation. In a civil case, the law expects jurors either to vote in favor of the plaintiff's case story or to give their vote to the defendant where liability, cause, or even duty are seen as less than likely. But in the minds of every decision maker considering the case stories, things are not quite so cut and dried. There will be parts of the criminal defendant's story that some decision makers may strongly dislike, or parts of the civil plaintiff's case the listener thinks are weak, are missing facts, or are carried by witnesses not fully credible. Yet there may be other parts of those case stories the decision makers find quite compelling. Just like the lawyers that carry these cases into focus groups, negotiations, settlement hearings, and trials, no one who hears and sees a particular case story believes 100 percent in every single detail of that case. Not even the lawyer. Like the lawyers, the decision makers can decide in favor of a case story despite actively disliking—or disbelieving—certain parts of that story. People can and do decide cases both because they favor one side's case or because they dislike the other side's; they can vote *against* one side's story even more than voting *for* the one that prevails on the verdict form. And in almost every instance, even in a case where a decision maker votes *for* a case story that she or he actually favors, that vote may still be in spite of parts of the story he or she dislikes or disagrees with.

The law makes strong distinctions between elements of a civil injury claim, dividing negligence clearly from cause of harms, and from damages in their turn. Human beings, regardless of the roles they play in the system, tend to blend the elements of case stories together, supporting one with another, or diminishing one due to their perception of another. Similarly, the jurors' and judge's impressions, perceptions, and interpretations of the messenger that brings the story, and of the story itself, tend to blend into one another. For example, all lawyers fear "breaking a promise" made in the opening statement, not because the evidence left out comprises the whole case, but because of the impression left by failing to deliver as promised. But how many professionals preparing case stories for presentation in court realize that the same damage can be suffered because of the way a juror or judge responds to the *tone of voice* in which certain questions are asked or statements entered into the record?

While the law likes to imagine clear separations between criminal and liability claims, between a document exhibit and a demonstrative aid, or between an argument and a statement, all human beings, regardless of their training, tend to blend the various parts of the process in varied and unexpected ways. So *how* a case story is crafted is extremely important in helping people draw their own meanings in the most advantageous way to the client. But it is important to realize from the start that the text of the story cannot and does not convince by itself. The *telling* of the story leaves inevitable marks on the meanings people draw from it as well. People blend all the elements as they create their own versions of the text, of the telling and of the teller. Ultimately, someone may prevail because the decision maker chose to vote more against one story than for another, despite what the rules specify about burdens and proofs.

Each listener formulates a personal version of the case story from what he or she *receives* of what was presented, and that always includes *how* the presentation was made. Though they do not appear in the *Pattern Jury Instructions*, or in any statute for that matter, the basic story elements of theme, scope, viewpoint, and sequence are essential in crafting a case story that is more likely to be appreciated as you would like it to be. There is another area in which professional practice has not caught up with the realities of juror and judge decision making, since facts are not a story in themselves, nor do they present a cohesive story in the aggregate. It is the *story* brought to bear delivering the facts, rather than the facts themselves, that most influences how any case is perceived, processed, and then decided.

1.4 Process of Story Growth

Because most early parts of the decision-making process are not accomplished consciously, the personal references come from what is often termed "implicit memory." The connections made to a case story from stored personal life experiences are never fully open to conscious review, though no less potent for this. So the understanding or reactions to the case story that drive each judge or juror in constructing his or her own theme, scope, and the like, could be called "implicit understandings." Though each decision maker is building a story to judge each case, the building process is never fully evident, even to the builder. The process isn't "reasoned out" along the way, but selections and associations are made more in ways that people will describe as "intuited" if pointedly questioned about how exactly they got to the position they have taken. The process can be traced, just not dissected.

The rough sequence of the building process is:

1. Presentation
2. Referencing
3. Selection (or Decision)

1.4.1 Presentation

Facts need to be delivered, as does the law that applies to them. However, the delivery communicates not only the words, but many other things as a result of what is seen, heard, and felt by decision makers while those words are being communicated. The means by which the verbal communication takes place, in writing and aloud, also influence development of the case story through reactions to the language and even the voices used. Everything the decision maker sees during the process, from facial expressions to demonstrative aids is factored in, as are the visceral and physical sensations experienced during the presentation. The way decision makers perceive the facts, the telling of those facts, and the tellers themselves all directly impact the developing story just as the words do.

1.4.2 Referencing

Just as most people will not be fully conscious of the impact of factors such as facial expressions and voice tones unless their attention is drawn directly to them at the time, so many elements of the process of referencing stored experiences are not consciously available to consider as they happen, or even on later reflection. Of all the memories, past impressions, emotional reactions, attitudes, ideas, and beliefs that are accessed by a juror or judge processing a case story, very, very few actually reach the conscious level. Yet, every fact written in the record, every syllable uttered, and every face focused on will be subject to this cross-referencing against the listener's own stored life lessons and experiences to draw meaning from the case. Many people presume that the more important or significant aspects of their own referencing process are always available to them in consciousness. This is not so. Many times, the most significant connections we make between what we bring to the story from our own lives and what we take in of the case stories presented are never reduced to conscious awareness at all, though there are often many verbal and nonverbal hints as to their general nature. But their specifics frequently never reach consciousness, and recognizing the sheer numbers involved—thousands and thousands of potential connections every second—it is easy to see why.

1.4.3 Selection/Decision

What *does* occur in consciousness is the connecting of reasons and justifications with the leanings that the earlier parts of the process create—mostly outside conscious control or recognition. Once the judge or jurors have begun to respond to their own story construction, they begin discussing that position privately and then aloud. This last general division of the judgment process has more to do with describing, assessing, and justifying these positions, consciously *recognized* as they emerge from the stories built or building in the listeners' minds, than with dispassionately weighing each in its turn. This does not mean that a final decision has been reached the first time a listener's story takes shape. Certainly, some jurors make quick work of the process. A certain percentage honestly attest that they have not even reached a distinct leaning toward one or the other side's case as deliberations begin, but the majority do. And even the conscious surveying of mock jurors involved in the process at each step of the way shows that the trend to reinforce the initial story structures they create is far stronger than reversing direction and rethinking that early trend.

Though written about here sequentially, these artificial divisions are contained in a more organic process in which, to some extent, the steps are more synchronous than sequential. But what is definitely sequential, and a major factor to which most trial professionals have yet to fully adjust their practice, is that every decision maker's story begins before all the facts are in the record, and usually long before. (This is even more true of judges and mediators, due to their earlier exposure to written references to the case story and greater experience with the process.) The story each decision maker constructs controls the sorting of facts by significance within that story; it determines how much each fact will be emphasized, and even which facts have more perceived *use* within the story constructed. First, the judge or jurors draw on their own references to build a story to find the meaning of the case story before them. The theme of that story allows them to infer the meaning. The remaining story elements, along with the theme, create the framework within which the facts and the law will be made use of by each juror or judge.

In their book *Minding the Law*,[2] Anthony Amsterdam and Jerome Bruner describe how the entire tradition of our courts "rel[ies] on storytelling, and how their stories change the way we understand the law—and ourselves." Using detailed examples from United States Supreme Court cases, they point out that the story and the law have always been thoroughly entwined. To better appreciate the nature of law's stories as stories per se, they propose sorting them into three fundamental divisions:

- Categories
- Narrative
- Rhetoric

The individual decision maker uses similar tools.

1.4.4 Categories

Each person, by referencing the story presented against her own life experiences and the beliefs attached to them, automatically *categorizes* the information, setting frames within which the story will be understood and acted upon. Here is where the theme is referenced and adopted.

1.4.5 Narrative

The *narrative* one then retells oneself about the case sets into motion the story elements of scope, viewpoint, sequence, and others to distribute meaning and significance.

2. Anthony Amsterdam and Jerome Bruner, *Minding the Law* (Cambridge, MA: Harvard University Press, 2001).

1.4.6 Rhetoric

The *rhetoric* used to deliver and color the case story to the juror or judge is incorporated on a subjective basis, and that influence then reemerges in discussion or deliberation by the decision maker.

When people begin processing a case story, they do so by reference to their own life experiences and the lessons drawn from them. Those lessons are themselves essentially stories we tell ourselves about the meaning of each of those reference experiences. They are variously identified in voir dire (examination of prospective jurors) and pretrial research as biases, prejudices, beliefs, values, or decision-making habits. What is not always appreciated is that to some extent all of them are applied to create a private version of a case story. Some biases certainly stand out over others, but they are all engaged within the process. Sometimes they are even set against one another by the story in each decision maker's mind. The perceptions experienced in the courtroom as well—all the sights, sounds, and sensations the juror or judge experiences—are part of the story-building process, as are all the experiences and lessons we draw from them.

My friend and vocal performance expert Leon Thurman provides a telling example of the power of the stories we carry with us, whether we know anything about them or not.[3]

You can test its value by lightly placing your fingers and thumb on either side of your larynx and softly humming first a very high note and then a very low note a couple of times. Notice if the throat moves upward for the high note and downward for the low one. It turns out that, physiologically, it is not really necessary in order to change pitch. Moreover, if it's done to extremes, it can actually hurt your vocal machinery. So why are you doing it?

It's a story. A story you told yourself. Leon explains that as we grow old enough to stand, we start to reach for things above and below us. As we learn to coordinate the concept and language of "high up" and "low down" with muscular effort to reach both directions, we also incorporate the language for "way up high" or "way down there" that we learn from those raising us. The connection made for one set of muscles is incorporated for a totally different set—in our throats. The cue is taken from language, but the meaning comes straight from the story we learned about reaching high up needing effort, literally or figuratively. And despite the fact that it does not help at all, we still do it because we all told ourselves the same story.

Trial professionals would be wise to note that this acquired story is not a consciously received message, though some of its components are. And it is reinforced outside of rather than inside consciousness.

---

3. Leon Thurman and Graham Welch, eds. *Bodymind and Voice: Foundations of Voice Education* (Minneapolis: VoiceCare Network, 2000): chs. 7–9.

The actual events that began the string of behavioral incorporation are not available to discuss or measure in a focus group or juror interview. And yet it is a story that is hugely effective, because it was established, reinforced, and maintained by other-than-conscious means.

When seeking out the values, attitudes, and beliefs most influential in a decision maker's story process, it can be helpful to keep in mind that these habits in our thinking are just that. Habits. They do not function by conscious will, nor did they get attached to our prior life experiences because we deliberately decided to pin them there.

Conscious inquiries in focus groups or jury interviews can produce answers related to the story-forming territory, and those answers can often point to the shape of the underlying stories that prompted those verbal responses. But it can be very important to avoid mistaking spoken answers for the whole story. It is the stories we have learned and stored outside consciousness, attached to experiences we have had but may not be able to recall, that drive the process that turns a courtroom presentation into a compelling story in our heads. Conscious inquiries have a good track record in collecting some of the categories of the respondent's stories, but not the actual stories themselves. Trial professionals who presuppose that anyone can have conscious access to the whole story-building process for the asking will miss a lot by attending to the answers more than to the implications of the stories behind them.

1.5 Seeking Out Stories

Cognitive science and linguistics recognize that our perceptions and references create stories that we use to make meaning in our lives. Narrative has roots not only in our cultural and language habits, but also in our courts and law. Jury researchers have settled on the point that juror decision making relies on case stories constructed by the jurors. So the story comes first, and no two are alike.

No one has conscious access to a majority of the parts of his mind used to recreate a story of the case, but neither is the process a complete black box. We do know that once the early part of the process is underway, it is not very easy for the lawyer or the listener to edit that story foundation and substitute a new one. Adjusting to this reality, it becomes an important part of the job of trial professionals to find out, as well as they can, how each case may invite certain kinds of stories to form over other kinds. Even more critical to the client's success, they must learn how best to present a story that encourages the decision makers to form their own story along similar lines.

The best way to influence their stories is first to learn how to craft your best story, and then how to communicate that story to the mediator, the judge, or the jurors. This is a lesson best learned from the source, rather than in the abstract, at a distance. You have to put the process in motion among real, live decision makers, and then try to learn as much as you can about their process as it happens. Naturally, this could end up being a very unrewarding process if you wait and use the *actual* decision makers in the forum of mediation, arbitration, negotiation, or trial.

Because the story-building process happens relatively quickly and substantially out of the reach of simple, direct questions about what is occurring, the sample decision makers used will need to have their process interrupted and explored along the way during the test case presentation. New input creates new references and memory of events that are not fully conscious, fades fast—supplanted by reasons given for a leaning in the mind, but not the process itself that creates the leaning. Because of this, inquiries held to the end of the day yield little significance about the early parts, where the story gets started. Thus, the most effective forum for this kind of exploration is a focus group rather than a mock trial, where participants simulate juror silence throughout.

To be most successful in exploring how stories are likely to develop for people considering the presentation of one particular case, it is helpful to keep certain presumptions about the whole process in mind:

Many stories	➲	Not one story
Inviting	➲	Not inserting
Inferring	➲	Not explaining
Beginnings	➲	Before conclusions
Story elements	➲	Over story typing

1.5.1 Many Stories—Not One Story

Even jurors who vote in favor of one side's story do not all hold the same story construct in their heads. And the stories they have constructed may share many similarities with those of the lawyer and witnesses presenting that case, but they will differ from them in significant ways as well. When learning how to craft the most effective case story for delivery to any decision maker, it is important to realize that you are not picking one story over another, which all the jurors or judges will then plant in their heads if they decide your way. Even when they decide your way, they each base that choice on a sometimes radically different version of the story. The process is more about discovering degrees, emphases, and possibilities than about eliminating one option for another.

1.5.2 Inviting—Not Inserting

We have left behind the old notion that facts are talkative and speak for themselves. Facts, once they have been dumped in decision makers' laps, do not provide a solitary, objective, and consistent story across the board. On their own, they provide little. However few legal professionals have fully adjusted to the many requirements that this fact imposes on their work of preparation and persuasion. One area that still needs adjustment for many is the assumption that story telling is a *declarative* action: a simple matter of clearly and confidently relating the evidence of the way things are. As the opening quote from Anaïs Nin smoothly points out, people do not see things as they are. Thus, an approach to building and delivering a case that aims to tell people how things are fails to convey the case story in the way most likely to succeed with the largest number of people over time. To do that, you must engage their story-making process at the earliest possible chance, and invite them by less direct and didactic means to build a story along lines you believe will be most productive for the client.

1.5.3 Inferring—Not Explaining

When eliciting how people are reacting to the presentation of a case story in a focus group, it is important to respect another well-accepted but widely disrespected fact about the process: it is neither totally conscious nor consciously controlled. Decision makers do not consciously select the life references and meanings to be associated with each aspect of the client's case story. To assume they do will prompt questions they cannot honestly answer, and answers you cannot fully trust. For example, a question like, "Why is that the strongest fact in the evidence you have heard for the defendant company?" presupposes full access to the process that created the leaning. The respondent is assumed to know all the references that *could* have been engaged, as well as the other-than-conscious selection process detailing *how* they were engaged. We know that neither of these assumptions is true. A focus group run more like a voir dire session—where no close-ended or exclusive questions are asked of the participants, but rather open-ended, inclusive questions about how they are perceiving each story element in their own context, rather than the context of the trial result—is what is needed to respect the way we know their minds are working. Not coincidentally, this generalized, implication-rich approach is also the best for beginning the actual case presentation.

1.5.4 Beginnings—Before Conclusions

One other fact we know, but that has not been fully adjusted to by professionals preparing cases for presentation in focus groups, is that *primacy* is a real factor among decision makers forming their stories. The earlier connections made by jurors or judges tend to stick, and they will influence much of the personal referencing that happens from that point on. Yet rather than exploring how many options for primary attachments, associations, and reactions might engage each participant's processing at the start, most professionals let that rich, early activity go by in silence. Instead of taking the chance to discover how many themes, scopes, viewpoints, and especially sequences every listener tries on at their early stage of story building, most professionals still invest far too much attention to the deliberations at the end of the day. Whatever is said then is being attested to by people with finished story constructs in their heads, and virtually no conscious means of tracking back to their sources, much less the inclination to do so. If we accept that primacy has a big influence on the formation of juror and judge story constructs, then focus group deliberations provide the *least* valuable information for tracking possibilities in that influential, early process.

1.5.5 Story Elements—Over Story Typing

When trying to harvest and understand the manner in which a group of people process a particular case story, taking shortcuts is always a temptation. For instance, when patterns in responses appear to be uncovered in an early push to see a product defect case through the lens of owner responsibility for maintenance, inspection, and repair, it is common to try to build a formula for predicting that response, instead of fully exploring how many ways it can be arrived at, packaged, and either encouraged or diminished in the mind's eye of the participants. Whether through sophisticated or garden-variety means, the shortcut to this sometimes difficult inquiry is simply to decide what "type" of people will tend to build that "type" of story. These typing rules all have exceptions, and sometimes fatal ones for the client's results. Just as human beings tend to blend rather than divide their thinking and impressions of legal divisions that the court draws inside the case story, we also know that human beings are capable of more than one perspective, driven by more than one bias, value, or belief associated with more than one demographic or social category. Just as all military people are not in favor of waging every war, neither are all "personal responsibility" stories found and identified within any particular cohort of race, religion, or socioeconomic status.

Are there trends? Certainly. *Are there exceptions?* Without a doubt. But the adjustment many professionals have yet to make has nothing to do with playing these odds, and everything to do with fully exploring the stories each individual can build from the case so that you are as fully informed as you can be. The alternative is to turn away from exploring the full story to reinforce pre-existing notions about types of people at the expense of bringing the most persuasive story to the actual decision makers. Focus groups can tell the trial professional the answers to two critical questions:

1. What is the case story?
2. How is that story best presented?

The analysis of any group's input is only as good as the information pulled from it. That requires some adjustments among professionals to respect the realities of what we know about juror and judge decision making and the stories they tell themselves. Setting goals and establishing procedures for focus groups that respect that process can produce some remarkable results. Failing to do so can produce some preventable disappointment. Simply learning and adhering to a style of questioning, in writing and aloud, that better respects the access a decision maker has (and may not have) to his own process can have an enormous influence on the results that group produces. This same style of questioning is also the most appropriate for voir dire, a side benefit of learning and practicing it.

Even the most rudimentary groups run by untrained attorneys without the aid of trial consultants, can usually produce three benefits if they demonstrate some respect for what we know about the decision-making process:

- They will reveal parts of the case story that professionals never found very significant but that many of the listeners do.
- They will reveal parts of the story the listeners find quite insignificant, which the professionals may have assumed would be seen as important.
- The attorneys will end up far better prepared to deliver that case in court than one that they never "focused" at all if the lawyers are doing some of the case presentation for the group.

To do this, one needs to blend two extremes of focus group structure, combining the informal, open-discussion model with the more tightly controlled, courtroom-style mock trial. Seeing how well participants blend all elements of the story across arbitrary legal divisions such as fault, cause, and harm; how their own life experiences and beliefs get so well blended with the elements of the case story before them; and how thoroughly one impression gets blended into another as the story takes shape and starts filtering the factual input, it would seem that efforts to blend rather than stick with arbitrary divisions are the order of the day. Turning attention away from conscious declarations and finished rationales leaves room in the exploration process to pursue the perceptions, impressions, and personal narratives that form the story that decides the case.

In any venue, what you can end up producing is a plan for the presentation of the case story most likely to be persuasive to whatever people end up hearing and seeing it delivered. Much can be learned along the way about how certain sets of life experiences jurors or judges carry can help or hurt their ability to build stories along the lines you seek. That information may help in selecting decision makers where that is possible. But it doesn't substitute for knowing the full scope of your most effective stories, who stands at their centers, what occurs from start to finish, and most importantly, what these stories will need to be about for the decision makers you invite to build them.

1.6 2015 Supplement

1.6.1 Of Two Minds

Since the original publication of *Facts Can't Speak for Themselves*, one area of a decision maker's mental processing that still gets very little respect is the dynamic between their consciously available thinking and that which is not consciously available. While almost all trial professionals will acknowledge the role of the other-than-conscious mind in legal decision making, they are acknowledging the concept only; their approach to focus group research and legal persuasion still will tend to play very much by the "rules" of the conscious mind. Yet, in everyone's brain there is a brilliant *common* dynamic at work that simply cannot be discounted (regardless of whether an attorney wants to) the very live dynamic between our coexisting conscious mental function and our other-than conscious mental function.

Most attorneys still act as if a suggestion has not been made or a question not properly asked unless it is made or asked specifically and directly. For example, in discussion with the venire panel, the direct question, "So, taking all those admissions into account, would it be a true statement that you cannot be a fair juror in this case?" will never be as effective as an indirect question, "How much will all those things get in your way of being as fair as you can be here, but not in *any* of the other cases where you could do the job of juror just fine?" Yet, the direct question form still dominates in courtrooms.

Language is tricky. Just discussing the two parts of the mind in this way can suggest inadvertently that there is a two-way street between them. There is not. The processing that takes place outside conscious awareness and direction is a one-way thoroughfare that delivers finished products to the conscious mind, frequently with little to no input from the conscious mind at all. The other-than-conscious mind perceiving and reacting to case facts and law:

- Responds faster
- Has the first influence on the stories decision makers are (re)constructing
- Has a much broader scope of activity than its conscious counterpart
- Results in perceived positions that are difficult to challenge, edit, or change

Not only are *legal decisions* actually (re)constructed and not "weighed" by *any* decision maker in the traditional sense, but, since 2005, a significant amount of research has shown just how much more of our mental activity, previously considered solid and discrete, is also more of a construction process mostly out of conscious reach.

In Chapter Three of the First Edition, I discussed how implicit memory drives the implicit understandings that lead to legal judgments about individual case stories. We know now that our *memories* (and the stories they reflect and carry) are not recorded and stored in a precise way, as mental audio and visual recordings or scrapbooks, but are constructed and reconstructed again and again, altered each time we simply seek to review them. Memories rely more on subtle implicitness than on literal "transcription." When we deliberately try to change, or ameliorate our memories of past events, we are rarely successful. Quite ironic, considering the fact that our memories are being altered constantly by indirect means.

Another process that has been revealed to be more of a construction process than an exact reflection is the *vision* we use to build and reference the mental imagery in our (re)authored legal stories. Vision, it turns out, is mainly a process of "filling in" sketchy sensory input, not the recording of discrete images we once thought it was. One of the most significant improvements to the techniques offered in the original publication of *Facts Can't Speak for Themselves* are more focused and refined direction for *managing* just how decision makers build, rebuild, and use internal imagery.

So, now we know that not only are legal decisions arrived at through a (re)building process that is each decision maker's private project, but the images used to (re)construct most of each decision maker's story of each case *and* the memories they use to hold and carry those (re)constructed stories forward are also less solid or distinct than once thought. Just knowing how much is going on behind (and *above*) the scenes of conscious awareness should provide more than sufficient motive for serious trial professionals to adopt methods of communication and persuasion that show more—not less—respect for the other-than-conscious part of the mind. Every perceived fact, every image, and every story frame remembered by a decision maker are not simply "received" whole from an attorney; they are all *(re)created* on the spot without conscious direction, then made available to conscious thinking shortly afterward.

Once these professionals are able to fully appreciate how little of any case story is fixed, objective, or discrete, dealing with the decision-making process can get really interesting. Respecting the fact that that mental construction is really *(re)construction* at work, we can appreciate more fully that decision makers don't just consciously sift through the bits and pieces of a case narrative presented to them by an attorney, responding to the bits they identify with here, and rejecting the rest there. The traditional thinking about objectively judging a discrete, unchanging stack of facts and rules of law really is no longer viable, because there is no *fixed* "as is" story there to judge. Instead, justice is wrought every day in the courtrooms, deliberation rooms, and mediations by legal decision makers building and *(re)building* their own versions of the case narrative or story line delivered to them by attorneys in the cases in front of them.

What makes the process even more interesting is that, once attorneys give up the old "deliver the facts, weigh the facts, receive a decision" model, a new door swings open: *collaboration* with the decision maker's other-than-conscious mind. Because facts aren't fixed and decision maker decisions derive from (re)constructing and (re) building during the case story delivery, approaching decision makers by means that acknowledge (and make use of) that process opens the door to collaborative input from attorney directly to decision maker. How so? Because being an astute nonverbal communicator allows for reflexive feedback about those efforts. Instead of being resigned to just "waiting" for decisions after presenting a case, attorneys can become active participants with decision makers during presentation, reading, and assessing the results as they happen in real time.

So, where to start?

At the beginning. The decision process starts on the other-than-conscious level, first. So, it must be addressed following the rules the other-than-conscious mind follows. And, when it comes to helping someone (re)construct a decision, that means aiming at influencing emotional reactions on the other-than-conscious level, first.

"Other-than-conscious" is a term I picked up from Dr. Dave Dobson[4] to refer to the multitude of mental functions that happen above, below, before, and beyond the reach of most conscious functions. He coined the somewhat awkward term to help avoid the unproductive reinforcement that the prefixes "un-" and "sub-" carry. Antonio Damasio, a significant player in the brain research community and dedicated to exploring the nature of consciousness chooses the word "nonconscious" to avoid further reinforcing poor framing.[5] Take your pick which one to start using, and begin employing it consistently. Remember, we get what we rehearse, much more so than what we intend.

1.6.2 Body—Brain—Mind Matters[6]

Perspective is a tough thing to "keep." If it actually were a "thing," perhaps we wouldn't "lose" it so much—but then, keys and cell phones are "things," and they get left behind all the time. For example, H.L. Mencken wrote an entire book, *In Defense of Women,*[7] promoting the premise that women are, by any reasonable measure, clearly the superior gender. But he then hastened to add, considering the nature and situation of *Homo sapiens* for one and all, women's superiority is really nothing to brag about. So it is too with the actual, physical parts of our older, more primitive brain that function as the "reptilian" mind (called the limbic system), sitting just below the mid-brain. The reasoning "higher" brain is found on top of the cerebrum, one of the latest parts of the human brain to evolve. So, configuratively

4. Dr. Dobson was a clinical hypnotherapist and trainer of nonverbal and implicit suggestion and communication.
5. Antonio Damasio, *The Feeling of What Happens: Body and Emotion in the Making of Consciousness* (Orlando, FL: Harcourt Inc., 1999).
6. Portions of these supplements have appeared previously in my newsletter, *The Mental Edge for Legal Communication*, available at www.eric-oliver.com.
7. Mencken, H. L. *In Defense of Women* (New York, NY: TIME Books, 1963 Edition).

speaking, the newest parts of the brain on top, are indeed "higher"—but only by mere inches.[8] The "higher" brain may actually be *physically* higher, but no "mightier" for it. In fact, being the newest kid on the brain's block, it almost always gets into the mental act *last*, after the so-called "lower" bits have already made their stage entrance. Brain function, including decision making, derives more from a "bottom up" than "top down" arrangement.

Just as car keys often appear to be lost just when needed most, often perspective too is easily lost when you most need it to consider how to approach the task of persuading the human brain. We may know what to do, but habit tends to make us do as we always have done.

"Framing" the *language* we use to discuss things amongst ourselves—like decision making—largely is rooted in the perspectives we bring to or adopt about the subjects of those discussions. For example, as mentioned above, the two most common expressions used to describe what goes on in the part of our minds that is out of conscious reach are "*sub*conscious" and "*un*conscious." However, each term is a significant misrepresentation of the factual basis of their function and encourages an insidiously dangerous distortion of actual experience.

*Un*conscious is the state into which you (i.e., the *you* that is your mind) can be rendered by the force of a blunt instrument or the anesthetic substances available in any hospital and most fraternity houses. *Sub*conscious implies mental function that is lower, and by implication lesser, than conscious mental processes, not directly perceived by the consciousness, from which memories, feelings, or thoughts can influence behavior without any realization of it. In their book *Reptile*, David Ball and Don Keenan[9] quote neuroscientist Joseph LeDoux[10] on the functional weighting of different parts of the brain as working either more consciously or more other-than-consciously: "The conscious brain may get all the attention, but consciousness is only a small part of what the brain does, and it's a slave to everything that works beneath it."

I'm not a fan of framing that suggests "enslavement" of one part of the brain to another any more than I am of framing that suggests some kind of "subterranean" source for brain function that, in fact, is primary, both in its proportion of active influence over our daily lives and our sequential functioning. Instead, I strongly suggest that attorneys who want their case stories to have greater persuasive effect may want to take the "whole brain" into account when developing—and especially when

8. Advocates for approaching decision makers mostly through the reflective mind would probably want me to point out that those couple inches of newer grey matter are the result of tens of thousands of years of evolution of the cortex, matched only by dolphins, bested only by whales.
9. David Ball and Don Keenan, *Reptile: The 2009 Manual of the Plaintiff's Revolution* (Atlanta, GA: Balloon Press, 2009).
10. Joseph LeDoux quoted in *Reptile*, author of *The Emotional Brain* (New York, NY: Simon & Schuster, 1998).

delivering—their clients' stories. This requires adjusting their approach to align with the fact that *most* of the whole brain works outside conscious reach and direction, and that it does that work first. The scientific evidence for this has been less and less in dispute since the early 1940s, and today the most advanced neurological and psychological research puts these facts beyond question. The last thing we need now is any further reductive thinking about how we think.[11]

If an attorney's goal is to persuade as effectively as possible, it would be foolish to ignore or discount any part of the brain's complex of functions, especially the most highly evolved ones. Yet, ignoring major chunks of these functions is exactly what most legal advocates do in most every case. Because each part of the mind plays by different rules to do its work, anyone wishing to engage, influence, or persuade that mind (or *any* mind) would be wise to learn enough about each of those sets of rules in order to act in ways that invite both the conscious and the other-than-conscious parts to come to the table.

1.6.3 Seeing It My Way

Consider illustrating the courtroom's "Golden Rule" from the perspective of persuasive efforts and effects. For the best of intentions, court rules prohibit trial attorneys from directly telling decision makers to "put themselves in the litigant's position and wonder what they would do, say, or feel under those same circumstances." However, everyone in the courtroom, especially the jurors, will "other-than-consciously" break this Golden Rule in order to process most pieces of the stories the attorneys in the matter are presenting.

We realize our moment-to-moment experiences by other-than-conscious *referencing* and in the process, our mind sorts through our own personal stored experiences to help us make sense of what we are seeing and hearing. In the case story (re)building process, the first context into which decision makers *all* put the experience of each party (and of most witnesses, lay and even the experts) is their own private lives. For a very brief moment, we plug ourselves into the closest reference we have in our own mind for that spot; then, we react, and we often consciously and reflexively interpret our reaction, as if actually aware of it. We identify with another's experience in order to relate it to our own, and to make our own sense of it through perceptions—not through emotion, or attitude, or belief—at least not at first. What we do know is that any *reaction* will be an *emotional* reaction. We also know that all legal decisions, even those rendered from a "professional distance," have an emotional basis.

11. Most astute neurologists, neuropsychologists, and various other practitioners tend to agree with such luminaries as Wilder Penfield, who asserted that no matter how much we can distill and refine about what we know about the brain, those facts can't illuminate our awareness or knowledge of what we have to call "the mind."

The authors of *Reptile* observed (with plenty of evidence) that a certain percentage of the American jury pool had been directed over many years to rehearse and internalize negative reactions to plaintiff suits in general, and personal injury suits in particular. They were asked to frame them as most likely "frivolous" as a group. This was an "emotional preemption" of the decision makers' first, fundamental response to a case story and the entire "system" depended upon doing so. David Ball makes a convincing case, confirmed by many observers from experiences nationwide with focus groups and actual jurors, that this initial framing sponsored by the Chamber of Commerce and its cronies has now become a generational "belief"—i.e., a fully incorporated anti-plaintiff cultural bias handed down from generation to generation. The truth is that decision makers must be allowed to be "encumbered" *only* by their own *personally developed* preemptions and predilections when hearing the case's facts, law, and narrative—breaking the Golden Rule as they go.

The *Reptile* thesis claims that visceral fear reactions have been reinforced in many potential decision makers' psyche (professionals included) and that many of them negatively equate (though unaware and unwittingly) that basic response of survival level fear to all successful plaintiff lawsuits. Imagine a cartoon dialogue balloon above each of these folks' heads, as if they could actually talk themselves into their preemptive emotional reaction to another "frivolous" suit by internally chanting to themselves, "Your lawsuit is going to hurt me, your lawsuit is going to hurt me." When actually asked to respond (out loud) in a focus group or voir dire session, that innate fear is framed (out loud) in phrases that are more anti-plaintiff biased: "That would never be me," or "If that were me, I'd never . . . ," or even, "He just wants something for nothing." Please note that these phrases would literally be *after*thoughts, i.e., feelings and thoughts that have never actually been internally articulated but are prompted by an already-triggered *emotional* response—before the conscious mind can catch up and try to interpret that other-than-conscious, nonverbal reaction.

When running properly, our legal system *does* take into account that individual bias is unavoidable and deals with them as shown by the exemplar voir dire questions above. What the system does not account for is preprogrammed bias, promoted *and* paid for over many decades, by just one side of the civil litigation community: the defense. So then, what fuels the "reptile" effect that daily turns "tort reformed" jurors into plaintiff advocates? Preempting a distorted or tainted emotional reaction with a more distinct and clear emotional reaction. As Dr. Dobson said on more than one occasion when talking about problems psychotherapeutic clients faced, "If *fear* is their motivator, then find a *better* fear for them to work with."

However we choose to level the playing field from its unbalanced current condition, the persuasive bottom line stays the same: when delivering a case story, the primary job of the plaintiff attorney is to evoke an emotional response as a foundation from which her decision makers can begin their story (re)construction jobs.

When it comes to the other-than-conscious mind, forewarned can be forearmed. If you know that a purely perceptual identification—not a rational or emotional one—will be happening, you can learn to invite it to work from one person to the next. But naturally, there is a catch. You can't extend this invitation through conscious, verbal means alone because the part of the mind that initiates and drives emotional responses doesn't play by conscious rules.

For instance, it does not work to directly invite a juror to identify more with the "one-in-a-million" injured person who is harmed by a manufacturer's neglect that lets this foreseeable harm occur only in the name of increasing "company profits." No one will break the Golden Rule just because you directly suggest they put themselves in that one-in-a-million position—if it means getting hurt in that scenario. You can't just tell jurors to *see* the way; you must *show* them the way.

How?

First, you must engage with them so they'll allow you to show them the way.

So, one might ask, "What is the minimal, necessary first step to approaching a case story that shows respect for *both* the conscious and other-than-conscious process of any decision maker I want to engage and invite into an emotional response?"

1.6.4 I've Got a Feeling

Exmovere is the Latin word for "emotion," but its literal meaning is to "move outward."

"There is no judgment, legal or otherwise, without an emotional basis at its heart," writes Antonio Damasio, hot on the trail of a definition of consciousness himself, identifying emotional reactions as the key to consciousness itself.[12] And, we know the first step to approaching the other-than-conscious minds of legal decision makers is to indirectly invite the desired emotional response to a case story. Easily done. Let's all break for lunch.

Or not.

When it comes to the law and emotion, many jurors (and some judges) misconstrue the "no sympathy" bias or prejudice rule to mean that emotion should be banned from legal decision making. Many lawyers think that emotional reactions simply play no role at all (much less a significant one) in the job of properly judging a legal case.

12. Antonio Damasio, *The Feeling of What Happens: Body and Emotion in the Making of Consciousnes* (Orlando, FL: Harcourt Inc., 1999).

And all would be wrong.

Here's what George Lakoff, an expert on frames of mind and the metaphors that support them, has to say on the role emotional reactions play in the real rational process:

> Real reason is inextricably tied up with emotion; you cannot be rational without being emotional. False reason thinks that emotion is the enemy of reason; that it is unscrupulous to call on emotion. Yet, people with brain damage who cannot feel emotion cannot make rational decisions because they do not know what to want, since like and not like mean nothing. "Rational" decisions are based on a long history of emotional responses by oneself and others. Real reason requires emotion.[13]

So, giving some thought to how to package your case story in a way that invites the decision maker to produce the most compelling emotional reaction early on is a good step to take. However, to do that, it's essential to resist the temptation to assume all emotional reactions are equally available to a decision maker's conscious scrutiny and experience.

They are not.

Damasio (and others like him in the field) put emotional reactions into three camps:

Primary—happiness, sadness, fear, anger, surprise, disgust

Secondary—social, i.e., embarrassment, jealousy, guilt, pride

Tertiary—background, i.e., well-being, malaise, calm, tension

When Paul Eckman, expert on nonverbal communication and detecting deceit, teaches people how to recognize the universal, nonverbal facial expression of each primary emotional reaction we are capable of, each of which expresses the same way other-than-consciously, he adds "contempt" to Damasio's list of six primary emotions.[14]

Note that the most basic survival-based drives and motivations, with their attendant pain and pleasure responses, aren't on the list. This is because most professionals investigating the field of human awareness and responses haven't placed the most basic drives the *Reptile* authors relate and use in their prescription for trial work into any of the categories of more evolved emotional reaction listed in Damasio's primary, secondary, and tertiary categories.

---

13. George Lakoff, "Obama, Tea Parties and the Battle for Our Brains," Monday, February 22, 2010, Truthout, www.truthout.org.

14. Paul Eckman, *Telling Lies: Clues to Deceit in the Marketplace, Politics, and Marriage* (New York, NY: WW Norton, 2009).

Whatever we call them, these basic emotional drives—along with the intrinsically fearful (or relaxed) sensations that accompany them—are what you want to start with when building the basis of the emotional components of your case story. "Whole brain"-friendly efforts to influence other people always start with addressing the other-than-conscious parts of the mind first—the order in which all human reactions occur. Least conscious first, most conscious last. What you are conscious of at any given moment exists only as a gift from your faculties outside consciousness. Had the gift not been given, you wouldn't be thinking, seeing, or feeling it. But how do you address a nonverbal part of the mind that functions more outside conscious reach than within its grasp?

First and foremost, know your territory. Again, here is what Damasio has to say:

> The pervasiveness of emotion in our development and subsequently in our everyday experience connects virtually every object or situation in our experience, by virtue of conditioning, to the fundamental values of homeostatic regulation: reward and punishment; pleasure or pain; approach or withdrawal; personal advantage or disadvantage; and, inevitably, good (in the sense of survival) or evil (in the sense of death). Whether we like it or not, this is the natural human condition. But when consciousness is available, feelings have their maximum impact, and individuals are also able to reflect and plan. They have a means to control the pervasive tyranny of emotion: it is called reason. Ironically, of course, the engines of reason still require emotion, which means that the controlling power of reason is often modest."[15]

Thus, you can override and rethink an emotional response, choosing not to act on it, if:

- You are aware of it.
- You're aware of it in enough time to redirect your response.
- You've had enough practice to overcome the force of habit driving that response.

What you cannot do, especially with the most basic, potent, and least consciously available, survival-driven emotional responses, is to try and choose not to have an emotional response in the first place. A major point about responses and reactions generated outside conscious reach is that the ability to discuss them does not grant the power to choose among them the next time out, nor to be in control of them. Thankfully, we tend to build habits in our emotional reactions as we do in all other things and situations.

---

15. Damasio, *supra*, n. 12.

Safety, sex, sustenance, shelter, procreation, and the like are the territory in which our most basic emotional responses reside. Fearful and comfortable are the two most common sensations you'll feel generated along the upper midline of your body when this level of response is engaged (at the times when you notice it happening). At this level, emotional responses are like blunt instruments and, when fully realized, take precedence over reactions generated by parts of the brain a few inches upstairs from where these fire off—that is, the "reasoning" parts.

Whether we notice or not, these are the emotional responses that push a person to respond in ways that completely confound a rational, objective observer listening to a juror justify a decision for the medical defense against a brain-damaged child, "because the parents are from outside this country and probably came here ready to file a lawsuit and get rich." It's hard to hear the unspoken preemptive emotional response behind that comment—i.e., "I'm protecting myself and my family from being hurt by your illegitimate lawsuit." Harder still, when the juror denies her own fearful reaction should anyone attempt to directly question it aloud in a post-trial interview. To get a worthwhile response, that kind of question would have to be asked of the other-than-conscious mind, but that part of the mind doesn't speak. That part of the mind just knows what it already knows, learned through experience.

How do you use the knowledge of a hierarchy of a handful of basic emotional responses to help you develop your case in discovery, client interviews, and depositions?

Begin by changing your own ingrained perspective on emotions by framing your language differently. Adding the word "acting" in front of, or "reaction" just after, any emotional term you are using (e.g., angry, fearful, joyous). Framing your own (and others') emotional reactions as what they actually are reframes every inner story anyone builds about what transpires after that reaction. Far from being temporarily "possessed" (for example, "Sorry, my temper-jealousy-pride-anger got the better of me . . ."), you can begin to see even tort-reformed jurors as capable of responding with the full range of their God-given emotional potential and will be that much more likely to *act* that way as a result.

Reminding yourself that emotions are not "things" that periodically possess us, but simply *reactions* among a number that are available at all times under all but the truly dire circumstances, can make the task of developing a presentation package aimed at evoking one reaction over another among decision makers that much more achievable in your own mind—and, consequently, that much more easily acted out, congruently, as must be done to effectively invite their collaboration in (re)building your case story.

Next, start at the survival-based level and work your way up. I highly recommend you give the prescriptions David Ball and Don Keenan offer a long look.[16] The most

16. David Ball and Don Keenan, *Reptile: The 2009 Manual of the Plaintiff's Revolution* (Atlanta, GA: Balloon Press, 2009).

primitive emotional responses in any human story are "reptilian": fear and comfort. The higher emotional responses include happiness, sadness, fear, anger, surprise, disgust, and contempt.

The basic approaches to appealing to our most primitive reactions are predictable: plaintiffs generally want to evoke fear and defendants generally want to ensure comfort. So, the question to ask (and have answered) in your focus group research is, "What is the emotional basis of the story of someone in my clients' position under these circumstances?"

If you aren't able to conduct focus group research, you can still ask people about your case. Reduce the five-minute openings to two minutes each (similar to the two-minute pitch in an elevator sales exercise) and poll your "Phil Corboy Cab Driver" research group.[17] Present a balanced pair of positions and don't push the emotional lever just yet. Wait to hear responses beyond the surface, too, because these reactions are usually described indirectly, without directly naming the emotional reaction—just as your questions about them ought to be phrased. Remember not to ever discount "surprise" as an initial emotional response in a plaintiff's case; it's often the one people go through first, before they fully comprehend what is being presented to them. Begin to recognize that one emotional basis alone almost never fulfils a decision maker's needs for fully appreciating and emotionally reacting to your case. You should always be wondering—what's the *next* strong emotional reaction here?

1.6.5 OK, Now Push the Emotional Lever

As a plaintiff attorney, you want to and try to evoke survival-based, other-than-conscious responses. The first step is to make the problem posed by the defense choices and acts *bigger* than the details of the case may objectively indicate. In voir dire, think about questioning jurors about their experiences regarding using, managing, and following safety rules. If the attorney is not thinking about a bigger case story, he may ask, "Who here has experience working as a journeyman millwright, using high-speed metal lathes, following all the safety rules that apply to them?" In such a line of questioning, there is no room left for anyone to relate *but* the plaintiff. This safety story is too small in scope, and consequently bereft of openings for emotional reactions for potential jurors. Certainly, there has been no window opened for those already wishing to emotionally connect with the "unjustly accused" defendant.

If you know you want to develop a story that throws the widest net possible over the perceptions and basic emotional reactions of your decision makers, allowing the greatest opportunity for any person approaching the story to be able to relate, what would be your next step?

---

17. The late Phil Corboy, a well-known Chicago trial attorney who reportedly always ran his cases by cab drivers for their reactions as an impromptu focus group.

I suggest challenging the long-standing, and mostly unthinking, habit of otherwise great trial attorneys of jumping directly to the rules and the defendant's violation of or adherence to them. Instead, I suggest you invite folks to ask, "What purpose does this rule/law/industry standard serve anyway?" Over the last decade or so, I've suggested my attorney clients ask, "What risk/hazard/threat *justifies* having a rule at all?" and "What danger is the rule in place to guard against?" Ball and Keenan say always stretch the perceived risk further by asking about the full extent of *all* harms that risk left unchecked *could* cause, perhaps beyond the extent a violation or dereliction of the rule caused in this specific case. They then invite you to take your witnesses one step more, asking for analogies to other harms caused in other situations when bad acts *like this one* are allowed. All this can, and will, invite emotional responses. You just need to know which to recognize and reinforce, and which to invite to be reconsidered before it's too late.

By making the perceived dangers and likely harms that attend them as big as possible in your story, that story is now well positioned to engage the survival-based emotional drivers that are each decision maker's default way of relating to any embodied, human story. This also helps decision makers identify with the risks present under the circumstances in your client's story.

So, now that the decision maker has been invited to identify fully with the Risks faced by anyone *like* the client in these circumstances, they have "bought into" the need for protective Rules. My suggestions here run very close to those Malone and Friedman wrote about in *Rules of the Road*[18] (another must-read for plaintiff *and* defense attorneys). First off, do the same thing you did with the "Risk that justifies the Rule" by making the scope of the Rule bigger and broader. Ask yourself (and your witnesses) in terms of the context or situation the case story presents, "What is the highest purpose this Rule serves?" Once the expanded risk territory is established, it naturally is the first place to start looking for or inviting answers:

> "Doctor, is it fair to say that a reasonable medical professional's highest priority, in these circumstances, is protecting the safety of their patient?"

Or, phrased in the pain-avoiding perspective:

> "Doctor, is it fair to say that a reasonable medical professional, under these circumstances, never needlessly endangers their patient's safety?"

The prescription always is to follow the brain's lead because the brain always moves from the most general (biggest and broadest) frame to the most specific (small and very detailed), no matter what the subject is, or what individual internal experience is available with which to relate. A standard "umbrella" rule, linked to

---

18. Rick Friedman and Paul Malone, *Rules of the Road: A Plaintiff Lawyer's Guide to Proving Liability of the Road* (Portland, OR: Trial Guides, 2010).

the most broad and general threat should that rule be violated or unenforced, helps decision makers draw their own sense of protection and self-preservation into the Risk and Rules frames of your story, starting from the most basic, most potent emotional level. Then, encourage witnesses during discovery to relate any specific rules, standards, guidelines, good ideas, and common sense choices of action to the collection of case specific rules you are compiling. Keep an eye focused on those that can be clearly depicted as having been violated in your client's case.

Next, address the functions of the mid-brain and those even a little higher up in the cortex in your story sequence. Be curious as to which of the six or seven primary emotional responses—acting angry, happy, sad, contemptuous, surprised, disgusted, and/or fearful—are most likely to prompt decision makers to internally build stories that lead from an initial, primal reaction of fear to "buying into" the *Rules justified by the Risks* present in the story's circumstances, perceiving those rules being violated and all the way to the "happy ending" you and your client most desire. Focus groups, moderated by someone trained to do so, can help you find the one or two primary emotional keys to play your case out as well as it needs to be done.

And finally, beware of settling. Many plaintiff attorneys have been taught to believe that an angry reaction is all they want—or need—to get a big verdict number at the end of the day. If your case story requires people to start at "surprise" and work through that to get to "angry," but you fail to build cues for surprise into the early parts of your case story presentation, don't be taken aback when decision makers can't find their way at the end to acting as angry as you had hoped. Your story, as developed, helped preclude this result. The emotional basis of the best decision was left half-developed.

Even though these primary emotional responses are closer to conscious awareness—i.e., more easily realized and discussed—*indirect* packaging of their parts in your case story is still the most elegant, and certainly the safest, approach to delivering your case story

For example, avoid asking witnesses, "How angry did seeing that make you?" Rather, allow the decision makers to follow along with a more experiential review of what was available to be perceived at the time, as if they had been there to witness the events as they unfolded. Ask questions that set the scene, both in the circumstances and events, as well as within the witness's internal state, so everyone can relive it as much as possible. "How big was the room? Where were you in it? What else was around? How did his voice sound? And yours, as you answered? What exactly was said, and what happened next?" gets you to the same place in the story you want to be, but is more likely to encourage emotional tailgating by decision makers when packaged in this step-by-step fashion.

In Chapter Four, I discuss the story element of *Point of View* and the position of the *Central Character* through which the case story's events are usually referenced. Once you've discovered the most productive point of view to build into your story, one that evokes the emotional reactions you are looking for, your witness questions in discovery and your work in voir dire and in your opening statement will be much easier.

For instance, fostering contemptuous reactions toward a negligent manager, inviting decision makers to act sad about significant threats that have been allowed to go on for years, or inviting surprised reactions toward a malingering plaintiff, can be attempted in two ways:

1. Directly—by seeking a conscious response
2. Indirectly—by inviting an emotional response to emerge from the way they perceive the context of answers

Asking an expert exactly what managing something well looks, sounds, and feels like, and then asking how far from that norm, in the specific place and time, each particular defendant act turned out to be, and with which particular people, gives that witness the best chance to actually *react* contemptuously and *model* that reaction for decision makers.

Or, you could just directly tell people how far off the reasonable path the defendant strayed and just cross your fingers that they build the emotional reaction (or any emotional reaction) on their own.

So, always address the survival-based emotional drives first. No matter how compelling the "higher" emotional chords you play in the story, if you fail to adequately invite the bottom-line drives into the story first, they can (and often will) override any other influences you may try to bring to the table to be judged. It is a risk you need not run. Package your case story to take care of decision makers' feelings *first.*

I want to reiterate what I began this supplement to Chapter One with: that because the two parts of the human brain, the conscious and the other-than-conscious, are not a balanced, two-way street, the actual experience of the legal decision maker arriving at a conclusion about a case story they are (re)constructing in their "mind's eye" is that of *realization.*

More than being *made* in the traditional sense, legal decisions actually *are realized.*

Chapter Two

Lives of Their Own

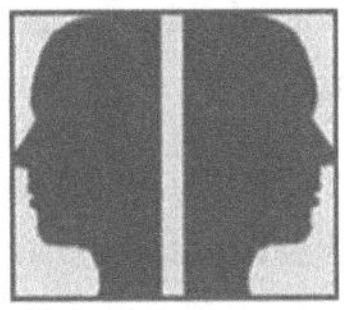

Justice is the giving to each of his own.
—*Cicero*

2.1 Tempting Types

When thinking about decision makers and legal case stories, it's tempting to see the jurors or judge as an audience more than as participants. But even an audience viewing a movie or play, with no legal duty to find justice in the story, is not nearly as passive as it can appear. Presuming that people not talking are not directly involved in the process is a risk trial professionals need not run. The public perception of the decision makers' role tends toward that of a passive receptacle, which gets filled with a story and then goes off to make determinations based on its response to the full account. Most people imagine decision makers responding more to background and prevailing beliefs than to a group process or even a determined individual effort. It is this mindset about the passive listener, reacting as much as deciding, that leads to a focus on "typing" decision makers, especially jurors, and to discounting the stories they author while judging a case.

It makes a certain amount of sense. It has long been acknowledged by observers of jury trials that each person sitting in judgment hears and sees the story differently. How they do that and how each decision maker's own life story fits into the case story prompts questions about what kind of person is between those listening ears and observing eyes. It seems almost axiomatic that personal differences must account for the differences in the stories decision makers construct from legal cases.

This notion helped support a stereotype of jury psychologists, who were once thought to be able to use research to type the "ideal juror" to hear a case for one side or the other. This outdated notion occasionally emerges today much as it was described in a televised account of Richard "Racehorse" Haynes's efforts with pretrial research four decades ago. Haynes told of the jury expert he hired to help him identify his ideal juror in the murder defense of T. Cullen Davis, a very wealthy and well-known client.

> He said what we were looking for was a black female, mid-30s, college educated—what else—oh, yes, divorced, Catholic, too, who read newspapers and periodicals from outside the Ft. Worth area. I said, "That's it, doc? For all that money, that's it? Well, doc, any first-year law student will tell you that in a capital murder case, a college-educated black female is a pretty good place to start. But do you know how many college-educated, black, female, divorced Catholic women we have here? None. We had one, but she moved to Detroit."[1]

And therein lies the rub. No matter how many variables you account for and test for, people always have more, and truly selecting any set collection of them is pretty much impossible.[2] Although research suggests that juror profiling for use in voir dire is not as effective as once imagined and a strategy focused mainly on peremptory challenges instead of challenges for cause is far less helpful in court, many in the public, and even many lawyers, still assume that picking the perfect panelist is the trial professional's primary job when it comes to getting a case story heard productively.

In one way of looking at the field, they may be accurate in the presumption. While profiling for the "ideal" juror is not happening much today, lawyers are still looking for decision makers with the potential for creating more helpful case stories because of their backgrounds and beliefs. "Just tell me who I need to be looking for. Who are my best jurors, and who are my worst?" are very common questions posed in trial preparation. Many consultants will point to a set of beliefs or known reactions of varieties that could help or hurt a juror's chances of appreciating one or the other side's story.

The juror profiling that Racehorse Haynes decried isolated a number of characteristics, stacking them all together in one ostensibly perfect panelist for any case similar to the one at hand, and then used that aggregation to try to guide juror selection, despite the fact that potential jurors can only be struck by attorneys or the court, never directly selected. Today, rather than trying to build and find a perfect profile from a large collection of thinking habits and experiences, many trial professionals research how certain types or categories respond to selected aspects of the case at hand. Instead of accumulating categories and types from which to build an ideal juror, they reduce the search to isolated parts of people, selected as important for categorizing or typing.

There is a great deal of research, for example, about a psychological category, a characteristic called "authoritarian thinking." This personality attribute has produced measurable results in many mock trial experiments and thus has received a

1. "Trial by Jury," *60 Minutes*, CBS News, April 22, 1984.

2. This is true in most venues if for no other reason than that the number of peremptory challenges (i.e., alleging no cause or reason) available to either side in many cases, especially in civil disputes, is quite limited and has been shrinking rather than expanding since the days when this stereotype arose.

great deal of attention in printed research results.[3] You will commonly find legal professionals examining this psychological category in case research. During voir dire, potential jurors may be reviewed for their alignment with the authoritarian or non-authoritarian camp along the lines for which the mock trial jurors, phone survey subjects, or focus group members were scanned. Not the profile of a collection of categories, but type by characteristic type that research showed might tend to help or hurt the client's case story, often sorted by strong presence or absence. Moreover, there are many divisions for categories beyond the psychological: sociological, cultural, decision making, and even the old demographic divisions.

Lawyers often hear consultants using typing techniques say things such as, "jurors who think that way" or "people who think this way." The objects of these sentences, whatever the people are really thinking about, are frequently split into either/or categories, such as authoritarian or non-authoritarian. The inquiry is usually focused on life story values, attitudes, and beliefs, referenced to elements of the case story, that can build camps of potentially helpful or hurtful jurors depending on what types of thinking these people are said to do. This strategy is not aimed at finding ideal jurors or targeting peremptory strikes against the non-ideal ones. Rather, it seeks a *cause* (in the beliefs and life lessons a potential juror carries) that would make the job of listening fairly to the particular story at hand, much harder for some types of people over others.

At a conference on focus groups, I once heard a consultant describe such a category division for the assembled attorneys in the context of medical negligence cases:

> We've learned there are some jurors who think of medicine as consumers of a product. In their life experiences, they approach buying medical services more like they would approach buying a product like a car, or a service like financial planning. They can be expected to comparison shop, to get on the Internet and research their own conditions. They will want more than one opinion, and they may be strong advocates for participating in their own treatment. On the other hand, we know there are people who think about medicine more as dependents, in a more parental framework. They tend to do as the doctor says with fewer questions, show up on time, wait for hours without complaint, and ask for second opinions only when the doctor suggests they should. You could have a person who thinks of medicine as a consumer as someone's daughter, while the mother was much more of a parental thinker.

If these personal background differences could indeed account for the differences in the stories we create as decision makers, then a lawyer representing a plaintiff in a

3. Two other juror characteristics receiving a similar level of research attention are perceptions as to whether circumstance or character primarily control outcomes in life (locus of control) and belief in a "just world," where actual outcomes are most probably "deserved" in some fashion.

case where timely diagnosis had been needed could have his case story put at risk in the hands of *consumer type* jurors, who prize second opinions and personal control of each stage of medical care. Similarly, an attorney representing the doctor in that case may not want a panel full of *parental* thinkers, who may just want to confirm that the plaintiff dutifully followed doctor's orders before finding in her favor.

Though typing seems to satisfy the understandable desire to find where personal differences may create differences in the stories decision makers build from a case, there is another view to consider. What if some of the ways people engage their own stories, while learning the story of the legal case, take precedence over their typing? If each judge, juror, or mediator makes up her own story about any case, as research and simple observation confirm, then it may well follow that people within the same category build their stories differently from one another in significant ways, despite having one or more measurable category types in common. In truth, the extraordinary event would be finding two individuals who actually craft the very same story in deciding a case.

Looking at the two patient types proposed above, many "consumers" and many "dependent patients" share a common theme for medical stories whatever their various backgrounds and attendant beliefs. If you ask them the question, "How do you know you have a good doctor?" seeking answers of a thematic nature,[4] you may well find an interesting trend. A large number of people with otherwise varied backgrounds and beliefs will describe some form of communication as an important criterion for a good doctor: "He listens to me," "Her office always returns my calls," "They always follow up when they say they will," or "He took extra time to make sure I understood his instructions" are very typical responses this question elicits. Asking *how* someone knows their doctor fits in the "good" category may open a window onto what they have learned in life about medicine, much as asking them to hum a higher note shows off what they have learned about needed effort. The most revealing parts of the response may not be those they consciously put in play, and so may be more true to their own life stories.

Or consider the story frame alluded to in introducing the two types of patient/jurors above. If you discuss the "business of medicine" or "healthcare industry" with potential jurors in focus groups or voir dire, without limiting their responses, you learn that the perception of medicine-as-a-business can foster some odd story constructions. For example, many people find a reason in that story frame to offer the benefit of the doubt to "harried and overworked" medical staff at the hands-on level of care. In a case where the claimed injury involved failing to catch a crisis as

---

4. If you presume a category of "bad doctors" and ask about the qualities that exclude physicians from that undesirable group, people will tend to offer suggestions on appreciating, understanding, and valuing medical care itself, personified by their own experience and their own history. This works far better than simply demanding the top five factors that make a good doctor. There is ample suggestion in the form of the question that people look outside their own experience, and no invitation to stick to personal references.

it developed, a civil defense attorney working for a hospital and its nurses may well worry that people could automatically assume that those closest to the injury, with a direct duty to monitor and observe patient condition, are the most likely to be seen as blameworthy. If this category of the medicine-as-business story frame were to be applied by either consumer or dependent-type jurors, building the basic theme of their own trial story, that lawyer would be assuming way too much. Other people considering the healthcare-as-industry framework, when imagining money as a motive, often see cost, not profit, as the prime mover of modern medical companies. A plaintiff's attorney arguing that the HMO or medical corporation had only "one thing on its mind: profit" might be planting motive seeds on rocks for those folks, regardless of their personal preferences. They could either see savvy consumers already aware of the realities of healthcare costs and prepared for their impact, or with equal influence, they could see their trusted doctors, hamstrung by fiscal pressures, still doing their best to offer help and care. Either way, the expectations of the listeners, regardless of their category type, would not be to invite images of patient deprivation by the profit motive.

When exploring the modern business of medicine, you may find that many people look at the duty of today's healthcare professionals as twofold, not just as the Hippocratic promise to "do no harm," which heralds many medical negligence cases each week. These folks expect doctors to do double duty: to help and not hurt in the process and at the same time. That is, to "provide the medical service I pay for, while doing all you can to protect me from danger." Any attorney who walks into court telling a story based on only one side of that double-barreled expectation, on either side of a medical malpractice case, could be telling only half the story his listeners walked in wanting to hear. And for every person who directly or indirectly reveals such a "help and don't hurt" position on the duty of doctors, can anyone judge from that response alone which type of patient owns it: dependent or consumer? Would either be OK? Or could the positioning that listeners adopt within their own stories sometimes supersede their typing?

Can you safely say if a consumer type would be more or less likely to use a fundamental medical theme such as "communication is care"? A consumer type might think of full discussions with the doctor about alternative treatments and multiple patient options, while a dependent patient could just as easily be recalling a long conversation about general health with no specific service in mind. Each would be finding effective medicine through the theme of communication. Will the person that has been diagnosed through focus group or voir dire answers as the type to put medical professionals in a parental slot see doctors and nurses as more, or less, responsible if they tell themselves a story that has *cost*, not profit, as the medical business's prime motivator? Will the consumer type put blame on the highest medical authority, on the hands-on worker, or on no one in a birth trauma case given those choices? And if either type sees the duty of medical professionals as requiring the provision of both the treatment purchased and caring protection in equal measure, will they read the patient's signature on the consent to surgery form differently?

Like Bruner and Amsterdam's *category* frames for stories in *Minding the Law*, many of these decision maker *types* are derived directly from the subject matter of the specific case being researched. Thus, they can certainly point toward themes that might surface, under the influence of that typing, as individuals create their own versions of that particular case story. But general category leanings do not necessarily show a trial professional how the *narrative* elements of that private story, or the *rhetorical* tools used to argue for it, will play out, even for the person who seems to show a definite preference between the two types.

2.2 Familiar Ground

Trial professionals using the typing approach base their groupings on either general case story frames (medicine: product or parent?) or general categories of belief (trust: no one or the doctor?). They are essentially still answering the same question as before: "What kind of person am I looking for on this jury?" Despite the shift to case-specific research—and to dividing up characteristics for use in selecting jurors instead of bunching them all into one imaginary perfect juror—dividing people into artificially discrete case story or reference-experience category types is still profiling. The temptation to type potential decision makers could lead legal professionals to take one or two answers as if they were a whole life story. Worse, it tends to distract from the stories these people are actually creating as you talk with them in focus groups or voir dire. "Less likely" to think this way or that does not mean "unable." A few people will create their own versions of a particular case story *against* type. Lots of story elements draw positive and negative responses regardless of typing. Many, if not a majority of all potential elements of case stories formed by decision makers, will not be attributable to any typing done in case research. There will always be many more categories and elements available in creating any juror's case story than there are measurable types to overlay.

Just as a juror or judge does with any case, so legal professionals make up their own stories regarding the fact that everyone makes up a story from which to build their judgments. In general terms, there are two competing trial stories at work today among legal professionals when it comes to dealing with decision makers, the case story, and judgments. If we were to divide them up by their essential elements, the older and newer trial stories could look like this:

Case Stories

How are they seen?

	OLDER	NEWER
THEME	**Interpretation**—*Who needs to see and hear this?*	**Construction**—*What most needs to be heard and seen?*
SCOPE	*One set of facts;* *One set of decision makers;* *Delivered and decided.*	*Multiple themes,* *Multiple interpretations,* *Multiple conclusions.*
POINT OF VIEW	*The Attorney or The Jury.*	*The Jurors or Their Stories.*
SEQUENCE	*Witnesses deliver facts;* *Attorneys deliver case;* *Jury/Judge delivers decision.*	*Attorney presents story;* *Jurors/Judge formulate stories;* *Multiple conclusions drive verdict.*

Figure 1

Starting from the demonstrable observation that each decision maker heard and saw the case story differently, previously it made sense to conclude that differences among the types of people making the judgments accounted for the differences in their versions. But today we are also aware that people, professionals and laypersons alike, are not just interpreting a set of predetermined facts and objectively applied laws and rules. Every decision maker authors his own version of the facts and legal rules, relating ostensibly separate elements of the case and referencing personal experiences, reactions, and attendant beliefs with little or no conscious awareness of that process. This all happens before anyone recognizes the results of the process, which are then available for reviewing and discussing, alone or with others.

At least one factor that kept juror typing popular was that it was not much different from what trial lawyers had been doing before the arrival of consultants and juror and decision-maker research. Lawyers had developed voir dire strategies from training, scuttlebutt, and habits passed down from one attorney to another over generations. For decades, lawyers were assessing what they had for the case and running it by friends, colleagues, and strangers to elicit opinions. They would then try to extrapolate characteristics and trends in those people—usually demographics such as gender, profession, and race—that could translate into the types of jurors they thought might help or hurt in court. What the new science of jury selection promised was a more efficient, more effective way of doing what they believed they were already doing.

This tack owes a lot to the older story, long told among legal professionals about decision makers and how they might be influenced, how they might work, and how involved they are in the process. But if legal decision makers are more participants than audience, then that older story used by so many to prepare and present cases may not be the whole story after all. Certainly, a person's background and lessons learned from life are going to affect how they approach the job of deciding a legal dispute. But what if that is not all? How easily can legal professionals make adjustments to a story they may have relied on, with little conscious scrutiny or consideration, for a long time?

One impediment to editing the former story about decision makers and case stories is the tight link between our thinking and our biology. Just as a part of our brains strives to keep our temperature, weight, and other physical features contained within a narrow set of norms, once established, so do our minds try to maintain the status quo. Homeostasis, the automatic drive to keep the status quo intact, works for our habits of thinking, our beliefs about the world, and our habits of communicating in that world around us just as it does for our temperatures. Once a pattern is established, it tends to maintain and reinforce itself in its own equilibrium.

One way an old belief is maintained is by selective attention. We tend to reinforce and emphasize the results we expect to see, and to diminish and ignore those we don't.[5] For example, to maintain a gambling habit, people tend to overemphasize recalled wins and ignore or discount losses. Reasoned thinking does not usually make much of a dent in this habit under ordinary circumstances. Empty pockets are rational proof, but they don't always convince.

The premise of typing people or parts of their thinking to anticipate a helpful or harmful verdict seems very reasonable, considering the impact our prior history has on our present situations and attitudes. But even if research seems to show that the successes were not really that spectacular[6] (like a psychic whose hits are applauded and whose misses are not recorded) if the professional has long treated the limited typing story as the whole account, she will tend to reinforce that belief more than rushing to reject or even adjust it.

---

5. Researchers divide the levers we use to maintain our selective attention in many ways. They propose many thought filters (such as authoritarian thinking) and functional processing filters—from the availability heuristic, through norming and confirmation biases, to the belief perseverance bias among others—to describe this part of our minds' means of keeping the mental status quo, just as it does with many physical processes. *See* Chapter Three.

6. F. Strier, "Whither Trial Consulting? Issues and Projections," *Law and Human Behavior* 23 (1999): 93–115.

Research has consistently shown, for example, that lawyers, like many other professionals dealing with people telling stories under great pressure, often deem themselves very good at sorting out truth from falsehood. But they aren't. Studies have shown that lawyers, judges, law enforcement officials, teachers, psychologists, and others in professions where interpersonal truth detecting can be at a premium all consistently overestimate their capacity to pick truth tellers from liars.[7] In fact, the numbers say that all these professionals fare no better than chance—a coin flip—at using whatever skills they believe they have acquired for differentiating the truth from the lies. Usually, when told of these results, most lawyers will agree that, of course, those *other* people get fooled a lot and it's a tricky task to tell who's not being truthful. But more often than not, privately, they exclude themselves from the no-better-than chance group. If they believed in their skill in the past, they will tend to persist in their belief despite hearing facts to the contrary.[8]

There is one sure-fire way that these professionals can realistically assess their current capacities, and it is to improve them and review their success in hindsight. Once they learn an alternative method that helps them demonstrate truth-detection success at rates greater than fifty-fifty, they can better acknowledge their former level of effectiveness in hindsight. The same may be true of trial professionals making adjustments to a different story about cases, decision makers, and judgments—once they put into practice a demonstrably effective alternative to the focus on category types. As the practitioners of neurolinguistic programming (NLP) were fond of saying in their early years: "If what you are doing is not working well, do anything differently now and think about it later." All that is required is a viable alternative.

The scientific method starts with the hypothesis of a different possibility than the one currently accepted. From there, practitioners design an experiment to test their hypothesis and prove it to be more or less true than what came before. To do an experiment correctly, researchers must first catalogue the *variables* that can influence the outcome so that they know what makes the outcome happen. Then, while testing the hypothesis, they must eliminate or control for those variables that are not relevant to their search. Once the rest of the variables are eliminated or well controlled, the test is assumed to be a valid inquiry into the variables that will affect the case outcome.

If you step back from the trial story territory described, you can see the trial professionals' older story at work in the forced dichotomies: the either/or framework that the act of assigning categories tends to produce. This "just two sides to every story" is a huge cultural bias that extends far beyond the scientific camp when it

7. *The Human Face*, The Learning Channel, Discovery Communications, September 2001.

8. This reaction recalls work on "locus of control" and attributions of responsibility or blame, mentioned above in connection with establishing the case story point of view. Many studies show a great discrepancy between what a person sees as the source of another person's misbehavior—that person and her character—and the circumstances they tend to blame for their own undesirable acts or responses.

comes to the themes and narratives we use. Note the two variables addressed so far in typing decision makers along either story frame or personal experience lines. The first is found in choices made by the lawyer through which juror categories and attendant values or beliefs are partly focused on, and then in how to make cause or peremptory strike decisions based on that focus. The second variable is the mental makeup of decision makers: the trends of thinking and reacting they bring to the story, learned from their life lessons up to that point. Whether based on the outdated idea of an ideal juror, or on a collection of pro and con categories that one could bring to a particular case story, these trends are usually depicted as a variable affecting the final verdict formed by the decision makers.

Thus, two general variables populate the older case story tale when it comes to researching where the advantages may or may not lie: lawyer choices and juror (or judge) characteristics.

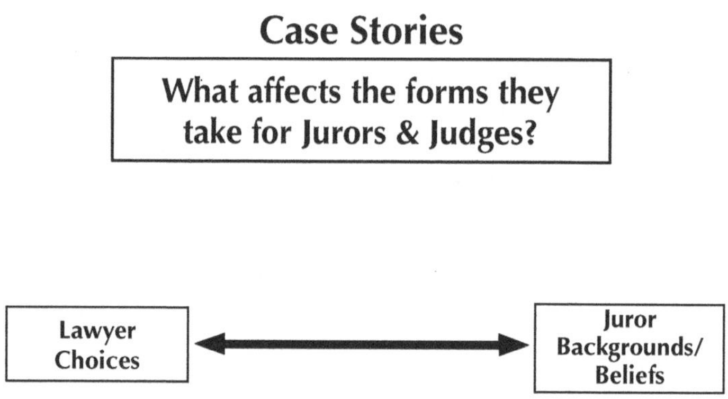

Figure 2

Typically, when trial professionals set about designing pretrial research for a case, they have to find a way of controlling input from the *lawyer variable* so that the *juror variable*, the one they want to test, is isolated. Imagine a horizontal line with arrows on both ends pointing to the lawyer variable on the left and the juror variable[9] on the right. If the lawyer variable is not eliminated or minimized in the testing, how would you know on which side of the line to attribute the outcomes of the research on decision maker differences? Which variable was the one influencing your results? So you standardize the selection process of your test audience in the room or over the phone, ensuring that the input your group receives is controlled to diminish the influence from the lawyer variable. This will isolate the juror variable as the active ingredient in the test.

9. Though the second variable will be labeled the "juror" variable for simplicity's sake, it refers to any decision maker's process, whether professional or layperson.

What are the hypotheses these tests should prove or disprove? Mostly the overall strength of the case. But many different aspects can be tested in focus groups, from the overall theme down to the value and staying power of a single demonstrative exhibit. Phone and written surveys are usually used to test the impact of community attitudes, values, and beliefs that jurors will likely draw on to appreciate the case story, while mock trials, also known as trial simulations, aim more at trying to read and assess the intersection of those prior beliefs with a thorough presentation of the specific case story in a trial setting.[10]

Presentation of the case story is a whole other consideration. Many of the results of pretrial research are used to rate the strengths and weaknesses of case facts, the legal positions, and of course, the monetary value of damages in civil cases where they apply. But it is important not to lose track of the fact that this rating commonly takes place only in reference to the *juror variable*. The older trial-story theme still applies, whether the outcome of research on the juror variable is to establish cause strike issues, rate the strength of liability facts, or test the impact of legal rules on cause of harms, or the relative strength of demonstrative exhibits or story elements on damages. Research results are assumed to reveal "people who think this way about the law or who think that way about the facts."

Focus group members for civil cases are typically asked to rate their responses to the plaintiff's side of the case, in writing, delivered in a controlled package, and often committed to videotape, so there can be no variation between delivery for one group and the next. Then they are exposed to the defense side and asked to rate that, too. In the process, people's particular leanings are elicited or emerge in various ways, and they are often surveyed about background factors and psychological, decision-making, and even cultural trends. Frequently, for example, everyone will be asked about the six major points in the plaintiff's presentation. They may have them spelled out, with a scale of one to five next to each major point, with instructions to assign a value to the importance, strength, or credibility of each point, along with an explanation of why a certain number was selected for each point. The results are then analyzed and correlated according to the categories, beliefs, or attitudes determined as the factors strongly affecting a person's view of the whole case, or the particular parts being tested at the time, such as, "People who strongly view medicine as a commodity tend think this way about these liability facts in this case."

2.3 New Ground

Although case facts or legal points may be categorized in the testing process for later use by the attorney in presentation planning, they are assessed only in direct relation to the juror variable: differences among decision makers. And, in

10. There is a lot of blending of these approaches. For instance, many people run a series of focus groups in lieu of a large-scale survey to seek out trends in jury pool attitudes in a community.

the vernacular of NLP, here lies the part that isn't working the territory as well as it can be worked.[11] The process is still producing piecemeal profiles of juror trends according to the construct that "people that think this way about those facts" or "jurors that think that way about this law" are good or bad for your case. But we know that the bulk of the science out there, so far, on jury psychology and trial work says that predicting verdicts based on Haynes's wholesale or even piecemeal profiling does not offer a huge return on the value invested.[12] Instead of searching for types of people, using story elements just to confirm them, the more productive priority may be to first seek out just how many possible stories people can create, and then relate any differences among the people to that collection of case themes, scopes, viewpoints, and plots.

The persistence of the older approach may have a lot more to do with a lack of recognition of viable alternatives than with the belief that testing the juror variable reveals the whole story. The seeds of juror and judicial decisions take root in the shared territory of both the conscious and not-so-conscious mind. And there may well be more going on in the minds of legal decision makers than a set of cause effect responses tied to previous life experiences dictating story forms. The differences in the case stories that grow out of those minds may be tied to more than just personal differences among people.

If you leave the realm of questions, answers, and specific responses and jump up a few logical levels to the category choices made to attempt to control the overall research process, you can easily spot the big missing element in the older thinking. What if there is another fundamental variable with a life all its own? A third, independent variable in the testing territory, besides the lawyers and the jurors, that can have an equal or greater role in determining the outcome of any given case? And what if that variable could be tested for its influence just like the juror variable has been, particularly in focus groups (though some traditionally prescribed methods might need to be set aside to do so)?

Imagine a point above the line drawn earlier, and set this third variable up there between the lawyer variable on the left and the juror variable on the right. Add two more lines, forming a triangle, depicting the *three* most influential aspects of decision-maker experiences, with observable impact on judge and juror judgments. The maxim in physics and in communication theory is that the element in a system with the most flexibility tends to control or direct reactions within that system. Our triangle is an interacting system. And possibly the most flexible, most changeable, most reactive variable is the *case stories* themselves—the case as it is perceived and

---

11. In addition to the "if it's not working" aphorism, NLP also relied on the observation that "the map is not the territory," referring to individual representations of reality versus the real thing. That trials deal strictly with re-representations of reality should be no surprise to anyone who's ever seen and heard one.

12. Strier, *supra*, n. 6, at 101; and Neil and Dorit Kressel, *Stack and Sway: The New Science of Jury Consulting* (Cambridge, MA: Westview Press, 2002): 130–135.

processed by each decision maker. Among the lawyers, the jurors, and the stories, you may find that the facts and the applicable law are the most flexible variable of all. It may just turn out that what people try to see as "established" facts and law are actually far from that when it comes to both their presentation by lawyers and their assimilation by jurors.

Case Stories

What affects the forms they take for Jurors & Judges?

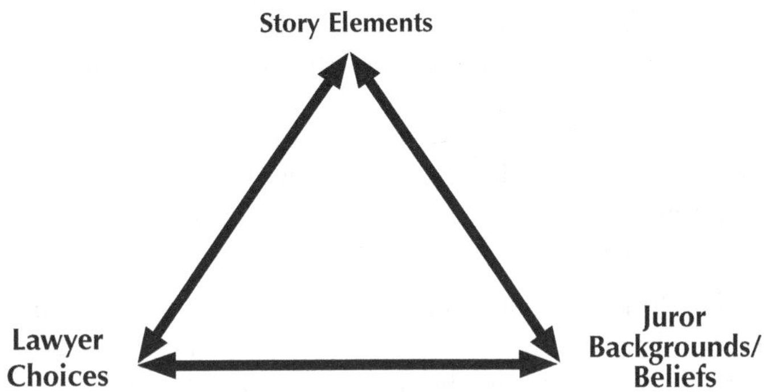

Figure 3

Most pretrial tests examine what a set of people think about what is assumed to be a predetermined case. What if the trial professional set out to more fully explore the whole range of stories each individual can build from a case? Instead of seeking out types of people, what if you were to seek out *types of stories* as the primary aim of the research, not just as evidence of juror category distinctions? As mentioned earlier, with this approach focus groups could tell the trial professional the answers to two critical questions:

1. What is this case story?
2. How would it best be presented to any listener?

If you start from the premise that there are two variables at play that strongly affect verdict formation—input from lawyer choices and juror backgrounds and attitudes—it is reasonable to try to put clamps on the first element and use research methodologies to objectively catalog the parameters of the latter. Just as it seems sensible to conclude that if decision-maker life experience and personal references make a difference in how they hear and see legal cases, then they should make *the* difference. Either/or.

Once case stories are introduced as a third, independent variable, the situation is no longer an equation where control can be exerted on one variable to test the limits of influence of the other. If the case story is truly variable and not fixed as most people like to presume, then there is a system of interacting parts at work among these three primary variables, not an either/or arrangement in which only the "or" side can provide answers on the value and strengths of a case. As radio personality Paul Harvey has said, this would be "the rest of the story."

How can a set of facts and points of law be so variable? By their very nature. The law and the facts in a case story have no independent, objectively fixed nature through which they are introduced to jurors in the box, mediators on a panel, or a judge on the bench. Even if a videotape of the event in question exists and is presented, which is a rarity, the actual events described by the facts of the case are not happening in court, they are being retold, recreated, or reiterated in written form. And the law that jurors and judges are asked to apply is by its nature conceptual, not objective, requiring jurors and other decision makers to provide uniquely personal meanings for every "reasonable," "preponderant," and "willful" in its text.

The facts and the law that make up every case story are not firsthand reality. They aren't even secondhand reality. They are third-hand versions, retold first to attorneys and then literally *re-presented* to the negotiating representative of the opposition, the mediators, or the judge and jury. That means that the third variable, the case story, is subject to unlimited, uncontrollable influence at each stage of the process that brings it to the ears and eyes of the decision makers. Behind the eyes of each decision maker, the case stories take on their own separate reality during the retelling, no two alike, and none fully predictable in the course it may follow.

The facts are distorted each time they move from one head to another in the discovery process, by both the vagaries of human communication, memory, and perception and by orders of the court regarding evidence. (The text a court reporter provides, of course, contains just the verbal referents for the facts, not the facts themselves, though many professionals keep remembering to forget this.) Expert opinions change and evolve over time, sometimes disappearing completely, but still leaving a trace in the way the story is carried on thereafter. And each witness whether live, on videotape, or entered by deposition, influences the nature of the facts by the many ways in which his presentation of those facts affects each listener's responses differently. None of this metamorphosing of fact perception and retention even begins to take into account the huge role of the first variable: lawyer input. Every part of the factual case is influenced by the choices a lawyer makes about inclusion, exploration, minimizing or emphasizing, visually supporting, verbally discounting, and even behaviorally (i.e., nonverbally) contradicting facts throughout the preparation and presentation of a client's case.

The law suffers from the same problems as the facts with regard to how variable this component of the case story truly is. The law is typically also a third-hand event in the minds of most decision makers. To appreciate even the simplest statutory direction, a normal human being first processes the general principle, ethic, or proscription involved, then tries to assimilate the specific language of the statute in its apparent meaning, and finally applies that personal appreciation, based on uniquely individual views, to the particular circumstances represented by the facts of the specific case. Each person does this just to understand the legal rules before applying them to the facts. And each person does this in a unique way, unreachable and uncontrollable by verbal or written direction from a lawyer, a court, or a professional researching juror attitudes, because the primary work is done outside of conscious control. Naturally, the more hardened biases about legal rules will be found among professional decision makers, if based on nothing but familiarity. But the blending of facts, perceptions, individual references, and legal concepts is a human part of the process, not subject to the roles those humans play. Legal professionals just dip into different pools of experience such as prior cases of the same general type, personal or third-party knowledge of the attorneys or firms, appellate hopes or fears, and the like, to do their private promoting of one story element over another.

The three primary variables are intertwined, reacting to and influencing each other. But the case story itself, the stack of facts and the legal rules to be applied to those facts, is a most potent variable in and of itself. The influence of the full scope and reach of the case story, and of the multiple shapes and forms it can and most likely will take, is a variable every bit as deserving as the other two of testing, scrutiny and appreciation by trial professionals hoping to rate and improve their chances of success. This is no less effective for success in mediation or negotiation than at trial. And that few people may have seriously looked at cases this way in the past makes it no less accurate.

The multiple case stories generated by jurors may be much more than evidence of measurable habits of thinking at work. Our emotional, behavioral, perceptual, and intellectual reactions could just as easily be proof of a story at work on us in sometimes very unaccustomed ways.

Let's look, for example, at a single fact taken from a single case story. In a focus group testing a case in which an electric company's stray power line burned down an unoccupied warehouse. The group was told during opening statements that the defendant company had already admitted liability and that their job was restricted to determining the true, fair value of the losses incurred in the fire. Another fact that was not in dispute was the time the fire burned: eight hours. Something that was very much in dispute, however, was the exact nature of the building's contents and how flammable they may have been. The group got an introduction to the process and their job, as well as to the law they would be applying. Each side was given just under ten minutes to provide a complete opening statement after which group members were individually surveyed in writing and then debriefed as a group by the moderator. Within the first few minutes of the debriefing, just after hearing both attorney's opening statements, one participant declared, "Well, it must have been really flammable, because it burned for a *solid eight hours.*" Less than two minutes later, another participant who sat facing the first acting as if he'd never heard the prior comment, said, "How flammable could it be? It took *eight hours* to burn."

Setting aside important considerations about expert testimony, input from fire departments and the like, as well as consideration of how "flammability" may be handled in the court's instructions, stop for a moment and consider what these two declarations about a single fact in this case story reveal about the third variable. Each person had just heard and seen both attorneys summarize their cases minutes before. Ostensibly, they had exactly the same input and based their responses on exactly the same messages about the case. Yet they each saw the same fact in exactly the opposite way from their colleague on the panel. Based on the older trial story, many people might be tempted to ask a question like, "What kind of person thinks of eight hours as solid, and what kind thinks of it as so slow?" Or perhaps they would like to know, "What percentage of people can I expect to see on a panel in this venue who are 'solid' thinkers, versus 'slow' ones?" Some might even go so far as to ask, "If I have a lot of 'solid' thinkers on my panel, what level of influence can I expect from that view, in the light of people who tend to think of corporations as strongly responsible for safety?"

Two questions might not be the first to jump to mind, but they could have a great deal to do with the huge range of possibilities that even a single fact holds in any case story, i.e., the third variable. The first question would be, "What were the focus group members asked that prompted their conflicting answers?" And the second would be, "What else did other people say?" The first answer is that they were asked, "What are your first impressions of the story you just heard?" The answer as to what other people said is little else about the flammability, and a lot about other things. As a focus of the case stories participants generated that day, "slow" and "solid" were not very important categories after all.

Knowing the presuppositions reinforced earlier in this chapter, it is not unlikely that many readers are now hurriedly rethinking the ways in which they had been figuring how to best identify "solid" and "slow" types. The "flammable" story was presented just now so that attention was likely to fix on that familiar either/or choice to engage life lessons that have encouraged and reinforced that mindset for many people. But this is a different approach, inviting professionals to ask in the future "What else is there?" more often than "Which is it?"

2.4 The Illusion of Control

The older trial story regarding influences on the outcome of a case is reflected in the first three "solid" and "slow" questions above, which deal with juror types. The question actually posed to the focus group, "What are your first impressions of the story you just heard?" heads in a somewhat different direction. If there are only two primary variables affecting a decision maker's responses, then one side, the lawyer variable can be controlled while the influence of proposed juror categories can be measured against the facts and law in the case. But if the facts and the law—the stories made up—are an independent variable in their own right, then acting as if they are not can prove very misleading. Our example of the two wildly opposed views of a single fact, in a single case, is just one illustration of how variable the case story will really get, once it's out of trial professionals' hands.

And that's just the start. Those who have worked to introduce material about decision-making research into the practice of lawyers trying cases deserve credit. The story model of juror judgment owes much of its existence to the research done on such factors as schemas, mental models, and all the other habits and patterns attributed to human decision making, developed over years of studying the judgment process. Likewise, there is a debt owed to those that have introduced the research on human learning and teaching, and how they apply to the development and delivery of case stories. What we know about how people do and how they don't learn plays a big part in appreciating the way case stories will be reauthored and reconstructed during the legal process. Categories, characteristics, and background still play significant roles. The myriad studies on these factors greatly contribute to the goals of trial professionals wanting to craft the most effective story for their listeners. However, the courtroom is not just a lab, a classroom, or a polling booth in the marketplace. And a legal case story is not just a stimulus, a lesson, or a measure of cause and effect.

From the moments before the case presentation begins, in voir dire or opening statements, there are factors at work on the case story behind the scenes in the mind of every listener. All these elements affect the eventual story structure, starting with the theme and moving through the others to provide the decision maker with a uniquely formed version from which a judgment will be drawn. Perceptions are an influence, whether of the story context and content, the messenger, or the message as it emerges in spoken, written, or visual forms. Personal references to literally thousands of life experiences—stored, reinforced, and then associated (or not) with the tale at hand by wholly other-than-conscious means—exert a massive influence on each individual case story. And finally, imagination in the form of the individual narrative drive—the scope, viewpoint, sequencing, and emphasis of one story element over another—will have its effect before anyone, including the owner, can consciously apprehend it. The theme comes from an appreciation of what this story is all about, not in any objective context, but in the context relevant to the mind dealing with it. It is that mind that will determine in which direction the story's fundamental meaning may lie, and that will point the rest of the listener's faculties in that direction, even if it goes against his or her character. One focus group member in a recent case, sounding nonplussed, said, "People who know me know I am never one to go along with what a doctor has to say—until now."

The following story illustrates how dangerous it can be for an attorney to ignore the fact that the stories jurors and judges build may very well have lives of their own:

> The case involved a plaintiff suing for injuries from the collision of his motorcycle with a school bus turning left in front of him at an intersection controlled only by a yellow caution light. In two short focus groups done primarily for educational purposes, the injured rider's attorney told the consultant, "I only want to test how jurors will value the damages in this case. I have no problems with liability. Though the injured plaintiff was not wearing a helmet in the crash, and jurors could find that a problem, I don't have that because the law in my venue excludes that fact from the case." One additional story fact might help in fully appreciating how much the impact of the third variable, the case story, could have on his client's chances of recovery at trial. Most of the severe injuries were to the rider's head.

The attorney in this situation felt himself reasonably entitled to ask for testing of how the juror variable was going to influence views of damages. And if the juror variable were the only one in play, then he ran no risks. But, obviously, the perception and processing of the omitted facts would pose a serious threat to the assumption that his case story had "no problems with liability." The question might then become, "Where do I put the focus: on the juror types, which may lead to stronger or weaker interest in the helmet, or on discovering the many ways in which the helmet itself (or its lack) can be perceived, distorted, and processed with the rest of the case story, regardless of what categories of thinkers are listening?" The situation in which an effort is made to exert greater control over the juror variable will often lead to even greater dispersion and unpredictability in the stories generated.

If the facts and the law were not a major variable, then the lawyer could be justified in presuming that jurors would not think about the helmet, either because no facts about it were presented or because the judge instructed them not to think about it, in accordance with the law. But assuming that human nature might make that kind of control over jurors' thoughts unlikely, he could still believe that the jurors' types of thinking, not the story itself, were the only significant variable. He might assume that facts are facts, the law is the law, and his case simply required him to test jurors' attitudes and beliefs against the helmet fact, even though it would not make a *formal* appearance in court, because it would emerge anyway. But how would that inquiry be controlled? What questions would you ask focus group or survey subjects? "How likely would you be to judge the case based on a fact you wouldn't be hearing, that he wasn't wearing a helmet?" Or what about, "On a scale of one to five, five being 'most likely' and one being 'never,' how likely would you be to ignore an instruction from the judge telling you to give no weight to the rider's failure to wear a helmet?" And how useful would the answers be, since they require speculation about processing that the jurors aren't really going to do and could not consciously control if they did?

Consider how many influences on the story itself can be gleaned from this very short example. In their discussion with jurors during voir dire and in their openings and questioning of witnesses, the lawyers will bump into the silent territory of the helmet over and over again. Is it hard to imagine the influence it could have on lawyer choices of how long to stay on certain subjects in discovery and at trial, how early or late in the story to bring up sections of the case, how to phrase questions to both friendly and opposition witnesses, and how to select language throughout the trial that will help all those other efforts? What about the judgments and choices the lawyer will be faced with when it comes to visual evidence and demonstrative aids? Even otherwise innocent questions such as "Which way was he *heading*" could cause distress for a lawyer acutely aware of the possibility of problems.

- And what about the jurors (and the judge)? What do they do with images they may generate of a rider with a helmet—or without one—while they await the details of that part of the story?
- How do they keep their minds off the obvious question, the longer it isn't answered? (How does one think of anything but blue when asked not to think about it?)
- How do they rein in speculation as to which side to attribute responsibility for what some may see as a pretty major, annoying omission?
- Will some discredit the court somewhat for the same reason? How do they fight those impulses?
- What about speculation on motives for keeping the fact out, regardless to whom the choice is attributed?
- How will jurors reconcile the rest of the story about the plaintiff's acts, aims, and claims in the light of their own imagined scenarios dealing with the meaning of the missing helmet?
- Will that processing be the same, somewhat different or completely different than it would be if the lack of a helmet were simply admitted up front?
- Who will even speculate about that quandary while trying to judge the facts according to the law?

Just as each individual person is not summed up by a collection of biases, beliefs, or background experiences, so a single case story is not encompassed by the list of witnesses, the statutes applied in verdict questions, or the transcript of the presentation. Some people will certainly display habits in their thinking, and categories in their experience, that can start the observant trial professional guessing about potential effects on the case stories those people might construct. For example, there are a certain number of people who, listening to almost any case story, are never likely to engage their imaginations beyond the basic story of a lawsuit being filed and tried as a sign of the system working. But even these limited constructs most often tell a tale of the system working badly.

Categories could just be the start of the inquiry, not its finish. To devote an honest effort to plumbing both the outer reaches and middle ground of the story territories that people's minds can devise with all their attendant tangents, distortions, and generalizations far beyond the scope of any legal matter, professionals may want to start approaching focus groups more like voir dire. That is, not only presenting parts of each side's case, but spending most of the time and resources inviting participants to bring all they have to bear on that beginning. In voir dire, it is improper to ask potential jurors which side they would prefer based on the revelation of a fact or two in a case yet to be officially opened. Instead, assuming cause strikes are the goal, venire people[13] are asked to fully explore their own experiences and related lessons as they may relate to the story they are about to hear, with a minimum of case facts—none if possible—being related at all. The case story topics would be engaged and expanded by each juror's own life references, not by inappropriately revealed facts from the case yet to be heard. Approaching focus groups in this way, as if asking participants about the case outcome before the end were an improper inquiry, might just reveal how much of the third variable people can give away, given half a chance.

Of course, the opposite would be true, too. Approaching *voir dire* a bit more as if it were a focus group could be very helpful. Rather than walking in assuming a known set of parameters, categories, and either/or types that the attorney must seek out and cull through, imagine how much more of the reach and shape of potential case stories could be revealed by acting as though the job were to walk into court and ask the venire people, just as in a focus group:

- What is this case story?
- How would it best be presented to any listener?

With *three* main variables affecting judgments in negotiations, mediation, and trials in the same way, the question serious trial professionals may want to ask is: "How safe it is to keep ignoring or minimizing the influence of the third variable when testing cases in focus groups, before stories are made up and judgments made?" The big question about the third variable could very well be: "Just how flammable can it be?"

---

13. The entire group of people called for jury duty and from which jurors are selected.

2.5 2015 Supplement

2.5.1 *Same as It Ever Was?*

Some things have remained just as they were long before this book was originally published in 2005—some trial professionals still wonder about the value of focus group work, that is:

> "Is what we're going to get from a focus group really worth the time, effort and money?"
>
> "Isn't a lot of what you're going to turn up what we—as the attorneys—already know?"
>
> "Aren't people just going to react the same way they always do?"
>
> "Isn't what you see and hear pretty much what you get?"
>
> "How much is going on below the surface, and how much can you hope to influence that anyway?"

For example, during preparation for a series of focus groups (sometimes referred to as "jury exercises" or "mock trials," though not by I) prior to a recent trial that would have nationwide repercussions for the client, one of the trial attorneys involved remarked:

> I disagree strongly that this is not about the lawyers. Of course one wants to develop good themes and arguments but real trials involve real lawyers and the lawyers make a difference. Some themes and arguments may be more powerful coming from certain people. And a lawyer must feel comfortable telling the story in his or her own voice. A jury exercise allows a trial lawyer to try out and test that voice. We all agree jury exercises do not predict results. They are meant to test themes and propositions and give the trial lawyers practice. [We've all] done many jury exercises, and there is no magic formula for these things. All exercises have their strengths and limitations and this one will be no different. [To suggest otherwise] is absurd.

The old, two-variable approach to understanding and appreciating juror[14] decision making clearly is still alive in this attorney's comments. Note that the decision-making world implied is still neatly divided into lawyer choices first and juror reactions after. The very idea that the case story itself could be (much less *is*) the most prolific element in the system is "absurd."

The danger of the two-variable approach is that it is actually limited to just *one* variable: the presumption being that juror reactions are predicated primarily

14. This applies in equal measure to all decision makers, no matter their professional background or the forum in which they will be working.

(if not entirely) on how an attorney chooses to "deliver the goods." Decision-maker reactions either will be prompted by the attorney's choices during delivery, or they won't. This "lock and key" metaphor still pervades much of the small group research being done on legal cases and, relying as it does on a rather overinflated view of the persuasive power of attorneys over decision makers, it bespeaks a condescending (never mind rather depressing) view of the decision-making potential of the "regular folks" that fill our venires on a daily basis. As NLP co-founder John Grinder used to say: "If you argue strongly enough for your limitations, you get to keep them."

The "lock and key" metaphor also supports the old approach to "typing" decision makers—whether the "whole person bias" version, or the relatively newer (though still in the "old approach" category) "case specific factor bias" version—and its discredited formula is still applied regularly by attorneys:

this type (of individual)

approached in *this way*

with *this type of story* (or portion thereof)

can be relied upon to react in *this way*.

But, once an individual's inherent creativity and imagination are allowed into this picture, there is a third variable that comes into play—that is, the effect of the case story itself in the decision-making arena. Because of its other-than-conscious nature, once "unleashed" into the equation, it is an unfixed and unpredictable variable taking on a life of its own separate from the decision maker's conscious intentions or efforts. What happens for each individual outside conscious awareness during the story (re)construction process dictates the shape of the stories used to decide the matter.

In a three-variable system, the kind of *control* imagined by those who wish to continue to work with just two is exposed as just that: "wishful thinking." While some trial professionals publically claim focus groups are "not rocket science," if they were willing to put in the effort required *and* at the level necessary, they'd find the truly effective ones aren't child's play either. Those willing to put in this kind of work preparing their case will be the ones to discover, develop, and ultimately deliver the strongest and most persuasive case stories.

If the variety and number of potential case stories being developed in each decision maker's imagination is as significant a factor as the attorney's choices and actions while delivering a story, *or* any decision maker's reactions to that multi-part process as it is happening, then the whole enterprise begins to look a lot more like "rocket science" and a lot less like child's play.

2.5.2 Persuaded Against Type

Let's take a closer look at how the old "typing" model would actually play out. Recall, earlier in this chapter, the comment made by the "nonplussed" focus group participant:

> People who know me, know I am never one to go along with what a doctor has to say—until now.

She had been participating in a group specifically aimed at supporting a mediation between a plaintiff patient's family and a well-respected local hospital. After the case stories were delivered by the attorneys—with periodic debriefs in lieu of deliberations—each participant was interviewed individually about their position on the case story and their perceptions of its value, if any. The "nonplussed" focus group participant went on:

> I'm saying I'd sign off on the $12 million verdict, but just this once. If they don't get the message and they make the same mistakes again, the sky's the limit!

This was after a morning during which a few times she proudly (and out loud) had "typed" herself as an older woman with a very conservative view against attacks on hospitals and corporations, and a tort reformer's view of plaintiff personal injury suits. The "doctor" of whom she said she would never be caught "taking him at his word" was an expert testifying on behalf of the plaintiffs. Prior to arranging the focus group, the plaintiff attorneys (who lived and regularly worked outside the venue) were repeatedly treated to defense attorney accounts of just this type of woman as the kind of potential juror in that venue who would "never vote for a multi-million dollar verdict against our local hospital"—and for supportive evidence they pointed to the fact that, indeed, no one ever had.

So, were the defense attorneys wrong to assume about the "types" of medical malpractice jurors who lived in that venue?

Was this older woman wrong when she identified herself as staunchly among that "type" and never likely to side with a doctor produced by a plaintiff's attorney?

Or does the most persuasive story, delivered in the most persuasive way help people of any potential "type" build their own versions in helpful ways—even if it means going "against type," just this once? Decision makers do not have to change their ideas, attitudes or beliefs for life—just in this case. Your job is to find the most persuasive invitation to encourage them to do it.

We all know that life experience is a profound teacher, yet efforts to "type" legal decision makers, far from creating accurate predictors, has only continued to demonstrate (particularly over the past decade or so) what a problem relying on demographic variables in a decision maker's background actually poses for attorneys. As often as not, it "backfires."

In the focus groups run to refine their *Reptile* model for case development, Keenan and Ball[15] found a certain percentage of previously "poisoned" tort reform participants could be counted on—with the proper persuasive approach—to not only vote "against type" but also to tenaciously stick to their unaccustomed guns throughout the focus group process. Additionally, they've publically recounted several attorneys' efforts at trial that bore out this same pattern.

So it was with the older woman in the medical negligence group because—she was not alone. The distribution of individuals across that group showed defense attorneys at the mediation that two-thirds to three-quarters of potential jurors in that "never gonna do it" venue actually were *very likely* to do it after all and do it against "type."

How so?

The stories participants generated for themselves, from those they were presented, overcame the prevailing attitudes they carried with them into the group. Apparently the majority of them saw stopping the hospital's negligent practices in this particular case as more important than *any* attitude they might have about lawsuits in general. A particular story can override general attitude.

Despite this kind of progress (which is well documented in the current annals of trial advocacy), I still am asked almost weekly, "Can you tell what *type* of jurors we'll want on our case?" Not long ago, an attorney I was working with spent a good deal of time telling me that, from her own experience with jurors and trials over the years primarily representing plaintiffs in workers' compensation and other personal injury cases, she'd come to the conclusion that women are never, ever good jurors for those kinds of cases, regardless of who the woman is (or even if the plaintiff was a woman).

In an appearance on *60 Minutes* in the mid-1980s, the late trial lawyer Harry Lipsig laid out the more conventional bias many attorneys have about women as jurors—linked to *other* women and their appearance:

> Women do not have the compassion for other women that men do. And, if I represent a woman, I fear the women on the jury. If she's good looking, they will hate her. And, if she's dashing, they will burn her at the stake!

Yet, when attorneys who've made a collection of such "types" to dread over the years are asked to "be more specific" as to these types, they all can tell you a story that proves the exact opposite—i.e., when they experienced a juror going against their supposed type.

The GM design engineer who decides against Ford in a product defect case.

The surgical nurse who decides against a doctor and hospital in a negligence case.

---

15. David Ball and Don Keenan, *Reptile: The 2009 Manual of the Plaintiff's Revolution* (Atlanta, GA: Balloon Press, 2009).

The human resources manager who decides against the defendant's HR department for their hiring and firing practices.

The white woman who decides in favor of the convicted felon caught carrying an illegal gun.

An experienced rock climber who decides for an injured iron worker who removed his own restraints before falling and getting injured.

The very factor that makes "typing" decision makers so tempting is also the very factor that proves it is a very dangerous game to play with client's lives. It is tempting to think one can draw a straight line of cause and effect between a set of demographic characteristics, a collection of life experiences and the knee-jerk reactions and judgments they are most likely to prompt—this is the heart of the impoverished "lock and key" view of persuasion with decision makers.

A part of the sample introduction to a focus group in Chapter Four reassures participants that not only are they not there to be "typed" as potentially "good" or "bad" jurors, but also to let them confirm for themselves how questionable that practice is, extending the reference to members of the military to make the point:

> Who here knows someone, close friend, family, or yourself, who has served or is serving in the military? Show of hands, please. That's seven . . . eight . . . nine total.
>
> Please keep your hands up.
>
> If your response to the following is that it's *not* true, you can put your hand down.
>
> *All* those people who have their hands up all voted the same way in the last presidential election, true?
>
> And, *all* of them are the same religion, true?
>
> And also, *all* are the same gender, true?
>
> Of course, the odds tell us that if we are looking at eight military members in a panel of forty-five potential jurors, then seven of those eight probably did vote the same way in the last election—for those who voted. But, knowing that doesn't necessarily tell me who any of the seven Republican voters may react to this case. For all we know, it's the eighth military juror who reacts more conservatively to parts of the case story than any of the other "conservative" types.
>
> That is why you are here and we are going through this exercise. People are too different to accurately predict what they've taken away from the life experiences they've had. People are more variable than a demographic formula can predict—and thank God for that.

> The only way you are going to find out what any particular individual may think or feel about a particular case story is to give them the story and talk with them about their reactions. Anything else is just guessing.

And, it's dangerously biased guessing at that.

Let's review the two-variable attorney's comments at the start of this supplement to Chapter Two. While that "typing" is more about "jury exercises" than about the "jurors" in them, the principle that dooms "typing" is the same. An individual's reactions to her own life experiences and the lessons she draws from them are too variable to know just by looking. For example, you can look at the eight military types in the venire, but until you talk to them you only "know" what you *think* you know about what's in their heads and hearts. Experience ends up teaching many lessons, too many to accurately predict by just looking at the person who learned them well before they met you.

So, if you think you know what "types" you are looking for to remove from future panels, think again. What we should be looking for is a human being who is ready to rebuild the client's case story in the best possible way for that client—and just because he may not look ready doesn't mean he isn't.

Chapter Three

In the Beginning

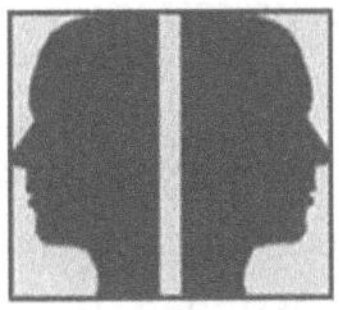

What a word is truth. Slippery, tricky, unreliable.
—*Lillian Hellman*

3.1 Roots of Story Growth

Since legal decision making in or out of court starts with stories "made up" by each party judging a case, volumes have been written about how we might construct these stories. Because the bulk of the process works outside conscious reach, speculation is the rule in these propositions, just as it is in the best focus groups. Research on decision making has developed models for appreciating the conscious/other than-conscious interplay that produces each private version of a case story. The research is worthwhile even though its target defies precise measurement or definition. We know that the story-building process happens, even if we can't be precise about exactly how. There are perhaps dozens or hundreds of stories/models that seek to determine how we might be building our individual stories of a matter put before us.

Alex Bavelas, for example, reportedly imagines a story-building model composed of four elements:

1. Behaviors
2. Procedures
3. Interpretations
4. Puzzles[1]

1. Karl E. Weick, *The Social Psychology of Organizing* (New York: McGraw-Hill, 1979).

He envisions a part of the mind approaching a slice of someone's life story as if it were a puzzle to be solved by observing and appreciating three factors:

1. The stuff people do (behaviors)
2. The accepted ways of doing that stuff (procedures)
3. The various possible interpretations of how stuff can be fit together in the current case

Bavelas proposes that we solve the puzzle by attempting to connect the various behaviors, procedures, and interpretations. Similarly, Bruner and Amsterdam might suggest that once the categories are assigned, the narrative can begin so that rhetoric can be used to justify the perceived conclusions of any listener.

Linguist Charles Fillmore sees a single sentence as the shortest form a story can take. He suggests this as the smallest, simplest, and archetypical example of a story, expressing interpreted connections among a subject, object, and related action. As more such sentences are generated about the inner version of the case story, more complete answers will likely emerge as to which behaviors should receive the most attention, which procedures prove the most important, and which interpretations are the most trustworthy. A subjective story built by any decision maker to reconstruct the one offered in court, mediation, or negotiation will ring true for its creator in all four of Bavelas's categories. Many students of rhetoric, such as Charles Faulkner, who steered me to this particular story-about-stories, would also suggest that:

> The very form of the individual sentences being used begins to create an effect on the listener, [and] when these rhetorical devices and the greater narrative are in concert, it is often termed art or at the least a compelling story.

3.2 Limitless Possibilities

There's the rub for the trial professional attempting to adjust legal presentations to the needs of a listener's story-making process. How *does* one go about making the "greater narrative" and the rhetoric used to deliver it work "in concert" for whoever is going to be hearing and deciding the next case story? The answer may lie in avoiding the powerful temptation to prematurely limit the many possibilities in even the simplest case story. The task gets easier once one gets used to thinking of decision-maker case stories as independent variables constructed from a huge range of possible story formulations instead of a fixed stack of facts and laws. If it helps to have a speculative model for how people may be starting their own stories about the case, the three above have much to recommend them. To act as if the process isn't happening, that the case stories themselves don't have lives of their own between the ears of every decision maker, and that those stories are far from fixed but are the most variable element among the three (presenter choices and acts, backgrounds of the jurors or judges, and the case stories) will achieve little more than a false sense of control.

When an attorney seeks the most compelling theme, scope, point of view, sequence, and all other components of a compelling case story from a focus group, a good start can be made by keeping in mind an updated model for case stories such as that suggested in Chapter Two, section 2.2, "Familiar Ground." Consistently expecting people to build independent stories and not just interpret a fixed set of predetermined facts and legal guidelines can quickly draw professionals to more expansive, inclusive approaches, rather than to reductive, limiting ones.

Instead of rushing to reduce input from each focus group member to a single conclusion about which side is winning the point, or to an either/or response between fixed choices (i.e., burning slow or fast? healthcare as consumer or parent?), professionals can be more open to the unexpected: the many ways participants can find significance where there seemed to be none or insignificance where obvious truth seemed to reside. You may be tempted to credit each person's imagination as much as the thinking, perceptions, emotional reactions, memories, and attendant beliefs it moves in unexpected directions, sometimes even against type and trends. You may soon discover that each person has more than one version of the client's story from which she can decide the case. Soon, each potential juror and each focus group participant may start looking not like the "type of person" that has one type of story to tell, but rather like someone that can build any number of possible versions of the client's story, some helpful, some not so, and maybe one that is quite compelling indeed.

By respecting all three major variables, trial professionals may discover that there is no right answer to the question, "Which of the three is the most influential variable affecting the construction of decision-maker case stories?" However, while the possible story versions may have many permutations, the outcome of the legal issue—whichever stories are built and used to judge it—is almost always an either/or proposition. Thus, at any given time, with any given judge, juror, mediator, or negotiator, any one of the three key variables could end up being the one that makes the difference. Devoting all the effort of preparing a case presentation to only one or two of those variables could be a very costly mistake. The lives of the stories themselves require at least equal consideration.

The Case Story

What affects its adoption the most?

☑ Decision-Maker Attitudes or Biases

☑ The Case Story Itself

☑ Perceptions of the Messenger and Court Environment

Since the decision is "Yes" or "No", *any* factor can be the most important with any given decision-maker, at any given time.

Figure 4

3.3 Common Bias, Experience, and Sense

To reveal the full range of potential stories a case can generate, the most useful habit to develop for voir dire and focus groups is to constantly recall that nobody can completely realize the process involved in story building. Most of the process happens before we are conscious of it. This is so challenging. Decades of research and trial work have relied on the unproven assumption that people can have access to their whole thinking process for the asking. An additional impediment is the habit of distorted thinking that most of us adopt when we hold a bias common to that held by the majority. People who hold a majority bias often don't see themselves as biased; they just see themselves as *right*.

The older, commonly accepted version of trial case stories is that there can only be one story per case, interpreted either well or badly by the decision makers, but never authored by them. It often takes breaking new ground through action to be able to recognize limits on thinking that were there all along. Einstein reportedly said: "The significant problems we face cannot be solved at the same level of thinking we were at when we created them." Yet, often it is only with the benefit of hindsight that our thinking catches up to the reality of our actions and their results. Attorneys who improve beyond the typical fifty-fifty performance standard in identifying credibility cling to distorted perceptions of their effectiveness until after they have done something to improve it. Building new thinking habits is easier than breaking old ones, but neither is really easy. Simple, yes. Easy, no.

3.4 The "Right" Way To Drive

The more integrated a perception or impression is in our life story, the *less* likely it is to be consciously noticed for its true level of influence on our thoughts, attitudes, acts, and feelings. Just as people can be blind to the real extent of a common bias, the influence of shared common experiences can prove quite strong in its effects on decision-maker stories long before these experiences ever make themselves realized. In legal cases, one example of integrated life experiences and attendant stories about their meanings crops up whenever the case deals with the "right" way to drive in traffic. Most people that drive see themselves as pretty good to very good drivers. They think this with little sense about the context for their beliefs, and many times despite a list of admitted weaknesses in their driving skills. If a person has had few or no collisions or other poor outcomes on the road, their personal context for judging their knowledge of, adherence to, and actual abilities to follow the rules of the road can often be quite distorted.

Jurors whose only life experience with anesthesia involves themselves or their loved ones going to sleep and waking up when it was all over can talk easily about inherent risks. However, the real threat those risks pose play little or no role in their inner minds, where case stories that lead to final judgments are created. It is the same with the stories jurors, judges, and other decision makers start to build about driving when their own subjective framework is free of the burden of a more dangerous, realistic perspective.[2] Modern trends in legal rulings that affect selection criteria for jurors and judges tend to suggest that ignorance of the case context improves objectivity. Often it can do the exact opposite.[3]

Experience will influence the context in which case stories are built for all decision makers. But having a common experience such as driving can produce a very objective or distorted context, just as the absence of driving experience can. One non-driver may not be a driver's best judge, but the next might. The way to find out is to discover what happens when their habits of thinking are exposed and alternative associations are presented. Again, any work dealing with the interface of the dynamic between conscious and unconscious processes is about the individual mind, rarely about a type. Exploratory efforts need to rely as much on implication and inference as on conscious self-reporting.

---

2. Very often, newer trial attorneys, with the least experience, perceive themselves as needing the least help in their preparation and presentation of cases. Alternatively, many civil plaintiff attorneys fear older people, who hold what is referred to as enriched experience, because they could be prone to folding one more story into their great pool of prior experience and jumping to a snap conclusion about its meaning before fully engaging the case story. That is, the same response for opposite reasons: stories built on either impoverished or enriched experience creating snap judgments.
3. For a full discussion of this presumption and how it inadvertently became a standard in American jurisprudence, see Jeffrey Abrahamson, *We, the Jury: The Jury System and the Ideal of Democracy* (New York: Basic Books, 1994).

When decision-maker learning about an unfamiliar road rule or standard is essential to the job of determining the truth of the evidence facts, and their perceived expertise might contradict that rule, the risk should be clear to both civil and criminal attorneys presenting to the group. When confronting a stated standard or rule of law that contradicts the world as it has always been imagined, the listeners' minds will start to work on the rule. This effort will not be conscious.

The three most prolific functions of our perceptual apparatus in such a situation are our abilities to:

1. Distort
2. Generalize
3. Delete information from the mix in our story-building process[4]

We will unthinkingly change, override, or "remember to forget" the conscious message so at odds with our unconscious life stories about driving. The profound effect on the case story based on a common bias about driving "expertise" and common driving experiences, can be nearly impossible for a listener to track whether asked to try or not. Since the beliefs are integrated in "driving according to me," the person is much less likely to realize that he made such a move at all. Because of the commonplace nature of this widespread thinking habit and its familiarity to the driver judging the case, the presenter of the case story should find a way to expose and reframe it before plunging the client's future into machinery in which the public, conscious contradiction almost always loses out to private, unconscious conventions. Conscious ignorance of the factual context might improve objectivity. But ignorance of other-than-conscious influences on story formation can completely negate any hope for it.

One way to interrupt this automated process just long enough to make a suggestion or two comes during questioning during voir dire. The questions can also be adapted for use during the equivalent period of discussion with potential neutrals or negotiators from the opposing side(s).

In either a focus group or voir dire, questioning might take the following form:

> Ladies and gentlemen, by a show of hands only, every person that drives any kind of vehicle regularly, please show me how many of you are willing to admit right here in front of everyone that you're a very, very, poor driver—a really bad driver? How many? [*Few to none is typical.*]

4. Joseph O'Connor and John Seymour, *Introducing NLP: Psychological Skills for Understanding and Influencing People* (New York: Harper Collins, 1993).

> Well, now, that's very interesting. Let me see if I can go at it another way. How many of you that drive know someone else that's a really bad driver? That many, huh?
>
> OK. Here's the last round, and I need you to be completely, brutally honest with us on this question, all right? If the persons you just had your hands in the air about—the ones you say are really poor drivers—were sitting here, how many of them would have had their hands in the air, only talking about you? They'd be pointing at you just like you were pointing at them?
>
> OK, while the laughter dies down, what have we learned here? Is it possible, just possible, that the way we see ourselves and the way we look at other people when it comes to something like driving may not be altogether the most unbiased, fair, and neutral subject in the whole world? Is that possible?
>
> [*When you get sufficient agreement, with or without attendant discussion, proceed to insert the following suggestion while the pattern is fully conscious, available, and most open to outside input.*]
>
> It's just not possible that everyone here is a really great driver that knows a really crummy driver, but when the tables are turned and we ask the supposedly crummy drivers, they all turn out to be the great ones and you're the poor ones. That just can't be, can it?
>
> Rather than fighting to be right, which is not really part of the best juror's job description, who here would be willing to put a question mark in front of whatever may have felt right to you about the right way to drive until this moment, here in this room today, just long enough to get curious about what the law/rules/official standards might say—those that the court will ask you to apply to your job here? Is everyone willing to try that? Who can tell me right now that he or she is not so sure you can do that? How so? Please say a little more.

Research and actual practice have developed many different models to describe the various functions of the story-building process that decision makers go through to judge a legal matter. They will be introduced later in the chapter. The theme suggested here for trial professionals to maintain when eliciting parts of that process out loud, is *expansion and inclusion* as opposed to *reduction and limitation.* The suggested action to use in pursuit of the many possible stories being formed is invitation, rather than instruction.

It is worth examining how the habit of thinking about driving is first brought out, then interrupted, and finally invited to expand by including other associations. The listeners are never directly told to reject or consciously try to eliminate a thought from their heads. Of course, that would be impossible. Asking someone to consciously overrule or wipe out a thought that they never consciously generated suggests to the listener not to expect anything of value to come out of your mouth anymore. People cannot consciously control unconscious thinking habits, regardless of whether they are aware of them.[5] So isolating unconsciously formed and maintained associations, only to instruct a person or group to stop using them, will fail in most cases and often make things worse because of the reinforcement the conscious attention creates. (*"Do not think of blue. If you think of blue, something awful will happen to you and yours. So don't even think about thinking of blue."*)

Look at the first two lines of the driving discussion's last paragraph, delivered after everyone has had a chance to produce, laugh at, and consciously acknowledge the possibility of the "punch line" of their own hidden bias about driving abilities:

> It's just not possible that everyone here is a really great driver that knows a really crummy driver, but when the tables are turned and we ask the supposedly crummy drivers, they all turn out to be the great ones and you're the poor ones. That just can't be, can it?

3.4.1 Attribution

There are several story-building factors and functions mentioned and/or utilized indirectly here. The first is the mental processing habit called "attribution" or the assignment of control or active-party status in a story by the decision maker. The entire discussion is focused on attributing abilities in driving to self and others. We asked them who they personally know is a bad driver, not to consciously assign that status, though some will certainly do so anyway, to join in. Most will have already attributed the skill—or lack thereof—in their own life stories, and will automatically draw from those unconsciously formed associations.

3.4.2 Availability or Norming

In utilizing the abilities of listeners to attribute good or bad driving to people in their lives, along with themselves, and then making that selection process more conscious, we move to another mental processing factor called "availability" or a variant called "norming." The question-and-answer discussion leading up to the suggestion paragraph at the end works as an invitation to the listeners to make this particular habit in their thinking more available to their conscious attention than it was minutes before. For many, this more-available arrangement of assumptions also suggests the "normal" way of their inner worlds.

---

5. This is a salient fact ignored by the judiciary in even the most progressive jury reforms being tested and put in place across the country. Plain English instructions, delivered in an exclusive and impossible-to-do fashion, are just as bad as the incomprehensible instructions currently being delivered in the same way by judges across the land.

3.4.3 Repetition, Reflection, and Reinforcement

When we repeat the conclusion or "punch line" of the inquiry in the first line of the suggestion paragraph, we start to use some psychological processing factors to deliver our invitation to the group. Among those factors are repetition, reflection, and reinforcement. The rhetorical question, "That just can't be, can it?" gives people a chance to openly acknowledge and identify with their own thinking habit just opened up for consideration, and to repeat its parameters to themselves as a question, one more time.[6] Now they are focused on their unthinking, but very real bias, and the lifetime of experience associated with it. Note how the examiner in our sample voir dire or focus group proceeds:

> Rather than fighting to be right, which is not really part of the best juror's job description, who here would be willing to put a question mark in front of whatever may have felt right to you about the right way to drive until this moment, here in this room today, just long enough to get curious about what the law/rules/official standards might say, those that the court will ask you to apply to your job here?"

3.5 Indirect Inclusion and Expansion

Here is where the theme of inclusion and expansion is served. Instead of doing the expected and leaving the thinking habit isolated while trying to get conscious agreement to refuse indulging in it anymore, we immediately invite the listeners to place two more topics on their plates, about which they also likely have strong, long-standing associations: defending perceptions of right and wrong and the job a "good" juror has to do.

The word "right" is deliberately offered to all as an ambiguous anchor[7] for all three versions of what was or is right for each listener about driving, juror jobs, and their sense of right and wrong itself. To do this well, it's best to introduce a certain vagueness as to just which "right" thing we are referring at any given moment. This makes the newly suggested associations a little more available to the listeners, just as their perceived driving expertise was, by itself, moments before. The feeling of being right about driving is all that anyone can consciously experience of an embedded

6. Questions asked rhetorically can often engage far more effectively than declarations, simply because the listeners have the chance to participate actively in both the query and certainly in their private response. Even if they don't speak their answers aloud, members of a group will still nonverbally advertise when their answers match or mismatch that of the majority of their partners in the group.

7. "Anchoring"—conditional reinforcement of certain associations, views, or feelings with certain verbal or visual cues—is a popular and effective tool for any public speaker, particularly for trial lawyers and consultants working with focus groups and jurors. See Chapters Four and Five for more specific examples of the use of anchors in the story-eliciting and story-delivering processes. *See also* Paul Lisnek and Eric Oliver, *Courtroom Power: Communication Strategies for Trial Lawyers* (Colorado Springs, CO: Professional Education Systems Institute, 2001).

bias such as the one just exposed when it is actually at work behind the scenes. That feeling, should it be noticed now or later during deliberations, is also offered as a kinesthetic anchor to remind jurors or group participants of what we've invited them to do with their old thinking habit:

> . . . for this moment, in this room today, just long enough to get curious . . .

That is, to "put a question mark" in front of it, not to set it completely aside and guarantee the court, the lawyers, and God that it will play no part whatsoever in your thinking about this case at all. Inclusion and expansion. Not reduction and limitation.

We give everyone a chance to publicly and physically identify with taking the suggestion and we include the option that they may opt out of the invitation:

> Is everyone willing to try that? Who can tell me right now that you're not so sure you can do that? How so? Please say a little more.

3.6 Presupposition

Note, we do not accuse the person of being unwilling to consciously choose to follow our invitation. We rather presume by the form of the final question that they are indeed willing, but may somehow be inhibited in their aim. This element of presupposition is yet another means of reinforcing one connection over another, without consciously demanding that either be excluded by the party inside whose head both options reside.

Common experiences can be associated with common and unthinking bias that are so well integrated that without outside help, we may entirely miss their effects on the stories we create. The opposite is also true when a subject area is utterly lacking in a decision maker's direct life experience—for example, skiing, reading a construction contract, or flying a helicopter. When story makers have no common experiences to reference in "making up" their versions of the case story, they do not stop making things up. Instead, they rely more on associations and connections far outside of conscious control to build their stories, and the distortion, generalization, and deletion begin in earnest. "I get the impression he was skiing too fast," "Those kids always go too fast on those skis," or "I don't recall them saying anything about skiers having a code to follow."

Always keep in mind that it is the stories constructed from the facts and the law, not the facts themselves, that determine the ultimate decision. So getting in at the beginning of the listener's story-building process, as much as that is possible, is critical then to finding what any client's story really is to decision makers, and how best to present it to others.

So if the bulk of the story-making process is not consciously available to the decision maker, how does she show the trial professional the lay of the internal land? As Bruner and Amsterdam say, by the categories, narrative, and rhetoric used to express how the story that originates outside their conscious reach. As Bavelas says, the puzzle is perceived to fit together. As Fillmore says, each sentence reveals the story. It can help to consider that each sentence, when focused on the subject at hand, is all about the story forming outside conscious reach, regardless of whether we know or choose to acknowledge it. Our implicit memories produce implicit suggestions in the stories they generate about the case stories we see and hear. By using focus groups more as voir dire than as a lab experiment, attorneys learn to pursue more possible permutations of a single aspect of any given story with any given participant, instead of taking any one answer as the whole story. What is said about the process and what is implied beyond the words is available for the professional to consider.

3.7 Getting Groups into Focus

If deciding cases is all about the stories being built outside conscious awareness and each person builds their own version, then what value is there in gathering a group of individuals together to consciously talk about their unconscious processing? Indeed, I received several unsolicited copies from trial attorneys across the country of a Slate article apparently asking that very question.[8] In posing the question, the article cites a couple of respected researchers telling consumer product makers and service providers that customers don't really know what they want. In fact, they are often inclined to lie about it in a focus group. They are said to lie because the questions are asked outside the actual buying context, because their motives for participation don't incline them toward open, honest responses, and due to placating or ingratiating responses offered to please the moderator or the imagined sponsor of the group.

To control for variables in the old, two-variable model, most of these concerns would have to be fixed on the side of attorney/presenter choices and delivery rather than on the side of participants' backgrounds and their attendant stories about life's meanings. If you approach a focus group on a legal matter as if all three major variables affecting story construction are at work and control is out of reach, then you might have enough spare time and energy to ask how these supposedly negative factors differ substantially from those affecting virtually every juror or decision maker.

- Aren't they all there because of outside impetus or pressure, whether they need the money, human contact, to answer a subpoena, or do their job?
- Aren't they all dependent on the presenters to get their job done?

8. Daniel Gross, "Lies, Damn Lies and Focus Groups: Why Don't Consumers Tell the Truth about What They Want?" *Slate*, October 10, 2003, http://slate.msn.com/ (posted 3:29 p.m. PST).

- Being human, aren't they all likely to form positive or negative associations with the presenter(s)?
- Aren't they all prone to speculate about larger, ulterior, unknown motives, factors, and forces beyond those being presented?
- Do they not all make every decision and choice based on a process that begins outside conscious awareness, not knowing how they end up knowing what they think they want?

So far, that doesn't sound so different as to disqualify focus group members from hearing, seeing, and reacting to a legal case story much as jurors or professional decision makers will.

What about when matters get serious? Won't these focus group strangers play poker, hide their full reactions, and offer distorted versions of their own thinking in a hundred different ways?

Some researchers suggest that presenters leading the group would have to invest huge amounts of time "building trust" to make participants feel comfortable expressing "heartfelt, brutally honest opinions," or else the respondents would simply censor their answers, giving incomplete, politically correct, or even false responses. Again, if this were all about measurable, repeatable material as in a lab or classroom, these concerns might be valid ones. But in court, mediation, and negotiation, how often are hours devoted to building trust, followed by floodgates parting to let the heartfelt confessions flow through? Professional decision makers are even less likely to meet this open-heart criteria, since most believe that doing their job well requires a clinical distance from the parties and an effort to maintain a professional reserve, consciously trying not to react to the presenters at all.

The Slate article's writer quotes author Gerald Zaltman, who delivers the big blow against focus groups: the other-than-conscious mind. In discussing the reputed industry standard, eighty percent failure rate of focus groups to predict success for cars, movies, or TV ads, he says:

> Contrary to conventional wisdom, they [groups] are not effective when developing and evaluating new product ideas, testing ads, or evaluating brand images. . . . Standard questioning can sometimes reveal consumers' thinking about familiar goods and services if those thoughts and feelings are readily accessible and easily articulated. . . . [But] most of the thoughts and feelings that influence consumers' and managers' behavior occur in the unconscious mind. . . . *Unconscious thoughts are the most accurate predictors of what people will actually do.* In the space of five or ten minutes in a focus group, which is the average air time per person, you can't possibly get at one person's unconscious thinking.

And so you have it. Two different sets of researchers condemning the focus group research method their colleagues use for pretty much the same reasons. To paraphrase: "You don't have enough time to find out what thoughts they really have behind the scenes."

What is the common story behind this sentence? What are the implied suggestions about the process of evaluating thinking in each of the critics' world models, as reflected by this "shortest of stories"?

- Unconscious thoughts can be separate entities from conscious thoughts.
- Unconscious thoughts drive our responses, while conscious ones comment on them, sometimes badly.
- Unconscious thoughts are the most accurate predictors of what people will actually do.
- Given enough time, you can hear someone's unconscious thoughts just by asking for them.
- You can "pull out" someone's unconscious thinking, but it takes a lot of time.
- There is only one set of "thinking" per customer.

I earlier suggested five presumptions about the processes at work in legal decision makers' minds:

1. *Many Stories*—not one story. Each person builds her own and has many at her disposal along the way.
2. *Inviting*—not inserting. Less direct, less declarative means are the most productive in influencing early story building, as well as in eliciting it.
3. *Inferring*—not explaining. When exploring how decision makers are responding to or re-presenting a case story, inference is what is best relied on in both listener description and presenter delivery.
4. *Beginnings*—before conclusions. The earliest process is the most important one to reach, and to attempt to recognize as it works.
5. *Story Elements*—over story typing. You can't "pull out" the one type of story or one "type" of person that "thinks that way," because there isn't only one there.

When eliciting how people are reacting to the presentation of a case story in a focus group, it is important to respect another well-accepted, widely ignored fact about the process: it isn't totally conscious and it is not consciously controlled. Decision makers do not consciously select the life references and meanings to be associated with each aspect of the client's case story. To assume they do will prompt questions they can't honestly answer and you can't fully trust. For example, a question like, "Why is that the strongest fact in the evidence you've heard for the defendant company?" presupposes full access to the process that created the leaning. The respondent is assumed to know all the references that could have been engaged, as well as the other-than-conscious selection process detailing how they were engaged. Neither of these assumptions is true.

A focus group run more like a voir dire session is what is needed to respect the way we know minds work. Questions asked to participants are not closed-ended or exclusive, but open-ended, inclusive questions about how they are perceiving each story element in their own context, not the context of the desired trial result. Not coincidentally, this generalized implication-rich approach is also the best one for beginning the actual case presentation.

3.8 The "Problem" with Focus Groups

The problem with focus groups has nothing to do with the nature of the minds at the table receiving the presentation of case stories from the various parties. The "problem" lies with moderators who ask questions of one part of the mind, expecting answers from the other. Each one plays by entirely different rules. It is also represented by researchers who deny that any valuable information can be gleaned about juror or judge story building until the brain learns to answer the questions the way the research format requires them to be asked: closed-ended with one or two choices and ranked on a scale from one to five. All in under ten minutes each.

As in cross-examination or deposition of opposition witnesses, when an attorney blames a witness, it is often the question that turns out not to be responsive to the prior answer. It appears that many researchers are blaming their subjects for their own inadequate methods of eliciting information. If participants can't answer a conscious, verbal question about an unconscious, nonverbal process (we already know they can't), then where else can you look for the response? Participants, jurors, negotiators, and judges all carry both parts of their minds with them at all times. When they go into their other-than-conscious thinking, they are not leaving the Earth's orbit. Both parts, conscious and otherwise, are active at all times a person is awake and responding to your questions.

The real question in determining the value of the discussion in a focus group may be: "Just how hard are you willing to look for the implied suggestions that reveal the implicit memories forming the story each person is about to use to judge your client's case? And what will you do when you find them?"

I once watched three attorneys deliver short opening statements in a civil case involving a couple that was out drinking in two bars through the night. They left the last bar at closing time.[9] Shortly thereafter, the driver wrecked the car, seriously

9. Names and some details have been changed, but the discussion is reported accurately.

injuring the by-then unconscious woman passenger. Along with the driver, both establishments were being sued for serving someone already intoxicated. At the end of the opening statements, the participants all filled out a short questionnaire that did not ask them their position toward the case, nor to rate the strength or weakness of any of the three sides so far. Then I stood up and asked everyone, in an unpredictable order:

> What are your first impressions of the stories you just heard?

Participants had previously talked about what "impressions" can include: attitudes, ideas, emotional reactions, and especially reminders of previous experiences from their own lives that seem to relate or just pop up unexpectedly.

One woman, pointing to the plaintiff attorney and calling him by name said:

> I was insulted by Mr. Manning. He said in his opening statement that it didn't matter if the driver himself was drunk. He said it was the same as ignorance of the law being an excuse. I found that insulting.

Her response prompts questions.

- While it is true that she has not and cannot provide us with a guided tour of her inner mental workings, is it really true that nothing of value can be inferred about the structure of the story she has begun building?
- For instance, is it a big stretch to imagine that the active party in the process she's engaged in so far is not any of the characters in the case story, but the plaintiff lawyer himself?
- From which point of view are the observations being made that she finds so "insulting," if not from the perspective of the drunk and apparently unrepentant driver?
- What is apparent about the scope of the story she is building? Is it dealing with everything that happened before, during, and after the event, or is it concentrating more heavily on the "after territory" to draw its meaning?
- Can anything be inferred about where in the sequence of the story she figures the driver ought to appear in relation to the two bars and their management or owners?
- Are we left clueless about what type of theme underlies the story she is starting to tell herself? Can we say with some confidence that whatever words she might use to express it—if she could— might have a lot to do with her suspicion of the system?

I wanted to find out, so I followed up by asking her how she had gotten the message that he was declaring that already being drunk was OK under these circumstances. She responded:

> Because he said it. He said, "Just because he was drunk . . ." he didn't . . . no, that he doesn't ". . . that just because you are drunk you *don't* abdicate your responsibility."

Rather than correcting her mistaken interpretation of her accurate restatement of the attorney's line, I asked her:

> *How so?*
>
> Because the way he said it, it was the same as if he were saying that ignorance of the law is . . . OK . . . is . . .
>
> *An excuse?* I asked.
>
> Yes. He was saying that being drunk didn't matter. "You *don't* abdicate your responsibility just because you are drunk." Same as ignorance of the law. I found that very insulting, because I believe it does matter, and ignorance of the law is no excuse.

Despite the researchers' claim that this woman would never be able to be brutally honest without hours of trust building on my part,[10] I wanted to keep a part of her mind open to other story lines for the next six or seven hours, before it was too late. Much like the experienced drivers looking at facts about traffic, here was a person who seemed to imagine that she had some expertise in the civil-injury lawsuit arena. She was not about to let herself get fooled about what was "right" with regard to suing. I wanted to interrupt the pattern and offer a new suggestion, without condemning her pattern or making her account for an other-than-conscious distortion in front of everyone, with only her conscious, verbal facilities available to use in forming an answer. We had all previously discussed the need for jurors to test disputed recall of the evidence against that of their fellows. ("If you are the only one out of seven who heard it or saw it that way, you may want to give up on your version.")

I turned to the whole group and asked [*note that I do not ask who agrees or disagrees*]:

> Who else had a similar reaction to that part of what the plaintiff lawyer said?

Several people suggested that they had heard him saying the driver still had responsibility. Being drunk was not an excuse. Out of politeness, group solidarity, conflict avoidance, or some other private plot line about potential mindsets, nobody openly told this woman she was wrong.

---

10. By that point, we had been there about an hour and fifteen minutes, it was her first chance to speak after the openings, and the attorney who "insulted" her was sitting right in front of her the whole time.

All that was left for me to do was raise the bar by invoking the higher criteria of the job they came to do, over the less critical job of hearing every word "just so." In generic, third-person terms, I repeated the agreement we'd all made to subordinate what we thought we saw or heard to any unanimous, differing version that the rest of group remembered. Nearing the end of the admonition she'd already heard and not directly addressing her, I looked her way as I ended with:

> . . . [You] may have to give up yours.

Without speaking, she nodded. Later she did "give it up" enough to focus her attention on other aspects of the story she was deciding.

One of the challenges of eliciting and delivering stories is that you are always going to be reinforcing something. And as this influence and reinforcement are produced, every part of your demeanor is in play as much or more than your words' meanings. An almost sure-fire way of reinforcing a reaction or connection a listener has built in his own mind is to consciously challenge it. Remember, it is at the intersection of conscious and other-than-conscious processing that your toughest choices need to be recalled and reinforced, and foremost among them is choosing not to demand conscious awareness of processes and story formulations that are out of conscious reach.

Could I have insisted she heard him right and interpreted him wrong? Yes. Did most everyone else in the room know this by now? Yes. So what positive purpose would be served for her, the group, or the attorney sponsoring the inquiry? Because she made her connections unconsciously, she does not know how they came about, nor how to correct that process. But she would certainly know how to feel very uncomfortable about that, and how to paste that discomfort to my face, were I to expose her in public. Instead, again, I made an effort to expand the subjects on her plate beyond the "insult," to include the job she was doing, the group's efforts, and her prior choices and commitments already made as a member of the group. Then I suggested they all (not just her) recommit to the group's perspective on the story over their own. Nonverbally, I just checked in with her at the end to see if she was paying attention to all the items included on the plate and she did seem to be.

Always remind yourself that for the purposes served in a focus group or voir dire, the answer, "This is how I always dress," to the question, "Is your appearance here subject to a subpoena?" *is* the right answer. The next question is what else do you want to learn about that answer?

3.9 How We Build Our Stories

The question is not whether there are stories building behind the eyes and between the ears of every person witnessing the case presentation. The question is how best to elicit all the possible story lines for each person before they settle on a finished product. Focus group critics confirm that assuming unconscious material can be elicited by conscious means alone won't work. We know that assuming there is only one fixed story per person doesn't help either. Neither does imagining a fixed and predetermined case story spoken for by the facts alone. It helps to recognize that any method used to explore people's stories, whether in a group or individually, written or spoken, instantly become part of the process and not a neutral, clinical measurement with no effect. That kind of imagined "control" slips away as soon as the case stories are recognized as the third, independent variable affecting decisions that they are.

The single-sentence summary of the focus group critique above ("You don't have enough time to find out what thoughts they really have behind the scenes"), and the story lying beyond the distorted opening statement sentence stored in the woman's head, offer two examples of how to infer certain story line structures, even the main story elements of theme, point of view, scope, sequence, active party, and more. Both highlight one way of imagining how the story-building process works outside of conscious reach. The researchers and the focus group participants each perceived a presentation, then referenced their experiences to begin assigning narrative and meaning to what they'd seen and heard, finally deciding on a judgment about how they imagined the story would end.

They created categories ("lying focus group members," "unconscious drives," "insulting attorneys," or "accountability in the system"), and started a narrative ("too little time to get inside people's heads" or "getting by with a serious breach of responsibility"). They also began using rhetoric ("customers don't know what they want" or "it's just like ignorance of the law") to express the stories they were each developing. We could also break down what we heard on the outside about both of these privately grown, inner stories according to the four determinants of behavior, procedures, interpretations, and puzzles. Many models could apply to the task.

However trial professionals choose to collect and evaluate the inferences expressed about the implicit memories at work behind the scenes—and the meaningful lessons each person carries with them—if the approach helps us appreciate the broad possibilities in the mind, it has value. Remember, just as in the best focus groups, speculation is the rule when trying to assess and categorize the story building process in the human mind. We know that it happens; we just can't know precisely *how*.

Following are two large groups of factors selected from among the many ways people have addressed the question of how humans develop stories that lead to judgments. Many trial professionals use these distinctions on a regular basis. Attorneys occasionally forget that the words in court transcripts are not the facts, just their verbal referents. When invoking any of these models for the mind's work, that fact can help us recall that these are all just mental models themselves, useful speculation and perhaps educated speculation, but speculation all the same. People do not really have a five-pound hindsight bias hiding behind their spleen or a fundamental attribution error in their liver. Knowing that, we may be reminded to focus our attention on the stories we are trying to measure, not on the yardstick being used. Someone once said that "Art, like morality, consists of drawing a line somewhere." Many of the models for assessing influences on our thinking and deciding have proven very useful at drawing some lines for many professionals across the globe for years. The constructs deserve some scrutiny if only to know a little about the territory people working with the mind travel. Plus, they can help draw some lines distinguishing one story line from another in focus groups designed to find them.

3.10 Perceptions and Their Influence

3.10.1 Other-than-Conscious and Conscious Interplay

The most basic dynamic at work in every person forming a judgment by building a story about the legal matter before them is the interplay between their conscious, verbal facilities, and the majority of their mental processes, which are not available to conscious review or direction. It helps to start noticing when you are asking someone a question they can't consciously answer.

This happens most commonly when an attorney or trial professional asks a mock juror (or real juror after the verdict is delivered) *why* he decided as he did and exactly how that process ensued. Nobody has anywhere near full access to that information, and repeated asking doesn't help bring it to mind. We do have references, since we draw on some of the memories being used to try to describe the story we can't fully grasp. But the paltry proportion of information available for conscious asking is something that trial professionals would best keep in mind lest they fall prey to taking one answer as the whole story one too many times.

Other-than-conscious/conscious interplay is perhaps the single biggest factor consistently forgotten or minimized. Yet, there is a fundamental dynamic between those mental processes in the decision makers' heads that play by conscious rules and those that don't. Because the latter are so much more prolific than the others, and because they do play by different rules, learning how to approach their intersection when researching case stories in small groups can be crucial to success. Respecting the limits when seeking direct answers about processing outside conscious awareness and control, can open up other ways to access the potential shapes of case stories brought out by a single client's situation. When will a person be forming meanings for a judgment with the least or most access to their thinking process? There are divisions to be noted among written, spoken, or seen messages. Written influence and responses favor a more conscious focus than some other types of messages. Some people call them "left-brain" input, though geography isn't a key. Your methods should always respect all parts of the minds you are working with.

> **Harvesting Stories.** Often when a decision maker presumes a fact or connection, or suggests something is obvious to her by using terms like "just," "clearly," or even "obviously," she has arrived at an inner storehouse of references and associations and is announcing that important fact.
>
> **Delivering Stories.** When confronted with substantial sets of associations of an other-than-conscious nature, avoid asking the person to rush to any conclusion. Ask short, general follow-up questions such as "What else?" which offer no direction and only presuppose that there is still more to come. In opening remarks, stick to the same, general territory. Expand and include.

3.10.2 Perceptual Preferences

In expressing thought and action, each person has a preference for one of the three major sensory systems (variously defined in different fields of study). Because of this, we also develop unthinking habits for what we tend to see first, hear most clearly, or feel most deeply within the full mix of sensory experience brought into our minds at the moment or through memories:[11]

- ➲ Do you like a good explanation or the big picture first?
- ➲ Can you plan something crucially important for your future without a pen and paper?
- ➲ Is eye contact something you can do without?
- ➲ Can you relive a gut feeling or just the idea that you had one?

Everyone has a full range of sensory perceptions operating in the mind all the time. We tend to express ourselves through one over the others as we grow up. As a result, we tend to favor or ignore input and memories contained in that preferred system over another.

Catastrophic injury cases often favor visual evidence of real and imagined forms—debriding burns, for example, if the event is not videotaped. But the person accustomed to visual images as the way to relate to the world may not be the one on the mediation panel most affected by the images in this story, on this day. This observable habit in our perceptual apparatus could alert you to that fact long before it is too late.

Evidence can have a bias toward imagery, words, or even just a sensation. Lawyers presenting cases each have and express their client's case story through this preferred filter of words, images, or sensation. If you are not aware of these differences, you

11. O'Connor and Seymour, *supra*, n. 4, at "Sensory Preferences."

may end up asking someone to "see eye to eye" who is far better equipped to "hear what you are saying." Appealing to the less-preferred sensory adaptation can dilute the subject's ability to receive the message and reply as well as he might. Because you can view burn photos and stay detached, you might presume listeners will react to certain images or written statements the same way as people who happen to be arranged the way you are—not the way your judge, mediator, or most jurors are in this instance. Knowing how to identify this perceptual filter operating on all our minds all the time, can help you plan the presentation of case stories to avoid those weak spots. One excellent area to practice observing this perceptual patterning is with focus group members discussing case stories.

Harvesting Stories. Focus group participants and voir dire panelists (and judges or mediators) will often demonstrate a propensity to emphasize or diminish whole tracts of a case story based on a sensory bias, filtering for visual, auditory, or kinesthetic input, or working to filter it out.

Delivering Stories. If you learn to recognize verbal and behavioral cues that advertise this constant filtering and practice delivering a message well in any one of the three basic sensory channels, you can adjust to do some good, either translating imagery to words, for example, or doubling up on the verbal packaging that is already part of your presentation.

3.10.3 Verbal and Nonverbal Messages

The dynamic between conscious and other-than conscious mental processing is subject to divisions by degree that are often much less solid than writing about them tends to suggest. Putting influences of spoken and written language in the conscious camp, and facial expressions, demonstrative graphics, voice tones, and gestures in an other-than-conscious one, is not a complete solution. Someone who can accurately recall long strings of attorney or witness commentary may have a more pronounced auditory set of mental muscles, but it could also be a tone of voice, a drop in volume, or even a facial grimace from a witness that "told" this individual which specific parts to recall so well. That cue may be lost to conscious review and evaluation, while the words it marked out take center stage for both the decision maker and the professionals questioning her. Most important is avoiding the temptation to only count and measure that which is most easily counted and measured.

For example, though the majority of people hearing a case story probably won't prefer visual processing, it would be a mistake to think that they are less influenced by demonstrative illustrations of the testimony. One well-known study[12] points out

12. Harold Weiss and J. B. McGrath, Jr., *Technically Speaking: Oral Communication for Engineers, Scientists and Technical Personnel* (New York: McGraw-Hill, 1963).

that average retention of presented material goes up dramatically, when measured after seventy-two hours, when the verbal message is supported by a visual element. Also, visual messages are retained somewhat better than strictly verbal ones.

So you know that matching visual aids to the key verbal points can help decision makers hold your key points in memory longer and they may, then, emphasize those points as if they were key to their version of your story. Discounting drafting, mechanical or medical drawing techniques, and principles of good design, how will you know which elements of the story to single out for visual representation and how best to present the visuals? Being prepared to search for and sort the visual, verbal, or feeling influences in people's expression of a case story can certainly point you in the right direction. This is true even when the people aren't conscious of the role an image may be playing in their own thinking, but are communicating it indirectly. They may be so wrapped up in defending a position that they fail to notice their own use of visual imagery and analogies as they paint their big picture for you. But you might just see the value of their nonverbal message very clearly indeed, as long as you are looking for it.

Harvesting Stories. One major key in tracking the other-than-conscious trends in a developing case story is to carefully observe nonverbal and implicit behavioral marking of points, concepts, or sections of the stories during the telling by the individual. Shifts in voice volume, tone or timbre, and velocity, and "physical marking" with head or hands of certain parts of the narrative trying to describe the story-building process going on inside, are all important to note and consider.

Delivering Stories. This overlap of verbal and nonverbal emphasis, whether positively or negatively positioned in regard to your desired outcome, tracks those points most strongly retained. Thus, it can often point out along with other indicators, the degree of importance assigned to those story elements by the individual. You can increase your sensitivity to these layers in communication by striving to balance your delivery to individuals and groups along nonverbal and verbal lines. Practice tracking each of the elements of behavioral marking listed above. This will help you gain confidence that you are using such nonverbal overlaps as intended, rather than as driven by your own inner processing at cross purposes to your intent.

3.10.4 Life Experience Biases

These are the more familiar "biases, prejudices, and sympathies" the court warns every juror to exclude from their decision-making process during trial and deliberations. Yet, life experience tends to reinforce a consistent set of attendant biases, attitudes, and assumptions to maintain an equilibrium rather than evolving. But they are not impervious to change. As the late Harry Lipsig said quite well about the ideal of the impartial juror and its reality, "The human being is never impartial. He is biased by everything he has experienced, suffered, and seen."

Our expectations of every event are affected sometimes deeply by the reference experiences we have stored as the sum of our lives to that point. Each new experience has the potential to change the arrangement in ways ranging from imperceptible to shattering.

These biasing habits in our thinking are not wholly driven by case story content. Yet, they may be activated by that content. Viewing a situation in hindsight will tend to make trouble on the approaching path seem more apparent. Seeing the outcome as more predictable or apparent at the time doesn't mean that one side only, say the defendant, will be seen as having the capacity to avert that outcome. In fact, a plaintiff who had something to do with his injury or had prior problems of a similar sort can suffer more from juror hindsight than the defendant in the same case. Similarly, attributing more blame to personal responsibility for harm than to circumstantial forces at work, doesn't always single out to which person—plaintiff, defendant, or third party—fault will be attributed. Each has a demonstrated trend, but not a universal one. Many defense attorneys run first to the personal responsibility well from which to draw a story decrying the use of lawsuits to get obscene, undeserved levels of compensation. But, plaintiff-leaning jurors can build stories against defendants who held prior knowledge of impending harms or abuses refusing to act responsible for their past choices, though they've been called to court to do just that. Meanwhile, the irresponsible third party can end up as the wild card for either side. (See also Hindsight Bias and Attribution Errors, below.)

Some suggestions can be made for approaching and dealing with habits of thinking formed by a lifetime's experiences and reinforced by the stories we tell ourselves to give them meaning. First, it is more important to notice them than to name them. It is very unlikely that you can get someone to consciously change such a life habit for the length of a focus group or trial. Yet, you may occasionally find a way to get them to use a different set of biases not usually associated with the kind of story line they expected to hear. One key to doing that is to start making distinctions that go beyond *how* someone may seem to use one bias or prejudice over another. Start looking for the degree to which that thinking habit, attitude, or belief is expressed, and how many others also seem available for use.

For example, in the focus group described earlier with the woman who felt insulted by the attorney, the invitation was extended to use her attitude toward being the "best juror" and doing the "best job" she could. Perhaps the degree of attachment she has to her beliefs about work and juries can help her hear something different as the case story is delivered. Most importantly, it is never a wise idea to mistake the *whole* person for one bias they may have learned, even a very strong one. They may have another, equally strong bias sitting right next to it waiting to help. Assume that there will always be more and consistently invite their inclusion in the process.

> **Harvesting Stories.** Do not overlook the obvious. Often the life story elements most heavily influencing a focus group member's or voir dire panelist's story building efforts are precisely those absent in self-reports of what stands out to that person. Their influence is so pervasive and common that it is more often presumed than consciously noted and declared. Generalized beliefs, attitudes, or values, for example, often exert strong influences on the basic story structure. Still, they never get verbalized since their influence is ubiquitous to the owner. Demanding names instead of narratives from focus group participants will not lead you to those beliefs.
>
> **Delivering Stories.** Become accustomed to looking for evidence between the lines where the three big filters—distortion, generalization, and deletion—are at work on the story context and its content. Practice following up by first exploring where you detect hints of these three filters in the broader story contexts, before you move to question the case or fact related specifics that may have provoked them. Avoid reducing to detail or single, closed choice options what can be included in larger frame questions and answers. It is usually more beneficial to exhaust the general discussion before descending into detail.

3.10.5 Private Story Structure

In *Minding the Law*, Amsterdam and Bruner offer this assessment of the fundamental role that stories play when justice is sought in America:

> Law lives on narrative for reasons both banal and deep. For one, the law is awash in storytelling. Clients tell stories to lawyers, who must figure out what to make of what they hear. As clients and lawyers talk, the client's story gets recast into plights and prospects, plots and pilgrimages into possible worlds. (What lawyers call "thinking through a course of action" is a narrative projection of the perils of embarking on one pilgrimage or another.) If circumstances warrant, the lawyers retell their clients' stories in the form of pleas and arguments to judges and testimony to juries. . . . Next, judges and jurors retell the stories to themselves or each other in the form of instructions, deliberations, a verdict, a set of findings, or an opinion. And then it is the turn of journalists, commentators, and critics. This endless telling and retelling, casting and recasting, is essential to the conduct of the law. It is how law's actors comprehend whatever series of events they make the subject of their legal actions. It is how they try to make their

> actions comprehensible again within some larger series of events they take to constitute the legal system and the culture that sustains it.[13]

The more you seek out how many different stories a person can generate prior to settling on her version of the case story, the more you will be ready to hear and see the unexpected story turn the next time. Listening to and inviting expansion of even the "single sentence stories" can reinforce the presumption that storytelling is a critical talent for trial professionals to appreciate in others and adopt for themselves. If you take Amsterdam and Bruner's observations to heart, you may recognize that everyone involved in a legal dispute applies habits of narrative. Even lawyers and judges steeped in years of work in the system still make sense of human stories first as human stories, not legal ones.

For the professional approaching a focus group who is wondering about the many ways a case story can be perceived and then processed by its members, the primacy of stories as the human means of dealing with our life experiences should be at the forefront of her mind. Anyone trying to make sense of the case story will first approach it through a theme.

Just as each new experience makes sense outside consciousness by referencing collected prior experiences, so a case story will be compared with hundreds of prior references for seemingly similar stories (to the listener), which are also outside consciousness, to start appreciating its meaning. The first stop on that search will usually be at the most basic story element: the theme. Many trial professionals have considered and accepted the idea that starting with a theme while delivering the story is a useful commitment. Not as many carry that notion to the minds of the decision makers, recognizing that, invited or not, they will each soon be starting to receive and rewrite your story through their own theme, too.

A problem emerges from the fact that themes truly at work in a listener's mind are rarely verbalized for easy reference. Quite often, especially early in the process, they can't be put into words. But they make themselves apparent indirectly. Fritz Perls and Virginia Satir, students of human relations, took serious note of analogous speech patterns such as "dim view," "blinded by," "just can't see," and descriptions of the family structure taken literally as a structure ("above," "on top," "outside," "under her wing") in order to question what people might not want to see in their lives, or where in relation to others they would be likely to keep "putting" themselves. These professionals had a huge impact not only on the people they worked with, but on thousands of others that learned from their examples and applied them independently.

Charles Faulkner, Neuro-Linguistic Programming (NLP) and systems dynamics expert, has made a habit of demonstrating how quickly central metaphors in individuals' lives can be revealed through nonverbal behavior alone, and through the

---

13. Anthony Amsterdam and Jerome Bruner, *Minding the Law* (Cambridge, MA: Harvard University Press, 2001): 110–120.

suggestions advertised in our speech.[14] One courtroom example of this metaphorical advertising could be a large organization's antitrust defense against charges of illegal fixing of salaries for certain job positions nationwide. If the case story deals with money being held back from what plaintiffs claim are fair salary levels, the defense probably doesn't want to show up in court openly denying that money is a central theme of their story. Yet hold up dozens of demonstrative exhibits, each a set of bar graphs depicting salary level comparisons and using cartoon stacks of cash for all the bars on every graph. The real theme leaks through the verbal denial.

Harvesting Stories. All the basic story elements of theme, scope, point of view, sequence, etc. are somewhat present in the direct and indirect references that each decision maker uses to try to describe the multiple and occasionally contradictory parts of the story that each must build to decide a case. This advertising will go on as long as the follow-up questions do.

Delivering Stories. Get in the habit of playing a game with yourself during focus groups. At the earliest stage possible and for as many participants as reasonable, assign a single-phrase theme (up to four words) to the story they are developing, based on the hints they provide. At the end of the complete analysis and reviewing all the members' input, do it again without referring to your original list and see how well you did. Be tough on yourself, insisting on close matches for a theme you identified early that did not change throughout the process. Take special note of those themes that surprise you, and those about which you were way off that remained consistent throughout. Note that if nobody is talking with the group letting them talk more than just listen to case input, this game will be very hard to play.

3.10.6 Sorting or Organizing Filters

These filters that NLP calls "metaprograms" offer certain gems by suggesting that people divide their perceptual experience along a series of dichotomous options. They habitually tend to favor one end of each continuum over the other, thereby changing the meaning of their experiences and eventually their expectations for new experiences. These patterns suggest an array of perceptual habits that we use to categorize our experiences. Some examples of these divisions can give you a sense of how many ways are apparently in use by our minds to filter our perceptions of a story, usually before we even start to think hard about it. Proposed metaprogram differences can include sorting more for one or the other of these extremes when motivating ourselves, or imagining others motivated to action:

14. Charles Faulkner, *Metaphors of Identity: Operations Metaphors & Iconic Change* (Lyons, CO: Genesis II Publishing, 1991).

Toward or Away	➲	Moving toward perceived benefits or from perceived losses
Internal or External	➲	Reference for motives, direction or control
Options or Procedures	➲	Increasing perceived options or adhering to order (i.e. to expand or to follow)
Similarity or Difference	➲	Aligning with consistency or with change
Specific or General	➲	Working up or down from wider to narrower scopes[15]

Another set of suggested filters deals with larger chunks of perception and experience that people may emphasize or set aside in processing case stories. This set can have a profound effect on the perceived meaning of a story through shifting the focus, much as a visual preference can turn attention from written documents to photographic evidence, by consistently weighting one type of experience within it, such as time, over information about the rules applied over that time. One attractive aspect of this perceptual habit (and its influence on judgment formation) is that it can be relatively easy to catch once a trial professional consciously seeks it, and it is also easy to direct in your own communication with others.

There are five ways that we filter the kind of messages sent and received in legal stories:

1. People
2. Place
3. Actions
4. Information/data
5. Time

Individuals and groups settled on their versions of case stories tend to show a filter dominating their expressions of that story. You may not think you know about these ways of filtering the communication we give each other, but you do. For example, we all have a "family historian" figure in our lives that sorts exclusively by people:

> You remember Charlotte, she's Dave and Reenie's daughter, her brother was Sam, who played football two years before you in high school.

---

15. Metaprograms can be fully reviewed in Richard Lucas and K. Byron McCoy, The Winning Edge: Effective Communication and Persuasion Techniques for Lawyers (Tucson, AZ: Lawyers & Judges Publishing Company, Inc., 1999), 61-69. This arbitrary selection represents those examples of perceptual factors affecting judgment that seem to show up regularly in focus groups and voir dire discussions.

His best friend was Donald, whose brother Derrick got you that job with Mr. Smith, who was so good to you all that time when . . . .

It's not that action, time passage, or information are not delivered by such sorting. It's that, as with point of view in a case story, when it comes to the action involved, this person prefers to get there through the people. Changing the filter (or the metaprogram) during the discussion of a case story can help change the whole story for some people, as well as offer valuable practice in the mechanics of storytelling.

Harvesting Stories. While even these partial lists can look overwhelming, you need not develop a profile of filters when exploring developing versions of case stories. What can be valuable to note is where each person seems most and least consistent in what are typically default arrangements of these other-than-conscious selections of what to emphasize in the inner story being created. Consistency can point to the level of personal investment or identification being brought to that part of story. Inconsistency can show a part of the story in flux or that is being dismissed.

Delivering Stories. Do not build a checklist or divide listeners into camps of "procedurals" who all move "toward" "necessity" while filtering for "actions" before "people." Instead, develop enough flexibility that with roughly the same number of words, you can describe any small part of a case story smoothly in the ways listed above. Learning to put stories across using any of these filters equally well can sensitize you to them coming back. Ultimately, you will occasionally find a very influential filter that you wish to plug in throughout the actual case presentation, or which can prove very helpful to note in voir dire or in selecting other decision makers.

3.10.7 Juror-Litigant Similarity or Dissimilarity and Attractiveness

This bias matches both gross physical aspects (race, age, gender) and more subtle cultural or ideological features *perceived* to be common (class, politics, religion). In practice, the biasing potential of this factor can prompt people to openly defy even the suggestion that it is in play in their minds. Interestingly, these denials tend to rise in vehemence in direct proportion to the apparent level of influence for some individuals, but not for all.

The research on this subject comes primarily from criminal cases in which juror and defendant similarities were considered, often on the subject of race. Though not unanimous, the results overwhelmingly support the observation that such a perceptual factor can provide a major influence on decision making in those trials. This can happen despite voir dire mention of such biases and instruction from the court to eschew any such reactions. All of these factors function independently of conscious attempts to impede, interrupt, or instruct them away. That's what makes them so valuable for trial professionals.

Because perceived alignment or similarity can be such a wedge by driving leanings of the decision maker out of proportion to any rational assessment of its value, it needs to be considered by those that professionally make the effort to persuade or influence such minds. Similarity of a nonverbal sort is regularly being used in depositions, focus groups, mediation, negotiations, and courtroom trials every day. This is the directed, intentional form of similarity marshaled by the technique of mirroring or matching the nonverbal postures and demeanor of the recipient of the message. Given the potential impact of perceived similarity, taking advantage of the chance to directly address its influence can become a significant tool for any serious trial professional.[16]

Another interesting habit related to appearance is observation about "attractive" and "unattractive" parties. The criminal defendant deemed attractive will be acquitted more often and fined less according to research. Yet, most of the people making these decisions will not be seen as similarly attractive by the average observer. Mock jurors in test cases also attribute incredible arrays of positive personal characteristics to the better-looking litigants, even when they never speak at all, but sit there as evidence is introduced around them. Any remaining doubts people have about how much of the story and decision-making process happens outside of conscious direction can be easily resolved by watching these kinds of connections being made in one focus group after another.

Harvesting Stories. There are two consistent ways these types of life experience biases indirectly advertise themselves:

In added story characteristics, event precursors and human qualities not present in the actual presentation, such as the personality enhancements provided to the silent, "good-looking" defendants. Do not challenge such additions, but follow them up.

The other common sign that a listener is identifying with their private references as if they were a given part of the story context is the persistence shown for an unsupported belief if it does get challenged. Despite rational, logical refutation from others, some people will defy all logic and cling to the additional constructs authored between their ears rather than by the facts. Again, these embellishments should usually not be directly challenged.

Delivering Stories. Each appearance of this perceptual processing habit offers further incentives to incorporate physical mirroring in all

16. For a full discussion of the technique of mirroring applied to legal communication, see Paul Lisnek and Eric Oliver, *Courtroom Power: Communication Strategies for Trial Lawyers* (Colorado Springs, CO: Professional Education Systems Institute, 2001): Chapter 3.

interactions in focus groups, and with jurors, judges, attorneys, and negotiators. Beyond this, it offers trial professionals the chance to practice a simpler, verbal form of reflection when asking for further follow-up from focus group members or venire people, by feeding back the exact phrases used to express the unconscious embellishments. When asking to hear more, be very careful not to rephrase the verbal anchors they use to announce what they've added from their own references.

When considering all the perceptual factors that can influence the construction of decision makers' case stories, trial professionals should start at the beginning. All stories are first perceived, then referenced, and then decided upon by means mostly outside of conscious reach. The primary source of expectations we bring to the next story in life is the vast pool of prior life experiences we store, and from which we find references for each new event or communication. The fundamental way those raw experiences are sorted is as stories from which we draw meanings, and that we later use to construct our values, beliefs, and attitudes—and judgments of legal cases.

Before the thinking processes described later begin, the perceptual processes have had their way with the context and structure of the case story. These processes will continue to exert their influence throughout, until that story is stored as a long-term memory and part of the reference structure applied to the next one. To take a measure of control, lawyers might expand their job descriptions to include being managers of *perceptions*, not just words, facts, and legal concepts. By managing the perceptual package within which a case story is presented, the odds of that story beginning with a helpful theme for each listener, traveling a productive sequence in their minds, and ending at a beneficial conclusion for the client, can rise dramatically. To reach that point more often, trial professionals can practice recognizing and responding with more respect to these perceptual processing factors. Fortunately, every focus group member offers us the chance, in every session.

3.11 Influence of Thinking Processes

After the case story and the messengers delivering it have begun to be perceived and the references from life experience and the stories that give them meaning have begun to be engaged by people deciding a case story, a whole other set of recognizable factors can be engaged by the mind, affecting the eventual shape and meaning of the versions of that case story under construction. Also variable in their degree of conscious availability, these mental processing habits can be distinguished from the perceptual patterns above as being factors that deal more directly with the private version of the narrative as it forms, rather than setting the perceptual context in which the listener's story starts.

Again, this is neither a comprehensive nor an exacting list, but one in which trial professionals can find frequent examples expressed in focus groups, as well as by jurors, negotiators, mediators, and judges. Each of these mental habits can be observed to affect the stories people build to judge legal matters. And with some familiarity, and practice, they can each be utilized by attorneys to present case stories with a much more compelling effect.

3.12 Decision Making Biases or Heuristics

3.12.1 Hindsight

Though hindsight works with memory, it becomes problematic because of "forgetting." Most people can't forget the known outcome of the events in a case story when going back and reviewing how those events first occurred. So when judging the actions or motives of people involved at the time, most listeners will tend to look at the parties' situation as if everyone could see what *they* now see coming down the road. That is when the luxury of hindsight can become a liability for those parties upon whom the decision makers impose unreasonable expectations to respond as if they should have been able to see into their own futures, as decision makers do looking backwards into their past.

When looking at civil injury cases and "foreseeing" the known outcomes, decision makers will tend to attach greater or lesser accountability for preventing the outcome to certain parties over others. If they are questioned about how the target of their concerns could have prevented the coming problem, much can be learned about the structure of the story they are building to judge the case. What the habit of attributing blame for failures to "prevent, protect, or avoid" often does is prompt the decision maker to seek out the *simplest fix*. The most easily accomplished action—or refusal to act—that would have kept the known outcome from ever happening. Note that this habit by itself neither favors the defense nor the plaintiff in a civil conflict. Yet, often because their actions or inactions are in question in the claims, the defense often suffers from the consequences of this habit working on decision-maker stories.

Research has been done on whether teaching jurors to consciously try to see things as the parties saw them "at the time" can help alleviate the effect of this biased view of the story, and it can.[17] In focus groups, much can also be learned about how to present the story by exploring the scope of the stories that seem to indulge in a lot of hindsight, looking for how many ways the simplest fix gets placed at the feet or in the hands of one party over another, in the minds of those unwittingly using hindsight to judge them.

---

17. M. J. Pitera (neé Stallard) Ph.D. and D. L. Worthington, "Reducing the Hindsight Bias Utilizing Attorney Closing Arguments," *Law and Human Behavior* 22 (1998): 671-683.

Harvesting Stories. When gauging the amount of hindsight at work on the stories that focus group participants are forming, pay particular attention to the elements of *point of view* and *sequence*. Note where, when, and how forcefully the notion of preventing, avoiding, or protecting people from the known harmful outcome is packaged indirectly and when the possibility is verbally addressed.

Delivering Stories. To invite listeners to *diminish* hindsight effects, point of view, and sequencing are important in your own delivery, and should be planned well in advance. It is not enough to tell people they must only judge events based on what knowledge, information, and choices were available to all parties "at the time." That phrase can be offered as an anchor, but you must establish the full context in sensory terms (sights, sounds, and feelings) for the party that you say could not prevent or avoid the outcome, as well as drawing a clear contrast with what was known later but was not available to use at the time. Whenever possible, it helps to suggest an alternate party with a greater chance to keep the known outcome at bay, and to sequence his, her, or their appearance far earlier. Whoever you want seen as more in control at the time should have their crucial choices and acts described in the *present tense*, while the other party's acts would come out best in the *past tense*:

> At the time, the plaintiff is refusing to answer inquiry after inquiry about their production quality dropping. By passing them off to lower level functionaries, they are missing the chance to do exactly what their own chosen contract language guarantees them the right to do: sit down face to face, talk things out, and jointly establish a plan to fix their dangerously slipping performance and keep their business with us. We tried for over a year to get that accomplished.

To *encourage* the use of hindsight, the sequencing prescription still applies: prioritize the party for whom you wish hindsight to be used and make a long list of protective or preventative factors available *at the time* very much in that party's control. Again, be sure to cover the other side, indicating how, whether later on or *at the time*, that element of control stays strong for only one party—the one you highlight first:

> You will soon learn that one of the highest priorities for any medical professional is patient safety. You'll find on this day, the professionals here each get all the information they need to act in plenty of time to give this patient a better than ninety percent chance at a full recovery. They each get complete communication, they have all the needed resources at hand, everyone is in the building, and the choices they have to make are explicitly dictated by the

> medical rules. All they need at the moment they each get the message is to act.
>
> In working to diminish or encourage the use of hindsight by a decision maker, avoid gilding the lily by overdoing descriptions of a harmful outcome early. Most jurors and professional decision makers are conditioned to push for a decision on fault first. Too much emphasis on a harmful outcome that is often self-evident can be felt as a delay or impediment.

3.12.2 Attribution

Attribution errors often have a lot to do with how we unconsciously view *cause* in the course of story events. In most legal contexts, that would mean the cause of some trouble. The *fundamental attribution error* is feared more by plaintiff attorneys because it helps a decision maker tend to underestimate the impact of circumstantial and situational forces, while overestimating the power of the person in the story to control their own fate. Many people look at others and attribute far more blame to that person's character, motives, or intentions than to circumstances leading the person into trouble. Yet when they imagine themselves in the same spot, they turn around and give more weight to the situation than is warranted, while excusing their own motives or choices as not a big factor. The "fundamental error" when things go wrong is overestimating the personal part for others and underestimating it for ourselves.

This is another form of hindsight. It works primarily on our fear and is focused even more on a person or persons in the decision maker's developing story. Where general hindsight seeks prevention in the simple fix and in the most likely person that we can imagine who "should have seen it coming," attribution allows the decision maker to inject a surrogate self into the mental process, projecting "What I would have done if it were me." Or he may inject what a person of better character and intent would have done, overemphasizing the person against their circumstances.

In both criminal and civil cases, motive is a big factor though the rules consider it a factor only in the former. In order to determine cause, people use what is called a "locus of control of the significant actions"—that is, who or what represents the active party or ingredient in the decision maker's story.

This comes out in the stories described in focus groups and voir dire in which people or things are selected as the active party/ingredient, and from whose point of view the stories are told:

- The pressure put on the drivers to meet their deadlines. . . .
- Long before the car was even purchased, the choice is already being made to leave the weakened parts in place. . . .

- The patient learns all the risks, gets all her questions answered, she asks for the most drastic surgery, and when the complication she already knows is a good chance happens, she turns around and sues.

Another attribution error that can typically swing toward the plaintiffs more than toward the defense in civil injury suits, all things being equal, is what is termed by author and researcher David Levy the "consequence intentionality fallacy." That is, the effect of a set of actions or events leads to presumptions about intention to produce those outcomes. Instead of counting how many people seem to unthinkingly adopt this tack during a focus group, much can be learned by fully exploring just how many ways participants can find to attribute intent that isn't actually in evidence, to how many others they might attribute it, and under what story conditions. This effort is especially worthwhile in matters dealing with miscommunication, misrepresentation, or the language of contracts and instructions.

Harvesting Stories. Keep yourself clear on the distinctions decision makers place between fault and cause. This thinking habit has more to do with how events come to occur than with who to blame. The form of hindsight used in this story construct usually includes an unconscious projection of the decision maker in the role of either perpetrator or preventor. Then, like "good" drivers seeing only "bad" drivers all around, the decision maker errs by deeming the incident a result of poor character or motive from which he doesn't believe himself to suffer. Typically, such a person begins with phrases like "If it were me . . . ." Take special note of both the point of view from which each listener retells their version of the story and who or what constitutes the active party/ingredient. They may not match up and they can tell you a lot about the story structure when they don't. In the example earlier about the woman misinterpreting the "Being drunk doesn't abdicate a driver's responsibility" line, the point of view of her developing case story seemed to be that of the drunk driver. However, the active party in her retelling certainly was the attorney himself. A story in which the listener's fault/cause focus is split between the drunk driver and the plaintiff attorney may be exactly the one the defense of the dram shop wants to learn all about. It is undoubtedly one the plaintiffs need to learn all about.

Delivering Stories. Once you explore which constructs lead to a party taking center stage and where the active party/ingredient lies, you can carefully invite someone/something else to take that position instead. Controlling your delivery of point of view can strongly affect who or what is seen as wielding control or causing events to occur. Do everything you can to attribute the active and reactive roles where they can do the most good.

> To encourage attribution of intent, motive, or cause to one party over others, be certain that you consider how many active choices can be linked to that party's position in your case story. Learn to use the present tense and the active voice when delivering that part of the story construct. Do it as early as you can and out of chronological sequence where necessary. Trial professionals often have trouble with "active voice" because they've practiced discussing every element of every case in a passive, clinically detached fashion. For the pros, people rarely kill someone. Instead, someone "came to be murdered."
>
> To discourage attribution toward one party, it is necessary to suggest that a substitute party, organization, or other entity take up the active, causal role early. This mental habit requires both distance and conclusions about each person's individual story. So consider how the overarching element of the theme can be used to help establish and reinforce the kind of connections needed to invite the use of this habit by the decision makers.

3.12.3 Assimilation

Forming our individual and multiple stories about what life's events mean, we all develop shortcuts for sorting them out. Psychologists and other researchers refer to one such shortcut as "schemas" or "mental models." If you imagine sorting stories into various categories or topic areas—romantic, dramatic, adventurous—you know exactly how schemas work, except that you don't need the conscious step you just took to build and use them. If you are asking a listener to see whether certain actions or events in a case story fall into the "right-thinking" or "normal-acting" category, usually your listener has already developed schemas into which the elements of the story can be easily assimilated. People find ways to assimilate facts and legal rules into the norms set by their own schemas, which often match those of the majority of "like thinkers" in society. We use our schemas as "script categories" to know what to expect from life situations. If we didn't, every situation would be unpredictable and new, like having to learn about a door to use it every time you stood in front of one.

In the minds of listeners, there is usually more than a particular way a case story can be assimilated, more than one category of habituated formulas for how it may be seen in relation to each listener's own perceived "way of the world" that exists in the listener's head. Because perceptual patterning is still at work behind the conscious, one version over another will tend to distort and rearrange the facts and rules in the case to make an even tighter fit with the schemas each listener brings to it. By letting yourself hear what you *least* want to hear from focus group members, and fully exploring what creates connections they see as "obvious" or "natural" against a certain party's interests, you can discover how other schemas might operate to make different connections "ring true."

Harvesting Stories. Schemas or mental models express the perceptual processing areas of life-experience bias and private story structure. Life story references and their related meanings establish, reinforce, and maintain the schemas we each adopt as individual norms, which work with and occasionally against culturally reinforced norms. The third big perceptual filter, generalization, can help you detect when this thinking habit is at work on the case story being considered and discussed. People will treat their "norm," as they see it as normal for all. And that allows expectations for likely story outcomes and for story characters' likely reactions and conduct at every step. So key in when people infer or declare that their prior, unspoken expectations have been met or violated. People will usually tip their schemas off by presupposition. Their comments and conclusions driven by this "private-story" thinking filter will either contain or betray assumptions about what should or should not have been seen, heard, and felt by the people in the stories:

> I can't see that he tried anywhere hard enough (according to "my standards" for enough).
>
> What they're saying is that she didn't care (according to "my rules" about caring).
>
> Why didn't they just go for another opinion? (according to "my norms" for medical care).
>
> I think this could be seen coming (according to "my views" of their foresight).

Delivering Stories. Presupposition can be a powerful tool in almost every area of legal communication. Listening to the myriad ways that focus group participants and voir dire panelists can assume the "right" or "wrong" direction in each step of their case stories can help direct you to presumptions most likely to encourage or discourage the application of certain schemas to your case.

One example useful in deposition and examining witnesses in a case presentation, presupposes that rules exist that "everyone knows." Avoiding verbal expression of such a rule by presuming it in your question forces the witness to position himself regarding the rule. By the time the answer starts, your presupposition has already had ample time to affect the references of each listener. This, while being less subject to critical scrutiny due to the indirect delivery.

Most listeners will take it for granted when making sense of the question and will apply their own schemas that take the presumption for granted. This does not mean they automatically agree with it. It just increases the odds. Particularly if the witness is forced to openly acknowledge the presumed rule, standard, or performance expectation just before admitting that he did not adhere to it, or conversely to admit that there is no such standard.

> Doctor, what did the rest of the pathologists in the group say when you told them about the prior failures you folks had recorded from all their labs?
>
> (Presuming these findings are normally always passed on.)
>
> How did these negative research results affect your rating of the drug's effectiveness?
>
> (Presuming negative results are normally taken as measures of drug effectiveness.)
>
> When you returned to the doctor because of the pain, what did he say?
>
> (Presuming anyone would do that, and there's something "not right" with someone who didn't.)

3.12.4 Representativeness

Akin to the maneuvers accomplished with assimilation in general, this shortcut is usually applied to the characters in a case story. It is used to match the parameters of each new person to a set of mental stereotypes, looking for matches among the categories of individuals stored there by the listener. An example would be similar to that cited earlier of an attorney profiling or typing a prototypical "good" or "bad" juror, although that process was done consciously. The way that professionals know their own prototypical types would be accomplished in the usual, other-than-conscious fashion of decision makers whether professional or lay person.

Harvesting Stories. When examining the many ways focus group members can stereotype the people involved in a case story, it helps to listen carefully to the hints they offer on how they know to attribute one set of expectations to "this kind of person," as opposed to another. They will direct you to what criteria fit that "other." Listen for the anchors they use in their language and the descriptive effects they have. Discovering crossovers and similarities in various descriptions of different categories of people among a whole focus group can aid choices on how to actually represent those people to the final decision makers.

A basic story element often used in applying this habit of thinking is sequencing. Listen to and explore how a focus group member or venire person knows to place certain people earlier or later in their discussion of significant parties and events. However, be wary of just asking them why this is done, as you will break up the story framework by insisting on reasons instead of the imagined, recreated experiences driving each decision maker's story line to its own end.

Delivering Stories. Often attorneys tend to use nouns where adjectives will do more good. This is never more evident than when a party, witness, or expert is introduced in the presentation. "You are a business owner, is that correct?" "She is a nurse." "They are all experts." Or, if they do use adjectives and other descriptive modifiers, they tend to pick one and ring that bell far too often: "You will learn that he is a very caring doctor."

When you find people fitting witnesses or parties into their own stereotypical packages, follow up until you get both a number of adjectives, and hopefully, an anecdote used to establish this person as representative of the same type. Then, in your descriptions of these people during voir dire, opening statements, and in your initial questions to them on the stand, use as many related descriptors as you can. You can also invite them to relate their own anecdotes, similar to those you've linked to better story references. Note that this process can be a negative or positive positioning effort with equal effect.

3.12.5 Availability

Experienced trial attorneys or consultants will recognize a very common question coming from the venire or focus group: "How many times has this happened before?" and its many other incarnations. The habit of thinking that drives this common curiosity can be evidence of the *availability heuristic* at work. When it is working most strongly, the question is never asked because the answer is simply supplied by the mind of the listener: they *just know* that most patients do (or do not) get second opinions for minor surgical techniques; they *just know* that auto makers do (or do not) dynamically crash test large numbers of each new model of car produced; they *just know* that accounting firms can (or cannot) fairly perform both auditing and accounting functions; or they *just know* that the Food and Drug Administration does (or does not) do years of its own safety research on new drugs.

Likelihood is a major conceptual element of many cases in trial and other formal dispute resolution forums. What is seen by each juror or board member as more or less likely is quite often a function of what they have seen before and stored away—but near the mental surface and thus available. The expectation of relevance is prompted simply by the ease with which that kind of experience can be brought to mind. The more vividly they can bring up the set of available experiences in a category, the more likely they will be to generalize from them, distorting their importance in the rest of the story to include them as basic story components, deleting others the attorneys or the court might find more important to the case.

For example, the number of witnesses for one side, on one topic was formally studied and showed a consistent influence despite direct instructions against allowing such influence to occur. Regardless of the *content* of the expert testimony on either side, there was a greater *number* of "heads" made available to the jurors on that story topic from one side. That tends to make a difference, no matter what they say. There are voir dire considerations at large here, but that is not all.

Harvesting Stories. While inquiring about the many ways listeners could apply availability to their case stories, a questioner might want to explore both sides of the stories: those that get all the attention, seeming most available, and those that get none. Ask a lot about what they seem to leave out completely. A few experiences might turn up that make those unmentioned aspects seem more likely to someone, by virtue of seeing them in ways that were overlooked at first. Remember especially early on that many more than one story package is available for each set of facts and law.

Delivering Stories. Keep your follow-up questions free of conscious direction. But it doesn't hurt to presuppose that there are more ways to see the part of the story you are discussing. "What else might cause that?" rather than "Is there anything else . . . ?" Tracking what's left out in focus group member stories may lead you to story packaging that invites decision makers to see parts of the case story as much more likely than they might otherwise have thought. You will never be as persuasive just telling them that they should.

If you review the earlier voir dire question-and-answer session on driving skills, you'll note another extremely valuable aspect of availability at work. If you want people to open certain parts of their life story references to curiosity about other potential connections and associations, it helps to be sure that the subject matter is foremost in their minds. Rhetorical and direct questions with open presuppositions can help listeners' minds engage topic areas so that suggested expansions can be more freely indulged.

3.12.6 Belief Perseverance

As the name suggests, the effect is that a belief, once built and in action, will tend to perpetuate itself, often in the face of direct evidence challenging or even decidedly refuting it. "*I just know* that a patient should not go into the hospital alive and come out dead, unless someone did something wrong." When examining the impact of this thinking habit while questioning a group considering a case story, be sure you don't accept evidence of a belief at face value. Some beliefs, for instance, have opposing partners nearby in the same head. "A doctor can do everything right and the patient *still* dies."

Harvesting Stories. Belief perseverance is usually described in terms of what people will deny, dismiss, or completely ignore. Again, note any deletions. Apparent drops of evidence or legal rules can become signposts for where to begin digging. Check for the strengths of the stated beliefs, but also add some descriptive effort on their context and character. This can be helpful when balancing which declared beliefs might be the best ones to seek out and reinforce among the actual decision makers, partly by how the case story is packaged to align or contrast with them. Here is where practice can also be gained in separating a single spoken answer from the whole inner story, because what is said about a belief is often far less compelling or apparent than what is done to maintain it in the face of challenges in a group discussion.

Delivering Stories. When interviewing potential jurors or questioning focus group members about beliefs regarding situations in which their belief could persevere, it can be helpful to play with the story element of scope. Factually or hypothetically changing the reach of time of stories can help loosen mental frameworks in which other beliefs are available. The exercise can also help uncover areas in which no amount of altering of the broad elements covered in the story scope seems to have any effect at all.

Another technique—"menuing"—can also help track some of the other-than-conscious sorting going on behind the scenes. It involves menuing a list of possible responses, values, or beliefs that could accompany the part of the story being focused on as each person is asked to consider and weigh the various items on the list. This is often a more productive option than asking how strongly someone identifies with a single statement of belief rated on a scale from one to five.

3.12.7 Confirmation

In the field of hypnosis, there is a phrase often used to link one event to a desired event in a hitherto unexpected cause-and-effect relationship: "the more . . . the more . . . ." For example, "The more you feel the book in your hands, the more you may find the thought of your skin of interest." *Confirmation bias* is about unconsciously finding similar links by sorting through a message for the "good parts," the parts that confirm what we already think we know. When you buy a new car, for example, and it is a model or a color you have never really considered much in the past, have you noticed how many of the same model or color cars suddenly seem to leap out at you from every intersection and at every turn? The odds are that they were there all along, but you had no prompting to confirm their existence and importance until you became a proud owner yourself, and thus sensitized to see what you had looked past before.

There are many values, attitudes, and beliefs abroad in the national jury pool waiting to be confirmed by the lawyers, parties, witnesses, facts, and legal rules in every case story. Some will be helpful and some will not. Suspicion of the legal system itself is a very pervasive attitude of many jurors. It can be confirmed and used to overemphasize certain parts of one side's case story. Unlike belief perseverance, the confirmation habit is typically described as helping the decision maker overemphasize rather than deny story elements. The question about suspicion is where and by what it will be confirmed. Since it is undifferentiated suspicion of the legal system, as a general attitude, perhaps whichever lawyer does and says things that confirm how much of a creature he is of that system gets the full brunt of some folks' suspicious expectations. But maybe the other lawyer can confirm something else about herself next.

Harvesting Stories. Watch for people in focus groups who appear to be agreeing with an answer that they seemed to know was coming. They probably did. Ask them how they knew to expect it and the possibility of confirming other associations will open up. They will often have a good number available. It is an unspoken confirmation like a mental, "See, I *told* me so." Such fundamentally strong attitudes often link directly to story themes. Ask how they knew that this was about the thing they knew it to be about. A rough version of their story theme will often emerge in response.

Delivering Stories. Encouraging the confirmation thinking habit, this sense of recognition and familiarity with your story, begins and ends with the number one element—the theme. The most important aspect in establishing, reinforcing, and maintaining a theme for the final decision makers is to pay more attention to the packaging than to the words you use to define it. Once you've elicited thematic input from focus group members,[18] sift through their contributions for experiential references, analogies, and descriptors that seem to ring common, strong chords. Note which elements of the case story they consciously cited in the process, and which stood out by their absence. Also consider that the jurors' stories end with the law, the instructions, and their verdict questions, so a familiar path to fitting them into the mix will need to be found.

18. See Chapter Five.

Then begin constructing a large number of ways you can remind the actual decision makers of all the things the focus group found familiar, in the most compelling sequence, from the most memorable point of view.

3.13 Psychological Factors

3.13.1 Primacy and Recency

The ideas of *primacy* and *recency* are well known to many attorneys, but most have trouble describing their actual nature. The typical description heard is that receivers of the story presentation will tend to retain and emphasize the "first and last things they hear." That is not accurate. The way this processing habit works is akin to confirmation and exception. The first point to hit home with a decision maker may actually be the third point made. But it matches up well with her prior experiences and the stories about their meaning. When something early in the presentation is taken as matching the listener's own experience, that part of the story will tend to get the extra reinforcement that primacy reactions bestow. If you question people near the start of a focus group about their views of the story, not the legal outcome, and do it again in a similar vein near the end, you will usually find more than half still using the same point of view, sequence, primary acts, events, and rough themes. Learning which elements of the case story seem to invite this treatment, or how they can be presented better to help them do so, is well worth the effort.

Similarly, the reinforcement afforded by the recency effect has less to do with the last point made in your presentation chronologically and more with which of the latter points stood out by its unusual or unexpected nature. The most exceptional point coming near the end of the line will get the same disproportionate emphasis as the first recognizable or familiar one does, assuming the listener is paying attention throughout. Since the court's instructions are unusual and come near the end, it is no surprise they often carry the recency effect within juror case stories and the decisions they spawn. Which instructions tend to capture attention near the end and how that can either be enhanced or diminished for the listeners can be learned from focus group participants.

Harvesting Stories. Learning as much as possible about the elements that seem to confirm people's world models will give the trial professional a chance to collect as many elements as possible for a primacy candidate in the final story presentation. Fully exploring which later points seem to be unthinkingly emphasized by listeners can help divulge what seems to make them "exceptional." Remember that the questioning can't be too direct, since conscious inquiry into even partially conscious patterns in the thinking process usually doesn't

> yield useful answers, if it yields any at all. "Please say some more," works far better than "Why did you say that?"
>
> **Delivering Stories.** Marking out the elements that you hope will draw on primacy and recency effects involves multiple tasks. You need to establish your entire case story plan with an eye to inviting the confirmation and identification that private story processing can garner. You also need to pay attention to every segment of every beginning and end the decision maker's experience. Plus, you need to ensure that you make the effort to invite primacy and recency effects at each opportunity, whether in voir dire overall, the testimony of the first witness, or the hour-and-a-half before the next break.

3.13.2 Reinforcement

The more a response, action, or perception is reinforced, the more of that you will likely be getting back in the decision maker's story. Reinforcement doesn't require an overt reward, as Pavlov's dogs or Skinner's pigeons expected, but outside input in the form of attention, confirmation, or affirmation all accomplish the same purpose. Referring to the person's point in front of the whole group, asking how many have similar stands, or simply noting how many others seem to agree, are all means of reinforcing a position available in any group discussion.

While you watch, question, and listen, remember that reinforcement comes in positive and negative forms. Strong denials or objections may be reinforcing something as much as strong assertions or confirmations do. Just as metaprograms suggest that some people *move toward* events, actions, or ideas as their habit of directing their own choices, others tend to *move away* from anticipated negative situations to get themselves going. Many jurors, and other decision makers can decide a case by voting more *against* one side, than for the other. Recognizing that this kind of negative reinforcement occurs should remind the trial professional to be vigilant for signs of this processing taking place behind the scenes of the focus group discussion.

> **Harvesting Stories.** It can be helpful to see which parts of the story and especially which individual life stories and experiences are getting active reinforcement by the people considering the case. This is where this phenomenon offers the greatest value in preparing a case story for presentation.
>
> What does this part of the story tend to remind people of? What pops to mind from their own life experience or lessons and is apparently reinforced by this case story or elements within it? How do those connections seem to be made? Over time in the discussion, does that reinforcement continue or do other things easily interrupt the connection?

> **Delivering Stories.** When you determine what parts of the case story are consistently reinforced and which are consistently minimized by focus groups, you will have a rough map to determine which elements of your story need special attention in your presentation and which you may be able to use as levers to advance them.

3.13.3 Repetition

What keeps coming up? Certain topics, points of view, time frames, or events seem to get repeatedly mentioned or implicitly referenced without direct commentary. Still others are diminished or ignored despite equal or greater importance to the case story you want to deliver. Rather than trying to question why, ask follow-up questions about *how* the repeated point draws attention to itself. Bring up other less repeated points and ask the same type questions about them. But do not try to get the conscious mind to answer how the other-than-conscious mind selected which part on which to focus repeatedly.

Learning theorists agree that repetition in presentation is a major predictor of success in adult learning. We know from focus groups that topics of importance, whatever purpose they mean to the listeners, tend to be repeatedly revisited once they appear, and this is one means of identifying the primacy effect being imposed by each person. It can be astonishing to discover how often over a full day's presentation and discussion of a case story, members of a group will consistently return to the same perceptions, concepts, events, phrases, facts, and legal rules to make their points.

> **Harvesting Stories.** When you experience consistent repetition among group members reviewing a case story, you can almost watch the process of how quickly the other-than-conscious faculties can assimilate new perceptions, concepts, phrases, facts, or legal rules into their preexisting mindsets. You may start to find clues on where to seek out more and different stories from these folks and their habits of thinking, stories that can complement or improve on the one that seems to be repeated.
>
> **Delivering Stories.** Note which story elements get repeated by which people and what each of their eventual versions of the case story lead them to conclude. This can help highlight which story aspects may need extra reinforcement with visuals, added testimony, or verbal anchors. It can be an aid beginning at voir dire and on through trial presentation. Collected anchors used by people forming particular versions of the story can later be used to focus on people in voir dire using similar expressions. This can confirm whether such a story structure may be likely to develop again and to express that position for all.

In doing a few such presentations and dealing with this phenomenon, you'll have the chance to discover the fine line between repetition serving to reinforce an idea, a phrase, or some factor in your story, and beginning to tear down those connections from overuse. This alone is worth the effort.

3.13.4 Reflection

This habit of mental processing emerges as "feedback" to another group member or the moderator. It emerges as what the *person who is being addressed by the speaker* just said, not what the *speaker* previously said. Interpersonal repetition: this sounds less like a compliment or critique and more like an acknowledgment or confirmation. It is repeating key phrases from the other person's remarks or questions. Many attorneys, salespeople, negotiators, and mediators are trained specifically to reflect back what they hear from the targets of their persuasive efforts, particularly what is said or alluded to on key points about goals, values, or aims within the message they are trying to reflect back. This is an attempt to improve rapport by "aligning" with the conceptual messages they are getting and it can help reinforce or start to clarify the reflected point further.

Many people are aware that literal reflection in the form of physical or auditory mirroring of some of the communication output of another party, is a potent tool for quickly capturing the undivided attention and interest of that person. How this tool ought to be used to further effectiveness in focus groups and in courtroom presentations will be covered later. For now, it is enough to point out that mirroring in its naturally occurring, unconsciously driven state of reflecting postures and gestures, is an invaluable tool for observing where attention is being placed by various members of any group before you, whether a panel of judges, a group in a negotiation, a jury, or a focus group. Even when people are not speaking, they are often giving away which people in the room have more of their attention than others. Often, this information allows some observations and conclusions that could never emerge from conscious questioning alone.

Harvesting Stories. As with those frequently repeating certain points, note and pursue the story elements and structures that are reflected between the members. This selective feedback can often reveal connections and constructions in the participants' versions of the story that you may have not previously noticed or considered. Again, be wary of asking for answers they can't consciously compose. "Why did you pick that to repeat?" for example, will not help you at all. The selection process isn't available for conscious review and discussion.

Delivering Stories. Alignment in all its forms can help decision makers identify with, emphasize, or confirm more in a case story than they otherwise might have. For decades, the "Pygmalion effect" has been confirmed by multiple studies after Dr. Robert Rosenthal's early work, which shows that the nonverbal or implied communication of an expectation of a type of response from another person greatly encourages that response. Initial work with schoolchildren raised and lowered supposedly "fixed" performance levels just from indirect suggestions that they were expected to improve or not. Subsequent work confirmed the same effect among adults in many contexts, including the law. One way to encourage the Pygmalion effect among group members or legal decision makers involves this interpersonal repetition or reflection. If you combine the skill of physical mirroring with the verbal reflection of story elements offered by a decision maker while adding a presupposition that links and includes more of your desired story, that implicit invitation may be accepted.

Group member: I think my company shows real consciousness of their duty toward safety by having the safety inventories done for every worker at the gate.

Company attorney: And a reasonable company would be conscious of their duty to safety in what other ways? (*introducing the "reasonable company" anchor and presupposing the participant's own company is part of that "club," asking for other criteria that he or she can immediately begin attaching to the label, which may also be able to be reflected back later, building up identification of the reasonable defendant company point of view along the way*).

Note that at trial and often in focus groups, the attorney could not "jump in" immediately as depicted here, unless in voir dire. But physically mirroring the person whose input is to be reflected and invited to expand will reestablish a constructive connection as a starting point for the next steps of reflecting and presupposing. If this were opening statement, the question could be raised rhetorically, then answered by the lawyer with a menu of possibilities that the group could pick from, since they can't answer aloud. The menu should come from focus groups, not just from trial professionals' input.

3.13.5 Identification

Some people tend to plug themselves into certain stories over others. It is axiomatic that everyone must process the story as they perceive it by referencing their story elements against many stored versions of their own experiences, real and imagined.

In this way, they take their perceptions of the early parts of the case story and the perceptual effects of presenter delivery itself, placing both into their own reference experiences and the many stories they have to explain what they mean. No one can hear and appreciate another's story without going through this process, albeit, mostly outside of conscious reach and totally beyond conscious control. Perceive first, reference next, and select or decide last. In this respect, we all identify with the story just to make any sense of it.

But as the story versions start emerging from this private referencing, it can be very instructive to notice which positions, characters, actions, time frames, events, ideas, rules, and such have emerged strongly, weakly, or not been incorporated. Often the position of a single participant in the case story is emphasized. This emphasis can frequently reveal the point of view from which the listener is going to see the entire case. Most presentations jump around in point of view unless the speaker has been trained to focus the delivery. Yet even in those mixed-up deliveries, one point of view tends to prevail. This habit of identification can give trial professionals observing the process early clues as to which characters are tending to take center stage in focus group member stories. If they also note which points of view were offered for decision makers to adopt, the learning can begin.

As with other models for factors in our story processing, guard against the presumption that all identification is positively inclined. A very common example that incorporates the habit of attribution happens when jurors or focus group members align their inner stories with the point of view of the injured, cheated, or otherwise allegedly harmed plaintiff and they reconstruct the case story strongly from that perspective. Yet, in their commentary they will often turn on the plaintiff harshly, and describe how in that position they "would *never have done* as he did," and decry the plaintiff's choices, acts, and intentions as anything from foolish to criminal. All the while, they are "identified" with the point of view in the story of the party of which they are most critical for playing the "role" so badly.

Harvesting Stories. In addition to noting and following up group-member identification with characters presented or added after the fact by the listener, save some attention for this thinking habit's effects on the story elements of scope and sequence. Scope can be portrayed in the number and quality of actions encompassed in the decision makers' stories, not just in how many people are touched by the story in a number of ways. Often you can note identification by tracing which acts are referred to when the person or persons are not mentioned. The acts mentioned earliest and most often repeated, provide similar direction for your inquiry. When following up, do not demand to know who is doing the acting. Instead, ask about the qualities associated with them. You may find more than an active party or point of view, you may gain valuable insight into the theme driving this person's version of your case story.

Delivering Stories. Refer to comments above under juror-litigant similarity, verbal, and nonverbal messages, reinforcement, and reflection. If you develop skills in physical mirroring and the expression of sensory preferences (visual, auditory, and kinesthetic), you can encourage a high degree of identification from the listener with you and your subject matter by reflecting back both their physical demeanor and their sensory preference.

3.14 Harvesting a Case Story

Most trial attorneys are always willing to learn the facts of the cases they build. Most spare little effort, often going to great expense to learn them. The more successful spend time and effort learning the story *best* suited to present that stack of facts. Tracking any one focus group member's "take" on your case story can provide ample incentives to join those few.

First, you will find evidence that the story presented is being worked on by the perception process, applied both to the message and the messenger. Then, outside conscious reach, the story gets referenced against a lifetime of experiences and stories about what they mean, at processing rates beyond measure. Then, starting with a feeling, an impression will begin to form, which is always generated outside conscious awareness.[19] That primitive feeling will trigger a set of reaction parameters. It is at this point, when decision makers start demonstrating curiosity, anger, or boredom, that the bridge to conscious awareness is opened and the version of the story in progress is revealed to their "thinking" parts. These thinking parts promptly start wondering, considering, and narrating, engaging all manner of other mental manipulations, developing a case story on the way to a decision drawn from that story's final form.

Knowing that every decision maker can't do her job without first going through the process of reconstructing whatever case story is delivered to them for judgment can encourage learning about how those stories are developed and applied and the many ways an attorney might have to influence the process as it begins—before it's too late. The perceptual and thinking processes outlined earlier may seem daunting in their reach and unwieldy in their numbers, but these are only some of the ways listeners perceive, reference, and eventually select the story from which they make their choices. Some lawyers may find exploring all these other-than-conscious processes worth the effort, even though the processes are only hinted at, suggested,

19. Paul Lisnek and Eric Oliver, *Courtroom Power: Communication Strategies for Trial Lawyers* (Colorado Springs, CO: Professional Education Systems Institute, 2001): Chapters 2 and 3.

or inferred by their owners. Nobody really knows exactly how all that processing works—least of all the person doing it.

There is a great deal of activity going on behind the eyes and between the ears of every person rebuilding the case story as they hear it. That process, however, is extraordinarily quick. Before the second witness takes the stand in a trial, most jurors and the judge have already built most of the basic elements of their stories: theme, scope, point of view, sequence, and so forth. From that point on, they engage the general mental functions of distortion, generalization, and deletion, and the other perceptual and thinking habits listed earlier. These serve to build up their versions of the case story in the direction they've already started, while changing or forgetting the pieces that don't "fit," and confirming those that do. Focus group work can show the interested observer exactly how hard it is to try to edit perceptions already established about a case story. It can even be difficult to alter the narrative being built to support those perceptions. Perhaps this is because the stories decision makers recreate are largely built by referencing their own experiences and their own stories about their meanings. It's more personal. This makes getting the story out right at first that much more critical.

Regardless of whether a lawyer is concerned about primacy, the facts about decision making as we can know them are in, and it is the story that rules the process. Unfortunately, there is always more than one story and each decision maker starts with several as they quickly narrow the options. To best influence the process, an attorney would need to know the width of the territory of those likely story options, where the worst pitfalls lie, and how best to present the case story—particularly the very early parts of it. This, to enable inviting the listeners away from those pitfalls and toward his best theme, most compelling scope, most persuasive central character, and all the story elements—big and small.

Judgments clearly do not live by facts alone. Everyone else will be speaking for the facts that do not speak for themselves. So learning about the *case story* as well as the *case facts* seems safer. But since the story-building process isn't open to conscious, verbal dissection, the lawyer seeking to learn the story of a client's case has few options. Trying to guess what would best serve the needs of the eventual decision makers is playing long odds, given the number of ways a listener can wander far and wide from what the lawyer finds compelling, persuasive, and true.

Mock trials allow the full story-building process to finish even before the first question is posed aloud. Surveying the venue by phone offers little or no chance to search beyond closed-ended answers to closed-ended questions.

That leaves focus groups to get the help needed in finding out what your case story may be to those who will construct it, and how best to turn around and present that story to them.

3.15 2015 Supplement

3.15.1 Bodies Build the Narrative

So, aside from sounding clever, or having Henry Kissinger's "added advantage of being true," what does it mean that *perceptions* of facts, and *not* the facts themselves decide legal cases?

Well, in the most literal sense:

The facts aren't *the facts*, the law isn't *the law*, case stories aren't *the case stories—until* they are perceived to be so—by any legal decision maker at work on any matter.

Just as emotional *reactions* don't fully exist until they are *expressed*, so it is with *perceptions* of facts, law, and stories. Our private narratives are only fully realized as they are expressed among others who will incorporate that expression into stories of their own.

Many brain researchers, psychologists, and even cultural anthropologists now agree that the fundamental bridge between the inner and outer realities we inhabit is a narrative. Science recognizes a narrative built of perceptions and molded by the sensory experience of our bodies, driven by metaphors also tightly linked to our physical presence in the world and how we express ourselves in that environment.

When developing your case story, once you're ready to address emotional reactions, the next step essential to respecting the whole brain of any decision maker is to invite him to pick or refer to the most useful or productive experiences with which to construct his own version of your case story. In Chapter Three in the section "How We Build Our Stories," I point out most trial professionals know that any legal decision maker (lay or professional) will filter or change elements of your case story in her head, then decide the case from the version she unknowingly altered for herself. One of the challenges of developing a story that influences the subjective (re)building process is that people don't wait for every last detail to be presented before they start working on their own story. So, early on, you need to give them some solid direction to lean one way over another (or others). And, because the brain always starts with the general and moves to the specific, follow the brain's lead in your delivery.

Instead of beginning with a myriad of disparate case story details (i.e., all the facts—as in "the facts can't speak for themselves"), imagine starting with the human body. Just as reason won't work right without an emotional component, just as the conscious parts can't function without the other-than-conscious ones going first, it turns out our mind won't work very well without relying on a strong perception of our own body either. This is especially true when you invite a mind to create a personal narrative using private reference experiences to (re)construct the stack of facts and law in your client's story in order to judge its merits. Consider the following research on the mind-body connection and the potential it reveals for developing stories that affect legal decision making:

Several studies by Yale's John Bargh and many others on the topic of "priming" show that subjects given a warm or cold drink to hold before being asked about their own relatives, being introduced to strangers, or being asked to judge the character of potential employees, all consistently rate the character of, and relationships with people (whether they know them or not), as "warmer" or "cooler," just because of the temperature their hand felt as they were thinking. Interestingly, people thinking of moments of social acceptance or rejection will consistently miscalculate the temperature of the room they are in by an average of five degrees: colder for those remembering rejection, warmer for those recalling acceptance. *Warm hands expect warm hearts? Cold shoulders?* You get the idea.

The same spots in the parts of our brain that process social rejection are the same spots that process experiences of physical pain. *A real slap in the face?*

When thinking of the future, people unwittingly but consistently lean forward; similarly, they lean back when considering past events. *Looking ahead? Looking back?*

People tend to place good, positive, or correct ideas higher in their "mind's eye," and to place ideas that are bad, negative, or incorrect lower down. *Higher purposes?*[20] *In the gutter?*

Just holding a heavier clipboard tends to invite people to consistently rate the material clipped to it as more important than the same material where no clipboard is employed. *Weighty subjects?*

Even with a measure for inches or feet in front of them, people consistently underestimate how far or close an object is in line with how desirable they find that object to be. The more they want it, the closer they think it is (and vice versa). *Within reach?*

Sitting at a dirty desk, or smelling a foul odor while being asked to judge a person's failure to return a lost wallet or to lie on a résumé, led people to consistently judge these actions as *more* wrong. The opposite has been found consistently to be true, too. Washing one's hands after experiencing the bad odor or dirty desk leads to less harsh judgments of the same kind of wrongdoing or transgressions. *Unclean hands? Clean conscience?*

There is a huge volume of similar research on this subject, called "embodied cognition" or which the phenomenon of "priming" is just a part. This is a fancy way of saying as primates, humans tend to position thinking through the body's senses, not just as disembodied ideas or concepts in the mind. The latest developments in the research have only revealed that this is much more prevalent than

---

20. Just some food for thought when designing effective demonstrative aids for court. When was the last time you put the data or images about the opposition above yours on a chart? Or, harms and loss information on top, and damage amounts on the bottom? *See also* Chapter Eight, section 8.12, "2015 Supplement."

previously imagined. In other words, not only will decision makers rewrite your story with their own personal reference experiences plugged in order to make sense of it, but those earlier references usually are built from chunks of body-based narrative—i.e., as seen through the eyes, smelled through the nostrils, heard through the ears, and felt through the skin of characters in the narrative. Characters like your clients.

At some point or another, decision makers all will violate the courthouse Golden Rule, whether they know the rule or not, or whether they know they are doing it or not: they will put themselves inside the story's general plot outline (and inside its characters) to try to see "from the inside." But when you invite decision makers first, to see a risk to anyone in the plaintiff's circumstances, our survival-based drives and more evolved emotional reactions will lead decision makers to seek protection from that threat, rather than to try to get "inside." When you show them *Rules* justified by that *Risk,* and how safety is preserved by applying those Rules the right way, decision makers can start to feel for themselves the emotional basis of the (re) constructed story they will use to judge the case.

We adopt the character's experience in order to appreciate his situation. And, we adopt the kind of situations surrounding those characters in order to start reconstructing our versions of the plot. Poor Golden Rule.

So, how do you package the start of your case story to most effectively invite people to break the Golden Rule in ways that help you most? Use *embodied metaphor* to guide their choices throughout presentation of story building material, while you still have the chance to most strongly and persuasively influence the process and outcome.

No matter the complexity of the legal matter, whether commercial contract conflicts, antitrust actions, even intellectual property disputes, people called on to resolve these matters will turn the facts and the law into a hands-on, usually face-to-face tale of human striving, struggle, or success. When our inner movies are about conflicts or problems among people, we draw from our most basic tool—our own bodies and our ability to project ourselves moving through space and time among other people—to filling in the "scene of the crime."

However, our processing isn't random. Even on the other-than-conscious level, as each decision maker begins to build a version of your case story, there is a method at work in her mind—her *whole* mind, that is. In the very earliest stages of individual case story construction, that method is *metaphor*. The categories of experiences we sort through to reference and begin to relate to the parameters of any legal story are, by nature of the parts of the brain working them out, more general than specific, more related to the body than to ideas, more experiential than rational, and much more visual than verbal. Approached with some respect for their natural attributes, these metaphoric categories decision makers are using to relate to your story are also wide open to your influence.

In 2003, George Lakoff and Mark Johnson codified the subject in their book, *Metaphors We Live By*.[21] Since then, Johnson wrote *The Body in the Mind: The Bodily Basis of Meaning, Imagination and Reason*,[22] which carries their observations about the power of metaphor to shape our mental relationship with the surrounding world even further.

If your case story deals with a claim of wrongdoing by a professional, imagine for a minute the implications of the "dirty desk, clean hands" experiment when it comes to a juror or judge unknowingly relying on such a metaphor to sort out their very first perceptions on just how wrong the acts or choices being claimed really were or weren't. In the tests, the body takes the physical experience of the foul odor or the dirty desk and applies the "disgusting" or "dirty" metaphor from the experience to the researcher's spoken description of the action of lying or cheating. The mental image of a greater wrong is drawn straight from the metaphor cued by their body's experience. Note: no rational assessment of the situation leads to a conscious mind saying, "Dirtier desk in front of me means dirtier deeds in the facts of this case." We don't "tell" ourselves directly what to think, and we resist when others try to as well.

This kind of progression among and between referenced experiences, actions, and metaphors is widespread and consistent. Experimenters in the Netherlands asked test subjects into a room with a long table and seated them at one end. There they conducted what appeared to be a study with this person, but this person was actually a distraction. The real test came when the subjects were rewarded with a very crumbly cookie to eat as they waited to be excused. Twice as many cleaned up the inevitable crumb spills, cued by a referential experience they were encouraged (or conditioned) to have outside the reach of their conscious minds. Did you guess? (I didn't). There was a pail of water hidden in the room with a bit of cleaning fluid in it. The cleanser smell was detectable by people walking into the room, but by no means obvious. But, when the pail was not in the room, the impulse to get "next to godliness" drifted away. People translated the physical "clean" smell through their stored reference experiences into the "clean" *metaphor* and into their actions to "clean up." This is other-than-conscious recognition of a smell, a metaphor, or an impulse to action at all. Similar experiments employing a "business is war" briefcase sitting on the far end of the table invited people to compete in an experimental contest much more aggressively. Similarly, if the "competitive" briefcase was instead, a more "let's all get along" backpack, people reacted more cooperatively in the same game. The objects—briefcase or backpack—aren't just seen at the end of the table. They are seen through their metaphoric properties, with observable

21. George Lakoff and Mark Johnson, *Metaphors We Live By* (Chicago, IL: University of Chicago Press, 2003).
22. Mark Johnson, *The Body in the Mind: The Bodily Basis of Meaning, Imagination and Reason.* (New York, NY: Basic Books, 1999).

effects in terms of choices and action. Embodied metaphors hold real power over our embodied thinking.

Our cultural and personal metaphors for major life experiences automatically are referenced to make sense of any legal case story. Time, money, power, control, emotional reactions, work, values, and so on—all are embodied referential experiences most easily accessed by metaphor first, and through the details of the facts and the law later. This mirrors the primacy of other-than-conscious functions over conscious ones in general, just as Amsterdam and Bruner[23] place Rhetoric last in their hierarchy, following the more general story Categories, and then Narrative. Researchers have even collected some basic metaphors for us to use to approach and influence decision-making minds with respect for the potent processing done other-than-consciously very early in the (re)construction process.

Ask yourself, "What is it I want my decision makers to envision when they first are presented with this story?" Or, "What do I want decision makers to see when they ask, 'Just what kind of story is this?'" If your answer is anywhere along the lines of, "A defective product tort action, wherein the defective design is characterized by a failure to adequately warn of reasonably foreseeable dangers, in marketing to and instructing the end users," you might as well just turn out the lights and go home.

Instead, use the following list of embodied metaphor categories and look for the closest match (occasionally two) for the kind of experiences you'd most like your decision makers to use to build their private versions of your case story. The list very closely tracks many of the same basics Johnson selected. I pulled it from the book, *Marketing Metaphoria: What Deep Metaphors Reveal About the Minds of Consumers*[24] (which came out much later than Johnson), because the authors, Gerald and Lindsay Zaltman, have confirmed these seven categories of embodied experiences are basic drivers of purchasing decisions of goods and services in the open market.[25] Over seventy percent of the time, the products or services that most closely met unspoken but clearly visualized expectations driving a decision to buy fell into one of these seven categories. Attorneys trying to "sell" a position on a case story that they'd like each decision maker to envision and "buy into" could make good use of these metaphors. The metaphor can invite the mental referencing that cues building private stories soon "realized" by decision makers as very public legal judgments.

23. Anthony Amsterdam and Jerome Bruner, *Minding the Law* (Cambridge, MA: Harvard University Press, 2001), discussed at length in Chapter One.

24. Gerald and Lindsay Zaltman, *Marketing Metaphoria: What Deep Metaphors Reveal About the Minds of Consumers* (Boston, MA: Harvard Business Press, 2008).

25. This is the very same Zaltman cited a couple of times in the original edition as a critic of the potentials of standard focus group work.

Each of these metaphor categories can, depending on the story, be the central goal or central hole in the story most likely to lead to the outcome your client wants.

- Journey
- Balance
- Container
- Transformation
- Resources
- Control
- Connection[26]

3.15.2 Managing Perceptions

In Chapter Three, I took on the three primary habits decision makers default to for structuring and populating stories as they (re)build them. This is in order of their influence:

1. Habits of perception
2. Habits of thinking
3. Habits of psychological or social behavior

How does this three-part hierarchy emerge in the mind of a decision maker?

Perceptual Process

Our perceptions carry our awareness in and out of the context of our current and stored life experience *context*. They come first in the line of our experiences. They are the most prolific of those experiences. And, they are those that work mostly at the other-than-conscious levels of our minds' functioning.

Thinking Habits

The "ideas, attitudes, biases, and beliefs" commonly examined during voir dire provide a narrative *content* within the perceptual *context* of any developing story. A big part of these habits of thinking, as seen above, is driven by embodied metaphors that fully inform our human narrative, before they even reach our conscious awareness.

---

26. See the full article, "Brain Friendly Case Stories, Part 1," in the Summer 2010 issue of *The Mental Edge for Legal Communication* at www.eric-oliver.com for a more detailed review of each metaphor.

Psychological Factors

As it emerges into our conscious thought process, our story (re)building efforts are further influenced by these more interactively based habits, like *identification* or *reinforcement.* As the inner (re)construction becomes more available for reflection, these habits affect our *expression* of both the *perceptual* context and *cognitive* content of our private embodied narratives.

In the original publication of *Facts Can't Speak for Themselves,* I introduced the idea that attorneys should consider managing perceptions as a necessary part of their "job." But I did not fill out the details of what that might entail, nor the benefits managing perceptions brings to the table. So, allow me to do that here.

There are three areas of human perception that you want to work to "manage" with decision makers, both in focus groups that help you develop case stories and in the delivery of your best case story to the final decision makers. These areas are rapport, narrative, and imagery.

You can be sure that in a book subtitled "Reveal the *Stories* that Give Facts Their Meaning," the concept of *narrative* was given the lion's share of attention. In the First Edition, Chapter Four showed how to engage decision makers' mental *story* building process. Chapter Five broke down the design of case *story* development for a focus group. Chapter Six extensively covered the *story* element review and refinement process. Additionally, the 2015 supplement to Chapter Five picks up where I left off in 2005, showing how the *story* sequence and frames that deliver it have been refocused and refined over the last ten years.

Thus, this supplement to Chapter Three concentrates on managing the remaining two factors of perception—rapport and imagery—that received much less attention in the original edition.

What makes this management task more interesting is that the source of rapport and imagery is the part of the brain that is other-than-conscious.

How so? Let's take them in order.

Rapport

In Chapter Three, I introduced a couple of critics of focus groups and their number one shared complaint about the standard focus group process: that no member of a standard focus group will ever be induced to give fully "honest responses" without "hours spent building trust" with them—and, of course, there is no time in the standard focus group format to do so.

Actually, the exact opposite is true.

Believe it or not, all you need is just a few seconds to build rapport with any decision maker, in any venue. Research[27] has emerged since the original publication of this book, revealing that rapport is not a rhetorical skill, but a physical one, and requires the ability to mirror an individual. As a matter of fact, research has shown not only that the rapport generated by physical mirroring is the most effective factor predicting success in interpersonal encounters, but that it is most likely the connection we indiscriminately refer to as rapport, and cannot be made at all without some form of physical mirroring, mimicry, or alignment, first.

Mind you, despite how quickly it can be established with another person, rapport is not something that is turned on or off like a simple light switch. Mutual connection, not just contact, is fundamental to persuasion. But, the less contact you make, the slighter your chances of being able to both fully engage a decision maker and to influence his or her decision making process. And, when your aim is to engage and persuade the parts of the brain that are mainly outside conscious reach, relying on your verbal delivery alone is not enough; not even close to enough.

How so?

Because our other-than-conscious processes always come first, preemptively coloring any and all communication, influence, and persuasion. Rapport is seen more than spoken, felt more than considered, realized more than rationalized.[28] Yet, it can be exquisitely memorable, standing out as a beacon among dozens of other types of interactions with people, lighting the way to achieving *real* human contact.

For any attorney interested in taking advantage of the single most compelling tool for building rapport currently known, the one point the studies objectively verify is that if you ever hope to establish fully engaged rapport with another human being, you only get there through mirroring. The proven fact is that any strong connection we've ever had, any strong experience of rapport we've ever felt, would not have happened without mirroring.

Neuropsychological experts like Nadia Webb[29] point out that the absence of functioning mirror neurons also proves this point. Patients with damage in that area of the brain are unable to maintain rapport with spouses and partners whose company they previously had enjoyed for decades. Attorneys can experience a break in rapport (without experiencing a brain injury!) by unwittingly mismatching

---

27. The acknowledged progenitor of all the research on mirror neurons is Italian neuroscientist Giacomo Rizzolatti. His work and others is discussed, along with some of its more intriguing implications, in UCLA professor Marco Iacoboni's book, *Mirroring People: The Science of Empathy and How We Connect with Others* (New York, NY: Picador, 2009).

28. Just as all decisions for all legal decision makers are more "realized" than "made" in the traditional, conscious sense.

29. N. E. Webb, *Differentiating PTSD from TBI.* (New Orleans, LA: North American Brain Injury Society, Sept. 2001).

posture, gestures, or movements of the other person. Too often, we communicate more with ourselves when we should be directing our attention and some of our actions toward those very people waiting to return your attention with their own just because you made those efforts. This is why the single and most important foundation of effective case story delivery to any decision maker, in any venue, is the rapport you build with her.

Consider what MIT's Sandy Pentland has to say on the subject in his book, *Honest Signals: How They Shape Our World*.[30]

> [P]eople have a second channel of communication that revolves not around words but around *social relations*. This social channel profoundly influences major decisions in our lives *even though we are largely unaware of it* . . . . These social signals are not just a back channel or complement to our conscious language: they form a separate communication network that powerfully influences our behavior. In fact, these honest signals provide a quite effective window into our intentions, goals and values.
>
> By examining this ancient channel of communication, for instance—paying no attention to words or even who the people are—we can accurately *predict* outcomes of dating situations, job interviews, and even salary negotiations.
>
> We have shown that people's behavior is much more a function of their social network than anyone has previously imagined . . . . What the sociometric data demonstrate is that this immersion of the self in the surrounding social network is the *typical* human condition, rather than being isolated examples found in exceptional circumstances . . . . We are familiar with many types of human signals; smiles, frowns, fast cars, and fancy clothes . . . .
>
> We are all conscious of these types of displays and often carefully plan to incorporate them into our communications. And, therein lies the problem: because these signals are so frequently planned, we cannot rely on them being honest. We need to look for signals that are processed *unconsciously* [*sic*] or that are otherwise uncontrollable, before we can count them as honest.
>
> Some people are experts at reading these social signals and using them to influence others, even though most are unaware of how they do it . . . . In both salary negotiations and sales, we have seen that *mimicry* functions as an honest and effective signal of the trust, as well as the

30. Alex (Sandy) Pentland, *Honest Signals: How They Shape Our World* (Cambridge, MA: MIT Press, 2008): Preface.

> empathy required for successful negotiations and financial transactions. What is particularly impressive is the effectiveness of the honest signal: unconscious [*sic*] automatic mimicry improved financial results by *20 to 30 percent.* The impact of mimicry on these financial interactions dwarfs almost every other factor that has ever been studied.

In the late 1970s and early 1980s, the NLP folks referred to their work modeling human performance and communication as the "study of the structure of subjective experience."[31] In that context, what you will discover by adding physical mirroring to your daily practice of persuasion, what the research has now determined: that the "structure" of rapport rests on a foundation of mutual mimicry called mirroring.[32]

Researchers from as early as the 1970s, such as the great Robert Rosenthal (who coined the term "Pygmalion effect" to describe how students would consistently produce performances beyond their measured abilities in response to indirectly communicated expectations of them by their teacher) have acknowledged that other-than-consciously generated mimicry, i.e., mirroring, is an objectively verifiable measure of connection between human beings. Since the discovery of *mirror neurons* (ca. late 1980s and into the early 1990s, and a subsequent wave of studies), automatic mirroring outside conscious awareness in dozens of different kinds of interactions involving decision making, has shown an irrefutable link to empathetic reactions. Consciously directed efforts to mirror by attorneys have proven equally effective with witnesses in deposition and at trial, with potential jurors during voir dire, with judges at the bench and elsewhere.

Empathy has been tied repeatedly to mirroring activity through the functions of mirror neurons, the insula, and the limbic system, collectively referred to now as the *mirror system.*[33] That area of the brain has been called a "biomarker of sociality and empathy" by UCLA's Marco Iacoboni, but in people with very low activity in that area, the disorder of lost empathy—a form of autism—shows up at a very high rate.[34] The brain chemical oxytocin, when released, induces a "connected" feeling, one of belonging and trust. This is a feeling very often referenced when talking about rapport.

In 2011, I was talking with a group of about 200 trial attorneys,[35] when I asked how many were able to recall within the last six weeks an experience of strong connection with another human being. By that, I meant how many had

---

31. Robert Dilts, et al., *Neuro-Linguistic Programming, Vol. 1: The Study of the Structure of Subjective Experience* (Soquel, CA: Meta Publications, 1980) (emphasis added).
32. Eric Oliver, *Persuasive Communication: 25 Years of Teaching Attorneys* (Portland, OR: Trial Guides Publishing, 2010): Chapter 1.
33. L. Cattaneo and G. Rizzolatti, "The Mirror Neuron System," *Archives of Neurology, 66*(5) (May 2009): 557–560.
34. Marco Iacoboni, "Imitation, Empathy, and Mirror Neurons," *Annual Review of Psychology, 2009*: 655.
35. The actual demonstration can be found on my DVD, *Delivering the Goods*, produced by Trial Guides in Portland, Oregon, www.trialguides.com.

rapidly developed a strong feeling of connection with someone, either personally or professionally, who they did not know well or had just met. About sixty percent of the group's hands went up immediately.

Stepping forward, I started eyeing folks in the rows nearer to me and asked something like, "Who can tell me specifically and precisely *how* you made that connection?" I quickly settled on an attorney about five rows in, and, holding my hand in the air much as he was, tilting my head forward slightly much as he was, I asked him about his experience.

He proceeded to relay a story about a woman sitting next to him on a plane who was returning from a hospital visit for diabetes. He told her that his father had lived with diabetes for thirty-five years, and *just like that,* they were off in conversation. How come? Because they apparently had connected at the *content* level of communication. I then asked him if he'd ever met someone who was diabetic but with whom he hadn't formed a connection, "even though you had talked about diabetes?" He agreed that he had indeed had such a conversation without forming a connection.

The next question was, of course, "So what was the difference in what happened? If the content of a conversation is the key lever, how come a connection wasn't made?" He made a couple ineffective efforts to explain that began something like "Well, we *just* . . . ." That is a very common verbal sign of the conscious part of the mind trying make up an answer for something the other-than-conscious part actually did. When we get to that borderline, where processing outside conscious reach is going on and we are asked to, or want to try to, talk about it, we all begin *guessing*—and the guesses usually starting with "I just . . . ."

I then explained to the group that "when I recognized that signal it was time to stop asking the question(s). Because, he *doesn't know*—nobody knows—what is outside their conscious grasp." I continued on, "However, people feel compelled to make up something, and if, for example, you are an attorney conducting a focus group, you'll write down the person's conscious guess, and think you've got the 'real' answer to your question—*don't do that!*"

The attorney I had called upon then agreed that at the moment we'd begun his hand had felt a bit "stuck" in midair as I stared at him, my head still arranged much as his was, my hand still lifted in the same fashion. What many in the group did not notice was that our hands stayed up *together,* until they lowered *together.* In retrospect, the most important part of this demonstration isn't what any person can easily validate at any time through their own experience with mirroring other people, i.e., that, whether rapport is achieved—or missed—how we physically act *and* react to and with one another takes precedence over the content of our communication. This is particularly true when it comes to the experience of rapport.

The primary point to consider is just how many people raised their hands when asked to remember an experience in their recent past when a rapid, strong "connection" with another person was made. If the science is correct, that means they were all recalling an experience when mirroring with the other party led to the feeling and experience of rapidly formed rapport. As you'll recall, out of the more than 200 or so in the room, at least sixty percent had a hand in the air within seconds. All were instantly able to recall this moment of "connection." Most followed the prevailing assumptions about the mind and framed their own "connected" experience as a result of what was being discussed—the conversation's content. Most also would have been reduced to guessing what kept them from forming the same level of connection in other conversations on the same topics. What was missing then? More likely than not, for one and all, it was mirroring.

Emotional reactions, especially the most primitive and visceral ones, are *preverbal* experiences. That fact does not change even when the top two inches of the higher cortex throw vocabulary into the mix. We can talk ourselves *out of* an emotional reaction, even a visceral "reptilian" one, under certain circumstances, but we can never talk ourselves *into* one. Nor, can we just talk someone else into one, either. Talking someone out of an emotional reaction usually is counterproductive, like screaming, "Don't panic!"

But, make no mistake, a *feeling* reaction is your goal.

That sense of connection that so many attorneys quickly remembered, and all the attorneys in that group identified with, though could not say how to make happen on demand, is experienced first and foremost as a sensation. The experts call it "empathic resonance."[36] Just as rapport is the foundation of the most effective delivery of your case stories, so is mirroring the foundation of fully engaged rapport. It is the feeling of rapport that is so easily pulled from our memories of interaction. And, mirroring is the path to invite or encourage anyone to (re)build a foundation of an emotional reaction.

Empathic resonance—the feeling of connection and sense of rapport—is a basic human response as old as the reptilian mind itself, but it is a product of other-than-conscious processing, and thus primarily a behavioral and nonverbal experience. If improving persuasive methods that are friendly to the thinking processes of any decision maker's whole brain is your goal, then the importance of this nonverbal primacy is incalculable. Although it is not available just for the *asking*, it is readily within reach for anyone willing to do some *acting*—not melodrama, just mirroring.

Imagery

The attorney taking on the job of managing the perceptions of decision makers needs to take into account the key role mental imagery plays in encouraging the story (re)construction process.

36. Iacoboni, *supra*, n. 34.

So, how, exactly, does one manage the pictures in someone else's head?

When it comes to which of our three primary sensory systems are used to process and "make sense" of any case story—1) words and phrases (auditory), 2) sights and images (visual) and 3) sensations and emotions (feeling)— it is the second one, visual imagery, that is the most influential when building the embodied narratives that lead to a particular leaning or eventual judgment. Although feelings provide an emotional basis for the (re)built story, the mental imagery triggered by metaphors and referenced life experiences carries the process on from there.

This, of course, makes complete sense. You really can't appreciate a human narrative without actually *seeing* the humans involved in the events. How many times have you thought "the movie wrecked the book," or maybe even the opposite, how the movie predetermined what you saw when you read the book.

Most people believe that they are "visual thinkers," i.e., that their thoughts are primarily constructed of images. And, most people would be wrong. While we seem to live in an increasingly "visual culture," that distinction is based on the input we are receiving, not how we are processing the input in our heads. In fact, we tend to make sense of the world by talking to ourselves about it, i.e., we "translate" all of our sensory experiences into words, first. So, why emphasize mental imagery so much? Although we have all three sensory systems working in our minds all the time, attorneys would be wise to recognize that the proportion between the three is different for each individual. Specifically, there are three types: people who respond first and best to verbal input (the largest group), people who respond first and best to visual input, and people who respond first and best to sensory stimulation of a feeling nature (the smallest group). However, when it comes to the mind, just because most decision makers prefer to think in words or phrases doesn't mean that images have a less powerful effect in their "mind's eye." In fact, the reverse is often true. The more a person tends to think in words, the more sensitive they are to effective visual communication.

Whichever sense system a decision maker might prefer (other-than-consciously), all three sensory building blocks—words, pictures, and feelings—inform the case story they (re)construct in their heads. It is the perceptions of the facts in a case, not the facts themselves, that drive any decision in every case. This is equally true for the professional legal decision maker as for the non-professional. Impressions always take precedence over interpretations. By the time we begin to interpret, our impressions have already created the framework that rules the mental territory where decisions are realized.

Images are a potent force that drive powerful reactions among human beings. Think of prejudice, for example. When you hear a claim made about a manager, administrator, or judge making a choice about another person based on prejudice, what comes to mind? What do you *envision*? Subjects in research studies see *something* that leads to an "unconscious (so called) bias" that produces prejudicial choices and actions, even as they are sincerely unaware of the tendency,[37] and though it is known to drive many managerial decisions and result in many lawsuits. In a 2013 issue of the journal *Science,* researchers reported on studies they did in "the board-room" using the same techniques they had used to ferret out "unconscious bias" to make predictions about the bedroom.[38] They found that people who, when flashed a picture of their fiancée momentarily hesitated before clicking on a reaction word like "amazing" or "awful," were more likely to have marriages that did not last as long as those who did not hesitate before clicking. What did the research subjects perceive to create such a measurable response? I think we safely can assume that it wasn't a hastily constructed list of "pros and cons" about their intended.

So the key is to ask yourself first, "What do decision makers need to see?" And then, even more important, "How do they need to see it in order to see things my client's way?" How can you most effectively persuade them? Just as you can't expect to succeed by simply telling people what to think, simply telling them what to see doesn't succeed either. It works much better when persuasion comes in the form of an "invitation" to look at things a certain way without directly saying the words that represent what you want them to see. Furthermore, demanding that someone "just look at it this way" can come across as rude and aggressive to a decision maker, thereby negating its effectiveness. But, *show* them what you'd like them to see, literally and/or figuratively, your chances of managing their mental imagery increases exponentially. You've invited them to *see* their way right into your client's case story and to "make sense" of it as you would most like them to.

Although not a guarantee, selecting words that are more likely to evoke the mental imagery that will help decision makers build a better story for your client is effort worth expending. Inviting the right image affects the value of the case story as it is constructed by any decision maker. As the mediator winking in the back of the elevator said (while tapping the charts tucked under the plaintiff attorney's arm on which the demonstratives for his client's case story were printed), "Good stuff. More money!" The plaintiff attorney's successful presentation had just led to overseas excess carriers being called on the phone during the mediation to bring the settlement value up to twice what the client had hoped.

Get it? Fewer words. More pictures.

Demonstrative visuals are not just for court anymore (nor were they ever). Opposing counsel, insurance adjusters, negotiators, referees, expert witnesses, lay witnesses, and judges all use mental imagery to build private versions of case stories in exactly the same way as anyone else: *other-than-consciously* and, at your most persuasive invitation. As the attorney in an insurance bad faith case discovered three days into

---

37. Charles Feuss and Jeremy Sosna, "Courts are Warming to Claims of Unconscious Bias," *National Law Journal* (Oct. 1, 2007).
38. Reported by Karen Weintraub, "Subconscious Relationship Doubts? Trust Gut Instincts," *USA Today* (Nov. 28, 2013).

trial, the opposition can comment derisively all they want on the images you've invited them to "see," doing so only sets these images more clearly (and firmly) in their heads. The opposing counsel for the insurance company literally laughed out loud when shown the plaintiff's demonstrative visuals, calling them "simplistic" and "completely unconvincing." But a few days later, when the defense showed up with their own hastily constructed versions of similarly "simplistic" images, they discovered they were too late to compete with the mental images jurors had already adopted.

However, we usually are far less inclined to respect the decision maker's internal image-making process than the words we use to try to persuade. Most attorneys, even if they have an image in mind, will deliberately withhold it from those who they most need to influence—the other side—in the mistaken belief they will lose that image's impact "when we get to trial." The unfortunate consequence of this way of thinking is that the one image that could perhaps "make it or break it" ends up being "saved" for the scant five percent of the time that case actually might go to trial. In the meantime, without that crucial image nagging at them, the opposition feels free to devalue your client's losses. Think how often you hear something like, "Does that sound right to you?" and how rarely you hear something like, "How does that look to you?" Yet, it is usually the latter that drives the story any decision maker (including other attorneys) (re)constructs in their "mind's eye."

We humans are very effective at conditioning ourselves to respond to certain cues in certain ways. We are also very adept at linking words or phrases to a mental image and then, other-than-consciously, using that perceptual pair to repeatedly produce the same response. Many attorneys know this phenomenon as the "anchoring effect."[39] In recent years, plaintiff attorneys have sought out big numbers to reference in their case presentations just so that they can invite that as an anchoring effect in decision makers' minds. For example, the hundreds or thousands of hours of plaintiff's suffering prior to trial, and many times that suffering to look forward to in the future. When it comes to using time as an anchoring reference for harm value in the case, the intention is to invite decision makers to associate and equate big numbers in hours with big numbers in dollars. However, most attorneys stop there, defeating the purpose. This tactic succeeds *not* just when the numbers are *heard* by decision makers but *only* when the attorney's verbal delivery of the numbers is linked to an *image* of the numbers (the right image, of course), creating a much more powerful *anchor* in a decision maker's mind.

Here is a good example. A medical negligence case dealing with a fatal error of delay in diagnosing a young mother's breast cancer. West Virginia attorney

39. Daniel Kahneman, *Thinking, Fast and Slow* (New York, NY: Farrar Strauss and Giroux, 2011): 119–129, 363–376; also excerpted in *News From the Mental Edge* (Fall 2012), available at www.eric-oliver.com/newsletters).

Jim Lees[40] told jurors a story using the big number portion of the anchor he had invited them to set: he counted out either the days or hours from the point when the diagnosis *should* have been made to the date and time of the start of the trial. By repeatedly making a verbal association between those calendar numbers and the daily fee of just one defense expert, he invited jurors to form an even bigger number in their minds. But was it just the two numbers that actually created a leaning about the magnitude of the value of plaintiff's harms? No, it was the image he provided with the story that pushed jurors to multiply—almost exactly—the amount of the expert's daily fee by the number of the plaintiff's lost hours and days in their final verdict valuation of the harms caused.

What was the image he invited people to use?

The plaintiff's four-year-old daughter repeatedly reaching to be picked up by a mother whose severely advanced breast disease (and treatment) forces her to look down at her daughter's little upturned face and outstretched arms and say, "No." Over and over again, she is forced to answer "No," at the same time as knowing how few days left to enjoy with her daughter were being allowed her by the defendant's negligence. In this case, the mental image of a "formula" would read:

numbers over time + image over time = value of loss over time.

When we use words like *justice, pain, fairness, family, negligence, fault* with phrases that also link to our shared emotional responses, we make sense of those words *not* by their objective definitions, but by the subjective imagery we attach to them in our mind's eye, not as if they were written in stone but rather, as if traced in shifting sand. When someone says, "I don't get it," they are actually saying, "I don't see it."

If you want them to get it then give them a way to see it. Using demonstrative visuals focused on illustrations as well as visually evocative language, to invite decision makers to create anchors for your key story points, is a good place to start showing instead of just telling.

3.15.3 "Bloody Mess"

An example of managing perceptions in a case story by reframing the images first and changing the narrative as a result comes from a retrial of a medical case involving a plaintiff mother's claim that her obstetrician performed an unnecessary hysterectomy shortly after the delivery of her child.[41]

In the first trial, in which the defendant doctor prevailed, the defense claimed to show "multiple medical problems" for a couple of hours following a c-section delivery. The plaintiffs did not thoroughly deny this and let "them" be referred to as

40. Discussed at the Louisiana Association for Justice "Last Chance" conference (Dec. 2011).
41. The negligence case against the obstetrician was lost, then re-tried, after an appeal about either an instruction or evidence ruling.

"multiple medical complications." Most urgent was the failure of the uterine muscle to firm back up, known as *atony*, complicated by excessive uterine bleeding that seemingly could not be stopped. At about 1:00 a.m., after a c-section performed just after 11:00 p.m., the alleged ongoing blood loss led to the doctor making the decision to perform a hysterectomy in the interest of her patient's safety.[42]

Focus group participants (prior to the retrial) who favored the defense, and some who favored the plaintiffs, made it clear what imagery they imagined was visible at the scene, at the time. "It must have been a bloody mess!" was more than one person's observation. They additionally imagined that the doctor's frame of mind must have been like being "at the end of her rope," trying everything possible, but nothing helping with the "multiple medical complications," the patient's still unrecovered uterus, bleeding out on the table.

One of the challenges to presenting a cohesive case story for the plaintiff's side was the "multiple problems/complications" imagery because of the many medical techniques and standards the jurors needed to learn about to determine for themselves how well the doctor and nurses followed the rules governing reasonable medical practice with patient safety uppermost in mind. That final point— protecting patients' safety—was the starting point for framing the plaintiff's story, in questioning each medical professional, both those at the scene and those hired to render standard-of-care opinions. The question can't be asked, or answered, without inviting the desired image of patient protection.

> "Tell me, doctor, is it fair to say that among the highest priorities, if not the highest for your job is protecting the safety of your patients?"

The key anchors helping to facilitate plaintiff decision maker reframing, again were in the form of images linked to key phrases. Almost a dozen different drafts of the demonstrative showing blood loss (and replacement) over time, from the start of the c-section until the time the hysterectomy began, were tried out and rejected before the plaintiff attorney was satisfied with the combination of a timeline that included a visual depiction of *manageable* blood loss using pictures of blood products pictured as larger or smaller beakers. The timeline showed just four blocks of time, through vertically shaded columns, the widest by far (covering about a third of the entire chart and the longest length of time) being the fourth column on the right, depicting the time elapsed *after* 500 cc of blood products were given to the plaintiff, and how much blood she actually was recorded as losing over that final stretch of time: a beaker the same size showing 500 cc. Because this was the smallest unit of measure on the chart, the beakers were both very small, and the final beaker looked quite small indeed, sitting at the bottom of a column spanning an hour and fifteen minutes which is shown as wide open space, with two clock faces

42. The rationale for the appellate court's decision to send the case back for another trial did not involve this evidence, nor this opinion of the obstetrician.

at the top, showing the passing time from the one on the left to the one on the right. See for yourself:

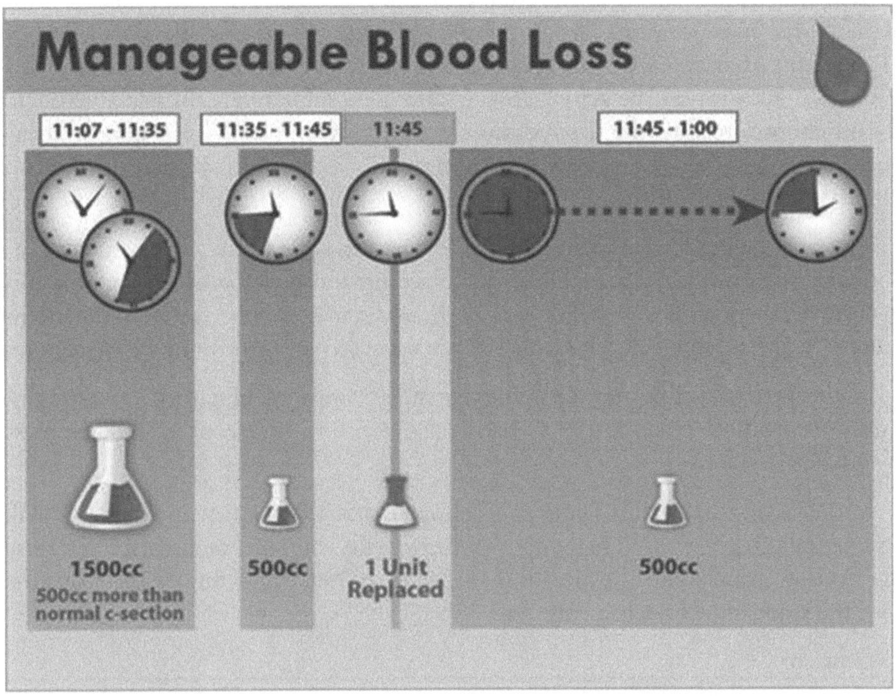

However, this carefully crafted visual would have had minimal impact were it not for the two verbal anchors the attorney adopted both to help jurors distill and understand the medical needs and procedures themselves, and to objectively consider the perception of the doctor as truly being at the "at the end of her rope." These two anchors used very general terminology from earlier in the trial: the *muscle* and the *blood*, but now in a separated context instead of the "multiple medical complications" including an unmangeable "bloody mess."

By dividing the world of seemingly endless, intractable problems—i.e., the "multiple medical complications," into just two complications—and a consensus of the experts from both sides that the uterine muscle did not perform its natural postpartum contraction and retoning and the allegedly "excessive" loss of blood, decision makers could assess how well the doctor applied her judgment and actions to just these two problems, at the scene, at the time.

It quickly became clear that while any reading of the reasonable care standards would say that she had used most of the ordinary approaches to help speed up the firming of the uterine muscle, she had stopped at the second of many required steps to deal with this kind of blood loss. After more than an hour of doing nothing to deal with the continued loss of blood, she jumped directly to the last and final resort, simply cutting out the uterine muscle completely.

With this consensus medical reframe in place and ready to be responded to by decision makers as they heard experts and treating professionals alike state—or have to concede—that as long as the blood loss is not severe and/or increasing (the little 500 cc beaker showed the actual slowing and acceptable rate), a reasonable doctor always chooses to give the uterine muscle time to come back, as it almost always does. "Give Mother Nature time to heal naturally" was a phrase (and image) used successfully by the plaintiff.

The final mental image invited for jurors was this: one of the very next steps in a normal postpartum situation, to alleviate bleeding and give the uterine muscle time to naturally contract is to tie off one, or both, of the major blood vessels to the uterine muscle. Sadly and ironically, this is also the very first step of performing a hysterectomy.

In the first trial, the prevailing mental images were of unnamed, innumerable "multiple medical complications" and the overriding image of a "bloody mess" everywhere to be seen.

In the second trial, after a concerted effort to actually manage the decision makers' mental images, they all had only two (now really relevant) pictures to pick from: the firming muscle and the clearly manageable blood.[43] Looking at the story that way, the professional neglect was clear.

How so?

"Blood" now didn't mean a "mess." "Blood" now meant neglected work and the excuse for unneeded surgical removal of all the future children this woman could have given birth to—as all could now clearly see.

43. We consciously emphasized the more static and objective phrase "blood" over the dynamic and scary "bleeding" in our trial vocabulary to help anchor the "non-messy" imagery linked to those phrases.

Chapter Four

Well Begun

In theory, there's no difference between theory and practice.
In practice, there is.
—Charles Faulkner

4.1 Preparing to Present

There are some hard and fast rules for preparing a case for presentation to focus groups that test the range and nature of the stories participants can build. The quality of your results depends largely on the quality of your delivery. While the situation is never going to precisely mirror that in which the actual case will be presented, that is no excuse for failing to provide the most professional delivery possible.

There are certain risks you do not need to run. For instance, presenting the facts sitting around a table with the group in a conversation adds a layer of distortion to the message participants receive, making it less like the one that might be presented in a more formal setting. Likewise, with stopping to question the group after only one side has opened. Jurors, judges, or mediators will not be asked to consider just one side's story at a time. You want practiced, adversarial presentations of each party's story prepared before the group arrives. Avoid having the professionals presenting the case facts also doing the questioning and moderating. It adds a layer of distortion to the actual situation, even if voir dire is allowed in your venue. In that case, a lawyer would not be representing the client one minute and dropping that role to have a chat with the jurors, judge, or mediators. The adversaries in the matter should be represented equally as well as at trial, rather than jamming three parties' case presentations into the hands of a single attorney for convenience within the group(s).

The person most familiar with the case, typically the attorney whose case is being tested, should present the side she opposes. The lawyer cannot hide her familiarity with the case and strong commitment to it. It will "leak" out in verbal and nonverbal ways during presentation.[1] The participants, perceiving that leakage often imagine a more credible story, and not just one with which the speaker is more familiar. You want any advantage this might produce to accrue to the other side, not your own. Your presentation of another party's case is hampered by your lack of connection to the case from the other party's point of view. Artificially strengthening your client's position further by having the most well-versed attorney sitting on his side is a risk you don't need to take in influencing the listeners' story building. In a related vein, the attorney(s) less familiar with the matter needs to be well schooled in the facts and coached to present their side's position well. The aim is to get both side's best foot forward in this abbreviated way. Aim to present the opposing story even better than what may occur in the actual presentation.

When deciding how many focus groups to run, consider everything from finances to the availability of discovery material. While Mies van der Rohe's dictum "less is more" applies to what's presented to decision makers, the opposite may be true regarding the number of groups you are able to run. In that case, more may well be more. Still, most trial attorneys that believe their cases warrant pretrial, pre-mediation, or pre-negotiation research are looking at a very limited number of projects. All the more reason to prepare to get as much as the participants will be happy to give, if they are approached well.

4.1.1 Packaging the Facts—Theme, Scope, Point of View, Sequence

When packaging the facts and law for a group, gather:

1. All the information of the facts most likely to be in evidence
2. The language of the laws most likely to be used in claims
3. The jury instructions and the verdict form

Many of these choices have to be made by educated guess, so the hard rule is always the same: If you are uncertain about a document, fact, or ruling, always err on the side favorable to the opposition and *unfavorable to yourself*. Do this only on the truly close calls. Do not unnecessarily weaken the presentation.

1. "Leakage" is a technical term describing the nonverbal, implicit expression of a position, perception, or leaning about the message the speaker holds, but tries to hide. Your attachment to your own side of the case will "leak" in many ways. Practice and effort can lessen the effect. Since the other attorneys presenting typically have less of an attachment to the matter, someone not in the firm or not connected to the litigation can have very little of this nonverbal "subtext" at work. They will be providing fewer misleading signals. It is advisable to take your bias and place it in the opposition's camp to at least blunt the impact of your leakage and draw on your superior familiarity with the case to bolster the implicit strength of that side and better balance the presentation at these levels.

Build a narrative description of the complete case story of no more than three pages. Try to incorporate the most significant facts, but start to shed needless detail.[2]

Cover the whole arc of the story rather than singling out one area.

Include a page or two to list all the weak spots and strong points for each side in your summary and the major points for professional and lay witnesses to make, and a brief account of the most significant documents likely to be in evidence.

Filter all this collected and distilled material into what you believe will be the most compelling story format.

Fit the narrative for each party's case into these story elements for your presentation using theme, scope, point of view, and sequence.

Theme

What one phrase most embodies what the story is about?

When you are establishing your theme phrase, be sure to anticipate the decision maker's task at the end, when it comes to the forms of the questions they will have to answer. Do not settle for a short version of the plot line or facts. Rather, find a phrase that encompasses their full meaning in the light of what you want the decision makers to do about either side's case.

Scope

Consider the time each story presented will cover; people directly or indirectly involved or affected; and actions, events, and numbers related in the stories.

In which areas is it broad, and in which not broad? For example, is it about one or two events or acts over a long period of time involving a few people, or is it about a single act that takes only a second or two but was repeated by dozens of different people? For each side, how far should this story reach?

Point of View

Who is the central character or what is the central point of reference in this story for each side?

2. Names, dates, and detailed qualifications of choices, acts, or events are not needed to put most stories across. While the principals' names need to be used, the name and background of the officer at the scene, the middle manager delivering the contracts, or almost any expert witness do not. Exhaustive steps in chronologies are another place where detail can be shaved, as well as technical descriptions of any ilk. The entire anatomy of the chest does not have to be related, illustrated, and labeled to express the dangers inherent in a punctured vein. Also, if you plan to try to change the names of any party, it is strongly suggested that you do a full dress rehearsal to get all the inevitable slips of the real names out and corrected, because suspicion of the system flows through these groups as well as through jury boxes, and you will only draw exaggerated attention to any changed name that slips out.

Which individual, organization, or entity is the one through whom all the others are best referenced? As a consequence, who are the less central characters, the lesser figures compared with the main one(s)? Look beyond just the choice between the parties themselves, as many times the most compelling story revolves around a third party (e.g., the end users of a disputed product), a group (e.g., all reasonable professionals), or an abstract entity (e.g., the law, common sense, the body, or its condition, time itself).

Sequence

This is a very important element to get straight and with which to be consistent in a focus group presentation. Which is the best point in time for the story to start to most effectively establish and support the theme? Quite often, the most effective presentation sequence is not chronological, though it is many people's first resort. The most persuasive beginning, middle, and end for your case story may very well not be in a calendar. It can be a story told backwards in time.

4.2 Video Testimony

Since the aim is to make sure that we get all the participants' possible stories straight (not overwhelm them with our version), they need ample room to let us know how those stories are forming. One way that can be achieved is to minimize the use of video testimony and allow group members time to discuss their versions of the various elements of the case story.

Video testimony from actual or facsimile witnesses tends to draw attention and have an impact disproportionate to those story elements and case facts that will not be presented on tape. Also, unless every tape you show has been produced for the group, consistency will almost certainly be lost in the questioning regarding the important elements of theme, viewpoint, etc. If you need to test head-to-head credibility of a couple of witnesses or if you have strong concerns about the demeanor of a witness in testimony, videotaped excerpts *can* help.

Still, a couple of hard rules should be in effect:

1. Keep them very short, aiming at five minutes or less.
2. Balance in the delivery has to be maintained, so if you bring a video of one witness from one side, corresponding witnesses must be produced for the other side(s).
3. To the extent possible, make sure the case story you plan to deliver is supported by the questioning on the tapes. Try to balance direct and cross-style questioning as you shoot live or edit from deposition tapes.
4. Wait to show them to the group until two jobs are done: participants all have the full gist of the stories from all sides and you have had time to find

out directly from the participants what they've done with what they've received up to that point. This way, the exaggerated and artificial impact of the tapes can be blunted somewhat, while still testing the strength of their content for effects on participant story development.

4.3 Visual Aids

Visual aids will either make the participants' lives easier or more complicated, depending on how they are designed and delivered. This is true for jurors, judges, and all decision makers. It is important to put together visuals designed exclusively for that group. You may find that those serve well as templates for the visuals to be used in actual presentation. Confirm that the language anchors and other reinforcement methods for all the story elements you've chosen to put across to the group are well served by every visual you present. Because of the summary nature of the presentation, visuals can be used to collect and summarize points that may otherwise come out in distinct parts and pieces. Be wary of the inclination to bury the group in boards or slides. That is not the most effective way of presenting a case story to elicit the most open and complete responses from the people you came to hear.

4.4 Small Bites

If you are going to get even a small window opened onto the process of the group member's story development, you have to interrupt yourself long enough to listen to them. Given that the process of building each private version of your case happens quickly, this applies particularly near the beginning of the group session. One method for respecting participants' perceptions and processing is to design the presentation to be delivered in small bites, rather than a half hour of uninterrupted narration for each side, with no intervening participant input.

Divide focus group presentations into several sections, alternating attorneys presenting their case stories with short written and ample verbal queries of the group. The typical arrangement has a very short opening statement from each side, followed by written and verbal feedback. Then a short portion of the evidence from each side comes out, followed by more questions and answers. That is repeated one or two more times until all the pertinent evidence for the test has been delivered. Videos, if needed, are inserted at this point. Finally, closings are followed by more written feedback, and then by deliberations of small break-out group "juries" selected from the larger group.

Primacy has a big influence on the formation of juror and judge story constructs. Tracking those early constructs becomes harder if you wait to start your inquiries until the end of the day. Thus, focus group deliberations provide the *least* valuable information for tracking possibilities in that influential, early process (*see* Chapter One).

However, if at the start of deliberations you first ask participants to summarize the significant or important elements of the case stories as they heard them, uninterrupted and without declaring a final decision, you often get some strong hints about recency effects on the stories they've been building all day.

In our groups, we have each side's attorney plan for a five- to seven-minute opening statement before we begin surveying the group members in writing and then aloud.[3] The structure of these openings gets more attention than any other part of the presentation preparation. This is not only out of respect for primacy and recency effects, but also because the task to be accomplished by opening these sessions is very different from the one practiced by attorneys introducing a case story in court. Since the decision maker's process starts at the level of perception—of message, messenger, and context—moving to a global referencing of stored experiences and associated life stories, we want to reflect that process with a presentation that also starts very generally rather than diving into all the factual details. This helps meet decision makers where they will begin processing: at the perceptual and unconscious levels, not the verbal and conscious ones.

In trial, the traditional job of opening statement has been to introduce the upcoming facts. In a focus group, the task is to avoid too many factual details letting the lawyer introduce the story:

- The theme
- The major and minor characters and actions
- The beginning, middle, and end of the sequence you've determined best expresses the theme
- The key verbal and visual anchors

All of these should be referenced through the point of view you want to test.

To accomplish that in only five minutes, you have to be selective about specifics by cherry-picking only those key facts for which detailed descriptions best illustrate and establish the story structure you want to present. It is our contention that a lawyer who can't summarize the full arc of his case story in five minutes or less is not ready to present that case for trial or for any other dispute resolution.

4.4.1 The General Approach Versus the Detailed Approach

This method of introducing the story and not all the details can't be done well without practice. Before learning to start focus groups in this way, most trial attorneys have had lots of practice in beginning trial presentations by censoring the

3. Aim for five and you'll usually hit seven.

establishment of story elements in favor of an overly objective listing of facts, repeatedly following the phrase, "the facts will show" or something similar.

Due largely to this practice of sorting to fine detail more in a list than in story form, most attorneys fall into what one lawyer we've worked with calls "detail spin." This in spite of their sincere efforts to avoid it. It is not unusual for such a lawyer to start her five-minute opening the first time, determined to get the whole story arc out, establishing all the important elements of theme, scope, point of view, and the rest, only to sit down fifteen or even twenty minutes later having been waylaid by detail spin at the halfway mark. Still, the lawyer is not yet finished. Regardless of our best intentions, when it comes to our habits in communicating, we all tend to do what we rehearse, not what we intend.

A quick review of some of the perceptual and thinking habits that jurors and group participants use to start their own stories, outlined in Chapter Three, can show you why a general, not overly detailed approach to getting out the full story of both sides is preferable in openings to groups.

1. Since we are dealing with the intersection of conscious and other-than-conscious processing, start generally and move to the specific, respecting the same kind of referencing happening behind the mental scenes by each listener to find references to you case story and to make sense of it.

2. To help overcome some of the challenges to receiving worthwhile information about the unconscious stories building in the group, it helps to try to engage people in the broader context of the story first, to allow as much of their own life experience biases and private story structures to engage your story in as many ways as possible at the more significant, perceptual levels.

3. As group members think more about it, this general approach allows room for positive outcomes to be invited from assimilation and confirmation effects and it turns reinforcement and identification to your aid, too.

It is far easier to meet the aims of expanding and including as many varieties of response as the group members can come up with if you avoid reducing the tale to the lowest level of detail from the start, limiting reactions to a short list of what you have already expected to hear. (If you are curious how reasonable the company's acts and choices will be viewed, never declare them to be so with detailed backup at the start.) These groups work best when they are filled with reactions and additions you might never have imagined. Your first presentation has to leave them room to develop. The longer you go on, the more likely people will finish the perceptual framing of their stories completely. They will shift into using habits like confirmation or norming to fix their attention on a single detail and filter everything else they hear and have to say by deleting, distorting, or generalizing in line with that one conclusion. This leaves their story construction far behind and farther out of reach.

4.4.2 Presenting the Opening

Regardless of whether we know precisely which stories are developing behind the conscious process, we can get many implicit suggestions about *how* people are doing it. Those suggestions will be found in and between the lines of their answers to our questions. Each person has to be given as much room and personal latitude as possible to engage the story we offer. In that way, they will find their own categories, build from their own life references, and attach their own narratives to the stories they start building to decide the case. This is a process better encouraged by invitation than instruction or declaration. Listing "what the facts will show" invites a disengaged, arm's-length perspective from the listener at the outset.

On the other hand, suggesting that—

> You may soon learn (or find, discover, or have revealed to you) how this person (or that company) chose to act (or was acted upon), over (this amount of time) by (such and such forces), leading to this/these outcomes, which the law says, as you may soon see, are well within what any reasonable customer can expect.

—is far more inclusive and likely to help listeners engage their own minds, rather than telling them to stand back.

It turns out that strong memory is keyed by emotional responses to the events or narratives we store as references.[4] You want to invite judges, mediators, negotiators, jurors, and focus group members to have the emotional responses necessary to get their brains (specifically, their amygdalas) to "mark out" your theme or point of view in their memories. It is easier to do this by allowing them every chance to fill in their early versions of your case than by trying to limit their options. Since they can't arrive at a decision without first building their own version and for efficiency, it seems wise to start generally, and move to the details later.

This form of presenting an opening, using less limiting assertions such as "you may soon discover" or "you will be learning how," still meets the needs of most court restrictions on opening statement language. It also allows you a better chance to meet the needs of the decision makers. Some people think that boldly declaring what the facts will prove helps the attorney appear more confident in the eyes of jurors and other decision makers. The people thinking this are almost invariably attorneys who wish to be seen as more confident in front of jurors and thus help perpetuate this myth. You do not invite people to engage your story by daring or ordering them to do it. You invite them to engage your story by lowering the perceptual and thinking barriers to that task as much as you can. One way to do this is to offer them the *illusion* of choice in the matter. To set the framework for this effort, use words and phrases such as "learning," "finding out," and "discovering,"

4. James McGaugh, *Scientific American Frontiers*, PBS (original air date March 2001).

which are activities few people resist and many enjoy. Remember, according to the best formal research over the last decade or more, one of the most common attitudes jurors bring into the room that colors their hearing of criminal or civil cases is suspicion of the system. Viewed in that context, telling people what they will be thinking about one fact or another in evidence, in order to make yourself feel more confident, seems to be inviting nothing but disaster.

The total time invested in the group needs to take into account the time needed to draw the most from what the participants offer. Not only does the presentation time need to be held down to a minimum, the time devoted to eliciting the group's input needs to be maximized. For a group of about two dozen people, this means a full day's commitment.

4.5 Focus Group Presentation Tips

Though the focus group setting is informal and you'll become familiar with "juror" leanings throughout the process, make every effort while speaking to the group to conduct yourself as if you are speaking to a jury in court. (Please dress for court.)

Avoid the temptation to "break the frame." Make no comment out loud regarding the time allotted for you to speak/present, or the process itself. Be sure to avoid any references to artificiality, i.e., "If this were real," "If we were actually in court." Do not "apologize" for any part of the day's events, whether for the presentation itself or any quirks related to the facility.

Balance in attorney presentation is essential for the best results. Balance between the stories the group is presented with, *not* between the strengths of the legal positions. However, it does refer to all the factors involved in presenting the facts and the law—time spent speaking, general number of major points covered, level of detail, emotional intensity, planned deliveries versus *ad hoc* commentary, use of visuals both in style and number, level of formality or engagement—all need to be as closely matched as possible. One side cannot overwhelm the other with exhibits, video testimony or overtly greater case knowledge if you want the best results. For example, if the plaintiffs use their fully allotted time at each opportunity, but the defense consistently comes in one-quarter to one-third short of theirs, then the presentation can be unfairly overbalanced, regardless of what is said. Likewise, if one side is closely adhering to the presentation plan but the other departs from it just to list answers to charges or serially respond to participant questions, then we aren't executing the best testing we can. "Freewheeling" in these groups can wipe out the reliability of our results.

Winning is not the goal for *either* side (this is *not* an effort to "test drive" the facts to a simulated verdict). If the groups deliberate and you prevail, great. If you do not, even better. The goal is to learn as much as possible about how your case story is likely to be *perceived* by an actual jury. To achieve this goal, it is still extremely important to give serious thought to exactly which points are your best points, and in exactly which order and in what way the group should be made aware of them. Equal—or greater—consideration must be given to the very best points of the other side's presentation in order for your client to gain as much as possible from the effort.

During the debriefs of the full group, you may hear a number of erroneous statements of facts or law from individual participants that you will want to directly address or "fix." You may even want to "argue" directly to them. Please avoid this; do not directly address individuals who raise these points. Instead, make every effort to incorporate the items you wish to correct, expand on, or argue into your evidentiary presentations or closing argument. During the debriefings, if you are suddenly asked questions directly, avoid responding except through the moderator, unless otherwise informed. Never come into a section on evidence with a list of answers to questions asked in the prior debriefs. Always stick with the presentation as planned.

Opening statements, as conducted in these groups, are the biggest departure from typical courtroom presentation; the need for balance is nowhere greater than in their delivery. There, you are introducing the *facts*. Here, you are introducing the *story*. Each side wants to make sure their theme is well established, to set up whatever anchor phrases, analogies, crucial visuals, etc. are needed to convey them. However, you want to avoid exactly what is most commonly practiced in court: backing up *every* assertion about the story with a list of detailed facts from the case. *Facts* are about specifics: dates, times, backgrounds, technical language and descriptions, processes, and people, including names, titles, and qualifications. *Story* is about the theme, the main characters and their actions, minor characters and why they are minor, the scope of the story, its general beginning, middle and end (chronological or not), using a minimum of detailed facts. In the focus group, detailed case facts should be carefully chosen and *very* selectively used to illustrate those story points. Where they are not *essential* to introducing the full spectrum of the story, avoid descending into detail; use as few full names as possible, do not use strings of complete dates, leave out lengthy witness qualifications, do not excessively define places, do not use full job descriptions or long citations from the statutes.

Don't waste time worrying about a panel becoming "contaminated" by the intermittent discussions between your short presentations. The panel comes "pre-contaminated"—as soon as the participants walk in with their values and beliefs attendant to their life experiences. Our purpose is to find out which kinds of contamination are likely to be elicited by your case presentation when it comes to each person's *perceptions* of the case stories; how likely these contamination(s) are to spread, and how tenacious each is when interacting with another.

Avoid worrying that your time is too short and that "If only I could say more, they wouldn't be thinking these things." After sitting through actual trials, regardless of length, most jurors express that they wish they had been given more information.

Summarizing your case efficiently, while still putting the best evidentiary foot forward, can only help you deliver a more clear and compelling case in court, or in alternative dispute resolution. If you don't mistake detail for specificity, you can be very clear and comprehensive in a relatively short time. In focus groups (and trial too), taking too much "time to explain" only compounds confusion and errors.

Witnesses often need to be tested, particularly if some specific problem like credibility is a concern. Please be prepared to produce a video of an *opposition* witness addressing the same or closely related topics as your own witness(es) do to keep the balance level. If an opposing witness is not available on video, you will need to create a video that accurately reflects that witness's sworn input, as well as her general demeanor and style.

Visuals can help a great deal, as long as they are not substituted for a planned presentation; they should *summarize* points that otherwise would be presented separately at trial. A *Reader's Digest* view of details you can allude to—not fully explore—by each general topic area. Excerpts from depositions and documents are better than page after page of blowups with lines highlighted. One visual with five or six culled-out phrases, covering all witness accounts, for example, is what's required. Remember, the number of visuals, like depth of detail, level of intensity, and length of speaking times in these presentations, needs to be *balanced* between the two sides. The number of visuals each side uses doesn't need to be precisely the same, but it can't be wildly different, either. The formats in which they are delivered must be similar, and it is best to think of *no more* than five visual demonstratives per fifteen-minute segment. Avoid handouts.

4.6 Ground Rules

When the group has been recruited, screened, surveyed, and seated, most are probably ready to participate.[5] Still, they will all be on separate pages and some probably aren't even ready to open the book. Human beings are not solitary entities. We've been herd, pack, or tribe animals from our beginning. Thus, there are libraries written about the influence of group dynamics on individual behavior. One recent study of jury groups suggests that even the potent pull of prior personal bias or prejudice can be measurably diminished by competition from the many influences we have on each other when we gather together in a group. Let's not forget that the same problems that individual jurors have in voir dire are present

5. There is a whole industry devoted to the recruiting, care, and feeding of focus groups for small-group research for legal and nonlegal purposes. One focus of this book is about how to approach the group and appreciate what they offer. For more information on how to construct groups and some of the ethical considerations involved, you may want to review David Ball's *How to Do Your Own Focus Groups: A Guide for Trial Attorneys* (Louisville, CO: National Institute for Trial Advocacy, 2000). Also consider looking at the Small-Group Research Standards on the website of the American Society of Trial Consultants, www. astcweb.org.

in varying degrees in focus groups too. Everyone hears how high the fear of public speaking consistently ranks among Americans polled on the subject of fear. People frightened of looking foolish or performing the task badly may have lots of other distracting things on their minds. They often would rather be anywhere else but for the subpoena that brings them to the jury box, or the fee they came for from the focus group.

On top of all that, one more major impediment to gathering the most useful input about their private case story constructions is that nobody sitting around the table knows how to do the job. Unfortunately, much like presuming their own "expertise" in rules of the road for driving, most of the focus group participants imagine that they do know. As the focus group critics say, some think their job is to provide the expected or politically correct responses, some think it is to give the answers they imagine the sponsor of the group would like, many act as if the job is to please (or antagonize) the moderator. Then some think their job is to either hide from or lead the parade—all day long. Of course, all these presumptions have their referents in how actual jurors approach their jobs too.

While the idea of building deep, personal trust with each person in a group of two dozen people in half an hour is farfetched, it is not required to do what needs to be done. As a matter of fact, playing the three kinds of influences listed above against each other—group dynamics, individual assumptions and fears, and the habits we have for following rules—can help invite participants to become more constructively forthcoming in very short order than some of them ever imagined they could be. Each person in your group, for instance, has several large sets of references that can be invited to the fore to be made more available by the trial professional moderating your group before the opening statements begin. They include:

- Prior experience with juries on TV, in movies or books, and in actual jury service
- Learned social habits, including the group dynamics mentioned above and other, more direct forms of peer pressure
- The more innate "herd instinct" we all possess, which drives people (especially in groups) to follow leads and leaders once they are established
- The "job frame": accumulated presumptions and habits for how a person approaches a job, wanting or obligated to "do their best"
- The "as if" frame: an effective tool that relies on the potent, persuasive effects of presupposition

In effect, people in legal focus groups do know how to do the job, since the "how I always dress" answer to the "appearance here today" question is still right. But they can be invited to know how to do it more productively before the lawyers' presentations start. As with opening statements and other persuasive suggestions, these invitations are often best made somewhat indirectly, rather than through a printed list of commandments. The areas of prior life experience and private parts of each participant's life story can be marshaled during the introduction to invite each participant to apply these resources in the most productive way during the group. Just as few people want to sit on a jury in a frivolous lawsuit, very few focus group participants want to spend all day making efforts they see as wasting their time. (The very few who get past initial screening can be weeded out.) Thus, most start positively motivated for the task at hand. So it is the job of the moderator to introduce the chance for each participant to take full advantage of these resources. This, in turn, will help them envision how a "job well done" depends on engaging the story more fully, then honestly revealing as much of his or her inner-story building as possible, although not in these exact words.

The tasks the moderator wants to accomplish to engage group resources during the introduction include:

- Establishing rapport or a useful connection with each individual by employing physical mirroring to establish more complete communication and matching each person's expressed preference for visual, auditory, or kinesthetic processing
- Approaching each person's responses by mirroring phrases, implications, frameworks, or perceptual preferences (where time allows)
- Spreading the "wealth" of the group's attention, establishing a pattern that leads to the expectation that hearing from more people is preferred to hearing from less, and that greater group input resolves confusion, conflict, and hard questions
- Setting frameworks to handle challenges[6]
- Building trends, demonstrating, and practicing productive responses using presupposition as well as open direction
- Dealing with fears, spoken and unspoken
- Shrinking the job frame to manageable size by setting a perceived limit on what is required from group members at any given time

---

6. Family and group therapy pioneer Jay Haley used to say that in order for the professional relationship established with clients to work, an unequal, one-up and one-down framework needed to be established and maintained throughout the likely challenges from the client. One of his contemporaries, Al Lipp, described the application of this frame to group work as requiring the leader to maintain control over the "contract, context, and structure" set up in the beginning, expecting challenges to the agreement parameters (contract), the course of the group conduct (structure) and what parts of members' lives (context) are—and are not—relevant to the work. Lipp called the process "an administrative battle for control of the situation in which, if the client wins, the client loses."

- Modeling humor
- Encouraging response potential[7]
- Meeting some expectations by setting schedules and other requirements and sticking with them, without turning the group over to any whim and a raised hand
- Setting anchors for life-experience content, rule adherence, and responsive reactions through verbal, visual, or spatial anchors or repeated indication of individuals who first produce certain responses as "anchors" for the rest

To get these resources up and running, the group needs to begin well before the attorneys are allowed out of the gate. It is imperative to invest some time setting up useful frameworks and expectations for the group's participation, since the primary discussion topic for the whole day is their individual imaginations and impressions. Plus, there are well-known conscious limits on both expressing and exploring them. This is very different from "making sure they get the story straight," as the old interpretation theme had it when it came to decision makers judging case stories. In a world where the stories are the biggest variable and every group member constructs his own collection right in front of you, the watchword is much more like "making sure we get all *their* stories straight." Less illusion of control, but potentially greater value in the end.

This juggling act with the group and its input can easily fall apart if members aren't given a useful mix of invitations and directions that enable them to do their jobs well from the start. Foremost in that effort is attention. That is the subject and the substance of rapport—not positive feelings, not agreement, not control or dominance, but focused attention. Coordinating the nonverbal and verbal message provided to each participant in the earliest stages can help invite more complete attention and a fuller engagement of their story building strengths from the outset. Where possible, acknowledging, and utilizing both perceptual preferences and analogies or examples from their personal life stories, as revealed, can extend the invitation further. Subtly sorting for difference in verbal responses a little more than for similarity can keep participants focused on answers to the "what else" question at the heart of the inquiry. Reflection and reinforcement, in some of the various forms indicated above, can help invite and capture the greater investment of participant attention needed to get the results you seek (whether by engaging availability, norming, identification or confirmation habits). Finally, repetition and simply forming questions well can drive the expanding and inviting posture most

7. There are many ways to build up participants' expectations to do well, including fostering competition, encouraging reflection within the group, and simple reinforcement of any and all moves in the direction you'd like. One example would be the suggestion some professionals make that the results of the group may be helpful in resolving the actual conflict later on.

helpful to drawing out the widest possible reach of the many versions of the case story available to hear and consider.

Does this effort eliminate confusion or distortion? No. Is it designed to control all possible inputs to narrow the field to a select few? No. It is a more complete job description and job training for the workers about to embark on the hunt with you, the professionals, leading and examining these folks for the gifts they offer the clients whose case story is about to be studied. So why not join in with the "workers" as it begins, rather than just declaring the job description process?

Following is a transcript of a typical introduction, which aims to inform, direct, and rehearse certain responses from the group to prepare them to do the best job they can with the case story about to be placed in their hands.[8]

4.7 Sample Transcript—Introduction and Job Description

> Good morning, my name is Eric Oliver. I'm not a lawyer. But there are lawyers in the building, and they'll soon be in this room. So take whatever precautions you think necessary.

These people are going to be asked to repeatedly jump back and forth between reacting as jurors and commenting on those reactions.[9] Technically, they are being asked to repeatedly engage in the process and then to "meta-comment" about it. Rehearsing that task can't start too early. One effective lever is to use unexpected humor. Jokes require listeners to take a "meta-position." Assuming most participants are somewhat anxious much like actual jurors and they are there to do a job but don't know the full description, humor can help them rehearse their first jump.

This also helps in setting the "as if" frame. I am not the lawyer, so this may not be the serious part, with less reason for concern about what we accomplish before we "really start." This lessens fears and still gets the job described and rehearsed.

> What just happened earlier—when we all waited for one person to return to the room—is a good example of what's going to have to happen for the rest of the day. If somebody's out of the room, you can't talk about what you came to talk about. Toward the end of the day, the last thirty to forty-five minutes will be spent in three different groups of seven people deliberating the case you are about to see. So look around the room and decide which six other people you least want to be on a jury with and you can bet that's who you'll be with, because

8. This introduction is for a civil case, but the same concerns apply to criminal cases, though the analogies clearly need adjusting. Presumption of innocence substitutes the "preponderance" of these beginning sessions—that is, the element of the juror jobs that requires the most attention.

9. That is, taking mental or "meta" positions outside their immediate circumstances, disassociating for the purpose of evaluating or commenting on that situation.

> I get to pick them. And when you're there, you can't talk about the case unless every one of you is there. You can talk about the lawyers, or me, or anything else, but not about the case unless everybody's present or you defeat the purpose of having a jury at all. Everybody has to have a full chance to hear and see and fully contribute for the jury to serve its real purpose. Does that make sense?

Spreading the wealth of attention to include every member. Demonstrating and practicing a productive response to a rule, while also raising response potential about the job. Using the participant's absence to model from the front of the room.

> Did I mention that you have to be unanimous? All of you have to agree on each question asked on your verdict form, in order. [*Long pause.*] We promised we'd get you out of here by 9:30 or 10:00 tonight, right? [*Participants are usually told 8:00 a.m. to 5:00 p.m.*] Unanimous means that on the verdict form I'll give you, you all have to agree on each question before you move on to the next. Those of you with actual jury experience will be pleased to learn that there are only six questions, not fifteen pages and forty-seven questions per page. It can get pretty complicated these days.

Referencing jury experiences, encouraging availability, and identification. Shrinking the job frame and a little more humor. "Future pacing"[10] the job at the end, while reinforcing acting as jurors would. Meeting some expectations, while setting the unanimity anchor and framing the structured rules with both implicit and direct suggestions about adherence as part of this job.

> Who's been on a jury recently? Criminal case or civil?

If you review experiences, find former forepersons and find out if jury service was a satisfying experience, and why or why not. Unsatisfactory elements provide a chance to reframe focus group experience from those parts of jury service. More life experience and job-frame referencing, while spreading the group attention some more.

> Who's here after talking with someone on the phone about this job? They asked you if you knew a list of people, organizations, businesses, law firms, and the like? How many of you recognized that as the same list you just went through on your background forms? Does any one of those names look familiar to you yet?

Wait till you connect with each party after each question. Note that including "yet" presupposes there will be a response.

> So, who can tell me what the job you all volunteered to do today is?

---

10. An NLP term for mentally rehearsing a future act, rather than simply intending to do it.

> *To give our opinions.*
>
> What else?
>
> *To listen to a legal case and give our ideas?*

Move regularly from those eager to talk to those clearly not, as you expand and contract the territory of "right" answers. Reflect and reinforce wherever possible. Leave the final answer open. Presuppose their versions are more important to hear, setting a trend of moving away from reduction and limits.

> There are a number of ways a group like this might be called together. Sometimes we do these groups for cases that have already been through trial. Why would someone do that?

Explore and validate answers, minimizing "appeal" and maximizing "education" responses.

> Sometimes a judge puts you here in what are called "mini-trials," "advisory jury trials," or "focus groups." They'll do this to encourage settlements in cases long before they might otherwise happen. If that were the case, these tapes we're shooting would end up on the judge's desk on Monday morning. Now, while your decisions would, of course, not be binding, you can bet everything that what each of you says will be taken extremely seriously.
>
> That leaves the most common reason someone would ask us to have you here: one or both sides in a case that has yet to go to trial asked you here.
>
> Now tell me the truth, what do you think someone who has yet to go to trial would want to get from a group like you about their case, whether it's one side or both sides sponsoring the event?
>
> *Strength of case; gonna win or not; how much?!*
>
> Yep. That's the number one answer. Are they going to win? Now, what if I were to tell you that you guys, sitting here on a Saturday and talking about your impressions of a case, are very good at doing a lot of things, but that one of the things you're really not good at is predicting precisely what a jury in a courtroom would do with these very same stories. And if you look around and think about it for a minute, you'll see why it's so hard for a group like this to be precisely predictive of an actual verdict in court. How might that be?

Eventually, through discussion, answers will form about the difference in the experiences in the group and those of a jury in court. Note the response-potential reinforcement, while widening presuppositions about what "right" answers could be, setting up the presupposition that the first, easy answers may not be the accurate ones. Leaving all these possibilities open on the menu helps divert attention away from the sponsors' motives and toward the process itself. It can help to slip into past tense occasionally throughout the day when describing the elements of the case or trial, in order to keep the detectives in the group reminded of the many options governing their positions. Also, note the fairly consistent attempts to deny or reverse likely prevailing presuppositions about both this process and the court system as a whole. Challenging these leanings early, offering "surprises" to what was assumed, can prove helpful later, primarily in keeping a higher level of engagement with the story than may otherwise have played out. All still in the "as if" frame, before the serious stuff starts.

> Exactly. The experiences you have here and the experiences the jurors in court have are so different, in so many ways, that there's no way you could guarantee from your experience what they might do. For instance, you know when you're leaving. You're being paid substantially more, less parking. You aren't seeing any (or most) witnesses, and those you do see are only short bits on videotape. How can you fully evaluate how they'll be taken if you aren't even going to see them? You have no procedures, no jury room, no bailiffs with guns, no bench conferences, and no objections or other formal nonsense that delay your day. All you have are the very best-foot-forward, *Reader's Digest* condensed versions of what it's agreed both sides can produce about the case in front of you. I promise, at the end of the day, I will tell you as much as I can about which of these brought you here today. Those of you that still want to play detective, be sure to look closely at what the lawyers wear on their feet, because I have it on really good authority that shoes are good clues.
>
> Now, if you're not here to predict a verdict, what else might you be here for?
>
> *Money, amounts.*
>
> Almost always the number two answer. Thank you for playing, but I'm afraid that ain't it either. The other thing this kind of a group is not great at predicting—and it stands to reason if you think about it—is the eventual amount of the verdict if the plaintiffs were to prevail. What else could someone want to get from you guys?
>
> *To pick the right jurors.*
>
> Again, a very good try, made all the more reasonable by the number of John Grisham novels floating around out there. Unfortunately, just as the experiences you have are so different from those of jurors in a courtroom, each person has way too many different characteristics from which to build a "perfect juror" to hear any particular case. How

> many of you know someone close to you who has served in the military? And if you look around at the hands, they all voted the same way, go to the same kind of church and are all the same sex, too, right? No, of course not. I'm afraid it just doesn't work that way.

By now, virtually everyone should have been connected with at least once, and both herd instinct and peer pressure should have been engaged.

> So back to the original question. What is the job you've volunteered to do today? You know it has to do with rendering your honest opinions, right? And you know they can't get certain things from you, including who's going to win, how much it's worth and who the right juror to hear the case might be. You can't say, and I won't ask.

> This job is to render your opinion about a legal matter. The upside of that is that since it's your opinion, anything that comes out of your mouth is on the subject. You can't possibly give me any opinion throughout the day that is off the subject. As a matter of fact, the more off the subject it sounds, the better, because the alternative is what I don't want you to do. Who here thinks it's just a great idea to rush to snap judgments in the American jury system?

Show your raised hand, and wait for follow through around the room. Shrinking job size, challenging presumptions, reinforcing job frame, and setting anchors.

> Would you want your own case handled that way? Somebody takes one look at you [*to a participant*] and says, "Oh, he's so guilty—just look at him." OK? If you think that's a bad idea in the jury system, then please don't indulge in it here, because I'm predicting right now that some might slip up. The lawyers are going to come in here in a few minutes. They're each going to give you five to seven minute opening statements, the gist of the story they're going to tell you during the day. Not evidence. Just the opening statement. What the evidence is going to show you. Then, after you fill out a little form for me, you and I are going to talk. Now I predict that you'll hear a couple of subtle, barely recognizable hints from a couple of people that might indicate that they've developed a little leaning on the case. They'll say things like, "I don't know what the heck this is even going to court for. They don't have a case. No business bringing such frivolous stuff to us—but I've still got an open mind!"

Take a position against the side you are working with.

> They haven't heard a word of evidence. "Oh, no, no, I haven't formed an opinion yet. I just think they're stupid for bringing the case, but I'll keep an open mind." Right? The object here is to get to deliberations with the most open mind. Not "I can name that verdict in three notes."

> That's not your job. "Rushing to judgment" is not what we're about here today. I'm not interested in and you'll never hear me say, "Who's ahead? Who's going to win? Who has the best case?" That's not what I'm interested in. You can't predict the outcome anyway. That's not your job. I predict your three juries at the end won't even completely agree with each other.
>
> I'm just interested in your impressions as the story develops. And I don't care how close or how off the subject they sound.

Declare main task anchor as "impressions," and immediately set parameters that aim at expansion, rather than reduction. Denigrate "solving" the case, and use an anchor—such as the not "rushing to judgment" that you get the entire group to publicly commit to—to reinforce that position. Contradict another one of their primary assumptions about their function to focus attention on the next step of the job description.

> Besides opinions, which we've already covered [*indicate the source of that answer*], what else can be covered by impressions? What else is the job about?

Elicit input, including attitudes, emotional responses, beliefs, and the like. Share the wealth and reinforce participation and varied input as much as possible.

> We're missing the biggest part of your job. I'll give you a hint. It's what jurors in both criminal and civil trials spend fifty percent of their time talking about during deliberations. What one subject do all jurors spend half their time talking about?

Here is the first real open-ended question that takes some effort. Model the presumption that it will be answered, while soliciting as many participants' inputs as possible, rejecting only the answers they can clearly see are either way off track or already covered. Here is where trends for the day are established and reinforced, practicing productive responses, while demonstrating that easy, quick answers aren't the goal. Start cutting off the chattier folks and selecting the quieter ones to confirm and expand answers. Contrast the aims of the job—and increased speculation and expansion of the story beyond the facts—with likely expectations, while at the same time using the group to rehearse a similar elicitation of multiple, differing inputs ending in almost all "correct" answers. Future pace to the end of the day.

> Yes! Their own lives. Themselves. It just makes sense. If you're going to make sense of someone else's story, you relate it to something from your own life, true? So your job of rendering impressions includes any and all of those things: attitudes, ideas, opinions, beliefs, and whatever pops to mind that the stories remind you of from your own lives. Again, it's not "name that verdict." Whatever pops into your mind, however off the subject it seems, is still right on target.

Let me give you an example: we were doing a case about a medical trial. That's not what this one's about. This deals with cars. The other case was about a surgery that went wrong. We were talking about it with a bunch of people like yourselves, and when the lawyers finished the opening statements, I stood up and—this is what we will do today, too—and I said, "What were your first impressions of this story?" And this woman said, "I don't know why, but the stories, they just started to remind me of the movie *Saving Private Ryan*." You find the connection. The closest I've ever come is, like, blood. That's all I can come up with. Those are the kind of answers I want—as long as they're honest reactions. I don't want you making up stuff to impress us. But if you honestly have something like Private Ryan pop into your head, that's what I want to hear. What I don't want is for you to try to "solve the case."

I repeat, please don't limit yourself because you think it's off the subject, or you think it's your job to solve the case. That's not what you're here for. I would rather that you get to deliberations with your minds completely open, not deciding one way or the other which way you should go before hearing from the other six people on the panel. Now, if you guys follow the national numbers, only one in five of you will honestly be able to say that. Some four out of five will go in with a leaning, one way or the other. That doesn't mean you're decided, but you know which way you're leaning. In juries they survey across the country, only one out of five people say they actually get to deliberations and have not decided—do not have a leaning either way—they want to hear what the other jurors have to say. Now, if you're one of the those people, I figure you've done your job. If you have a leaning, great, that just means you match the numbers. So either way you can't miss, unless you've already decided the entire case before you hear any evidence. That would be the one way to screw up.

The only wrong answer you can give today is to have an honest impression and not tell me about it. That would be the wrong answer.

Now, unlike the experience those of you that have served on actual juries may have had, I'm not going to wait till the very end of the day to give you instructions on how to handle the stories the attorneys are about to deliver. That's like, "OK, here's a pile of parts. Please take them and build a microwave oven. Before you start, I want to make sure you recognize that the future of her [*pointing*] life or livelihood depends on the kind of job you do. I'll be back tomorrow with the instructions—have fun." That's the way some court systems work. We're going to turn that on its head a bit and give you the main instructions right now to apply to what you are doing here today. So you know what to do with the facts as you get them from the attorneys.

Backtracking, the job description has now already gone from alternately commenting on and acting like a juror, deliberating as a full group, to applying instructions throughout even more than an actual jury might be asked to. Participants have acquired "special" knowledge about courtroom processes and might use it to raise the value of the current experience in their mind's eye. All the while, we've simultaneously expanded the simplified job of rendering impressions, inviting all manner of responses, while presupposing that "verdict answers" are the only ones to avoid, reframing preexisting notions about both focus group and juror "jobs." If you have woven nonverbal connections and overlaps into the verbal discussion with individuals, while accessing all of their references for juries and examples from their life stories about that "job," the first round of mental rehearsal for the day's efforts will have been successful.

> What's the difference between a criminal and a civil case? Ground rules. You're the jurors. You have to decide a civil case today, not a criminal one. What's the difference?
>
> *One is about money and one is about freedom, maybe life.*
>
> In a criminal case, one of the parties pulls the jury into the courthouse. One of the parties brings the jury into court. They're the ones filing the complaint. In a criminal case, who is that? Who brings you to court?
>
> *Various answers.*
>
> The prosecution, and they represent the people, the State, and they say you broke a criminal law, this set of rules over here that you can't break. If you do, we're going to give you criminal penalties if we can prove in front of a jury that you did.
>
> There's also a set of civil laws. Who brings the jury to court in a civil case, who is filing the complaint?
>
> *Various answers.*
>
> The plaintiff, from the root of the word "to complain." Whoever makes the claim, either in the civil case or in the criminal case, they have to bring the jury because, of course, they're the ones that say there's an injury. The criminal people say there's an injury to society as a whole. The civil people say there's an injury to my company, my person, my property and they deserve to pay, and you guys get to decide that. And if I'm making the claim, if I'm pointing the finger, then I'm bringing the jury to court. [This packaging can be used to explain affirmative defense burdens as well.] And then, of course, I obviously have the burden of proving the case.

Start from their baseline of criminal case awareness, set anchors for the burden. Include the name and the labels, as well as modeling from the front of the room, i.e., pointing a finger, setting spatial anchors for the two sides, etc. Note that having shrunken the juror job frame, we now reverse course and start acting as if they must adhere to the same serious burdens and instructions actual jurors must. The "as if" frame will likely start to lower a bit for many participants at this point, as they start taking the instructions they need to apply to their "real job," now that its parameters have been simplified, elicited from them, and set. Here is where peer pressure, herd instinct, and group dynamics will come to the fore, and challenges to the structure of the "contract" for the day can surface and be handled, along with remaining outstanding fears and doubts. Be sure to watch for any hints of separating from or disagreement with the group in this section, reengaging those individuals immediately. Set both visual and spatial anchors[11] in front of the group for the discussion about civil and criminal similarities and differences. Again, there is repeated modeling of sorting a little more for difference in responses, than for similarity.

> OK, if I'm the prosecutor, I have to prove this case to a jury of twelve people of your peers, because we're not going to throw this person in jail or give him a lethal injection unless you say it's OK. It's not just me declaring him guilty; it has to get past you. So I make the complaint, and then I have to prove it. The same thing in a civil case. The plaintiffs say they have an injury, whatever it is, physical, financial, whatever: you hurt my business, you kept me from getting into the market place, there are a lot of those kinds of cases, contract problems, you defrauded me, you misrepresented yourself in a contract, you did not pay me, I was your construction worker, I was your accountant. They make the complaint because they say they have an injury. They have to prove it to the jurors in order to get any kind of recovery. Are you with me?

Check in with at least three people in different spots.

> What do you call the person over here that the prosecutor brings to court? The defendant. What do you call the person over here that the plaintiff brings to court? The defendant. That's why it can get confusing. Same name in both situations. The person, people, or institution(s) that either the plaintiff or the prosecutor file the complaint against is called the defendant.

---

11. Setting up a cue for participants, jurors, or judges to condition their own responses relies primarily on timing and consistency. The cue is an invitation to mark out a response and link it to your proffered gesture, phrase, spot on the floor, point in space, tone of voice, etc. You must first time the introduction of your cue to the appearance of that response in the group. This is true whether they spontaneously create a response you wish to invite them to build an anchor for, or whether you elicit that response purposely. From then on, it is incumbent on you to recreate the verbal and nonverbal package of your anchor as consistently as you can in order to maintain the integrity of the connection you want to encourage. See also Paul Lisnek and Eric Oliver, *Courtroom Power: Communication Strategies for Trial Lawyers* (Colorado Springs, CO: Professional Education Systems Institute, 2001): Chapter 3.

In a criminal case, what does the law say a juror has to be thinking about a defendant as the trial starts?

Treat everyone equally. Innocent until proven guilty.

You'd be surprised how few people actually act that way when they get into court. Most people act as if he's guilty if he has been arrested, and he has to prove why there's a good reason he shouldn't have been arrested. They turn the whole system on its head.

Check group for nonverbal agreements.

In a civil case, it's a little different. You come at both parties on a level playing field. There's no presumption in favor of the defendant. There's no presumption in favor of the plaintiff, the party claiming to be injured. You have to treat them both equally, all the way through their stories.

The main question you have to decide in the civil case today is negligence. But who here knows the rule you have to apply to determine if someone is negligent?

Reasonable.

Yes, you know it's the "reasonable" manufacturer. But how do you determine whether it's been proven? In a criminal case, it's easy. The rule you apply is easy. How sure does the prosecutor have to make a jury before you throw someone in jail or take away a life? What's the rule?

Reasonable doubt.

Beyond a reasonable doubt? [*Wait for active signs of near total agreement.*] So you have to be pretty darn sure if you are going to take away someone's life or freedom. Why? Why would they make it that hard in America to take away someone's freedom? First, you have to presume the defendant did not do as the prosecutor says he or she did, and on top of that, you have to make the prosecutor convince you beyond all reasonable doubt. Why do we raise the bar so high to prove a criminal case?

No mistakes. It's most important.

Yes, the Constitution. What value in America is higher than liberty and personal freedom? According to the rule book, it's number one. Life and liberty are the highest values we have in our country. "Life, liberty, and the pursuit of happiness," correct? So if you are going to take away freedom, you'd better be darn sure before you do it. The party pointing the finger in a criminal trial has to make the jurors pretty much as sure as they can be. In some places they say "Beyond a reasonable doubt, to a moral certainty." What's that? [*Elicit a couple of responses.*] So, we all agree, if you're taking their life or freedom, jurors have to be made very, very sure? [*Wait for full acknowledgment.*] That is the theory.

Meeting jurors or focus group participants at their model of the world, not the legal model, requires acknowledging the widespread existence of a criminal mindset in experiences, attitudes and ideas about court matters, affecting views much more far-reaching than burden of proof. Allowing people to try to imagine the steps by which they would actually employ a presumption of innocence can get folks to the next step of personalized responses of a non-formulaic nature as the job training continues.

Now, what does the defendant in a civil case stand to lose? Their life?

Money.

Money. What else?

Reputation. Property.

I assure you, you will not be called on to do that. There's no slot on the verdict form that says remove your good name—and your dog, too. Just money. You value the loss. You don't even say where the money comes from. Just this loss is worth this much. That's what your job is. There's no slot on the verdict form that says we take away fifty pounds of respect. But you're right, if they lose a case, loss of respect may be another result, but that's not in the jury's power to take away. The only thing a defendant stands to lose in a civil case is money. The job of the jurors, if you get that far on the verdict form, which is not guaranteed by any means, but if you get there, your job will be to put a cash value on the losses you may have said the defendant caused. That value must be found in the facts in evidence before you, not just feeling badly to yourself and trying to put a price tag on your own bad feeling. That's not your job. But nobody talks about money unless you get over the first two hurdles in the first two questions.

Start reframing the distractions possible with damages, while inviting focus on the primacy of earlier concerns. Simplifying the job description more. We know that *all* decision makers will blend story and case elements, bootstrapping views of harms with perceptions of the level of fault, for instance. But, the criminal mindset pushes many people to act as if finding fault were their only job, so emphasizing all the questions to come at the end can help by presupposing that this won't take place, while bringing the full sequence of verdict questions to the fore.

So here we go, this is your job, how sure does the jury have to be in a civil case, where the defendant only stands to lose money as opposed to what we value most highly in America?

A preponderance of the evidence.

You would be surprised how often I have to pull teeth to get this phrase out. Preponderance of the evidence. What does it mean?

Elicit a good number of reactions. Reject only those answers they see are clearly off track or already covered.

More evidence than not. More sure than not. You have to be made more sure than not by the party pointing the finger. How much more?

Beyond a reasonable doubt.

Nope. Beyond a reasonable doubt is criminal. That is the murder standard, the lethal injection standard. This is civil. Preponderance of the evidence is civil. What I want to know is, what's the difference? According to you, how would you know the difference between being convinced beyond a reasonable doubt, and being made more sure than not—because that's the rule you have to abide by in this job today.

Set visual and verbal anchors for that job to use later. Spreading the group attention, while inviting expanded, inclusive answers. Some may take a little time, but they will eventually come. Setting prior expectations in the context of the rules to follow. Reinforcing the job frame and norming responses.

Beyond a reasonable doubt: no question in your mind. Preponderance of the evidence means there's more evidence against the defendant than not.

Right. How much more evidence against them than for them do you need in order to find for the plaintiffs, against the defendant, the person they say injured them, in a civil case? How do you know how to do it?

More than fifty percent.

That's right. More than fifty percent, according to me [pointing at the participant]. Of course, you also have to get six other people to agree with you. It's more sure than not sure. You have to feel more sure than not that the plaintiff's claim is accurate, that the defendant was negligent, because there was a defect and it didn't meet the standards and it did make the injuries worse. If they can prove all those things to you, then the defendant deserves to pay compensation to the person they've injured. But they have to prove it. And you, ultimately, are still the only one that knows if you've been made "sure" more than you've been made "not sure," aren't you?

> Here's the hard part: most jurors do not like that standard, because we're not trained that way. We're trained in our culture to like absolutes, nothing but absolutes. We do not like ambiguity—more likely than not, more sure than not. I do not like that. I want all or nothing. I want them totally guilty or totally innocent. I do not like this "maybe" stuff. If you're going to ask me to hold a company, a hospital, a doctor, or a driver responsible for paying monetary damages, you should have to make me, the jury, just as sure as if you were accusing them of a crime. Right? How so? [Get at least some acknowledgments, if not explanations.]

Having established both spatial and verbal anchors for the two extremes of the two standards across the front of the room, you now make them explicit to fully aid people in making the separation.

> We are over here today. You have to be more sure than not, according to you, that they did not act reasonably. That's your job. You have to be more sure than not, according to you, that there was a defect. Are you with me so far?
>
> So how will you know if you're more sure than not? How will you make that decision? I'll tell you what, it's much easier to catch people when they're switching the standards. Here's the problem. What most people will do is shift back to an absolute standard because it's so hard to stick with more sure than not. So what they'll do is say, "I have to be totally sure." Here's what you're going to hear, and I want you to police each other and if you're lucky you'll catch yourself saying it, too. I promise you, at least one of the juries is going to have somebody who'll flip back to a criminal, a murder standard, just because this one's so hard. They're going to say things like, "I'm not totally convinced." Now is that "more sure than not," or is that "beyond a reasonable doubt?" "They haven't completely convinced me. I'm not 100 percent sure. I'm not certain. I'm not absolutely sure." When you hear somebody say, or God forbid, when you start saying this to yourself, "I'm not 100 percent, absolutely, totally, completely certain or sure," here is what I hope you say to that person: you go, "Whoa, jump back and take a breath, Sparky. Relax, it's OK that you're not 100 percent, absolutely, totally certain—you don't have to be. All I need to know is, are you more sure than not, because that's your job. Your job is to be more sure than not."

Modeling with a participant, face to face. Check for acknowledgments in the group during and after, setting the framework to challenge contrary positions by presupposition and by appealing to the simplified job frame, herd instinct, peer pressure, open acknowledgment, availability, and norming.

> That means there are two ways the defendants get a verdict in their favor here and only one way the plaintiffs do.[12] The defense gets a verdict if the plaintiffs come nowhere near making you more sure than not. The plaintiff didn't prove the case to your satisfaction. "No, you're not negligent. No, you did not cause the harm, go away." Right? If, on the other hand, the plaintiffs make you much more than just a little bit more sure, then certainly they deserve the verdict. Here's my question—and we'll find out how well you guys are ready to do your job. Here's your first test. What if somebody on your jury says, "I'm kind of in between, I'm kind of in the middle, you know, I see where the plaintiffs say this, and certainly they would have those problems with that design, and obviously that's going to make things worse inside that car. But on the other hand, I can also see what they say about . . . what the company says about, you know, the state of the art, the engineering . . . they met the rules of the time. So I'm kind of like in the middle, I'm on the fence, 'I've got one foot on the platform and the other foot on the train.'" Who does that person on your jury have to vote for? Who must they cast their vote for if they stay in the middle?
>
> *The plaintiff.*

Wait for more than one response and gauge the rest of the group as well. Move forward if the majority disagree with the "plaintiff."

> No. The defendant. Are you more sure than not if you are sitting on the fence? I want to make sure that everybody understands they have to make you more sure. They just don't have to make you 100 percent sure. You can't be in the middle, perfectly balanced, "even-Steven," torn between the two, because if you are, that must go to the defendant. The plaintiff has to prove their case. They have to make you more sure, and if you're sitting there going, I see both sides, you're not more sure. Are you? Right? [*to the person(s) answering "plaintiff"*]. If you're even, it's a defense vote, even if you feel very badly and agree with a whole lot of the plaintiff's case. If the plaintiff fails to prove his case to you at all, it's a defense vote. If the plaintiff makes you more sure than not, even if it's only 50.1 percent, that is more sure and it's a plaintiff vote. You don't have to be 110 percent sure in order to find

---

12. This "two ways to a defense verdict" and strong emphasis on presumption of innocence are two parts of the introduction that would be reframed introducing a civil case tested for the defense. Also, adding reference to "punishment must fit the crime" to leverage the criminal mindset to the advantage of the plaintiff side can help, as well as talking more about the instruction about "a cause," not "the cause," required to find that element. Be careful about inviting suspicion by too openly minimizing the plaintiff burden of proof, i.e., "only a preponderance" while implying that the claim being made is valid. These are ways to tip the balance toward the opposition and hopefully counteract some of the inevitable pro-defense leakage in the lawyers' presentations to follow.

> for the plaintiff. But, you may still have a lot of doubts when you do vote. Are you with me? Questions?

As in voir dire, strive to avoid the phrases, "Any questions?" or "Does anybody . . . ?" as we all have reinforced the answer "no" through simple usage, when the question is phrased that way. Always presuppose there will be questions, input, and expansions, and there will. That is, unless you don't want questions, in which case be sure to ask if there are any questions.

> Those are the two rules you have to apply. You compare the reasonable standard of an ordinary company following the rules to what this one did. And you decide, have they made me more sure or not that they broke those rules. All right? Questions?
>
> Now you know who has the burden of proving things to you, and to what standard you're to hold them when they try to make those proofs. So how do you decide if somebody is negligent or not? The rule you have to apply is pretty simple. Here's the deal. You can't apply the rule of the world's greatest manufacturer and you can't apply the rule of the world's worst manufacturer. You apply the rule of a reasonable, ordinary manufacturer with the same amount of information at the time, under the same circumstances. That is the standard that you hold up to judge this defendant's behavior. That is how you determine if they were negligent. Did they act the way a reasonable manufacturer would? Did they not do the things a reasonable manufacturer would avoid? If the answer is yes, they're not negligent. If the answer is no, that they acted differently than a reasonable manufacturer would, then they're negligent. It's up to the attorneys to show you what those standards are. That's why they have experts—to tell you what the rules are. Because you're not assumed to know the rules for surgery, for example, just because you showed up here to listen.
>
> The next question you'll need to answer if you're made more sure than not that the manufacturer is negligent, is did his negligence cause the injury to be worse? Who here has ever accidentally run a stop sign? [*Raise your hand and wait for participation.*] I said "accidentally run," so how would you know? [to any without a hand up, one by one]. Now, who here that has most probably accidentally run a stop sign has hurt or killed someone doing it? [*Usually, nobody. If there is, you work from that point.*] So you can break a law or a legal rule by running the sign, but that doesn't necessarily mean someone gets hurt because you did it, right?

Again, reinforce full-group participation on each question. Get more than one verbal answer to those questions that require them, moving past the most eager ones to those that are less so. Rehearse as much responsiveness as you can. Use the second follow-up question. If possible, jump from shutting down an overly talkative member to one who hoped to get through the whole day without speaking a word. The first, potentially personal life question goes by quickly, but people still recognize it.

> So question one will be about negligence—acting in ways that you find to be in line with the reasonable, ordinary way or not. Then, if you find there was negligence, the plaintiffs still need to get past question two—was there any harm caused as a result of that negligence. You could have a foul, but no harm, see? [*Wait for majority acknowledgment.*]
>
> Now the day is going to be broken into basically two kinds of pieces. Some of the time the attorneys will be talking to you. During that period when an attorney is standing in front of you, you have to act as if you're in court. That means you don't talk to each other, and you don't talk to the lawyers, don't ask them questions, don't make comments to them. Take as many notes as you like. If they say hello, you can say hello. The same thing applies in the hall, just as in court, when you're out in the hall, it's just as if you're a juror. That means you can't talk about the case among yourselves, you don't come to any final or finished opinions about the evidence until all of it has been presented to you for your deliberation. Thank you very much [*acknowledging recognition from a panel member*].

Use every chance you can to use reflection, reinforcement and the other psychological principles discussed in Chapter Three to establish connections and responsiveness from each juror at least once during this session. Also, if you know the mirroring technique, be sure you are using it, at the same time checking for nonverbal responsiveness with every person.

> Don't talk about the case when you're out in the hall. Your job is to render your opinion, here today. If I don't get it recorded by that thing [indicate camera], or by her [*indicate reporter*] or by both, then your job hasn't been done. If the best of your opinions get exchanged in the bathroom, we've failed. We may have to activate the bathroom cameras if you don't follow this rule. If you're outside smoking, and you're talking about this case and you come up with stuff you wouldn't say in the room, we've failed. You've failed to do the job you volunteered to do, and I miss the best of what you came to give us. So, please, you can talk about anything else, but don't talk about the story you're going to hear unless you're in here, or you're in the room deliberating when we break up at the end of the day.

Imply common group goals and reinforce group affiliations and self-policing on an easy issue.

> Who here is congenitally shy? Can't talk in front of other people? Because you're in the wrong room. You took the wrong job. There are a couple of rules. One of them is, if I ask you for your impressions, you will have one. OK? The words "I pass," do not pass your lips today. Anybody have any difficulty with this rule? If you do, it's a nice sunny day out. You still have plenty of time to go out and enjoy yourself.

Reframe choice to participate as choice to answer, with full group as leverage.

> The other rule is, of course, that no one agrees with JoAnne. Why don't you agree with JoAnne?
>
> *Not her opinion.*

Lowering pressure and pushing for differences in responses against the natural tide pulling toward consensus.

> Yep. Is it even possible for anyone else to have JoAnne's opinion? You can have a similar opinion to JoAnne all day long if you like, but you're never going to have her exact opinion, because you don't have her experiences, you don't have her beliefs, you don't have her values. You didn't walk the path she walked to get here, so you can't have her head. When you go, "I agree with her, I have her experience," what you're telling me is "I have her brain." That ain't true. What it really is, is you going, "I pass, leave me alone, I don't want to talk, so I agree with her, whatever she said; I don't even know what she said, but I agree with it." So "I pass" and "I agree with so and so" are not acceptable answers. However, you can say, "I think very much like JoAnne, only I like it a little faster, I like it a little more blue, I like it upside down." That's great. But I want to hear the differences between your similar opinions. And, of course, it's not just JoAnne, it's anyone else in the room, she just happened to be here [*stop to acknowledge her*].

Again, shifting the "agreement" framework toward difference and away from similarity. Presupposing the target of the inquiry is the personal associations, personal life-story territory, not the objective alignment of opinions. Reestablishing the primary goal of story elicitation through impressions, in an expansive framework, now that the questions and concerns are past about how the final decision making will be structured.

> What you're about to hear is the CliffsNotes version of the trial. The lawyers will come in and give you short bites of the stories it is agreed are each side's absolute best foot forward, pared down to the simplest, straightest answers about what happened here for both sides. And that's agreed for both sides. Every piece of evidence the attorneys put in front of you is sworn testimony from this case. So if you see a document that says "The doctor says . . . ," "The EMT driver says . . . ,"

or "The police officer says . . . ," you can take it as the gospel truth. Someone, somewhere, put their hand on a Bible and swore to tell you that truth, that whole truth, and nothing but that truth. Now that is still the truth as that witness sees it, but I don't want you to waste time speculating about the sworn evidence or the documents here. Please don't waste your time wondering to yourself when the attorneys are talking about evidence, "Gee, I wonder if he really said that, I wonder if he's exaggerating, that's just the attorney talking, I bet he didn't really say that."

Speculation about attorneys is one thing. You want to know how to catch your speculation when it's happening? Two phrases. I bet. "I'll betcha what really happened is this . . . ." Or my favorite, "Maybe . . ." [*emphasizing tone on end*] ". . . maybe he didn't do it exactly that much, or that long, as he says." Then, there's putting them together. "Well, I'll betcha, maybe what really happened is . . . ." I don't want you speculating about what the facts in evidence are OK? [*Wait*]. But I invite you to speculate as freely as you wish, as rampantly and rabidly as you like, about what the evidence could mean to you, or you, or you. 'Cause, you know it can't mean the same thing to any two of you, don't you? [*referring to JoAnne*]. In here, with me, feel free to speculate wildly. No rushing to judgments, but free speculation about meanings.

We'll never ask you, "Is the plaintiff right?" or "Is the defendant winning?" But I'll be asking for impressions and then questions all day long. So in here, feel free to speculate. But once you get to your jury room, in deliberation, then you're stuck with the facts. No more speculation. No more, "I'll betcha, maybe, what really happened is . . . ," and so forth. You'll have to police each other. But in this room, anything goes, OK?

The reason why I have just the attorneys doing this is because they can do it all in thirty minutes, over one day, if it's just them. If they had to bring videotapes of every witness in the whole case, we would be here for three weeks. Anybody want to volunteer for that? [*One hand up*.] OK, but you only get paid what a normal juror would get paid. [*Hand down.*]

Would you like to know how the day's going to go? In about three minutes, I'm going to sit down and the lawyers are going to troop in here. They're going to start their opening statements for you. They'll introduce themselves. They'll tell you who they're representing, and for about five to seven minutes, they're going to cover the whole gist of the story from their side. Then I'll give you a piece of paper to fill out. After that we'll talk for the longest break of the day, because early on you know, first impressions, all that kind of stuff, that's the best stuff. Subsequently, every time one of us gets up to ask you questions—you can start looking forward to this now—it will be for a shorter and shorter time. But the imagining and speculating won't be any less.

I'll allow some time for certain questions, but remember, the first thing we always want to hear is all about your impressions of the stories as they come out, bit by bit. Any and all, small or large, relevant or irrelevant—your impressions. The only wrong answer is to have one and not let us know about it, OK?

The lawyers will then get up and give you half the evidence. It will take them about fifteen minutes each and that doesn't sound like much. By the end, I predict you will be surprised by just how much information about these stories you've really gotten. By the way, there's no allowing anybody on your panel to say, "Well I just don't have enough information to talk about that." That's the single most common complaint I get from actual juries, when I interview them after trials that have gone on for months. They'll say, "I wish I had more information," "I wish I had more facts about the case," "I wish I had another witness to talk about this." These people are not missing facts. What they've got is this illusion of certainty. Boy, if I had just one more fact, pow, it would be perfectly clear, and I would know what justice was. If it could be that clear, it would never get to court. Forget it. So, it's a cop-out for somebody to say, "I don't have enough information to address it." You will have enough information. It's just a hard job, OK? Don't let anybody get away with that. After we talk, there's a second round for the rest of the evidence.

Then, the lawyers get to give you a closing argument. Now, the whole time, they're watching, they're listening to your commentary. They're listening, so here's the interesting part about this. Unlike in court, the lawyers get to hear what your concerns are as the story is coming out. So they are going to stitch stuff in. If they have facts to answer a question you've got, or a worry you've got, or a concern you've got, they will put it into the next session, or the session after that. If they have the facts to address your problem, they'll come in and address it. But here's their problem. I won't let them address you directly, because that's not like a jury. They don't go around talking to each jury member out in the hall—"By the way, you had a question . . ."—because they would never know. So the way that the answers you want will come out is that they'll just weave them into whatever they were going to say anyway, so you have to listen carefully. But if you have a concern and they have the evidence to address it, trust me, they'll bring it to you either the next time or the time after that. So, if you have

> a question, listen for the answer because they'll bring it in. They just won't say, "Hey Michael, you wanted to know this, here it is." That's not what they're going to do. All right?

Helping increase both the weight of their role and their response potential and attention.

> So, quick review. No passing. No agreeing with JoAnne or anybody else. Impressions first, then questions. Reasonable, ordinary. More sure than not.
>
> Last, but not least. Once in a while, I'm going to go around the room and ask each one of you the same question. It usually happens toward the end of the debrief sessions. At that point, I would like all of you to resist another human tendency called herd instinct. The way to resist this is when you first hear me ask the question, jot down a word or two of your answer. For instance, at one point during the day I may ask you the question that will probably go something like, "Of all the people involved in this case, who would you choose to talk to? If you could talk to one person?" You would be surprised what people will say. Sometimes they will say, "Well, I want to talk to his wife, the injured guy's wife." If she was in the car. I don't even know if she was. I don't know the story very well, but if she was in the car it makes some sense. Sometimes she's not and they still want to talk to her, because they want to find out if he was really hurt. But somebody says, "I want to talk to the wife, not an engineer, not a design expert, not a person who built the car, nope, I want to talk his wife."
>
> Now let's say that Sharon has decided that is who she wants to talk to. And I start over here with JoAnne, and I go down the row here. And she says, "I want to talk to the car company's safety expert." And the next person, Betty, she says, "The same guy, car company's safety expert," go to Linda, "Car company's safety expert," James, "Car company's safety expert." About that time, what is going on in Sharon's head if she is like most people? Why am I thinking about the wife? Obviously I missed something. I don't know . . . And she changes her vote. Don't do that. Stick to your guns.
>
> How many of you remember the first, O. J. Simpson trial, the criminal one? I know it was a long way back. How many of you remember the O. J. Simpson criminal trial? The first one. Some of you? Did you know that on that panel was a woman who had been on a previous murder jury? Who, when they did their first vote, was the one vote for conviction. There were eleven other people that wanted to acquit this person, and she was the one person who wanted to put him in jail for life. One. Eleven to one. And by the end of that deliberation, she

had turned all eleven other people around for conviction, and they put him away for murder. How did she do that? I will give you a hint: automatic weapons were not involved. As a matter of fact, life threats didn't even enter into it. How did she do it?

She talked them into it.

Of course. How else? That is all she had. She had to talk them into it. But how did that work? Did she just wear them all down? You've got eleven people who are tired and want to go home. I can see it with maybe four. But eleven? [*Wait for acknowledgments.*]

It didn't go that long either. The deliberation wasn't like weeks and weeks and weeks, where maybe you could say they were all fatigued and gave up. All eleven of them surrendered. Screw justice. Let her have her way. I don't think that is what happened. What had to have happened?

She convinced them.

How?

She stuck to her beliefs about what she heard.

Uh-huh. Now think about this. They all heard the same case, from the same people, in the same room, at the same time. She heard the case differently from everybody else. And she was able to show them that the way she heard those facts differently made enough sense that eleven people, who were ready to let the guy go, put him in jail for murder instead, based on the way she alone saw it differently. That is what you're here for. I want your different opinions. So don't run around agreeing with everybody willy-nilly just because we happen to be herd animals. And the problem is, as you all know, that Sharon, after about the fourth "safety expert," starts to go "Hmmm," doubting her own position. Stick to your guns if you have an opinion, I want to hear it. And I don't want to hear it just because six other people have told me the same darn thing. Got it? You may each get to be the one in eleven at some point today, I'm hoping. If it's in your head, it's on the subject, so stick with it until I hear all about it.

Step-by-step rehearsals emphasizing priority of individual opinions over consensus, presuming full participation, and full consideration of perceptions of the situation, at the edges, instead of majority consensus as the presumed aim. Presumes that minority views overtaking the majority view can be a part of the job. This can slow the trend somewhat toward assimilation, norming, and defaulting to preexisting leanings.

Who has questions about the process? OK. When the attorneys come in, it's just like court. Do you need a break before I let them at you?

> You sure? I need two more hands. See all the friends you've got? Back in your seats in seven minutes.

At this stage, assuming the job of recruiting, screening, and herding the group together was done well, you can feel fairly certain that you've helped the participants draw on their own reference experiences for jurors and their jobs, jobs in general, and more ingrained habits regarding leading, following, and group dynamics. This will, in turn, help them be as ready as they can, under the circumstances, to expand their impressions of the stories presented and to relate the possibilities as well as they can of the stories they are already beginning to create.

4.8 2015 Supplement

As described previously in Chapter Four, there are a few significant differences from "standard" practices to consider when mounting focus groups aimed at eliciting the broadest array of possibilities from each participant in terms of (re)constructing your client's case story as it is presented to them. However, I did not provide a succinct list of these differences in the original publication. I'm taking the opportunity now to provide one that has been refined by use over the last ten years.

- **Live, Adversarial Attorney Presentations.** Chapter Four already details the pros and cons for taking this tack. Despite the artificial environment of a small test group, it is important to match as closely as possible the way actual decision makers will receive actual case stories from actual attorneys.

- **Short Openings.** The purpose for short openings during focus groups is discussed at length in this chapter. However, besides inviting participants to most fully engage with the stories they are privately (re)building, developing brief but comprehensive five-minute openings allows the attorneys to refine their own appreciation of their cases *as stories.*

- **Long Debriefs.** Talking with a full group of participants at specific points throughout the presentation helps to delay "group" trends toward consensus or distortions, and precludes focusing too much on distractions or minutia. More than any other approach, it also prevents the group from "rehearsing" reinforced differences within their responses, thereby helping to reveal *all* of the stories that give facts their meaning.

- **No Position Questions.** Story (re)construction is a different process from making editorial comments *about* a story. The former is a much closer match to the actual experience of a legal decision maker; the latter, in fact, has very little to do with that experience. Asking people to jump out of the story (re)building process to render opinions about the case or a fact in it or inundating them with serial hypotheticals—or worse, forcing them into your own predetermined "either/or" choices about their process—will stop the (re)construction process completely and changes the game for good for the research group as a whole.

- **Small Bites.** Pouring a half an hour, or even more, of details into the minds of participants at each debriefing juncture undermines their processing. It already is hard enough to access hints, implications, and suggestions of their story (re)building process when they are asked to handle short bursts of information. Don't hamper the participants with even more.

- **Limited Witness Videos Late in the Day.** How to construct these short witness videos was originally covered in Chapter Four, but I now have an additional ten years of experience that confirm their benefits during the course of a day-long focus group. When saved for the end of the day, prior to deliberations, these videos are best used to invite shifts in stories already (re)constructed by the participants, much like the use of "shadow jurors" at trial. The use of the videos should focus on the processing of impressions, not the "outcome" of participant opinions about a specific witness's "importance" (or ranking factual details from testimony on a scale of 1 to 5). Witness demeanor on video is as much a factor as what a witness says; delivering evidence through witnesses on video is not what you should be after in their use here.

➲ **Avoid Consensus—Reward Exception and Difference.** We are herd animals: we seek consensus, and trying to preclude group participants from doing so is ultimately futile. However, the inevitable *can be* delayed—and *should be* delayed as long as possible if the fullest value is to be gained from each group. Encourage participants to change position and reinforce changing positions. This means that the moderator occasionally will be called on to "push" positioning of the group away from consensus as it almost certainly will begin to form early in the day—regardless of around which parts of the facts or law they are coalescing. And this is also when an effort to be less direct and more suggestive pays off the most; asking serial counter-examples and forced choice "either/or" questions will likely undermine this process.

➲ **Reinforce Process over Outcome.** At the outset of a focus group, actively *downplaying* the perceived value of their verdicts at the end of the day *increases* the value of the process of getting there.

➲ **Minimize Written Surveys.** Participants' written input is valuable, but not as valuable as their well-moderated participation—very similar to the difference between juror questionnaires and open voir dire. A survey form doesn't provide a format for the proper follow-up questions—"please explain" is a good example.

➲ **In Court and Out of Court.** Though I did not emphasize this in the sample introduction in Chapter Four, this little distinction has often proven to make a very big difference in the quality of interactions among participants during debriefs. The more the attorneys and moderator work to segregate the "in court" activities (deliveries) from the rest of the day's activities in their language, demeanor, and conduct, the greater the chance participants also have to intuitively divide their "juror" jobs from their story (re)construction discussions. It is important to consistently convey that you really aren't interested in their verdicts.

➲ **Demonstrative Visuals.** Each side should have an abbreviated set of visuals designed to provide a storyboard for the key frames in their story's sequence. These need to be produced for the group and balanced in every way. The intervening years have shown me that the visuals for all sides need to be designed and produced by one source, applying the basic rule of *balance* among all of them.

- **Questions.** The early part of Chapter Four covers this area well, though I would like to add that when asking positioning questions on the strength of evidence or on the verdict, close-ended questions and those starting with "Why?" or "Does anybody . . . ?" should be avoided. When "polling" the group, always reflect and emphasize the minority responses by avoiding follow ups with the majority of those raising their hands. This is essential to the task of delaying consensus.
- **Preparation Time.** One thing that has changed significantly since the First Edition of this book is how we prepare for focus groups. With very few exceptions, experience has shown that a long-distance approach to preparation via only phone conferences and email exchanges just can't get the job done properly. Nowadays, we reserve a full two-and-a-half days prior to the focus group, in person at the venue with an attorney(s) and team, for preparing the presentations. Just as with the resulting input from the group's participants, the time invested with attorney team members produces presentations for the group that are far higher in quality and far more persuasive.

There are still many trial lawyers who question the value-to-cost ratio of devoting this much time and this many resources to preparing and presenting focus groups. But, if the objective is to obtain as much value as possible from the resources the actual participants of the group represent, anything less than this really *is* inadequate.

Focus groups ought not to be thought of as a way to *confirm* your assumptions about "your case." They should be thought of as a way to *undermine* any or all of those assumptions.

Careful planning can help you avoid the common group "research" habits of limiting and reducing input from the participants that you most need to hear. Consistently reinforcing the need to expand and invite participant input beyond your expectations throughout your planning can help with your delivery of the case *as a story* in some crucially important ways:

- You won't be as tempted to tell them *what* to think.
- You will be less likely to tell them *how* to think.
- You will find out how many ways they *can* think about the same case story.

Given a decent chance, they will surprise you every time.

Chapter Five

Open Wide

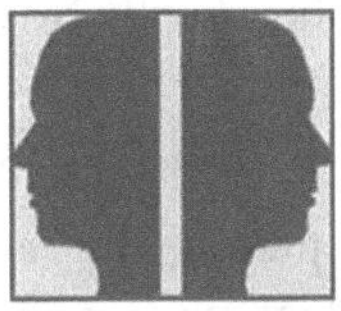

Form follows function.
—*Louis Sullivan*

5.1 Inviting Stories to Grow

When the introduction and job description are done, the frameworks set, the connections made, and everyone is sitting ready to start the focus group, we close the "as if" frame, reinforcing confidentiality and group participation at the same time:

> If the following statement is true, please raise your hand and keep it up until the camera has recorded you agreeing that "I read, understood, and signed the confidentiality agreement you gave me in which I promised to keep everything I hear and see here a secret." If that is true, raise your hand and keep it up until the camera gets around to you. We'll talk more at the end about what you can safely say about what you did here today. For now, we go to court. That means no talking to each other, no talking to the attorneys, but feel free to take as many notes as you like. We'll talk again when the attorneys have finished.

The seemingly more serious, courtroom stuff is about to be introduced. All the while, the hard work of preparing the participants to react as openly as possible with their impressions, ideas, and experiences as their stories develop has been done under the auspices of the not-quite-so-serious yet "as if" umbrella. After all that work, many trial professionals ask why the group should immediately be turned over to attorneys to run rampant? After all, this work is referred to as small-group research in professional quarters, isn't it? What do trial lawyers know about research protocols? They are advocates.

There are a number of arguments against having lawyers involved in the presentation process. The lack of the illusory control prized by traditional research methods runs through many of them. Lawyers can have memory slips, unintended gaffs, or unexpected gaps in the presentations they've prepared, just by being human, whether control of the lawyer variable in story formations even gets mentioned. They are prone to argue too much, slanting the story the group receives. Many times, the other party's attorneys are recruits from the same firm or from outside, and have no stake at all in the case at hand. They may not have chosen to familiarize themselves with the case enough to make the best showing possible for the party(ies) they represent to the group. Prepared or not, they are unpredictable and could jump off the planned track (because the spirit moves them or they see some response they like or fear) and head for rhetorical parts unknown. All this usually by way of detail spin. For any of these and other reasons, it is asserted that the critical goal of a balanced presentation can be poorly served by letting the advocates into the room at this early stage.

If you insist on having lawyers present the case stories for the parties, they ask, why not at least put them on videotape so you can edit to eliminate slips, gaps, and argument, and plug in the equal balance in each area so important to getting the most effective group responses? Better yet, why not dispense with the layer of contamination provided by live attorney presentations altogether and go right to the source of all risk of harm to any case in any venue: the jurors, judges, mediators, arbitrators, and negotiators that hear and decide the case—or their reasonable facsimiles in the focus group? Isn't that what they are here for?

In a word, no. Not if your aim is to test the stories these people can create. Their versions of the case stories and the potentials of those various versions is the territory these groups are designed to explore. To do that even a little bit well, trial professionals can't safely presume the existence of a fixed and predetermined stack of facts and law called "the case" or "my case." Here is where the remnants of the old, two-variable style of thinking tend to reassert themselves, sometimes with tenacious strength. You either continue to pretend there are only two active variables—lawyer choices in action and the influence of decision makers' backgrounds and attitudes—or you don't. If you allow the third variable of case stories with lives of their own into the mix, then the ability—actual or imagined—to control all relevant factors except the one you wish to test goes out the window. It may have been out there all along.

Does this mean trial professionals should throw up their hands and say anything goes? Not necessarily. There is a pragmatic way to increase the chances that group members can build the best case story constructs of possible, and can then be invited to relate those stories in writing and aloud. Despite the fact that this is primarily a consciously run inquiry into mostly unconscious processes, it is still an achievable goal. One big job required to balance story presentation and elicitation in focus groups is the same one needed in court or alternative dispute resolution: managing perceptions.

1. First, the stories delivered have to respect the nature of the decision makers' story-building process (see Chapter Four).

2. Then we have to deliver on the promise of the introduction/job description suggesting that participants' input will be the major factor in the day's efforts.

3. We would not want the presentation to be thrown too much toward the defense or the plaintiff side while testing a civil matter. By the same token, neither can we allow the day's efforts to lean too far toward the ostensibly objective parts of the inquiry when the subjective process is so clearly important, too.

5.2 Invite Input

It is important to invite and expand participants' verbal and written input. But what is implied, what is deleted from their consideration, and all that is strongly marked out by nonverbal means should be noted and factored in as well. The presentation can't be focused on the conscious minds working on the story. Neither should it be trying to map only the other-than-conscious terrain. While what is said and not said is very important to track, so is how it is said. Pretending that stories revealed by verbal and nonverbal means aren't a major factor in the decision-making system is no solution at all.

If the private stories decision makers author on the way to making judgments are ever the most influential factor in the process, then pretending they are beyond our reach or not worth the effort to explore is a dangerous risk you don't need to run. It comes down to choosing a method. Common bias and experience have tended to lean toward the comfortable image of control that we've thought we ought to be able to have by trying to objectively measure only certain subjective processes. You can always count on getting measurable results if you only count those results you can measure. Arguments about the quality of one method over another are then safely restricted to who counts better, not how much of what was sitting right there wasn't measured or counted at all.[1]

In trying to nail down the precise impact attorneys have presenting live before a focus group, the potential test results might be meager, but they aren't the whole story. Just working to deliver a case story more effectively to the people hearing and reacting to it can be a huge boon to lawyers unschooled in that part of their practice. A course in managing perceptions is not offered in most law schools or continuing legal education programs yet. Much like the decision makers, who can easily be invited to suspend their disbelief about the process and take it seriously, lawyers soon find that when advocating before a room of live people, their spinal columns and glands don't really go along with the conscious part of their heads claiming it isn't real. Affecting or improving the lawyer choice and action variable is much better done by live rehearsal. When the subject is behavioral change, you get what you rehearse, not what you intend. If trial attorneys are going to become polished practitioners of effective story delivery, they need practice. Conducting voir dire,

---

1. Lawrence LeShan on objective versus subjective measurement bias, *The Dilemma of Psychology: A Psychologist Looks at His Troubled Profession* (New York, NY: Dutton, 1990): 34–45, 49–75, 80–88, 100–111.

where available, more like a focus group means that actual participation in some focus groups is mandatory. But that's just a start. How the groups are handled is still an open question.

All three case story variables—stories, juror contexts, and the tellers' choices—are operating at all times. Each operates with varying influence for each decision maker in any room or focus group facility in which they might hear the case. People build their responses to all three variables through perception by building story versions from which they consciously reveal leanings that they've already begun forming behind the conscious scenes. If that is the way it will be done in court, in mediation, in arbitration, or elsewhere, why leave out one of the three variables—the lawyers and their choices—when trying to assess what stories may emerge to drive the decisions down the road? Just as with ignoring the value of the story-building process, isn't this a risk you need not run? Seeing that participants receive the message in the group as closely as possible to the ways in which the eventual decision makers will get it, seems only prudent.

If testing the range of story development is the aim, not winning or losing a focus group, and if the early (primacy) part of the day offers the most valuable input to harvest from a group, then mock trials featuring "jurors" silent until the end can't be the preferred method. Expanding and including as many different perceptions and personal references about the case stories is the goal. Inviting any topic or tangent they imagine is one way to do that if that aim is to be met. You can't have them sit in silence, writing answers to predetermined questions that can't possibly anticipate and follow up where their personal twists and turns may take them. There are no follow-up questions on a preprinted form addressing the many possible directions their first answers set in motion. You must talk with them early and often, in a way that allows the most open input about the perceptions and thinking behind their eyes. And if you want to test these case stories in an environment closer to the one in which eventual decision makers will receive case stories, the delivery will best be made by lawyers that look and sound like attorneys, with trappings more adversarial and less clinical, and with periodic pauses "out of court" to invite multiple and variable responses, through conscious self-reporting supplemented by implied suggestions and presuppositions.

Formally divide the case delivery and participant questioning portions of the day's activities and keep them as separate as possible. This provides some reference in the group to the adversarial package that will carry the actual story to its decision makers. Why would you choose to deliver the stories you want tested in a form less like the one they will actually take? What value can there be in adding more distortion to an already distorted message in an admittedly artificial environment? Because voir dire, opening statement, and the first witness are rarely left out by either side in court, your initial inquiries to the group should be made after both sides have had a chance to open. (Stories aren't delivered and deliberated in court one at a time. If there were just one story of "my case," fixed and objective in fact and law, this would not be advisable, because under those circumstances, you might be able to track a group of individual responses to the first half of the one case story at hand. But that is not the situation.) The focus group is here to help you learn what your case is and how best to present it.

Attitudes cannot be plucked from the participants independently from the stories each generates early on to categorize and narrate their private version of the matter. People use their minds to blend, not separate, elements such as the message itself, reactions to the messengers and the surroundings, or the vast array of life experiences and meaningful life stories they bring to bear on decision making. There is no neutral position possible for the people delivering the case story, nor for those eliciting responses. They are always inextricable, influential parts of that process, big or small, but always a part.[2] There is no objective means of eliciting and precisely categorizing the factors that influence each person's unconsciously developing case story. Yet, distinct and discernible clues abound when you talk to people about all the thoughts they are privy to along the way—this is, if you ask the questions well. People are usually of more than one mind, which makes reductive inquiries in formulations such as "either/or," "on a scale from one to five," or "who has the stronger case?" less helpful in determining all the possible tracks a case story can travel once it's out of your hands.

These days, for example, in the story category of business life, anchors such as "highly competitive" and "global-free market influence" are very common, often presuming a distorted Darwinian "survival of the fittest" theme when it comes to success in a "tough environment." That frame for approaching and building business stories can cut either way. Either side in civil or criminal business cases might benefit from stories spun from a top-down view, with control centered on market forces more than on personal efforts within the marketplace. These positions taken toward the "jungle out there" theme would suggest that business people act in response to the larger forces actually in control, "doing whatever you have to" and "having a right to do business." The locus of control is on the market, and the business or business person is reactive, not proactive. But a position focused on individual accomplishment, expressing an "Everyone can't be a winner, but we are" position, is equally possible starting from the same theme, by shifting the viewpoint and party status to reside with the winner in the story. Starting from that popular theme, the "fittest" could be seen as either party: those that reacted well to how the market forces control all, or those that stood firm and turned those forces to their own will. In the first, top-down framework, parties' stories would tend toward following rules that allow the kind of responsiveness the "tough environment" requires. But in the bottom-up stories, claims would center more on individuals seeking or taking some kind of unfair advantage.

By merely collecting answers bearing that common attitude toward business in a focus group inquiry, how can you say which decision maker is more likely to swing their story's active party and point of view in which direction at trial? More

2. That influence is frequently not reachable to be accurately tracked, but it is often quite clear in nonverbal marking, presuppositions, and other less consciously formed messages.

importantly, without asking, how will you learn the most and least effective ways to get decision makers to make the shift, or to shore up the original position instead? Have you learned what all you can from them about the survival theme simply by recording the fact that they uttered it?

What is less conscious, less able to be written down or articulated aloud, can often be the more influential and accurate measure of influence within the private stories people build to decide legal matters. Be sure you build a format for exploring these stories that gives you ample chance to assess the implicit factors not just those that are more easily cataloged in simple self-reporting.

5.3 Reality, What a Concept

We know formal mock trials are inadequate for fully exploring the range of case story creations in a test group. However, they can serve to test the impact of a single factor such as including or dropping a witness, evidence, or jury instruction. They even provide hints about likely trial outcomes, given really big groups and thorough presentations.

There is another form of group that is as informal as a mock trial is formal. It has been growing in popularity with some trial professionals doing small-group work, especially attorneys with a do-it-yourself bent. This format mirrors the traditional look of a focus group such as the one George Stephanopoulos can be seen hosting on TV during any election cycle. It consists of eight to twelve randomly selected citizens, sitting around a table chatting with a moderator.[3] While such groups may serve a purpose in harvesting possible themes, viewpoints, and story scopes before discovery begins, they offer little value in eliciting a real range of story constructs from a group, especially the more creative and sometimes dangerous tales people can build that end up driving actual decision makers.

You may know how these groups are run. The moderator gives a bit of background, emphasizing the need for open, honest responses, and begins by examining baseline beliefs and attitudes. Very general questions are asked about the idea of civil lawsuits, such as with medical malpractice suits or suing a surgeon, for instance. Civil process, evidence rules, damage-claim elements, and other concepts are broached one at a time to test the limits of attitudes people bring to the table. Once the territory of applicable biases and beliefs is mapped out, the moderator gradually introduces a significant fact or small set of facts in evidence one at a time, the individual standards to judge the facts, or maybe the instructions to answer verdict questions applied to them. There is a pause at each stage to thoroughly explore input from each person in the group. Each new set of concepts about each cherry-picked fact is exhausted before the next bit of the case story is introduced.

---

3. The American Association for Justice (formerly the Association of Trial Lawyers of America, or ATLA) refers to these groups as concept focus groups.

Often, the limits of a participant's position on a particular item are tested by pushing the envelope of the conditions that preceded their response. If they insist a second opinion should have been sought by a patient, changing the facts to include one, asking, "What would you think if I told you . . . ?" and adding third, fourth, and even fifth opinions to the "record" to see how strongly the participants might hold to their initial responses, and what they may say if they shift.

These groups seem to offer a controlled approach to discovering what every participant has to offer in terms of their ability to fairly hear a case. The illusion of control is never more apparent than in an earnest trial professional chairing such a concept focus group. They are missing the main ingredient: a common origin from which the participants' story building can start. The method relies entirely on the assumption that the only operative variable to test is participants' attitudes, and that the story is fixed and external to them all. The method does not consider that each person authors their own story version. It relies on the unadapted thinking that the jurors can only react to a predetermined stack of facts, and that a case story is only what a lawyer gives them. This method makes questioner and participants alike unsure of what exactly is being questioned and assessed. Because the true story-building process doesn't wait for anyone to say "Ready, set, go," the eliciting of input about general, disconnected fragments almost guarantees that all the participants' created stories will be on different—sometimes very different—pages.

Decision-maker case stories start out two or three times removed from the reality of the actual case events. These concept groups eliminate a common introduction to the story elements from each side. Given no common starting point, listeners unleash their imaginations disconnected from any common ground to "focus" what is at best, a sometimes wildly unpredictable collection of perceptions and references leading to decisions. Any tenuous ties to the second- or third-hand version of reality where the case story begins are blown to the four winds.

So what is the appeal of this method? Some of it may emerge from the combination of common-life experience and common biases, just as with the personal driving standards people don't always realize they hold. As in that example, bias often operates above the conscious radar of the owners. Consider the possible connections:

> **The appeal of apparent control over moderator output and participant input is reinforced by the illusion of testing just one thought or concept at a time.** This presumes a person makes no connections and authors no personal narratives until instructed, can build on only one factor at a time,[4] and only one operative variable needs to be tested: preexisting juror attitudes.

4. While it is true that the conscious faculties tend to handle only one thought at a time, the parts of the mind outside conscious reach suffer no such restrictions. There is no dispute about this. But if you want to believe you are covering every conceptual base possible, in a verbal inquiry into mostly other-than-conscious processes, you have to try to forget that fact.

The appeal of measuring. By presuming that only the currently selected topic is active at any time in the minds of all concerned, the moderator may assume he can accurately measure the relative strengths of attitudes about each isolated topic in line, as if each would have the same level of influence when perceived as part of a whole story, in an adversarial context, later on.

The appeal of traditional thinking. The approach presumes the old interpretation theme for each decision maker, a singular scope for the facts, a point of view fixed on the attorney as the active party, and a very traditional sequence of how things happen: attorney delivers case facts, jurors then return a decision (based solely on reactions to those unwavering facts). The notion of a fixed, predetermined stack of facts and law called "the case" is preserved by this approach, making a sense of control over the sometimes scary territory between decision maker ears, seem less frightening and more manageable.

The appeal of apparent objectivity. Perhaps the most unfortunate presumption fostered by these groups is that each participant has all the mental access they need to self-report the relevant connections and associations their minds can muster, if they are just repeatedly asked. There is no credible evidence that this is true, or that even the most important ones might somehow be more likely to pop out.

Don't overlook the obvious. Concept groups can be run with little expense, and the moderating job is comparatively quite simple. Attorneys can easily learn the questioning technique and dispense with high-priced, non-lawyer consultants, a bias still popular in its own right.

Perhaps experiencing what it is like to ignite your listeners' story-building processes with no common starting point can help demonstrate the value of working up carefully crafted, five-minute openings to do that job well. Here is an exercise that can help you.

Figure 5

This image was used as demonstrative evidence in a personal injury lawsuit.

To do this task well, think of the suit from the perspective of the attorney representing a man injured on the job. You are to imagine and construct a plausible, compelling story justifying his making this claim. You can consider manufacturers, manager, company owner, and anyone else when building your case story against the defense. You can consider anything that will help you build a compelling case about how this man's injuries suffered on the job while manipulating this dumpster built to be carried and used with his forklift could and should have been prevented. Once you are satisfied that you have constructed the best case with which to persuade a judge, jury, or other decision makers of your plaintiff's case—that there was both duty and fault present for the defendant(s), and that the defendant(s)' fault caused the preventable harms—then you are ready to fill in the major elements of your private story in their appropriate slots. Write them down. Please read no further until you have done so.

1. **Theme.** The theme of a story provides the means to determine what is important, what is and isn't a priority. What is this story really all about?

2. **Scope.** The story's scope covers the complete context of time, actions, places, numbers, and individuals involved. How far does this story reach?

3. **Point of view.** Through whom (or what) should the listener be encouraged to reference the entire story? Who (or what) is on center stage?

4. **Sequence.** What exactly went on here? What went well, and what did not? What happens—beginning, middle, and end—in this plaintiff's story that justifies the suit?

   1. __________

   2. __________

3. ____

____

____

Now, take a look at the end of section 5.9 for another image from this trial (Figure 6). This graphic depicts the standard rules for using the dumpster, which the plaintiff was taught and agreed he knew. The behavior in the first image, reaching between the uprights of the lift, is also prohibited by a sign posted on the uprights of his forklift, facing the injured driver.

Now that you've seen the second graphic and read two more facts, go back over the story you made up when you had only the first image and a very general framework to go by, just as a concept group member does.

- How well would your story stand up now?
- Would it persuade judge and jurors in light of the new evidence?

If you are the rare individual who anticipated these hurdles and prepared for them in your story crafting, congratulate yourself. If not, you have just joined the ranks of thousands of concept group participants working busily every day, revealing reactions to stories about events found practically anywhere but near the actual case.

Consider just how many different ways the impressions you formed while building your imagined story could mislead a trial professional that collected them from you as a group participant:

- Who was the main actor and the minor actors in your story then?
- How broad were the scope of actions, choices, and events in that version?
- What came first in the sequence of your old, imagined version?
- Look at the theme you proposed. Knowing only two more things about the actual story, how far did your theme stray from what any trial professional would need to learn from you in order to build a powerful presentation?
- What chances would a plaintiff have whose attorney presented a case based on the version you outlined above, if the actual decision makers started out knowing what you know now?

Now, here comes the fun part. Forget the whole story you built, completely. Eliminate any influence it could have on your views, memory, or unconscious associations and references now, in the past, and the future. As the court says, disregard it completely and give it no weight. This is what trying to edit already formed perceptions is like. And that's for yourself. Imagine trying to get it done inside someone else's head, when the whole creative process sits outside conscious reach. One reason adept presenters always start at a general level, avoiding lower levels of detail before their audience seems ready, is because of what happens when you contradict a perception or concept already in those heads. For instance, if you were to think of a big, jiggling bowl of Jell-O and consider where you would place it in your mind's eye, noting how the light looks coming through it—that *lime* Jell-O—you'd likely know what a contradicted perception feels like, unless pure chance happened to have you seeing and reading the color, green, by dumb luck.

Imagine actually setting aside all the thinking-process factors you've already engaged in, including:

- **Primacy** (it is the first story you created)
- **Reinforcement** (putting it together with a purpose and trying to forget it both reinforce it)
- **Availability** (you put it on your own mental front burner)
- **Confirmation** of your own associations

Try to imagine how one would even start to unring unconscious bells you can't even find—the lifetime of references and stories you used to build your story. Remember all those personal associations are now linked (anchored) to the sight of the dumpster, the word "forklift," and every word or idea you've heard or thought about it until this very moment. All of that is more reinforcement, just as telling yourself to forget it is.

Assuming that focus group members can drop one story midstream in favor of another ignores the well-known process our minds use to generate the stories that are the forerunners to all legal decisions. That assumption seems to be made by professionals running these groups in the vain hope of gaining some hypothetical control over a known uncontrollable process. As the exercise you just accomplished reveals, something valuable gets lost choosing a method that denies how the mind works. If the participants' responses haven't been strongly encouraged to start from a *common point*, as each side portrays it, you can't trust that the answers offered will have anything worthwhile to say about what eventual decision makers will most likely be seeing, hearing, and feeling when it counts. The story building and story-delivering variables are set aside pursuing juror backgrounds and belief in this way.

The responses collected in these "kitchen table" groups are easily measured, often limited to counting up stronger/weaker extremes in answers. They are focused on participants' reactions to bits and pieces of a case story tacitly presumed to be fixed, unchangeable, and outside those people's heads. You've just demonstrated that those easily measured and categorized responses have no verifiable connection to the same person's views of the actual case story once they are placed in the proper context.

The concept method forces participants to be farther removed from associations growing from a single legal story in favor of widely ranging speculation that is more about the experience of answering questions in a focus group. With no common story, that *is* the participants' primary experience. Biases prompted by identifying with the case story presented by two advocates are sent far to one side, while biases about doing well in the group around the table take over, affecting participant responses in both major and minor ways. This is the very situation the anti-focus group critics decry.

The major danger is that you can't really tell the difference judging solely from the answers gathered in these kind of groups, between valuable offerings and input pointing you 180 degrees in the wrong direction. You saw the second picture and read the extra news about the warning sign. But as a group participant, how many answers might you have given tied to a personal story that was completely off base with respect to what you feel and think now?

Most courts don't allow attorneys to change half the facts in evidence to match the misleading package their concept groups told them to present. Given that the responses invited in these groups rely on beginnings randomly generated in each person's imagination, out of all conscious reach or control, they are unreliable in measuring strong and weak points of the case story as it needs to be presented to the final decision makers. They can certainly show you a wide range of possible biases and life experiences people are bringing to the general topic at issue in the case. The stories generated from those randomly begun reactions, however, may have nothing to do with the best package for actual decision makers.

People using these groups apparently believe that each person listening to a case story has only one way to respond, one set of relevant values and beliefs, and are one "type" person. If each participant is merely a vessel, regurgitating the exact same beliefs or values to any story about work injuries, then it won't matter how many different facts about such stories they hear, in whatever order, or how randomly arranged. If you only have one set of responses, you would have only that set to offer, no matter how, where, or when you are approached. Just say "work injury lawsuit" and start the tape recorder, and that type of person can be counted on to say the same things, with the same associations, feelings, and only one set of reference experiences engaged from an entire lifetime. According to this method, that's just the type of person you always are. Unless the mind is a bit more variable, reactions a bit richer and more unique than this method can handle. Therein may lie some of the appeal.

You might have found yourself wondering who the defendants were, how exactly the plaintiff was injured, and what the claims of wrongdoing are. They still haven't been revealed. You could be eager to find all that out because of the value of knowing enough of the particulars to make intelligent, informed judgments. And that is the point. Without a common beginning set of general elements of the actual story, there will still be no lack of answers offered, still no lack of judgments being formed. What will be missing is reliable input giving a trial professional some kind of direction in designing and delivering the case story presentation. Lots of reactions, but no reliable help for the story. Participants' input and output will be as organized and as easily controlled as the average herd of cats.

Linguist Charles Fillmore might seek the one-sentence story about these concept focus groups in the verbal tool they liberally employ: the hypothetical counter-question or counter-proposal. This question tends to assume the same kind of perceptual editing you just proved impossible can always manifest itself at the drop of a moderator's voice tone. They begin with phrases such as, "What if I were to tell you . . ." and "Let's assume that . . . ." Then they go on to contradict or rearrange story elements the participant has already revealed and discussed, usually at some length. Besides providing more reinforcement, this ignores each "author's" simple pride of ownership in the stories already formed. An implied message to each person is, "That's enough about your reality, let's talk about mine."

NLP co-founder John Grinder used to decry the old method of teaching foreign languages in our secondary schools and colleges: the days of the "language labs" where students would walk into classrooms divided into walled-off, soundproofed cubicles, put on headphones, and rehearse translations from English to another language for a couple of hours a day. He said, "If we had set out to fail in teaching a useful, functional language, we could not have done a better job than these cubicles. Each student in them, over a course of a semester, learned several hundred words in German, French, or Spanish, all of which meant 'sound-proof tile'—because that was their sole experience while picking up the words."

Likewise, this is true with concept group members who are offered no common chance to engage a story being offered in an adversarial context, as persuasively as possible, as a brief introduction to the territory they are to be judging. A flat recitation of ostensibly neutral facts is even less like what they would hear in a courtroom or elsewhere in deciding a case story. Their common starting ground is the table, not the tale. And, they will respond in kind.

Make no mistake, hypothetical counter-questions will get answered. In fact, most people find them easier to answer than questions calling for an extensive search of their reference and story structures. That's because counter-questions require mainly conscious reflection, asking the person to step out of the story she just went to the trouble of building, to speculate about its reach, source, and persuasive power from a mental distance. While it is true that all comments in any focus groups will be made from some psychic distance, the moderator's job is to lessen that distance, not increase it. The same problem crops up when asking someone for reasons instead of references. They still know their own Jell-O isn't grape, but they can't consciously say precisely *how* they know that. Conscious inquiry into unconscious process. The method invites them to increase the distance from the parts of their process that start, reinforce, and maintain all the perceptions, references, and selections that produce decisions. Now they're just talking about the process, because the question as asked requires them to disassociate from it just to answer.

The other-than-conscious mind won't wait. It works at an incredible speed and volume every second. It is always making up, remembering, and reinforcing something. Most of that unconscious activity is not directly reached, much less measured, just by asking.

These groups multiply risks you need not run if your goal is seeking out the stories people make up to decide a legal case by:

- Choosing not to start with the best communicated stories you can muster for each side, delivered adversarially in a more formal way than the interspersed feedback discussions;
- Offering only an informal, roundtable chat as the primary context of participants' experience; and
- Testing just one of the three major case story variables: juror backgrounds and beliefs.

If there was no value to be gained by exploring the stories jurors can generate from a case and if the sole variable to test were an unnaturally limited piece of people's preexisting attitudes, then there would be no reason to reconsider the use of such roundtable groups.

The reality of the need to test more than just preexisting attitudes of people hearing a story and to elicit as many of the versions as possible of the stories they each will author on their way to a decision requires some adapting to a method designed for that purpose. If taking full advantage of all the resources present in a room full of people is the goal, you need to start with more of a story to get at all of their stories.

5.4 Planting the Story Seeds

Since our starting principle for eliciting personal versions of case stories is that the answer "This is how I always dress" is correct, then all forms of questions you choose to ask a focus group participant must adhere to that principle. If you want counter-example scenarios, you must ask questions that allow participants the option to generate their own scenarios. Avoid limiting them to your choice, excluding all other possibilities before knowing what they might be. They could be quite illuminating. Exploring how someone can't come up with a counter-example on their own from the positions they've produced may give you more valuable information for your presentation planning than mistaking any one answer for the whole story.

A story used by the late Milton Erickson, MD, to discuss a similar dynamic with his clinical patients in his world-renowned psychiatric practice can serve as a guide to keeping the process on the most productive path. Given that he was raised in Midwestern farm country, this story dealt with his youth among friends in that country.

> On this day, Milton and his friends came across a horse near the road, chewing grass in a field while dragging its reins on the ground, alongside its head. The young men slowly surrounded the horse and Milton grabbed the reins and swung up on top of him, turning his head toward the road as he did. As they got to the edge of the field, he let loose the reins and the horse, after momentarily hesitating, turned left onto the road and kept walking. Milton secured the reins and used them to keep him on the path till they approached an intersection, whereupon he let them loose again. The horse barely paused before turning and continuing.
>
> They made their way a few miles in this fashion: at every intersection or turn, Erickson let loose the reins till the horse chose a direction and then secured them again, keeping the horse moving down the road. Eventually, it turned into a long dirt drive that ended in the yard of a farm house and barn.
>
> A man emerged from the barn, wiping his hands, pointing at the horse and saying, "That's my horse."
>
> Erickson, dismounting and handing over the reins, replied, "I kinda thought so."
>
> The farmer asked, "Where did you find him?" Erickson said, "A few miles east of here."
>
> The farmer, looking up, says, "How did you know to bring him here?" to which Erickson says:
>
> "I didn't know. The horse knew."

But first, you have to get the group focused on the road.

The hands come down from the videotaped confidentiality commitments and—inviting focus group participant stories to start in a context as closely matched to that of the eventual decision makers' as the artificial process allows—the moderator asks:

> Counsel for the plaintiff, are you ready?
>
> Yes, sir.

Please proceed.[5]

Good morning, ladies and gentlemen. My name is Pat Martin, and I represent the plaintiff in this case, Sara Holbrook. Ladies and gentlemen, when we are sick, we entrust our lives to doctors to help us. Now, in placing our lives into the hands of doctors, we trust that those hands will be gentle and the doctors will act to help us. Not to harm us. In the case of surgery where there are known risks, we trust that the doctor will act reasonably and carefully to provide for our safety by preventing those known risks, provide for our safety by detecting when those risks occur, and provide for our safety by protecting us from the harms that those risks can cause. We ask that they exercise reasonable care and take reasonable measures to prevent, detect, and protect. Now, when I say "reasonable measures," I'm not talking about heroic measures, extraordinary measures, or superhuman measures. Just reasonable measures that other doctors would take when performing that surgery.

Now, I'm sure all of us here are familiar with taking reasonable steps to provide for our own safety.

When we drive a car during the day, we watch the road ahead of us to make sure that we know where we are going and that our car does not stray from the road and hit something. At night, we take greater steps to provide for our safety by turning the lights on in our car when we're driving down a dark road. We turn the lights on in our car because we want to be able to see the road. We want to be able to see what's ahead of us, and we want to make sure that our car does not stray from that path, leave the road and hit something. You will soon hear that surgeons must provide for the patient's safety and they must take reasonable safety precautions to prevent, detect and protect for the patient during surgery.

Now, the law says surgeons must act as other surgeons would ordinarily act when performing this type of surgery. It's what the law calls the standard of care. Now, the standard of care is not something that's embedded in a statute. It's not something that's written down that says when this surgery is done, you have to do X. What the standard of care is—and there's an instruction that we have in the law in this state, and you will see it. But the standard of care is that degree of learning and skill which surgeons ordinarily perform under the same or similar circumstances. That means when doing a surgery, you must do what other

5. This is a transcript from an actual group, with identifying information altered or removed. See Appendix Three for examples of other lawyers' efforts to meet the requirements of a five-minute opening that is strong on story elements and short on detail spin.

reasonable surgeons would do to insure the patient's safety, to prevent injury, to detect injury and to protect the patient when a risk occurs.

If a doctor does not follow the standard of care and harms the patient, you will hear that the law says that doctor is negligent. And that doctor is responsible for all the harms caused by his negligence. The greater the risk and the severity of that risk, the greater the precautions the doctor must take. And that means at the important steps of the procedure, when the risk is at its greatest, the doctor must take extra care to provide for the patient's safety.

Now, in this case you're going to hear about a surgical procedure that involves known risks. You will also hear about what the standard of care is when doing that procedure so that the surgeon will prevent those risks from happening, so that the surgeon will detect when the risk occurs, and that the surgeon will prevent the harms from that risk. Safeguards that you're going to hear about that can be taken by the surgeon in this case are safeguards that are available in every hospital, safeguards that do not cost any more money, and safeguards that do not prolong the surgery, safeguards that do not provide any additional harm to the surgery or any additional risks at the surgery.

The surgery involved in this case is called the placement of a hemodialysis catheter. We'll shorten it to a dialysis catheter. A dialysis catheter is something that is inserted into someone's chest and into the main vein called the superior vena cava so that the dialysis machine will perform the functions of their kidneys when their kidneys shut down. That's what dialysis is. Placement of a dialysis catheter is a minimally invasive surgery, which means a small incision is made somewhere on the body and instruments are then inserted to create a path so that the catheter can be advanced by the surgeon into this large vein that then leads directly to the heart. The surgical placement of a dialysis catheter has known risks, risks that every doctor knows about, every doctor is aware of, and every doctor should be trained in how to prevent. One of the risks is the puncture of that very large vein that I call the superior vena cava, a very life-threatening injury.

Now, since this is a minimally invasive surgery, one incision is made somewhere on the body. Then these catheters and the instruments have to be advanced over into the chest, this long . . . this large vein called the superior vena cava. The doctor cannot see with the naked eye how things are advancing, to see if they're staying on their path. It would be like driving at night without your lights on. But there is something called "fluoroscopy." Fluoroscopy is like a video. Fluoroscopy allows the doctor to see inside the patient and allows the doctor to see how he is advancing these instruments, some of which are very sharp, and make sure they are following their intended path, not leaving the path, and everything is going where it's supposed to and there is no injury. The fluoroscopy is much like the lights on your car when you are driving at night. Fluoroscopy is completely safe for the patient. Fluoroscopy is available at all hospitals. Fluoroscopy does not cost any more to perform. And fluoroscopy does not make the surgery last any longer. It is a reasonable safety device to prevent injury. You will hear in this case that fluoroscopy is the standard of care. It's what a reasonable physician does when performing the placement of a central catheter to prevent injury.

Now, my client's husband, Leo Holbrook, in March of 1999 was admitted to General Hospital because he had acute renal failure. That is different from chronic renal failure in that acute renal failure you will recover from with the use of dialysis. Mr. Holbrook needed a hemodialysis catheter to be placed. And the defendant, Dr. Clark, a general surgeon, was asked to place that. Dr. Clark has done these surgeries before. And Dr. Clark knows that fluoroscopy is a means of preventing injury to the superior vena cava when you're performing this surgery. Dr. Clark knows that because Dr. Clark arranges to use the fluoroscopy during the surgery.

Now, I'm going to explain exactly how this surgery is performed later. But it is a very regimented, step-by-step procedure. It doesn't take very long. It's performed every day in hospitals all over the country. It is not life threatening or a serious surgery. Dr. Clark does it. His assistant is a first-year resident. He even allows the assistant to do the first part of the surgery. For the very first part of the surgery, when he's inserting the first, dull instrument, he uses that fluoroscopy and he sees it. But then Dr. Clark with the push of a button turned that fluoroscopy off. And he now cannot see. And at the next critical point in the surgery when he is inserting very sharp, pointed objects, that fluoroscopy is off. Because the fluoroscopy is off, Dr. Clark cannot see where those objects are going and if they are following their intended path, if they're staying on the road to the superior vena cava.

Well, the evidence is going to show that while inserting these sharp objects, Dr. Clark perforated Mr. Holbrook's superior vena cava. Blood started rushing into the space. It wasn't going to the heart. And when blood's not going to the heart, it's not carrying oxygen throughout the body. And when it's not carrying oxygen throughout the body, the oxygen is not going to the brain. And when oxygen's not going to your brain, your brain is dying. It's like if you held your breath, you're not getting oxygen. And there's nothing you can do about it.

After placing the catheter, at the very end of this procedure, Dr. Clark turns the fluoroscopy machine back on to see if the catheter is where it's supposed to be. At that point he sees the catheter is out of place and is sticking out of the superior vena cava. He knows that it's a life-threatening event that needs immediate treatment, because the blood is going in the wrong place. But Dr. Clark doesn't act at that point. He's suspicious of a puncture of the superior vena cava, but he wants more information. He wants to confirm if it's out of place.

So there are two ways to detect whether the superior vena cava's punctured, two ways that are available right there. The first way is by dye contrast. Dye contrast is dye. It's right there in the operating room. You place it into the port of the catheter. It takes seconds. You put it in there, and it's going to show up on the fluoroscopy if the dye shows up out of place. That means there's a puncture of the superior vena cava. The other way of detecting this injury is by ordering an X-ray. It can be ordered stat, which means an emergency, I need it now. But if you order an X-ray, you have to pick up the phone. You have to call the radiology department. A radiology technician has to push a portable X-ray machine to the operating room, into the operating suite, put it under the patient, take the X-ray. The X-ray has to be taken to the radiology department where it's developed. And after being developed, it then has to be taken back to the operating room. That takes, according to Dr. Clark, three to ten minutes. And of those two choices, the immediate dye contrast or the X-ray, Dr. Clark chooses the X-ray. While he is waiting for the X-ray to come back, waiting for more information, Mr. Holbrook's blood pressure and his oxygen levels drop to critically low levels. He's told there is an emergency by the person monitoring the vital signs. And what does Dr. Clark do, he picks up the phone and calls a thoracic surgeon to come help out. But there is a lull there. There's several minutes that are not accounted for in the operative record, in the anesthesia record, time that we're waiting for the thoracic surgeon to arrive to be able to cut open Mr. Holbrook and repair the suture.

Now, you're changing procedures from this placement of a dialysis catheter to this procedure of cutting open the body and fixing the vena cava. It takes about five minutes to prepare the patient for that. You will see in this case that nothing is done during those five minutes while Dr. Clark is waiting for the thoracic surgeon to arrive, even though Dr. Clark has assisted in over fifty of these procedures.

The patient is not turned on his side. His back is not scrubbed with Betadine. Nothing is done to prepare him. And so several minutes are lost while they're waiting. And all during that time the blood is leaving the vessel, is going into the lung area, and it's not going to the brain.

After everything's done and they repair his superior vena cava, Mr. Holbrook's condition is terminal. Tests show that he no longer has brain function. He is on a respirator. And the doctors say that he's never going to wake up. And they break the sad news to his wife, Sara. She has to make the decision to let her husband die with dignity. And so she makes the decision, after letting days go by to see if there's going to be any change, to turn the ventilator off and let her husband die.

When her husband died, they were getting ready to celebrate their fiftieth wedding anniversary. They were three months shy of making that wedding anniversary. And that was one of the most important things to them. It's all they could talk about for months. They were married almost fifty years. They were best friends. They spent all their time together, meals together. They slept together. At a time when Sara should have been preparing to celebrate their fiftieth wedding anniversary, instead Sara was making the decision and signing the order to terminate her husband's life. When they used to eat meals every day together at the same table, Sara now eats alone. When they used to sleep together every night, Sara now sleeps alone. All the things her husband used to do around the house as her handyman, she now has to either hire out or they just go undone.

Your job as jurors in this case is to decide whether Dr. Clark acted reasonably and complied with the standard of care to provide for Mr. Holbrook's safety during the surgery, surgery that had known risks, surgery that . . . risks that Dr. Clark knew about. You must decide if Dr. Clark acted to prevent those risks, if he acted properly to detect if those risks occurred, and if he acted properly to protect Mr. Holbrook from the harmful effects of those risks. After making these decisions, you're going to have to decide what damages Sara Holbrook has suffered as a result of the loss of her husband of almost fifty years and what that damage is worth to her. Thank you.

Presented Theme	➲	***Surgeon's job to prevent, detect, and protect***
Presented Scope	➲	Place, person, and time = Narrow
	➲	Acts and numbers = Broad
Presented Point of View	➲	Third person/jurors
Presented Sequence	➲	1. Duty of reasonable measures to protect surgical patients.
	➲	2. Known risks and available safeguards with the procedure.
	➲	3. Turning off the light. Blood, brain, and O_2. Prevention before and protection after, both denied.

Counsel for the defense, please proceed.

Good morning, ladies and gentlemen. My name is Chuck Jones. And this morning I have the honor and privilege to represent Dr. Barry Clark, a board-certified general surgeon who lives here in Our Town, and practices here in Our Town. On May 24th, 1999, Leo Holbrook underwent a common, yet dangerous surgical procedure known as a central venous catheter placement. It's common, but nonetheless extremely dangerous. You will see in the evidence that the literature says this. All of the experts agree to this. It is just the simple truth of this procedure, that it can be a life-threatening procedure and is a life-threatening procedure, as common as triple bypass surgery, as common as lumbar laminectomies, cervical diskectomies, cataract surgeries, hysterectomies, as common as those surgeries, but equally as dangerous. As Mr. Holbrook and his wife understood prior to the surgery, the surgery not only carried with it risks, but real potential for complication to occur during the surgery.

Later on, I will talk with you about the specific complications. One of them that you will see throughout the medical literature on central venous catheter placement, and even in the handbook that tells doctors how to do the procedure, is perforation of large vessels, perforation of the superior vena cava. It happens even when everybody does everything right. You will see that in the medical literature. You will hear that from the experts who will come and testify on behalf of my client. You will also hear that admittedly from the experts who will come and testify on behalf of the plaintiff in this case. In medicine, like life, there are no guarantees of a perfect outcome. There are certainly even no guarantees of a good outcome in medicine. That is why it is called the practice of medicine. This is especially true when the patient is undergoing a surgical procedure like a central venous catheter placement. Make no mistake about it. Anytime you're putting something in a patient's body, particularly in their vascular system, like the blood vessels, like the superior vena cava, like the subclavian vein, it is no doubt a serious, life-threatening procedure.

Now, why was Dr. Clark in the position to have to place this central venous catheter in Mr. Holbrook? He was a very sick man. He had acute renal failure, acute pneumonia. He had a condition related to his acute renal failure known as rhabdomyolysis. He also suffered from a condition known as atrial fibrillation. He was critically ill at the time of this surgical procedure. There is no dispute that the procedure was indicated. It was the best and most effective way for Mr. Holbrook to obtain the medication and the fluid that he so desperately needed to treat his critical conditions. There is no dispute that the approach that Dr. Clark used in this case, the subclavian vein entry as opposed to the internal jugular vein entry, is appropriate and is a physician judgment call. Either way is OK. The experts will tell you that. The medical literature will support it.

What are the risks associated with this common yet potentially life-threatening procedure? Bleeding, infection, pneumothorax, hemothorax. We'll explain what some of these things are a little bit later. Thrombosis, or blood clotting; laceration or puncture of a vessel, including the patient's artery or vein. I'll talk with you during the evidence about Dr. Clark's education, background, and his experience with this particular procedure in detail. But what I do want to let you know is that the evidence will show in this case that Dr. Clark as of May 1999 had performed more than 200 central venous catheter placements without complication. Since the placement of Mr. Holbrook's central venous catheter, more than 600 central venous catheter placements, and no surgical complications. The literature will show you that the complication rate associated with this procedure is actually anywhere between one and fifteen percent. The evidence will show that Dr. Clark's complication rate is far below that as accepted.

But you will also hear from the experts in this case and some of the treating physicians that there is no consensus as to the use of fluoroscopy. Now, Mr. Martin talked about this light that can be used during this process. The fluoroscopy, what is it? It's an X-ray. Make no mistake about it. It's not just a video. It's an X-ray that shoots into the patient's body. So think about that when plaintiff's counsel tells you that there are no risks associated with continuous use of fluoroscopy during a procedure. What you will also hear during the evidence is that there is no national set standard for the use of fluoroscopy or the approach used in the central venous catheter placement procedure. You're going to hear from plaintiff's experts, and they're going to tell you that they believe that continuous fluoroscopy or at least the use of fluoroscopy when the dilator is introduced is the standard of care.

Well, you're going to hear from highly qualified experts on the defense side that I brought in to testify on behalf of Dr. Clark who are going to tell you that the exact way that Dr. Clark did the procedure in this case is the standard of care. It's the way they do it. It's the way that they teach and train the doctors of tomorrow to do it. It's the way that Dr. Clark was taught and trained to do it. It, unlike plaintiffs' contention, is the standard of care. You're not just going to hear from experts, though.

You're going to see in the training handbook for the placement of these specific catheters—they're called "Hickman Catheters"—nowhere in that handbook does it say the continuous use of fluoroscopy or the use of fluoroscopy when the dilator is being introduced is the standard of care. In fact, what you're going to see is it doesn't recommend the use of fluoroscopy or radiographic imaging at the time the dilator is introduced. There is no consensus on the standard of care. It is a physician judgment at the time of the operation as to what approach they're going to use, both in the approach of the vein and in the use of fluoroscopy. You will see that physician judgment has a big role in surgical procedures.

I will show you the consent form that was signed by the Holbrook family when a nurse by phone talked with Sara Holbrook about the procedure and obtained consent from her. And you'll also see that Dr. Clark signed the consent form when he explained the risks in detail to the patient before the surgery. You will see in that consent form that the patient gives a surgeon extreme . . . extreme deference and judgment in the surgery to do certain things. For example, to go and do some other procedure if once they're inside they see that something has occurred, to use medications, different medications than what are originally intended to be used, if it is necessary. You're going to see that physician judgment in these types of cases is paramount.

There is no dispute that during Mr. Holbrook's central venous catheter placement a complication occurred. A tragic, yet unavoidable, complication. What is in dispute, ladies and gentlemen, is whether or not that complication could have been avoided and whether or not Dr. Clark, my client, fell below the standard of care. You cannot equate a bad outcome with negligence. That's not the standard in the . . . this state. Dr. Clark wishes every patient that he sees—and you will hear this from him—has the optimum, perfect outcome. That's what all doctors hope for. But it just isn't reality.

In the end, ladies and gentlemen, the questions that I hope that you will ask when you are deliberating this case—there are three of them. What did Dr. Clark do to prevent Mr. Holbrook's surgical complication? What steps did he take? We're going to go over that in the evidence. And I'm going to do my best to show you what steps he took to prevent the surgical complications. The second question is, what did Dr. Clark do after he recognized the surgical complication? We're going to go through that in some detail. The third question that you need to ask is, was Dr. Clark wrong in taking the steps that he did, based on his education, his training, and what is out there in terms of telling doctors like Dr. Clark what is the standard of care? Those are the three questions that I would ask that you consider. I ask that you listen to this case with an open mind, that you are guided by the evidence and not your past experiences or your emotions. That is what Dr. Clark asks of you. That is what I ask of you. And really, it's what the plaintiffs are asking of you as well. Judge their case on the merits. Thank you.

Presented Theme ➲ **Complications happen (especially to such sick patients)**

Presented Scope ➲ All areas = Broad

Presented Point of View ➲ Third person/jurors

Presented Sequence

➲ 1. Common, yet dangerous procedure. Life threatening because complications happen.

➲ 2. Very sick man versus better-than-average surgeon. Critically ill at the time versus two hundred procedures and six hundred after with zero complications.

➲ 3. No standards/requirements for fluoroscope. Used as taught, as still taught. They knew and agreed to risks.

These openings were the attorneys' best efforts to follow plans based on the following story suggestions made in their focus group preparation.

THEME SUGGESTIONS

Plaintiff

"Greater Risks Need Greater Protection"

In this case, I'd suggest a theme of "greater risks need greater precautions," to take advantage of the likely defense postures and see how well we can reframe them.

I'd also be sure you cover two other basic story areas very well. First, the juror/patient expectations of doctors these days is not just to be protected from harm, but also to have the service that they need provided. The expectations are that docs will not just "help," but also avoid "harm" while they do it, usually in that order. Second, because this guy was well along, and quite ill, you definitely want to allow enough time to get a fair reading on what these people think of each of the "soft" or noneconomic damage elements you claim with the evidence that will accompany them. As I said, it will be very important to provide a few succinct lay witnesses, above and beyond the wife, to testify to the value both of her losses and of the lost chance as far as he was concerned. Her testimony alone is not really likely to be seen as adequate.

Defense

"Accepted Medical Risk"

For the defense, I'm suggesting a theme of accepted medical risk, to take advantage of the two big medical land mines most likely to appeal to defense-oriented participants: the informed consent agreement and that the known, inherent risk of the procedure could result in one of the foreseeable complications. (Just as the plaintiffs want to stress that this is "surgery," the defense may want to avoid that term. But the defense certainly will want to take advantage of the term "complication" either way.)

STORY SCOPES SUGGESTIONS

Plaintiff

People and Numbers—Narrow

Start with a generic, step-by-step description of the standard done well to a satisfactory conclusion, but with little widening of the frame beyond this event and these players; stress more the reasonable rules governing this unreasonable doctor's conduct at the time. Try to hold a tight focus on the rules for this event and the full scope of just this event through the first two steps of the sequence. Even the prior history should be packaged as "at hand" information for the doctor.

Time and Actions—Broader

While we do want to diminish the reinforcement of too much attention fixed on the patient's prior history, we want to be sure to expand the time line forward, and then a little backward, as the harms are brought into focus. Also, the choices and acts by the doctor at the time need to be expanded to their fullest extent.

Defense

People, Actions, and Time—Broad

Since the theme is about dropping this one event into the entire pool of the hundreds of procedures this man has performed, and the tens of thousands others have, all under the anchor of "medicine" in the legal context, the wider the focus on these factors, the better. Also, simply by cataloguing the many difficulties this patient had before the procedure, whether directly related to this particular health concern or not, and whether directly related as a cause or contributor to the claimed harms or not, you can help people maintain a broad view of both parties, and invite a more dispassionate, disengaged approach to the particular intervention in question. After all, there was a lot of "medicine" there that was successfully done.

Numbers—Broad on the standards, expertise, and protocols followed.

Narrow on the event itself. It needs to be seen as one, well-known complication within several successful placements.

POINTS OF VIEW SUGGESTIONS

Plaintiff

Reasonably careful surgeon.

Defense

Third person, either emphasizing the generic "medicine" world view, or the legal limits to which the jurors need to adhere.

PRESENTATION SEQUENCE SUGGESTIONS FOR OPENING STATEMENTS

Plaintiff	**Defense**
Step One—Surgery, Risks, Required Precautions	***Step One—Professional Care and Inherent Risks***
Medical needs met by the catheter	Protocols: what is and is not required
Standards, rules, and reasonable precautions for insertion	
Step Two—Derailed Treatment Plan	***Step Two—Treating Patient Needs***
Patient's prior course, current needs, and reasonable prognosis	Path to the procedure
	Complications happen
All harmful choices and acts (specifically prohibited or not)	
Step Three—Wrongful Death and Lost Chance(s)	***Step Three—Medical Realities***
Immediate injuries, consequences (ensuing harms/declines), permanent losses	Follow the rules and stuff still happens
Preventing disease and protecting patients from harm	

The efforts of the attorneys to develop and introduce their stories, following the plan, can easily be traced in what the group participants heard and saw during the openings. The participants then fill out a short survey to establish individual baseline records of their initial reactions to the two sides' stories.[6] Now the discussion begins.

5.5 Seeking Signs of Early Growth

Primacy is so influential and the later editing of established perceptions and stories is a monumental challenge. Because of this, the first open debrief session with the group is usually the most significant input offered all day. How people are approached and how well they are questioned can make all the difference. The goal is to elicit as many direct and indirect hints as possible about the story-building process going on in each head, while avoiding pushing participants to hasty conclusions, consensus, or solitary positions. The introduction has helped establish their job as avoiding rushing to

6. See Appendix One for sample survey forms typically used in these groups. The following chapter addresses input from these surveys.

judgment and accepting differences in responses from everyone, rather than snap decisions and unthinking consensus. The group will automatically begin challenging the order before the lawyers even stand up. Hearing and seeing those lawyers revives many unhelpful anchored responses. Because of this, the way the participants are approached at the beginning can prove critical to eliciting the broadest range of stories and allow them to continue to develop over the longest period of time.

By the end of this first debrief, almost all participants will have built the basic frameworks of their case stories: the elements of theme, scope, point of view, and active party or ingredient, sequence of main and minor acts/events, and so forth. Most of the rest of the day will be spent building on that original, personal model, just as the remainder of a trial will be somewhere after the end of the first cross-examination. To better fill out their initial versions, decision makers will tend to generalize, distort, and delete the remaining input from the messengers and the surrounding situation, the stories themselves, and their own backgrounds and beliefs far more often than they will completely rewrite the basics they establish at the beginning. That change can happen, but not very often.[7] .

Participants already have ideas on how these groups are supposed to work, from actual experience, through TV experience, to extrapolations from school, business meetings, jury service, or a hundred other reference experiences, real and imagined. They've also rehearsed the introduction's directions and suggestions on how the question-and-answer sessions will go. They must be shown that the way the job was described and rehearsed, not the way they may have anticipated it, will be the way it will actually be done.

One of the hardest rules to follow during questioning is that the moderator should assiduously avoid asking who is winning or who should. Do not rush to invite judgment by even indirectly asking participants to rate the strength of either side's case against the other side or against its own side (e.g., "What was the strongest point for the defense so far?") Plus, the moderator must be ready to keep from hearing who is winning even if the participant declaring her opinion wasn't asked for it. Moderators must be alert to voluntary input that offers or implies such a rating of the strength of case stories. Watch for answers and questions focused more on the outcome of the lawsuit instead of the story elements. Answers with an introductory phrase such as, "Well, I think the plaintiffs are in trouble if. . .," may seem innocent

7. Jurors and focus group members alike are prone to report that they often "changed their minds" during deliberations, and the one in five who say they haven't developed a strong leaning before deliberations start are trying to be truthful, too. But what people are changing their minds about is the decision, not the story built to produce it. By and large, as far as anyone can tell, the basic story elements do not alter once they are set. Changes of direction for the verdict questions have more to do with a story structure that will allow that kind of latitude, such as in the variable positions available through the "tough, competitive market" theme example discussed above. People can maintain their basic "fittest survive" theme, but shift another element like point of view to "change" their ultimate decision without changing their story's foundation.

enough, but they are not. Moderators must be ready to jump to stop that sentence midstream and remind the group that, "We are not ready for any decisions yet. That part of your jobs comes much later on. This part of the process is all about impressions, only, of the stories you've heard so far." The basic question throughout this debrief in our central "What else" vein is just that, "What are your first impressions of the stories you just heard?" Each person in the room gets a chance to answer that question before this debrief is done.

If a participant establishes a position that predicts his decision even indirectly, the story building has slowed or stopped. Rationalizing his choice will kick in strongly from that point on. Not only will the learning, expansion, and inclusion get cut off for that person once an outcome-focused opinion or answer is fully formed, articulated, and accepted in discussion, but the process will also likely end for several others listening, too. People don't usually like indulging in ambiguity, unresolved conflict, and unfinished stories. Many prefer to get to the end quickly as the work on civil burden of proof during the introductory job description demonstrates. Focus groups are an artificial environment, but that environment can be managed to maximize the chances that each participant has to expand and not limit their unique story-building capacity.

One way to help keep the introduction's framing for the discussion strongly in place is to avoid the horse race perspective. Inevitably, someone will want to comment on strong or weak points in either an attorney's demeanor, or the effect of an attorney's case facts or positions on the outcome of the claim. These offerings all need to be stopped short and either restated if they deal with impressions of the story, or held in reserve until the final written surveys if they deal with the advocates' presentation skills. The consistent invitation to the group needs to be focused on exploring the elements of the story from both sides, as they have perceived and rewritten it so far, after hearing the introductions to each side's story during openings. The varied definitions of what makes an "impression" will be reinforced. Speculation about the final outcomes and decision must wait. Speculation about elements of the story, no matter how seemingly far afield, are welcome.

Instead of the lawsuit outcome, the target of the focus group inquiry is what each participant has learned about the story so far, what they each think they know (distortions included), and all they can imagine from what they've learned. The position for all the debrief questioning is simple and very consistent. In one way or another, we usually want to know answers in the "What else?" vein when it comes to impressions of the story, as defined during the introduction and job description.[8] As the day wears on, the positioning of the inquiry should toward a central question such as "How so?" but only after participants have formulated more complete stories of the case.

8. In voir dire, the form and style of the questioning ought to be very much the same. But since the focus will then be more on the stories being tendered by the jurors than for them, as in a test group, the central question would shift more to something like "How so?"

5.6 Debriefing Participants

To fully explore the stories being formulated after opening statements, there are some general debriefing rules that can improve results:

> **When asking about first impressions after the openings, try to keep the questions and initial responses in the present tense.** Slipping into past tense early encourages distance and reflection when you most want to invite full engagement in each participant's own story constructs.
>
> **Be ready to explore each of the major topic areas from each side's story as delivered.** But do not spend too much time on any specific topic, regardless of the group's enthusiasm for it. For example, after the above openings, the first debrief could easily have stayed fixed on the choice of "turning on the light" or not. That did not mean the group didn't have plenty to say about older patients with several prior conditions, surgeon experience and success, consent forms, unwritten standards of care, and many more things.
>
> **Avoid going around the room in sequential order.** Arranging the group so each person can see the others, as in a "U" configuration, helps cohesion, but constantly running up and down the rows in sequence can defeat it.
>
> **Seek out deleted topics and subject matter and explore them.** There are often many "forgotten" topics. Invite people to relate or oppose them to subjects that have garnered attention and energy. "Did I hear one of the attorneys say that X, Y, Z happened?" is one way to introduce a deleted topic. Or in the midst of a related topic's discussion, you can insert, "What about X?" But avoid direct challenges to any open concerns, as if one point were right or wrong, proof or not. If you see such either/or positioning developing on one of these topics you introduced, back out and revive the original position right away.
>
> **Be ready to continually remind folks that this discussion is based on a general preview of the full facts.** Remind them that we are at a very early stage, before any facts in evidence have even been heard. Presuppose and even state directly that many parts of their stories will change as more is learned later. Use phrases like "later on," "so far," "up until now," "at this point" to keep the reminder alive without disrupting the discussion's flow.
>
> **Emphasize that people need not hold themselves to their initial impressions.** Consistently encourage them to focus on alternatives and expansions at each stage. Also reinforce the anchors set during the introduction for leaning toward difference over similarity (or consensus),

for encouraging speculation until deliberation, and for avoiding an absolute standard (unless a criminal case is being tested). Imply and declare that people's stories will change, and reflect and reinforce input that demonstrates that. Repeat often these are "first" impressions, with many more to come. Encourage writing notes about yet-unspoken responses for future exploration.

Be prepared to ask for alternatives to apparently strong positions taken in the group, asking what evidence people could be shown, could hear or have given to them that might make them even a little less certain of any strong leaning. "If you can make up any answer, regardless of whether the lawyers actually bring you that evidence, you at least know your mind is still open on that point. And the goal is to get to deliberations with the most open mind." Participants that are able will provide their own counter examples, rather than having them planted from the front of the room.

If a participant starts to advocate a right/wrong position, using absolute and generalized terms to back it up, i.e. "Anybody that has ever been to the hospital knows you never do X, Y, Z," interrupt their flow, reminding all of their jobs to provide impressions, not decisions, and to hear out both sides, "At least into the beginning of the facts they have in evidence, if not all the way to the end of the stories you came to hear before judging them." This is one place where a direct counter-example question can help, such as "Under what circumstances would that not be so?" or "What evidence could the attorneys present that might make that less important in this case story than another?" Push them to make up any plausible answer as a demonstration of lingering open mindedness.

If a strong counter-example to a popular topic in discussion has been presented in one side's opening statement, feel free to ask about it, but not in an adversarial "But what about this?" package. Wait for an opening in which the opposing position can be naturally introduced, a little uncoupled from the previous topic.

Try to keep their stories from rushing to their own ends too quickly. Be ready to regularly back out of the content of any set of answers into the broader context, with a question addressed first to one and then all, such as "What makes it important to know that at this stage?" followed up by the baseline "What else?" Statutes, standards, and legal rules should not be imposed, but explored as they come back from the group, in whatever form.

Resist the strong urge to reduce and exclude possibilities in people's responses. Participants can be just as likely as attorneys to indulge in detail spin. But at the early stage, the widest frame of inquiry and answers is still the best, since, once you descend too far into details, you can't go back and start over with a clean slate, as you and the dumpster just proved.

If the reluctant participant tries the "I need more facts before I can say" dodge that is so common in voir dire panels, take full advantage of the chance this tack provides to reset anchors established in the introduction. Agree wholeheartedly that, at this point, no facts at all have been delivered, only suggestions about those facts to come. Remind them of the "dangerous jobs" they volunteered to do, of all the particular factors that compose impressions from ideas to emotional reactions, and then give the reluctant person another chance to answer. Never let this kind of challenge to the group's structure and contract go without reimposing that structure, immediately.

Act as if you are learning the story while they are. Avoid letting the moderator be seen as equally knowledgeable as the attorneys presenting. Keep the perceived distance between the formal, legal presentation and the informal debrief sessions as distinct as you can. On topics large and small, the consistent attitude to portray is not only that you do not know "the" answer, but rather that you assume there will be many more than one to each and every question. Then act accordingly.

5.7 Polling Questions

At certain stages, you will want to quickly poll the entire group for closed-ended answers about certain subjects as they arise. Here are some ways to make this most helpful:

When likely areas of potential bias from previous life experience related to the story come up, it is time to poll the group. But wait until these areas of likely bias emerge in the discussion, rather than trying to inject them. "Who here has also had experience with a doctor placing a catheter?" or "Who else has signed a surgical consent and read it first—or did not read it first?"

If two or more strong positions seem to be coalescing naturally and are indicative of areas where prevailing attitudes or values can exert telling influence on perceptions and positioning, stop and use a show-of-hands poll to rank responses by the rest of the group.

When the opposite condition occasionally happens and you find multiple topics on the floor spreading the group too thin, you can back up, summarize them all in a list, and devise a poll question on some point somewhat common to most of them. Be sure to follow up extensively, however, as you must avoid the trend to consensus this can invite.

You can use a poll to encourage reluctant group members to start participating in an easy way. Following up with them can help push the expansion and inclusion goals for story content, while spreading the wealth of the group's attention at the same time.

Shift the first poll question on any subject up to the most general category divisions first. You can always get more specific later, but you want each person to have a chance to find their own Jell-O flavor before you ask and end up assigning it.

When the discussion turns toward choices made in the case story by any major actors, there may be a chance to ask a poll question if it can be phrased generally. For example, you would not want to ask, "If the fluoroscope was available, was the surgeon's choice to turn it off less responsible than leaving it on?" But you could ask a more balanced version, such as "If you had to choose, and you do, which job for a doctor comes first for you up to this point: following proper surgical technique or employing every possible safety device?" In that way, you could keep the participants' choice point closer to the general level of surgery versus safety concerns.

Ask the opposite legal side of every poll question possible. In this case, the follow-up poll to the question above might be, "Answer yes or no. Do patients still have a right to sue if they know all the common complications of an operation, sign the form, and then end up with one of them?"

As in almost all questioning of the group, avoid absolute language such as "Who agrees/disagrees with Fred?" or "Who thinks that is right/wrong?" Use rather, "Who has a similar view, more or less?" or "Who leans more the way Shannon does? And a little less?" To maintain and expand the leaning toward difference, always start with the minority views in following up on poll questions.

If one person has tried to dominate the group, a way to refocus everybody is to poll on a point she made, not only cutting that person off, but again engaging folks in such a way that disagreement is safe and invited.

If you are using a tripod-mounted camera, not a fixed one with a full-room view, be sure that hands stay up long enough to pan the room so you can count them when reviewing the tape.

5.8 Cultivating Story Growth

Each person's processing of the case story and its presentation begins with their habits of perception and then moves into their thinking habits.[9] Given that, let's review some methods for managing perceptions with the group first, and then how to ask questions in ways that can help manage thinking processes to encourage full participation and input from every member.

FOCUSING ON PERCEPTUAL HABITS
RECOMMENDED QUESTIONS

Open-Ended Questions

With the exception of full-group polling on subjects that warrant it, the questions you ask would best be open ended, that is, requiring a description or elaboration, rather than a "yes" or "no." The habit of starting with "how," "what," "who," "when," or "where" can help. The most productive of these are "what" and then "how." Be careful when you ask a "how" question that the answer given is not to "why." It is simple to identify and be quick to interrupt if the answer starts with "because." Just say, "No, not why, though I might want to know that later, what I'm curious about now is how you came to see it that way?" One elicits an experience-based response, while the other is just a reason.

Positive and Negative Anchors

"So what is it about that kind of irresponsibility that gets your attention?" When they are produced by the group members, during the immediate follow-up questions you ask, be sure you adopt the same phrases, rather than reframing or restating them. This form of verbal mirroring is almost as effective as the physical variety, and you will risk shutting

Questions or Instructions Phrased in the Negative

Avoid them. "Let's not think about the verdict," or "Who thinks the patient's wife has no role in keeping him safe?" may better be presented as, "Before you get to making a decision, what else is important here?" and "How do a patient's family members factor into his medical safety—or do they?" Follow up with "What else?" to keep the ball rolling.

"Why" Questions

As in voir dire, unless you want to find the specific arguments someone will try to use to defend a position, or you want to harden a preexisting bias, avoid the "why" question, as with the hypothetical counters. Since the aim is to invite people to engage all their story constructions and expansions, asking questions that force a listener to find reasons about the part of the story under scrutiny tends to stop the construction at that point.

9. *See* Chapter Three.

down the window into the perceptions of the speaker's model if you pick terms you personally find more palatable, descriptive or eloquent.

Presupposing More

Keep in mind that the object is to elicit more perceptions of various positions on and within the stories these people are building. Ask questions and make statements that presuppose there is usually going to be more to see and talk about. Rather than asking questions that exclude possibility ("Does that change your view?"), presuppose that additional positions are there to discuss ("How could that change your views?").

Owl Questions

To maintain the ongoing presumption that there will almost always be more responses to whatever question you ask or proposals you make, ask "who," as in, "Who here, Who thinks, Who sees, Who heard it, Who feels, Who else?" This will also help you avoid the conversation-killing "any," "anybody," and "anything else," which can be safely eliminated from your repertoire. If you are interested in counting reactions, then use "How many are there that . . ." (an owl question, once removed).

Story Elements

Just as with positive and negative anchors offered within the answers participants give, note and adopt the evident elements of stories they are building. These would include scope, point of view, visual imagery, and verbal anchors, especially the sequence that they may reveal they are relying on to see, hear, and feel their way through the story constructs. In follow-up questions, find what switching one element or another might do, if anything, to the basis of those accounts with their authors.

Menus More than Prescriptions

When alternatives are proposed, be sure there are more than two where possible. Avoid implying a single right answer among the choices. If the list is stated more than once, make an effort to scramble its sequence. "So it could be time considerations, it could be other, more critical concerns, it could be the rules, it could be efficiency: who feels strongly about one of those or another possibility here?" Avoid "So with a duty to patient safety, do you have an opinion as to which one was more important at that point?"

FOCUSING ON PERCEPTUAL HABITS RECOMMENDED CONDUCT

Mirror

Use this technique to fix attention and enhance responsiveness with each person in the room. Constant mirroring throughout a question-and-answer segment is not required.[10] But reflection, in all its forms, including the fundamental, physical one, can help maintain and improve the level of participation from each group member.

Visual Aid

Help people expand descriptions during speculative or hypothetical points by using a visually biased presentation style, including visual phrases, gestures, and even eye movements, while acknowledging and drawing the speaker out. This helps particularly when the speaker is describing a fact-based part of the story in his or her head. Starting with visually biased elicitation, then moving to what was heard, said, and felt aids memory and construction far more than a strictly verbal approach.[11]

Story Scope

Encourage participants to go beyond the boundaries of what they know so far, and let that search go backward

Matching Perceptions

If the question is "What is still bothering you the most about this story?" and you have the training, be sure to model a kinesthetic or "feeling" posture, gesture, and eye movement to go along with the words and help the participants being questioned sort for that portion of their own kinesthetic referencing, in the same way as with visual references, and with those subjects dealing with recalled conversations or written records.[12]

Premature Deliberation

Stop short any attempt by participants to bypass the moderator and jump directly to talking to each other, typically when in disagreement. Indicate to all that "This is called "deliberation," and you'll all be doing it soon enough, but not now." Offer to place the two people on the same jury panel at day's end, just before you remind one and all that their verdicts need to be unanimous.

General Before Specific

Decision-maker stories usually begin at the largest chunk, the theme, and work their way down to the details,

---

10. For further specifics on mirroring within the group, see the section in Chapter Eight dedicated to the use of presentation plan results in voir dire.
11. To learn more about the technique of cleaning up sensory expression in your communication and leading others to do the same, see Paul Lisnek and Eric Oliver, *Courtroom Power: Communication Strategies for Trial Lawyers* (Colorado Springs, CO: Professional Education Systems Institute, 2001): Chapter 3.
12. *Id.*

and forward in time, as well as throughout the scope of people, places, actions and events involved. For example, you could ask, "Is this about these kind of procedures, or more about this one operation?" or "Where do patients and families fit in here—in any hospital?" Then, in follow up, concentrate on speculating "Where could that lead?" and "Where does that come from/get started?" helping people steer toward imagined extensions beyond the limits the openings implied. Life experiences, brought out as illustrations, can be similarly expanded early on to keep the broadest scope open as stories develop and inevitably contract.

Interrupt Internalizing

If you identify a person disassociated from the group, with his attention more focused on internal dialogue (private editorializing) about the process, situation, or even the story, take the opportunity to interrupt that private conversation and make it public. Long internal discourse tends not only to wipe out group process, but it helps people rush to judgment. Once the silent talker has spoken aloud, he can be asked follow-up questions designed to help expand and increase the parameters of the position thus far.

though the process happens in the mind so fast that some details make themselves known very quickly. It is still wise to start with the large frames and categories and fill various positions in at that level, before shifting down to more and more details in accounts. This means lots of gearing up and down, because participants will be working at whatever level of detail they choose at the moment, and you need to try to match that. But stay most responsive to the group, which overall needs to start at the general and move toward the specific throughout the day. Periodically summing up and pulling the conversation back to the large chunks helps broad parts of some peoples' stories get covered, where they might otherwise be missed. Resist the drive to finish a point off too soon, because it is the stories, not the opinions, that you seek.

Verbal Waterfalls

On occasion, a participant will not be able to stop talking, jumping from topic to topic with little real story engagement, much like racing through a grocery store yelling out the names on the passing cans and boxes. Walk toward that person, gesture up and lead his eyes and head upward while summarizing his listed points in one or two general phrases. Then, throw the initial question back to him, tagging the question with an invitation to pick among the items for an answer. Do not argue, move, or ease up until that is done.

Shift to Neutral

If you know the method,[13] ask follow-up questions that lead to yes or no answers without giving any nonverbal signs or directions at all, in neutral. Where there is doubt about the participant's commitment to her response, ask a short follow-up question, again with neutral demeanor, and gauge the match or mismatch between the verbal and nonverbal parts of the message to get a reading on the degree to which the person believes what she says.

Although the perceptual packaging people create for the personal case stories that each builds is not always spelled out for easy access, it can often provide invaluable clues as to how a story may be experienced by decision makers. Since perceptual responses are more immediate and basic to early story constructing, hints of their influence and forms are usually more apparent earlier in a group. If you are paying close attention to nonverbal marking and other hints in the participants' demeanor and to the implications about the story structures in their heads between the lines of their spoken and written answers, a perceptual factor occasionally emerges that can prove decisive.

For example, in a plaintiff medical neglect case, the infant involved was well under a year old. Part of the early story of his situation included descriptions of repeated visits to the doctor and hospital with infections involving his ears. The applicable professional standards dealt with selecting an unusual diagnosis from the symptoms and signs available to the professionals throughout those visits. Two perceptual factors turned out to be extremely influential to a large part of a group during this post-opening period: common experiences in memory and the perceived age of the child.

At one point, while following up on descriptions from about nine participants, it became clear that many of them had very similar histories of frustration in treating ear infections in their young relatives. The process in emergency rooms and over the phone with pediatricians and their office staffs as described by one person was acknowledged or repeated by the next. By watching the indicators in people's gestures toward their imagined children or grandchildren, the focal points their eyes fixed on and the like, it also became quite apparent that something else was shared in the references these people were strongly imposing on the subject of the treatment in question. It appeared they were actively substituting, not just identifying, their children for the injured baby. And it was also apparent that none of the kids they were envisioning and superimposing on the story line in their own cases was a small baby, less than a year old.

---

13. *Id.*

Taking the risk that most may have had conscious access to the mental imagery they were displaying in their behavior, the group was asked for a show of hands of those that were remembering these kinds of repeated emergency room visits with ear-infected children. Nine hands went up, among them all those that had been singled out with the nonverbal indicators. These people were then asked just how old the child was in their mind's eye. Ages from three to nine years old were easily related, often by people again staring at the spot in space before them where they were replaying their own experience, in lieu of images more directly related to the facts in the case they were deciding. Next, the whole group was asked to reinsert their own image of the child at the proper, very young age in their mental movies or snapshots. Finally, they were asked whether the child they now saw seemed more or less vulnerable to harm from illness. Almost to a person, they spontaneously replied "more" aloud, still staring into space.

Had the plaintiff attorneys not been forewarned to make sure to use compelling demonstrative aids, anchor phrases, and gestures consistently during the early hours and days of their presentation to the actual decision makers, they would have walked right off a perceptual cliff. Decision makers in this particular story needed help maintaining an accurate image of the child at risk as they started building the most influential foundations of their nascent case stories. The very common experiences of parents or relatives, who might otherwise identify with the plaintiff parent's situation, could drive them to unwittingly substitute much older and hardier children for the actual infant in the case. That view, out of conscious reach for the most part, could severely alter the sense of urgency or duty these people might impose on the medical professionals, possibly before they had even heard about the standards of care required.

Or consider the case in which a defendant plant owner was sued by the guardians of a former contract maintenance worker, who along with six others, had been working on platforms and scaffolds surrounding a giant vessel in an area where occasional clouds of toxic, but sometimes odorless, gases drifted by. Of the seven workers on the vessel, one was overcome and died, one passed out and was revived, and two were mildly affected. All but the deceased visited the nearby emergency room and were quickly released. The worker who passed out was suing for ongoing harms attributed to the gas and neglect of safety precautions and procedures by the owners and management of the site.

During discussions after openings and beyond, a remarkable consistency showed up at the perceptual level among the participants. The worker who died and the one who passed out were located on two different spots on the same level of a platform. As time went by, it became clear that regardless of the rationales being offered for finding greater or lesser fault with the defendants, there was a distinct division based on the pictures in people's heads. Those that were using phrases such as "right next to him," and often gesturing a few feet in front and down as they spoke, were finding fault very easily. Those that were saying something more like "a few feet away," accompanied by more oblique gestures, were not.

By reviewing the video and written survey responses, the implications they contained added enough clarity to draw a definitive distinction between what seemed like a very subtle distinction in the self-reports. While the man who passed out was not in an enclosure but just next to a curved section of wall forming a shallow depression, his position put him out of the line of sight of his colleague. Though not being able to see him from where he stood, about eight to twelve feet away, did nothing much to affect the movement of the gas cloud, it did a lot for those that built their own stories having him in sight and those with a more accurate inner vision of him around the slight bend, out of sight. For them, out of sight somehow also meant out of reach of the deadliest harm, and much more likely to be a part of the crew that recovered, not the part that perished. Naturally, this factor would need to be subtly presented at trial, but imagine the advantage lost had this perceptual gem remained unrevealed to the defendant.

FOCUSING ON THINKING HABITS
RECOMMENDED QUESTIONS

Specific Personal Analogies

Especially when the speaker is focused on legal elements of the story such as duty or fault. Ask what it is like, what it reminds them of, what they know from their life that fits the assertion they've made. This happens pretty frequently without prompting, particularly in discussion of harms and damage.

Attributed Rules and Standards

Seek out the personal references and standards from the life stories the participants bring with them, as they are related to the story. Avoid the temptation to settle for collecting a list of topics when you can pursue the perspectives that house their private standards. Explore what limits, if any, each can imagine could be placed on the rightful imposition of those standards. And keep the official standard in mind for some kind of discussion when several are eventually on the table.

Counter-Example Questions or Proposals

As noted above, counter-examples can be found, but only to topics the group itself produces. The format for eliciting them begins "When/where/under what circumstances would A, B, C be important or not?" As soon as one side of a perspective has been established and members of the group have had a chance to weigh in with their versions and additions, ask for counter-examples. Avoid asking for negation or deletion of the subject or position, but rather how it would be seen under alternate circumstances, criteria, or conditions within the frame set up by the original observation. "So what would make it still OK to sue, even though they had signed the consent form? Anything? Nothing? What else?"

FOCUSING ON THINKING HABITS
RECOMMENDED CONDUCT

"As If" Frames

When possible, note and adopt the assumptions about the world contained in people's answers or questions as a frame for the whole group to pursue. "Right, so if the doctor had a long discussion like Sam says, what do you think about that? What would you expect as the doctor? The patient? The family?" Repeating this suggestion helps aid in the natural suspension of disbelief in which many will indulge, and that aids the process overall.

Verdict Job

As the day progresses, keep the verdict job in mind. Periodically ask about the significance of various story perspectives to people's personal views of the job of determining or applying standards, duty, guilt, breaches, or of valuing harms. Do not, however, reiterate instructions or details of that final part of the job before you discover how they currently perceive those things.

Surprise

Involve everyone. Relate and reflect some people's comments to others as bridges. Jump around the room so your next move isn't telegraphed. Switch topics abruptly on occasion if the group seems to be falling into a patterned response of leaders and silent members.

Some answers reveal thinking processes without a lot of work. For example, after the opening statements above, repetition, reinforcement, and assimilation were all evidenced in the ready adoption by many of the "turning on/off the light" anchor proposed by the plaintiff attorney. By the end of the day, many were using it exclusively instead of the actual name (scope or fluoroscope). Finding anchors that work so well can be a real benefit to the eventual presentation, as when the judge adopts them simply describing or discussing the case story during voir dire in front of prospective panelists.

Another example of thinking habits at work, providing attorneys with some invaluable persuasive help, came during the later debriefs of a plaintiff medical neglect case. As with many such cases, participants had superimposed some personal themes or standards of communication on the conduct of a number of doctors regarding messages needed to take treatment action for their neonatal patient. The doctors had each revealed that, not only did they not recall the conversations they'd had a few years before during the critical night, but they had no specific notes to either confirm or deny whether certain facts had been passed to them, as the surviving mother claimed.

In hindsight and exhibiting effects of other thinking habits such as identification and confirmation, one of the participants speculated that the doctors had reacted in extraordinary ways after the baby had died from the claimed delays in treatment. He pointed out that, in his world view, a conscientious medical professional would immediately sit down and review all she had done in order to make sure any such errors would never be repeated with future patients, to assure herself that all that could be done was, and that (a point with which everyone else agreed) it should have been done if only to cover her back. Now the hospital had a risk management policy that required doctors to do this very thing, but by itself, it did nothing to expose the possible motives that this participant's hindsight perspective did. As a matter of fact, presented alone, it had appeared likely to smack of reaching or technical finger-pointing by plaintiff lawyers. But as the end of a line of reasonable personal possibilities, the hospital's rule now helped a doctor's review and recording session take on a very reasonable appearance. Moments before, with only the risk management rule as a goad to filling in the record, the benefit of the doubt for the doctor's omission stood out. But in the context of the last reason in a line of reasons to do it, only the benefit of actually having done that part of the job occupied most people's attention.

5.9 Harvesting the Whole Story

The one thing all the examples but the "light" have in common is that they were not produced in the first answer to any single question. A conscious inquiry into mainly unconscious processes needs to keep scanning, both for what participants are aware of and what they aren't clear other parts of them are aware of, too. Implied information about implicit memories and perceptions can be just as important to the final presentation of a case story as the more available, more accessible input that groups are happy to give. But the less conscious material obviously isn't often self-reported.

So we divide the day into a number of short, formal presentations by the attorneys, adding evidence to the full stories they introduced in the openings, punctuated by lengthy debriefs to give participants every possible chance to offer us an insight into what they're each doing to the story between their ears. When we get to each individual, one question typically isn't enough. As with voir dire, which, by practical definition, doesn't start until the second follow-up question, so it is with the answers or input central to the stories group participants are building. It takes more than one "What else?" or "How so?" to get as full a representation of the inner process as any person can give out loud. The second follow-up, or the third actual question. The first usually fixes or catches attention, the second sets the parameters or subject matter in relation to the person speaking, but it usually isn't till the second follow-up question that values, beliefs, and individual stories get related to any real degree. This does not apply to all people in all circumstances, but it does for most in these groups, and certainly in court.

Do not settle for single questions. They just produce an inventory of answers skimming the surface of the stories being built by group members or venire people. Learn how they got on that track of looking at the part of the story that, at this point, has captured their attention. Then learn what may be associated with it in their heads. Wait till you hear fully represented, visual, auditory, and feeling references slipping out to ensure that the person talking is fully engaged in the story he is authoring. Listen for the implied or flatly declared rules or standards for others' actions and intentions, and look inside the personal analogies for the structure of fault, guilt, duty, burden of proof, cause, and harms values, which otherwise will stay unexplored and unused. The second follow-up question is the single most effective, simple tool to help you elicit all these things and more.

For example, a group was being conducted on the aftermath of a wreck in which a passenger bus left the road, broke through a fence, and fell off an embankment, coming to rest in a stream. The group was hearing about an older woman with prior back troubles who was claiming to have sustained three years' worth of extra back trouble and pain, until the results of the impact on her previous problems were corrected. The venue was more rural than cosmopolitan, and the jury pool was rather conservative in general about personal injury lawsuits. Suspicions of plaintiff injury claims ran pretty high, especially those with a lifetime of only three years, made by a woman that was indisputably better off now. In that context, consider the following exchange between the moderator and a young woman group member. The question on the floor is a full-group question, asked of each participant at the end of the first debrief following opening statements. It is, "If you were held to only one question you could get answered, what would it have to be?"

Moderator: Wilma?

Wilma: I would like to know more about her prior medical history. You know, what she has had prior to that, just to help me decide whether or not some of these injuries in the wreck are exaggerated.

Moderator: What's important to you about that? Or how is it that comes to mind?

Wilma: I guess, just because I know some people are money hungry.

Moderator:	OK, so . . . finish the sentence.
Wilma:	Just the fact that, you know, I feel like the injuries probably are real, but a little exaggerated, and to the point of, because of this, because of my injuries, I can blame it on this and maybe get something in return."

First, note that asking the second follow-up question requires no rhetorical legerdemain. The young woman had finished her sentence, but was perfectly willing to expand on it when approached well. More importantly, examine the difference between the story view attributable to this young woman after a single follow-up question and the second one. She was among the minority in the room that actually began the day imagining "real" injuries happening from the bus crash, without many doubts or suspicions on that point. This took her out of the realm of potential decision makers that don't accept that basic, causal link in their stories about injury claims. But that point, though hinted at in her first answer, was buried behind a suggestion of a very strong, anti-plaintiff bias at work in her second. Had the connection been broken off there, the resulting perspectives on the story(ies) she was apparently working from would have been quite distorted. The plaintiff's case facts were very strong on the value attributed to the harms, and with limited potential for "exaggeration." Knowing this, that clearer view of early positioning, of how she built it, and how similar building could be encouraged for others in the final presentation became that much more important to learn, and could so easily have been left unsaid for want of one more question.

Since nonverbal communication is a two-way street and the moderator cannot maintain a truly neutral posture, strive to maintain balance in the presentation, even if you have to push one side or the other in front of the group to do so. Remember, in the final outcome you seek, a tie is better than a landslide, indicating that everyone in the room was able to find something to identify with in the story as offered by all sides in the conflict. When a big, unbalanced consensus appears, bring out counter-example questions or appeal directly to the opposite perspective to find out what parameters, if any, will support the contrary view for parts of the story many people find compelling. Contrasting two related possibilities, both with some consensus, in an either/or way can help postpone consensus.

> OK, everyone has to vote. Even if it's not fair, if I asked you to choose between the one thousand successful surgeries done the same way, and the availability of the fluoroscope, how many would say that experience is more of a factor for you, and how many would lean toward the machine?

These forced-choice questions should be avoided during the first, post-opening debrief, but can be helpful nearer day's end, when the central question shifts from "What else?" toward "How so?"

Make an effort never to lose track of a basic framework. It is a poorly kept secret that many trial professionals approach participants in focus groups, like the decision makers they represent, in an adversarial light, as if the group members were out to harm the client or attorney who is sponsoring the group. To work as well as possible, the relationship cannot be adversarial toward the group. The question professionals involved need to be asking isn't "How can they hurt us?" but rather, "How many ways are they going to help?" They are not there to be thwarted in their harmful aims, nor to have their biases overcome. They can't be. Biases and beliefs, just like story-building capacities, aren't brought to an end in court or in a focus group. They aren't finished, extinguished or eliminated. They can be illuminated and then used for whatever help can be drawn from them in learning what the case story may actually be, and how best to present that to whatever group of decision makers may eventually hear it.[14] Groups enable participants to lavish those gifts on the professionals running them, who in turn collect them and put them to good use in planning the presentation of the case for mediation, arbitration, negotiation, or trial, using every gift given.

At least once in each debrief session, you may want to get an answer from each member to the same questions. Preface them with a reminder of the herd-instinct warning from the job description, so that participants know to add enough detail to their own answers to differentiate them from similar ones offered by their colleagues. These questions would best be designed to elicit particular case story features, assuming the individual case stories will be more and more fully filled out as the day progresses. Below are four questions we typically ask in most groups, though they are really only a guide. There are any number of creative ways to take the temperature of the state of the participants' stories by how you ask the question, and when you choose to ask it. You'll see that the examples below progress from the assumption that there are large holes in the case stories at the start, through a general thematic inquiry, and ending by asking for exceptions or "outlier" perspectives on a presumably settled story structure. Questions can be framed to lean responses more toward or away from elements such as rules over actions, standards before motives, but they need to be very carefully phrased to stay as general and as widely open as possible.

These questions get far better responses if you work to build a context for each, rather than dropping the interrogatory on the group cold. For example, in our initial, "one question only" query, we ask the group first to imagine the possibility that they are going to get to leave hours earlier than predicted. But that means they will have to deliberate to unanimous verdicts with only the information they've received after the openings. And if that were the case, and they could get only one additional question answered before they had to deliberate to the fairest decisions they could, what

14. David Wenner, one of the designers of the unfortunately titled ATLA seminar, "Overcoming Juror Bias," has been an active promoter of the shift from trying to overcome to effectively using preexisting bias where it may be found among jurors.

would that one question be? Encourage folks to write a word or two down as they hear the first iteration of the question, so they will not only remember their own response, but be better able to fight off norming-biased herd instinct.

1. What one question would you ask, if held to only one?
2. Who would you choose to talk to/question privately, of all the people involved in this story?
3. What is this whole thing really all about—answered just as if I were your best friend?
4. Of all the things that could, what is bothering you the most, still, about this story?

In the focus group opened above, the first debrief ended with just such a round-robin question, giving people the chance to consider what one answer would help them fill out their already formed story foundations more than any other. Here is what they wanted to know, at that point in the process. Note those items from the two stories that are significant by their absence. That is not because they may not be critical to a judgment for one side or the other down the road. But knowing how they came to be omitted or superseded here could be the decisive factor in the role those story elements end up playing.

Moderator:	If you could get only one question answered before you had to go do justice to this case, what one question would you have to have answered?
Wilma1:	Why did he turn it off if he turned it on to begin with?
Fred1:	It's pretty much why did he turn the scope off if he had the option to use it?
Wilma2:	Why didn't he go for the dye instead of the X-ray?
Wilma3:	Why did he turn the machine off? How's he going to see?
Wilma4:	Mine's the same. Did he need the light?
Fred2:	What happened in the five minutes? There was a five-minute span between the time . . . .
Wilma5:	Mine is what did he do to prevent complications or did not do to prevent?
Wilma6:	Mine's pretty much her saying . . . knowing

that—I'm going to bring the pneumonia back up again—because as the man got weaker and everything else, the light should have stayed on. Why did he turn it off, knowing it would be a higher risk?

Wilma7: Why didn't they have better facilities for what the doctor needed, the X-ray?

Fred3: Well, I was concerned about that time delay. He said there was three minutes' to ten minutes' time delay. Hey, a person can die in that length of time, easy. Why was there such a time delay?

Fred4: Did the doctor perform all the procedures to protect the patient?

Wilma8: Did the doctor specifically do something that caused the patient's death?

Wilma9: Were all safeguards used in this procedure?

Wilma10: Did the doctor perform the standard of care that was necessary for the procedure?

Wilma11: I think they kind of go together. I guess timing with the procedure after he saw there was a problem. What did he—why did he not do the things more quickly?

Fred5: On the 600 procedures since this incident, how does he do it now?

Wilma12: Mine was were his standard procedures followed to the letter and doing everything he could with the standard—what was standard to do in this operation?

Wilma13: After he made the puncture wound that caused the bleeding, what did he—why or what did he do to stop the bleeding?

Fred6: Well, first of all, why did he turn the light out? They didn't really say exactly what did happen in the surgery.

Wilma14: Was the doctor overconfident?

Fred7: Of the 200 previous, had he used the scope on each one of those?

Fred8: The time element. Did he make decisions in a timely manner for the procedure?"

Time pressures, alone, make it unlikely that many more than one or two of these "round-the-horn" question sessions can be done. In a large group, the time to answer may run as high as twenty to thirty minutes. Be sure you vary the starting point for each round so that one person isn't always first, or last. Pay special attention to these full-group responses in analysis, as they can help you vector each party's positions over time in the group, against the private, written responses at the start and end of the day and positions taken in deliberation. Some private trends can be amplified or diminished by group involvement, and whole aspects of the story, or subjects such as people, events, or legal rules, may wax and wane along lines these trends can make apparent, where they might otherwise pass unnoticed. Following up on some of these answers can provide big dividends.

Verdict forms for deliberation must be as simple as promised in the job description. Reiterate earlier instructions, and then have the groups break up. Because people have revealed thinking habits, perceptual habits, and other connections and predilections all day, you can choose to sort the "juries" according to a wide number of criteria in order to track the influence of any trends you might see. Our default arrangement is to put the people that take strong positions the earliest in one group, those that exhibit more deliberative, procedural, or right/wrong processing in another, and those expressing "wild card" or follower habits in the third. But the choices are as unlimited as the stories they can generate. You may want to avoid homogeneous groups along plaintiff and defendant lines, aiming at a mix for each "jury."[15] Deliberation rules and format are variable, though it has proven interesting to suggest that each foreperson allow group members to summarize their positions on what was most important to them, or struck them the most about the full case story, uninterrupted, before the verdict form is tackled. This can be justified in the instructions under the notion of respect for the group conscience, first brought out in the job description, and it gives you one last take on each person's story view in a more intimate setting, free of the moderator but in the face of the pressures of a verdict. What sticks and what slides off at that point can be quite instructive on occasion.

---

15. Group size varies, for many different reasons, but we aim for a group of twenty-one, which provides three juries of seven at day's end.

Gather the full group back together, have the various forepeople share their panels' verdicts for the record, reiterate and reinforce confidentiality commitments, and exchange the remaining written survey forms for payment. Wish all a safe ride home.

Figure 6

Additional demonstrative visual used for personal injury lawsuit introduced on page 173.

5.10 2015 Supplement

Less is More.
—*Mies Van Der Rohe*

5.10.1 Framing and Story Sequencing

A significant change to our case story presentation planning and delivery recommendations since 2005 is a more precise recommendation for plaintiff case story sequencing. Although I still suggest attorneys develop and deliver a story that has three basic steps (as all good narratives do), I did not fill out for the reader what has turned into a much more complete rendering of a basic plaintiff story. This story sequence provides a "default" starting point for my clients, and these days I often include it in my training presentations.

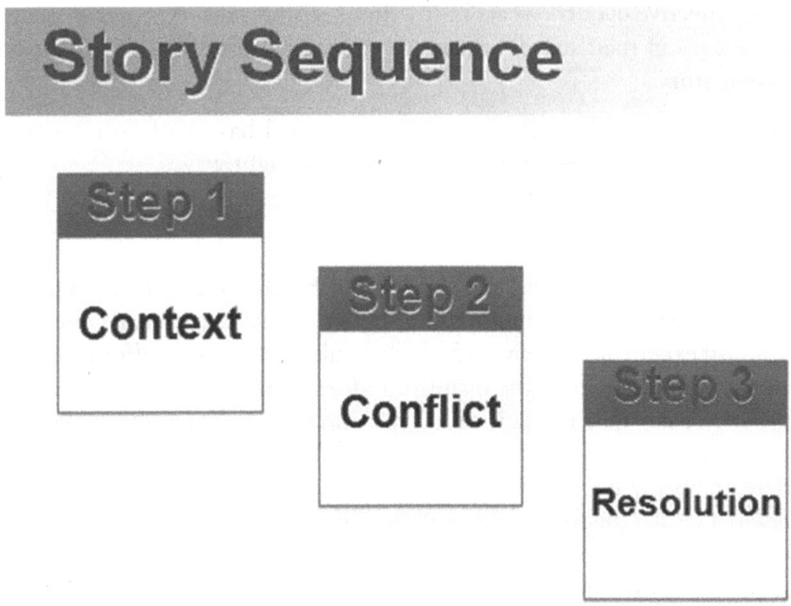

The first step of a narrative is what I call "context" (the law might call it "same or similar circumstances," and the screenwriter might call it "setting and characters"—i.e., the first act in which the main conflict, characters, and setting are "exposed" or revealed). However you choose to label it, you get the idea that the first step of delivering your case *as a story* sets the scene for everything to come after during trial.

The remaining two steps can be called "conflict," the middle step covering the major actions in the story and what they caused to happen in the immediate aftermath of those actions, and "resolution," the final step covering the consequences of the defendant's actions to all the characters and what losses and harms are caused by those negligent acts. The one difference between the three steps in a legal narrative and other forms of narratives is that the third step, resolution, has two parts to it. First, the expected one: what happens to the characters in the story? Second, exclusive to the plaintiff's story: what do you want the decision makers to do about that?

Readers will recall that I discuss setting up key story frames within each of the steps of a planned story presentation. However, where I previously advocated that the number of frames could reach as high as twelve, experience since then has taught me that the range of frames needed to construct a persuasive plaintiff's case story is only seven to nine, and no more than three frames per story step.

When your three-step case story narrative is defined, each step can more effectively deliver the whole story to decision makers if there are two or three smaller story topic frames within each step. For example, in many plaintiff cases, particularly injury and professional negligence matters, a trio of smaller frames has proven to be quite effective over the years in inviting decision makers to compose the first step of the story in their minds and trigger continued productive private rewriting of the whole story.

In order to successfully carry and deliver context, I have settled on a potent trio of initial story frames three frames: risks, rules, and right way.

Risks

In a plaintiff's case story, the "risk" is all of the hazards and/or dangers (actual and potential) that exist in a specific situation under similar or the same circumstances as the plaintiff experienced them, and which would be a hazard and/or danger to anyone in a position like that of the plaintiff. Rather than directly jumping into laying out the many rules that the law, industry standards, and/or professional practices dictate (to which both plaintiff and defendants alike must adhere), decision makers appreciate first being introduced to (and are better equipped for their decision making "job" as a result) the full extent of all the risks involved and the actual likelihood of one or all of those risks being realized that justify having such rules in place at all. Experience has shown rules mean little to decision makers unless they are justified in their own minds by a risk with which they can personally identify. Once visual and verbal anchors for the risks are provided, decision makers can, and will, better identify with the need for protection from, or prevention of, needless harms.

Rules

The "rules" are those rules that apply to these circumstances and are justified in terms of the "risks." Once decision makers have had a chance to personally identify with and understand the risks involved, the rules established to legally address them will have much greater import. Decision makers who are able to (and do) imagine themselves, their family, or their friends at "risk," will more easily find those rules legitimate, reasonable and, most important, absolutely critical to enforce. As Friedman and Malone recommend, starting with a very general "umbrella" rule under which all the other rules fit can be extremely valuable.[16]

Right Way

Often, the culminating third frame, the "right way" frame is left out entirely by attorneys when planning and delivering their case story presentation. The "right way" is a generic depiction of the exact "right way" under the circumstances—*sans* the defendant's actual bad acts. Without the concluding third frame of the right way, the rules justified by the risks can't be followed all the way to the happy ending the plaintiffs can then be perceived to clearly deserve. Asking witnesses step-by-step questions about what it looks, sounds, and feels like to see, speak, and move through events, threatened by risks and following rules those risks justify, helps decision makers to imagine as vividly as they can how that story should have played out—barring defendant negligence. For decision makers, this frame particularly benefits from a careful effort to manage the visual imagery being suggested to them. Managed well, a persuasive delivery of the "right way" frame not only seals decision maker perceptions of defendant negligence, but also multiplies damage values because of the gap shown (and perceived) between proper and improper conduct under the circumstances.

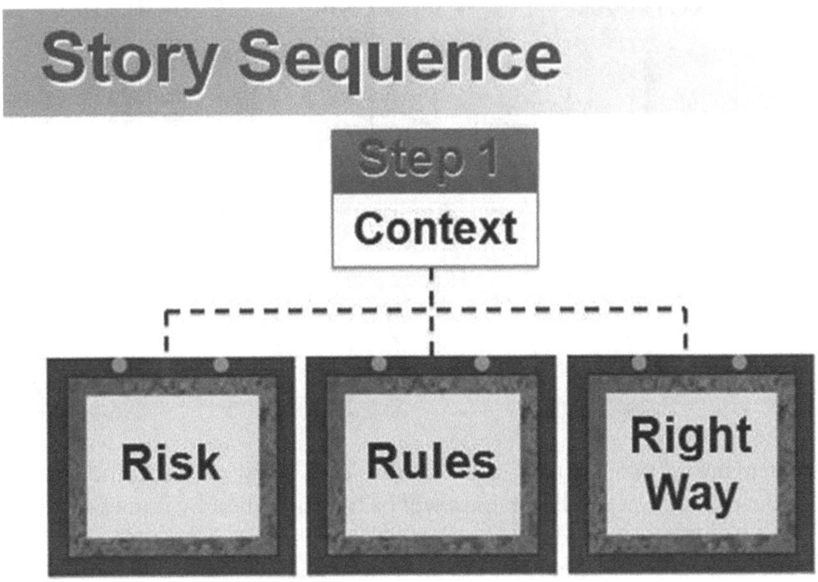

16. R. Friedman and P. Malone, *Rules of the Road: A Plaintiff Lawyer's Guide to Proving Liability* (2d Ed.) (Portland, OR: Trial Guides, 2010).

To maximize the engagement with—even identification with—the three story frames that make up the first step (context) of your client's case delivered as a story, I highly recommended that you work to actually dehumanize the characters of the case story, especially your plaintiff if you are representing one while you present these three frames.

How so?

The more general or generic the delivery of the risks, rules, and right way are, the more room is created for decision makers of any background to plug themselves, close friends, or family members into this first step of the client's case story. In several successful trials, I've recommended and then observed openings delivered without even mentioning the plaintiff's name in this first section (or referencing the defendant without any specificity as well). Consider what advantage you can grab if you wait to begin being specific about the particular characters and facts surrounding them until you get to the delivery of the second and third steps of the story sequence.

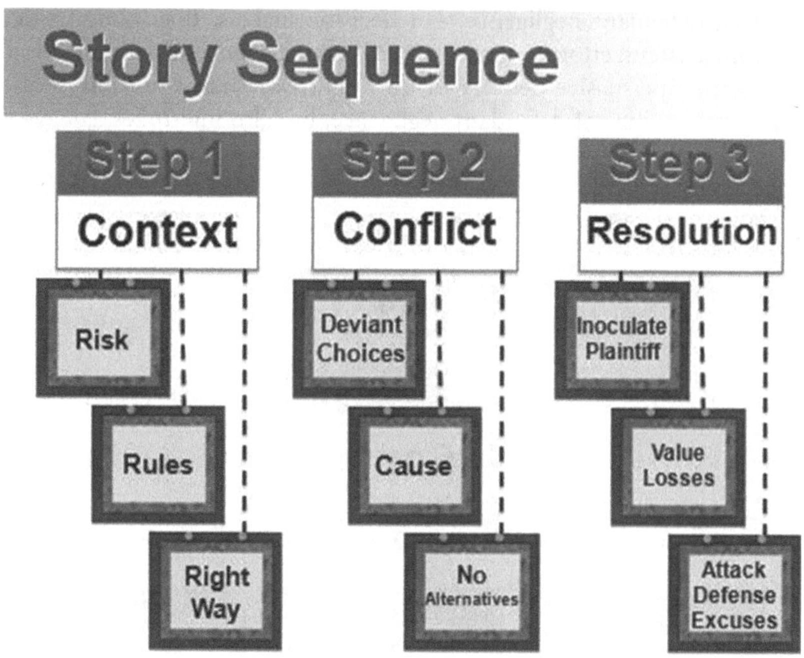

The remaining two steps of the plaintiff case story, conflict and resolution, each also carrying three smaller frames, will be portrayed best by frames that include:

- The bad or deviant acts
- What negative results they cause
- What other alternative causes of those results can be safely ruled out

- How to inoculate the plaintiff's problems in the story
- What the plaintiff and others are now deprived of
- And importantly, what attacks to mount upon how the defense is likely to excuse their behavior

This general list of smaller frames are now, after years of honing, the default suggestions for filling out the middle and final steps of a plaintiff's case story. It provides an additional benefit for the attorney presenting that story—selecting frames to be introduced by visual and verbal anchors in a carefully built sequence creating the opportunity to invite decision makers to reframe your weakest case points as strengths (as long as the reframing fits within the overall sequence of anchored frames your story has produced). Reframed weaknesses, delivered and perceived inside a complete story sequence, tend to stick in the minds of a wide range of decision makers. Without this kind of narrative context, you run the risk of reverting to the ineffectual, "just think of it this way" approach to attempting to reframe your weakest story points in any way you can.

Depending on the case facts, frames like Inoculate the Plaintiff or No Alternative Harms Causes, can be optional. As well, the sequence of certain frames, especially the Harms and Loss Values with the Attack on Defense Excuses also are case story dependent. Overall, some frames may need to be changed, or added or dropped, based on the requirements of the stories produced by the focus group participants. You will need to be both critical and creative when making the determinations.

Experience has shown me that this basic sequence provides a much more effective and persuasive "package" within which to deliver a case story—and using it to prepare focus group presentations can add even more value for lawyers who use it regularly. Keep in mind that this is a suggested format to help you analyze and arrange your presentation of your client's case *as a story*. The format—except for the first three frames[17]—is not set in stone, nor are all the subset frames necessary to fill out the delivery of every case. For instance, the No Alternative Causes frame is usually more applicable to a toxic tort or medical neglect case. Similarly, the Inoculate the Plaintiff frame is less applicable when comparative or contributory fault is not a significant issue.

A note to keep in mind while preparing for focus groups: defense case stories need sequencing, too. By default, it is particularly necessary for the defense to stick to its particular narrative (read: to stick to their guns). However, for most defense case stories the necessary frames do not significantly vary in content so much as in required sequence. For example, in the initial context step of the story sequence, many defense injury cases can be presented well by taking the risk frame and dropping it from the first spot to the third, making the order rules, right way, and risk. Of course, the risks

17. Barring rare circumstances.

in a defense case story would not refer to any hazards as being present for anyone like the plaintiff, but rather how "risky" this particular plaintiff's actions were or, just how his particular situation turned out at the scene, at the time. Short-changing the value of a focus group by not presenting the most strongly developed defense story possible is a mistake I see plaintiff attorneys making almost every week.

5.10.2 Look at It This Way

For any trial professional or decision maker in any venue, the primary dynamic in legal communication is the one between what is *other-than-conscious* and what is *conscious*. Inevitably, because that dynamic is so far reaching in its effects on perceptions of the stack of facts, and of the legal rules applied to those facts, what is verbal and what is nonverbal, is also a significant, far-reaching factor to take into consideration when managing the perceptions of your client's case story by decision makers.

If a part of your communication is not verbal, then logic dictates that if it isn't being heard, it's being seen—if only in the mind's eye of the decision maker. Aside from the impact of indirect suggestion by analogy and metaphor, nonverbal communication is almost wholly visual communication—no words, no sounds—just imagery, primarily the mental images created by decision makers. A mental image can be prompted by demonstrative visuals; it also can be evoked by painting a mental picture with words and gestures by the most powerful piece of demonstrative evidence in any legal venue: the attorney.

The bridge the brain builds between an anchor (similar to a cue, but more) to which we have conditioned ourselves to respond, and a frame of collected perceived experience that gives anchors meaning, is best composed of two parts: 1) a paired phrase and image (for a good demonstration, see the example of the image of the four-year-old child, the phrases "pick me up . . . no, I can't" and the big numbers to be linked to them in the conditioned responses of decision makers referenced earlier in the Jim Lees cancer misdiagnosis case).

Big numbers presented on their own, without an image, won't focus decision makers' emotional responses and therefore produce a less persuasive effect. Big numbers delivered with imagery will "delivers the goods." Without visual support, attempts to invite the reinforcement or conditioning known as *anchoring effects* often will fall short of your intended outcome.

Managing mental imagery during focus groups can help in several ways to increase the effectiveness of a group.

Packaging Questions

Visual language coupled with a visual delivery invites more imagery to come to mind for each participant—imagery that is then communicated back to you in their responses, if you are ready to read them. Their story frames come laden with images, and you'll want to know them.

Internalizing—Interrupt or Redirect

The reason it works to approach someone lost in internal dialogue and direct their eyes upward using image-laden terms is that it draws their conscious attention away from thinking only with words and redirects it toward thinking with images. If you are paying close attention, you will find that this imagery likely includes prior visual references for you to connect with in this participant's (re)construction job of your client's case story.

Ignoring Landmines

If you have a way of seeing how the story is being visually (re)constructed by decision makers and you track what they are referencing visually when certain topics drop off their screens and don't return as factors in their version of your case story, you can start building a very reliable list of landmines you may not want to directly inoculate against, or even address directly in your ultimate presentation for the resolution of your clients' case. Worrying about all the "what if's" is a bane of trial attorney existence. Knowing in advance which "what if's" don't count can provide a huge advantage—and relief for the lawyer presenting the case story.

The goal of appreciating how the story is being "seen" is to be able to recognize which landmines are so "remote" when the story is (re)constructed in certain ways, that they likely are unimportant—maybe even irrelevant—to decision makers, to risk reinforcing them by bringing them up. (See Chapter 6, "Point of View," section 6.9, the example of the car wreck is depicted strictly from the two drivers' viewpoints, rendering the coefficient of friction a distant third in the mental landscape of focus group members. The prior mental images rendered the later expert numbers less important to the stories they'd (re)built.)

Reframing Expectations

With one eye constantly on mental imagery as equally important a factor as what you say or hear during case story delivery, certain assumptions (often made without thinking) can suddenly be seen in a very different light. Consider the attorney fearing contributory fault being assigned to his plaintiff who had been involved in a wreck but whose blood alcohol at the scene was one one-hundredth over the legal limit. Multiple witnesses at the scene, including paramedics and cops, did not describe him as "not drunk," but rather as clearly "sober." The verbal part of the attorney's mind wanted to take advantage of a motion in limine to rule out any discussion of his blood levels (even though drinking testimony was coming in).

However, the "manager" of his own mental imagery realized the solid possibilities for reframing a weakness into a strength inherent in the picture of the attorney and his client "embracing" the "flaw" by adding it to the image of his proper conduct despite the indictment by "technicality." Of the many professional and lay witnesses at the scene, nobody saw intoxication as a factor. Letting the blood reading in, and adopting it as part of the plaintiff's story, fixed attention on what was witnessed at the scene (by so many) and not on the infinitesimal amount of blood that was read in a lab so much later, could actually strengthen the perceptions of responsible, not negligent, actions at that scene where so much good was observed by so many.

5.10.3 One Last Word

I have learned from experience, during the ten-year interim since I first published this book, that a warning I sounded in this chapter in 5.8, "Cultivating Story Growth," may require some clarification.

It is true that moderators conducting focus groups and attorneys conducting voir dire (or client interviews) usually are tempted to ask direct, conscious questions like:

- Why do you feel that way?
- Why should the defendant prevail?
- How exactly can you "set all that aside" and be fair?

The point that was not made clear is, because these questions address the part of the mind that is other-than-conscious, they cannot be honestly, thoroughly, accurately, or even approximately answered. These direct questions address the verbal, left-brain part of the mind that cannot produce these kinds of answers.[18] However, these kinds of questions almost always will get answered, and more's the pity. The pressures of social context reinforce our natural reaction to guess, to make something up on the spot, or to speculate wildly. The conscious effort to guess at what's out of conscious reach is so habituated that when they feel put on

18. This concern is not by any means limited just to focus group questioning. It should drive your strategy for design of questions in voir dire and early discovery (written and oral), and most certainly should be a guiding principle in depositions and witness testimony at trial.

the spot, most people won't even hesitate to answer. Furthermore, after the fact, they will defend their guesses as the singular truth.

Trial professionals must be constantly vigilant as to which part of the decision maker's mind they are questioning and which part is actually answering the questions. If you get a fabricated "just because" answer, you have only your inartful technique to blame. Be aware that their guesses are not referencing their (re)constructed case stories because they can't, given such directly posed questions. Learn to recognize quickly when it's time to rephrase, then follow up thoroughly.

Chapter Six

Refining the Story

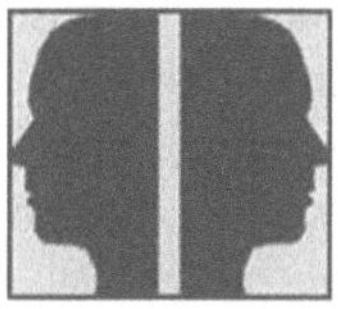

A point in any direction is the same as no point at all.
—*Harry Nilsson*

6.1 Bringing in the Crop

Chronology can be an ally when culling through the results of a focus group even though it is often a liability for a case presentation. Start with the transcripts of how much of the group you had recorded word for word. This is a matter of choice. We recommend transcribing at least what the lawyers have to say, since what they intended to say and what they actually produced often share little resemblance. It can be helpful to have an accurate record of what the group was actually told by each lawyer. Also, a transcript of each full-group, round-the-room question session offers hints about where each participant was in their own story building relative to each of their colleagues at select points during the day. So their inclusion is highly recommended.

Include the written surveys. The final pre-deliberation survey form we use (see Appendix One) includes a question about which way the participant is leaning, the first and only question of that nature asked throughout the day. We use those answers to divide the forms into plaintiff/prosecution versus defendant/defense favoring groups, with the occasional undecideds forming a smaller, third pile. Dividing all the prior survey forms along those self-declared lines of preference allows you to create a chronological record of clues about each participant's story building efforts, divided in the whole record of the day's work by the party(ies) they came to align with by the end. The aim is to record the many potential directions each participant's story might have taken, as well as the one it eventually did.

Adding the transcripts of deliberations if you choose to produce them, finishes a written summary account of the day's process from opening statements through deliberations, in order and filtered for defense or plaintiff, prosecution or defendant leanings in the group's written input. Written responses to any witness videos, or special input offered the group before closings, would be slotted into their appropriate places, too.

Now review the videotapes, especially those parts from the debriefing sessions after openings and following each evidence section. If the camera was handled well, you will have a record of the nonverbal marking, sensory-system advertising (i.e., visual, verbal, feeling), and other behavioral clues to each participant's story-building process. Plus, you will have the added advantage of replay, pause, and slow motion that reality doesn't offer during the actual session. You will also have all the polling-question results there to collect: the raised hands, cross-room eye contacts, nonverbal lobbying, or editorializing. Tapes of the participants can provide invaluable help. Since the focus group remains primarily a conscious inquiry into other-than-conscious processes, if you were forced to choose between the transcribed, written input and the parts of the perceptual and thinking messages caught on tape, there would be no real contest. Seeing shows us believing a lot more than just reading about it ever could.

First piece together a chronological record of everyone building their versions of the case story as its sides were presented by the attorneys. You will have a rough indicator of group members' final positions regarding the outcome based on personal their declarations at the end. That can show how balanced a response the attorneys' stories obtained. Sort more by the personally announced leanings on the final survey forms than by the votes taken in deliberation to account for balance in the group outcomes.

While collecting the material the group has provided and putting it in order divided by participant leanings, there are some general factors you can start to recognize. Those people that came to common conclusions about the case in their leanings toward statutes or verdict questions, arrived at their individual ends by building and following different story paths.

Often you can see, at first glance, how many took fairly consistent paths to reach their leanings. Were the common ends reached by consistent, somewhat consistent, or inconsistent paths? This is all grist for the presentation plan mill. One way this can affect attorney choices about the eventual presentation in mediation, arbitration, negotiation, or trial is to recognize that there may be a difference in the strength of the story from her side as heard by the group. This is represented by the amount of consistency with which people reached leanings for a particular side. Since we know that one legal or story element can often be used to bootstrap appreciation of another, plaintiff attorneys often look to this cross-story consistency as one sign of how much leverage actual jurors may give to perceived fault, neglect, or liability in their later damage value assessments. Civil defense attorneys looking for ways to minimize or eliminate damage numbers can find some equally valuable input from such a broad-stroke review of story consistency.

The term "consistency" is used here in the sense of whether each person's story is more or less similar in its basic elements of theme, scope, point of view, sequencing, active party or ingredient, major and minor events, and the like. For example, in favoring choices defendants have made, are participants generally telling stories about "no fault," or are they splitting their constructs between that position, alternate causes, defendant efforts to "do all that was possible," blaming the plaintiff(s), or even blaming outside forces or agents beyond the parties themselves? All those options can lead to a story that favors the defense. But a lot of different spokes on the story wheel rather than a consistent few, make a world of difference when considering how well a case story may be received by the eventual decision makers. They will have to build a group consensus based on describing and defending their individual stories. A more consistent starting point among the group usually heralds a more consistent end, and vice versa.

Inconsistencies can sometimes point exactly to where compromising will have to be accomplished among the various versions of decision-maker stories, when they try to negotiate their differences and draw a consensus conclusion. For example, let's say the defense in a civil injury case wants to push jurors toward a no-cause finding. Yet, in the focus group(s), a significant number of people resisted such prompting from their colleagues and the attorneys in their discussion. They all seem to prefer building stories more about fault and the defendant doing all she could under the circumstances. You may do well to get curious about how the stories constructed from these facts warranted that move for so many people, since appealing to both trends may not be possible if you want a coherent story to present at trial, mediation, or arbitration. Finding how best to relate one tack to another could be the most viable move. First, you have to be alerted that the second trend will likely emerge, and how strongly.

Try to remember that every person's story construct is still third-hand reality. The actual events are not what they are referring to, nor are they directly processing what the attorneys retold to them as the story any more than the words in the transcript are the actual facts. What they are constructing are a number of possible stories referenced to their own experiences and beliefs against a secondhand account of the actual case events and contentions. Work to assess each person's position as independently from your version of the case facts and legal rules as you can. That way you will be less prone to try to correct or dismiss positions due to their poor fit with your model of the world. You can also get a better glimpse of their perspectives. Whenever the choice arises, choose strong implications over direct assertions as they are closer to the primary source of influence in everyone's mind: that which is referenced outside conscious reach. Avoid the temptation to revert to acting as if the case story is just a stack of facts and law, fixed, predetermined, and outside the decision makers' heads. Likewise, avoid taking one declared position for anyone's whole story.

The raw numbers of people who declared a leaning for either side are another broad-stroke indicator if the nature of the inquiry is kept clearly in mind while reading the tally. The most effective outcome, of course, would be a tie, which indicates that all sides adequately backed their claims or positions. It is landslide judgments at the end of a focus group that must be eyed with suspicion. Is it really safe to take a landslide result and assume that nobody that hears and sees the other side of the case story presented will find anything in it more compelling than anyone in the group? How much of a factor was the *way* that side's story was presented? Before counting the numbers of people aligned against it, the trial professional should make a careful review of the strengths and weaknesses of the presentation to the group with the one-sided outcome. Perhaps one side was all that was presented—in which case the numerical measure is accurate, and completely misleading about the next set of decision makers down the line for this case.

Tracking general trends in focus group participant stories can reveal elements of the legal case structures, which usually provoke some trends over the time the group provides responses. For example, in the early debriefs people are usually more interested in setting contexts and placing actions and interactions among their stories' characters and events within them than they are tuned into motives or intentions. This is true even in criminal cases, where motive frequently plays a key role.

Noting what is not there is often helpful in drawing this kind of inference from the group's input. Deleting a major legal element, such as reliance on material representations made, or direct contribution to harms, for example, can be very telling in certain cases. It can reveal inadequacies in how the case story was put across and the occasional inadequacy that can't be fixed.

In reviewing the wealth of material for these general trends, note how early or late certain story elements such as active party/ingredient strongly appear. Note the level of presence they retain over time in peoples' output or how soon they fade from the group's reported radar screens. This can prove very enlightening in discerning how people arrive at the points they do. This is also true for proofs in evidence, facts, or legal points that don't stick, no matter how many times they are thrown against the wall of listener attention.[1]

Another result of a preliminary review of the group's offerings is a rough sense of which legal and story elements presented by each (or all) sides, seemed to emerge as the strongest or weakest parts of those stories for the full group. What was the most compelling aspect of the plaintiff's case story based on its repetition, its incorporation, and its role in the stories these decision makers authored? Was the theme proposed by the defense story directly or indirectly adopted and adapted by the majority of people from the start? Did it come to the surface after

1. In the Round Robin responses, herd instinct is surely a factor to be wary of when finding seemingly "strong trends" that fade when the group is questioned around the room in the other direction or when people's individual input isn't taken from a line of responses to the same question. The work done during the introduction/job description to establish and model a preference for differences within participant responses can pay off well here, especially if the moderator continues throughout the session to work at reinforcing that initial push.

several false starts or never rise for the majority of listeners? Particularly telling in many cases will be the story element of point of view, especially very early in the group session. Did many people reference their stories from the position provided them? If so, how did they express that positioning? If not, how did they indicate what led them to put another party, process, or organization on center stage in their stories?

These initial, general reviews of the material are easy, even if the trial professionals pull their observations from an instant review of the groups' offerings, just after the folks leave the room. You can track the development of stories both individually and within the group's interaction. Look for strong trends that stayed strong throughout and diversions that worked for the people that produced them. Bear in mind that these overviews often end up being overwhelmed by other, less apparent gifts those people left behind in the record.

Because this is a conscious inquiry into an other-than-conscious process of story building and decision making, only the professional with the shallowest appreciation for people's thinking processes would assume that "everything we need to know was all there in what they said." That is the rare exception, not the rule, which only stands to reason.

Consider fading story elements, which appear but quickly drop off the majority of radar screens in the group. If that untenable element is a legal rule or set of facts that the attorney considers essential, that trend needs careful review. Hints about how that element can be bootstrapped by changes in the sequence, what it is linked with, when or if a visual is needed in support, or if the language involved isn't helping fix the point, will only emerge from a more focused review of all the material collected, in print and especially on videotape. As with jurors or judges who form equally crucial associations from their perceptions of how a message is delivered as from what specifically is said, the astute trial professional can glean the same significance from the demeanor of the receivers of the parties' messages in a focus group. That is, at the time they hear and see them delivered (if the camera is kept on them) and as they discuss their story building efforts a little later on.

If the perceptual reactions, internal referencing, and other-than-conscious processes producing leanings were all consciously available, focus group participants could fax or phone in their answers and the sponsors could save the cost of feeding them lunch. That kind of surveying is helpful for rating very broad, general attitudes over a large population. Yet, it will not open any substantively useful doors to how eventual decision makers are likely to build their own versions of the client's case story. Neither will it reveal how to package and present a story that encourages the best results from their efforts.

Implicit memory builds unconscious understanding that helps all decision makers author their versions of any case story. These understandings need to be elicited directly, where available, and implicitly where not. Determine which implicit suggestions are essential to delivering the story you distill from the whole group's input. Many of the needed suggestions will be self-evident or show up in these broad stroke reviews of the material. The rest requires a little reading, listening, and looking at the participants.

6.2 Bridging and Blending

Participant input can be sorted into three basic categories:

1. Nonverbal
2. Verbal and written
3. Verbal once removed

Examples of and suggestions for dealing with each appear below. But it may help to have a couple of fundamental maneuvers in mind when considering how best to deal with each flavor of information that a focus group provides.

Just as attorneys try to balance their presentations to the group, balance is also a major factor in dealing with what the groups produce. The major variables affecting decision-maker judgments: lawyer choices and actions, juror habits and beliefs, and the elements of the case stories themselves, work synergistically within their three-way system. They work together without codified cause-and-effect signs. Each variable contributes to (or detracts from) others in ways that can only partly be tracked by verbal means. Implicit memory builds implicit understandings.

The same kind of balancing act will confront you as you start to piece together trends in the formation of the case stories that emerged from the group, building up to each participant's eventual judgment. Two big, intertwined and interacting packages for the stories in pieces before you are the stories' context, or perceptual structure, and content. Context includes the stored mindsets and sensory representations in images, sounds, or sensations that dominate the individually selected collections of story elements provided by each participant. This provides the story frame works which make some reactions and story meanings more or less likely to happen. Content is the selectively perceived references and narratives that relate all the words to the life experiences of the listeners. This allows them to see meaning through the characters, scenes, and action over the wide or narrow scope of their versions of your case. These two major factors, context and content, have a constant influence on one another. Neither is fully available to conscious inquiry or review, but content is the more consciously biased of the two. Pulling the strands of context and content apart will not work as well as seeing how they balance or tip certain parts of the story over other parts.

Once you know where the strengths and weaknesses in context and content lie in the stories, you have a key to the eventual presentation. Partly due to its greater remove from conscious discourse, strength for one side's story found in the context is usually best challenged indirectly in presentation through the content, rather than head on.

Fight fire with water:

- If they use the big picture—counter with details.
- If they concentrate on meanings and language—use actions and events.
- If they rely on theories—resort to practice.

Watching how these elements play out in the group can often provide a more persuasive solution to a tough problem than had even been considered before the group sat down. We can't always know or predict the range and staying power possible for various contexts and content in the stories human beings will build to appreciate a legal case.

Since all decision makers tend to blend elements and specific factors within their case stories, search for where that blending occurred for each one or for all if their stories are consistent. An almost inevitable result of finding where people blended legal fair play with notions of hard business realities, or fault with harms, for instance, will be the revelation that many factors they place on center stage have only a glancing or no relationship to specific proofs required by specific claims or elements in the legal case. Like walking on stones across a quickly rushing stream, you will find that most listeners build versions of the case story that demand that a rock or two be placed between the required stepping stone proofs of duty, breach, cause of harm, and damages, for example, in most injury cases. They may need you to extend these steps where the client would most wish them to cross. To get the required elements proven, focus group participants almost inevitably show trial professionals some extra elements within the facts or their implications that they will also need proven to their satisfaction, in sequence, along the way. Sometimes these added factors will have no direct bearing on proving a legal element in the case, though they are part of the evidence. In this respect, they fall under the heading of two of the three fundamental benefits any focus group will provide: things participants found unimportant, which the trial professionals found crucial and obviously true; and things the group found critically important, which the trial professionals found inconsequential prior to running the group.[2]

An example is the focus group that heard a contract dispute case. The element many in the group insisted on adding to the case was competition, though no claims had been made for tortious (implying or involving tort) interference, blocking the

2. The third, guaranteed basic benefit accruing from these groups, you'll recall, is that the attorney that participates in their presentation will always be better prepared to deliver the case at trial, in mediation, or in arbitration than if she had not participated.

market, or other unfair competitive acts. In fact, the case dealt with a standard of both parties expecting and producing behavior that was required in their supply contracts in order to meet the legal and industry standard of "honesty in fact." The claims inferred a certain need for the parties to rely on each other's commitments as honest and that such reliance took place in good faith. Neither reliance or good faith needed to be strictly passed in the official proof of the case.

Yet when considering whether one party had failed their obligation and dishonestly breached their agreement, the majority of focus group members inserted a new stepping stone—competition—between that honesty standard and a finding of fault. This happened whether they were experienced in this particular field, or with contracts of their own, or neither.

Many people set up an implicit understanding of the situation in the case that almost eliminated any duty to back up promises in the contract if the perceived level of market competition seemed to make a move appear helpful to the party accused of breaching the contract. For some, the context of perceived competition trumped the need for honesty in the content of the parties' written commitments. Most people that produced stories with competition as their added active ingredient did not appear conscious of how they overbalanced the contract commitments with a new element, which they held up as almost overriding the contract so that businesses can stay very competitive. This distortion went on behind the eyes and between the ears of many of the group members, despite the fact that it coexisted with their conscious and even stated awareness that they were there to judge the claim according to the legal rules, not by placing it in a subjective context where those rules may not need apply!

Moreover, as an example of "the best of what groups can offer" being hidden at first glance, the added attention that the competition factor received was not lost on anyone that listened to the group. On closer review, it happened that how an individual characterized the competition factor turned out to be a strong indicator of his eventual leaning in the overall case story. Those characterizations were found in modifiers, written adjectives, or associated phrases, or they came out between the lines in their verbal offerings on tape. But they were not apparent at a first look. That type of information can prove valuable in voir dire and in the vocabulary used with witnesses on the stand. It can also be valuable when consistently used in statements to the jury and judge. The plaintiffs in the contract dispute case needed to know how to stay dry as they led the decision makers down the desired path. Meanwhile, the defendants needed to know where the path was most easily cut off from a complete passage.

The basic message is the same with all similar factors as it is for dealing with the large-scale divisions that participants make between story context and content. That is, if people are going to blend one element of their story into another, or demand a bridge be added between two where the trial professionals or law anticipated none would be needed, then you are going to need to plan for building bridges and blending factors in similar ways in the eventual presentation for those decision makers set to receive it, regardless of their ostensible profiles.

Following are some examples of what these groups can provide to the conscientious professionals willing to unpack them.

6.3 Nonverbal Input

As with the group cited earlier whose members kept envisioning imaginary (remembered) children much too tall to safely represent the injured plaintiff's infant in the case, people will freely provide connections to their inner worlds by nonverbal means. They usually do this with no conscious awareness. Reading the interplay of the nonverbal packaging in which a yes or no comment is delivered can, to the trained observer, reveal what extent the speaker actually believes what she is saying.

People who use a visual strategy to successfully sort complex case elements that others have trouble relating to by verbal or written means give away a huge advantage for the eventual presentation. This is especially true if the attorney is schooled in congruent behavioral expression of visual messages and their verbal and physical counterparts. Mirroring, when tracked among group members or with one presenting attorney, can show the focus of participant attention more reliably than reading other signs such as eye contact. In voir dire and focus groups, people constantly convey their desires for allies, confirmation, or conflict and contrary editorial positions, without speaking a word. (Note that "people" in this case includes all the professionals in the room and any behind a bench.) Watch some of the rest of the room while the camera pans slowly from face to face during an around-the-room group question session.

It can show you—

who had never thought of what was being said before,

who may have similar or radically different ideas from those being expressed, and

who wants to see how many others do or don't agree

—all without a word.

It can also show how a seemingly hot topic among the group isn't really catching on with the overall group. That "hot topic" is thus likely to be less of a factor in the final stories generated by those people.

This is often the kind of event that misleads the professional placing too much value in what is too easily attained.

All these types of input and more that may be unique to a particular group presentation are available at no added cost by the participants in *any* focus group.

True, some of these indicators take special training and practice to identify on a regular basis, but many just need some time and attention. If they are ignored, an accurate and available explanation for a result in the group may well be drawn from totally different and often erroneous sources instead.

For example, in a small group done primarily for educational purposes, a non-verbally expressed source of a reaction that the plaintiff would value highly could easily have been misattributed to an appealing, but mistaken source. The case dealt with whether a woman in her early sixties received appropriate medical care in the treatment of her chronic sinusitis in which a mechanical instrument was used. The judgment of the doctor using the device to clear the patient's sinuses was in question. An eye injury occurred due to the proximity of the device. Injuries of this type are a known complication of the procedure, which is understood by the patient at the time.

One specific medical judgment in question was what the doctor saw poking through between the wall of the sinus and the orbit of the eye. It was called one thing in some records, another in others. But the primary questions of neglect or common complication revolved around whether the doctor would have known and been warned, from seeing that substance and correctly identifying it, as to whether to leave the tool where it was or move it. Many injuries along similar lines had been recorded from these tools in the medical literature, but the precise mechanism of harm proposed by the defense, as an alternative to a negligent act, had not yet been seen or recorded, though its possibility had been written about.

The plaintiff claimed, among other factors, that the doctor had expressed an eagerness to move past the work in the sinuses and on to another procedure during the same session, implying somewhat of a rush. The plaintiff's injuries were substantial. Her efforts to recover enough use of her eyesight involved more than just her eye. It extended into chronic neck and back problems. Problems that, from three years prior to the date of the focus group, had kept her from working at her chosen profession and many other jobs, due to her frequent need to rest to relieve discomfort associated with her eyes and her back.

Here is a partial, abbreviated transcript of what the five-person group, three men and two women, had to say after hearing initial presentations from both sides. Note, that because of the group's small size, very short time frame, and educational purpose, the moderator is not as gentle in efforts to keep some balance alive within the group's positions. Also, this group was not privy to the full introduction and its embedded rehearsals, so it tended to rush to judgments far more quickly than a group begun more carefully might have.

Moderator: If a medical stop sign isn't there to see, then the doctor can't know to stop, can he?

Young Woman: Preliminary looking—he did all the X-rays for her—he didn't look enough before.

Older Woman:	Would have been paying closer attention—if [he] did his job would have seen the abnormality and paid attention.
Young Guy:	He assumed that all odds were more or less equal—that there was a "stop sign" there.
Moderator:	He's already done a thousand—never happened before—should he have to be looking for every possible abnormality, every time?
Older Woman:	Yes. Your eyes are very important to you. If he doesn't do enough preliminary work, how can he do the job properly?
Moderator:	But how do we know a CAT scan is even going to show this orbital fat?
Older Woman:	We don't. Just have to take his word for it.
Young Guy:	The last explanation was that it's the patient's fault for not having enough eye fat around her orbit.
Moderator:	Wait a minute. His own expert says he's looked at her and she does just have a tiny bit of this stuff, instead of what you'd normally expect. What makes it up to the point of "blaming"?
Other Guy:	He should have been more careful. Knew that there was less fat.
Older Woman:	They knew.
Moderator:	What do we really know? What do you think you know?
Other Guy:	Some fat observed—he then changed his mind—the way he wrote it the first time.
Older Woman:	He had a nightmare, and then he changed it.
	[*Moderator describes burdens, criminal versus civil.*]
Young Guy:	Preponderance is just a hair over 50 percent. And a tie goes to the defense. The way they get me over the hump is by the doctor's credibility—the truth about the note.

Young Woman:	He said himself that he lied—or that he "accidentally wrote something down that wasn't correct." That he didn't mean. [*Ticking on fingers.*] Her eye is damaged. He lied on the report. And there are no previous happenings on the record of the muscle being sucked through (without negligent incursion of tool) and cutting itself.
Moderator:	The literature that says it can happen.
Young Woman:	If he does the wrong thing, it can happen.
Other Guy:	[*Indicates agreement.*]
Moderator:	He's saying he didn't do that, though. That he never got the instrument through there. [*indicating illustration*] Then he's not negligent.
Young Woman:	Yeah, he's saying it magically got sucked through the other direction.
Older Guy:	Damning that he changed his story, but I don't see enough positive evidence to push it over the line.
Moderator:	Where would you look?
Older Guy:	I don't know.
Younger Guy:	Other changed note.
Other Guy:	Other problems in the past.
Older Guy:	Possibly.
Younger Guy:	That anyone has a sufficient warning sign for any doctor to see—no matter their genetics or anatomy—inconsistent story from defense about the so-called problem. It's a tool that had a camera attached to it—they may not want to show us everything, but what was there?
Older Woman:	Other source about the construction of her eye—would tend to believe defense a little more then.
Other Guy:	How abnormal is this condition? It seems like a whole lot of unnatural, abnormal things

	have to be happening for the defendant story to be believed.

[*This complication happens a lot.*]

Young Woman:	In the other direction it happens a lot, but not coming at it this way, by itself [*indicating illustration*].
Older Woman:	Complications with the eye are the same? I'd demand to see the photos, video—I want to see what he saw.
Young Woman:	Rarity of this happening is enough—combined with him lying.

[*Discussion about adding notes, addenda, and changing story.*]

Young Woman:	Especially when it's something like, "I saw fat" and then changes that.
Younger Guy:	I'd have to see him explaining himself. He says he felt something different—what was it exactly that he thought he felt at the time? The doctor says he stopped when he felt something "unusual"—unusual how, specifically? What truly prompted him to stop and was that a truly novel experience?
Young Woman:	He says first [*indicating*] he's sucking up regular stuff, like snot, and then suddenly something thick. He's saying it's her fault for having a thin layer of this stuff, but he's also saying he knew he felt something wrong.
Moderator:	But that's not necessarily negligent, is it?
Young Woman:	[*Visually pantomimes the event from surgeon's viewpoint, as having happened before.*]
Younger Guy:	[*Synopsis: wants another "objective" physician to relate the exact same experience to this type of "one-time" event.*]
Older Guy:	He knew something was different at the time—he should know the value of vision better than anyone—should have stopped right there and not gone beyond that,

	regardless. Has to verify exactly what was amiss here before he moves on to next procedure and he didn't. [*All agree.*] He needs to know what he's done before moving on.
Older Woman:	So, if it comes up again.

DAMAGES

Young Woman:	Defense is wrong saying she can get some other job. How bad is it to expect her to work when it's two to three hours she's able to use her eyes, and she has to turn her neck like this [*modeling movement*] to be able to see what she's looking at. I wouldn't hire you if you had to stand there like this and sit down every couple hours.
Younger Guy:	I need expert testimony quantifying kind of life she'll live.
Young Woman:	[*Lists deficits: single, can't cook, can't drive, etc.*]
Younger Guy:	[*Synopsis: plaintiff attorney is overdoing the "never seen this before"—twisting the truth—discussion: lawyers are all used car salesmen, we expect to be spun by lawyers—so he shouldn't be reaching so far.*]
Moderator:	How will you put a value on the loss?
Younger Guy:	Her describing her life.
Young Woman:	How painful it is [*tipping neck again*]?
Older Guy:	Just her confirming, but also a third party, like a treating doctor, too.
Older Woman:	I understand how the injury is—I want to know how it bothers her—some people have headaches and they make them cry, others can do their regular things. Different tolerance for pain. She's raised four kids.
Other Guy:	Quality of life with the kids and grandkids. If she's not having the same . . .
Young Woman:	They could be looking at having to move her into their house—loss for them.

LOSS

Young Woman:	Losing your senses. Not like an elbow.
Older Guy:	Lost a lot from her work alone.

QUALITY OF LIFE

Younger Guy:	Fact that it will never improve. No repair techniques to end or improve today.
	[*Likelihood of treatment or recovery.*]
Younger Guy:	What did she want to do with the rest of her life? [*She had attended professional school late in life.*]
Older Guy:	Life expectancy.
Young Woman:	What she expected she could do.
Older Guy:	What was she used to? Lavish or minimum?
Young Woman:	That says a rich person's life is worth more.
Moderator:	If she makes less money, is she worth less?
Older Woman:	No. But that's how women are treated!
Young Woman:	She has things to see still. Children. New career, things still to see.
Moderator:	A plus for starting a new career? [*Some acknowledge yes, others no.*]
Other Guy:	Her relationships, quality of them. Harder if she has to lay down every couple hours. Potential relationships are very much a part of quality of life. Barrier. Burden. [*All generally agree.*]
Younger Guy:	I need lots of measures—more than one—if not driving, than some other dollars and cents things: transportation, lost wages, grocery shopping, and other accommodations—but also emotional qualities—but if they give me at least two or three measures, that would be the best way to determine quality of life—I don't know how much difference I'd put on them, but XX million dollars, I don't think it's worth that much. If doc was unable to make his case and I found for the defendant, I'd say . . .

Moderator:	Hold it. Assuming the plaintiff proves his case as he says, then [*asking all*] what is this worth?
Older Woman:	How old is she?
Moderator:	In her sixties.

AMOUNTS

Younger Guy:	$250,000 to $500,000.
Older Guy:	$500,000.
Older Woman:	They don't realize everything that's lost.

The two women place a much higher value in the "harms" category in this plaintiff-friendly group. If not carefully considered, that observation could carry an assumption into the courtroom and into jury selection. The active ingredient at work in this panel, as advertised distinctly in the nonverbal and implicit behavior of the two women and some of the men, was not gender. It had to do with point of view, which could support a gender-based distinction, except that the man labeled "older guy" swings his position around almost to the viewpoint of the injured woman, while the "older woman" comments are made more from a third-person position than from any direct identification with the plaintiff.

No, the factor that made the difference here for the two high-end women jurors, who both crossed the million-dollar barrier in their mind's eye, was the eyes in their minds—their visual sensory experience. There are references in the spoken text for the behaviors modeled on the tape. Only one of the two modeled a substantial use of the visual as a major sensory habit in her regular thinking. But if you replay the transcript, paying attention to how much more the visual aspects of experiences are evidenced, even the written text, without being able to see it modeled by the speakers in their gestures, actions, and visually oriented eye movements, shows you this factor at work.

Certainly in a case of this nature, many will use the words "see" and "look" more than usual, but giving primacy its due, look where they both start out in the early part. The older woman packages the doctor's job standard as "paying close or more attention" and "seeing an abnormality." "Attention paid" in this context has nothing to do with *listening* closely. It is the act of *watching* and *looking*, that she envisions as his job. Meanwhile, the young woman peppers her statements with visual predicates, expecting him to "*look* enough," before first noting that the "eye was damaged," and that there were no previous medical records of "the [eye] muscle getting sucked" into the machine.

These perceptual moments are brought to you courtesy of vision. She is not *listening* to the muscle getting "sucked into" the tool. Her frequent pointing, drawing the eye on the flip chart, are visual indicators with her hands and fingers, as a reference point.

Next, the older woman states, "Your eyes are very important to you," and shortly thereafter uses a visual metaphor describing the doctor's failing, "He had a nightmare, then he changed it." While some people could have nightmares about telephone conversations, this one more likely had stronger visual components at work in her mind. Now the young woman has the doctor crossing the fault line, stating, "It happens if he does the wrong thing," in response to the reminder that the literature says the complication can happen without a negligent act. (Note also her spontaneous use of both active voice and present tense.) Once she remarks on the difficulty the woman has seeing, having to twist and turn her body as demonstrated in the attorney's presentation, the young woman rarely mentioned harms again without twisting her own head and neck at the same time.

The older woman says at the end, "They don't realize everything that's lost." Again, a deep structure in her language linked to visualization.

The central image a trial professional could infer that was driving the older woman's story may be the initial sight of the loss she referenced in both how important your eyes are to you and her final remark. There may be some support for this found in the most revealing remarks by the older guy, the author of the story version placing the third highest value on the loss. He said, "He should know the value of vision better than anyone—should have stopped right there and not gone beyond that, regardless. Has to verify exactly what was amiss here before he moves on to the next procedure and he didn't. He needs to know what he's done before moving on." Again, these impressions of the direct contribution of the doctor's acts to a loss he calls "the value of vision" are all visual in their perceptual bias. And they probably constitute this man's central story image.

The young woman's likely central story image also provides readers with a good example of a focus group participant bootstrapping from fault to valuing harms, just as the older woman showed a more distinct harms package and the older guy blended harms and their cause. The young woman *sees* the injury itself happening and visibly marks out her modeling of the effects with her own eyes and neck from shortly after she makes that point aloud on throughout the session.

So what's the value and where's the potential harm in drawing the observable conclusion that inner visualization, and concentration on imagery, led to greater valuing of the plaintiff's injuries and harms than the shared factor of gender? Look near the end of the older woman's remarks, where she shouts out that women are often treated as "less valuable."

Someone assessing this group while ignoring the nonverbal and implicit messages threaded through it might be slightly more inclined to find significance in the gender difference just by hearing and processing that remark and not paying careful attention later on when looking for the "best type of plaintiff damage people." Such people may well exist for this case. But they will be found by seeking people using their *mind's eye* and their *visual senses* in a certain way when reviewing those harms, not by their estrogen levels.

There is no definitive checklist that will flag and categorize the significant nonverbal input in the group because of the individual nature of the input. Trying to build a uniform filter to measure nonverbal messages in any group falls prey to the same weakness that a written questionnaire does when trying to pose follow-up questions, which by definition must be unresponsive to the previous answer because a printed form cannot respond accurately to that answer.

The list of basic perceptual categories in Chapter Three can provide a tickler list of areas on which you want to concentrate as you review the videotapes. Have the camera person keep at least a couple of people in-frame to either side of the individual talking, and "pull out" to encompass as many people as possible when the person talking is in the front of the room. That way, you'll have the maximum amount of input with which to work. As in voir dire, you may find that the non-talkers are revealing much more than some of the talkers.

Sensory processing and other forms of nonverbal marking can be a major component to track when searching for the influences that people used to build the stories they eventually settled on to make judgments. This is partly due to the fact that the world of references in every person's head is constructed from nothing less than blocks of sensory experience. For these purposes, especially sights, sounds, and feeling sensations.

You know some forms of evidence or testimony are biased toward a particular sensory system (e.g. accounting, auditing, and bookkeeping toward the auditory, and catastrophic injury toward the visual), but some stories, overall or in major portions, appeal more to a visual, feeling, or verbal reconstruction process. Retention, emphasis, sequencing, and major actions can all be greatly affected by the perceptual packaging the receiver imposes on them. And with certain compilations of facts and legal rules, this fundamental perceptual factor can actually make all the difference in many people's ability to see eye to eye with your client's view or hear things the way they need to be said. This does not mean you need to run voir dire as a desperate hunt for jurors that are visually biased. It means, however, that you may need to be prepared to shift toward or away from a visually biased presentation for the description of the surgery and the consequences of its injury.

When sifting through nonverbal expressions in the group, seek indicators of intensity in the response. Whether associated with imagery in the story, phrases, verbal content, or the overall message of part of the case, the degree to which someone has a belief, feeling, or other response tightly attached to part of your case story can be hugely productive in tracking that story's likelihood of encouraging similar responses in others. If you know how to read full congruence in visual, auditory, and kinesthetic re-creations, you can track who may or may not be inclined to revivify certain parts of the story.

Anytime someone is fully or mostly congruent in their re-creation of the story (that is, they review certain imagery, then continue to relate auditory features of the same event, and express how the experience must have felt to the person or people at the time), that internal representation is usually far more memorable for the speaker. If they are fully representing some scene in your client's story, they have found a path to identification at that moment. It may be a connection you want to explore in their responses before and after for hints on how such a response can best be encouraged or deflected among the eventual decision makers. (Note that this does not necessarily have anything to do with the emotional content of the particular part of the story being represented.)

Another way of reading intensity of fixation or belief about a subject under discussion is to test for levels of nonverbal agreement or disagreement accompanying their verbal expression. For some, a yes answer is just being polite. For others, it may be taking a stand. They will not always be able or willing to let you know the difference aloud.[3] Don't overlook the value of tracking intensity by commonsense means, through confirmation, reflection in the group, repetition, revival of topics long past, and return to a chosen anchor to add similar intensity to another, different topic under discussion ("I just want to know why he turned off the light").

Moshe Feldenkrais wrote a book called *The Elusive Obvious*, and often that is what the material found at the nonverbal and implied levels of focus group offerings provides. I recently heard a trial consultant tell a tale that should help keep professionals from jumping to the easy, compelling, and wrong conclusion.

> In a Texas courtroom, the final strikes were being made by the plaintiff attorneys this consultant was working with, and a woman was being discussed that had several life experiences and voir dire answers that made her a likely candidate for a peremptory strike. Suddenly, a young lawyer on the team piped up and expressed his absolute conviction that the woman was clearly in their camp, particularly on the issue of harms, evidenced by her nonverbal actions. He had caught her wiping away a tear at the exact moment that the worst of the harms were being discussed. Nobody else had seen this, but he was adamant. The consultant, with his many black marks against her, was overruled based on her nonverbal sign of sympathy. And that woman went on to lead that jury in a very decisive judgment against the plaintiffs, occasionally wiping her eyes with a couple of others in the room that also suffered from strong allergies.

---

3. Paul Lisnek and Eric Oliver, *Courtroom Power: Communication Strategies for Trial Lawyers* (Colorado Springs, CO: Professional Education Systems Institute, 2001): 67–71.

6.4 Verbal Input

Verbal input is the largest category from which value from focus groups will be drawn, if for no other reason than that there is so much of it. In addition to obvious verbal references to story elements such as point of view, scope, and the sequence each person chooses for the events, it can be useful to track what is and isn't present between the lines. The value of presupposition as a persuasive force in language has been mentioned several times. A different kind of presupposition, equally powerful in persuasive effects, is implied suggestion. One question trial professionals want to keep close to the front of their minds as they read or listen to verbal input from focus group members is, "What has to be true about the world as this person sees it for him to say that, in just this way?" This is not necessarily a technique to try to broaden the scope of the person's statement or question, but rather to encompass more of its potential meanings and avoid supplanting too many of your own. This can prove quite helpful when assessing the thematic structure of each person's case story, since that is not scripted, even when you ask for it as directly.

Tracking presuppositions can help professionals identify some of the most significant mental structures that are influencing people so much that they don't even remember to list them as influences at all.

Listen for implied or presupposed messages within direct utterances. This is important because the more well integrated an experience, perception, or impression is among all the references of any person's life, the less likely that view or position is to be consciously cited for its influence on someone's judgments. Like the personal traffic rules most drivers carry around, their influence on perceptions is presumed more than it is consciously announced to themselves or anyone else.

Take a look at this transcript of the round-robin theme question[4] collected from a focus group on the case discussed in Chapter Five, in which a construction worker was injured by inhaling gas while working on the outside of a large metal vessel, where a coworker out of sight was killed by the same fumes. There were two defendants: the company owning and operating the plant and the subcontractor providing the workmen in the crew involved. Ask the "What has to be true?" question about each of these responses.

Question: Answering me as if I were your best friend, what is this thing really all about at its heart?

Betty: Money.

4. This question is usually asked toward the end of the second debrief of the day, after much of the evidence has been presented to mix in with the initial impressions formed after openings. By this stage, most participants have settled on their models of their case stories.

Betty2:	Whether or not this guy was actually injured.
Barney:	Money. But I want to add, I would be embarrassed about my money answer if the damages being sought are strictly for medical and improved safety at the plant.
Betty3:	I would say safety in a plant and who's responsible for it.
Barney2:	I mean, I would come back down to worker safety . . . as it safe, were procedures followed . . . and liability.
Betty4:	I would say it was about lifetime, knowing this man would be taken care of. That he needed that assurance that whatever state he was in, he would be able to take care of himself for the rest of his life.
Barney3:	Who was negligent.
Barney4:	How much one should drink before climbing on a platform.
Betty5:	I think it's responsibility. Who's responsible for themselves. The individual or the supervisor or the owner of the plant.
Barney5:	Who's going to pay.
Betty6:	I'm telling you the first thing that went through my mind, OK. It's about some kind of depressed dude, you know, that didn't want to work a job in the first place in a hot factory, like none of us, you know, trying to figure out a way to sue his employer so he can retire for the rest of his life. Boy, would I like to do that, too. The American way, yep.
Betty7:	I think [the plaintiff] saw some dollar signs.
Betty8:	A man who felt his employer had screwed up. Well, no, his, like, employer, like the big company, the one he's suing.[5]
Betty9:	[Defendant Corporation] and [Defendant Subcontractor] messed up.

5. Many times, the second or third sentences in these answers resulted from follow-up questions that are not recorded.

Barney6:	Irresponsible management.
Betty10:	I think [the plaintiff] saw an opportunity where there was loopholes on both [Defendant Corporation] and [Defendant Subcontractor], and it was a great way to sue.
Barney7:	Money.
Barney8:	It's not really a hard question . . . somebody asked me what it was all about . . . just a guy got hurt on the job, he's suing.
Betty11:	Crazy man trying to get paid.
Barney9:	Well, I'm kind of herding it.[6] Financial security from a terrible accident.
Barney10:	Easy money for worker's responsibility.

The following are some comments pulled from the report to the attorney on the implicit messages about where authority and responsibility were being envisioned by some of these folks. Note that more input than these answers alone is referenced in the comments and that the attorney represented the large business owner, not the subcontractor providing the work crew.

> These four answers in a row are instructive for one of our big story-element jobs at trial. Encouraging separations in how people see the three parties is the job at hand. Betty8 sees responsibility in one set of hands, but easily transfers it upstairs. Betty9 sees no distinction between the companies. Barney6, we know, sees only the top dog, though he can include the [defendant subcontractor] for some blame if needed. And Betty10 makes little distinction between companies as targets of unfair claims. Our story needs to separate and distinguish the three potentially responsible parties in every way possible. Trying to do this between the two defendant companies alone won't work in this story, as too many people have too many associations for at least some form of responsibility being accounted for at the "hands-on" level in this particular case.
>
> The answers this question provokes can provide some rough approximations of themes driving individual participants' stories.

General sorting by stated topics shows:

9 [citations] mostly about money

6. Referencing the instruction to avoid herd instinct in answering.

5 about pursuing a lawsuit

4 about responsibility

4 about wrongs or violations

1 about the injury

Putting a finer point to the legal claim framework alluded to in these remarks, you get:

6 on negligence (with one on company duty)

6 on anti-plaintiff tacks (with one on worker duty)

3 on money damages alone

2 on harms and damages

6 on negligence (with one on company duty)

1 on neglect and damages

1 on cause and harms

> This group leaned toward questioning the validity of the lawsuit, in part because they were not flooded with reinforcement presupposing a physical cause at the job site at the time. Because of this detached view, a total of fourteen fixed on non-story-related topics, a trend that could bring some danger at trial.[7] Participants ultimately ending up in this territory are not awful for us; however, that leaves few focused on a strong, arguable defense story to counter the seven people in deliberation that are still focusing on responsibility and wrongs and maybe presuming a large measure of control belonging to [the corporation]. Relying on incoming, pre-existing bias over a compelling case story delivery is almost never a wise trade-off.
>
> One disturbing trend is the blending of emotional harms into acceptable stuff for damage compensation: the "injury equals some fault" position implied to some degree between the lines of at least four answers. This highlights the need for a different kind of separation job in the story on the purely emotional source of his now-dramatic complaints—distinguished from a past physical injury caused by a physical source of gas at the job site at the time as the only fair road to awarding compensation. Attitudes and conclusions start to consolidate around

7. This comment was made before the perceptual connection had turned up for the line-of-sight criteria envisioned between the dead man and the plaintiff. Those who imagined the death occurring within the plaintiff's line-of-sight were far more likely to have placed some fault on the corporate authority.

> this time, as you can see from the move of sixteen out of twenty to fix the scope of their responses on the time of the accident or after—not in the relationship and duties established long, long before.

Other presupposed or implied suggestions about individual participants' stories between these lines could include views of the first and last line of protection or defense, who may be responsible for enforcing or maintaining it, and how it is controlled. Certainly, the hands-on or personal responsibility viewpoints are evident here. The injury-compensation territory and its legitimacy and the automaticity with which a few people seem to travel from one to the other are hinted at more than once. What do you perceive to be true behind the eyes and between the ears of the people in order for them to say what they did, in the ways in which they said it?

It's possible to construct any number of standard filters to sort out verbal input. One example follows. Because presupposition and implied suggestions are potent factors for eliciting and delivering stories, some of their attendant and related features deserve attention. They can be one of the most potent influences in establishing and maintaining mindsets. Reviewing the group members' use of presuppositions formulated and discussed in their versions of the case story can reveal the forms those stories end up taking. Perceptual positions, thinking habits and biases, and psychological factors affecting judgment[8] can be expressed by presupposition in people's story descriptions and in their comments about their version of the case contrasted with others.

For example, if you see hindsight in the presuppositions someone expresses about the easily foreseen outcome at issue, by examining their follow-up answers and the questions they themselves might pose on the subject, you can get a working view of the structure of the story package that most or least supports such a distortion and/or generalization.

Causes, motives, exceptions to standards, and perceptions of duties fully met can come across as other crucial story points will, behind the lines in statements and questions that group members (and lawyers) express. Locus of control (choice versus circumstance), active or passive voice, tense shifts, and first- through third-person accounting can be vehicles carrying forward a presupposition about the case in someone's speech. Every basic story element, from scope to point of view, can be found in these references. The answer to the question, "What would have to be true in their world model for that to be seen and said just this way?" can direct your attention to many fundamental assumptions at work.

---

8. *See* Chapter Three.

6.5 Oppositions and Linkages

Noticing subject matter or chosen topics in context instead of as a disparate list, can reveal all sorts of story terrain that might otherwise go unnoticed:

- What seemingly unrelated points or subjects get butted against one another for this person or that one?
- Where does this person find a sequence—logical, physical, moral, or otherwise—in linking this event to that one?
- How does this person shore up an assertion about the major importance of one document, one statement, or one omission by referencing a completely separate piece of evidence and finding or forging a meaningful connection where one may not have been imagined before?

These unplanned linkages are akin in potential to noting what parts of the story people leave out in providing valuable guidance for the eventual structure of the case story for presentation.

6.6 Degrees of Judgment

Assumptions about right and wrong are a form of presupposition. Yet, in the case of lawsuits or criminal trials, they can provide special assistance when trying to craft the most compelling presentation of the facts and law. Listen (and read) closely for presumptions of the "one way" or "wrong road" as they emerge. There will be many nonverbal clues to follow and there are linguistic signs too. These include universal quantifiers ("all, everyone, totally, never") and modal operators of necessity ("must, gotta, have to, should") to season the straightforward right and wrong language that points to judgments about the story other than the final one, but which can make or break that final one before it's ever reached.

6.7 Written Input

The common wisdom about written input from focus group participants or potential jurors on pretrial questionnaires[9] is that they may be more forthcoming and responsive when they are able to write down their impressions, attitudes, and opinions. Written survey questions asked immediately after opening statements and before discussion takes place with the group members do offer the trial professional a baseline set of observations from each participant, which are mostly unaf-

9. Supplemental juror questionnaires can be a very useful tool, and much has been written about their best uses in selecting juries. A fundamental resource is the National Jury Project's *Jurywork: Systematic Techniques*, eds. Will Rountree and Elissa Krauss, (Deerfield, IL: Clark, Boardman, Callaghan, 1983). See also the website of the American Society of Trial Consultants, www.astcweb.org, for resources on the subject.

fected by the group. This initial, individual written sample can be referred to for trends, resilient and fading factors, and any unique perspectives as verbal and other written input emerges. While different habits of perception and communication go into writing than into talking, the most common feature in comparisons of participant written and verbal input will be their consistencies. That helps highlight the differences, which can make all the difference.

The following vignette is divided into plaintiff and defense leaning groups. These leanings were self-declared at day's end. The answers come from the first written survey question asked of the group that heard the two opening statements in Chapter Five. Each set of answers is followed by some comments to the plaintiff attorneys that presented to the group. Before reading them, you may want to refer back to refresh your memory on the story elements the focus group plan called for the lawyers to present. Also refer to the commentary attached just after the openings, assessing how those elements seemed to emerge in the lawyers' efforts. See which fundamental story elements you find that appear to have been adopted, directly or between the lines, in these first impression statements just after openings concluded.

6.7.1 Survey Question One Vignette: Plaintiff-Leaning Participants

Moderator:	What brought about this lawsuit?
George1:	Death of patient.
Jane1:	Death of patient.
Jane2:	A supposed wrongful death and negligence by a doctor.
George2:	Poor judgment by Dr. Clark, which resulted in patient's death.
Jane3:	Error in procedure.
Jane4:	The patient dying.
Jane5:	The client dying.
George3:	A question by the wife of a gentleman who was having a surgical procedure done and died in the process. The question concerned "standard of care" and were standard procedures followed during this surgery.
George4:	The death of Mr. Holbrook.
Jane6:	The death of a patient.

Jane7:	Holbrook—was it caused by natural causes or neglect.
George5:	Death of patient and perception by wife of negligence.
Jane8:	The death of the patient.
Jane9:	Plaintiff feeling ripped off by doctor.

Note some signs of suspicion for the plaintiff position carried by phrases such as "supposed," "client dying," "a question by the wife," "perception by wife." Some typical arrangements at this early stage in the concentration on the patient and the death, all using arm's-length perspectives. Actions, in terms of violations, are an element we can use to develop our story, or as you can see here, that the jurors are likely to build on in their general packaging—"negligence," "poor judgment," "error," "neglect." If you divide their chosen subjects into two camps, "acts/judgments" and "standards/rules," the acts and choices drew more attention in today's group than generalized citations of "the care standard" with little real story material underneath. (About a 50/50 split today, as opposed to yesterday's group.)

People seem to be packaging negligence, cause, and harms separately. Our story can help them blend these elements, highlighting the two safety jobs the reasonable medical professional would have been concerned with here, creating two active sins that account for injury and avoidable harms. The cause part about blood and oxygen deprivation was an important missing link both days. This can be amended with more effective sequencing of the mechanisms of the two harms, the safe standard, and then the actual chosen acts discussed in the previous day's report.

6.7.2 Survey Question One Vignette: Defense-Leaning Participants

Moderator:	What brought about this lawsuit?
Jane10:	Main vein bleeding.
Jane11:	The death of a loved one believed to have been as a result of surgical procedures that did not include standard of care.
Jane12:	The family of Mr. Holbrook, the patient's complications set in.
George6:	Perforation of vein by doctor during procedure causing eventual death.
George7:	Death of a patient of Dr. Clark while in surgery.

George8: Money.

Jane13: Death of a patient.

Mostly "complications just happen" territory, with all third-person perspectives. We need to be clear that the initial introduction of the puncture injury isn't so clinically detailed—out of context from the hazard itself and the standard to avoid it—that the active party source of the puncture can be lost by those inclined to misplace him. It is no coincidence that, as neglect is taken off the table in these people's stories, cause questions and "complications happen" positions tend to replace them. Case story point of view and the language filter of actions need to be carefully linked throughout. Otherwise, some will see perforations as things that simply can't be violations, since they are listed with the known complications. A cure could be the harm-mechanism/safe standard/violations sequencing of the story on both sins ("two sins" referred to above). Jurors can't be allowed to lean more toward seeing a cause that is free of the active choices to neglect commonsense safety.

On the following pages, you will find some story elements and other factors that we typically sift from the group's input on forms and in the transcribed parts of their verbal input. They would be used to sort through these answers, and all others on the first survey form, in more detail. This is an arbitrary selection of factors, though they were picked with an eye toward pulling out what seem to be the most influential indicators of story building trends over some time, with multiple groups. There are always going to be more choices than time, energy, and resources will allow. Art, like morality, consists of drawing a line somewhere. Here are some we draw for each and every written section of the group's input. Some or all of these factors will be sorted from each set of answers to each written question, as well as, at the least, from each set of around-the-room answers.

We also sort the input from the attorneys along these same lines to be sure that presuppositions about what the group was offered are eliminated from our reviews, as much as possible, as a factor.

For unfamiliar terms, refer to the Glossary in Appendix Two.

THEMES:	SUBTHEME(S):				
SEQUENCE:	1. 2. 3.				
POINT OF VIEW:	3rd PERSON:	3rd (PLAINTIFF LEANERS):	3rd (DEFENSE LEANERS):	PLAINTIFF:	DEFENDANT:
ACTIVE INGREDI-ENTS/PARTY:	MAJOR ACTS/ CHOICES:	MOTIVES:	SIMPLE FIX:		
MAIN TOPICS:	DELETIONS:				
LEGAL ELEMENTS CONCENTRATED ON:	RULES/ STANDARDS:	NEGLIGENCE:	CAUSE:	DAMAGES:	
LANDMINES	BIASES:	DISTRACTIONS/ DISTORTIONS:	FILLING DEFECTS:	MISSING LINKS:	UNSUPPORTED CONCLUSIONS:
CONNECTIONS	MADE:	NEEDED:			

CONTRADICTIONS:

CENTRAL IMAGE:

PERCEPTUAL HOLES:

SCOPE:

TIME	**PEOPLE:**	**NUMBER/ACTS:**
BEFORE: DURING: AFTER:	**BROAD: NARROW:**	**BROAD: NARROW:**

ORGANIZING FILTER:

ANCHORS:

PICKED UP / REPEATED:	**SUGGESTED:**	**METAPHORS / ANALOGIES:**

LANGUAGE:

ABSOLUTE / NECESSITY:	**GENERAL / POSSIBILITY:**

IMPLIED SUGGESTIONS:

VOIR DIRE TOPICS:

SUMMARY COLLECTIONS

TRENDS IN MAJOR ACTS, MAJOR CHARACTERS AND MEANINGS:

PARTS OF STORY PEOPLE HANG ONTO:

PARTS OF STORY PEOPLE DROPPED:

SIGNIFICANT DIFFERENCES BETWEEN PLAINTIFF AND DEFENSE LEANERS:

WHERE CONTROL/CAUSE IS ASSIGNED/PERCEIVED, AND WHERE NOT:

VISUALS NEEDED:

6.8 Tell Me a Story

Once the nonverbal, verbal, and written sorting is done, compile all the observations into a coherent guide. Make choices regarding:

- What to push forward or hold back
- Where to start and finish
- How to say what needs to be said and what language to avoid
- Who the central character and active party or ingredient are
- The selection of all other story elements and components

As you progress through the day's group offerings, move back and forth between the self-selected plaintiff/prosecution or defendant/defense favoring groups. You can start to widen your frame of reference, as you did with the initial, bird's-eye view before the material was fully compiled. Now, the aim is to begin to hone the material into a single story.

To organize and refine the large amount of input you've received, use a shortcut sketch or preliminary story outline. We developed this method for cases in which a focus group's input wasn't possible due to budget or time constraints. The added perspective on likely landmines and strongest story elements has to be provided by the consultant.

With this preliminary or speed assessment outline, the elements included are arbitrary selections and a matter of choice for each trial professional to make.

1. **Biggest Landmines.** Of all the impediments to a decision maker building the case story closest to the one you want, which is the one fact, impression, perception, legal reference, image, bias, distraction/distortion, filling defect, missing link, unsupported conclusion, or other factor (or top few) that could derail that process?

2. **One-Topic Voir Dire.** If for any reason you were held to twenty minutes for the voir dire examination of the panel preparing to hear the case presentation, what is the one topic you would have to discuss to get any sense at all of who could not hear the case fairly, based on what they are bringing to the table? (This may relate to the top landmine, but usually does not.)

3. **Three Visuals (Sequence).** If you were to divide the story as it appears to be formed most compellingly into three big steps, in or out of chronological order, how would you illustrate those steps on individual demonstrative exhibits? Are there other factors within the story more important than those three for people fully appreciating the whole arc of the client's

story from the most helpful perspective, or do they fairly represent the beginning, middle, and end of that story? How did the group see the story arc progressing, and what demonstratives, in what order, best codify that progression visually?

4. **First Witness: Story Requirements, then Presentation Strengths.** If the story sequence as represented by your three key visuals is the order of your proofs, then who must be the first witness in order to best establish at least the first step, if not more, of that sequence for the decision makers? Sort first by who can best address the early sequence requirements of the story as you've organized it, and then by who among those people can also present themselves best to the decision makers. A great presenter that can't set up and reinforce the story as the trial professional has learned that it needs to be delivered is not the first choice for the start of this particular case. Maybe second or third, but not first this time.

5. **Central Image (Actions, Choice, Event).** If you think of the story as a play, a movie, or a book, what is the one scene that focuses the whole story's impact? Is it a solitary decision being made, a wreck, or a conversation? It is not always, nor even mostly, found in the purported bad act, although murder cases are usually an exception. What is the point in the story to which those people keep returning who see it as you'd most wish? Is there even a person in the picture at that point, or is it something else?

6. **Active Ingredient/Point of View.** Often, the active ingredient will be associated with the central image of the case story, the locus of control, whether circumstance or personified act, that in some decisive way produces the events now in conflict. Who or what is that actor? Just as importantly, there is another factor that emerges in this same point in the refining process: who is the central character or thing through which this story will best be referenced throughout in order to produce the most compelling version possible for the decision makers hearing and seeing it?

7. **Scope.** This story element, although very general and not steeped in detail, doesn't often emerge immediately from a consideration of the material from groups or just from the case itself. It is also very vulnerable to a trial professional imposing what he or she presumes is the best scope, rather than what may be right there waiting to be seen. What is this story's reach: broad or narrow, long or short, many or few, or just one?[10]

---

10. A professional's presumption about the scope of a case versus the best one suggested by a group or the facts and law themselves was never better expressed than in the comment by a lawyer at the end of a group on a complex medical case. As the group was still filing out of the room, the attorney was heard to remark, "Thank God discovery is still open. We thought we had a case against the doctor. Who knew it was really against the nurses, first?"

8. **Theme.** The theme, although the first, central, and overriding element of any case story, the one that must be consistently established, reinforced and maintained by all the other elements during presentation, is also often the most problematic. That is why it comes last in the string, instead of first. On occasion, the theme clearly and easily emerges during the early part of the analysis. Other times, it is still unclear until very near the end. Always be wary of preselecting, consciously or otherwise, the territory in which you believe the theme will be found. Stories can be "typed" by experienced professionals, with results that are equally disappointing as those sometimes produced by trying to type decision makers.[11] What is this whole thing really all about? And always remember to keep one eye on the language of the questions decision makers will be required to answer at the end of the line, as the theme will need to account for or anticipate that as well.

This condensed story outline can prove very helpful when poring over pages of transcripts and hours of video. Just as the five-minute openings serve to focus the story-building talents of the group members, so that they aren't allowed to wander too far from a central focus to spark their perceptions, imaginations, referencing and selecting, so a set of necessary and essential story elements can help the culling process for the professional attempting to sort out the wheat from the chaff (or the high explosives) in the mass of available material at hand.

6.9 Packaging the Full Yield

The complete outline of the presentation plan we use has eleven elements. A couple of these, such as the sensory bias, are not always incorporated into every presentation plan for every case story. For some stories, such as the sinus surgery situation related earlier or for an attorney skilled in the congruent expression of sensory-based messages, that element can be very useful or crucial. In the majority of cases, that final element will not be as critical to prepare and present as the top five elements. Everything still flows from the theme. Each story element serves to either establish, maintain, and reinforce a theme, or it works against that end. If something being said or shown from the podium or the witness stand doesn't serve to reinforce the case story's theme, then it doesn't belong in the presentation (assuming the proper theme for the presentation was derived).

6.9.1 *Case Presentation Plan—The Elements*

The path to refining and distilling the most effective theme from the material is often indirect. Because of the nature of the decisions, which have to be made from

11. This thinking habit accounts for much of the high levels of functional bias observable in professional decision makers, compare to lay jurors.

the stories reauthored from the ones presented, the first step in this presentation planning process should be focused on what to avoid, not what to emphasize. The stepping stones that seem the most solid or expeditious often hide major impediments. Alternate routes for the journey must be found. First expose and analyze problem areas to identify the safest path for the story theme.

Landmines[12]

Obstacles to a favorable judgment come in many forms, including:

- Pre-existing biases
- Legal points or rules
- Reactions from a decision maker to your preferred case story
- Troubles with language or imagery
- Case story elements

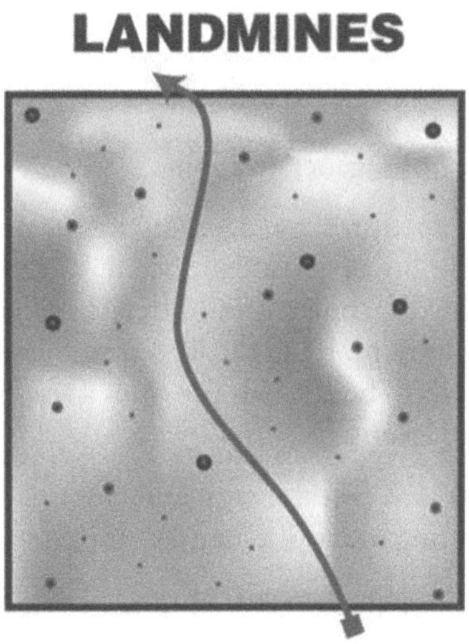

These landmines of varying severity are scattered across the territory in which you must deliver your client's story, carrying the decision maker(s) with you and holding your strongest story points in the foreground. The story delivery needs to help decision makers avoid engaging, reinforcing, or even stepping near most landmines connected with the story. Having a map of landmines from which to steer clear, can illuminate the safest path to a judgment.

12. Although it is in wide use, I first heard this term used by lawyer and trial consultant Rodney Jew to describe impediments in fact, law, or perception to a productive appreciation of a legal case story.

Landmines can be anything.

- ➲ Single facts
- ➲ Word choices
- ➲ Perceptions
- ➲ Values, morals
- ➲ Points of law
- ➲ Verdict language
- ➲ Story position
- ➲ Group of acts
- ➲ Problematic phrase
- ➲ Common analogy
- ➲ Likely impression to be formed
- ➲ Life experiences, witness's experiences
- ➲ Distortions, deletions, generalizations

Anything that by itself can distract a decision maker from a preferred leaning. The aim of compiling the list of most significant landmines is not to develop a corresponding list of "answers," but rather to devise a plan for presenting the case story that avoids eliciting or reinforcing the largest number of them, while reinforcing the positions we'd prefer. The list also provides a useful backdrop for planning voir dire and some witness exams.

To keep it manageable and focus energy and resources, we divide the list into three categories in descending order of potential impact:

- ➲ **Severe** Will lose case if allowed to play a significant part in juror case stories.
- ➲ **Serious** Can lose case if allowed to play a significant part in juror case stories.
- ➲ **Singular** Can lose one juror (or more) if this element is allowed to draw attention.

Additionally, the factors found in the group that correspond to each of the three levels of possible impact are divided into the categories in which they appeared and were sorted out from the group's input. Those we typically focus on include biases, distractions/distortions, filling defects, missing links, and "unsupported conclusions."

In reviewing the material from the case before the group, you can see plenty of landmines by yourself. More surface in discovery and early settlement talks. Your witnesses and clients will provide a few, too. Still, the focus groups will reveal most of those and many more you might not have imagined. (Focus groups will also find several strong points that you either overlooked or hadn't yet interpreted as quite so strong.) When we help plan a case presentation, the first pages are devoted to a list of potential landmines. That's because there is never a shortage of material to select among for most of the other story elements.

Themes are everywhere. If you don't provide one well, several will be provided for you uninvited. Points of view can abound. Sequencing the story, not just the witnesses, can start, end, and meander all over the map. There are at least five different ways to filter the words you use to deliver the package. It's important to know as many of the potential landmines as possible associated with revivifying the events within your client's case. This helps you pick among all the other case presentation choices in ways you now know can have a bigger impact than if you hadn't identified the mines in the field ahead.

Many lawyers look at the landmine list and think of cross-examination. They see a need for a specific answer to remedy each and every problem listed, even including biases from the jurors' own upbringings that could be lit up by the story's retelling. That is understandable but misleading, and a risk you need not run. The real task is to devise a way of presenting your client's story so as to diminish or avoid altogether as many landmines as possible in the decision makers' minds. Not because they have each been directly dispelled. Rather, because the version of reality you have offered them is compelling from a perspective so far away from the territory the biggest landmines occupy that whole sections of the list simply don't come to mind. This happens whenever you succeed at inviting people into the model of the world you are presenting, to engage the story you distilled and now delivered in its most effective form. So the more you know about which landmines the case story might encourage or invite to the fore, the better. The longer the list, the easier your task. This process guides the exclusion and reduction of the sometimes overwhelming number of possibilities with which you can effectively draw attention and responses toward your version of reality, and away from the territory in which you'd rather they never set foot.

Theme

The exclusion and reduction process continues. You now know several directions your most easily accepted story should avoid. Though you may not be able to put it into words yet, sorting the territory the story theme will occupy is the next big cut to make on the material at hand.

THEME

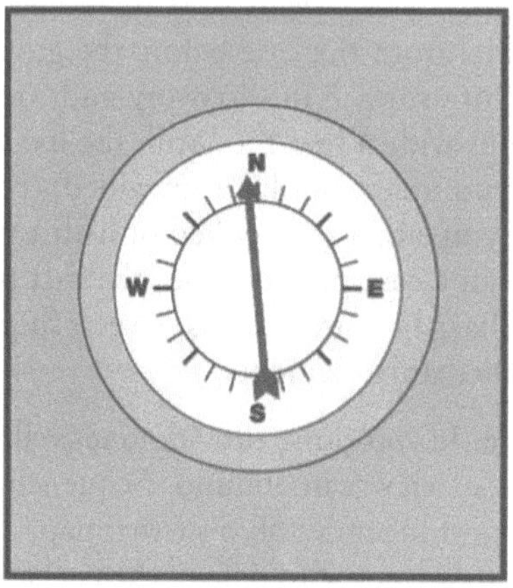

Sometimes the theme can be derived by approaching the case stories participants produced in a top-down manner, putting the context first, and sometimes from the bottom up, working through the specific content first. Sometimes it has to be almost a process of osmosis to locate the most effective, compelling, and memorable theme. It helps to be familiar with the nature of themes, as they are being applied in this endeavor.

The story theme provides a moral underpinning for the story about to be retold. It serves as the foundation on which the decision maker's edifice is built, the scaffold from which it is hung, and any meaning it will carry. As such, it has nothing to do with details, but is by nature very general. Since many attorneys have a habit of mistaking detail for specificity, this can prove problematic, leading trial professionals to substitute case theory for a theme. They are not the same: the theme is more important in court, mediation, and negotiation. The theory, the stack of facts and law, is more important to getting there. When asked the theme of their case, many trial professionals offer short descriptions of their theory. Hoping to persuade without a clear view and competent delivery of a theme is the same thing as waiting until the end of trial to instruct jurors on how to apply the law to what they've heard. They are moving ahead with no direction—lost, but making great time.

Knowing your case theory, the facts, and the positions people have taken regarding them, helps you distill a theme, but it is no substitute for one. The ten-word-telegram technique is a great way to develop a concise presentation of the stack of facts. It can also set you on the road to a theme. Developed as an aid to telling the story of the case with a distinct beginning, middle, and end, the telegram is a tremendous help in sorting out the story you're retelling in court into a consistent, human form.[13] It turns the lawyer's focus to issues typically forgotten in case preparation, for instance the impact of the sequence of the story on the jurors' appreciation of it. It reminds you to stick with a message that's ordered and complete. The whole story arc, all three steps, in ten carefully chosen words. Yet, the telegram it is still not a theme.

The theme is the foundation upon which the entire presentation is built. Delivering your case presentation should represent more specific ways of establishing, maintaining, and reinforcing the theme. It can roughly be thought of as the answer to the question, "What is this whole thing really all about?" Typical thematic territory for plaintiff injury cases is prevention or protection. Often, defense themes are drawn from the "act of God" or "stuff just happens" territory, or the area of personal responsibility. Commercial disputes often pit success or progress themes against following the rules and general welfare packages. If a statement, visual, or question is offered from your side of the room that is not in support of or directly derived from your theme, it doesn't belong in the presentation.

Consistency and the Theme

Consistency in your presentation is the hallmark of credibility for the receivers. Themes need not be stated aloud, but they are the foundation for everything that the decision makers hear in testimony and in your opening. The theme must anticipate the jurors' end-job of reading and reacting to language in the verdict form and instructions. It must be as useful there as in the beginning. If it gets across well, it will provide the meaning for the entire case story at any stage listeners select. Successfully delivering each presentation step, detailed below, when it is set up in voir dire, previewed in opening, and broached with each witness requires the attorney to begin each statement and question from a consistent base.

The best theme incorporates the most significant elements and factors emerging from the groups' collection of stories. When all is pruned and pared, this usually amounts to six to twelve items. These key story points can emerge as a bottom-up drive toward an eventual theme, though sometimes a top-down approach is dictated by what comes out of the group's yield.

When many trial professionals are asked for a theme (if they don't recite the theory instead), they often respond with the thesis or justification for the case position. The thesis is important, but it is not a theme or substitute. It is the easiest among theme, theory, and thesis to distinguish. It is the answer to the question, "Why should any juror agree with our position?" Or, from the decision makers' viewpoint,

13. Alan Blumenfeld, Katherine James, and Joshua Karton are credited with developing this telegram technique. Blumenfeld and James are available through Act of Communication, Culver City, California, and Karton can be reached through Communication Arts for the Professional, Santa Monica, California.

whatever completes the sentence, "That side should prevail because . . . ." The explanation often produced in professional negligence cases is that "they did/didn't do their best." Note that the thesis, "Doing your best—or not," works almost independently of the facts in evidence. The thesis really comes into play farther along in the case. It is an argument: a rationale for a mental position each decision maker must adopt about the legal rules and facts. It presumes a thematic position has already been built so it can be backed by this reason.

Still, rationale doesn't come first; positioning does. Once decision makers start to learn the story (theory), they come up with the reasons why the leanings they've built are the right ones. Before they can begin to accept the elements of the story, the theme colors them all. If you fail to offer a theme at the outset, one will be provided for you by whichever randomly accessed life experiences light up in each judge, juror, or other decision makers' minds at that moment. The *theme* determines how the newly reconstructed case story is seen and heard. The *thesis* offers reasons why that mindset is right. The theme is the compass; the theory, the map, and the thesis justifies the journey. Perceive, reference, and select or decide. Categories, narrative, and rhetoric.

Themes are not found in words nor limited by them. Rather, the case theme is the unifying image, idea, or concept each person uses to remind themselves what the story is about. Research is almost unanimous that any decision maker, in or out of courtrooms, lay and professional alike, will determine what the theme of your story is fairly quickly. Very little can change that determination once it's set. Distilling the best story and presenting it as well as possible early on can be the most critical part of the whole case presentation.

Some of the more tenacious confusion about the nature of themes has to do with their function, not what composes them. While they are utilized to bring meaning to the cases each juror hears, themes are not the reasoned conclusions this observation could imply. They can be expressed in words, but are not bound by them. Themes also lead to reasons to lean toward or against your positions. They function much like funnels or magnifying glasses, filtering years of life stories and beliefs about their meanings into those that appear most relevant to appreciating a certain story before us. Earlier, the case theme was described as each decision maker's private compass, pointing the direction to best grasp the elements of the case being heard. In truth, the theme is less the instrument and more the magnetic pole that empowers the compass to work.

So if a case theme is more subjective than objective, more perceptual than verbal, and more experiential than rational, what business do such amorphous things have in a legal case? The same as inherently ambiguous human beings do. Neither is optional. Your case will always have a theme in the mind of each person to whom you present it. To attempt to appreciate the cases being presented to them in court or elsewhere, all decision makers will use a theme.

While themes are not optional, choosing to try to influence them certainly is. Rather than devising and declaring a single theme, it helps to approach the theme presentation less as declaration, and more as invitation for each decision maker to draw up one of their own.

Being subjective, themes are private. Constructed from our own responses and understandings of our own life experiences, even themes defined by the very same words will have wholly different meanings for the people using those words. Take another look at the answers to the rough theme question from the construction accident/injury case above. Naturally, we get many politically correct answers to this question. So there will always be lots of minimally revealing answers, such as "Who was negligent?" "Who's going to pay?" and "Money." Other answers don't just serve to fill the blank and pray the moderator moves along, and these often prove very revealing. You might wonder, for example, what the differences between "Who's responsible for themselves?" "A man who felt his employer—no, the big company he's suing—had screwed up" and "Irresponsible management" say about the meanings of the case stories between the respective speakers' ears. How are perceptions of authority mixing with perceptions of safety? Where does action taken on either count start? In the notes excerpted from the attorney's report about the problematic blending of all the parties in participants' minds, note how the point made is evident even in what these three general statements imply or presume.

Many in this focus group were not thoroughly engaged in the case story as presented. Yet, it provides value for the trial professional analyzing it afterward. From the position of the defendant owner of the plant, based on these results, is that a posture you want to encourage or discourage in the final presentation? Another part of the answer was provided by the chance to place this verbal input up against the perceptually based material about the "in the line of sight" factor. On balance, though disengagement of decision makers is often a position from which civil defense attorneys will benefit, this case could be an exception proving that rule. It is hard to distinctly and strongly distinguish one character from another in a story with which someone is barely engaged. The impact of having someone out of view diminishes in direct proportion to how well you are actually motivated to look as the story plays out in your mind's eye.

When you review all the collected responses to the "What's it all about?" question and extrapolate what must be true of the individual stories each holds to produce their particular answer, certain trends usually emerge. As you compare and contrast those trends with other verbal, written, and nonverbal input, other connections can become apparent.

Each trend line will often have many aspects of the story being processed consistently by some faction in the group.

- On whom does the story center: for each of those factions or individuals? Who acts upon whom, who is acted upon, and who is either observing the action or out of the picture?

- ➲ Which elements of the case seem primary to the folks for whom safety is associated with the higher authority, compared to those that draw no distinctions among authorities, and those that start at the hands-on position when it comes to safety?
- ➲ Is the cause proof more significant for one group than the other, or is it negligence that their stories revolve around?
- ➲ What analogies from their own experiences do the factions rally around, cling to or reject out of hand?
- ➲ What catch phrases, imagery, and other anchors get the biggest response from one or the other?
- ➲ Where does one group's story seem to start and end? Is that significantly different from the other group's sequence for the case?
- ➲ What reasons or justifications do they later offer for why they found certain parts of the story more important than others?

All that and more flow directly from the theme each person recreates in their head as they see and hear the case story unfold. Because their private stories are internally consistent, their private themes underlie every aspect. That is why so many things have to be diminished, distorted, or deleted in each person's recall as the case progresses. That is also how certain facts, pre-existing attitudes, and rationales take on huge significance for certain people as the case presentation proceeds. Biases and decision-making habits such as attribution, hindsight, or perseverance adhere to the theme once it's engaged. They all lean toward each juror's private North Pole, though they may not if the juror is successfully invited to find a different direction. This funneling or focusing also starts very early in the process.

This is why a few select words alone, repeated often, are not up to the task of effectively delivering a case theme. That doesn't mean it won't encourage developing some themes over others for some people some days. It means that the attorneys that imagine their task with the theme is one of getting every juror to fill in the blank with the phrase, "If it doesn't fit, you must acquit," are imagining the wrong goal. They can all get the phrase and still build themes that lead to conviction. The phrase is not the theme. But the phrase can help reinforce and later reveal the theme. When reviewing all the focus group responses, collect every significant word indicating positions on what the stories discussed may be about at heart or what drives them. But when preparing to present the case story, stand ready to deliver the meaning that seemed to permeate those accounts, more than just those words that trailed them.[14]

---

14. *See* Chapter Seven.

In *Courtroom Power*, Paul Lisnek and I discuss the theme reportedly used by Michael Ciresi and his troops in the Minnesota tobacco trials. Mr. Ciresi described the driving theme of the case with the phrase, "Legal Product, Illegally Sold." Their pretrial work helped them determine this as their most effective case direction. He describes how after arriving at that theme, all document discovery and deposition questioning moved strictly in the direction that theme pointed. Granted, if sufficient other evidence emerged to change the story entirely, the theme could be dropped. Until that choice was made, adherence to the theme was the rule. This is how decision makers use their case themes. Following the shortest distance, straight-line principle, it would seem the wisest course to do when presenting to them.

Scope

Once you've made the first big cuts dictated by the landmine list, identified what directions or constructs to avoid in the story, and decided which direction to move toward by your sense of the theme, the remaining story elements usually become easier and easier to isolate. Just as decision makers' stories are internally consistent with their themes, so will yours need to be. Knowing where you can't step and the general direction for where you most want to step tend to winnow the field of options among the remaining material from which to construct the case presentation.

As with any element in the case story, consistency carries the most credibility. With the story scope, it is often the indirect reference in your choice of pronouns, tenses, singular or plural references, and other modifiers that connotes how broadly or narrowly the case story will be drawn by the listeners. Knowing exactly where you want to be consistent while presenting the reach of the people, acts, events, numbers, and time involved is the purpose behind carefully crafting and delivering the element of the story's scope. As you determine from the group's input, how broad or narrow the story's reach needs to be in each of those categories, hints, or directions for the point of view, active party, or ingredient (and the presentation sequence) will all become clearer.

What is most important to bear in mind while reviewing the material for building the most compelling package for the story scope is that each category involved—time, people, acts, places, and such—can be presented in a broad or narrow frame. It is not an all-or-nothing deal when it comes to delivering the story scope well. Review both scopes that were presented by the attorneys in the two opening statements in Chapter Five and those that were recommended. Notice how they divide the broad and narrow distribution to achieve the most memorable and persuasive arrangement.[15]

Story scope usually has an influence on the weighting of the context/content factors that decision makers will likely take from a presentation. Specific content tends to require a narrower reach in many areas. If you determine you will need to rely heavily on content-oriented packaging for your major story points, you may need to pay careful attention to how people with favorable stories dealt with any broad scope packaging. However, a class action dealing with a specific problem affecting many individuals could still have broad scope packaging in time, place, people, and some numbers, though it would be hard pressed to pass up a narrow scope on the choices and acts involved in creating the specific, now widespread harm. That critical content could lose traction if the plaintiff attorney forgot to reign in the scope of that part of the story. Of course, broad scope in applying those actions to many narrow aspects, isolating and distinguishing individual people, separate places, and different times, is exactly what the defense would want to proffer to counter an effective story scope for the plaintiffs when their turn comes along. That is the essence of the defendant's story scope in many pharmaceutical products cases, for instance, when a tiny percentage of adverse effects is often contrasted with millions of doses safely consumed.

Scope is not just about the scope over time; that is, does the story concern the events over thirty years' development and distribution of a product or the momentary decision process at the start of that line? No matter how it is delivered, some people will adjust the scope of the story to increase or decrease the events covered by the tale, the significant scenes where the action took place, and what actions are and are not important, in order to understand the story and how many people are involved, directly or indirectly, by the acts, intentions, or effects related. Is this a "big" story about culture and people at large, or a "little" story about a particular event affecting just a few people, or just one? Are these actions cultural trends, or individual heroics? Did this story take place over many times and settings, or can it

15. See Appendix Three for a number of other samples of actual openings. Before reading ahead to the end of each example, make an effort to pick out the scope, narrow or broad, as it was expressed for each of the main categories of time, people, actions, numbers, and sometimes places involved.

best be understood by consistently associating it with one locale and one particular moment in time?

Listen to the level of detail and logical levels of the language people use to describe the elements inside those other distinctions. Are they talking generically about concepts or about particulars? Do they jump from an action to the motive to the overall moral, or do they tend to keep bringing that kind of higher order discussion back down to the specifics of the single event? How broadly are they packaging a sense of duty or fault? Do they extend the image beyond the actual parties or not? And if they do, what kind of package do they use to do so: legal, moral, community, family, or what?

Point of View

Once decision makers know what the case story is about and how far it seems to reach, they will want to determine which character(s), groups, processes, or things to place on center stage. The eventual presentation should maintain a consistent perspective in each segment regarding the position on which you want the story to be fixed. This is all about the mental position of the "camera" serving each decision maker's mental TV screen. In reference to which position, and not necessarily person and/or personality, is attention to be primarily, consistently focused in the stories you've collected and are reviewing? Or over whose shoulder is the camera shooting other characters?

There are multiple options for viewpoint in even the simplest events, such as a phone call. Is the call being retold from the viewpoint of the caller, the receiver, the subjects of their conversation, the person in the room with either of them, the operator listening in, the phone itself, or the fly on the wall at arm's length from all the action? Practicing delivering point of view consistently can be enhanced by collecting such different references for the central character, object, or process in each participant's story.

When presenting it is not necessary to use the name or label of the subject referenced by point of view in every sentence or question you utter. All other people and processes would best be referenced consistently through their relationship with the party, company, object, standard, or event selected to keep a consistent point of view on the case story. This is true whether it's the hospital's doctor, the patient's disease, the defective part, the written rule or contract clause, or a time before the disputed events. Everyone and everything else needs to be represented in relation to that reference point, rather than as separate subjects in stories all their own.

The second, around-the-horn question we often ask participants is: "If you could only talk to one person involved in this case, who would you choose?"

People do not always pick their central story character, so the trial professional collating those answers seeking a point of view for the story may be misled. Usually that question produces the person people would most like to cross-examine about potential exceptions to or redirection of the stories they've been building. The list of answers may not deliver a viewpoint vectoring between who must be the central character(s) and which people they most want to cross-examine, but it can provide strong hints about the element most closely related to point of view: the active ingredient or active party in the story. The central character may not always be the same party or ingredient that controls the central action. Remember the locus of control dichotomy between choice and circumstance when seeking out point of view and active parties. If the client is vulnerable to perceptions of greater or lesser control, finding a suitable active ingredient far from the client's hands in participants' stories can prove quite valuable, even if it is an angle not previously considered.

The perspective from which your story is best going to be told is not always the one you might initially assume. Reviewing the material for point-of-view and active ingredient associations can serve as another reminder to be on guard against preexisting presumptions. An exercise for gaining greater flexibility in delivering multiple points of view in a single story is to partly or completely summarize the case story in a few sentences. Do this using no more than six sentences. Then retell that same story line from as many points of view as possible, being careful to remain consistent throughout each telling, just as with the phone conversation.

There are some commonsense patterns that most attorneys recognize when they appear in the transcript or on the focus group forms. People who initially see the case through the eyes of the family of the plaintiff, particularly if there's been little presented about the family, tend to end up being strong damage advocates. Conversely, those who see the case through the eyes of the legal system are often strong for the defense. This is perhaps because they keep at arm's length, maintaining their perspective of the story as a lawsuit first. Those who maintain a complete distance, seeing the story through the distanced view of observers of the legal system, are tough on plaintiffs as a group. As always, individual differences will occasionally override the trend, depending on the story, the person, and the delivery. If you compare all the recorded comments and early written survey responses with eventual leanings for the defense or plaintiff, prosecution, or defense, there are often some revealing patterns in the perspective each group develops early on.

In a recent demonstration of focus groups conducted on the subject of low-impact auto crashes for an organization of attorneys representing injured plaintiffs, the potential impact of a strongly delivered point of view was memorably illustrated. It helped undercut the jurors' likelihood of accepting or discussing the defense scientific evidence regarding G-forces, similar "safe" impacts in daily life, and injury probabilities. The attorney representing the injured, rear-ended plaintiff began his presentation making an effort to handle the common bias jurors hold about the accountability or personal responsibility of less critically injured plaintiffs bringing lawsuits for money damages. He spent some time introducing his client by listing many actions the young man had taken to discharge his responsibility to care for himself and get on, as well as possible, with his life. He referred to the young man's active role in his medical care, efforts the young man made to return to work and to which his doctors were originally opposed. The attorney identified areas in which the client had independently handled costs that arose from the wreck's aftermath, all the while stressing that his client was not seeking compensation for these items from this jury. Note that this approach violates the common wisdom about primacy, sequencing, and point of view for plaintiffs, which suggests always starting with the bad acts of the defendants, in context, first.

The attorney maintained the viewpoint of "the driver" as he switched to the defendant and her irresponsible acts, including her failure to acknowledge liability for the wreck itself (despite sworn statements to that effect) until the eve of trial. By the end of his five-minute opening, he'd established a consistent perspective of the whole case from the viewpoint of both drivers inside the vehicles. As many lawyers will, the defense attorney made an immediate effort to declaratively respond to everything. In doing this, he abdicated his only chance (according to research[16]) to strongly establish a consistent and compelling alternative point of view. He conceded and also reinforced the plaintiff's "both drivers'" viewpoint by listing answers to each claim about his client followed by harmful facts about the plaintiff driver he

16. While numbers from mock juror research by the Trial Behavior Consulting Institute (TCBI) indicate a majority of jurors form leanings farther along in trials than traditionally imagined, decision-making patterns like hindsight and norming biases clearly show that a person's initial impressions of the story line will tend to filter all the rest of the incoming information in a way that confirms that leaning far more often than it will change it completely, once it's formed. And people form impressions instantly, referencing sometimes millions of associations a second to make sense of any message.

planned to introduce. He "answered" every detailed charge, but built up the opponent's preferred viewpoint as he did it.

By the time he got to the strength of his story, the scientific material from reconstruction, human factors, and physics evidence, the damage was clearly done. This was evident from the participants' almost complete deletion of it from their spoken and written commentaries—even under direct prompting during the process. They apparently had no room left in the movies in their mind's eye to alter the perspective they'd developed just to incorporate what seemed like less relevant, "technical" items, based on the point of view of most of those mental movies.

There were a few exceptions to this trend in the group; one was a safety design engineer. His own personal viewpoint would certainly be expected to override that proffered by a plaintiff's lawyer seeking damages. But for the majority, with the story being viewed and retold only from the perspective of the car occupants, G-forces seemed less relevant than they might have if the viewpoint of the car, the investigators, the law, the biomechanical engineer, or the reconstructionist been offered early enough to help them switch their psychic camera angles.

Sequence

Any lawyer that focuses too much on the shape of the story according to her own memories, and too little on the open eyes and ears of the individuals struggling to remake a story, will tend to fail to give their perspective its due. One of the first casualties in that conflict is the sequence of the story the decision makers hear, the true order of proofs.

SEQUENCE

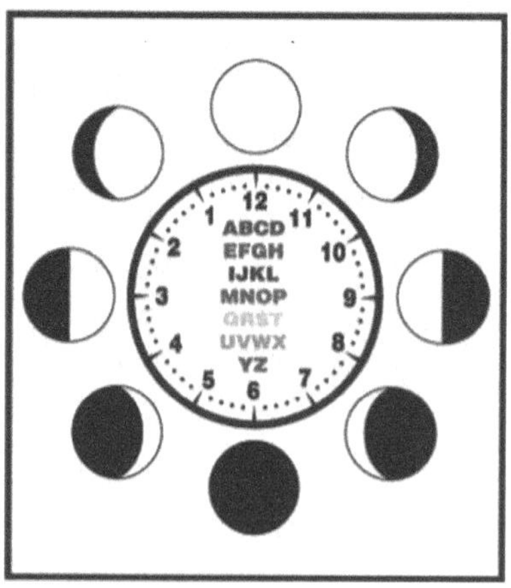

Returning to the well-documented story model[17] and the ten-word telegram that can clarify your client's particular story line, the simple start is at the beginning, the middle, and then the end. A lawyer overly familiar with a client's case often leaps back and forth between the three steps as the mood strikes.[18] This can lead to a severe case of juror psychic whiplash. If they are lucky enough to have a solid theme established, they can comfort themselves with the notion that they are still in the ballpark. But that is small comfort indeed when they find they don't even know the game being played there.

David Ball, a trial consultant and dramatist, frequently points out to lawyers that if you go back far enough, the paths of jury trials and theater intersect at what he calls the Greek "juristors."[19] The first trial was a play. It was this observation that prompted me to start looking for the average number of steps, or chunks, into which most trials could be divided, as if they were acts in a play. Most trials, like most stories, seem to fit well into three sections. However you choose to characterize the steps of your case, it is worth the time to discover what they are and how you would best articulate them in court.

As far as analyzing the focus group's input is concerned, the sequence of events in each person's story is often quite apparent, though few could ever articulate it if asked directly. Note where each person starts their commentary about the events, if they maintain that starting point, or if they move their story's sequence later to a different spot. Note what they stick with most as their primary and final points about the story. Beware of the habitual temptations of chronology.

Sequencing the case story is not just listing the order of the witnesses, but establishing the consistent order of the story to be retold by all of those witnesses. The idea is to learn where to break the entire case presentation into three, clear steps—beginning, middle, and end—though not necessarily chronologically. This is one of the most effective ways to establish a compelling theme for the jurors early on, then develop and maintain it throughout the evidence presentation. These steps should be mapped out well enough so that jurors know when you're moving from one time frame to the next, whoever's on the stand, wherever they are in their testimony. Carefully designed and well-utilized visuals make that possible, providing a key visual anchor for each of the three story steps.

Each witness will address whichever steps of the case story they can, but they should address each step in sequence. This order should even be followed, to the extent possible, during cross-examination of opposition witnesses. Careful

17. W. Lance Bennett and Martha S. Feldman, *Reconstructing Reality in the Courtroom* (New Brunswick, NJ: Rutgers University Press, 1981): 94.
18. Time is not the guiding principle in sequence. It is often a liability.
19. David Ball, *Theater Tips and Strategies for Jury Trials* (2d ed.) (Louisville, CO: National Institute for Trial Advocacy, 1997): Preface.

consideration should be given to the order of witnesses, so the strongest voices for step one come before those for steps two and three, and so on. Ideally, the first three witnesses would be the individually strongest voices for each step of the plan, in order, though this does not always work out. Once you have determined the most effective sequence in which to deliver the story, use it to outline the major evidentiary and legal points, step by step.

This outline almost never need exceed two or three pages in length. It will tend to determine the order of your witnesses, more than they should be allowed to determine its content and sequence.

More Possibilities, Less Certainty. Those are the top five case story elements to be drawn from the groups or whatever case material you may have at hand. When determining how to best use the input of focus groups to identify the best case story structure, there are a few more factors to bear in mind as guides to the sorting, paring, pruning, and gleaning process.

Narrative Factors. Patterns and trends in the way the story is related can help you rate the importance of various content elements and detect which context or perceptual structures are primary in this account.

Deletion, Distortion, and Generalization. All three of these basic perceptual trends can reveal hints or patterns of a group member's mindset about the case and related aspects of their world. If they are followed up as they appear on the tape or in their subsequent written comments, you will be surprised by how much of the inner version of the story that they construct can take shape. Often, these mindsets will also point you toward areas of life experience or life stories that are available to explore in voir dire discussions.

Frequency. Repetition is a well-respected tool in early childhood and adult learning. When people try to educate a deliberately "slow" moderator or their colleagues in a focus group about their own positions on the case before them, they tend to hit the same few points that originally struck their fancy, over and over again. This is more evidence that the early impact pointed to in the primacy effect is always important to track. After all, what you want to learn is which parts of a large bunch of facts and law in your story need to come first and be repeated most often, so that your chances of encouraging the learning you want are enhanced as well as they can be.

Primacy and Recency. If you fill the first open debrief of the group with the "first impressions" discussion, then you have a way of returning to each member's initial reactions and thoughts for comparison with what was declared or agreed with in public discussion and what was initially written in answer to the first questions on the survey. Responses at the end of the debrief to the single question participants would want answered about the case give you yet a third vector for assessing how well they were actually able to report their initial impression, and how that impression, and others, began to develop through their own "primacy portion" of the case story's emergence and consolidation.[20]

The same kind of packaging for recency can be found at the end of the day by vectoring among the positions taken on the last written form before deliberation, the summary of the most important or significant factors at the start of deliberations, and the positions written about on the post-verdict form. Comparing the elements emphasized early with those emphasized last can be productive, particularly when seeking anchors or other packaging for damage testimony, as well as for information about sequencing such material.

Analogies. Personal analogies can lead you to a treasure trove of metaphor, related life experience, and perceptual structures beyond the analogy itself. These can be useful in the packaging of your case story and the strategy for voir dire should a jury be involved. There are a lot of other areas, besides their personal experiences and what you offer them, from which people will draw analogies to guide their storybuilding process—primarily from the culture and the world around them. It can prove valuable to observe an early appearance on the tape and read and listen to later answers, questions, and assertions to find referents for those analogies, personal or otherwise, that landed for some folks, and began sending out roots and feelers in certain telling directions as soon as they did. Similarly, when you hear an attorney or group leader use analogies that you slaved over in preparation, only to see it die gasping in the middle of the floor, this too is good news for your later efforts.

Filling Defects and Counter Factual Constructs. Every narrative by its very nature will convey more holes in its structure, as it is perceived in the mind of listeners, than even the finest orator can fill with words during the telling. The filling of these gaps by the listener in the perceived story is often referred to as resolving "filling defects." Most of them never reach the level of consciousness. The mind simply fills in the defect with references and meanings the listener's head deems appropriate to this story, at this time. Finding trends when they are offered for how these holes are being filled, and what may or may not contribute to such a trend being expanded or curtailed, can be of inestimable value to the eventual presentation.

"Counter factual constructs" are a specific kind of filling that tends to supplant some actual evidence with more compelling material spun from the decision makers'

20. A phrase I first heard used by Howard Nations, referring to the period of trial starting with the first moment of voir dire and ending approximately with the first witness's cross-examination. The equivalent period in these groups is roughly from the introduction/job description through the end of the first debrief following openings. By then, you will discover, most case stories are sketched out and the filtering process has begun.

own minds. These often follow phrases in verbal responses such as, "If only . . ." "I'll betcha . . ." "Well, maybe what really happened . . ." and the like.

Anchors. Terms of art aren't the only verbal anchors available in a story. Sometimes colloquial anchors become so entrenched, so quickly within the package of a case story that they almost become terms of art specific to the case at hand (i.e., "What made him turn off that light?"). Pay attention to who creates such anchors and who adopts them. Notice which ones end up associated with responses other than those intended to be linked with the phrase (i.e., "I'm wondering if he's really hurt").

Legal Elements and Proofs. All this sorting and associating effort needs some direction or the amount of information and possible connections will overwhelm. The needs of the statutes, verdict instructions, and verdict-form language are an ultimate guide to valuing the various verbal inputs and perceptual structures of each individual or group-endorsed story. Also, keeping in mind the major legal elements of the legal proof can help shape your review of all the ways the story has been reauthored by the group.

Attitude Factors

- The decision maker is your friend. The decision maker is not an adversary to be deflected, dismissed, or overcome.
- Review and select as much as possible from the point of view of the decision maker struggling to build a coherent model of the stack of facts and law. [Temporarily] forget what you may have believed about what evidence needs emphasis or what points of law are obviously controlling, and consider how the story is best received rather than sent.
- Think "opening statement" all through the process. This will help you avoid drifting into the common trap of arguing the end of the story before discovering where it begins, who or what it features, its size, and what it's about.
- Think and collect information more in possibilities than in conclusions. Even as the process shifts toward reduction from ever-greater expansion, be on the lookout for windows opening onto new perspectives.
- Because they say it or write it down doesn't mean that's all that's on their minds. Avoid taking one answer for the whole story.
- Just because it isn't named, doesn't mean it isn't there. Most growth happens below the surface.

6.10 2015 Supplement

6.10.1 What Have We Here?

The old, two-variable thinking discussed in Chapter Two is most dangerous at the outset of analyzing the input from a focus group because trial attorneys have spent lifetimes reinforcing that what you hear is all there is, and that any statement a participant makes can be taken at face value and is complete for the record. This encourages the trial professional to revert to thinking of the old, two-sided equation between attorney choices and actions based solely on the perceived influence of juror backgrounds and beliefs. This is when making practicing managing mental imagery a habit comes in so handy, so that the third, most flexible variable in the system, the stories themselves, can be placed where they belong—at the top of the analytical pyramid—so that the input of focus group participants can be properly filtered.

It is important to recognize that although each variable in the three-variable system (one, two, and/or three) has distinct characteristics, it is still a system of interacting influences. No variable works independently of the other two any more than the two parts of the mind do. In fact, the best reminder to avoid limiting and reducing your analysis to the impoverished two-variable system can be found in the dynamic between what's conscious and what is other-than-conscious. Keep that in mind while reading the following; these are the two most misleading and inaccurate remarks I've heard trial attorneys make following a focus group or voir dire:

"*Everyone* talked about that so it *must be* important."

"*Nobody* talked about that so it *must not be* important."

The driving bias example from Chapter Four also can be a helpful reminder that some of the most influential mindsets are so deeply ingrained in our thinking that we just don't think of them consciously anymore. But they still fully inform our presumptions and the mental imagery and analogies we consistently express. The most common input from focus groups on civil personal injury cases is a good illustration. When the theme question, "What is this whole thing really all about?" is posed, that common answer is almost always "money." The follow-up question answers can range from, "Because they need help caring for their child," to "I want to know whose ad they saw on TV that told them they could get money," and from, "That is the only way left for the defendants to compensate," to "When your chance comes to grab some, go for it." Just like the conclusions drawn when looking at a member of the military in the venire, surface assumptions are never helpful, because, truly, you can't judge a book by its cover. What you see does not show you what you'll get.

One big change in my practice analyzing focus groups since 2005 is the choice of story element with which to begin developing a case story. An implicit suggestion throughout the First Edition was that theme is the story element to start with (although there were a few case-specific suggestions which required that the theme came last in the presentation plan).

Experience has shown me that it works more effectively to begin by determining the strongest basic story sequence and let the rest of the story elements emerge from there. Beginning with steps one, two, and three—context, conflict, and resolution—and their attendant frames, including the first step's important "set-up" trilogy (i.e., risks, rules, and right way), tends to clarify a great deal of the rest of the stronger story components learned from the focus group, including pointing toward who (or what) would provide the strongest point of view. This approach has confirmed for me that starting both competing—plaintiff and defense—case presentations for focus groups with the story sequences is more effective as well.

By starting with the sequence of the story frames in their three steps, you may find that elements like point of view often become clear just through sorting the order of the narrative. Sequencing also enables clear choices about witness order (or even the need for one or more of them), as well as starting the ball rolling immediately as to what visuals you will need to most effectively invite decision makers to most effectively anchor that story sequence by storyboarding it for them.

A few guidelines to keep in mind:

- Always work from the most general factors to the more specific.
- Beware of the "only what's said is important" bias.
- Ask: "What has to be true for that mind for it to be said that way?"
- Ask: "What has to be true for that mind for it to be seen that way?"
- Regarding demonstrative visuals, ask: "What has to be seen for them to see it our client's way?"
- Avoid easy conclusions. Seek out collected possibilities, then combine them, rank them, and review the effects of participant interaction on video.[21]
- To help develop metaphors and analogies, listen carefully whenever someone likens a story factor to something else—i.e. "It's like holding a hand of cards close to the vest."
- How do those differ from what they were "like" to you at the start?
- Look for "if this, then that" equations in people's thinking. For example, in a breach of contract case an unpopular local plaintiff company was seen as

21. We record the entire day's proceedings with cameras pointed at the group, not the moderator or attorneys, in order to better review their reactions as "advertised," but not spoken.

"OK to sue" *if* it fulfilled its side of the contract, a position spontaneously generated and returned to in various ways throughout the group.

Or, the worker on the far side of a door being installed, holding his hand opposite the drill his supervisor is holding on the other side. *If* the hand had to be there, *if* the drill never should be pushed all the way through, and *if* the hand could be seen or reasonably envisioned from the supervisor's side, *then* the fault could be seen as being on the part of the supervisor's.

Or, the contractor in charge of the chemically contaminated work-site. *If* there was simple clean up fix available, *if* the contractor knew of the long-standing, widespread contamination, *if* the danger was denied or minimized, and *if* there was financial incentive to avoid cleanup, *then* the contractor should be punished.

6.10.2 Order in the Court—and Elsewhere

As might be expected, ten more years of experience has shown me that certain story elements have sustained themselves while some have not, and at least one that didn't appear in the First Edition has been added to my standard list of case story elements included in every focus group analysis.

Two that are still important, but no longer included in the standard roster are *organizing filter* (sorting the content by *person*, *place*, *actions*, *data/info*, or *time*) and *sensory bias* (finding a perceptual bias towards one of three sense systems within the packaging of the story). The former tends to be more of an adjunct factor, only occasionally proving to be a major persuasive lever for story delivery. The latter requires a good deal of additional training to apply well.[22]

Additionally, there are two elements I have added to the list in Chapter Six of essential story factors to consider when analyzing focus group results to include in your case story presentation plan for mediation, negotiation, or trial. The first element is the *central image*—the fact-based image that best supports and reinforces the theme. While it was described and recommended in the original edition, the central image has emerged as a much more "central" element in a strong case story (no pun intended). Consider for example, the dangerous doctor who is maintaining privileges at one hospital while having them denied at another. How does this doctor (and his situation) have to be seen for decision makers also to see it from the injured patient's position? What primary image—fact-based and linked to the theme—will best encourage, all at once, imagery that generates powerful, personal analogies to experiences of the medical system, diseases, and doctors? How about as an "infectious agent" within the otherwise "healthy system" of the hospital itself?

22. *See* Eric Oliver, *The Persuasive Edge for Legal Communication*. Video training series. (Portland, OR: Trial Guides Publishing, 2014), www.trialguides.com.

The second element that has become standard fare in the interim is the *operating metaphor*. It—and its relevant value to a client's case story—is covered well in section 3.15, "2015 Supplement."

6.10.3 So, What's Your Plan?

The condensed *Case Presentation Plan* outline described in Chapter Six of the First Edition still proves quite helpful, especially for cases that are on the verge of being presented for resolution or when time (and/or resources) for a formal focus group are in short supply.

However, since the original publication of *Facts Can't Speak for Themselves*, I have developed and begun to use a *working presentation plan*. Long before a case heads to mediation or trial, often before it is even filed, a working plan that is used as a *guide* for story development (often before discovery begins, and as it unfolds) has proven extremely valuable. The effect of consistently treating a case *as a story* in discussions and written communication with the opposition, and even the bench, can't be underestimated, according to my experience with countless attorneys since 2005.

And, something inadvertently omitted from the original edition was a comprehensive layout of a full Case Presentation Plan. I am rectifying that now with two examples:

1. A *completed* Case Presentation Plan for trial in a case referenced in section 2.5, "2015 Supplement," when an ironworker disconnected his safety line, then fell and was paralyzed completely in the process.[23]

2. A *working* Case Presentation Plan for a case involving a less experienced doctor inserting sharp instruments into a patient at his supervising doctor's order—who then left the actual medical intervention illegally unsupervised, resulting in a very bad outcome for the plaintiff.

23. *Ron Bayer v. Panduit, et al.* tried by plaintiff attorneys Jay Luchsinger, Michael Carter, and Clifford Horowitz.

COMPLETED CASE PRESENTATION PLAN

You will recall, our "bottom line" framing question before the focus group was, how would the ironworker's disconnecting get perceived as moving, *at most,* toward safety and, *at least,* away from danger? This group indicated the best answer is to invite decision makers to see only a *false choice* of all workers on site being forced to directly violate a safety rule or do nothing because of a number of illegal choices the contractors made long before. And, according to what these folks gave us, here are the story elements of the presentation plan most likely to help decision makers (pros or jurors) build a story that positions those choices that way.

THEME—*what this story is all about*

Elimination of any safe choice for workers

- Instead of doing all they reasonably can to provide a safe working environment, contractors create and maintain an unreasonably dangerous work-site
- Removing promised safety plan and adding needless hazards
- Workers work the iron, contractors control their work-site

CENTRAL IMAGE—*the fact-based image that supports and expands the theme for decision makers*

The two companies "cutting corners"

- The visual that invites and supports this image is our stud installation image, surrounded by the OSHA prohibition language, the low bid language, and the "on board" memo/email language

POINT OF VIEW—*the case story's "central character" through whom or what the case story is presented*

The two contractors (and their sub's safety plan)

- There was an unintended benefit of the choice in the plaintiff's focus group presentation to keep the defendant contractors essentially anonymous during the delivery. What this group revealed was that calling them "they" and "the two contractors" makes it much easier for folks to attribute joint motives, bad motives, and joint bad acts to them
- Once that attribution is positioned in people's skulls, it's a local call to relegate subcontractor to the role of "their sub" bringing along "their sub's safety plan"

STORY SCOPE—*the reach or "size" of the story in numbers, time, actions, people, places, etc.*

Broad—on all workers, all job sites, all rules and regulations, and time frames

- Beware of jumping to specific individuals on this particular site—good or bad—too early

ACTIVE INGREDIENT—*the driving force we want decision makers to see behind the story's events*

This project is six weeks behind schedule for the two contractors

- This is so important that you want to be careful to introduce this fact at the very same time you introduce the two contractors and their sub, when you transition from the "right way" frame to the "deviant acts" frame (step one to step two) in our story sequence

OPERATING METAPHOR—*the metaphor(s) that best drive the case story narrative*

Resources and Control

- Extremely important to guide your use of modifiers, analogies, and metaphors in opening, testimony, and argument

- Sticking with this kind of language in your delivery is the key to successfully inviting decision makers to see the critical issue of "choice" the way we'd most like them to. It's very important to get to the point where we're using universal or absolute language on the elimination of choice for workers down to "commit a safety violation or nothing"

- Here is where the choices the two contractors make can capture the "choice" frame early and keep it where we want it by one of the two ways they made knowing choices: known enforcement refusals and knowingly crossing the line by violating OSHA's installation prohibition

STORY SEQUENCE—*the order of proofs three times: voir dire topics, opening, and with your first few witnesses*

There are two contractors in this case who completely controlled their work-site

- First, they refused to deliver any of the safety equipment or practices they had promised—and as legally required—in their plan for their site

- Next, they cut the ironworkers' walking work-site area in half, and on top of that, they illegally tacked on three catastrophic tripping hazards to the walking, working surface of their iron

Now, what do you think happened next?

STEP ONE—CONTEXT

Risk—the ordinary *risk* of the work—even when it's done well

- It's not the fall; it's the landing
- Construction sites have many hazards—always at the top are falls
- Iron is a construction site, too—with a *particular* fall hazard that can't be eliminated, only prevented, by establishing and maintaining the safest possible environment for the workers
  - Ironwork is done on top of the iron
  - "Walking-Working Surface" (OSHA)
  - This job = no different
  - 50% of the time—walking and working on the iron (without "tethers")—by necessity
- Naturally, biggest risk to these workers, like all construction workers, is falls
  - Up thirty feet, still no equipment demanded
  - Due to nature of the work and risks that the work carries
- Full scope of connector's job (in general)
  - *Beams can't come down straight* "tutorial" (with visual support)
  - When you unhook, when you don't (and where—i.e., perimeter)
- Fall "causes" (avoid linking to bad acts, yet)
  - Beams, equipment, other workers—where you have to look, first and last
  - The last place a reasonable ironworker looks . . . is down
- Tripping hazards—particularly dangerous—recognized as such, specifically
  - Specifically prohibited hazard = one in this case
  - Full scope of this tripping hazard and just how it produces the kind of injuries like those claimed here
- Falls lead to landings—landings cause injuries
  - Deaths (numbers annually: area, state, region, nation)
  - Broken bones and limbs

- Damaged, destroyed organs
- Brain and spine injuries

Rules*—protection *now* requires prevention *before

- Protection, at the time, at the site, demands prevention by design, ahead of time
  - Resources and control
- (Can't always, but . . .) When equipment can be used, *proper* equipment is essential
  - Lifelines and proper tie-off points for them (sequence is important)
  - Lifelines two ways—stanchions and/or perimeter lines
  - Tie-offs two ways—short and retractable lanyards
- With all equipment (not just fall protection equipment), must follow all manufacturers' recommendations and warnings
  - Tip-over risks—uneven ground, obstructions, 500 to 1,000 depending on extensions
  - Must follow all OSHA, ANSI rules and regs that apply
  - Must have—and must follow—own site plan for safety compliant with OSHA, et al. (*attorney to hold up plan at this point during delivery*)
- Must *enforce* all safety rules, and proper use of safety equipment, every day
  - Supervision, inspection, oversight (*contractors' complete control*)
    - The sub doesn't control the owner/contractors
    - Especially on safety
- Reward proper actions—punish improper actions (no defense witness can disagree)
  - Cite contractor's expert's article
  - Anything less = maintaining *unreasonably dangerous* work site for workers to walk-work on (despite duty to provide safe work environment)

***Right Way*—supervise and enforce**

This frame must be delivered "as if" they had planned to do it right on this site. That way, when it's revealed how badly they deviated from the *right way*, the positioning can have maximum impact for decision makers

- Full scope of this job site—planned construction *and* safety planning (again, wait on any violations)
  - The two contractors and their subcontractor
  - Proper use of lifelines (two ways), lanyards (two ways) on this site
  - Proper use of lifts and other equipment—on this site
  - Proper enforcement for 50% of time, workers tied off
    - Movement is a constant fact
    - Equipment, material, and workers move every way, all the time
    - Ironworkers must move, too
  - Proper maintenance of safety—meetings, documents, etc. (oversight)

STEP TWO—CONFLICT

Two contractors create and maintain unreasonably dangerous work environment

Consistently choosing unreasonable dangers for all workers (danger by design) and leaving them no safe, legal choice

- Contractors' roles
  - No other contractors/work going on—nothing else to see/watch
  - Open site photos (walking on top)
  - Email on tripping hazards
  - Shop prints
- Contractors' project is already six months late
  - Make themselves the general (don't have to pay)
  - Shop weld studs (don't have to pay workers—at higher rate)
  - Withhold any trained, competent safety managers (don't have to pay)
- Most significant "bad act"
  - Build-in studs—prohibited trip hazard
  - OSHA prohibition
  - Low bidder includes (prohibited) shop installation
  - "On board" memo/email

- Eliminate promised, planned, and required safety systems and equipment
  - Lifelines—two ways
    - Stanchions can't be placed over pour stops and studs (without welding)
    - Columns have holes—but no cables threaded through
  - Leave *all* workers with *no* safe, legal choice
    - Misuse of equipment—two ways
    - Lift as anchor point = improper use (re: maker)
    - Lift used to build-make connections = improper (and physically impossible)
    - ANSI Rule—*one choice they left him*
    - Misuse of lanyards, two ways
  - Sequence negligence
    - Wall put in too early
    - Iron outside bay (needless overhead threat)
- Take out workable safety plan—replace it with nothing
  - *100% production—0% safety*
  - Delegation area contract—"All production—no safety"
- How their illegal tripping hazard works on this ironworker (present tense)
  - Ron the *hero*
  - Ron is tripped by a shop-installed stud
    - Traps foot—falls off the building head first
  - Neck is broken on a wall on the way down
  - Initial injuries (subluxation, etc.)
  - Consequences: paralysis—spinal cord severed
    - Brain injury
    - Chronic pain (even with paralysis)
    - Bowel, bladder, sores, infections, etc.

STEP THREE—RESOLUTION

Hazard realized: worker's life ruined

- Losses created—debt owed
  - Wages
  - Medicine
  - Normal life
  - Pain and suffering

Attack defense excuses (inoculate the plaintiff)

- Safety responsibilities
  - Both corporations claim they have none
  - Both contracts say they control it (use their logos)
- Both corporations claim all manufacturing warning and instructions must be followed every day.
  - Lanyards warnings and lifts warnings were violated every day
  - Evidence will show that
  - Photos will show that
- Re: corporation's "ignorance" of hands-on site situation
  - *Visual* contract change orders with studs (*all* defendants sign off)
- 90% of these construction jobs use shop-welded studs (area erectors 100% of their stuff is shop installed; other guys say 90%)
  - Direct quote from OSHA
  - Direct quote from guy who lost bid because he wouldn't do it. Violation of OSHA safety regulations and his companies won't do it (expert witness)
- Architect versus shop print. Original design shows it to be field installed
  - Shop prints (contractor's hands say shop installed)
  - (Logos with architect's logos underneath)
- All plaintiff's "oath" violations—personal responsibility to care for himself
  - Expert's article—top down—"teaching" unsafe practices by poor control and enforcement
  - "He broke his 'vow' to always use safety equipment we promised and refused to deliver 100% of the time"

- Witness admits supervisor is there to enforce contracts including safety rules
  - Supervisor says in twenty years haven't read it. Don't know about safety
  - Witness says I sent no one out there for safety
  - Contractor says they know the contract required us to follow safety. But we delegated it
- Contractor's expert report contradicts . . . and attacks general contractor
- Show jury both labels from the two pieces of equipment are violated
  - Both defendants say they are following all manufacturer's instructions and warnings
- Both defendant's logos. Their consistent claim will be that plaintiff signed off on their 100% tie-off above six feet rule and would not be injured if he had kept his word
  - The six-feet, 100% tie-off applies to stanchions, and they were withheld on this site
- The two contractors claim you can make any connections on these beams from inside the basket.
  - Of the dozens of photos they produced, none show this
    - Coworkers' and other photos show multiple violations—OSHA
  - Expert's drawings—"What's missing from this picture?" (delete all worker connectors)
    - Have to "erase" people to get it
- It doesn't qualify for fall protection if 1) it's prohibited for that use; 2) it will let you hit the ground or a wall, beam, basket; 3) it will swing you into greater danger; 4) it will trip you; 5) it will fall with you; 6) you have to leave it to do the job.

Knowing better all along

- How do we know that they knew what they were doing all along?
  - Because they predicted this type of problem in writing beforehand
  - "Our long-standing safety plan was in place"—just as soon as you sued us and not a moment before

- Consciousness of guilt—credibility challenges
  - "Nobody needed to get out, don't know why he did"
    - Coworker testimony compared to "staged" photo of process on the job
  - "Will provide stanchions"
    - Excerpt of plan compared to photos of the iron at the site
  - "Can build all from lift basket and tie off to them, too"
    - Excerpts of testimony compared to other staged photos (outside baskets) ending with the suspended beam overhead
  - "The contract between the two defendants assigns safety responsibilities to contractor but retains the role of controlling contractor"
  - If any of contractor's safety reps or officers see you performing anything unsafe they will remove you from the site. Knowing all this, defendants still may try to claim their subcontractor "controlled all safety measures on the site"
  - "Lift baskets never move—or tip"
    - Excerpts of testimony compared with manufacturer's warnings and 5,000-pound rule
  - "He's an OSHA 'competent man'"
    - Excerpts of documents/testimony claiming this compared with excerpts denying
  - "Nobody *ever* walks these beams"
    - Excerpts of testimony compared with 50% statement and their staged, coworker photo
  - Supervisor claims he didn't know about safety or that the studs would be shop installed
    - Not only will you find many change orders for technical changes including an order for thirty more studs to a beam even before the job started.

ANCHORS—*the key phrases making the strongest vocabulary for this case story's delivery*

- Knowing two ways: known OSHA violation by shop installing studs and knowing that once installed they block themselves from enforcing lifelines and stanchion, according to plan
- How do we know they knew what they were doing all along? They predicted it in writing in their "on board memo"

- The only choice left is to commit a safety violation or nothing
- The "on board" memo
- The after the fact "lifts and lanyards plan"
- The two contractors (and their sub's safety plan)
- 50%
- 5,000 pounds versus 500 pounds, 1/10 the safe amount
- Six weeks behind schedule
- The specifically prohibited installation
- The low bidder includes known violation
- Conventional fall protection versus 100% fall protection
- Lifelines two ways, proper tie-offs two ways
- Perimeter lines—just left the holes without threading the lifelines through them
- Thirty feet untethered versus six feet "full protection" = false choice
- How can't he see what's right in front of him? The last place a reasonable ironworker looks *is down!*
- "*Hooked on safety*"

FRAMES—*the key case story topics, like the underlined frames in the above story sequence*

- Entire case must be framed "as if" we're talking product defects—i.e., unreasonably dangerous for the end user—the difference being only that this is a work environment/site
- Supervise and enforce
- Unreasonably dangerous work environment/site
- Defense excuses and credibility are both suspect
- *Protection at the time, at the spot, requires prevention by design long ahead of time*
- *Must* show purpose for the OSHA studs prohibition—e.g., trips already caused not just a "violation" by itself
- Need/gain framing damages versus loss framing (*not* where he is—where they have left him)

- Knowing what they were doing all along
- Pain "two ways"—in the neck and neurogenic throughout the body every day for the next thirty years
- Workers work the iron—contractors control their work-site

VISUALS—*the demonstratives that help "storyboard" the presentation*

- Walking-Working/safe work environment
- Harms and losses
- The big three sins now will be divided:
  1. The prohibited installation with OSHA prohibition, lowest bid, and "on board" memo
  2. Withhold lifelines two ways—with "compared to what's"
  3. Leave workers one false choice: commit safety violation or nothing
- The big three "full scopes":
  1. The full scope of the connector's job (any connector on any job)
  2. The full scope of this job—both building and safety plans
  3. The full scope of mechanics of how this tripping hazard works
- "Credibility?"

This board worked very well. We will want to select and then expand each critical item. Will want to actually use photos, head shots, and quotation excerpts to create a left-to-right "compared to what" from the lie to the truth.

- "Nobody needed to get out—don't know why he did"
  - Coworker testimony compared to "staged" photo of process on the job
- "Will provide stanchions"
  - Excerpt of plan compared to photos of the iron at the site
- "Can build all from lift basket and tie off to them, too"
  - Excerpts of testimony compared to other staged photos (outside baskets) ending with the suspended beam overhead
- "Lift baskets never move—or tip"
  - Excerpts of testimony compared with manufacturer's warnings and 5,000-pound rule

- "He's an OSHA 'competent man'"
    - Excerpts of documents/testimony claiming this compared with excerpts denying
- "Nobody *ever* walks these beams"
    - Excerpts of testimony compared with 50% statement and their staged coworker photo

- New risk visual—"It's not the fall, it's the landing"
    1. Numbers of deaths
    2. Broken bones and limbs
    3. Damaged, destroyed organs
    4. Brain and spine injuries
- Supervision and enforcement. Three sections: supervisors, inspectors, contractors
- Lifelines and the proper tie-off points for them two ways: lifelines with stanchions and shorter lanyards, *or* perimeter lifelines. Also, longer retractable lanyards anchored above you
- Lifts ***misused two ways***:
    1. Tie-offs (against manufacturer's recommendations and warnings, and tip hazard—5,000 pounds)
    2. Trying to build connections inside lifts only (impossible and dangerous—load overhead)
- Three "talking heads" visual: Talon rep, defense excuse witnesses 1 and 2
- Coworker staged photo proving his lie compared to what he claimed happened (*see* "Credibility?")
- Same pattern with all staged photos—i.e., violation in almost every one, greatest ironworker danger possible shown in one of them, and almost every lie illustrated in most
- Collect and highlight their "100% fault protection plan" photos to illustrate our "commit safety violation or nothing" anchor
- "*Hooked on safety*"

VOIR DIRE TOPICS

- The comparative fault—damage amounts sequence
- Any legitimate way to sue contractors or companies if worker in dangerous job causes or contributes to his own injuries (one hand—other hand)
- Even if you have to sign off on tens of millions of dollars for it?
- Worker's comp, insurance, liens, perhaps all taken "out of your hands . . ."
- Who already has a limit, no matter what
- 50% of the time, at elevation working without any tethers-tie ins. Who can't see it all the way through, if this juror job demands you accept that as a "norm"?
- Construction work experiences professional or personal, safety enforcement experiences professional or personal, ironwork experiences professional or personal
- Walking working surface and employer provides safe working environment
- Personal, professional experiences with catastrophic injuries?

ADDED DEFENSE EXCUSES

- (Picture of whom we can attack, perhaps defense experts?) *They had a plan in place*, and then show the contradictions
- Contractor CEO would expect them to inquire about shear studs
- Supervisor, on ground, says nope
- Supervisor says: I know nothing, not safety expert, not my job
- Supervisor is contractor's global construction contract guy. He admitted coworker was there to enforce contract, make sure all provisions were enforced, including safety provision
- Coworker came in and said: I wasn't there to enforce safety, I don't know anything about safety
- Supervisor says they had safety responsibilities. Then sends out someone unqualified
- Defense is saying we are misreading the plan. This was an option. All ten fall-protection devices were options
- Defense used one that wasn't a fall-protection device

- 90% shop weld
- Contradictions between defense witnesses
- His experience and history on the job—no falls, no serious injuries
  - Comparable to, in context with others on these two contractors' work site
  - *False choice* left to them all = commit safety violation or nothing to protect
- "De minimus" = no excuse (witnesses)
  - Relies on conventional fall protection as in their plan
- Blocked themselves from using from first, prohibited install on
  - Not only not 100% above six feet, less than 50% at all—usually violating manufacturers recommendations and warnings to do so
  - Contractor's attack on general contractor
  - Plaintiff not doing leading edge work
- "Lifts and lanyards plan"
  - Didn't exist before this injury is caused
  - Devised after-the-fact to defend a lawsuit
- Contractor claims no safety responsibilities
  - *Yet* contractor had all these safety rules
- Contractor says nothing to do with safety on the job
  - Contract speaks to safety

LANDMINES

- "Why did he untie?"—"How was he permitted to untie?"
  - These are equally bad perceptions of our story because they reflect the biggest landmine—perceptually—this case story can offer decision makers, i.e., the presumption early in the process of inviting decision makers to build a helpful case story that 100% tethering is "the norm"
- "The accident." You can say injury they caused, you can say threat they produced, you can say anything but "accident," because an accident has no active party producing it. Learn it, live it, be it

- Control. After the openings in the first debrief, the respondents divided themselves 9-6 against our guy in terms of "who had control of the situation." This was a clear result of our presentation as it came out, and it shows power of one of the biggest landmines this group revealed: that narrowing the scope to this worker, this work-site, and these specific circumstances will kill us
- Stud photo looks unflush
- Personal responsibility (like focus group participant asked)—"Why was he untied even if . . . ," "Nobody untied him, he did it to himself" [do not allow this "norm-ing"/seatbelt analogy to take hold too early]
- The "usual suspects" list: drink, drugs, wind, rain, sun, other people [eliminate quickly and early]
- Putting stanchions first before lifelines
- Jumping to too narrow of a scope—this worker, this site, these bad acts, etc.—before the big, broad scope
- The three big scopes missing: connectors job scope, construction and safety plan scope for this site, mechanics of fall and landing on this site (visual support essential to make these points)
- Not just safety scope—is clear down to the level of both construction and safety plans for this site
- Weight and diabetes traps (see attorney's solutions)
- 100% fall protection gets credibility instantly unless we institute up front 50% untethered as the rule *by necessity*
- Filling defect = perimeter lines (Rx = lifelines two ways anchor)
- Job or death choice cannot be allowed as a consideration
- *Must* show purpose for the OSHA studs prohibition trips already caused not just a "violation" by itself
- Need/gain framing damages versus loss framing (nothing but need framing in the focus group, because habits fade slowly)
- How "can't he see what's right in front of him"
- "Our studs for money" email has to become the "on board" email or it becomes a weakness, not a strength
- Workers work the iron—contractors control their work-site

WORKING CASE PRESENTATION PLAN

THEME

- Wrong medical professional
- Wrong medical procedure
- Will get the wrong medical outcome for your patients

RISKS, RULES, RIGHT WAY

- The number one rule is: all responsible medical professionals will choose to move towards their first priority, doing all that reasonably can be done to ensure their patients' health *and* safety.
- Never miss a chance to link the practitioner with the procedure: untrained, improperly supervised PA *trying* (never say *provides, delivers* or even *does* in reference to the procedure) a dangerous and outmoded procedure is, ipso facto, a "demanding" procedure—even with a doctor in the room.
- Any procedure you try when you are not properly trained or supervised to do is automatically a "demanding" procedure, true?
- (Shifting onus back to doctor, immediately.) The least you could have done was to be there to directly supervise a demanding procedure like that, right?
- You'll note I've shifted from "risks and rewards" to "first priority of patients' health *and* safety" because the framing effort of perceived legitimate—versus false—choices is better served by the latter phrase.
- Medical professionals can never put their personal priorities or personal preferences ahead of their very first priority: protecting the health and safety of their patients.
- "Moving." Divide it up to make the sin bigger.
  - Moving anywhere after you've confirmed the proper placement is bad.
  - Moving forward into the spinal column is the worst.
  - *So, what is the safest way to ensure you are not moving?* (Healing arts expert's bottom line of extender plus fluoroscopy as the bottom line.)
- Not looking. I'd characterize as both "closing his eyes" and "turning off the lights" analogies.
  - The phrase "selective cervical" is a big deal. We don't want decision makers fuzzy at all about the completely improper application of this

procedure at that spot—by doctors, much less untrained and unsupervised nurses.

- Cervical procedure no doctor tries—for diagnosis or treatment.
- Cervical procedure tried by a nurse—when no doctor even tries it there.
- Cervical procedure tried by a nurse untrained and without direct supervision.

INJURY CAUSED

- Link the patient's speaking out on her own behalf at the moment (despite any masking of overly generous painkillers) to the husband's need to hold her up on her failing leg at the time, with the unfortunate and curious lack of pictures that could confirm he had positioning the needle as he has now claimed he did, after the fact.

WHAT TO AVOID

- "Complication(s)." Unlike Harris, this result can't afford to be called anything but a needless injury.
- "Crossing a line." This case story does not lay out best as a violation of a bright-line rule. It seems to work much better as a story about *direction and progress* (a "journey" metaphor). Nobody does this thing in the neck at all—no doctor, *much less* a nurse, and much, much less an improperly supervised and untrained PA at that. There is no good, patient-centered reason to go backwards to a more dangerous, less effective procedure when you can move forward toward better health and better safety.
- "Choice(s)." We want to undercut the perception by the decision makers of these actions as valid "choices" at any time under these circumstances. They are invalid, at the least, because they do not put the *first priority* of patient health *and* safety first. Success setting up and reinforcing that frame will allow us to show that the real "choice" operating here that produces the needless injuries was a "false choice" of placing medical professionals' preferences and priorities ahead of their absolutely first priority.
- Other invalid aspects of the false choice: in the neck (wrong procedure for that); by a nurse; by an untrained nurse; no real distinction between diagnostic and therapeutic effects (since it's the wrong procedure for that spot); ultimately, you cannot just *choose* not to look at what you are doing and still claim you hold patient health and safety as your first priority.

DEFENSE EXCUSES—REFRAMES

- Just "pushed pause" on this improper use of personnel and procedures until the lawsuits resolve. No intention of not continuing to put medical professionals' preferences ahead of their first priority of patient health and safety.
- GP's damaging attitudes and conclusions must be reframed as we discussed, by letting the defense call her. That can also be bolstered by linking her "defense advocacy" to the "pushed pause" image of immediate and ongoing intent to threaten the patient population in the future.
- "Pre-damaged goods" so bad she was willing to endure injections.
    - It was bad enough for her to be willing to endure injections into her spine. Reasonably expecting they would be done the right way, at the right spot, by the right practitioner, whether they worked or not. Never was willing—and never asked—for improper procedure, at the improper spot by an untrained nurse without a doctor even directly supervising.

SOME LIKELY VISUALS

- Number of procedures possible to do when it's just the doctor, and under these negligent circumstances. Title: Personal Preferences
- Three "plane" fluoroscope images (illustrations) next to a black box, representing his "closed eyes").
- Illustrations of the two immediate signs (her pain and husband's needed support) with excerpted testimony, next to a third image of a chart page with a blank spot circled in red.
- Exemplar pictures of proper placement, next to the same black box used to show "closed eyes" to show how these objective images that *could* exonerate him have "not yet been produced."

Chapter Seven

What's Your Story? Voir Dire and Opening Statement

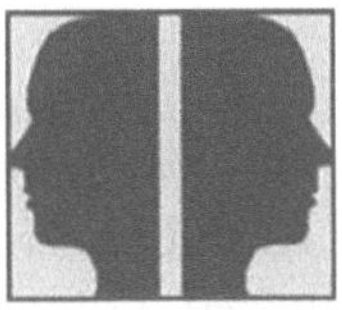

A human being is never impartial. He is biased by everything he has experienced, suffered, and seen.
—*Harry Lipsig*

7.1 Plowing—Voir Dire

7.1.1 Surveying the Ground

George Santayana reportedly said, "We look for similarities in differences and differences in similarities." In approaching voir dire of prospective jurors, cover the similarities with your focus groups first, then handle the differences. Trial professionals have had to relinquish the false sense of certainty in the old notion of a fixed, predetermined case story. But by now, the focus group(s) have provided a refined version of the most effective case story to present. Potential jurors' responses can be considered against this story for similarities and differences in the story elements and structures they are most likely to produce. Instead of seeking out the right type of person to hear a supposedly fixed story, at least part of trial professionals' attention can be invested in watching and tracking all signs of implicit understandings and memories revealed by the verbal and nonverbal responses of venire panelists. Valuable to listen and watch for are comments and hints indicating people beginning to engage in building a story similar to the one that will be presented in opening statements and evidence, sometimes despite the type of person revealing them.

One of the most uncomfortable and important ways in which voir dire needs to mirror a focus group is in the clear message attorneys must convey from the start to every member of the panel. That is, whatever panelists have to say about the beliefs, attitudes, and experiences they walked in the room with, no matter how challenging or difficult to the client's positions, "Those are the responses we need to hear—in full." As in a focus group, you must establish that the only wrong answer is to have a response and not to mention it.

David Ball describes this essential task as "Lowering the bar to the worst answers."[1] Taking that one step further: once you get the worst answer, always follow up with "What else?" and then "How so?" Answers to "What else?" questions net the most expansion into the panelists' personal stories, and "How so?" answers let you focus more on the context or references, and the emergent story structures that attend them.

The same focus group rule to invite expansion and inclusion in panelists' responses applies here, in the beginning, for each person, as they address each topic question. Hunting for story elements and structures that panelists are likely to use requires getting enough uncontaminated, minimally influenced input from everyone to make some well-informed judgments about what they say, how they say it, and what's most likely true today about the world between their ears from which it came. To accomplish this, attorneys need to hold back the temptation to lead the panelists as they would a witness. The most effective model for voir dire is that of a conversation with the world's best listener—as far from cross-examination as human discourse gets. Unfortunately, in a world in which people get what they rehearse, not what they intend, the temptation to cross-examine venire panelists often prevails.

Consider this example of the best of intentions for an open-ended inquiry getting turned (driven) from the many directions the panelists are free to take into a forced choice between two conclusions introduced by the attorney asking the questions. The case dealt with claims of professional neglect by an in-home healthcare agency and its employees working with an older person with a number of preexisting health problems. Trial professionals planning voir dire initially proposed this introduction to a discussion of one of the basic, hot topics contained in the case story suggested by the focus group.

> Home Healthcare, Incorporated. The question is, how do your life experiences and the values you've built from them tend to make you look at these in-home healthcare companies? For example, if we were to say you had to pick between two options [anchored spatially, side to side] to describe which best fits your view of "in-home healthcare companies," which option would you tend to lean toward? Do you look at them mainly as companies sending healthcare professionals into homes for patient care, or do you see them more as sending people to serve primarily as companions, housekeepers, or even "babysitters" in those homes? What leads you more to that view over the other? How so? Tell me more.

---

1. David Ball, *David Ball on Damages: A Plaintiff's Attorney's Guide to Personal Injury and Wrongful Death Cases* (Louisville, CO: National Institute for Trial Advocacy, 2001): 176. *See also* David Ball, *David Ball on Damages: The Essential Update* (Louisville, CO: National Institute for Trial Advocacy, 2005).

The plan, after eliciting a number of responses and follow-up answers, would have been to question how seriously people that took the "babysitters" route might handle the idea of professional neglect as a legal claim applied to such a job.

Both story frame anchors—health professionals and babysitters— affecting how people look at the job called "home health aide" emerged from focus group work prior to trial. This proposal for questioning highlights the very real danger of just how easily old juror typing habits and habituated bias toward cross-examination of panelists can combine to reassert an unadapted *interpretation* theme for case stories for the team planning their voir dire. That attitude shifts the focus remarkably quickly from a search for people's apparent qualifications to *construct* case stories favoring the most effective models emerging from focus group work right back to a model of the world in which jurors are assumed to fall into one or two limited types of people who think in one of a very few predetermined ways about select aspects of a case story that exists in a fixed, unchangeable form far outside their heads.

An alternative, open-ended inquiry might start with a general case fact (in-home healthcare companies), then shift immediately to pulling out as many different responses as possible, rather than assuming we already know how many of every variety of response and association about these jobs the whole panel walked in with before we asked. Even if the group eventually settles on the choice forced on them by the first example, we will have had time to discover much more revealing information about, among other things, the means by which people learned those distinctions (every variety and association); how long they have held them; what alternatives they also hold; to what degree their attitudes are fixed, strong, or positional in ways directly affecting the building case stories in their heads; and the distribution through the group of these notions and experiences. Also, the panelists will be treated to the experience of a lawyer apparently valuing and respecting their individual points of view, and reinforcing the critical idea that panelists' views are the subject of the inquiry, rather than the forced choices from a lawyer-generated menu of just two items, in the lawyer's language, with no discussion or exceptions allowed unless a panelist wants to openly buck that implicit trend. The following is a good example:

> Ladies and gentlemen, you've heard that this case will involve evidence about what are called in-home healthcare agencies. First, just a show of hands, who here has any firsthand experience with these companies—they send employees into the home to help out with usually older people who need assistance due to past health problems? Firsthand experiences, either in your home, or that of a close relative with whom you were—or are—involved? Now, what about secondhand experience with these in-home healthcare companies—that is, a relative that is not so close or so nearby that has used them, or maybe a friend or coworker that has? And how about third-hand experience? That would be those that have read or heard about this kind of work being done

for people in the home, and so you've got some ideas about it, but nobody you know closely has actually used it. Third-hand folks that have learned about these services somehow, but not from the experience of someone you actually know who had them in his or her home?

OK. Let's start with the people who have just heard about them through reading or discussion with other people you know, or maybe TV or radio accounts, but you have no real hands-on connections to this kind of business. Remember, the subject here is you and your own ideas and experiences, and the only wrong answer is holding back one you honestly have. We're all bound to learn a lot from a lot of sources about this kind of work as we go along here, but I'd like to hear your honest impressions about this kind of home service business now. Those of you who have third-hand experiences[2] [*refer to a few by name or by indication*], what is it you've heard that these companies and their employees do for people, by and large, when they go into their homes? How'd you come to that view? What's important about it to you, so far? What else? Please, say some more about that.

If you take a moment to analyze and compare the first proposed set of questions with the more open-ended example, you can see the differences:

- In the first, forced-choice version, who controls the assignment of the terms of the job in question?
- Where is the inquiry steered almost immediately toward explaining why a position is held, or describing its context and development for each panelist? Who is the more active party in the discussion?
- Which is aimed more at discovering the story elements within responses, and which is targeted more toward typing the panelist?

---

2. When identifying influential experiences in the lives of voir dire panelists, it is often very important to distinguish beliefs, attitudes, and positions derived from firsthand experience over secondhand and third-hand varieties. In many cases, firsthand experiences are richer, more variable, and less polarized in the mind than those held by someone that has arm's length experience, or that has just heard of the experience but has not been more involved with it. However, whatever positions that person has adopted will almost undoubtedly be used as a yardstick by fellow jurors in deliberations with the more experienced, juror "expert." This often holds true even when the panelist has no direct experience at all. Unfortunately, because these connections to beliefs about the valuable or heinous nature of the experience at hand (dentistry, police conduct, surgery, accountant audits, construction contracts, etc.) are founded on the strength of a personal link to the source of the secondhand or third-hand accounts (best friend, big brother, Aunt Kate, Rush Limbaugh), not directly on the experience itself, these positions are often both much more impervious to change and much less accurate in their depth and detail. This makes people with second- and third-hand experiences sometimes more dangerous juror "experts" than those with actual, hands-on connections, but both are influential.

- Which is more likely to deliver open windows onto the referencing and story building parts of the panelists' minds that you came to explore?
- When the time comes to ask people to excuse themselves from serving on this trial, based on beliefs and experiences that could lead them to prejudge parts of the case one way or another, which group will be more likely to acknowledge that influence: those given only two choices, or those asked to explain their own situations, their own way, in their own words?
- Is it less controlled and more challenging to do? Yes.
- Is it worth it? Results will tell.

Consider our earlier example of the gas-inhalation injury case. After refining the focus group input, the defense of the plant-owning company had distilled about a half-dozen story-centered topics for exploration with potential jurors. One such topic would be "authority and responsibility on hazardous job sites."

Such collections of voir dire topics directly related to the structures and elements of the case stories need to be placed, as a group, near the beginning of the inquiry, but usually not at the very start. Other, more easily addressed questions, such as hardships, knowledge of parties, and the like, can help set the group at ease and prepare them for the most focused part of the enterprise: the hot topics derived from the case story structure itself and its many possible alternative versions.

Theme. Going in, the trial team knew that the theme for the case story, from the plant-owning company's position, not that of the company supplying the contract workers, was *abandoned safety*. This theme had multiple, helpful reference points within the case facts and the story line of events for inviting views of control over the outcome, which viewed in hindsight, found that control elsewhere.

Scope. The story element of scope required a consistent and disciplined broadening of perceptions of everything: from the workers on the various giant vessels and scaffolds seen as a group, not isolated, to the numbers, acts, and people involved in similar kinds of tasks in many big plants, over many years and a variety of risks—long before this day.

Point of View. The point of view for the best case story was that of the second defendant company linked directly to its contract crew that day, but neither of them by themselves. (You'll recall that focus group members blending the two defendants together, or looking for responsibility in an either/or framework only at the top or the bottom of the ladder, worked out stories that did not help the defense much.)

Sequence. The sequence derived from the focus group work needed to invite decision makers to start stories in and around the broad arena of job risks, generally, and risks for these large plant sites, specifically, so that the standards established, applied or *abandoned* would carry the most weight later on in the stories they built as the presentation progressed.[3]

So as the topic of authority and responsibility on job sites is introduced, the defense attorney needs to be very careful to lower the barriers to the worst answers about those story elements themselves, not just the words tipping toward one verdict outcome over another. Those eventual verdict decisions will first have to travel through a unique, private version of the case story for each decision maker in order to come out with their final word.

> So we know who here has some personal experience with work on big petroleum, chemical, or steel plants, or knows someone else that does. We also know who's got some ideas about that work from what they've learned, heard, or read. Can we all agree that there are hazards to health and safety for the workers out there, in all these kind of plants? [*Wait for and acknowledge the responses.*] So here's the question. Who has a hand in, or *who's in charge* of safety out there? How do you think that works—or should work?"

As the discussion ensues, the tip toward the top of the ladder implicit in phrasing the question as "Who's in charge?" suggesting a single, higher authority character for the job, needs to be sought out and reinforced among the early responses, and all follow-up answers that reflect it. Also, the defense lawyer needs to be wary of jumping to highlight and reinforce answers that she would most like to hear: those concentrating responsibility nearer the bottom of the ladder with the work crew bosses or the hands-on workers themselves (note the characterization "for the workers," not "the workers have"). Those story structures and the elements of point of view, scope, and active parties that they reflect can wait.

First, what needs to be invited to expand are all the many possible tracks a story could use to run away from those desirable ends. It's hard to march through the minefield without a map. It's equally hard for people to turn down the juror job if they are not clearly aware of the barriers they carry to a totally evenhanded hearing of all the parties' stories, all the way through. The more they reveal to us, the more they reveal to themselves, too:

---

3. Civil and criminal defenses, which usually go second in courtroom presentations, need a story package that can be readily and effectively adopted by decision makers—in or out of jury boxes—perhaps even more than their colleagues preceding them. If all they do is sit back and attempt to deconstruct their opponents' stories while presenting, they've abandoned the more effective choice of providing an alternative story for decision makers to use in forming their judgments. Since the story comes first and picking one apart only serves to reinforce it as you go, the need should be obvious. Voir dire, opening statement, and many cross-examinations are vehicles to reinforce either your story or the lack of one. No third choice.

> What is it about the company that owns the plant that gets your attention here, Mr. Rubble? What led you to that way of looking at it? How is that important to you? Say a little more about that, please.

Rather than interrupting the third, fourth, and fifth person's version of this top-down view of safety authority and responsibility on the hazardous site, the attorney should be interested in turning up the *elements* of the stories or story fragments, referenced for their similarities or differences from those already determined through focus group work to be the most helpful. How is the way this person is structuring stories reflected in or between the lines they say? Along the way, verbal and visual anchors, life-experience analogies, and other valuable gems will be offered for free, as long as the follow-ups continue, just as in a focus group.

For instance, in the plant injury case, we know that a person that automatically sorts the people in his stories into distinct viewpoints, instead of blending two or even one big conglomeration, is potentially more helpful to our ends—this, no matter what he says in the abstract about the nature or particulars of any of the distinct character's safety jobs. Separating instead of blending characters' roles is the story-building strength we are seeking. There are equivalent strengths to be sought out as they relate to every element and factor present in the final presentation plan.

Note that this kind of advantage disappears quickly if the attorney slips into detail spin: the potential decision makers start building inner tales more from the case specific facts, rather than recalling them from their own life references. Thus, you would never isolate one kind of plant at this point in your questions, when three or more kinds can be consistently menued for inclusion in the panelists' reflections. As long as the topic is authority applied to safety in *any* hazardous job site, you can more safely rate the indications you get back about panelists' life references, while lessening the temptations for them to build and comment on detailed versions of this story too soon. Just as in a focus group, *balance* is a key feature. Offer enough of a story to focus the discussion where we need it, but not so much that the personal stories are eclipsed in panelists' minds by speculation on the trial facts to come.

The ideal for which to aim is voir dire free of case facts. Shaving off as many specific factual details as possible in favor of specifics drawn from the actual lives of the panelists—relevant and related to the case by their structure—is a more beneficial goal. Voir dire is all about what the panelists are bringing to the table, just as a focus group is. It is thus less effective the more it becomes a list of cherry-picked facts presented as either/or referenda for panelists to pick between. It discloses little of what might have contributed to their selection in the artificial, forced choice, while boxing the speakers into preselected types. Trial professionals going into voir dire focused on the case stories jurors are likely to begin building are less interested in relating trial facts, and more interested in hearing all about the facts of life in the stories each person relates.

Milton Erickson rode the stray horse all the way to its home because he never fooled himself into thinking that he knew the right direction to take before the horse did. In voir dire examinations based more on life stories than the lawyer's case story, panelists will often let the attorney questioning them follow them right to their own cause strikes, as long as the attorney demonstrates the awareness, in word and deed, that it is *only* the panelist who knows where they are.

7.1.2 Mining the Mindsets

The territory to be explored here emerges from what could be called the current *mindsets* of the panelists, as they relate to or engage with those major topics of your case story selected for use during voir dire examination. Mindsets, for our purposes, cover the mental waterfront, from habits in perceptions and stored life experiences outside consciousness, through the thinking and psychological habits used to reinforce and maintain them. They are not just biases or beliefs, but the whole mental construct that enables them to work, establishing and maintaining certain stories about the life each person experiences as more prevalent than others. They can cover everything from the habits that create story categories, through those that generate their narratives, to the rhetoric with which the stories are expressed, explained, or defended.

For example, a few years ago, a Dr. Ronald Glasser wrote an article[4] describing five mindsets that he perceived as popular, if not dominant, for a great number of Americans when the topic was medical care, and especially managed medical care. Before the backlash from some of the public against managed care institutions, Glasser contended that these businesses sold themselves by helping build up mindsets, or story lines of expectations, including:

1. All doctors are rich and omnipotent.
2. The operation is [probably] unnecessary.
3. The doctor is like a mechanical device.
4. Patients love to go to the hospital.
5. Sickness is the patient's fault, and death is a preventable disease.

Each of these plot line summaries, much like a thesis statement for a case story, were filled out with accompanying facts and stories, appealing to some of the public's life experiences, to be used as reinforcement. For instance, sickness could be seen more as the fault of a patient who failed to exercise; who indulged in known risk behaviors such as smoking, drinking, and overeating the "wrong" foods; who failed to take care of himself in any number of ways, and yet acts surprised when his

4. "The Doctor Is Not In," *Harper's* (March 1998): 35–41.

"unnecessary" illnesses, perhaps "self-imposed," are not immediately cared for and cured at cut rates by a system overburdened by thousands of similar personal-care slackers.

By now, the appeal to certain thinking habits such as hindsight, norming, availability, and attribution, to psychological habits such as identification, and some references to images of personal control and responsibility (*active party*) from the point of view of the patient should be fairly easy to pick out of the messages above. An implicit theme suggesting *scarcity of available help* can raise fear and self-preservation drives as the story is presented in press releases, magazine show exposés co-written by medical businesses, printed feature stories and editorials, and talk radio broadcasts. Many people engaged by such presentations establish, maintain, and begin reinforcing their own versions of expectations (*mindsets*) about medical care based on the line these stories follow.

Of course, nobody made the five story lines quite as obvious as Dr. Glasser, because the implied message is always more effective than the declared one in a fair fight. Implicit messages inspire implicit memory to build implicit understandings. Judgments are formed from the stories that result. And the majority bias is rarely seen as a bias, just as "right" by those that carry it.

It is unrealistic for a trial professional to walk into a courtroom[5] expecting a nicely detailed review of the pedigree of the story lines he may face behind the eyes of each venire member. But there are many different ways, illustrated in Chapter Five, to tease out indicators of the whole story behind the mental scenes, and almost all can be applied in voir dire with little change, until the cause strikes begin to be set up.

One tool not explored in great detail so far would be *anchors*, whether verbal, visual, or even of a feeling variety. Anchors are conditioned or rehearsed responses to perceptual cues:

- A phrase
- A voice tone
- A mental image conjured from memory
- A marked-out gesture
- An image on a chart

Everyone builds their own to reflect their own inner world's arrangements, and also adopts anchors liberally from the thousands afloat in our environments. Among

5. Throughout this section on voir dire, observations about mindsets, their effect, and how they are best elicited by less direct means are also applicable to those that would be confronted in negotiation, mediation, or arbitration.

other functions, they can cue the imposition of one mindset over another, when the connections they each reinforce are brought to mind, i.e., "babysitter" versus "health professional."

7.2 Medical Loss Ratio

Were the voir dire examination to require input from the stories each person had about managed medicine, there is an anchor phrase quoted by Dr. Glasser in the same article that could be used to scope reactions to the "medicine is scarce," "doctors are greedy," and "other patients are undeserving" theme reflected earlier.[6] That verbal anchor is "medical loss ratio," a technical term that serves as an anchor for initiated professionals. The term is an arcane, annoying curiosity to the rest of us. The wise attorney consistently sandwiches such terms between two iterations of its plain English form, particularly during a first encounter with potential jurors. More particularly since suspicion of the legal system can be inflamed by the indiscriminate use of private anchors of lawyers.

"Medical loss ratio" is the term the early HMOs used to describe the actual outlay of cash for a patient's treatment—a loss to the company and its shareholders—money lost to covering medical care. Cost consciousness, not profit, is where many first look when thinking about the healthcare industry's relationship to money. Introducing that term to a panel primed by discussion about their own experiences with the rising costs of medicine could provide insight into the stories driving the responses offered to explain the value or meaning of the term. The professional should pay attention to the point of view and active ingredients reflected directly or implicitly in the emerging hints about stories. So the answer to the question "lost *to whom*?," could be revealing—revealing enough that you may not want to lead that answer directly during the discussion. Opt instead to follow up repeatedly with people whose revelations about the stories driving their answers are at odds with the one you came to court to tell.

Mindsets within the jury pool are a constant subject of survey and focus group research and are a never-ending discussion in trial lawyer organizations and publications. From primarily the 1980s into the late 1990s, some in the plaintiffs' bar researched and wrote a lot about the negative mindsets of jurors often referred to as "Gen-X" jurors.[7] Because many "Gen-Xers" attested to beliefs that prompted

6. Note the commonalities with the "fittest survive" theme cited for stories about business in general earlier. It is in our nature as creatures of habit to build perceptual and mental habits, and then use the same ones to respond in many, many areas of our lives. For example, operating metaphors of sports, games, or war are ubiquitous.

7. Lisa Brennan, "Pitching the Gen-X Jury," *National Law Journal* (June 11, 2004): 1. Demographically speaking, Gen-Xers were in their twenties during the Reagan era. It was followed by Generations Y and Z. Although biological generations are measured in twenty- to twenty-five-year chunks, this cultural division is closer to ten years.

more suspicion and less faith in societal and cultural institutions, many plaintiff attorneys feared their thinking patterns. Gen-Xers, however, have been found to reveal life-story structures that may actually *favor* some elements of plaintiff cases—for example in valuing damages. Many younger jurors (Gen-X is now one or two generations older) have little attachment to the traditional link between money and character or status and virtue associated with more positive views of cultural institutions. Many see money and success as a market commodity or product acquisition. Their personal stories don't necessarily put obstacles in the way of assigning cash values for harms that more engaged relationships to the meaning of money often do. Assuming that a plaintiff lawyer is able to reach a person with such mindsets in a case presentation on liability, the numbers for valuing the harms are no less likely to ring true for that person because of their otherwise negative life stories. Such mindsets could make a strong damage juror, but by different means than the person that identifies intrinsic life values with cash amounts.

7.3 The "Criminal Mindset"

Today, one mindset all civil attorneys will confront during a voir dire interview is the "criminal mindset." Most potential jurors have more familiarity with criminal legal procedure (largely because of popular culture) than they ever will with civil procedure. This doesn't mean they are free from leanings about civil cases. The majority surveyed imagined they would be a defendant, not a plaintiff, if a lawsuit were ever to befall them.

It means that all things being equal, most potential jurors during voir dire tend to:

- Look for a higher standard of proof against the alleged wrongdoers ("beyond a reasonable doubt").
- Seek out just one source of wrongdoing even among multiple defendants and plaintiffs.
- Expect proofs about intent or motive to harm as part of the case story.

Assuming that the expectations this exclusive mindset fosters featured strongly for a potential juror, imagine how it could affect perceptions and narratives responding to an instruction in an injury case that asks for "a cause," without requiring that the cause be proven as being "the" cause of the claimed harms.

Trial professionals know from experience that absolute positioning on singular fault and exclusive views of the cause proofs are important to the reauthoring of the case story, which depend more on multiple, even ambiguous, sources of control. A version of our job-description inoculation against burden-shifting by jurors in Chapter Four could be of use in this situation. The needs of the particular story will dictate when in the hot topics sequence it should come up, and how much attention should be devoted to its discussion with panel members.

Keep in mind that the other-than-conscious mind is present and never asleep. The story construction process begins in earnest just as the attorneys stand to introduce themselves if not before. As the focus group critic Gerald Zaltman assures us, "Unconscious thoughts are the most accurate predictors of what people will actually do." In examining panelists, the attorney should invite the most relevant parts of people's life stories to surface and be fully referenced during discussion about the major topics of the case (expansion and inclusion). Reveal as much as possible about the unconscious mindsets that will affect the rebuilding of that case story in each of the actual jurors when opening statements begin.

7.4 "Kill the Lone Gunman"

For an effective voir dire examination of even the smallest panel, the job is too big for one person and one mind. For one thing, it's too much work for one person to take adequate notes about the questions and answers passing back and forth between the lawyer and the panelists. Here is a partial list of other issues that can emerge from every one of these interviews that make the lone gunman approach very ill advised.

Poker playing. Every person in a courtroom inquiry will be playing poker with their questioner to some extent. Despite good intentions, they will move to suppress their responsiveness in the words they release to you, the engagement with which they do so, and in their affect just after answering.

You can't see me. As with many people in public group settings, if a person is not talking, they often act as if they are invisible, not simply silent. This cures the poker-playing problem. If there is someone with an eagle eye scanning those people near the panelist answering, she will be rewarded with multiple nonverbal cues (signs of agreement or disagreement, editorializing, signs of confusion, and emotional reactions) emanating freely from the silent partners of the poker-playing speakers. The lawyer with the seating chart who is doing the talking can't look away to check other reactions.

Cataloguing characteristics. For every panelist who speaks, some basic factors need to be collected, considered, and recorded. These factors include reactions and input on story elements and story topics about which the attorney interviews folks. When "on topic," it is asking a lot to expect the attorney to stop and take verbatim notes of the critical answers to cause-strike related questions for later use in making those strikes. Each party advertises his or her sensory preferences (visual over auditory, words over feelings, etc.), which by now may be known to be a major lever in the processing of the case story at the primary, perceptual level, before the thinking habits of narrative even take hold. Associations with the major story topics reviewed, whether directly or indirectly addressed, need to be noted for every panelist. If the observers possess the skills, noting how each panelist expresses distinct agreement and disagreement nonverbally can be useful in tracking his or her early responses to the case stories to be presented to the panel.

"Juror seeking juror." Relationships develop, sometimes quickly, inside the jury box and in the halls outside. It is too much to ask the trial professional to observe, track, and record the verbal and nonverbal development and advertising of such connections for future use.

Maintain close contact with the people at the table assisting counsel in tracking the course of all the communication (spoken or otherwise) offered during voir dire. The assistants can help track two important issues: who to follow up with on the panel and who has yet to be invited into the discussions. Evenly dividing attention and reinforcement among panelists is as effective during voir dire as it is at the beginning of a focus group. Before beginning with the panelists, it helps to review the lists of prior references and tasks for the moderator from Chapter Four, as most apply equally to voir dire interviews run as focus groups, rather than as cross-examinations. They all help encourage and engage mindsets of value to voir dire.

Prior life references to elicit, make more available, and reinforce:

- Prior jury experiences—actual or imagined
- Social habits, group dynamics, and peer pressures
- Herd instinct—following leads and leaders
- The job frame
- The "as-if" frame

Attorney (moderator) tasks at the outset:

- Rapport/mirroring—physically and of nonverbal marking through voice and movements
- Matching responses—key phrases, implications, story frames, subjects, and perceptual preferences (visual, auditory, or kinesthetic)
- Spreading the wealth of group attention ("more input is better," group input as a resolving force)
- Setting frames to handle inevitable challenges to the conduct and context of the interview ("I'd need to hear the facts first.")
- Building trends, modeling helpful responses, and using presupposition
- Dealing with spoken and unspoken fears

- Shrinking the job frame
- Introducing humor
- Encouraging response potentials
- Setting anchors for helpful life experiences and references, rule adherence, and responsiveness
- Teaching the applicable rules

7.4.1 Logistics

Before these tasks can begin, there are some logistics to be sorted and dealt with by the trial team. Take the last item on the attorney's task list first. Voir dire on the critical instructions must not be curtailed, so clear beforehand with the judge how far the attorney can go in such an inquiry.

Instructions. Bowing to the assumption that any juror will follow any instruction from the bench, is not acceptable. These people have volunteered to do a job that requires them to apply the law to the facts they hear, see, and try. If someone is more or less constitutionally able than the next person to follow those rules, then one is less suited for the job that requires a particular rule to be applied. There is no more relevant area of inquiry in voir dire than that of the individual panelists' abilities to follow the instructions they will need to apply to the facts in evidence. So be sure you know exactly how that inquiry should be conducted, in discussion with the judge. Be sure you've learned from your focus group which instructions or verdict question phrases on which that inquiry would best be concentrated.

Time. Next on the logistics list is time, a major bone of contention in courts across the land. Judges must balance the right of every litigant to a thorough and probing voir dire of the potential jurors with the right of every litigant to a speedy resolution of their case. Attorneys and trial professionals should avoid easy pitfalls. When scheduling the time in advance, avoid settling a deadline, such as by noon or by the first afternoon break. Rather, get specific commitments to the number of hours that will be afforded each party, so that lengthy motions, scheduling discussions, outside interruptions, or unexpected delays don't turn a three-hour voir dire into the last twenty minutes before your lunch deadline.

Questionnaires. If supplemental juror questionnaires will be used, the logistics dealing with their production, distribution, collection, and disbursement among the parties and the bench, and the processing time allowed, all need to be thoroughly covered before a single panelist's pen is put to paper. These tools can increase the efficiency with which voir dire examinations are run. Handled poorly, they add a layer of confusion and consternation to a process they can help streamline. Just be sure every step the paper will follow is well traced and rehearsed before the actual event. Do not assume you can burden the court clerk with this task.

Attorney-Conducted Voir Dire. Some courts have had little experience with attorneys skilled in the art of conducting a voir dire examination well. Many courts and many lawyers suffer the mindset fostered by the powerful perceptual habit of deletion, unintentionally imposed by a legal education on many practitioners even years removed from law school.[8] Law schools train lawyers in cross-examination technique in the rules of evidence and the arcane language of the law. Yet, they ignore focused practice in wide-ranging, often intimate conversation. Therefore, many legal professionals discard the need for the latter, in favor of the familiar former. Other-than-conscious convention overriding conscious exceptions, once again, produces voir dire as cross-examination.

Without thinking of the implications of what he was saying, a judge was once heard interrupting an accomplished trial attorney after his very first question, before an answer was even voiced. The question began: "How do you feel about . . . ?" before it was loudly shut down from the bench. Then, in front of the panel,[9] the judge said, "Counsel, you know better than that. I'll have none of that here. Ask your questions in the proper form or not at all."

After a short bench conference, the court made it clear that it's idea of proper form for voir dire questions used to elicit mostly inarticulable beliefs, attitudes, and inclinations was to use only closed-ended questions, which can all be answered with either a yes, no, or a show of hands. Were the court to avoid even accidental contact with a potential juror's true mindsets, it could hardly have done better except by eliminating voir dire altogether. (Something else, incidentally, to get straight before you start. In federal court in New York City, recently, a judge made the whole effort moot by starting voir dire, on the record, declaring she had "no interest in hearing about the jurors' beliefs.")

If necessary, be ready to show the court using examples from prior voir dire discussions or those generated in focus groups, what purpose is served by a series of open-ended questions in this conscious inquiry into other-than-conscious processes. Also show the opposite side, filling in the "compared to what" answer. Show exactly how closed-ended questions can't determine who is best equipped by their backgrounds, their beliefs, and their story building proclivities, to fairly hear and judge both sides' stories all the way through the presentation process. Nor can close-ended questions determine who is better equipped for the same job in a different

---

8. Harvard Law Professor Arthur Miller is often credited with calling the fruits of a legal education a "special form of insanity."

9. Research on courtroom communication has been filled, for more than a decade, with examples of how nonverbally expressed expectations from the bench influence jurors. All the more reason for the advocates—who have greater opportunity to influence, and whose job descriptions require it—to pay attention to how that influence is passed not just by what is said, but often much more by how. *See* A. J. Hart, "Naturally Occurring Expectation Effects," *Journal of Personality and Social Psychology*, 68 (1995): 109–115; and Peter Blanck, ed., "Interpersonal Expectations in the Courtroom," in *Interpersonal Expectations: Theory, Research and Applications* (New York, NY: Cambridge University Press, 1993): 64–87.

case, with different story elements. Be sure the question of a person's intrinsic fairness is not allowed to be set up, since in most cases that is not the issue.

In civil cases, the basic issues are:

- Bias about people, institutions, organizations, acts, situations, or circumstances involved
- Bias about the cause of action
- Bias about damage elements claimed

Be sure you have developed a way for each party on the trial team doing the observing and recording to note their observations and get them communicated among the team in the most effective way. This means staking out a place to talk on breaks and deciding which person will ride herd on those conversations. Before the day of trial, choose an acceptable method for collecting, considering, and acting on everyone's input.

Pretrial Motions

Tasks to accomplish in pretrial motions include approval of visual aids to be used in voir dire, opening, or during trial, and agreements about how the trial team will be addressed and dealt with by the other side(s). If the attorney plans to bring a consultant into court during voir dire and/or the rest of trial, agreements should be elicited that grandstanding through blackening of the consultant won't be a part of the opposition's performance for the panelists. If the attorney plans to use a consultant and tries to hide that fact from the opposition, make sure the input the consultant can provide isn't lost because nobody found a secluded place and arranged time to compare notes.

Biases

As the juror job interviews begin, remember all three major story variables are in play:

1. The influence of potential juror backgrounds and beliefs
2. The influence of the teller, and the telling
3. How the telling is referenced and imagined

The most dynamic of the three, the potential and eventual case stories to be built by these panelists, are ever present. Each person's storymaking machinery will be engaged to some extent during the process. For many, their private case story construction will start as soon as the questions and answers do. Knowing how important the early stages of that process are to each person's production of possible story lines, down to the one to be used in final decisions, great care needs to be given to how the process is approached and conducted. If you are to learn as much as you can about how each person may start leaning in their story-building efforts, you must lower the bar to bad answers and avoid leading questions on your follow-ups. Plus, you must lower the bar to getting full answers to personal questions despite the impediments inherent in a big group of strangers, sitting in a court of law. Fortunately, you have a script to follow for a good deal of that process and its primary points are discussed in Chapter Four. There are, of course, a few big differences that need to be addressed up front as a supplement to the focus group introduction.

The point of voir dire interviews, how they fit into the trial process, and how each panelist can do the best job all need to be clarified by whichever attorney wants the benefits of the effort to fall his way. One way to start is to be direct.

> Ladies and gentlemen, we are starting a process that will take up a fair amount of time, probably into the afternoon, because it is the first, important step of many in this system we Americans have for holding jury trials to resolve our disputes fairly. This significant first step, as the judge just told you, is called the voir dire exam, or interview, or discussion—pick the term you like. It is one of only a couple of times when we attorneys will be talking directly to you folks, and it is the one and only time you will have a chance to talk back to us lawyers. Some of you, I'm sure, will want to take full advantage of any chance to talk back to lawyers, and you should know that we welcome the input.
>
> So what are we going to talk about? Who has some ideas about what this voir dire interview is meant to do?
>
> [*If there are simply no responses, you can do one of two things: pick a likely subject to start with, or back up and menu a few possibilities and then ask again.*]

Panelists' backgrounds, life experiences, and beliefs built up from those unique sets of experiences need to be brought out and reinforced for the whole group. Before examining those experiences and how they seem to be aiding the construction of story elements, reinforce some of the basic frames for the enterprise. Do this by raising the profile of the job, while simplifying the task at hand and expanding the options to more than this case in this room.

> So you know this is all about what *you* are bringing to the table, and not yet about the facts of the case or the particular law the judge will give you to apply to those facts—not yet. Why is it so important for a jury of someone's peers, as you said [*indicating*], to get their backgrounds and experiences considered, and especially the lessons they've learned so far in life, before they eventually decide for themselves—yourselves—just who would be best suited by those experiences to sit in judgment of this case, and not best suited to some other case down the hall? One answer is that in the American system of justice,

it is exactly that mix of all sorts of different experiences that makes *all* the difference if justice is the goal. In America, we put our trust in common sense. And we expect that living your life has given you a fair share of common sense, so far, true? [*Some more than others. Yep, I agree.*] The whole point of having juries made up of one's peers is to allow everyone on the panel to pool all their experiences and what they've learned from them, and to apply what you've each learned from life to help each other resolve the conflict in front of you. We trust your accumulated pool of knowledge and common sense to be the very best way of determining justice. That's our system.

So does it make sense that getting to know a bit about each person's experiences, ideas, and beliefs about some of the subjects this case will be touching on is a wise thing to do before the case begins and the facts start getting delivered?

[*Wait for agreements. If shaky, invite questions or disagreements. Either way, move to the "as if" frame next.*]

Before we get started on the individual questions and your answers, there are a couple of things I want to get solidly understood with everyone. So, please, by show of hands if you would, please, answer this question, "If you were to end up on the jury panel for this case, can I take it as a given that you would try your very best to be as fair as you could in making your judgment? Who here, if you end up on this jury, would try to be *as fair as you can be* doing this job?"

[*Wait till all hands go up. Identify any reluctant or confused panelists.*]

Great, so we know that if you are seated on this jury, every single person here will try their best to be as fair as they can be doing the job, right?

[*Hands again. Acknowledge a few responses—track agreement and disagreement signals.*]

OK. So let's move on. Again, please answer by a show of hands, how many of you will agree to be as honest as you can when answering the questions we lawyers have for you during this part of the day? Who here, in line with the oath the judge just took from you, agrees that you will be as honest as you can in answering these questions?

[*Wait for all the hands. Acknowledge several.*]

So we know everyone will be honest answering these questions, and we know everyone will *try* to be as fair *as they can be* if they end up on the jury panel itself. So why do we need to ask any questions at all about what your ideas and beliefs are right now?

[From the discussion that ensues, the attorney can segue into the section about the "only wrong answer" and other baseline frames from the focus group introduction.]

This "fair and honest" framework can be used to accomplish three crucial tasks with any venire panel:

1. It can justify the inquiry by acknowledging those that speak up and agree that some people may have biases and attitudes that makes them prone to prejudge one kind of case over another. So they may be less suited for this case no matter how hard they'd try to be fair compared with their neighbor.
2. If the attorney is challenged by the "I'll have to wait and hear the facts" dodge, she can refer everyone's attention to the initial confirmation that "This part of the day is all about what you are bringing to the table," not about the facts yet to come.
3. This early confirmation can be used with any participant as leverage in setting up a cause strike.

To expand the positioning, the attorney can tell the panelists that cherry picking a couple of the best facts for just one side, completely out of context and without the witnesses themselves, would be inappropriate and unfair. It would be trying to push a potential juror to start making a decision when he or she hasn't even been sworn in yet. That reframe can revive the job interview frame and the chance to reinforce the *panelist* as the active party in the choice of this case over the next case as the one for which they would best be suited. Be very consistent with this indirect message throughout: *they* are doing the selecting when it comes to *this* job among many others.

In effect, they *are* interviewing themselves for the job. This is the basis of a voir dire strategy steeped in the story building predilections of the panelists and focused on maximizing cause, not peremptory strikes.[10] By this indirect method, we've invited the panelists to acknowledge and affirm their own unique collection of experiences and life stories that, based on their content, make each of them biased toward or away from certain case stories. It also confirms that they are intrinsically fair and honest people.

---

10. As noted earlier, peremptory strikes in most civil venues are few, averaging about three strikes, and the current trend is to reduce if not utterly eliminate them. However, many people that advocate reduction of peremptories would require a corresponding increase in the effective use of cause strikes. *See* Jeffrey Abramson, "Abolishing the Peremptory but Enlarging the Challenge for Cause," American Psychological Association, *APA Newsletter* 96(2) (Spring 1997): 114–126; *see also* Neil and Dorit Kressel, *Stack and Sway: The New Science of Jury Consulting* (Cambridge, MA: Westview Press, 2002): 211–231.

As in the focus group introduction, the framework of the choice to stay or go is not based on how fair a person I am *willing* to be, since I didn't choose my background. Rather, the choice to stay or go, when placed in each panelist's hands, is based on how *able* their circumstances and unique life lessons have left them, when the object is fairly judging a particular story, with particular topic areas. We are publicly presuming that the influence of their background circumstances is the active ingredient at work, and that the panelists are honestly and fairly in charge of rating their job prospects for this case based on that influence. Of course, the focus of attention is now turned toward examining that potential impact as the story subjects and topics are presented for discussion. Review the remainder of the focus group introduction for items that seem most useful for the voir dire in each particular case, considering logistics such as time, the number of other attorneys who will be speaking, and what may have been covered badly or well before you get to speak.

7.5 Bending the Branch

The purposes of voir dire seem to depend heavily on who is doing the defining. For some, the purpose is to quickly seat the first six, eight, twelve, or fourteen jurors. The first goal is having no clear and obvious connections to the matter at hand, nor any overwhelming sympathies, biases, or prejudices directly related to the outcome. For others, voir dire establishes a connection with the panelists and the prospective jurors. Many people think at least one big purpose voir dire serves is as a means to educate the panelists about the nature, if not the facts, of the case they will be judging. Others find education, along with rapport building, to be inappropriate efforts for these interviews.

There are two other goals to be at least partly achieved by the voir dire process—the answer from the panelists' perspectives to two familiar questions.

1. What is this case story?
2. How would it best be presented to any decision maker?

The questions and answers will now be less direct and more focused on the dynamic between two contexts simultaneously at work: the life stories of the panelists and the story structure that the focus group work provided. The overall thrust of focus group inquiries is embodied in the "What else?" question.

During voir dire, seeking identification with or alienation from a distilled set of case story elements, the inquiry may start with "What else?" but will turn quickly toward "How so?" questions in order to draw some distinction as to what the answers suggest about the world between those ears. One purpose of voir dire is to find what kind of versions of the client's case story may be nascent among the panelists—which are likely or unlikely to emerge as elements of their stories once the presentation starts. If the panelists are to succeed in educating the trial team about how well they are equipped to build case stories, how will the attorney best educate the panelists about the case story that emerged from focus group work to obtain that input most clearly?

Trial professionals should remember that the influence of values, attitudes, and beliefs is not a constant, but rather a waxing and waning effect over time. Even the most cherished, consciously desirable values are subject to unwitting change. If that were not true, the Roman Catholic Church would never have had to consider how to deal with "loss of faith," and no marriage vow honestly taken would ever get broken. Some beliefs are fairly constant, some come and go, and some are transient.

While the answers are coming in, people cannot accurately assess the experience of their own life stories, beliefs, or biases in the present or projecting into the future. This is important to keep in mind. As with all other aspects of human awareness, these drives make themselves known only as memories and thoughts after the fact, as we live through each minute. For trial professionals in voir dire, this means that the people reviewing their life experiences for you are looking in a rear view mirror as in hindsight. They are required to sort through their life seeking nonverbal, unconsciously moving trends that they are asked to reduce to words. They also required to act as if each belief were a discrete entity, complete, and in their control to assess and project its total influence on a story heard in court. That is only part of what they are asked to do. Plus, we are asking them to do it all in hindsight.

If the nature of these parts of people's lives is as a part of their *past*, then discussing them as things they have experienced, felt, or thought "so far," "up till now," "in the past," and so forth is only polite. That such an approach may also enhance chances of hearing more about each topic area from each person is an added benefit. If you are going to ask those people that remain to suspend some of their prior beliefs about lawsuits, business, or the world at large, discussing such beliefs as if they are safely behind us can only make suspending them that much easier.

7.6 Your Story

You now know exactly what the story you will present is like, and you have a decent idea of what the opposition will bring. Now you want to get some sense of the elements of certain life stories that people brought to court so you can see which fit with the two presentations better than others. Since you can't review the life story of each panelist, nor deliver your whole case in voir dire, it helps to have a cleanly organized presentation plan with a strong theme and hot-topic selection that you can explore in the allowed time. You can get reactions to your case theme without describing the whole case or any specific part. You can get references for most elements of your case story without detailing specific case facts by references to the panelist's experiences. You can get a sense of how these people respond to the general territory occupied by your story by reading the connections they do or don't develop for the story's general content (theme, general topics, other story elements) and the tenor of your own communication with them (through which the story will be received).

To do this well there are certain ground rules for the inquiry, which are similar to those used with focus groups:

- Mirror selected verbal and nonverbal output.
- Keep the subjects more general than specific, especially at the start of each topic.
- Listen much more than you talk.
- Detail only as many specific case facts as absolutely necessary.
- Remember, real voir dire doesn't start until the *second* follow-up question, on any topic, with any person, with no leading.

Too many attorneys mistake indoctrination for education during voir dire, much as some mistake detail for specificity everywhere. Refining a single, comprehensive theme for your case story allows you to be selective in the handful of major story topics that you need to explore most for their fit with the multiple stories jurors bring with them. Jurors will form their subjective, individual versions of your case story early by building a theme. In deliberations, it is the themes they bring, and those they have built for your story, around which discussion revolves.

Voir dire gives you a chance before too much internal construction starts, to assess some of the themes they have most readily available to them at that moment. Themes are manifest in the partial descriptions of the life stories of each individual in the box.

- Which of these themes seem broadest?
- Which seem less comprehensive?
- Which are likely to fit well with the story you're bringing, and which won't, as with the blended or distinct points of view reflected in the gas-inhalation injury questions and answers?

If your inquiry barges too quickly into asking for reactions to multiple details and facts in your case story, or tries to pin down forced choices *you* provide, potential jurors will simply start building their final versions of your story on the spot, and you will be unable to get what you came for.

7.7 Distorted Judgments

Many plaintiff attorneys have indulged an old habit of getting commitments on damage element numbers, pending proven fault and cause, while their defense counterparts worked just as hard to contract for zeroes. Not only is this tack ineffective, it shifts the focus of the inquiry drastically. When you inject too many details and start asking people to take conditional positions, the beliefs being scrutinized belong primarily to the lawyer. Panelists can just confirm or deny the lawyer's presumptions about their *expected* reactions, not those they actually had a chance to generate on their own. Exploration has stopped.

Not only do people rightly say, under those circumstances, "It's not fair to ask until I've heard all the facts," but they have started building your case story from a distorted, piecemeal version of the best your client will offer. They cannot stop that process once it begins, nor readily be talked out of its fruits. This is not investigating the influences of various references and mindsets panelists may bring to certain topics related to a case. This tack actually precludes such an inquiry by rushing people into distorted judgments.

Imagine a civil defense attorney with a client accused of delay in a professional duty: delayed medical treatment, delay in responding to a question, an emergency, or a contractual obligation. Imagine that the delay is substantial: five hours.

> If you were to learn that my client failed to respond within five hours and the plaintiffs hire an expert to tell you that's four hours and fifty-eight minutes too long, how are you still going to arrange to hear my client's story as fairly as the plaintiff's? Can you commit to waiting till our experts have spoken before you decide what's too late or not? Won't we start out just a step behind in your mind? How about a half step?

Or:

> The subject of doing a job *in time* may well come up here. Each side may have different ideas about what that means. Who here has had situations in your life, at work or at play, where getting something done *in time* is important for safety, success, or saving money? What was that like for you . . . for you . . . for you?

Then, second follow-up questions would be "How is that important?," "When would it be OK for *in time* to be longer than usual?" "When would it not?" and "How would you know for sure?"

One inquiry is about what the panel members know, have experienced, and may believe. One is all about what the attorney *expects* is in their minds. The search for life experience themes has been reduced to an either/or, yes, or no proposition about reactions people have not yet had, to a story they have not yet learned.

Done effectively, the indirect education jurors receive can be more compelling than specific declarations and demands about particular case facts and legal points (and hurried argument about them) could ever hope to be. If you stick with the world models of potential jurors when discussing their influence on the selected hot topics covered in your client's story, relying on the panelists' personal examples throughout the discussion, the lessons learned will be more personal, memorable, and persuasive because of their origins and your openness than anything you could throw in from outside their heads. The horses know.

Regardless of whether you believe the surveys that place fear of public speaking at the top of the public's fear pile, venire people are usually uncomfortable when called on to discuss their inner lives. There is one aspect of this situation that often goes unnoticed. Part of what makes probing our own guiding principles in life so hard is that what we call values, beliefs, or biases don't start out as words, aren't encompassed by words when they operate, and won't ever be fully encompassed by words in reflection after the fact of their lifetime influence on us. Combine that with the pressures of sitting in a courtroom quizzed by attorneys on such subjects and lawyers may begin to recognize that, however uncomfortable with voir dire they may be, potential jurors are probably even more uncomfortable. These subjects simply are not part of daily discourse on the job, and as many people have accurately said: "It's hard to put something like that into words." But it's not just because we rarely try putting them into words that makes the effort such a challenge.

As with all human reactions, whatever we choose to call these responses that intersect the perceptual, thinking, and psychological sides of our inner life, the reactions explored in voir dire are not conscious functions. They are not derived and built by conscious means, nor reinforced consciously. And their action is neither cued nor executed by any manner of conscious will or choice. We don't pick our beliefs, or decide where to employ them. Since speech is a major function of consciousness, it is important to recognize that the words said about biases and beliefs have no necessarily direct connection to them. Just saying "You have my sympathies" does not mean the speaker knows where she may have gotten them, what parts of her life contribute most to their continuation, nor anything at all about what might make them stronger or less so in the given situation. The words declare the territory a belief may occupy, but they do not define it. When it comes to these conscious inquiries into other-than-conscious territory, speculation is the rule. Implicit answers to indirect questions are the rule, until it's time to get specific about cause-strike answers.

Since perceptual habits get first sway in the story perceiving and story reconstructing process, if the attorney wishes to help manage the perceptions being offered panelists in the courtroom, wouldn't starting perceptually work best? Physical mirroring can establish a connection with each person addressed in less than ten seconds, smoothing the way for verbal exchanges to come. In those questions, starting at the most general, least leading level, with a manageable handful of hot topics derived from the case story to be presented, you can give panelists the greatest latitude and ease in bringing all they know and have experienced to bear on those generalized topics.

7.7.1 Nonverbal Mirroring

Nonverbal mirroring among the panelists, especially when they aren't seated directly next to one another, can be tracked for helpful potential down the line, though very large panels make this more a diversion than a help. As relationships develop, they are often advertised by behavioral indicators in an individual's attention by "mirroring" (imitating) the other person in postures, gestures, movements, or physical alignment.[11] Spontaneously talking just after the person is another sign, though less reliable. As the panel gets winnowed down, watch for blocks of such advertised connections forming among the panelists. Often these nonverbally expressed connections predict verbal connections to come or relationships just starting.

Sometimes, based on verbal input you get during interviews, they can suggest where a lawyer may or may not want rapport to continue.[12] Always be aware that the biggest talkers are often not the biggest leaders, but the person that most people follow nonverbally usually is.

Another problematic aspect is the interesting, almost inverse relationship between what most people can say about their beliefs and the relative value their influence holds. The more valuable the part of life being questioned, it seems, the less adequate words are at accounting for that value. So someone may find it easy to try describing attitudes about driving over the speed limit. But to wax eloquent on the subject of what a patient has a right to expect from the medical caregiver could be tougher. If a lawyer were to confuse the mere number of words easily invested in one topic over another as a sign of their relative value to the speaker, she could be misled.[13] Values and beliefs aren't installed by direct, conscious means. Nor are conscious, direct answers to case specific questions the best means of developing a full appreciation for the influences working on any given person at any given time. It can help to remember that the greater the influence and implicit perceived value, the less open it will usually be to conscious, direct inquiries.

---

11. *See* Chapter Eight.
12. We know research has shown that even somewhat powerful biases or prejudices can be muted by the pull of group processes at work. But biases can also be amplified by a block of likeminded individuals within the group.
13. Some studies have actually been conducted trying to assess leadership in groups by counting the number of words each person uses and anointing the most verbose as the leader. You can always count on getting measurable results if you only measure what you can count.

After mirroring words and demeanor, and staying purposely general while exploring story topics, the remaining ground rules can help ease the way for the panelists to respond as thoroughly and honestly as they can. That is, by listening more, aiming at an ideal of a case discussion that is free of the case facts, and especially, following up with minimal leading for each person on each response. Keep the horse Erickson rode back to its home in mind when the understandable desire to fix or redirect a panelist's response crops up.

7.8 Priming the Pump

All the possible biases and beliefs a person is capable of using are present all the time. Some are used more frequently than others. Yet, like the part of the mind that first generates them and maintains and reinforces them for the conscious mind that points them at the world, they don't leave for a vacation when they are offline. How best might an attorney approach potential jurors to get the broadest possible access to that whole pool of constructed responses, some of which may be those most amenable to constructing the most valuable case story from which to decide? In addition to the ground rules stated earliest, and all the elicitation techniques, verbal and nonverbal, suggested in Chapter Five, there are some other simple tools on hand.

7.8.1 Poll Questions to Open Topics

Beginning a topic area discussion with a poll question is a useful way to engage people in a safe response, by getting their hands in the air. Follow-up questions after that initial moment of volunteering information via a raised hand usually begets greater responsiveness.

7.8.2 Dead Air

Thanks to a number of generations raised on radio and then on TV, the experience of "dead air" (silence) where a broadcast existed a moment before is almost excruciating for some folks. If you ask a question such as, "Who else?" having just seen several nonverbal responses, simply shifting focus from one person to another can often prompt a response. This tendency can be enhanced further by asking, "Who else?" or "What else?" with a flat or sustained inflection, instead of the typical rising inflection with which most questions should be delivered. The extended tone connotes an expectation that there's more to come for many listeners. You can increase responsiveness even more by mirroring the silent objects of your inquiry as you move from one to the other. Piling up these influences—silence following a sustained tone when combined with mirroring—compels many people to speak up.

7.8.3 Presuppositions

Presuppositions have as powerful an effect in court as with focus groups. Like presuming the attorney and the panelists are in sync when actions are discussed by shifting to "we" instead of second person pronouns.

Never ask: "Could you?," when "How can you?," "How many ways can you?," or "How might you?" will work more effectively.

Always presume the worst answers are there. If topics need to be pressed, bring up someone you know who has similar attitudes first. Never ask someone to try to extinguish a thought when you can presume there are three more productive ones available waiting to redirect his attention. In every way possible, act, and talk as if you presume they each have something more to say.

Presuppositions can quell or swell participation. After asking, "Does *anyone* have *anything* else to say about that?" and getting thirty seconds of silence from a full voir dire panel, the attorney felt a tug on his sleeve from his cohorts and got a whispered message. Rising to face the panel, he then said, "OK. *Who* has something else to say about that?" and four hands promptly shot up. If you can be that effective with a single word, imagine what you can start to do with whole sentences.

7.8.4 Owl ("Who") Questions

These are just as effective in voir dire as they are in focus groups. Asking *who* thinks, feels, likes, dislikes, worries, holds the thought, carries the opinion, has a similar or slightly different take, and the like helps people a great deal.

7.8.5 No Fences

Avoid exclusive frameworks for questions to individuals or other verbal means of boxing someone in before they've answered, i.e., "Who else can't be fair?" versus "Who else might have some trouble with that?" Similarly, be careful about judgment loaded terms such as "right" and "wrong," "good" and "bad," "agree" and "disagree," when less restrictive ones will do. Never try to lead or force people into their own story, when it is only they who know the way.

7.8.6 Linkage and Anchoring

If during the course of each hot topic being discussed, you hear panelists use anchors, analogies, or metaphors that match or are close to those you plan to use, be sure to quickly pull yours out and link them up with those coming from the panelists. ("Who else thinks, like Ms. Rubble, that not watching everything there is to watch can be like closing your eyes or turning off the light?") That kind of linkage for the key phrases you've chosen to deliver your most persuasive story can prove priceless. Their analogy or anchor phrase came not from you, but from their own midst, and that counts for a lot with many people.

7.8.7 Act Interested

- It doesn't matter if you "are" or "aren't."
- "Acting" interested even when you aren't *works.*
- Many attorneys aren't interested.
- "Acting" is both more accurate and easier to swallow.

By the focus of their attention, the pace of their follow-up responses, their posture, their means of acknowledging potential jurors, and a hundred other ways, some attorneys advertise a very low level of interest for the personal information offered them in voir dire. Many act as if they could care less. If you are not really intrigued by the responses you are getting, you might ask yourself why in light of the impact they hold for your client's case. Perhaps it's the kind of questions you may have settled for in the past, equivalents of the "Yes, I can be fair" confabulation. Aim at asking the second follow-up question as often as you can and see how different the process becomes.

7.8.8 Psychological Habits

Utilize psychological factors such as reinforcement, reflection, and identification. When you get the first, usually tentative response, stop and acknowledge that person's input verbally and nonverbally. Make no comment on the actual answer, merely that it came out and it is exactly the type of thing we all came to discuss. Reflect the position of what the process should be in order for jurors to do their jobs well and for justice to eventually be achieved; that taking the chance of speaking up first in a group and being open and honest is exemplary. Emphasize that message, especially when the position revealed is most likely in the minority for the panel. Time and attention are the keys here. So be certain you've gotten advance agreement from the judge on the former, and you have practiced ways of expressing the latter that will serve you best. (This may involve fighting for time with almost every judge you meet.)

Reinforcement doesn't always come as a reward. Jurors take the job seriously, and challenging their unconstructive work is also effective.

If you've asked an appropriate, non-case-specific question and you still get the "I'll have to hear all the facts" response, that answer is being employed as a dodge from a sworn duty. Respond by reminding the person that you presume he is fair and will try to be objective throughout the trial. The subject of this inquiry is not the case facts. If your question made it appear so, apologize for that.

Rather, it is about how lessons from people's personal experiences have left them more or less prepared to judge a case related to certain parts of these other lives and the law. The problem, therefore, is not the facts of the case. We assume you'll try to be fair when you hear them. The questions are about what you bring to the table from your experiences before you even hear the facts.

> Since the subject matter is your own opinion, every answer is right, as long as it's honest and complete. The only wrong answer is having an impression and keeping it to yourself.
>
> [*Confirm that he understands. Then ask the question again.*]

7.8.9 Expand and Include (Initially)

Expand any inquiry before you narrow it down. The more you help someone articulate their personal references and elements of their own stories, the more they will personally be able to acknowledge their undoubted influence on their world views and your client's story, should the need arise. You must encourage a biased response to help the potential juror overcome the pressure of the easy "I can be fair" evasion. If you need them to stick around, you can always do your own rehabbing before you move on by asking a couple of pointed "why" questions about the value and purpose of this belief. Remind the person of her overall fairness in general. Covering this step at the time you've engaged her and have the greatest rapport with her can leave her more amenable to fully reviving the bias when asked, as the other side or the judge tries to help her deny its influence. Either lock or prop open the window to her bias before you leave.

7.8.10 Sensory and Nonverbal Preferences

If you have practiced recognizing sensory preferences for thinking in pictures or words or feelings, as well as identifying nonverbal "tells" (behavioral tip-offs) for agreement and disagreement, voir dire can be a profitable arena within which to use these skills. By reading the congruence in a person's reactions discussing visual anchors or imagery strongly entwined with a hot topic, you can find people who can clearly see those images in their own mind's eye. Depending on whether your client's story requires excellent or poor inner vision on a subject area, you can gain a great deal of information about how strongly this person may be prompted to respond to those pictures when they emerge later on. Also, it can help you know how much help you need to provide him in that effort should he remain on the panel.

A person that claims to be recalling a conversation addressing one of your hot topics, yet who continually moves his eyes to their right while doing so, may well be making something up in his recitation.[14] If you know how these signals work and you are attending to the full answers offered, you will be alerted to some possible deception, hidden agendas, or simple misconceptions in time for you to do something about them. If you are able to read and catalog signs of agreement and disagreement in people's demeanor as they speak, you can put yes and no follow-up questions to one of their few good uses in confirming the *degree* to which certain biases may be driving an individual's responses.

7.9 Sequencing Hot Topics

Sequencing of the voir dire interviews can be as powerful a tool as it is in the case presentation itself. The sequence settled on after focus group work for the most effective story progression allows you to pick out major topics, such as the "in time" topic cited above. You can fairly easily find three or four major subject or topic points for each of the three sections of the story sequence (from nine to twelve points) as you have outlined it for presentation by the witnesses, and by the attorney in opening and closing remarks. Make an effort to either select the strongest of the nine to twelve points or to combine topics to produce a total of about six of the most critical areas in which panelists' reference experiences and private stories may hold the strongest sway. Be sure they each can be packaged as "case fact freely" as possible. Rather than asking about "material misrepresentation to this buyer" or "good faith reliance by that contractor" as they may be applied to contracts or agreements at issue in the case, find generic ways to present those story lines and work to elicit personal mindsets regarding each, derived from the factual experiences of the people talking, which drive their beliefs far more than case facts.

Once you have your top six or seven hot topics, present them as questions for discussion in voir dire, in the same sequence in which they will emerge in the opening statement depicting your case story. For example, if you are thinking about presenting alternate causes as the bulk of the second step in your presentation, be sure they aren't discussed first with the panelists. Note that it will be the rare voir dire that doesn't dedicate at least one or two of these hot topics to discussion of the instructions or case law language the decision makers will be required to apply, and how well or poorly they may each be equipped to do so. Also, for plaintiff attorneys in injury suits where jurors must value the harms claimed, expect at least two of your hot topics to be focused on that territory. Panelists won't necessarily recognize that their own input was sorted into the same order of the case story presentation that they hear next in opening statement. That is because one concentrates on facts from

14. Eye movements can reveal the eidetic or memory process or the constructive or imaginative process at work. Never challenge nonverbal incongruence out loud. Confirm and record it instead. Paul Lisnek and Eric Oliver, *Courtroom Power: Communication Strategies for Trial Lawyers* (Colorado Springs, CO: Professional Education Systems Institute, 2001): Chapter 3; *see also* Paul Eckman, *Telling Lies: Clues to Deceit in the Marketplace, Politics and Marriage* (New York: W.W. Norton, 1992): Chapters 2, 4, and 5.

their lives, while the other is centered on the particular facts of the case. However, the order of the hot topics to which they contributed will seem familiar at some level. In this arena of persuasion and other-than-conscious processes, familiarity often reads as credibility.

When you engage people in discussion of your story's hot topics in the same sequence of your planned case presentation, do not allow housekeeping or procedural topics to interrupt the flow (hardships, witness connections, related life experiences, professional links, etc.). Once you start the sequence, go straight through without interruption. As you move through the hot topics, always start each round by eliciting the worst possible answers, following those up, inviting as many "bad" answers as possible, *before* allowing movement toward positions more helpful to your case in the panelists' minds. When you make these shifts, just as when you ask for initial responses, imply that there are many available. "Who here has a similar or slightly similar view?" is more effective than "Who agrees with Mr. Casey?" It lowers the barriers and takes personalities farther out of the mix. One step farther back from directed, closed-out responses would be to add "may" as a qualifier, "Who may have a . . . ?"

7.10 Effective Education

The pattern of moving from alignment first with the opposition's positions, through engagement of people's own beliefs and attitudes, and toward attitudes better aligned with your story, can serve as a rehearsal for the eventual jurors. People are paying attention to your inquiry and their colleagues' answers during voir dire. They are learning and starting to construct their own foundations for the eventual case story they will use to decide the matter. They are learning to recognize a soon-to-be-familiar story sequence and pattern as each topic comes up *inside* that sequence. In the end, it always seems to resolve in your favor. Indirect questions lead to implicit understandings. Implicit understandings lead to direct decisions.

7.10.1 Sowing Hot Topics

Pretend you are handling a prescription diet drug case for a plaintiff with heart problems. The focus group work you've done suggests that a theme such as "clashing priorities" is due north (theme) for your case story.

The hot topics for discussion will be derived from:

- The story elements that proved most problematic for the focus group(s)
- Those factors that kept dropping off the radar screen for certain people
- Parts of the story to which panelists consistently returned when justifying or ridiculing various positions on the case

This is not a comprehensive list of every topic for jury selection. They are the core topics to decide *who* is most likely to appreciate your case story's elements or to use similar ones of their own making. Let's say those topics included obesity bigotry, rating government oversight, corporate contributions overall, vague causal links, personal responsibility, full disclosure, caveat emptor or "stuff just happens," big damage numbers, and statistical danger signs. Let's say that, in line with the theme, decisions were made as to how the story would be sequenced. So it begins with the corporate decision making and information control, moves on to acquired knowledge and actions from each party over time (drug company to doctor to patient), and ends with the contrasting outcomes for the company and for the patient. That would mean the topics list would have to be changed to reflect that sequencing for your voir dire hot-topic package.

Reflecting the sequence the story line will follow, the topics would be discussed in this order:

1. Corporate contributions overall
2. Rating government oversight
3. Statistical danger signs
4. Personal responsibility
5. Full disclosure
6. Obesity bigotry
7. Caveat emptor, or "stuff just happens"
8. Vague causal links to harms
9. Big damages

Say that your pretrial research also revealed that those versions of your client's story that concentrated a point of view on her, rather than on the drug company, produced poor results (even those couched in very sympathetic terms). Also, you found that a subgroup of people that retold your client's story as being all about *her,* also had entrenched, poisonous reactions about the whole weight-loss thing in general, particularly with regard to women. Then how would you sequence the story topics for voir dire? Sometimes, despite the coming presentation sequence, the voir dire interview sequence needs to be adjusted to the requirements posed by the uninitiated decision makers being interviewed for the job. Particularly when time for voir dire is short.

You could consider doubling up on some of the topics. Presenting opposing topics in questioning is a good way to obtain more complete answers from potential jurors. You are constantly trying to adhere to the compass heading of *clashing priorities*, knowing what the presentation sequence will be, and having the additional information about hardened positions around patient-centered and weight-centered points of view. Where can you combine topics within the overall story sequence, discussing two at once, to greatest effect? Consider this arrangement:

1. Personal responsibility versus corporate contributions overall
2. Obesity bigotry versus full disclosure
3. Government oversight—adequate versus overrated
4. Statistical danger signs
5. Caveat emptor or "stuff just happens" versus big damage numbers
6. Vague causal links

So, with an eye to the north star of *clashing priorities*, for both parties, you could start a string of direct questioning (needed for shorter voir dire) with a set-up such as:

> To do your jobs well, there will be several factors you'll weigh in testimony. One question you'll have to answer is what's *reasonable* to expect, both from people that make pills and those that buy and take them. For example, you'll hear a lot about how my client decided and went about getting prescriptions from her doctor to lose weight. On the other hand, you'll also learn a lot about this drug company, their many products, and the millions they've helped. Before you hear any evidence, I'm curious how you handle those two notions—somebody's desire to take drugs to lose weight, and any company's aims in making such drugs—what's reasonable to expect from each?

Follow-ups to explore thematic, scope, and active-ingredient references that jurors bring to the company, plaintiff's motives, and standards could include:

> What worries you either about her taking the drugs or even about their making them? What will be important to hear and see? What would make it hard for you to give a fair hearing for either my client's or the company's story?

Most people tend to answer only one side of the question. Having first recorded their predilections, always follow up with the other when they're done:

> I've heard that some drugs had to be pulled from the market, that's true, sir. And that might make it harder to hear things from their side, true? But what about my client's or anybody's decision to take weight-loss drugs? How does that sit with you, going in?

Any time discussion settles on one party too long, steer your questions to the other side. There is a greater chance that people will be prompted to express themselves and the context is far more realistic when it comes to the eventual context for every decision maker's story-building, and (re)building, processes. This gives each person a chance to reorient to their preferences between both *if* the follow up questions are more neutral than leading after each topic-centered question is posed and reposed in follow-up.

Jurors have the widest latitude to hint at and even admit to biases, since the context is never just about one side or the other, but rather one side *in reference to* the other. This is how it actually will be when they hear the case framing, and forming their own versions of the story. Bias against obese people could be discussed separately, approached indirectly, but as with all biases, that would be totally misleading. A biased position exists only in the context of dozens of others, connected by the strains of the tunes this person's life experience has taught him to sing. When this particular bias is strong and is invited to surface for certain people by this story, you tend to lose. So dealing with it early, in a context truer to the one that will confront the jurors' process seems wise.

Having also learned that a strong tendency to hold a plaintiff-oriented point of view is trouble, you can keep your ear cocked for those perspectives, advertised in the responses to the initial questions offering them *both* parties from which to select. Also, in whose hands, if either, is *control* assumed to reside by how each person answers? The questions and follow-ups will focus on the parties' priorities, that involved them in the story at the starting point of the coming story line: taking and making weight-loss drugs. A sequence hinted or declared in answers that put the drug user at the forefront would certainly be of interest to defense attorneys.

The same kind of one-hand, other-hand arrangement can be used to plumb the positioning of potential jurors on the next hot topics in comparison: obesity bigotry versus full disclosure. In the story structure for which you are laying a foundation, this is a step further than "Meet the characters and guess their motives." That was the game for the first topics. This one is more, "By their acts shall they be known." So offer up your client's role with the smallest barrier to attacks on it, on the subjects of weight, weight loss, and the success (or lack of success) of obese people's losing weight. When their answers invite it, reveal that some testimony may concern information on control: what the company knew, when they knew it, and what they did with that knowledge regarding the reasonable expectations of their products' end users.[15]

On these topics, where the human references are closer to actions than intentions, anchors you plan to use later can be deployed. From the plaintiff's perspective, you might start repeating ". . . if she did everything she could . . . ," on the one hand, and " . . . what they revealed, and what they may have concealed . . . ," on the other.

---

15. This is in reference to verdict questions again. Linking their jobs and the standards they must apply to them with the hot topics of your theme and case story is an essential part of the process.

Note that the basic pull of *clashing priorities* is never lost. As you discover who is most prepared to utilize such a theme today, you establish and begin to reinforce the main player, basic sequence, and ultimate theme of your case story.

This more directive version of questioning is not the ideal, but when time is short, with careful management of any leading in your follow-ups, it can be very effective. Here is how a less directive, more open-ended process on the same subjects might begin:

> Who here has ever heard a doctor say, "Stop smoking" or "lose some weight"?
>
> [*Wait for multiple acknowledgments.*]
>
> When the idea is losing weight, where would you first turn? Where did you get that? Who else here would go to a doctor first, if you were serious about losing weight? Who would make that the last resort, or at least farther down on your list? How so? Say some more about that, please.

Then, awhile later:

> You know this case deals with a drug company, a weight-loss drug, and the harms this woman claims were caused by that drug. Those of you that would think someone wanting to lose weight would be better off starting somewhere other than in a doctor's office, what do you think of weight-loss drug prescriptions such as the ones in this case?"

And so on.

Note that the active factor here is the person "wanting to lose weight," and where "they start out," pushing the panelists away from friendlier packaging for the plaintiff at first. That can allow for a more distinct shift when the inquiry moves from the first half of the hot topic, "personal responsibility," to the other, "overall corporate contributions."[16]

While the more overt packaging of the story elements here favors defense positioning as it should, note the implicit suggestions at the start that address the panelists' own life experiences directly. The context is their own their family's doctor and includes a second factor—smoking—a universally acknowledged health hazard. (At the time these interviews were conducted, obesity had not risen to similar status in the eyes of government health police. Smoking held a far stronger consensus as a threat.)

---

16. The second follow-up question allows potential jurors the time needed to reveal their private viewpoints, themes, and centers of control that simple mirroring may mask in a single, initial response.

Norming and availability bias, in addition to reinforcing a common, personal experience, invites people to story build by seeking answers from their own inner movies about "good" medicine. Since the coming inquiry was centered on finding those that could spin personal stories that made weight loss more or less of a medical concern, the implied invitation to open up those private doors into those personal references seems only prudent, particularly if primacy effects are to be respected. Despite adding the overt suggestions for anti-plaintiff leanings, the implied suggestions about a linked, common hazard within visions of their own doctors' offices could help panelists draw the mindsets and references we need to explore for their value to the upcoming trial story. This illustrates working to access both sides of the most basic, conscious/other-than-conscious decision-maker dynamic during voir dire interviews.

7.11 Winnowing the Panelists

When the attorney for the plaintiff had ascertained that one of the panelists was a former patient of one of the defendant doctors, he assumed he would need to work toward a cause strike and began to do so:

Q: Ma'am, you were a patient of Dr. Borden's for how long?

A: About two years, from '96 to '98.

Q: And you stayed with him as your internist for that whole time?

A: Yes.

Q: . . . And what prompted you to leave?

A: We moved.

Q: Well, would it be fair to say that, since he was one of your own doctors for a couple years, sitting here listening to a case against him by a party who claims his injury was caused by your doctor's negligence, would it be fair to say you would have a harder time than someone who had never seen him professionally, listening to that case?

A: No, I don't believe so. I think I could still listen.

Q: Well, put it this way, would my client, the plaintiff, start out at any disadvantage in your mind because of your prior relationship with the doctor?

A: No. I don't believe so.

Q: Well, would Dr. Borden start out in your mind, even before you've heard all the facts in evidence, just a little ahead in your mind?

A: No, I don't believe so.

Q: Not even a little ahead? One step, maybe?

A: No, I don't think so.

Before he could sit down, the consultant, who had been observing the young woman's nonverbal behavior, whispered something to the attorney, who spun around and said:

Q: Ma'am, would the doctor start out a little behind in your mind?

A: Oh, yes—*definitely!*

This example illustrates three principles:

1. Assuming that you know which bias is driving a set of answers isn't always right.
2. Losing a "good" juror isn't always bad.
3. Relying on the opposition to strike or not strike someone is hardly ever a good idea.

The plaintiff's team was rightly convinced there was something going on with the young panelist. They wrongly assumed it had to be bad for the client, based on the doctor-patient association and its length. She was incongruent in how she said what she did, but the observable polarization was the reverse of the expected one. Despite asking a question that exposed a positively biased panelist, the plaintiffs held ground.

The doctor in question was the middleman in a string of three physicians accused of neglect. His entire input during the events in question had been at the other end of a telephone line, in one call. He was also the best looking among everyone seated at the defense table and acquitted himself very well during deposition testimony. In that context, a profoundly felt indictment from a former patient of two years' experience in front of the whole room of potential jurors made the voir dire panelist into a good plaintiff witness. Of course, the defense took her off with a peremptory strike, although relying on the other side to do something in selecting jurors is still a risky proposition.

7.12 "Please Excuse Yourself Now"

When establishing the groundwork for panelists to excuse themselves from a trial's job pool, shifting to eliminate the panelist should not make the relationship adversarial. Too many people working for a particular side in voir dire unthinkingly hold mental positions of fear or hostility toward potentially unhelpful panelists.

7.12.1 Keep It to Yourself

Remember that what we consciously or unconsciously feel or think tends to leak out in our external behavior, through eye focus, shifts, voice tone or volume shifts, awkward phrases, and a hundred other little ways that telegraph our animus.[17] Considering that the attorney is about to ask these people to voluntarily give up a job, which may involve seeing themselves as a somewhat less fair person than they may have thought walking into the room, there is a potential downside to approaching cause strike efforts in any adversarial way.

7.12.2 The Jury "Pool"

The first task in helping strong positioned panelists excuse themselves from the job hunt is to widen the scope of the job frame. From the start, keep the panelists' focus on juries, trials, and courtrooms in the plural form, not the singular. Consistently refer to this case as one among many on which they could be qualified to serve (as if it were a selective process that just happened to have begun in this courtroom). They are there to match up their life skills and beliefs against the needs imposed on all potential jurors by the particular arrangements of this case story. Invite them to broaden their scope.

Directly and indirectly avoid framing their declarations as admissions, confessions, or surrendering. It is after all, "Perfectly OK for people, maybe many people, to hold the same or similar beliefs." This statement must be heard as true, despite what it means to an attorney's case to be contemplating a juror or two with those "OK" beliefs deciding his case. It is expected that some people can, will, and should be able to hold beliefs inimical to the outcome desired by one or the other side in the conflict. Be cautious about accusatory postures, gestures, or other flairs as the cause questioning begins in earnest.

Be sure the reframing of panelists as being "blocked from better intentions by unfortunate fate" has been well invoked. Remembering the prior discussion about

17. Robert Rosenthal, A.J. Hart, and Peter Blanck are at the forefront of researchers confirming this effect in the courtroom for more than two decades. Data from more than one study show that a fairly high degree of accuracy can be achieved in predicting jury decisions in criminal deliberations based solely on the nonverbally communicated leanings of the judges while they instruct the panels. Trial professionals need only recognize and respect these facts to find all the needed motivation to develop skills in presentation of a case story commensurate with their craft in preparing the legal case.

locus of control, the fundamental attribution error, trial professionals can see what an easier task it is for a panelist to be invited to view *circumstances* over *character* as the reason she might not be the best equipped by life to hear this particular case with her fullest fairness.

If the court requires that a set of specific words or phrases be used before a cause strike can successfully be made, allow the panelist to link the meaning of his own phrases to those required by the court. Modeling with the attorney's demeanor, indicate that the real reasons are associated with the words chosen by the panelist, and the technical language is just pro forma. Be careful not to make the intoning of the words of the court sound more serious, delivered in a more grave voice than the actual words offered by the person in front of the whole panel. Their words are the "real" ones. The use of mirroring at this point can raise the level of success achieved by means of a behavioral lever. As the panelist is invited to mouth the magic strike words, the attorney draws her attention with a broad arm gesture, more toward the bench than toward the lawyer as the cause confirmation is made by the panelist. Prior mirroring will have encouraged greater *following* of the attorney's lead, directing the panelist to, in effect, make the cause confirming statement right to the judge.

To guard against the rehabbing efforts of the court or opposition, offer at least some of the panelists the opportunity to rerun the original "fair and honest" frame set back at the beginning. Establish the distinction between his or her being an honest person in their answers and one who would try to be as fair as possible if empaneled. Mark out the big distance between being an *otherwise* fair person and the specific declarations they freely made as honestly as they could. That reveals how much less fair they would be hearing this case than some other. Also, in bench conferences (where the term "admission" *is* a useful anchor), this tack can be used to challenge any attempt to rehabilitate a panelist in general, but not for the very specific admissions he or she has already put into the record. You can't generally rehabilitate a specific admission of bias by invoking generally fair inclinations or intent. If you want to rehabilitate that, you have to go back and ask the person to reverse their specific, honest admissions already tendered to the court.

Do not finish with such phrases as "would you feel uncomfortable . . ." or "wouldn't you feel more comfortable if . . . ." The individual's personal comfort isn't at issue. It is his ability to act fairly and treat each side evenhandedly, all the way to the end of each side's presentation despite certain well-traveled, personally important views, gleanings, or positions. Such views would make that task difficult or impossible for any reasonable person.

Once or twice during a voir dire session, when seeking a cause-strike confirmation from a panelist that turns recalcitrant or hostile, be prepared to use the impossible question. The question cannot be answered honestly by anyone, because it requires the respondent to try to answer with one part of the mind on behalf of the other, which works out of reach of the conscious part that fields the question.

Q: So you say that, despite the fact that you have long held the belief, and hold it to this day, that nobody should be suing anyone for money damages over a death, that you could still set all those parts of your life's experience to the side, and sign off on a verdict form that contained a very large sum of money if that's what the evidence was proven to warrant?

A: Yes, yes I can.

Q: You could set aside everything you've ever seen, said or heard that has led you to believe as you have for at least what—ten years—or longer that money damages for wrongful death claims are wrong? You could still set all that aside?

A: Yes.

Q: Can you please tell the court exactly how you would go about doing that?

The typical fallback for those who don't surrender immediately is to proclaim their good intentions, "Because it's important to be fair," or "I'll just do it." To either tack, you quietly agree, and then reasonably repeat the request for a specific description of how this person will consciously set aside unconsciously formed, maintained, and executed beliefs of a lifetime just because he or she wants to. This question should never be used as a first resort. It risks rapport with others besides the speaker and it destroys rapport with him. Once per session is the reasonable limit. Also be selective and careful with which person you first choose to close the deal on a cause strike. The rest of the group will likely take that success or miss as their model, encouraging or discouraging further voluntary exits from the job interviews.

For those that remain, be sure you engage in some juror job training with the last of your allotted questioning time, inoculating them and eliciting agreements to "police one another" as in the focus group introduction on burden of proof. There will be other instructions, depending on the case or the likely caliber of deliberations, on which you may want to focus this "all for one" attention:

- Proscriptions against consensus verdicts
- Averaging, halving or horse-trading damage amounts

- The territory the sympathy instruction does and does not cover
- The actual meaning of the proven by evidence and circumstantial instructions
- The notion that all jurors should be heard from during deliberations

These are all parts of the job that could end up being very productively discussed here at the end of the beginning, rather than saved till far too late in closing argument.

7.13 Planting—Opening Statement

7.13.1 First Things First

Facts *can't* speak for themselves and they don't decide legal cases. Once the judgments are made, you can count on facts getting blamed for the decision by its authors. Some researchers try to reassure advocates that juror deliberations are "fact driven." The topics discussed in deliberation do center on facts in evidence and some that were not. This points more strongly to the power of the story with which those facts are delivered. No research claims that jurors weigh every fact equally, nor that they make an effort to discuss all the presented facts. Much the opposite. People pluck the facts from their versions of the case story to offer to their colleagues as proof that the story supported by those select (often distorted or disproportionately valued) facts is justified. This applies to all legal decision makers, professionals, or lay people, making decisions alone, on small panels, or in jury groups.

7.13.2 Silver Bullets

The attorney armed with a refined case story who is standing to present it in opening remarks, knows that this is likely the most open-minded moment the decision makers will have. After this, they will be getting more involved in the story construction and fact-filtering process as time passes. The attorney should be aware that opening statement is not about providing an inventory of case facts. It is more the first (second, if *voir dire* was allowed) and best chance to engage the decision makers in the story they will use to sort, select, and argue the facts. Richard Crawford, in his book *The Persuasion Edge*,[18] referred to the first few phrases delivered during the first few moments of opening statement as the advocate's "silver bullets," to encourage attorneys not to hold back strong story elements and to fire away at the start while the mental irons are hottest. In light of the fact that whether standing or speaking

18. Richard J. Crawford, *The Persuasion Edge: Winning Psychological Strategies and Tactics for Lawyers* (Eau Clair, WI: John Wiley and Sons, 1991).

or not, each attorney is always reinforcing some response for the decision makers, this could be a very smart move.

The story elements in the completed Case Presentation Plan outlined in Chapter Six can be used to fit any venue within which trial professionals find decision makers: from a twenty-minute narrative in a facilitated mediation to a trial schedule of two months or more. Some attorneys have found in negotiations that instead of being driven by the numbers, delivering the theme, scope, viewpoint, and sequence of their best case story in pieces, forces a more focused reaction to the case story than their opponents may have expected. The story package emerging from focus group work is the same, no matter how, when, or where it is utilized.[19]

Attorneys need to consider certain realities before opening remarks:

1. The bulk of the early story-building process is not a consciously directed or accessed activity.

2. The sequence in which the many early stories and eventual single story from which judgments are drawn begins with decision makers' perceptions. It then moves through habits of thinking or cognition and psychological reactions to produce the categories, narrative, and rhetoric of each individual's final version.

3. Perceptually, people will first use deletion, distortion, and generalization to find references for a thematic context in which their story building will happen.

4. All manner of other mental habits will take hold in the process. Almost all this activity is neither within reach or direction of their conscious parts.

5. Lastly, realization that some construction has already happened begins to seep down into conscious awareness. At this point, language is latched onto to begin mostly private deliberation of the meanings that the partly constructed story has to offer on the way to fitting in all the remaining facts, testimony, witness communication, and exhibits.

To approach the decision makers' processing with respect for the way it works and create a hospitable environment in which our own version of the case story can take root, know that acting as if there is more than one story in between each set of ears at the start, is only wise. Then the approach would be to concentrate on invitation and inference, on encouraging beginnings over conclusions, and on the elements of the story we came to deliver, not its type or detailed facts.

---

19. This includes discovery motions, depositions, and pretrial motions to extract and/or plant seeds of the most effective story and determine where to invest—or withhold—resources in the preparation of cases.

Case Stories

How are they seen?

	OLDER	NEWER
THEME	**Interpretation**—Who needs to see and hear this?	**Construction**—What most needs to be heard and seen?
SCOPE	One set of facts; One set of decision makers; Delivered and decided	Multiple themes, Multiple interpretations, Multiple conclusions
POINT OF VIEW	The Attorney or The Jury	The Jurors or Their Stories
SEQUENCE	Witnesses deliver facts; Attorneys deliver case; Jury/Judge delivers decision	Attorney presents story; Jurors/Judge formulate stories; Multiple conclusions drive verdict

Figure 7

The general rules for such an approach to opening up the case story follow:

Actions—before Words. Because there are three variables at work in the room and the messenger and her telling of the story are influential in their own right, attention to demeanor, conduct, and overall communication style are most influential at the start.

General—before Specific. Because the attorney wants to preserve the widest latitude for each decision maker to draw on her own references and concomitant life stories at the start, detail spin is to be avoided at all costs in the beginning.

Implications—before Explanations. In a fair fight, the implicit suggestion always beats the explicit one. The rule is that the more one wants the point to take hold, the more one makes it by implication first.

Perceptions—before Conclusions. The early, lasting appeal in legal persuasion is always an appeal first to perceptions. By the nature of the mind, it can be nothing else. Trial professionals must first manage the perceptions of their story, then argue for the conclusions that may develop.

Who, What, When, Where, How—before "Why." The way to accomplish this crucial task is similar to the way opening statements are best developed and delivered to a focus group. Develop a statement that adheres to the major story elements elaborated from focus group work: theme, scope, point of view, active ingredient, party, and the steps of the story sequence that can be delivered specifically in *five minutes or less.* If you cannot yet do this, the story is not ready to be delivered. When you can do this, you can safely expand the package somewhat. But to adhere to all the basic rules of legal persuasion from the start and demonstrate respect for the workings of the minds we attempt to persuade, less is more in opening remarks.

7.14 The Story's Central Image

Serious consideration needs to be given to the perceptual element of the story's *central image* in the presentation of a story in opening statement. To make sense of anyone else's story, all humans need to reference that story against his or her own. In doing so, whether they are consciously aware of it or not, most people end up selecting a central image, usually coincident with the central point of their own narrative. This image is usually set in human as opposed to conceptual territory. The imagery associated with it will be those references from the listeners' own lives that compare well with the imagined images they draw for themselves to represent the stories of the people involved in the case. This image is not always logically derived, but it is frequently associated with the locus of control (active ingredient/party) and its effects within the story context.

The moment in the story line that people select for their central image can differ wildly: some sort for the earliest, significant scene, choice or act; some for the penultimate event or action; and still others for the most compelling portrait of the aftermath, sorting backwards from there to fill in their own conclusions. The opportunity that opening statement and subsequent presentation of testimony offer to *suggest* such an image for the decision makers should rarely be passed up.

A central image doesn't need to be announced. During the story introduction sequence where all your prior work indicates that the most effective central image may reside, make the effort to fully depict that scene so that decision makers can make most pervasive use of it thereafter. That means marking out that section of the story in opening using both the verbal and behavioral means discussed in Chapter Three. Bridge visual to auditory to feeling phrases. Fully fill the sensory palette on which listeners can build. If you have acquired the skill, mirror perceptual preferences with your gestures and appropriate eye movements as they are delivered. Develop a compelling perception of the story's central image.

Consider our two running examples: the catheter insertion and inhalation injury cases. From what you know about each case story—the plaintiff's medical-injury position and the plant-owning company's defense position—what would be the most effective central story image?

While people could differ on this, if you thought about the image of the doctor "turning off the light" at the critical moment when the sharp instrument is pushed forward, or the inexplicably influential image of the worker that passed out being "out of the line of sight" of his fatally injured team member, you may be on a productive track. Can you see how much of each case, as the helpful members of the respective focus groups saw them, can be seen to revolve around each of these central images of their respective story lines?

To develop the most effective central story image:

- Determine your most persuasive central image.
- In the agreed-upon sequence of your opening remarks, deliver it in the most fully represented form.
- Avoid attaching descriptions of your own meanings or drawing unsupported conclusions for the jurors about why that image is so important.
- Make sure it is most likely to be noticed and retained by those you came to persuade.

With regard to sequence and the decision makers' visual facilities, opening is a powerful place to help listeners adopt visual anchors. Each step of the three-step story sequence ought to have a key demonstrative exhibit. That is, a demonstrative visual that either points to, summarizes, or describes in some way the central point of that particular step in the story sequence. They may make their first appearances in opening to double up the perceptual channels observers are invited to use to process and remember your story and to help mark one step from the next as they are introduced to your story sequence directly for the first time. (Voir dire will have introduced them as the sequence of the major topics, but not as the steps in your story's narrative order.)

- If you are not using visuals during voir dire, produce the "invisible exhibit," using these three key visuals as examples.
- Move to the spot where the visual will be displayed.
- Mark it out with your gestures as you describe the general appearance of the board and its content in line with the story introduction that opening provides.
- Link or associate key phrases (verbal anchors) you would like used with those points, factors, or whole story elements conveyed by each board.

When the time comes to actually produce the three-dimensional version of the board, it needs to match your description and be placed in the spot in which you asked folks to rehearse putting it if you want to avoid sowing confusion where clarity could grow. PowerPoint slides are not adequate for this task. Hard boards are.

7.14.1 Seeding Growth

You are entitled to a theme. If you desire but do not provide one, one will be provided for you (and it won't be one you like). When most trial professionals read those lines, their first guess about who will do the providing is often mistaken.

It is not the opposition or the judge in a jury trial who will be offering the alternative themes should you fail to carefully craft and deliver one. It is each decision maker who will do the job. In truth, they will anyway. The advocate's job is to provide an effective enough invitation so that each decision maker will draw their own themes from story territory that the focus group work indicated would be best for the desired outcome.

7.15 Unsupported Conclusions

Avoid the flat assertion or projected conclusion unsupported by a part of the story being introduced. Citing reasons early why a vote would best be for or against your client is no substitute for establishing a theme. It is understandable, but a nonetheless ineffective attempt to defy the decision-making process itself. When judgments are undertaken in the human mind, reasons come at the end of the process, not the beginning. Perceptions come first, followed by referencing, reactions, cognitive impressions, and reasons. When lawyers trumpet conclusions or reasons with no thematic rhyme and no established story line to allow decision makers to use their own decision-building processes, they risk planting every seed thereafter on bare rock. In essence, they are saying, "I'm telling you now what your opinions will be, and there's a good reason why. I know you'll trust me when I tell you what conclusions you can draw, because, as you all know, I am a lawyer." Instead, to aid the decision-making process, state the reasons last.

Many trial professionals believe that the right way to integrate a theme during the early presentation of a case is through theme repetition. While a proven tool in learning and persuasion, repetition is not the most persuasive choice for introducing and reinforcing the theme of a case story during opening statement. There are a number of ways to invite decision makers to establish, maintain, and reinforce a theme for themselves close to that which you've determined will be most productive. While none of these techniques (i.e., repeating a theme anchor phrase) will fully contain your theme, all will inspire theme adoption and reinforcement.

Themes are not contained in words, listeners are likely to start with a theme regardless of whether you try to suggest one, and all cases are decided by the caliber of the story constructed about them by decision makers. So consultants and lawyers need to be clear that themes can be *suggested* by the words you choose, but never *contained* by them. The themes are the meanings accumulated from privately held life experiences, bumping into the classic and obscure templates of culture, mixed up with your immediate attempts to persuade and the listeners' efforts to do the right job.

All things being equal, it is often better to imply your theme than to state it aloud. This is due to language limitations and strengths of our imaginations. To put a theme across implicitly, to have that meaning suffused through every statement, every deposition transcript or video, every question, every heading on every visual you many not ever actually print the word or phrase that you personally prefer for expressing that meaning. That way, should each juror have a better word, a worse word, or even the same word, they'll all have the freedom to put the *meaning* first in their own minds. They should never be forced into a conflict between the meaning you want to convey, and the idiosyncratically unacceptable word you may have chosen to describe it. This is a distraction to avoid, particularly early in a presentation. The theme cannot be left behind, nor tacked onto the stack of facts and law (theory) as an obviously awkward afterthought.

Advocates run a risk declaring their themes aloud, especially early in opening. While the temptation could be strong to declare, "This is a case about abandoned safety," in the inhalation injury story, or, "This is a case about erring on the side of danger—twice," in the catheter-puncture matter, it may be the wiser move to resist.

By nature, themes are more—

subjective, perceptual, and experiential

than—

objective, verbal, and rational

and—

are never fully expressed by words.

As a case begins, themes can be easily distorted or wiped out by trying to corral them into a single phrase, a phrase that has productive clear and present meaning to the case story only for the one speaking. It is the anchor for the theme of the story that so much work and resources were invested to produce. Don't go so far and fast in trying to declare a theme that you prevent jurors from processing it in ways that work as well for them, as your phrase, patiently developed, now works for you.

Since the theme must be incorporated into all parts of the trial to provide direction throughout, the more varied the ways it is expressed from the start, the better. The fewer ways you use to try to put it across, especially more obvious ones, can limit your chances of influencing the formation of the juror's themes and emerging stories. Explicit rendering of that one phrase can run afoul by the one juror who takes exception to your phrase. It's akin to settling for anger as an answer to the question, "What drives large juror verdicts?" Yes, anger is one possibility. But why would you choose to settle for only one? Or on the defense side, why would you try to insulate against anger alone, when you could wipe out many more paths to an award instead?

In a fair fight, implied suggestions are always more powerful than explicit ones. Once you have derived your theme from the focus group work, the sowing of as many different seeds as you can in its direction is most constructive. Use the phrase you settled on sparingly, don't use it at all, or reserve it for closing. Begin by recognizing that establishing a theme for the story, for every decision maker, is accomplished by different means. The job is to establish and then consistently reinforce a perspective on the meaning of the case. It is not to plug one phrase into one, three, six, or twelve heads. Trial consultant Amy Singer has long held that "jurors deliberate in themes." They can't form their own versions of your story until they have one. They will always reference that theme when they discuss any part of the story they've built. If that's where the jurors start, is it wise to skip over the effort to establish the theme as you begin your case story? How do you do that, if not just in words? By consistently coordinating your words, the mental imagery you invoke, the actual images you display, and the actions you and the witnesses take to convey the story. All can be harnessed to fix juror attention on the idea, image, or concept of what this story is about as they listen to that story unfold.

Methods to invite jurors to adopt their own versions of the preferred case theme have many forms, but here are a few of the more common ones:

- Rhetorical questions, proposals, and devices such as the rhetorical rule of three[20]
- Demonstrative images (imagined or actual)
- Other visual, verbal, or experiential anchors
- Linkages, such as "the more . . . the more . . ." suggestion, opposition, or juxtaposition of subjects
- Summary/menu lists, statements, or phrases
- Reframes and catch phrases
- Analogies, metaphors, and similes
- Quotations

Consistency in development and delivery of a theme determines its credibility for the jurors. Yet there seems to be an inverse alignment between the times in trial when an attorney is most likely to jump off the theme-driven presentation, back to

20. For instance, that people prefer their groupings of topics or references to come in threes rather than twos or fours. Best example—the original Churchill phrase was "blood, sweat, toil, and tears," but people insist on hearing only three items in the list.

old habits, and when jurors most need the attorney to stay the course. The effort to convey a case story theme is frequently hampered by an ironic impediment: knowing the case so well, it is hard to deliver it to uninitiated decision makers. Anchors, positions, and story sequences can easily be dropped over time, then revisited from your knowledgeable perspective. Abandoning the theme to pursue a challenging expert far away from your story can do more harm than good. The juror, can't make the same jumps because of unfamiliarity with the story territory. Starting with one set of anchors, then adopting a whole new set during any witness exam without linking them to the originals, is backsliding, not progress.

Trials are rife with tangents, interruptions, and distractions from the cohesive, compelling presentation of a case story. The risk for experienced trial attorneys is greater because distractions and distortions of a carefully laid out presentation plan have become routine. One insidious example of this is the many and varied ways in which legal procedures are placed ahead of people from minute to minute in courtrooms. If the "story is all about what it spends its time being about," then there are dozens of temptations to make the story more about the legal system than about the case story. This is more problematic for professionals than lay jurors.

As the focus group presentation tips suggest, openings conducted in these groups are the biggest departure from typical courtroom presentation. There, you are introducing the *facts*. Here, you are introducing the *story*. Each side wants to get their theme well established and set up whatever anchor phrases, analogies, crucial visuals, and the like are needed to convey them.

What you want to avoid is precisely what you've practiced in court: backing up every assertion about the story content with a list of detailed case facts.

Facts are about:

- Dates
- Times
- People (including names, titles, and qualifications)
- Background specifics
- Technical language, descriptions, and processes

Story is about:

- Theme
- Main characters (and their actions)
- Minor characters (why they are minor)
- Story scope

➲ The general story beginning, middle, and end—not necessarily chronological—a minimum of details

The presentation of a case story is an appeal to both the conscious and the primarily other-than-conscious facilities of decision makers. *How* you deliver your opening and the rest of the story through the witnesses is often more important than the specific words you use. If you're talking in a monotone about the fuse—the murder suspect burning down and about to explode—don't calmly turn to the judge and ask about mid-morning breaks in the same cadence. To deliver a theme about time running out, don't ask for early breaks and take days qualifying a minor witness. Never take it for granted that you will get back to the demands of your presentation plan when this half-day of procedural nonsense is over. You may, but the decision makers won't.

7.16 Tracking Growth

It is not always necessary to directly use mirroring to reap benefits for your client. Watching ordinary mirroring among others in negotiations, meetings, or the jury box can provide much valuable direction. Opening statement is an excellent time to track connection building among and between jurors. It is also an opportunity to track individual responses to the emerging story.

This point was made to a roomful of attorneys attending a professional conference a few years ago. They had been introduced to nonverbal techniques such as mirroring earlier in the day. That afternoon they gathered to watch a mock jury deliberation on a closed-circuit TV that had sudden audio trouble. While the glitch was being fixed the attorneys observed the group selecting seats around the table before beginning deliberations.[21]

One of the gathered attorneys pointing to the soundless video running shouted to the nonverbal communication instructor, "Hey, tell us what they're thinking!" to a small chorus of giggles. Several lawyers near the trainer turned. The trainer, still facing the silent screen, spoke with four of them seated in front of him:

> I can't tell you exactly what they're thinking, but I can tell you this. The woman in the gray coat will be the person to direct all the activity. The young man across from her (a law student, they had all been told) will probably be suggested as the nominal foreperson, but he will still defer to her directions. The woman to her immediate left will be the one to talk first on most subjects. The younger, dark-haired woman directly across from Ms. Gray Coat will typically speak last. The older gentleman to her left will have to be prompted for any contributions, and

21. *Trial Diplomacy Journal*, 19 (1996): 299–307.

> Ms. Gray Coat will have the last word announcing a consensus, after which deliberations will come to a quick halt, within five minutes.

Shortly after the sound came on and over the next forty to fifty minutes, as each predicted response appeared, the lawyers would turn and stare more. Later, the attorneys said they were most impressed that the information had been gleaned mostly from watching the jurors speak with no audible words about things like sodas and seating arrangements.

The lawyers assumed, as we all are inclined, that the subject matter of a discussion somehow controls the outcome. We presume that concepts drive our interactions: "Tell us what they are thinking, so we may know what they will do." More often, it's "Watch what we *do* to learn about our thinking."

7.16.1 Connections

What drove the speculations that proved accurate about the mock jurors was what they did *without thinking*. They advertised connections, which in turn predicted alliances. They did this by virtue of the sequence in which people repeated their response patterns with one another and the topics they had previously verbalized in voir dire, the sequence in which the topics discussed would be introduced and disposed of by the group. Most of the connections were visible by watching who was mirroring whom—the sequence of who consistently shifted posture or gestures after someone else showed the order in which people would most likely speak when deliberating. The way Ms. Gray Coat invited people to speak or stop simply by moving the focus of her attention, without necessarily speaking, suggested strongly who would be directing things once we could again hear the conversation.

Mirroring allows you to track responses. For example, jurors can be seen adopting the postures and gestures of certain people in the courtroom with whom they've developed connections. They don't all just mirror each other. Although not confirming agreement or affection, this signal does confirm who currently has that person's least-divided attention. In one of the earliest post trial interviews I ever did, one juror repeatedly modeled the actions of the plaintiff's attorney when describing his personal thinking process in arriving at a plaintiff's verdict, as well as when we discussed the attorney's attributes and presentation. But he displayed this distinct behavior at no other time during the hour-long interview that was videotaped for later review.

7.16.2 Mirroring Among Jurors

When observed over time, mirroring among jurors often shows the sequence in which people repeatedly respond to things they all hear and experience. That order almost always transfers to the jury room when they begin deliberating. Knowing the predilections of jurors that will probably speak first, second, and last is an opportunity to craft your case presentation by taking advantage of that sequence.

For instance, in the silent video example, if you could see after you had observed the order of the group's mirroring that Ms. Gray Coat's friend on her left would lead each subject, and you knew what the hot-button biases and issues were for her in voir dire, you could form strong guesses about which portions of the case story would most likely be brought up first in deliberation. If those portions are not your particular strengths, you might want to shore them up more strongly in opening and during testimony along the lines of Ms. Me First's prevailing biases. Or you could choose to offer different, stronger parts of the case, reframed to be more acceptable to those attitudes. At a minimum, you would know that something would have to be done, for whom and when. How exactly to go about it would depend on the specifics of your case, your presentation style, and the witnesses' talents.

When dealing with biases, knowing which juror is more likely to fully attend to which other jurors is a priceless chance to suggest and reinforce alternative biases to one or both parties to overcome prevailing leanings in deliberation. For example, after watching who shifted first, second, third, and so forth in a focus group on a medical neglect case, it seemed apparent who would be directing one group's deliberations. While the rest of the panel had strong, conservative leanings regarding the practice of suing doctors, one young man brought his prevailing beliefs in personal responsibility and the doctor's failure to "do all he could to protect the patient" out early. This shifted the tenor of the whole panel's discussion. The person that had followed him most, nonverbally, spoke up next, adopting the preventability language herself. The second person to speak after her, who was mirroring the first woman, was also following the young man. In court it will be the lawyer or a witness addressing the "leader" member, along lines they've declared important in voir dire or on their questionnaires.

Verbal matching of hot topics that are most meaningful or available to certain jurors can be ratcheted up in impact by matching a portion of that person's demeanor before broaching the subject in opening or later with a witness. Eye contact isn't even required for the effect to be achieved. People associated with certain hot topic areas of the story line during voir dire can be referred to nonverbally by a slightly sustained look or an imprecise gesture as the point is addressed during opening or testimony. This helps that individual and all present to more easily focus on what linkages are being made and what factors are being reinforced or challenged. We can envision their minds (as if run by verbal means) saying something like, "OK, yeah, Fred's the guy we all already have associated with 'safety on the job.'"

Rhetorical proposals or propositions of a yes-no nature can be tracked among decision makers throughout opening statements, in any venue, for the unspoken responses they get, before it is too late to address them should the wrong ones pop up. The horse knows, and given half a chance, will show us where to go next.

7.17 2015 Supplement

7.17.1 *What's Your Story?*

There still is no better heading for this chapter than the one I used in the first edition of *Facts Can't Speak for Themselves*, and in many significant ways, voir dire is truly a return to the very start. And, as far as this book goes, the "very start" is still encompassed by two questions:

1. What is this case story?

2. How is that story best delivered to any decision maker?

During voir dire, you are given the opportunity to learn, for the first time, how decision makers are reacting to your client's case story and what their perceptions of its parts are—only, this "focus group" really counts. As you know now, the people sitting in the venire are the ones who will (re)build your story in their own way. You should be ready to spend your time with them asking them indirectly, but with as much accuracy as "indirect" permits, exactly *how* they are most likely to go about that "job."

Experience has shown me since 2005 that the general attitude I proposed to you then with which to approach your potential decision makers can now be safely laid out much more directly. You want to voir dire on your case *story* far more than you want to voir dire on your potential jurors' backgrounds, attitudes, ideas, and beliefs—*except* as they relate to the case story. Your inquiry should be governed by the amount of case specific facts you allow in. And, the prescription today is still the same: as few as possible.

If the goal is to voir dire on the story, you cannot ask direct questions of what "someone" might think of each fact in your case story. Not only is that legally inappropriate, it's also highly ineffective. Instead, consider discussing only the bare minimum of case specific facts in favor of filling in each step of your story sequence with related facts from the prospective juror's own life story—each frame of the story should be filled with *their* "facts," not yours. That's how you'll find out who is ready to (re)build the story you need, something you can't find out through bombarding them with the facts and asking how biased they are about one or the other.

As much as we might struggle against it, we know perfection is unattainable, but we still give it our best shot. In the same way, it is unlikely that you will ever achieve a perfectly "case fact free" voir dire. However, when you reference the key topics in your client's case story sequence as generally as the facts allow, in order to invite potential jurors to inject, as fully as possible, references from their own life experiences, that is as close to perfect as you can get. Use specific case facts only as needed to focus people's self-referential search. That is the most effective approach to take, and the added benefit is that it inhibits an attorney's natural inclination to argue the entire case during voir dire, before the jurors have been seated.

Also, in 2005, I mostly focused on what *not* to do during voir dire, but didn't specify exactly what *to* concentrate the bulk of your efforts on. Now, I'm able tell you that ninety percent (or more) of your efforts should be devoted to discovering the story-building potential of each person in the venire. During whatever time you are allowed, find out who among the group is most ready to (re)construct your client's case story the way the results of your focus group and your presentation plan say will be most likely to achieve your client's desired outcome.

How to do this? Frame by Frame.

In addition to the frames you've developed for your case story,[22] add two more frames that are exclusive to voir dire:

1. *Burden of Proof*
2. *Damages* (amounts, categories, purpose served)

Then, in the same sequence that you will be presenting your case story during opening and then again during testimony, engage potential jurors in an open and honest discussion of each frame as they relate them to the "job at hand"—i.e., the job they are "applicants" for—*and* the job they are allowed to turn down—i.e., the job of juror in a plaintiff's case for money damages.

The challenge is to avoid introducing any of the frames like this:

> Ladies and gentlemen, you'll learn that my client, Fred, was employed for six months as a welder at this company's airliner construction plant, and he was subjected to several hazardous conditions on a daily basis that, while he had some responsibility to handle on his own, were ultimately in the complete control of the company in charge of his work-site.

Don't argue your case before it's time. Instead, ask about people's experiences, ideas, and attitudes in terms of how they frame the *risk* on their *own* job sites (former, current, future—and those of close friends or loved ones) and ask:

> Who here—yourself, a close friend, or family member—has ever had to deal with any kind of significant risk, danger, or hazard on the job or in a work context? You? Please, tell me about it.

---

22. Risks, Rules, Right Way, Bad Acts, Cause of Injury, Harms and Losses, and Defendant Excuses; *see* Chapter Five, section 5.10, "2015 Supplement."

Just as Friedman and Malone suggest, when establishing a complete list of "rules"[23] for a plaintiff's case, always start with the most general and move to the most specific. Their prescription works because our brains happen to function the same way, from the general to the specific. Cast the widest net, so nobody feels left out. Find the version of each of your story frames including *burden of proof* and *damages*, with the broadest scope, and start each topic with a question parallel to that scope of inquiry. You are interested in the stories jurors are primed to tell, so by all means, leave your client out of it all at this point.

You should constantly and exhaustively seek out the life experiences that mirror the frames in the case story you have prepared. Potential jurors won't realize you are examining them in this way—i.e., that you are trying to plumb how closely pieces of their own lives can relate to pieces of your client's story they will soon perceive in opening statement and in testimony by witnesses. Until then, you want to open the door as widely as possible to invite them to relate their own life experiences, as fully and as thoroughly as possible, as they perceive, in turn, each frame in your case story, all while you are talk only about themselves. Again, just as the brain does, always begin with the general and move toward the specific.

The more an individual juror can recognize any of their own life experiences as a personal example of *risk* and/or *rule* recognition, the more they have injected their own experiences into the frames of your case story. And so, soon after your opening begins, when they start to perceive (and remember, they are doing so primarily other-than-consciously) the same sequence of frames, they will feel a certain familiarity as in voir dire. And now, for the second time, those parts of someone else's life story have been *specifically* related to the frames of your client's case story. Now, indirectly, but all the more persuasively as a result, they feel invested in perceiving your client's story as something more than a lawsuit. Now, these story frames are not just concepts obviously designed to elicit emotional reactions, but because of the recently shared, honestly acknowledged (by you), and revivified life experiences (by them), they are now likely to elicit powerful "gut" reactions to your client's story.

This approach actually serves the federally sanctioned purpose of a "thorough and probing" voir dire far better than heavy-handed attempts at pre-trying your case by browbeating "commitments" from potential jurors ever could. Or, you could waste time and squander rapport by asking them what they think about "tort reform," "litigation lotteries," and "obscene multi-million dollar verdicts in the frivolous lawsuits that so overwhelm our courts today."

In voir dire, when something is important it needs to be acknowledged early. Doing so, by using the "on the one hand/on the other hand" approach, is

23. Rick Friedman and Patrick Malone, *Rules of the Road: A Plaintiff Lawyer's Guide to Proving Liability*, 2d Ed. (Portland, OR: Trial Guides, 2010).

most likely to encourage a judge to allow cause strikes based on responses from potential jurors.

How so?

There is no argument to be made that you "misrepresented," "segmented," or "cherry picked" information during your inquiry.

How so?

The extremes of both sides of the topic(s) have been laid out for jurors to consider, offering a complete range of possible reactions, and any response they have will fall within this range. Later, when discussing cause strikes with the judge, there can be no suggestion that you were strategically slanting your questions.

Here are some other suggestions for voir dire that can produce equally valuable results.

- If your goal is to maximize strikes for cause,[24] then conduct yourself throughout voir dire as if you have no peremptory strikes available to you.
- Always ask questions that presume an answer—e.g., "Who here feels at least a little like that?" or *"Who wants to go first?"*
- Never ask questions that presume you will receive *the,* or even, *a* "right" answer to your question—e.g., "So, you would agree that if a company did this then they'd be responsible for what happens, right? Am I right?" (This has proven to be an ubiquitous habit of attorneys that is very hard to redirect.)
- Employ the "on the one hand/on the other hand" scenario or the "my friend John . . ." technique whenever possible. After introducing a frame of inquiry like *burden of proof* for plaintiffs, set up two diametric positions:
    1) Unfair because it's too *easy* on the plaintiffs
    2) Unfair because it's too *hard* on defendants
- Follow up with the defense-leaning folks first, exhaust their input, and gain cause strikes. Then talk to *your* "friendlies."

24. It is a sad fact but true that some attorneys who disdain (read: "fear") talking directly with jurors during voir dire actually hit the podium circuit ("Coming soon to a conference near you!") admonishing their colleagues to shun any and all voir dire strategies designed to maximize cause strikes because of the "potential loss of rapport" with the entire panel due to just one juror's negative response, because it's "just never worth it."

While at first this might seem anathema to almost any attorney—i.e., inviting someone to expose attitudes that are "friendly" to your case in front of the panel and opposing counsel—this strategy is critical to building a perceptual foundation for any venire panel that improves your chances of success.

How does this work?

Because Pavlov and Skinner were right. If there is no credible reinforcement early on of the frames and anchors (a phrase and an image) tied to your client's case, there will be nothing for decision makers to build on throughout the trial, *and* nothing for *your* case-friendly jurors to reliably draw on during deliberation. Talking with potential jurors friendly to your case can cause real consternation for a defense attorney who is expecting to walk in to voir dire and hear only the defense-leaning people speaking up—plaintiff attorneys generally fear exposing even a single person friendly to their client's case. But, by eliciting plaintiff-friendly comments based on a potential juror's life experiences, ideas, attitudes, and beliefs about each frame in your case story sequence, those perceptions are being actively reinforced for the panel, and plaintiff counsel can cement this advantage by acknowledging and reinforcing perceptions that come directly from the panel and not from an attorney. These perceptions will form the foundation of each case story (re)built by the jurors who remain. If you want that foundation to be available to you, you must give potential jurors the opportunity to lay it down in their discussions with you.

7.17.2 Rapport with Jurors—Voir Dire

In 2005, I pointed to decision-maker *attention* as the primary result of physical and verbal *mirroring*. However, the intervening years have confirmed how much more mirroring to achieve *rapport* with an individual, or a group, can actually help you accomplish. The research shows efforts to mirror not only "invite" decision makers' attention, it actually can produce reciprocal engagement. Mirroring is about making a connection—a reciprocal connection— in a matter of moments with anyone you want, whenever you want, with or without the use of spoken language.

Since the late 1980s when Giacomo Rizzolatti's neurological researchers in Parma, Italy, discovered what they termed "mirror neurons," literally thousands of social, psychological, and other research projects have been conducted which have confirmed that there is a direct connection between mirroring and the establishment of rapport. MIT social scientist Sandy Pentland, in his book *Honest Signals: How They Shape Our World*, wrote:

> [U]nconscious, automatic mimicry improved financial results by *20 to 30 percent.*
>
> The impact of mimicry on these financial interactions [sales and salary negotiations] dwarfs almost every other factor that has ever been studied.[25]

Many of the studies on mirroring and rapport say one can't be achieved without the other—that is, if there is no mirroring, there can't be any rapport. Neuropsychologist Nadia Webb points out that the opposite situation is also true: when you have achieved rapport and you eliminate mirroring from the relationship, the rapport disappears also.[26] She was referencing happy couples in which one partner suffers an injury to the part of the brain that houses the mirror neurons—now sometimes called the *mirror system*—who then consistently experiences a loss of connection with their spouse along with the loss of those brain cells.

The 2015 supplement to Chapter Six includes the case presentation plan for an ironworker's suit over a work-site injury due to safety equipment that was withheld by the contractor, resulting in the ironworker being paralyzed. In the venire panel, there was a rock climber—with well over twenty years of climbing experience who was proud of his injury-free record and knowledge of safety equipment that had helped him build that record. But, before the details of his rock-climbing experiences came out during voir dire, the plaintiff's attorney spent a few seconds tilting his head, arranging his shoulders, and nodding along with this rock-climbing person in the venire. Prior to mirroring in this way, the answers he was getting were of the "yes," "no," or "maybe"—i.e., "I'll have to hear the facts"—variety.

But, as the attorney continued to mirror this potential juror's demeanor while discussing the risk frame of working in very high places, the rock climber spoke sincerely about how he felt *personally* responsible for taking every action necessary to keep himself safe while climbing very high on the rocks for all those years. But it was *how* he said what he said next that made a big difference.

He said that, as a rock climber, fully cognizant of rock climbing's inherent dangers, not only does he rely on—and actually has no other choice but to do so—a "double redundancy" in safety equipment, such as two safety lines, but also on the fact that he *gets* the safety equipment from trusted sources. This was absolutely key: that it when it comes to safety, it was not just him acting on his own behalf while climbing.

Can you see the parallel between the story of a contractor/owner removing promised safety equipment and the proudly uninjured rock climber who relies on

25. Alex Pentland, *Honest Signals: How They Shape Our World.* (Boston, MA: Bradford Books, MIT Press, 2010) (emphasis added).
26. Nadia Webb, PsyD, made these comments while presenting at the annual convention of the International Brain Injury Society, March 21–22, 2014.

the caliber (of the "doubly redundant") safety equipment he gets from others? Now, here is where voir dire can really pay off for your client. If the discussion were to end there, based on the facts of their own lives, any rock climber in the venire might well have seen the ironworker as acting irresponsibly by disconnecting his safety line. In fact, this rock climber used the phrase "personally responsible" in discussing rock-climbing safety. Yet, his take on "personal responsibility" for safety notwithstanding, he is still a perfect example of being able to bring the personal experience of a potential decision maker to bear on the task of (re)building the case story *your way*.

As it was, this gentleman became the foreperson for the trial and led the jury to a state record verdict for this type of plaintiff personal injury case. Had he not been mirrored by the plaintiff attorney during voir dire, we would not have heard anything about the parallels in his experience with a crucial liability frame in our case. Once rapport with him was established, he revealed that he was ready to (re) write a story about a company that takes safety equipment *away* from its workers.[27]

7.17.3 Opening Frames—or "Framing Openings"

Quick, think of someone who is rolling his eyes.

How many meanings came to mind just then, solely from your perception of that one gesture? Now, think of as many different situations in which someone rolling his eyes could be important, or—not.

The "or—not" is an important concept here because prior "mindsets," or frames of reference, stored in our cache of experiences—along with their meaning and importance to us—are accessed by *anchors*. Anchors are images and verbal expressions that trigger specific frames of reference in our own personal storage, which, in turn, give those images and words their particular meaning and import for each of us.

Any single image or phrase, when we are conditioned to respond to them, can evoke a "frame of mind." We have conditional responses linked to many anchors that can evoke both general *frames* (outcome and process, prevention and protection, risks, rules, right way, etc.) and specific *frames* (judging someone by appearance, driving standards for professionals, factors making a lawsuit less legitimate, etc.) for the person seeing or hearing them. Focus groups allow you to harvest the most potent of these anchors related to your case story (as revealed by participants) and can serve to guide your use of them with any legal decision maker.

Imagine the frames of mind common to most attorneys that could be evoked by the following images and phrases to which they've developed conditional responses.

---

27. The outline I provide to attorneys who have trained with me in this approach to voir dire appears at section 7.17.5, "Voir Dire Practice Plan," below.

- ➲ A juror in the top row, staring the lawyer down, with arms crossed and lips set.
- ➲ "I've tried all those tricks taught in the CLEs, but the jurors in my state are just too poisoned to reach, no matter what you try."
- ➲ A substantially overweight client, in ill-fitting clothing, sweating visibly at counsel table just before you rise for opening statement.
- ➲ "This judge has been against us from the get go."

You can demonstrate this for yourself, right now. Imagine, as vividly as you can, giving your opening statement to an openly hostile judge. How do you feel? How does your voice sound? Where is your gaze? Where are your hands? What is your posture? Now imagine giving your opening to an adorable eight-year-old. Get it? What *you see* is what *they get*. A difference on the inside (within *your* mindset) dictates how you come across on the outside, which, in turn, directly affects your audience's mindset.[28]

Let's consider an example common to many negligent labor and delivery cases: how the needs of the baby and mother can seem to compete or be at odds with one other depending on how their stories are framed during your case presentation. If the story focuses on risks to the mother because of prior health problems (obesity, high blood pressure, etc.) and how they magnify the real hazards of surgical delivery by C-section, significant attention can easily shift away from the other important patient—the baby—when judging the conduct of the medical professionals at the time.

How so?

The inevitable breaking of the Golden Rule by decision makers inserting themselves into a story where all their personal experiences as, or with, patients (such as themselves, their close friends, and/or family members) tends to draw their focus *away* from the baby *toward* the mother's situation. Decision makers who (re)build the story from the mother's point of view first, are likely to frame the primary patient concerns as linked to the mother. But, what if the story is framed at the outset from the point of view of the baby? The ever-present danger of a brain deprived of oxygen—and the lifetime of disability that deprivation presages—would inform all of the related actions, talk, and choices in the story, while the mother's situation

28. Linda Trickle-Degnan and Robert Rosenthal, "The Nature of Rapport and its Nonverbal Coordinates," *Psychological Inquiry* 1(4) (1990): 285–293, cited in Daniel Goleman, *Emotional Intelligence: The New Science of Human Relationships* (New York, NY: Bantam, 2007). Since the First Edition of *Facts Can't Speak for Themselves*, I have seen this validated by dozens of attorney groups across the country. Try this exercise for yourself in front of an actual group and see how differently they perceive the two performances. Interestingly, the research agrees that just putting yourself into a "professional" frame hurts your ability to even connect well with other people you may wish to influence.

by default would take a back seat in decision makers' minds. "Oxygen deprivation" and a brain starved of oxygen are the phrase and image that anchors for decision makers the mindset that everything now has to do with babies, protection, and the need to *prevent* injuries through actions taken well ahead of time. The frames rule the facts.

So, how does an attorney increase the chances that the anchors she uses most likely will bring up the frames of mind she wants decision makers to use? Rapport. When we are in rapport with another person, that person is much more likely to adopt similar anchors and frames to the ones driving the story being related at the moment. If you mirror an openly hostile judge, you actually can achieve a *stronger* connection—and rapport—regardless of his attitude. But, if your frame of mind isn't tilting toward a productive one for the situation—i.e. "helping," "educating," "informing," or even "relieving" the judge in that judge's mind under those circumstances—you may fall into a less productive frame, exemplified by: "But, your Honor, you *have to understand*!" Any rapport you've established to that point will be broken by the demeanor driven by this unproductive frame of mind. For you to present congruently and in a way that maintains your rapport with decision makers, the first frame of mind you want to manage well is your own.

However, having an awareness of the most productive frame of mind for you to adopt is valuable, but it isn't quite enough. You want your invitation to others to adopt that same frame (or frames) as you to be as compelling as possible. Framing *will* happen, with or without your help. Imagine what other-than-conscious images and experiences would go through your head as you approach the bench of a hostile judge if you don't intervene consciously to preempt them. It's very unlikely that internal dialogue like, "He's going to screw me again!" is going to bring up a frame of mind that allows you to present (or to be seen) at your very best. Attorneys who have observed how focus group participants (or mock trial jurors) respond to frames that, at the time, felt "right" to them but turned out to generate nothing helpful at all from the actual decision makers, will have no trouble adopting a demonstrably more productive frame. (By the way, this is one of the most valuable uses for focus group work.)

One caveat to bear in mind is that the process of setting up frames for yourself follows the same rules as trying to reframe someone else's experience. It takes more than conscious lip service—i.e., "just think of it this way!" If you want to adopt a "relieving" frame of mind with which to approach a judge, you must relive a few experiences of your own when you actually did relieve something from someone. Anything less will likely be perceived by decision makers as if you were saying yes while shaking your head no.

No matter how much you practice coordinating your verbal and nonverbal responses, if your *own* "mindset" is not on board, your audience will pick up the incongruence. If when you are saying yes, but your audience experiences no from *any* level of your delivery, you lose credibility. When decision makers experience incongruence, they not only associate it with the case story frames you are presenting, but they particularly associate the incongruence with *you*.

This means that every time they see, hear, or experience your delivery in any way, your credibility will be in jeopardy. So, it helps immensely to appreciate that the most effective way to influence or persuade others is to literally "step inside" the most helpful frame of mind yourself, first. Only, now *you know* how it is that you can't fake it.

7.17.4 Hold Me Down

I've suggested that the path to any *frame* in a case story leads to (and through) an *anchor* (or anchors)—i.e., a phrase and/or image to which we are conditioned to respond. We all have anchors and attendant frames to which we are preconditioned. But, because the process works so well, an attorney with rapport can quickly invite an individual or a group to create one of Pavlov's *conditional responses* from a new set of cues, linked to a new set of experiential frames.

A good example is the visual anchor David Ball proposes to plaintiff attorneys in order to "make preponderance work" for them.[29] He suggests using a more carefully executed version of the old "I'm a Little Teapot"-outstretched-arms depiction of the scales of justice. David's version brings the attorney's hands in very close to the chest, making a very small movement up and down to indicate the tiny standard of preponderance. Here's another example of the value of congruence between delivery and the frame you want to invite.

Any decision maker faced with an attorney pantomiming justice's scales with arms *fully outstretched*, tilting their *entire* body this way or that in order to physically communicate the "tiny" difference of evidential preponderance immediately will perceive two things:

- Based on the physical modeling, the actual burden of proof must be massive—perhaps even greater than the criminal standard.
- The attorney appears to be an idiot—or actually is one.

Holding two hands, mid-chest, raising one hand very slightly (the same hand each time) shows what the "tiny" standard really is all about. Asking, in voir dire, who thinks such a tiny burden is "unfair" and is "too easy for plaintiffs and too hard on defendants" only improves an attorney's credibility.

This seems to work so well that in a focus group in San Francisco that I was conducting a few years ago, a woman who had seen me model David's "preponderance hands" and then saw it modeled a few more times again by the plaintiff attorney

---

29. David Ball, "Making Preponderance Work," *Trial* (American Association for Justice, March 2008).

during his seven-minute opening, actually repeated that gesture when *she* was talking about a "standard." But it wasn't the preponderance standard; within a matter of minutes, she had attached the physical anchor (i.e., hands forming a scale) associated with the legal standard to the standards she knew (i.e., the standards of the real estate profession). She was unaware that her hands were "illustrating" (other-than-consciously) with the same gesture she'd just seen and was *deliberately*[30] using it to express her frame of mind.

What this woman actually was demonstrating was what the grandfather of anchoring, Ivan Pavlov, termed "translation." Though he had many, perhaps Pavlov's greatest talent was observation. What he noticed in his intentionally conditioned German shepherd dogs was that, after they had learned (other-than-consciously, of course) to link the smell of meat powder to the sound of the ringing bell, nobody told the dogs that the research had been concluded. They kept conditioning their responses to more and more cues all on their own. Pavlov's genius was that he noticed that the dogs kept the conditioning "train" rolling on—i.e., they:

- Salivated when they anticipated a bell *would* have been rung in the past
- Salivated when an experimenter entered the room *as if he would* ring a bell
- Salivated at a particular time when a bell *might have* been rung

"Translation" is the talent we have for transferring one anchored effect—a conditional response—and attaching it to another cue entirely. So, in our negligent baby delivery example, the "protection" response can be primarily linked to the mom in fragile health, but it can be transferred to the baby having oxygen withheld, too. Same "protection" response, two different cues. For example, the lady realtor in the focus group "translated" the preponderance hand pantomime to another related area of her life experience without consciously realizing she'd done so—all within about forty minutes.

Any attorney who has seen multiple focus group members consciously and other-than-consciously repeat and model the "hands" standards they were first introduced to at the start of the group all the way down into deliberations when arguing for (or against) applying the preponderance standard can begin to appreciate how far this phenomenon of anchoring really can affect your persuasive impact with any decision maker, in any venue. But, anchors work far better among people who have established rapport. And, the frames you want anchors to invite to the forefront in any decision maker's mind are much more likely to be used if the attorney already has adopted that frame of mind before they begin.

Anchors bring up *frames*. Frames rule *facts*. But *rapport* must always come first.

---

30. John Grinder, PhD, co-developer of the Neurolinguistic Programming Model, was fond of saying about such activity that "[i]t was not conscious, but it was deliberate."

7.17.5 Voir Dire Practice Plan

VOIR DIRE PRACTICE PLAN

AIM

- To maximize strikes for cause
- To identify and confirm the most crucial candidates for peremptory strikes
- To support the use of statistical profiles to their best advantage

MEANS

- Only ask questions that lower all barriers to the worst possible answers to case story-based attitudes, ideas, and beliefs.
- Follow up each "worst possible" answer at least twice with very short questions (How so? What else?) while avoiding the temptation to add information, advocate, or argue your positions).
- Encourage elaboration on the basis for each "worst possible" answer from each venire person.
- Exhaust all holders of such ideas or beliefs on each of the selected key topics (scripted for each case).

PROBLEM

- The "fairness question."
  - "Despite all your admitted biases, can you still listen to all the facts, apply the law as it's given to you and *be fair*?" (If you need the answer to this question to be no for a biased juror to be excused, you will get it nearly as much as you need.)

SOLUTION

- Frame all the questions you ask in a way to invite an answer more like, "Yes, I can be as fair as I'm able to be as a juror . . . but anywhere else, just not here."

FRAMES

- Ready—because summoned
- Willing—because showed up

- Able—the essential point of voir dire inquiry
  - At start of discussion: "Who here promises to be as fair as you are *able* to be if you end up sitting on this jury panel?"
- Being a juror is a job
  - A job among many jobs, and you have more than one from which to choose.
  - Everyone wants to do the job *as well as it needs to be done.*
  - You want to be as fair as you are *able* to be.
  - Each case presents different issues that could get in the way of doing the job *as well as it needs to be done.*
  - Things can get in your way, stop you, and even block you from being as fair as you are *otherwise* able to be and doing the job as well as it needs to be done.
  - What can stop you are the things *you* bring to the table from your life experience (attitudes, ideas, beliefs, life lessons that cause you to pre-judge certain situations or circumstances).
  - Honesty in answering every question is all that's needed to determine *where* you can do the job best, and be as fair as you are able to be.

  Then, at the end of setting up those frames up for the discussion:

  - "Who promises to be as honest as they can be, to take each question seriously, and to answer all that apply to you? The only wrong answer is the one that you keep to yourself."

FOLLOW-UP QUESTIONS

Follow-up questions are the key factor to success or failure in maximizing cause strikes. Follow-ups can all be done with only three questions:

1. What else?
2. How so?
3. Can you please say/tell me some more?

But, if you haven't asked of each potential juror of interest at least two short follow-up questions after the first question on each major topic, you will not be getting enough input to make successful cause challenges—or to identify the most important candidates for peremptories either.

HANDLING INPUT

- If jurors ask a question in response, either answer with a question, i.e., "How is that important for you to know?" or "It sounds pretty important to you. How did you get there on this particular subject?" Or, rephrase the original question for them. Avoid adding any information, advocating, or arguing.
- If jurors claim, "I'll have to hear the facts first," remind them what the inquiry is all about and that the job requires them to recognize, *before* they are sworn in, whether what they are bringing to the table will make it harder—maybe much harder or even impossible—for them to do that in this one case, but not in any of the dozens of others out there available to sit on.
- Thinking or feeling you can be fair, but then finding out halfway through the trial that you can't be as fair as the job demands, will be too late. That's why neither lawyer will cherry-pick a couple of their best facts and argue them now; it's not appropriate. First, they have to determine who is best suited to judge this case or who would do a better job on some other case among all those out there.

SETTING UP STRIKES

When the answers have revealed a strong enough attitude or position to warrant the effort, work to get the potential juror to "invite themselves off the panel."

- Who is already beginning to believe this may not be the job for you? How so?
- If these are the rules you have to follow as a juror in this case, who is already starting to think some other case, with some different rules you must enforce, is a better fit for you?
- Would it be fair to say that any case that doesn't throw up these obstacles is one where you would be better able to do the job as well as you can do it?
- If you were to stay here and try to deal with these obstacles, would it be fair to say it would be hard in this case, if not impossible, for you to do the job of applying these rules considering these obstacles?
- The ideal response, especially when questioning a potential juror's ability to apply the law, is: "If that's the rule/law I'd have to apply as a juror here, I would have real trouble with that . . . find that hard—if not impossible—to do that job here."

Chapter Eight

Start, Look, and Listen: Visual and Verbal Aids and Evidence

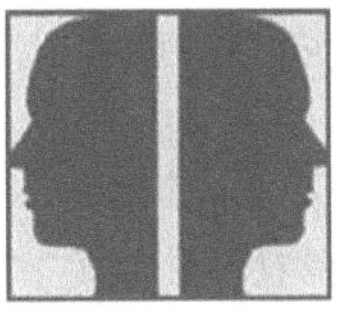

Every picture tells a story, don't it?
—*Rod Stewart*

8.1 Feast Your Eyes

When a person closes his eyes, there is a huge surge of electrochemical power in the brain, because the complex activity of seeing things around us uses so much energy. It can help if trial professionals constantly keep in mind that many of the images that make the most difference to any decision maker already reside in the brain. These images are composed of millions of stored pictures in memory and the thousands we then construct using those references to help make sense of everything during the experience of a single day. This could also include a case story presentation. All our remembered images are actually constructs, too. Each time an image in memory is accessed consciously or otherwise, it is altered during the process by the interface with newer, current input.

Memory is not fixed; it is malleable. Imagery is less insubstantial than recalled words, and is often used as a first step in retrieving our stored references. If you imagine all your experiences stored outside conscious reach in a series of file cabinets, and each cabinet drawer you open is filled with manila files, with locator tabs at the top, the label on each of those tabs that you use to open the memory file very often comes in the form of a picture, an image.[1] Interestingly enough, even though retrieval may start with images, a majority of people processing those

1. I first heard this analogy about the role imagery plays in perception and recall from hypnotist and psychologist, Dr. Dave Dobson. It refers to a phenomenon of images and retrieval of memories less cut and dried than a real file cabinet, though the sense of the strength of a memory does rise with its association to an image. The inability to distinguish between actual and constructed "memories" also rises with the intensity of the perceived visual image. Francis Crick and Christof Koch, "The Problem of Consciousness," *Scientific American*, 12(1) (2002): 10–17; and Dan Schacter, *Searching for Memory* (New York: Basic Books, 1996): 23, 47–48, 69–73, 86–88.

references from which the raw material of decision-maker case stories are drawn, do so through auditory, not visual means. We may get to our references by images, but the majority of us process and make sense of them auditorily once a mental file is opened and in use.

An appreciation of the story-constructing role each decision maker plays demands adjusting to managing perceptions while delivering a case story.

Then what are trial professionals to make of ubiquitous pronouncements on the subject of one particular perceptual channel?

- We live in a visual culture.
- Most people are visual learners.
- Television-taught decision makers expect a more visual presentation, whether they know it or not.

Trial professionals regularly hear all three of these statements. They serve as goads to produce and present cases with a lot of exhibits, demonstratives, and every available bauble and whistle. Many are beginning to suspect that it's going a bit overboard to truck in ten boxes of foam core boards for a three-day trial or a week-long arbitration. In most cases, the problem does not lie in bringing too many visuals into mediation or court. Disaster is invited when too many of the wrong kind and too few of an effective form are produced. The visuals produced are frequently presented counterproductively for the purpose for which they were designed. These major errors in presentation bespeak a fundamental failure to appreciate and accommodate effective, respectful communication of a story at the visual level. Managing perceptions means managing visual and verbal channels in equal measure. They are both unquestionably used in equal measure to build case stories. There's good evidence to suggest that the pictures may actually come first.[2]

We know that the story-building process begins from the first moment in presentation long before evidence is broached. We know legal presentations are referenced against each person's prior experiences and their attendant, unique life stories. And we know unconscious selections from that constructive process produce stories leading to final decisions. The first part, and all the larger parts of this work done by every decision maker, originate and are reinforced and maintained outside conscious reach. It can't be directed by simple declaration any more than it can be fully revealed by direct questioning.

2. Modeling and expressing the third sensory channel of feeling is essential to a completely congruent message, but balancing the visual and verbal channels is challenge enough at the outset. *See* Paul Lisnek and Eric Oliver, *Courtroom Power: Communication Strategies for Trial Lawyers* (Colorado Springs, CO: Professional Education Systems Institute, 2001): Chapter 3.

Since the earliest steps of story building have a bigger influence on the final outcome, the job of managing perceptions delivered to decision makers will be most challenging and rewarding nearer the beginning. How the earliest parts of the case story presentation are perceived can have a huge, sometimes disproportionate effect on the final versions built to decide a legal matter.

Nobody can manage what is done inside decision makers' private, perceptual processing. Once underway, it is rare that they can be induced to even edit a set of emerging story elements. But a great deal can be done by managing how decision makers are invited to perceive your case story elements while they are being delivered. This is truer at the level of visual messages than at the verbal level, partly because so few professionals make a real effort to present a message that is as consistent and balanced in material and mental imagery as it is in words. This is often because they have yet to learn of the need to do so or how best to go about it.

Images play such a primary role in getting the perceptual referencing process underway, and the mind works in its own way regardless of whether trial professionals make an effort to influence the imagery it employs, that the question arises: "How safe is it to neglect the visual channel of communication when delivering the case story as the focus group work has suggested?" If we are going to show respect for the way case stories are actually judged, the answer is, "Not very safe at all."

Even today, when PowerPoint rules the legal landscape, very few trial professionals approach the minute-to-minute delivery of a case story as a chance to provide a balanced presentation to spark the decision makers' referencing with verbal and visual delivery streams. Yet that is what is required by the reality of a decision-making theme based on constructing a story to judge, not on interpreting a predetermined stack of facts. The delivery of case story elements must balance their visual and verbal packaging.[3] A well-managed presentation offers more to the receiver than a preponderantly verbal experience with some appended visual support.

Just as it is true that *how* something is said can carry more weight than what the particular words mean, how something is *shown* can outweigh its seemingly objective content. Overall story constructing puts our perceptual, thinking, and psychological habits in play. So do all the specific factors provided to decision makers so they may see, hear, and learn. Even though most people process information primarily by auditory means, trial professionals should recognize that all decision makers see as much as they hear. They also look to their seen and stored images to heard and stored words to build their versions of the case story. Balance between the verbal and visual delivery is not an option.

---

3. One more advantage to be garnered from the adversarial presentations in focus groups will be the chance for the trial professionals involved to practice balancing the verbal and visual delivery of a case story in real time, with real people.

8.2 Common Problems with Exhibits and Visuals

So which exhibits/visuals are the "wrong kind?" How is a "good" visual sometimes delivered in a manner that undercuts its intended effect?

It helps not to overlook the obvious. As some jurors could attest, most visuals delivered in case presentations are usually too busy or wordy. Exhibits saturated with multiple images spread edge to edge, or composed of a single image drenched in detail from top to bottom, bearing many colors, all perched atop a nine-foot-long time line, is too much information for the average brain to absorb. The same goes for a flurry of three dozen almost identical boards or slides depicting prior testimony in the record, contract paragraphs, or leaves from the book on industry standards in any matter. It can be hard to tell from whose position to read all that stuff, or what relation the twenty-third page shown this hour has to the overall theme initiated yesterday.

The majority of demonstrative or evidentiary exhibits also suffer from the verbal side of the "too busy" syndrome. They are too wordy. Think from the decision maker's viewpoint. If half the text on a slide or board requires more explaining or qualifying to properly appreciate and place it within the story elements it is intended to reinforce, there may be too many words on it. Especially if, as in most cases, more than half of the words do not even directly address either the particular point of the board or the overall theme on which the case story is based. All the extraneous verbiage just happened to be there in the document and got blown up, too, as all the unnecessary body parts and their labels show up just because they were part of the generic diagram from which the surgical visual was drawn.

Producing the demonstratives and exhibits too late is a risk. That does not mean a recess must be called while your boards are noisily unwrapped and sorted, before you discover that the final set of changes you called in last night were never made. Be prepared to present by taking the task more seriously. "Too late" in this case refers to those boards, overheads, and PowerPoint slides that were not developed until twelve days prior to the mediation or trial.

The visual channel of your message needs to be designed and integrated along with the verbal one to expand and support the growth of stories you hope their balanced delivery will impart. That means harvesting the suggestions and directions for their inclusion in the story package at the same time the verbal message is gleaned from focus group offerings. Just as you work out what each story element of theme, scope, viewpoint, active ingredient, sequence, and so on will be composed of—and which facts and opinions in testimony will go where, in what framework, to best carry those elements into each listener's private referencing—you also must be on the lookout for how each major topic or point needs to look inside their heads to do the same job. Every head watching and listening to the presentation has an almost unlimited storehouse of mental imagery, actual and imagined, with which to build and reinforce a story more or less like the one that you would prefer be built.

Leaving that imagery to be formed by random association or chance is every bit as dangerous as leaving the words to be selected with minimal or no direction. You are entitled to a theme. If you desire but fail to provide one, one will always be provided for you, and almost never in the way you would like. In cross-examination, the old saw reads, "One question for one fact." With the use of exhibits, demonstrative aids, and their visual delivery by the lawyer, the dictum could become, "One image for one story point."

Many attorneys succumb to the "I got it in" habit, which allows disparate, disjointed testimony to be introduced to confused or distracted listeners, who have no idea of what the full message they were supposed to hear among the bits and pieces. There's a visual version of that "I got it in" routine wherein images are expected to educate, persuade, or emotionally move people just because they are held in front of them. They will persuade, alright. Still, without some direction that influence is just as likely to move people farther from the story element you wanted them to see.

In a recent focus group, for example, five sections of five different documents were displayed for the participants, much as they would be in court or arbitration, using highlighted sections run through a video presenter. Late in the day, during a group building their private versions of a wrongful death story involving a residential care home, which had allegedly allowed a resident to wander off the premises to an early demise, it was apparent that the majority of the group was still vague on what exact duty the caretakers had toward residents. This, despite the fact that it is incorporated in a single, fairly clear phrase, "protective oversight," later defined as "constant awareness" of location and condition of the residents. Each of those phrases had been duly highlighted and displayed on the screen. So had three other sets taken from other sources, such as brochures, expert reports, and instruction manuals. The attorney involved, recognizing what a hard time the participants were having grasping the rule that seemed so simple and obvious to him, appeared frustrated at the participants' apparent inability to absorb basic concepts and messages.

Yet, when he was invited to see the story delivery from their perspective, he easily understood where they had been let down by the professional at the visual level. Though the represented documents were clearly accurate copies of the actual pages from the five original sources, the anchors the professionals already had for them could not have been more different than those they invited the participants to build. By showing them all in the same format, in a sequence and verbal package that made no strong distinctions among the five bits of type highlighted in yellow and flashed one after another at the crowd, the primary packaging invited the same meaning to be drawn for all five: black and yellow words about the rules. Though some people had drawn the proper verbal distinctions, calling the two key phrases "the law" or even the "statute language," the homogenizing force of the mushy visual delivery took far greater hold of the referencing and imaginations of the majority in the room. They had been *invited* to mix them all up. And, for the most part, they all accepted the invitation. No matter what was said about the five exhibits, they responded more to *how* they were shown, losing the significance of the key phrases.

So how do you know which kind of images to bring and in what numbers? More importantly, how do you go about presenting them in such a way that their impact is most compelling for the decision makers?

Many experts (notably Edward Tufte, whom the *New York Times* calls the "Leonardo da Vinci of data") write and present to all manner of professionals on the development and design of visuals to best portray quantitative information. Many others work exclusively as/or with legal professionals to assess, integrate, and produce the visual side of a balanced case story.[4] Just as there are businesses dedicated to the corralling, care, and feeding of focus groups, there are companies dedicated to the production of visuals for legal case stories. Accordingly, this chapter will focus more on the "how they are best shown" side of the task, rather than the "what they show" aspects. Once you have your story, how is that story best presented?

8.3 Visuals: So How Are They Best Shown?

In terms of demonstrative visuals, there are a range of typical problems to avoid:

- Illegible from more than three feet away
- Too few
- Too many
- Too busy, wordy, or data dense
- Too distracting (color schemes, number of images, number of points illustrated)
- Too dissociated from the theme and story elements, and even dominant facts
- Too disjointed in content and context from one another (especially if experts bring their own)
- Too heavy with irrelevancies (to the story, if not the evidence)

You may need outside help with the most effective design choices in support of the story elements you need to deliver. But if you have a case theme, theory, and

4. Four such resources are Rodney Jew, Corporate Design Strategies, Palo Alto, CA; Samuel Solomon, DOAR, Inc., Long Island, NY; James Gripp, Legal Arts Communications, San Diego, CA, and Arlington, VA; and Robert Bailey, Trial by Design, Sebastopol, CA.

thesis formulated, the scope the story must occupy, the point of view from which the story is best perceived, the active ingredient or party that drives the action, and the sequence in which the story unfolds, then you have all the necessary elements to test the content of any exhibit, model, or animation you may wish to present. Quality control for the kind of language you use or discard, images that will help and those that won't, comparisons and contrasts you'll want the visuals to highlight, the perspective from which they'll be drawn or shown, when to show them, how to show them, what words, gestures, and witness statements to associate with them will all be much more apparent if you've planned the presentation of your case as outlined in Chapter Six, with one eye fixed on the visual delivery channel.

The general design of all your exhibits will need to be somewhat consistent in both the form they take (color, size, text, delivery methods), and the function they will serve in expressing, maintaining, and reinforcing the theme that should be binding your case story together from start to finish in the decision makers' mind's eye. But be wary of settling for a single format, when an unfamiliar one may serve the story delivery much better. DOAR's Sam Solomon suggests equal attention be paid to six typical formats for visual design:

- Time lines
- Relationship charts
- Rating charts
- Comparison charts
- Process charts
- Decision trees[5]

Avoid getting stuck delivering only one or two formats by simple habit when the story could be served much better by a change.

8.3.1 Mental Multitasking

Anyone who watches the news on television is familiar with the graphics that accompany stories, which usually appear just over the talking head's shoulder for almost all of the twenty to forty in-depth seconds of coverage any story receives. If you look only at the speed with which such images are flashed at the average viewer, you may succumb to the logical, but erroneous, conclusion that people are now processing those images at a fantastic rate of speed. Culturally, the analogy would be the myth of mental multitasking or the more accurate descriptor: attention dividing and diluting. Note that not infrequently, immediately following a news story

5. Samuel Solomon, *Visuals and Visualization: Penetrating the Heart and Soul of Persuasion* (Long Island, NY: DOAR, Oct. 2002).

about how we, as a visually saturated people, are now able to absorb, process, and incorporate visual input at a previously unimagined rate (primarily delivered to our living rooms by the very same networks reporting the increase) will often come a story reporting on the diminishing attention span of the average American—with no irony intended or even perceived. These contradictory factors are well known to trial professionals across the country, but no matter how fast the images are tossed out, when it comes to referencing them, or processing them with any significant meaning attached, progress is still pretty slow for most individuals. And in a teaching/learning environment such as arbitration or trial, the amount of time needed to help any single visual or proposed mental image carry the desired impact is still closer to ten minutes, not seconds.

People will give the images offered them, or those they are invited to construct internally, the attention needed to form associations as you would desire—if they are not distracted or sedated by how they are presented. That someone *can* shift their attention every ten seconds doesn't mean they always will, or should be asked to. This is one of the primary negative aspects of PowerPoint presentations: the inevitable temptation to work at the rate of the machine when building and then displaying slides in massive numbers and rapid-fire cadence. A trial attorney's job in presentation is to first capture attention and then direct it to incorporate and use his message to build the most compelling version of the case story possible. Visuals drawn and delivered in the most effective way are not optional in that effort. That anyone may ever have thought they were doesn't make the former statement any less true.

8.4 Gleaning Images

Focus groups indicate where visuals are most needed, or where the ones you thought would be useful are in need of redesigning or a different delivery. When reviewing the offerings harvested from a group, start by sorting in four fundamental areas for hints about where a specific image or exhibit or an indirect suggestion to start employing a mental image could prove most valuable to decision makers building their story versions.

8.4.1 Significance

You will always get feedback about aspects of the case story you found significant that participants failed to and vice versa. Often, in the former case, that means coming up with some visual lead-ins, emphases, and/or follow-ups that convey the significance you need. Strong points confirmed as strong, whether predicted or not, also probably need to be made visually, to help assure similar responses from the actual decision makers to those you received from focus group members.

A problem for participants in this category of the story context, such as the slow grasping of the "protective oversight" rule for residential homes described earlier, would point directly to a better marking out of the visuals addressing those rules, and a more prominent placement for their delivery, so they can truly serve as aids to memory and meaning rather than impediments dropped onto the video presenter.

8.4.2 Juror Jobs

There will almost always be two areas in which demonstrative exhibits will be of assistance to jurors and professional decision makers. First, to help them place some limits on their natural speculation about what they are here to do, in this case, setting a job frame much as in the focus group introduction. Second, to help show how, exactly, they are supposed to do that job, in this case. Visually mark out both the scope of their task and the rules by which they must play that task out. In planning a visual channel of presentation, this category of potential guidance may be very important away from the jury box as well, in mediation or even arbitrations or bench trials, where the decision makers are presumed to be fully familiar with the legal rules governing their jobs. However, the design and delivery of the visual messages used there may require more circumspection.

In civil cases, using visuals to refine and focus what parts of all the various facts are most relevant to inquiring minds, can be very productive. But no more than the statutes, instructions, and verdict form questions when the outcome is based on a clear understanding of the legal rules decision makers are asked to apply. Standards in both the world they are asked to judge, such as contracts or medicine, as well as guidelines in the legal world they are asked to judge within—both foreign to the average juror—can use a lot of visual help in being conveyed. It stands to reason that this is one place where balancing two out of the three perceptual channels available might be pressed to good service for a case story.

8.4.3 Education

Knowing the designations of the professional standards applicable to certain civil cases is kind of like a spelling bee for many decision makers. They know the sound of the word and can memorize its spelling with visual assistance, but may have no notion of to what those letters and sounds are best related in forming a helpful case story. With professional decision makers, this problem can be exacerbated by their very familiarity with the terms of art, and their tendency to have already placed them in private reference categories that are not helpful to those called for by the particular story. Consider the term "negligence." Alone, it will surely prompt as many different connotations as there are jurors or judges on the panel—multiplied by the number of seconds they have available to reference and consider it throughout a trial. Different heads will always produce different meanings. Nothing a lawyer can say or show will change that perceptual basic, but that does not mean you can't herd most of those meanings in a particular direction.

In one case, a general practitioner's actions over many years with certain select female patients were called into question in a civil suit. Focus group work suggested it was very important that jurors be able to easily collect all the widely varied wrongs being claimed under a general umbrella termed "negligence." They needed some sort of solid pattern they could all appreciate—regardless of the entry point their own life experiences provided when confronting a story about abuse of the doctor-patient relationship.[6] They had to easily be able to group the disparate claims inside the context of medical rules of propriety, while simultaneously instructing themselves a bit on the legal standards they were being asked to apply to that package of professional standards.

The doctor's conduct over many years with many women patients was questioned in several areas: he physically handled certain women in some "funny" ways during various kinds of exams, including physically "punishing" them for their resistance. He made verbal comments that were, by almost any standard, inappropriate. Plus, his habits of referral, prescription, and counseling were all questionable in different circumstances, with different patients. Focus groups found these sins of omission and commission too diffuse to hold up to a legal neglect standard with any real assurance of doing the job well. A visual representation of the various alleged wrongs seemed in order, grouping and reframing them for emphasis.

We came up with a list of three topics to be drawn out by the plaintiff's attorney in opening statement, emphasizing verbal anchors she'd already established extremely well during voir dire. The headings, on a chart, which could easily have been titled "Doctor's Bad Acts," were "Language," "Conduct," and "Treatment," with subheadings under each major heading providing an easy and clear number of groupings for the otherwise distracting and diffuse laundry list of claimed harmful acts.

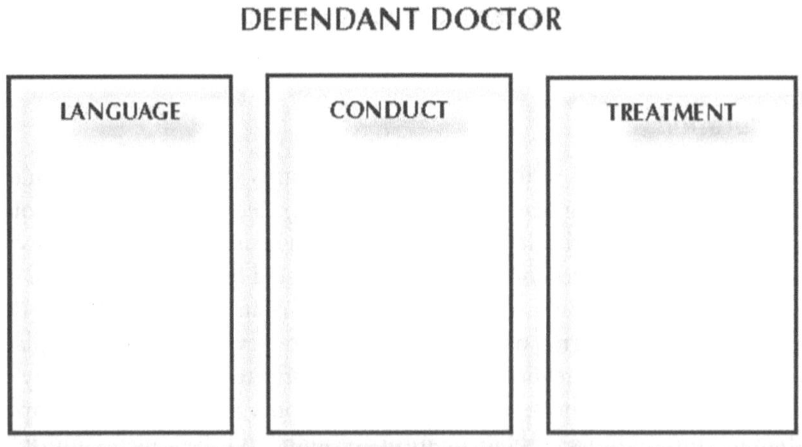

Figure 8

6. See Chapter Nine for a more complete discussion of the development and delivery of this specific case story.

We had learned that the biggest perceptual hurdle all the focus groups had to cross in building a clear vision of negligence was the inclination to divide and disperse the many odd, poorly related, and uncomfortable claims of the plaintiff patients. Over and over, groups produced people ready and willing to "Yeah, but . . ." each woman's individual claims to dust, before ever getting a chance to view the full picture presented by their uninterrupted accumulation. Point of view and active-party status in their individual stories needed help getting shifted away from the plaintiffs themselves long enough to allow medical and legal rules to be held up to a clearer package of the claimed wrongs. A simple group of three headings on a flip chart provided that help.

Having already established the basic rules by which a physician plays, the proud duty a physician has to patients in a necessarily subordinate position, respecting their rights in the three areas in question—language, conduct, and treatment—allowed the swarm of problematic choices made by the doctor to became a fairly indivisible whole within which each plaintiff's complaints could reside. The three phrases were displayed while the highest duty was described and reinforced, and thus took on some of that mantel. That duty then had a fair chance of being viewed in the context of all the myriad complaints over the wide scope of time, people, numbers, and acts the story contained. Any act outside the lines drawn, no matter how odd or distracting, could now be sought and found in evidence in one of just three ways. Having heard the three phrases already, seeing them at the outset of the case presentation, helped the grouping and contextualizing purposes the focus groups revealed as so necessary. One page of one flip chart leveraged the advantage of the primary demonstrative in the courtroom: the attorney's.[7]

8.4.4 Story Elements

The fundamental gift received from focus groups are the answers to:

- "What is the case story?" and
- "How is that story best presented?"

In the element of story sequence, the Case Presentation Plan shaped by the group's input will have three steps: a distinct start, middle, and finish. However, keep in mind these three stages may have little—or nothing—to do with sorting—or sequencing—the case story by time. Once that division is made clear from the perceptual and narrative needs identified for a case story by focus group work, then you can begin to ask what one key visual (or mental image) will be needed to help decision makers anchor or condition themselves to each of those three basic steps overall, so they can't get lost during any point of the presentation? Along with the mental version of the story's central image, distilled from the versions offered by

7. Attorney Elizabeth Kuniholm, *Baker v. Evans*, Wake County Superior Court, Raleigh, NC, November 1999.

the panelists, these three "solid" visuals can actually provide the much-referenced, but rarely seen "mileposts" along the journey throughout the story's delivery (though referencing them as such is greatly discouraged).

An attorney was preparing the visual portion of a presentation plan for defending a driver in a civil-injury claim arising from a wreck. His client, on the job, was pulling from a parking lot into two lanes of traffic and was hit by the plaintiff traveling in the inside lane. In most traffic case stories, the factor of juror common experiences and common biases needs to be carefully considered.[8] The defense, sometimes perhaps even more than the plaintiffs, needs to maintain a rigidly disciplined approach in the early going of any trial or other legal presentation, taking every single opportunity to establish and reinforce the elements of the defense case story independently of the other side. (This applies to both civil and criminal defenses.)

One of the essentials of achieving a story helpful to the defense was to invite the expansion of early story building by decision makers, away from the limited time and place involved in the wreck itself. The defense had, at best, a difficult message to get across on the subject of fault if isolated to itself. In making decisions about how to sequence the defense presentation—in light of both the known needs of the best story formation and the likely offerings by the plaintiffs in voir dire, opening, and with their early witnesses—we had initially concentrated in a common area: the onset of claimed injuries suspiciously later than the event itself. We aimed to introduce, early in the sequence of the presentation, a time frame much *later* in events than the collision itself. As we began sorting out the numerous medical reports to establish when the first of an increasing number of different, more severe damage claims began, it appeared that, in this case, a number of years had elapsed before the plaintiff had ever actually lodged a complaint with any medical practitioner about any of the mental or emotional harms that, by the eve of trial, now constituted the largest values in the losses being claimed. Until trying to put the visuals together, nobody had noticed in the whole record how late the onset of those claims really was.

We began setting up the visuals to help reveal the scope of the defense case to be set up in the first step of our story sequence. In order to ensure complete accuracy with the record, which had just revealed one surprise in the four-year gap preceding the biggest claims, we searched for any such mental or emotional harm claims ever made by this woman.

A remarkable thing happened. It seems that, if one were to look back, rather than ahead, in the medical story of this injured plaintiff—though the four years following this accident produced no such claims of harm—they all were clearly in the record, in remarkably similar form, only not in 1998, when this wreck happened, but rather back at the end of 1975 and the beginning of 1976. Many of the

8. *See* Chapter Three.

current medical records, produced during treatments following the wreck now in question, had remarked on this prior wreck, but had all indicated no such harms were associated with it in the next line on the page. However, a more detailed search of the records from the mid-seventies revealed a much different story. With this information and some carefully prepared and well delivered visuals, the defense was now prepared to use their story sequencing to widen the scope of the case story far, far before and years after the single collision itself. In this way, until some questions raised were satisfactorily answered, prevailing attitudes among jurors such as suspicion of the system might well play to keep their story scopes from shrinking back to the most narrow and most risky arrangement: in the moment, at the scene.

Even in this effort, however, sequencing of the revelations for the decision makers had to be carefully considered, and the visual presentation had to be fully utilized to minimize distortions or confusions. With a story that was now twenty-seven years long, yet somehow still about a car wreck, that task had to be done effectively. The first boards had to establish the time line in a way that concentrated on similarities, not differences, so that the time gap could be accepted and used most easily by the observers, instead of questioned by them. Fortunately, the similarities were apparent.

TWO ACCIDENTS, SIMILAR CLAIMS

	ACCIDENT 1975 / 1976		ACCIDENT MAR/ 4, 1998	
	YES	NO	YES	NO
SEVERE HEADACHE	✓		✓	
BLOW TO BODY	✓		✓	
CERVICAL DISK DAMAGE	✓		✓	
VISION PROBLEMS	✓		✓	
NECK / SHOULDER PAIN	✓		✓	
BACK PAIN	✓		✓	
LOSS OF CONSCIOUSNESS/ " BLACK-OUTS"	✓		✓	
CONFUSION	✓		✓	
SPEECH PROBLEMS	✓		✓	
MEMORY LOSS	✓		✓	

Figure 9

Then, to support the fault-finding area of the decision makers' emerging stories, the effort in the visual case had to incorporate the elements of both point of view and active party. At the scene of the wreck, there were only three candidates for active-party status: the two drivers and a third vehicle that affected visibility by its presence, and whose driver may have contributed to some of the choices made by others at the scene. For both juror and judge, the focus of story building needed to be effectively invited to shift to the plaintiff driver as much as possible in the early stages of the presentation sequence. And there was something, it turns out, over which she exercised almost complete control: the passing on or withholding of information about all those very similar prior claims. The list of her treating medical people, her medical experts, and those from the defense that examined her produced a common thread when it came to depicting who was in charge of revealing or concealing the earlier claims.

MEDICAL FACTS

Concealed, Denied, or Deleted

		Prior Mental Problems		Prior Car Accident/ Head Blow		Prior Cervical Disc Injury		Prior Seizure Concerns		Prior Loss Speech/ Impairment	
Date	Doctor	REVEALED	CONCEALED	REVEALED	CONCEALED	REVEALED	CONCEALED	REVEALED	CONCEALED	REVEALED	CONCEALED
March 4, 1998	Dr. MacA		X		X		X		X		X
March 6, 1998	Dr. T		X		X		X		X		X
July 27, 1998	Dr. R		X		X		X		X		X
Sept. 1, 1998	Dr. O		X		X		X		X		X
Sept. 30, 1999	Dr. M		X		X		X		X		X
May 28, 2000	Hospital		X		X		X		X		X
Jan. 8, 2002	Dr. A		X		X		X		X		X
Feb. 4, 2002	Dr. N		X		X		X		X		X
Feb 21, 2002	Dr. O'L		X		X		X		X		X

Figure 10

Blending of legal elements—for instance, using injuries or the cause of lasting harms to raise or lower perceptions of fault—is inevitable with every decision maker, regardless of background. Given this, the perceptions offered by these two boards, delivered in proper sequence, suggested a whole other story at work than one about a car wreck. This story had the plaintiff herself as both the central character and the active force, in a story whose scope was twenty-seven years, involving many more doctors and hospitals than a several-second-long crash and the medical care it needed afterward. So, with those elements of viewpoint, active ingredient, and scope delivered in the visual channel, taking advantage of the early positioning in the sequence of the story presentation, can you begin to imagine decision makers building themes far different from those their common experiences with driving and common biases about rules of the road may have inclined them toward as they walked into the room?

8.5 Handling Imagery

In a professional negligence case, the defense lawyer knew that a major hurdle his presentation had to clear was the tendency focus groups demonstrated to leap to seeing the level of gross negligence quite quickly in their stories, rather than viewing the gap between negligence and gross negligence as a longer trip. Whenever he mentioned the term "ordinary negligence," he held his open hand about chest height, palm down. But when things in the conversation rose to the level of gross negligence, so did that hand. It stayed palm down, but traveled way up over his head. Unlike in the focus group work without this visual aid, the actual jurors had a hard time reaching all the way up to that level. In fact, they never found that the case did. Did this image override the evidence of the severity of claimed neglect? No. But without it, observable trends in both perceptual and thinking habits proved likely to undercut the very same message in the stack of facts.

Please be wary of emulating the small child, who covers her face with her hands and then shouts, "You can't see me!" The ground rules for inviting establishment of verbal anchors—full attention on the receiver's part, consistency in your delivery, and isolating your efforts to the cue and response alone, free of any other potential attachments or associations—apply even more to the visual conditioning you invite during the presentation of your case.[9] The most prolific, active, and potentially effective demonstrative aid in the courtroom will always be the body and voice of the attorney delivering the case. If you look past the mental hands we often put over our faces, you can play that role strongly at each stage of the delivery, especially with witnesses. The task is neither to just tell a story, nor to just show a story's elements, but to balance both channels in delivery. When most effectively done, the attorney invites the decision makers to recreate certain realities associated with the case story elements in such a compelling manner that the invitation itself is almost transparent. (Focus group members discussing the level of neglect adopted the same hand gesture without consciously indicating it was a deliberate move.)

9. *See* Lisnek and Oliver, *supra*, n. 2, at 75–78.

This could serve as one example of the conclusions reached by Albert Mehrabian years ago when he was studying what happened when someone perceived a conflict between what a person said and how it was put across, nonverbally and tonally. In his much misrepresented experiment, Dr. Mehrabian found that the receivers of a message perceived as conflicted between the content of the spoken words and the visual and tonal package that delivered them, would opt for the part they saw and the tones they heard up to ninety-three percent of the time, even if it meant utterly discarding the actual words said.

One common way this conflict is modeled for jurors by the demonstrative aid known as the attorney comes when the lawyer shakes his or her head no, advertising the message she most fears, while asking a venire panelist or opposition witness a question for which he or she clearly would very much prefer a yes answer. Many, if not most people, just like those that unthinkingly adopted the "gross negligence" hand gesture, may well respond to the visually loaded side of the conflicted message with the questioning lawyer's advertised, feared no answer. On a more positive note, venire people can be visually encouraged to increase the chances that their reasons given for cause striking will be better accepted by the bench. This is done by the attorney nonverbally drawing their focus toward the judge just as he or she asks the follow-up question to elicit that confession, which may then be made more directly to the decision maker behind the bench.

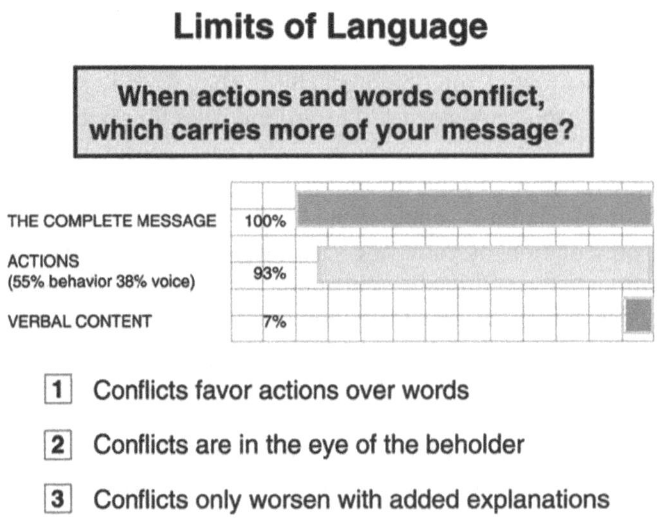

Figure 11

There are far too many images rushing about in the stored life references in every decision maker's head for anyone to censor or control for any length of time. The only real option is to first capture the decision makers' full attention, then balance the invitation to build story elements from two parts of their heads (visual and auditory) instead of one, to help them encode[10] a compelling and memorable association for that story point. Then, repeat the process for the next element in the story sequence you've already presented at least once in opening remarks and, where permitted, in voir dire as well. Throughout, it can be very helpful to bear in mind that all the images people create case stories from are mental images—all constructs. No objective pictures external to their mental process will be used to build the stories that lead to judgments. The transcript just contains verbal references for the facts, but not the facts themselves. The images, actual and imagined, generated from the presentation are equally unique to the mind's eye of the observers. If remembering this fact helps a professional regularly check in on how well decision makers appear to be receiving their invitations to generate mental imagery and personal narratives, without conflicts between the visual and verbal channels, it will prove well worth the effort.

Pay attention to the message sent by how visuals are being handled. You literally can take away more impact by handling your exhibits and aids poorly than even the best designed ones can provide. Pictures, while not exactly like facts, also cannot speak for themselves, though they are potentially far more evocative than any verbally delivered fact, however probative.

Where you choose to place an exhibit or a set of exhibits, in relation to another, counts. When and with whom you display them, as well as how long one versus another may be displayed, are all questions you should be able to answer for each exhibit, before the presentation starts.

How they will be organized, how they are arranged and displayed when you are not using them, how you put them up, and how you take them down are all questions you need to answer in advance. Where you look and invite others to look while a visual tip is up, no matter who is talking, is all part of the job.

There is a time when, ideally, nobody should be talking at all: the first few moments after you put a visual up and decision makers are reading with undivided attention. Avoid the manner of a criminal defense attorney in a police brutality trial who held a street-map diagram turned toward the witness, with its—and his—back to the jurors as the witness drew on it. The two men were shielded from having to view the jurors by focusing on the board, and they carried on almost a private little conversation about the marks the witness was making and discussing, and locating in space and time for their private edification. All this took place far from the jury box, with most

10. Schacter, *supra*, n. 1, at 42–64, 81–86. One way to help encoding is to sort out the sensory language depicting sights, sounds, and sensations in the statements made and questions asked. That is a good start, but the more compelling package is to actually model the full expressions of visual, auditory, and kinesthetic processing through the use of eye movements and gestures lined up with the appropriate words at the appropriate times. Lisnek and Oliver, supra, n. 2, at 61–66; Richard Lucas and K. Byron McCoy, *The Winning Edge: Effective Communication and Persuasion Techniques for Lawyers* (Tucson, AZ: Lawyers & Judges Publishing Company, Inc., 1999): 12–13.

sight lines blocked. Finally, at the unveiling, it was revealed that the diagram consisted of blueprint-sized pencil lines, visible only up to about eighteen inches, with some red spots in the middle, the results of the witness either drawing with a red marker on it, or perhaps having smashed a bug on it, while people couldn't really see. It was all gone and forgotten in a flash as the board was unceremoniously dumped by the lawyer, out of the jurors' view, on the ground behind the witness stand, never to be seen again. Implicit messages, intended or otherwise, often carry far more weight than explicit ones. Advertising to decision makers how seriously visuals are to be taken is basic.

8.6 Visually Seeding Perceptions

Perceptions preempt thinking in the story-building process. So how best can you approach the perceptual processing habits of decision makers by utilizing the visual channel? First, by committing a similar amount of time, energy, and resources to the visual level of the presentation plan as you give to the verbal level. Many professionals are familiar with these statistics:

> People recall only ten percent of the words you tell them, twenty percent of images you show them,
>
> but—
>
> over sixty percent of the combined package, three days after its delivery.[11]

Along with all the common presumptions about speed of image learning and attention span, the three-day retention conclusions have something accurate to point out about the value of a visually balanced case story presentation. Two channels of a head are better than one—if invited to work well together. The begged question is, if sixty percent is *always* available, which parts of a case would a trial professional choose to sacrifice to a twenty percent or ten percent comprehension and retention rate among decision makers? Which case story elements, and points within them, do not deserve a balanced delivery in both verbal and visual channels?

Think of the definition of demonstrative evidence, also known as illustrative evidence. "Evidence in the form of objects (such as maps, diagrams or models) that has in itself no probative value but is used to illustrate and clarify the factual matter. Evidence that aids by its ability to demonstrate."

The functions the visual channel serves, whether through two-dimensional images or attorney behavioral illustration, are crucial to decision makers hoping to collect and recall the pieces of testimony and the bits of evidence they are being asked to contextualize and form judgments from. Nothing in the definition restricts

11. Harold Weiss and J. B. McGrath, Jr., *Technically Speaking: Oral Communication for Engineers, Scientists and Technical Personnel* (New York: McGraw-Hill, 1963).

this illustrative function to paper, cardboard, or PowerPoint slides—hands, eyes, and evocative language are not excluded. Illustration is essential in providing a framework for the story in which piles of disparate, evidentiary bits can start to make sense. There is no guarantee that simply because you put up a board or slide every twenty minutes, you will accomplish any of the functions the decision makers each need. In fact, you are more likely to impede their processing if you're unsure of the purpose each visual would best serve and the way in which it needs to be introduced and displayed to maximize chances for that success. And success, in a world where trial professionals have fully adapted to the fact of a story construction theme, rather than a story interpretation theme, involves the expansion of the presentation job beyond the spoken word into the task of managing at least one more perceptual system in the story delivery.

First and foremost, you want the visual package to convey the message as clearly and compellingly as it can. Just blowing up a page of a contract, medical chart or a letter will hardly ever do that, unless the message is for the decision makers to take a break from what's being said in opening or from the stand for the five to ten minutes it takes for each to read every single word on that page, down to and including the watermark for the more suspicious folks looking for hidden clues and excluded secrets.[12] A couple of examples follow of visuals that were produced with a particular case story message in mind.

The late Larry Lee, a trial attorney from Colorado whose experience included many auto injury trials for plaintiffs with soft tissue injuries, noted a recurring difficulty conveying the real impact of ongoing medical care on many injured client's lives. Because of the nature of the treatments, their lack of emergency status, and the likelihood that, at some time, many jurors had similar medical work done for themselves, the message about the time, struggle, and pain involved was frequently minimized by most decision makers, lay or professional. Also, had his client ever been to a chiropractor or a physical therapist prior to the wreck, that minimizing was often ratcheted up to a virtual conspiracy to grab money for treatments the client "would be getting anyway"—perhaps "unnecessary treatments," too.

Larry's solution to passing the message he wanted to get across—that his client's lives were altered by both the required time and physical needs of treatment—was ingenious. He took a piece of paper and drew a row of thirty-one small blocks, left to right, across the top. Then, just below that row, a row of twenty-eight small blocks, and so on till he had a years' worth of empty little blocks, twelve rows high covering the page. He made a few copies. Then, each year got the appropriate blocks filled in according to a color scheme that included a color for "regular doctor's appointments," "leg treatments," "physical therapy," "hospitalization," "outpatient

12. The *National Law Journal's* survey of juror attitudes, published in the November 2, 1998, issue, indicated that "suspicion" of the process was the prevailing attitude brought to courtrooms by jurors in all trials.

surgery," "rehab," and so forth. The two or three years before the crash and the months and/or years following, depending on the plaintiff, were then markedly set apart from each other in the jurors' eyes. They could not only see the difference since the wreck, but they could also easily total up just how many hours and hours during the marked days the person was now required to be making medical efforts rather than living his former life. Many of them also found themselves wondering just how much all those colored boxes would cost, at the rates their own doctors charge, and how many would not be covered by insurance.

This visual actually allowed Larry the opportunity to present medical treatment as a "double loss," when the factor of time, a story element attributed to scope, was fully engaged by the decision makers. People don't automatically consider what time in a day is used for, much less what it could have been used for after it is involuntarily committed somewhere else. Larry was able to simply describe what his clients did with their time before the wreck, and what time was taken up by all the various colored-in blocks on the year charts. This allowed the jurors or judge to extrapolate for themselves how the treatment was not only not something they would have sought, but also, in each passing minute, a drain away from the life each plaintiff had every right to expect he could have been leading. Time is not usually a commonly presumed element of harm, unless one can see it. And a timeless focus on suspicion and other biases, in the face of this visual reference within a day-to-day time frame, can prove much harder to sustain.

Note how the desire to maintain a plaintiff-oriented viewpoint by defense-favoring jurors, to support themes in the personal responsibility territory, can be undercut by this approach, as well as the redistribution of the active ingredient to injuries, treatments, and healing processes outside the reach of any personal control attributable to the plaintiff. Attribution habits and the assumed "norms" they might be based on can be all but eliminated as strong points in deliberation by these simple calendars. And perceptual distortions aimed at minimizing the harms could prove quite difficult to support, too, in the face of all the colored boxes.

An attorney defending a doctor and hospital in a suit arising from a birth trauma described a different, common problem also having roots in decision maker perceptions. As in many such cases, a great weight would be placed on the fetal monitoring strips, showing the baby's heartrate experiencing late decelerations or other abnormalities on the ubiquitous strips of graph paper. The attorney's concern was that, in order to defend against the careful selection of particular pieces of the strips presented by the plaintiffs, he felt he had to drag yards and yards of strips in front of the decision makers that showed functioning in the normal range during the birth, and to risk boring, overwhelming, or distracting them from the point. The "too busy" mistake.

I pushed his problem one step further by pointing out that he also risked helping the plaintiffs make a much stronger presentation with the complete strips than the one he feared from the excerpted bits. I suggested that, were I working with his opposition, I'd hand the attorney a red felt-tipped pen and suggest he give it to his expert on the stand. Then they'd proceed to set up every single defense exhibit with strips on them, chronologically, wallpapering the whole room. During their discussions about decelerations, their cause and impact on the child, how they appear on strips, and so on, I'd be sure the expert was liberally marking points here and there on each and every board—even if it were only times, or peak ranges, not necessarily the decelerations the plaintiffs had been exclusively focused on before. By the time the lunch break rolled around and the expert returned to the stand to finish up, the decision makers would find themselves seated in a room surrounded with defense provided strips covered in red marks by the plaintiff expert doctor. As he imagined the scene in his mind's eye, the defense attorney shook his head and closed his eyes.

Then he opened them, saying, "That's a problem I always run into. They get to pick and choose the sections of the strips they want to use, and the only way to show jurors that the vast majority of the time the strips were in the normal range is to overwhelm them." There is an alternative. One demonstrative visual with two sections of strip blown up on it, one sitting right above the other, both shoved far over to the left side of the board. On the top, an exemplary section from the records showing the fetal heart tones in the normal range. On the bottom, an example of the type of abnormal tracing claimed in the case. Then, positioned to the right of the top one, a big, brightly colored bar graph extending horizontally to the right. The bar on top would be far, far longer than the tiny little bar placed next to the excerpted strip on the bottom, as they would depict the overall time the strips looked like the one on the top, versus the total number of minutes or seconds they appeared as they did in the bottom example.

In the case we were discussing, the second bar would be very thin indeed, virtually just a pencil-thin line, compared with a seemingly two-foot long green bar. Here, the elements of scope, viewpoint, and active ingredient can all be influenced very strongly in the early stages of the story-forming process by this one visual. And the thinking habit of hindsight bias can be turned radically around to favor the side it often hurts in such cases. The bar graph, though visually presented, appeals to auditory processing, which can help draw people's attention away from more dramatic internal visualizations, which—all things considered—most people may wish to avoid completely in such cases, regardless of any sworn oath, sincerely taken.

Then there was the message an attorney was having trouble getting across about the overprescription of steroids his client had suffered, over about three years. With the medical rules for long- and short-term doses very vague in their verbal form, the plaintiff's attorney needed to find a visual way to overcome the strong possibility that jurors and judge would resolve their difficulty in handling medical rules in the simplest way—deferring to the defendant doctor's judgment—using hindsight, life experience, availability, norming, and confirmation biases, as well as identification habits to shore up the precipitous position. How could we get across, all at once, how two or three years' worth of prescriptions far exceeded what the doctor and his expert witnesses would all declare to be just separate, "short-term" amounts, particularly since the prescriptions had varied in that time, and we couldn't point to any set amount over a set time? An image would work, setting a visual anchor up against the opposition's verbal ones.

This chart had three broad vertical bars graphing three years' worth of dangerously repeated "short-term" steroid prescriptions. Only these bars weren't made of plain ink in a solid color. Instead, they were built from little red dots. Each dot was about three times "life" size, representing one pill the doctor had told her to take. There were a whole lot of dots. Out of court, we called it the "Pile o' Pills" board, and it carried the message quite well. In court, the lawyer supplemented the chart with a huge jar full of red jelly beans in the exact amount prescribed.

It may be helpful, when considering how best to put across your own case specific messages visually to take note that all three of these examples, the before-during-after calendars, the monitor-strip bar graphs and the Pile o' Pills board required little, if any, added explanation to make their points. Their image is the message, and all demonstrative images end up as mental images. As defined, they demonstrate the significance of the evidence accompanying or following them.

When it comes to forming a judgment, to making a decision about the competing messages in a courtroom, a clear, compelling perception of the message one side brings over another can make all the difference. Judgments in legal cases are formed the same way they are formed elsewhere: first, an impression based on perceived experience referenced against stored experiences; second, a reaction; followed, eventually, by several reasons why that was the right response to have. Impressions based on perceptions are far more easily accessed if you use two of the three main perceptual channels—verbal and visual—rather than just verbal.[13] The task is not to counter and defeat the perceptual, thinking, and psychological habits described in Chapter Three, but rather to marshal them to your purpose through the story you invite decision makers to construct.

8.7 Visually Seeding Narratives

If an exhibit, a demonstrative or an illustrative behavior doesn't support one of the aims listed below in relating your theme and its story elements, that visual display probably has no business in your case presentation. That applies especially to randomly acquired, unproductive habits in demeanor while presenting. And, in two-dimensional form, to a pile of boards or slides carried in by an expert, having been used for several years, but never in this case, which is visually inconsistent with

13. Written messages are processed auditorily, as if heard. There is no basis for the myth that reading and writing words are activities of a visual nature, with the possible exception of some visually based, rapid reading techniques.

the other exhibits you've developed, and for which decision maker(s) have already formed ongoing associations during your prior presentation time. After you consider the perceptual demands the focus group work placed on your story presentation, you must consider how best to utilize the visual channel to meet the narrative needs of the decision makers reauthoring your case story as they hear and see it. There are several narrative purposes to consider when developing the visual delivery.

The case presentation remains an arena in which the focus group invitation to expand and include is still alive, but the invitation must be more focused. And nothing helps focus like a mental image, or a series of well-crafted and well-timed images. By making a real effort to balance the verbal and visual depiction of each major story point within each of the fundamental story elements, the trial professional effectively ends up with two chances, not one, to make each point well. And research says that this increases the odds that each point will be accepted and recalled when needed by decision makers by a minimum of forty percent more than if the effort wasn't invested. After the perceptual framework is considered, the narratives of each decision maker should be offered visual input among the following areas as the presentation is planned for delivery.

8.7.1 Emphasize

This is the fundamental purpose of visuals accompanying your case, whether evidentiary or demonstrative. Help decision makers attach significance to the point being offered by adding a visual dimension to that point. Often, the opposite aim is also served. That is, by successfully emphasizing a point you wish highlighted in the jurors' thinking, you may also diminish the impact of a related or contrary point proffered by the opposing side or by prevailing assumptions.

Here's where the crimes of busyness and wordiness can really hurt. If everything is emphasized, nothing is. As blues singer David Bromberg told it:

> He'd given her a copy of Kahlil Gibran's *The Prophet* with all the significant passages underlined. Every line in the book was underlined.[14]

Learning what your theme is, and what the scope, point of view, and sequence of the case story need to be to successfully establish and convey that theme, can help you isolate just which points to build up and mark out for people. Knowing how to do that for all decision-makers without asking is not possible. All your exhibits and your behavior will emphasize something. Use the rest of this list to consider exactly how you want that emphasis to be accomplished. Otherwise, you're sure to fall back on the habit of highlighting every word in the transcript, and shoving each page after the other under the video presenter, wiping out most worthwhile distinctions in the process.

---

14. David Bromberg Band, "How Late'll Ya Play Till?" (Fantasy Records, 1977).

8.7.2 Provide Context

Many times, it is a challenge for decision makers to stretch their imaginings beyond litigation in order to put the story of clients' lives in the appropriate context—that is, something different than lawyers, in a room, just talking about past events. Engaging decision makers in the story—even when the story on which you want them to focus actually is the litigation—requires a compelling invitation to the viewer and listener. Photos, calendars, before and after representations, and vividly drawn visual descriptions can all help decision makers see the world being discussed in a framework more conducive to your message.[15]

8.7.3 Summarize

The influence visuals have on individual story building provides a cure for both verbal and visual versions of the lawyer-centered "I got it in" habit. Visuals that list or otherwise depict the accumulation of several points, parts, or conclusions in testimony—whether about rules, actions, or their successful or harmful consequences—are essential to decision makers in building narrative connections that professionals might otherwise assume (due to a private familiarity with the case factors, as in the example of the obscured "protective oversight" residential home rule above).

8.7.4 Group/Isolate

Similarly, there may be particular points among many that you want the decision makers to associate with each other or individual points you want isolated from the herd. Showing them together, or alone, can accomplish this purpose before (and after) anyone says anything about them.

8.7.5 Compare/Contrast

Sometimes groups of points from both sides need to be related to one another in ways that carry through the theme underlying your presentation. Whether the comparisons are intended to be favorable or not, the points are better made, and more easily recalled, by illustrating them as well as by just talking about them.

8.7.6 Instruct/Rehearse

Whether you are emphasizing the standards applied, the order in which things need to be done, the verdict form, a differential diagnosis, the meaning of reliance,

15. Note that a particular design category, like a time line, may or may not be the best choice to help listeners set up and reinforce a context in the narrative drawn from the story as it's introduced. The design categories should always serve the narrative factor needed, never the other way around. For example, for a longer-scope story, a horizontal time line applies, whereas when a shortening of the scope of time is required, a vertical chronology is much better.

or a value-assessment instrument, if there is a process a client, witness, or juror is asked to follow, it's very helpful to have that process made visible to the people judging or using it. This cannot be simply a transcript of an expert's arcane language. At least translate it into English. Better yet, relate the points creatively in the visual channel. Think how useless it is when judges resort to simply rereading instructions to jurors in the name of "clarification" if you are tempted to succumb to the same obscuring sin here.

8.7.7 Link/Anchor

Artfully presented images are far more effective than plain words in helping people form solid, reusable associations for impressions, perceptions, or ideas. Think of them as visual bells, prompting mental salivation—anchors. Also, these anchored responses can then be linked to each other in ways that would not necessarily flow naturally or automatically from the narrative alone, making them a most powerful tool to establish, reinforce, and maintain a story sequence throughout a lengthy legal presentation.

8.7.8 Reframe

Next to anchoring associations, an effective reframing is one of the most potent purposes visuals serve. The Pile o' Pills board reframed the phrase "short term," the fetal-strip bar graph reframed the message from one being all about information to one all about time, and Larry Lee's calendar reframed a message about damages in court to one about life outside it, changing the context for the jurors. Reframing is like argument, only it's usually not prohibited, and it's far less likely to be critically challenged by the decision makers when delivered well in the visual channel.

For example, the terms "material misrepresentation" and "reliance," like all terms used to delineate legal lines, mean something to each of two contracting companies as well as to each and every decision maker reviewing the story of their claim. But if the first of the PowerPoint slides (Figure 12) were to be shown as the representations and reliance were first being described—not only as the relevant rules to be applied in judgment, but also as the particular meaning to be drawn from those terms in this construction-contract story—then decision makers would all be a lot closer to the "same page" in their heads when contemplating what the plaintiffs claim they were told about how many other contractors would be on the same job site, during the same time. Switching to the next slide (Figure 13) then reframes whatever expectations observers may have had about a "close call" or an "honest mistake" if the defense truly knew, and held back, how many other crews would be trying to work in that same space at the same time. Just reciting the two sets of numbers—three and forty-six—can never really accomplish the same persuasive end as two images do, yet, in truth, the words and the images both ostensibly present the very same fact.

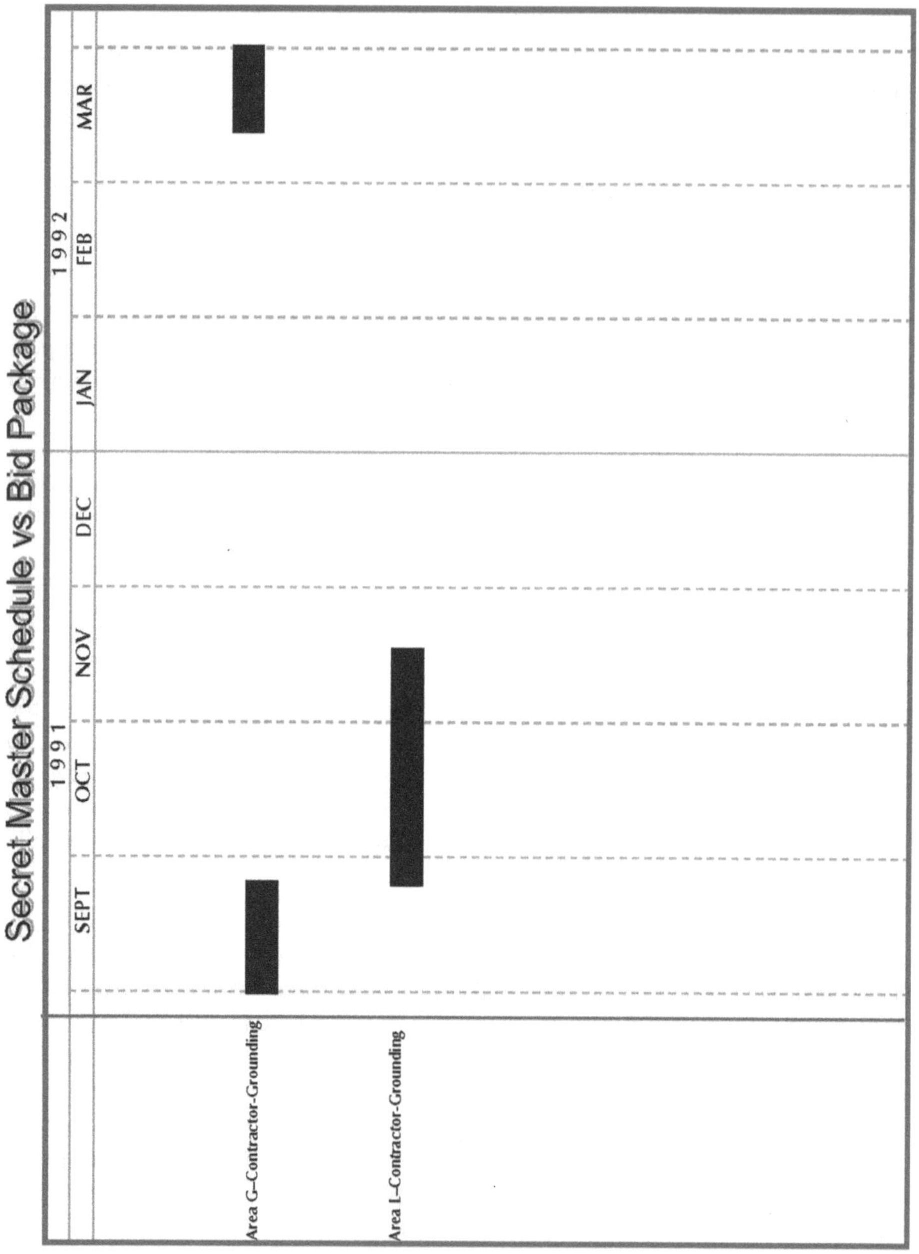
Secret Master Schedule vs Bid Package
1991
1992
SEPT
OCT
NOV
DEC
JAN
FEB
MAR
Area G–Contractor-Grounding
Area L–Contractor-Grounding

Figure 12

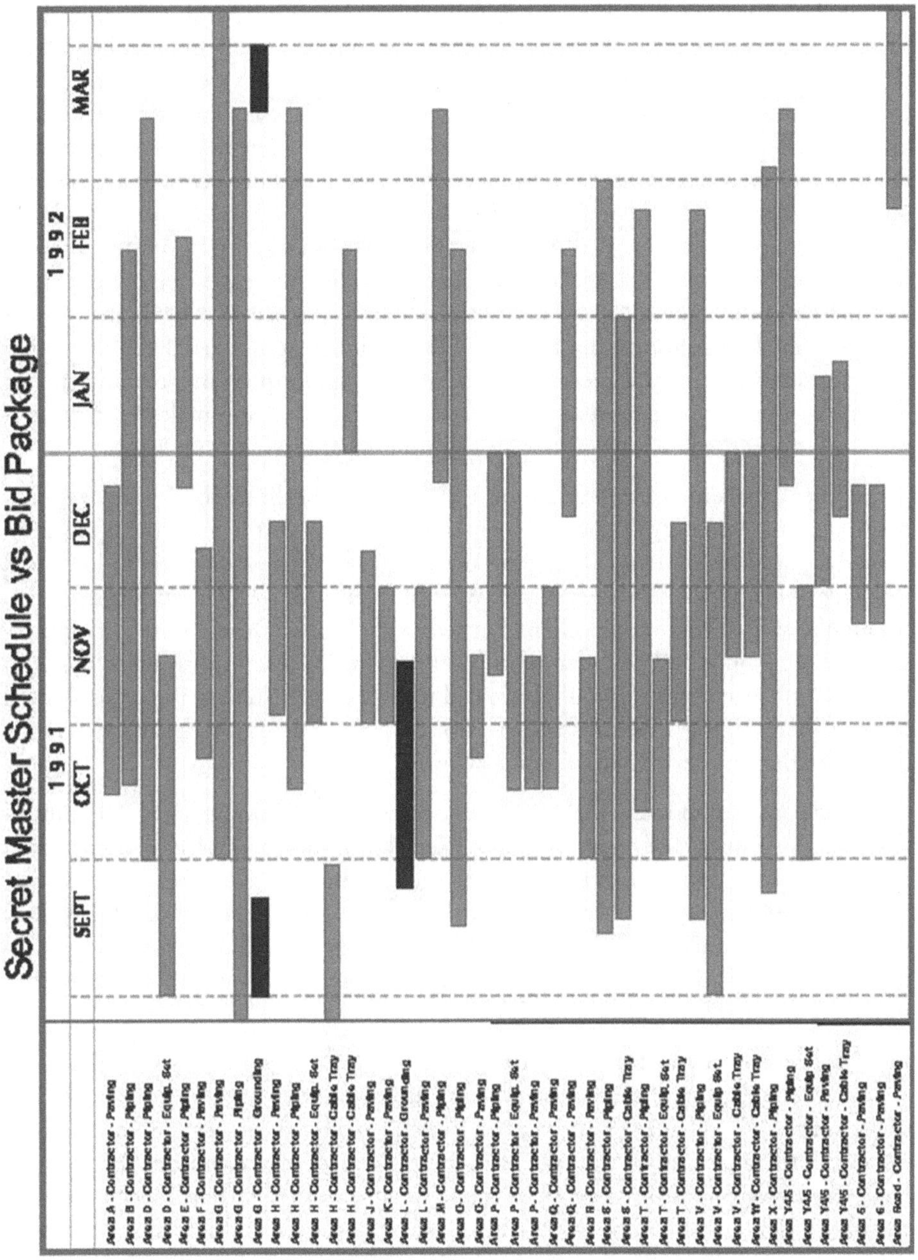
Secret Master Schedule vs Bid Package
1991
1992
SEPT
OCT
NOV
DEC
JAN
FEB
MAR

Figure 13

The list of aims above, though not comprehensive, can filter out the knee-jerk, "We better blow that up" inclination many trial professionals know all too well. If you actually consider which of these purposes (or how many of them) the visual you are contemplating may serve in the presentation of your case, you will rarely find yourself leaving the courtroom or negotiation with a large file or stack of images nobody ever even glimpsed. Less can, well, be more. As many people have pointed out, a well-developed, integrated set of visuals can easily become a working outline for your case presentation. This outline will work just as well for you, the presenter, as it will for the decision-makers there to learn and build their versions of your story, and the witnesses providing the narration. Presenting a set of coordinated visuals and behavioral illustrations, built to serve the specific purposes listed above—rather than one tied to a private piece of paper, atop a private podium, reading private messages—opens up the presentation of a story so that decision makers can accompany you along the way, rather than just waiting to hear what is said next.

Another excellent use of reframing can be accomplished when designing and developing the visual story channel by taking images or words from the opposition and recasting them to help deliver your own story. An attorney headed soon to trial sent some videotapes for review. Some were of focus groups filled with people that seemingly wanted his injured client burned at the stake. Others were surveillance videos those groups had just seen of his client ostensibly accomplishing things with her hand and arm that she should have had trouble doing. In fact, the tapes showed hours of her walking around, standing around, and in a couple instances, actually demonstrating the very disabilities she claimed.

But the opposition knew the value of context and pre-framing. They knew, intuitively or consciously, that most decision makers, lay or professional, have hundreds of hours of viewing of such tapes embedded in their memory by TV magazine programs, under the tagline anchor of "waste, fraud, and abuse." That these tapes didn't show any fakery wasn't the point. They were anchors for lots of stored references all presuming fraudulent behavior, and judging from the focus groups' vehement reactions, they seemed to be succeeding at pulling those references to the surface.

This case involved a doctor injecting something in a hand that harmed the hand, and over time, harmed parts of the patient's arm, shoulder, and portions of the rest of her system. The plaintiff's attorney had several exhibits he planned to use to show the initial treatment errors and the advancing progress of the injuries through her body. Since the opposition had been kind enough to offer us hours of full-length, face-front views of this nice woman walking toward their hidden cameras, I suggested we should select and capture a still from one of their tapes, one that was repeated often throughout the hours of taped surveillance, and use that image as the basis for every single treatment and progressive injury diagram, demonstrating and hopefully associating each and every harm as they progressed from the initial negligent acts. That is, use their image of the actual woman, instead of the archetypical, female line-drawing figure, for all our injury and advancing harms visuals.

Little red dots and lines on one image concentrated on her hand, with the doctor's name, his negligent act, and the date across the top. Next to that board (cited as coming from the secret tapers hired by the opposition), the next in a series, with more red or green marks superimposed on the photo, showing the next stages of the deterioration. Collect all these boards in a line, left to right. Finally, as her disabilities were discussed toward the end of opening and in testimony, I suggested the attorney show short, clear excerpts from the long, mostly boring, tapes and then freeze, giving anecdotal evidence—provided by and credited to the defense's stalkers—of the very problems the focus group jurors chose to overlook when they linked older tapes in their heads to the unadulterated surveillance films here. Still images from each of these "greatest hits" moments showing the very harms caused by the defendant, and denied by his attorneys in their claims, would then be reproduced as charts for later periods of reinforcement in testimony and closing.

The aim was to take key portions of the surveillance tapes and turn each image into a visual anchor linked to a point in the plaintiff's case. Assuming voir dire was allowed, this process could actually begin that early, since prevailing feelings about injured plaintiffs surreptitiously taped were obviously a source of potential bias in this case. Done well, the borrowed images serving as plaintiff story anchors would turn any attempt by the defense to play the very dull tapes in their entirety into an opportunity to reinforce every visual anchor set up by the captured excerpts and used to both diagram the disorder and highlight the disabilities the defense claimed didn't exist. I envisioned a juror turning to a partner and whispering, "Here comes my favorite part." After seeing some examples of the visual presentation to come, the defense tapes never even made it to trial.

Of course, it's not necessary to wait for surveillance tapes to use opposition input, in the form of their words, against their intended purposes. In the first Fen-Phen case that the pharmaceutical defendants allowed to go to verdict, the plaintiffs used visuals and defendant statements in opening remarks as a PowerPoint slide show. Before trial, in addition to the usual cutting and editing, the slide-show topics covered by the multiple defendant statements were placed in a manageable number of groups, five, and sequenced in line with the demands of the story suggested by focus group work. The case story theme was (Incompatible) Priorities, and the key anchor and central image dealt with the drug maker choosing to either reveal or conceal information, based on priorities that were antagonistic to those held by the doctor and his patient, now the plaintiff. Each of the five sections of comments on the slides was linked to the questionable priorities of the maker and seller of the drugs. Thus, the slide show became an outline, built exclusively from defendant statements, for the presentation of the plaintiff's case. And each aspect of that outline, verbally and visually, from the very beginning, was linked up to the theme, by way of our "revealed/concealed" anchor.

One slide in the bunch provided the fundamental anchor from which the entire priorities theme was built through the trial. It was a simple comparison, visually stark, again drawn exclusively from defendant statements, of the amount of money spent over a single year to keep a stronger warning label off one of the drugs and the amount spent over the entire lifetime of that drug for research on its safety.[16] This visual served triple duty as the key anchor for the second step of the case story sequence, and, for at least some observers, the story's central image.

8.8 "Sightlines"—Conscious and Other-than-Conscious

Every decision maker, even a blind one, has a visual cortex that is working all the time. Just as every person receiving your case will provide a theme, so will they also associate thousands of mental images with it from the very start. Each decision maker must be invited to see her way clearly toward the ends your case story requires. So attending not just to the invitation process but to all potential and unexpected impediments to it falls under the task of managing the perceptual presentation.

Start with the literal sightlines involved. Be sure everyone can not only hear well, but also see well. Be sure the images and words you bring are big enough, close enough, and up long enough to be fully appreciated. One extremely common and easily avoidable mistake is taking images down too quickly, when they can be left in view to be used for both conscious referencing and unconscious assimilation and anchoring instead. This is particularly true for the three key visual anchors linked to the three steps of the story sequence, and the mental imagery associated with the story's central image.

Remember that people read from left to right and from top to bottom. Not only on a single page, but among the pages, screens, or boards you display. Give some careful thought to the placement and packaging of every image or exhibit you are going to invite people to review and use in order to build their stories. For example, in preparation for a medical negligence trial, five illustrations were reviewed of individually claimed surgical errors a plaintiff was going to show to a judge and jury. The illustrations were all essentially of the same location in the abdomen, though one was a side-view and the rest were frontal. But, for reasons that had nothing to do with helping decision makers build effective versions of the case story, two of the front-facing images were drawn upside-down compared to the other three. The people producing the exhibit drafts did not consider this an error since they used their own points of reference, and not that of the decision makers. Once straightened out, these five images were set up on easels—after graphics had appeared higher and to the left side of the room on a projection screen, showing the applicable "right way" standards and illustrations of the expected and unnecessary

16. The first figure was in tens of millions and the second was zero—a sharp contrast. Also, the drug requiring the additional warning label, a "black-box" warning to be placed in drug literature and the *Physician's Desk Reference*, was actually a newer version of one of the "fen" drugs known as Redux.

outcomes. In this way, the key images of the appropriate and the actual outcome could be contrasted there, where the rules were associated, on the screen, while the more "tangible" five failure boards were placed closer to the jurors, in their proper left-to-right sequence.

If you learn about the perceptual functioning that is advertised, in part, by the preponderance of peoples' eye movements toward points above, along, or below an imaginary line crossing their face at the ears, you can start taking advantage of another powerful, less literal sightline. People, regardless of their particular preference for mental processing among visual, auditory, and kinesthetic modes, will more easily access images if they are looking up at them, and more easily appreciate the emotional content in a message if they are invited to look slightly down and to their right. Words, written or spoken, are more easily processed if the eyes are invited to stay at the vertical middle, passing from left to right. Memory can be enhanced by placing images to one side of the observer, and imagining or construction can be enhanced by shifting to the other.

So if an attorney wanted to draw attention to a time line of events and their progression in the defense of a university's psychological team, accused of bad practices over a long period with many people involved, she might resort to bringing an extremely large exhibit into court. This purposely large exhibit creates a new "wall" in the room, right next to the jury box, set up in the only available spot, closing the panel into a much closer space with the second attorney to speak, which just happens to also force them to look up (visual) and to their left (visual memory, not imaginings) to even see what the subject under discussion is.

Or perhaps in the defense of a criminal case, where the woman defendant is the only one of ten board members (all the others men and prominent citizens) on trial for the failure of a travel service business, the attorney might want to invite the jurors to project the "ship"—on which all the board members were previously anchored to a chart with their names appearing in their seats, with no visual distinctions between the well-connected men and the legally isolated woman—in midair, above the rail of the jury box, as it is launched on its doomed voyage. And, naturally, as he describes the development of the ill deeds done as the woman tries to stem their consequences (by herself), he might draw the jurors' attention to the invisible boat moving from left (past) to right (future) over their heads—sufficient that the federal prosecutor involved might just surrender after the mere vision of the trip in opening statements.

Then, again, you could pick the more direct route when circumstances demand it, as when the attorney in a medical neglect trial was brought up short by the expert that refused to agree with him that there were holes in the charting in the medical records of the baby's delivery. Here, it was all about the words, and the verbal anchors the doctor-expert inadvertently invited everyone in the room to associate with the sounds emerging from his mouth:

Attorney:	Doctor, would you agree with me that there are some holes in this record.
Doctor:	No, counsel, I disagree with your characterization of them as "holes."
Attorney:	So, if you don't want to call them holes, what would you call them?
Doctor:	Err . . . Um . . . I guess, spaces?
Attorney:	Great. Spaces it is. Let's talk about how many facts are missing in this particular space, first.

Artistry can begin to enter our efforts when we develop the skills to coordinate the verbal, graphic, or written invitation to build an image, recalled sound or phrase, or sensation with the physical modeling of that neurological process, in action, at the very same moment the invitation is made.[17]

If certain words on certain slides, pages, or boards are very important and if the court allows, give individual copies out. But be sure the page received exactly matches the blown-up version used with the witnesses, or the linkages invited can get muddied.

If you've learned how to recognize the other ways in which people reveal their preference for processing sensory input among the three major sense systems: pictures, sounds, or feelings, you can start making more complete, constructive judgments about how, when, and where to present and discuss visuals with those individual juror biases in mind. Just as with witness testimony, you can actually begin to target certain visuals—and the points they emphasize—to particular individuals in the box, at selected, hopefully propitious times, and check for results using nonverbal indicators alone. The story itself often dictates when enriched delivery in one or more sensory channels can prove most effective and, given the opportunity, the lawyer's behavioral illustrations can help invite those enriched responses strictly from a visual-level effort, with little or no added verbiage needed.

Because consistency in the delivery of a story carries so much of its credibility, it is worth the effort to make sure decision makers see consistent uses of color, key phrases, fonts, and type sizes in the basic design of all the visuals that lend themselves to such treatment. This is especially helpful when you jump from one medium to another in their presentation, such as charts and PowerPoint slides. Also, if your presentation plan is developed around a comparison format—on the one hand, but on the other—you can separate the images instantly into the first and second camps by carefully controlling these factors, as well as spatial separation and location.

---

17. Lisnek and Oliver, *supra*, n. 2, at Chapters 3–6; Lucas and McCoy, *supra*, n. 10, at Chapter 4.

If you keep the requirements of each decision maker's direct and indirect sightlines in mind, the documents, deposition cull-outs, instructions, definitions, graphics, photos, videos, and illustrations you offer will be far more likely to be accepted and appreciated as you'd like. And judgments about whether to use individual copies of pages, overheads, solid blow-up boards, PowerPoint slides, animations, or models will be easier to make. First, the focus group helps you establish the theme, the scope, a viewpoint, and a sequence for the presentation, so you know which elements and their establishing points require visual support the most. Then, you vet the decisions about the choice of each exhibit through the earlier lists of perceptual and narrative purposes it must serve. Next, run through the sightline requirements of the people in the panel, again in light of the theme, perspective, and sequence of the story you want received consistently in the visual channel. Naturally, this all assumes your visuals are already free of all the common problems outlined earlier.

That packaging process should help you determine the most effective medium and design formats for the images that must carry the message across to the jurors, including those that will only exist in the attorney's demeanor or descriptions. Often, the process will produce a far lower-tech answer than you might expect. As one example, remember the sightline mentioned earlier—processing time and attention spans. If the point you need emphasized is a reframe, a grouping, or a comparison of real significance, why would you have it only momentarily flash by on a PowerPoint slide or in an animated form that decision makers see for only a few seconds? Establish that visual anchor at the start of its sequence within the case, leaving it out and prominently displayed (off to the left, up high) so everyone can constantly refer back to the fundamental image you've worked so hard to provide. Or, alternatively, if the image is a part of a slide show, bring the greatest hit back in summary form on a single hardboard the jurors can use as a reference point for all they saw in that show. Typically, the final slide in many evolving displays contains the full amount of data to make the story point, which, if shown in total from the first glance would be way too busy and wordy. But now it can serve as an anchored reminder of the process viewed in the slides, with a solid, easily referenced incarnation that offers the luxury of time and personal choice to the viewers using that visual reference again and again as statements or testimony continue. The hardboard produced provides and reinforces the highlighted part of the case story context and/or helps observers anchor the desired responses linked to it in words.

Remember, the legal presentation is a dynamic process rather than a series of discrete admissions you "get in" to the record. Thinking about the figurative "sightline" of memory for your visuals, and how the images will be oriented to one another accordingly during presentation, is worth the time invested in preparation. For example, the five images in the medical case mentioned above were illustrative of five alleged failures of the laparoscopic surgeon. The images were not best presented chronologically—that is, at the time each omission or negligent act supposedly occurred. Rather, they were oriented to each other differently to best support the theme and central image in that case story, and to add to the impressions of the scope of the accumulated failures.

You can add or subtract images from their original orientations over time in the presentation. Set up one demonstrative as an anchor; then when more information is added in the case, you can add images to be associated with the new material. Think about whether you want to add the next visual before, during, or after the point is spoken about. Is it better that decision makers see this point before they hear specific evidence, or that it is revealed to them simultaneously with the verbiage—or even afterwards, in reframed reflection? Each makes a difference in terms of the attention, presumptions and processing. Rodney Jew is known for building a series of boards, typically three in number, designed to build on each other as they are added during trial. Often, his initial "anchor" board sets the context of the subject for the jurors, his "link" board establishes the rules or standards within that context, and his "payoff" board shows the behavior of the party in light of those contextualized rules.[18] Naturally, consistency in the look, language, and physical and verbal presentation of these three boards is vital to their successful application.

8.9 Behavioral Illustration

If the board "speaks" pretty clearly by itself, like the Pile o' Pills board, you may wish to set it up slowly, in silence, before the witness is asked a question about it. Let the significance begin to be assimilated without verbal direction. Then, what is said can come more as confirmation for decision makers of attachments they've already begun to make. If your visual is text heavy, or the goal is more in line with instruction or other explanatory functions, you'll probably want to find an early spot during testimony or near its end to offer that piece of your message. And be careful to guide the images that the words suggest in the appropriate direction when they are not as easily discerned, automatically, by those whose mind's eye you wish to engage.

Remember that the primary demonstrative exhibit in any trial, for better or for worse, is the attorney handling both words and images. Just as in the verbal world, if not more so, when it comes to offering people images to carry the points, how you show them often means as much or more than what is actually shown.

8.9.1 Handling

Sort them before you get there. Hold them as if they are important, before and after their presentation. Limit and censor their availability to enhance their impact, rather than diminish it. That means putting anything you don't want observed as

18. Rodney Jew, "Motivating the Jurors: A New Paradigm for Trial Communication," reprinted in *News From The Mental Edge* (MetaSystems, Ltd., Spring/Summer 1997).

part of the ongoing message away, where it can't be read, and preferably can't even be seen.

8.9.2 Moving

Move to where the exhibit and observers have the best chance of connecting, even if it's awkward for you and/or the judge. Plot out the choreography and placement before you start each half-day of trial. If someone else will be running your slides, overheads, or placing your boards, rehearse it at least once with them (mentioning, discussing, or talking through do not qualify as rehearsal). Act as if all the visuals have the same level of importance when someone else is handling or moving them as they would if it were you.

8.9.3 Speaking

Not only is censoring your own speech useful as you first place an exhibit up for the jurors, there are times when you will want to avoid talking as you or a witness moves toward or away from the visual. But there are also times when talking through that approach—at the penultimate moment in cross-examination, for instance—can provide the most effective redirection possible of decision-maker attention.

8.9.4 Consistency

Much like assuming the impact of the board itself, many people assume the conditioning aspect of anchoring just happens by default. What is being connected with mental imagery for decision makers can spin far out of control if the attorney abandons the invitation process. If you want to associate a key phrase, person, period of time, or anything else in testimony with a mental image, or a collection of visuals, it is the concurrent behavior of the presenter that will either enhance or distract from those associations being made. One or the other. No safety zone.

One of my favorite examples of the attorney-as-demonstrative comes from my colleague David Ball's book, *Theater Tips and Strategies for Jury Trials*,[19] wherein the attorney's consistency in handling a prop—in this case a thin red file—invites the best chance for an anchor to be set in the minds of the jurors. The lawyer planned to pick up the file, look inside, and ask the important question apparently related to something in that file with each witness the opposition put up. If he failed to handle the file the same way each time, pause the same way, place the file back in the same position, at the same time, with each iteration, the impact would be diminished according to each inconsistent move.

---

19. David Ball, *Theater Tips and Strategies for Jury Trials* (Louisville, CO: National Institute for Trial Advocacy, 2003): 33, 93.

Recall the use of the "invisible exhibit" suggested for voir dire in Chapter Seven. In courtrooms or hearing rooms where demonstratives aren't allowed in opening statements, it can come in very handy. Picking the appropriate spot; positioning yourself most effectively; using terms, tones, and volumes as they will later be repeated; and utilizing people's advertised perceptual proclivities to help them better envision the upcoming exhibit exactly as it will be displayed before it ever actually appears can very often be more persuasive than having the exhibit there from the start. But all that effort and potential impact can and will be lost if you fail to repeat all that spatial and behavioral packaging when the real thing arrives, or if you fail to invite the jurors to "see" the invisible version of the exhibit in such a way that differences in the actual version jar their prior expectations of it. When you get comfortable with this technique, you can use the spot in space, a tone, or gesture, or all three to refer to that exhibit far more frequently, accumulating its effects, than you would ever dare do with the fully visible version. This also helps when exhibits must be taken down before their full impact is established for decision makers. Carefully "reviewing" them invisibly can often invite an even more intense response due to the greater investment coming from the decision makers participating in the review.

The spot on the floor itself can become an anchor, if you so desire and work to establish it. The actions you use to throw observers' focus toward that spot or to a particular spot on the invisible version of the exhibit can be writ as large or as small as you want. A hand gesture, a finger, and eye or head movement, a tone, a posture, or a pause and a look can all become anchored to the point you established while repeating them earlier. Many attorneys have big areas of the floor in court dedicated to various segments of their case stories, such as liability and damages, or guilt and punishment. Each side is addressed only after it is occupied physically, or at least indicated for the jurors somehow if running there isn't appropriate at the moment.

There are hundreds of examples of the attorney-as-demonstrative, in conjunction with other visuals or standing alone. The hand rising only so far for "negligence," but consistently far higher to indicate "gross negligence." Another hand rising to indicate "big numbers" in voir dire, but never quite reaching those heights of such unacceptable amounts as it is used to describe actual damages numbers in the case at hand for those panelists selected as jurors. Ranking of three parties by their true importance with an invisible letter T, placing the least important party, by name, at the viewers' right of the crossbar on top. Then, when describing the actions of all three, descending in importance to that least-involved party's acts, again "shown" at the bottom of the upright of the invisible T—each and every time the three are contrasted (left and right from the jurors' perspective, not the lawyer's). Two fists can become two vertebrae, slowly being ground back and forth in front of the jurors—but only in the same spot, with the same orientation, and the same verbal packaging attached. A cheek, pressed down atop a podium, with shoulders slowly twisted down ninety degrees to that cheek still pressed to the podium, can illustrate distress far more effectively than a diagram in the right circumstances.

8.10 Offering Visuals with Witnesses

Visuals can help fill a collateral cross in which questions focused on other aspects of the witness's testimony, not shown on the chart, can only reinforce destructive impressions. A "collateral" inquiry leaning more toward the elements forming the context of your story, while avoiding the content of the oppositions, is very often the wisest course for your efforts. Visuals should often provide an outline for you to follow in such cross-examinations, where the point is more how the witness is forced to answer what you ask about on the board, than to contradict other things said during direct examination. The added value of using visuals in this way is that the attorney will know when the end is reached and be less tempted to venture on.

You can use the emergence of a key word, phrase, or point from the witness as your cue to turn to a visual or retrieve one you hadn't expected to use here. You can make a rhetorical proposal or ask a rhetorical question, and then, as its possible answers are being contemplated, you can pop up the slide or image with the answer you hold to be most accurate. If that answer, perception, or impression is not quite solid—for instance, if we aren't sure decision makers can easily distinguish between two different knee X-rays—the procedure can be run in reverse: popping up the image first and using the rhetorical devices to shore up the associations it offers, instead of opening the mental floor to wider speculation by leading with the words. But, again, these considerations must be handled in advance of the presentation.

Silent emphasis can be achieved anytime by placement of visuals alone. Consider a list, such as the handwritten "Language, Conduct, and Treatment" list mentioned above in the paragraph on Education under Gleaning Images. Let's say it's placed about five steps away from the witness stand, to the left of the jury box. Especially at the start of the education process, while experts instruct judge and jurors how certain behaviors done with any woman patient are out of bounds, the board can be used to invite the jurors to get in the habit of grouping, contextualizing, and reframing otherwise disparate points. As a type of language, or a variety of behavior or a lapse in treatment is mentioned, pause and walk to the board, indicate that category and ask a loopback question. Pause again, and then return to the witness till the next chance comes up. When jurors start looking at the proper category before you reach the board, maybe silently mouthing the term, you've confirmed that the board is serving its full purpose. There is no need to read off the category aloud, or to make the connections to its significance aloud—just physically gesture and loop back the witness's previous words. Anything more could be overkill.

If you've learned how to read the degree of bias that jurors express nonverbally, as assertions are made from the stand or in attorney remarks, you can tailor this nonverbal give-and-take to a fine pitch using your visuals. Again, you can then start targeting pieces of the message, doubling up on the perceptual channels used to do so, to the jurors most likely to be helpful to you in that effort.

Many of you will note that this pattern is a version of David Ball's red file prop. In this case, where the point is part of education more than persuasion, the written portion needs to be made more explicit, not hidden. The theme of each case story, the scope it reaches, the point of view from which it is best related, and the sequence through which it unfolds can always cue you on how best to utilize the emphasis visuals are providing. Of course, that takes some planning. Would you rather invite the jurors to speculate, or memorize? Positioning alone will either help or hurt that processing.[20] The simple act of planning where you're going to put a visual during testimony will either add to or detract from its persuasive potential.

Visible behavior on the attorney's part, in this case the technique of physical mirroring, also emerges as a very potent tool when witnesses begin taking the stand. To be more effective in using visuals and verbal anchors to invite strong associations with certain points, mirroring can help you capture and confirm an observer's full attention before you introduce the demonstrative aid or the key phrase. Establishing that connection first can make a big difference on the receiving end of the communication. Likewise, when you use any other communication techniques, you are more likely to succeed if you've first worked to invite the person's full attention. Without applying mirroring before trying these techniques, your chances of failing rise, even with simple techniques such as rhetorical questions or rule-of-three groupings.

Mirroring or matching some behavior of your listeners is the most effective means available for capturing and then directing full attention.

The technique takes ten to fifteen seconds, does not depend on any spoken words, and yields a far more complete connection to the listener's mind than spoken messages alone. The connection thus achieved, often called rapport, is a function of perceptual habits, more than of either thinking or psychological ones. By mirroring a listener's gestures, movements or other physical arrangements and their subsequent reaction, you can establish a connection with them that invites their full attention, though the person may be consciously predisposed to disagree with your spoken message. Nevertheless, if you approach your listeners with some respect for the real nature of attention and its unconscious and then conscious layering, your listeners can be invited to offer your points a fuller range of their attention, despite contrary conscious biases and habits. Do not expect the same attentiveness if you fail to mirror first.

Here's how New Jersey trial attorney Tom Vesper once described such an encounter at deposition:[21]

> In a case involving a defendant previously deposed by my co-counsel, described to me as the most stubborn, hard-to-understand witness he'd

20. Lisnek and Oliver, *supra*, n. 2, at 67–71.

21. Tom Vesper, "Stories About Mirroring," *News From The Mental Edge* (MetaSystems, Ltd., Spring 2000).

> ever deposed, mirroring worked a "miracle" of clarification. The defendant's prior deposition read like a bad *Tarzan* script—"Me defendant, you lawyer." I decided to re-depose this individual, disregarding my co-counsel's caveat that this was a waste of time. I was warned that he was a former Nazi . . . who didn't understand English, was difficult to understand, and [it was] basically like talking to a wall. I arrived at the deposition early, and even before it started or the defense attorney arrived, I greeted the man. He stood and formally bowed to me. I formally bowed to him. I immediately commenced mirroring as I got him a cup of coffee. He sat down, folded his arms across his chest, and leaned forward; so did I. He then took the oath, after which he placed both hands on the table, and we were off . . . .
>
> This defendant, who had expressed difficulty in understanding basic questions at his first deposition, immediately admitted to me that he had taken several days to prepare his written answers to interrogatories as best he could with his wife; he also quickly admitted that he had performed an installation contrary to manufacturer's instructions and further admitted he had never gotten the manufacturer's instructions. At a time when the project was nearly over, he took them to the general contractor (another defendant in the case) . . . and was told by the general contractor to "ignore them!" Obviously, defendant's counsel and defense counsel for the contractor were stunned by the flood of information I was getting from this presumed "Berlin Wall."

Vesper said that mirroring led the defendant to give more honest, detailed answers that went well beyond the scope of the questions. At one point, defense counsel tried to stop him from answering a question by grabbing his shoulder. The defendant just pulled away and continued talking with Vesper.[22]

By mirroring both a witness and a juror in proper sequence—juror, then witness, then back to juror—you can actually invite a witness to "target" select pieces of testimony to a particular juror, assured that the juror will give his or her full attention to that specific piece of the witness's message. You mirror the juror as you begin your question, passing focus to the witness as soon as you see a response. Then, as the answer is about to start, having mirrored the witness through the middle and end of the question, you are ready to "throw" the attention you've captured from the person on the stand, back to the person whose attention you confirmed at the start, just as the answer begins.

It is not always necessary to use mirroring directly to reap benefits for your client. Often, just watching ordinary mirroring among others—in negotiations, in

---

22. *Mercer v. Weyerhaeuser Co.*, 735 A.2d 576 (1999). No names have been used. Tom Vesper can be reached through Westmoreland, Vesper, Schwartz & Quattrone, in West Atlantic City, New Jersey.

meetings, or in the jury box—can provide a great deal of valuable direction for your efforts. When dealing with biases, knowing which juror is more likely to fully attend to which other jurors on the panel can provide a priceless chance to suggest and reinforce alternative biases to one or both parties in order to overcome some prevailing leanings in deliberation. Combining the observation of these advertised relationships of juror attention with conclusions drawn about thinking habits and attitudes from voir dire can actually lead to some strategic planning for targeting of visual and testimonial input.

In the prior example, after watching who shifted first, second, third, and so forth in a focus group, there was a strong indication of who would be directing one group's deliberations. So, even though the rest of the panel had some strong, conservative leanings regarding the practice of suing doctors, this one young man was able to bring his prevailing beliefs in personal responsibility and the doctor's failure to "do all he could to protect the patient" out early, shifting the tenor of the whole panel's discussion. The person that had nonverbally followed him most spoke up next, and adopted the same preventability language herself. So did the second person to speak after her, who had been mirroring the first woman, who in turn had been following the young man. At trial, with the same circumstances present, knowing how to most fully arm the presentation with the most compelling testimony and imagery on the duty to "do all that could be done" may well have proven decisive. Observing that sequence of visible signs of attention within relationships can be of tremendous value, and it's there to use in every single case.

After capturing a witness's attention by mirroring, you can invite that witness to either enhance or inhibit memory, as well as the intensity of their expression of the memory. This is done by adding such aspects as fully represented sensory language—weaving sight, sound, and sensations together—and directing the witness's eye movements to areas where recall of information or emotional responses are easiest. Eyes up and to the left, for most people most of the time, helps remembered images emerge more clearly. Eyes up and to the right, on the other hand, tends to foster constructing or imagining images. There are eye positions for each of the three major sensory systems, advertising which one each person happens to be indulging in at any given moment. If you mirror a witness, he or she will tend to follow you even more than people ordinarily follow the human object of their attention. By looking up and to the left, or just raising your head or hand slightly in that direction, while asking for memories of sights or images, you can nonverbally invite the witness to improve both the quality of the memory, itself, and its subsequent expression in court. (Of course, the process can work to inhibit memory retrieval and expression if you invite a witness's eyes to search for information through an inappropriate access.) Practice in mirroring anyone over time automatically heightens your awareness of these and all other movements they may make.

If you first confirm the witness's full attention by mirroring, a whole array of methods is in reach to help them tell their truth in the most effective way possible.

If you use mirroring well, you can begin to confirm within seconds whether you have, or have lost, a witness's, judge's, or juror's full attention to parts of any message in time to replay them.

8.11 One Story, Many Mouths

For attorneys adept at crafting and delivering persuasive openings and arguments, the transition to testimony is a very common trouble spot at which they are likely to be tempted to abandon the words and actions needed to reinforce a solid theme. As a matter of fact, were the trial actually a road we could map, that spot should have a roadside shrine commemorating the thousands of presentation plans and themes that died an early death there.

Many attorneys, in both direct and cross-examination, will unthinkingly drop the phrases they have determined are best for their case story in favor of those a witness happens to use. Rather than following the direction that focus group work determined should be advertised consistently to decision makers, common "herd" instinct can stop many professionals from leading with their own anchors, following their own sequence, and using visuals consistently to reinforce the story they came to deliver on their client's behalf. Any answer from the stand can be reframed in follow-up to continue the story's reinforcement for the jurors. Any anecdote the witness tells can be linked to the appropriate parts of your client's story line simply by one extra question. And because witnesses are human and follow the herd just as lawyers do, carefully using your own anchor phrases in your questions will help each witness follow suit on direct examination—and many on cross—without even thinking about it.

Witnesses are the main delivery vehicle for the case story, after the attorney that questions them. Every story element will either be reinforced or diminished during each witness's stint on the stand. Because people tend to follow the person on whom their attention is fixed, whether they are consciously mirrored by that person or not, many witnesses will simply adopt phrases and gestures the attorney uses as the questions are posed. In this way, language and anchors associated with the thematic points, scope, viewpoint, and active party or ingredient can all be reinforced by simple discipline on the attorney's part alone.

Preparing for and video recording of depositions provides the raw material from which trial stories will be filled in during their eventual presentation, wherever that may be. That being the case, that process will produce larger potential results for trial professionals that have already established some or most of their case story from focus group work before discovery is completely closed. Big surprises emerging from the last witnesses deposed might necessitate renewed focus work. But, usually, having the basics of your presentation plan in hand as you videotape the last of the discovery witnesses offers the invaluable chance to use all you know about delivering a compelling case story from witnesses—on tape—as if they were in trial, not deposition. While this may require some big readjustments in professional schedules and expectations, the potential rewards are worth the effort.

Sequence is a key element to successfully delivering a case story, and requires some serious thought when it comes to planning the order of proofs and witnesses. One formula that often works well is to divide your witness list by the strongest person addressing each one of the three story steps, and make these the first three to testify. This can help decision makers cover the strongest testimony over the entire story arc, in the sequence determined to be most helpful for this presentation. Naturally, most witnesses will be addressing more than one step in the sequence, and there will often be many more than one witness contributing evidence on one of the three steps. However the mix is worked out, the sequence of the story must be consistently delivered. Each person on the stand would best start as early in the story sequence as his or her testimony allows, and be led through their part of the story in the order decision makers have been invited to adopt for it, with attendant visual and verbal anchors and behavioral illustrations used fully. This applies to the fullest extent possible to early cross-examinations by the defense.

Witnesses that come out of sequence are always a big distraction from the consistent presentation of a case story. Sometimes that can't be helped. What can be done is to mark out where in the story line the witness's account belongs by referencing the verbal anchors you've established for that step, or by showing visuals previously associated with it—or both—as he or she arrives. Rather than questioning witnesses in ways that build a consistent version of the case story, some attorneys fall prey to breaking up the carefully planned sequence wildly from one witness to the next. In cross-examination, where a certain amount of bouncing around is recommended, particularly with experts, marking out the proper sequence of the responses just before or after, just as you would mark out an out-of-sequence witness, is still required so the decision makers follow as well as they can. Very often, however, preoccupation with the immediate task leads attorneys to dump their story entirely, sometimes for hours at a time. The more experienced an attorney is with courtroom routine, the greater this risk of overlooking the fact that the first task is always establishing, reinforcing, and maintaining the theme throughout the delivery.

Preparation with experts can be done in such a way that several goals are accomplished simultaneously. Once the story is set up in the presentation plan, revise the five-minute opening to reflect that plan, as if another focus group were being prepared. Then, expand some of the areas to introduce a bit more detail on the key evidentiary points that focus group work indicated would require the most reinforcement. Plan the insertion of the visual channel in all forms—exhibits, demonstratives, and behavioral illustrations—in the outline at their appropriate spots to achieve the needed balance in verbal and visual delivery. Then, call the key experts.

Using them as your sounding board, live or by conference long-distance, run through the beefed-up opening. Aim to stay within twenty minutes whenever possible. Solicit input from each expert about their contributions in light of the whole story sequence and package they are all now focused on. Correct misconceptions and misrepresentations, but also elicit reactions to the whole presentation package, keeping the input from group participants very close to the front of your mind. Some suggestions for how these professionals can better support the case story's delivery will almost inevitably emerge, frequently from the witnesses themselves. And you can invite any inconsistencies in how they will shortly be carrying their part of that story to the decision makers to be displayed and dealt with before it's too late. The professionals planning the case get some educated feedback, the experts all get to land squarely on the same presentation page as the rest of the trial team, and the attorney gets to practice delivering the story he or she has thus far only seen on paper and talked about in the abstract. Everyone gains from the exercise.

While presentation in voir dire and/or in opening remarks sets up and establishes the elements of a case story, it is through the effectively balanced visual channel of exhibits and demonstrative and behavioral illustration, and the verbal channel of questions and answers of witnesses, that the story is most likely to be reinforced and maintained to the end by decision makers, in or out of court. The visuals are the bread crumbs on the trail, the outline of the whole story, in sequence, to be followed backward and forward by decision makers. They can be anchors for everyone, including the presenter, to keep on the track of the story suggested by focus group work.

One other potent verbal tool to help the visuals achieve their greatest effect is presupposition, a factor mentioned several times earlier and a skill worth the time invested to fully develop its potential. Indirect suggestions, delivered well, are almost always more potent in their effect than their more direct counterparts, if for no other reason than that they are less likely to be singled out consciously and scrutinized for their persuasive intent by the listener. If you want people to see a certain relationship as important, a certain set of conditions as a precursor to other events, a set of factors as controlling an outcome, or a set of questions as still open or as fully resolved, you have two choices in the questions you ask witnesses about all these things. You can ask them directly about the level of importance, the precursor role, the level of control, or the closed or open nature of the questions. You will, where rules of evidence allow, get answers that directly state the status one way or the other. But if you were to presuppose the status in a way helpful to your position, while directly asking about some other related part of the evidence, it is often the case that listeners will adopt the presupposition contained in the question, while consciously processing, questioning, and considering the more direct subject addressed in the answer.

Let's look at our two running examples one last time: the "turned off the light" catheter placement and the "out of the line of sight" industrial injury. The attorney in each case could choose to directly ask questions about these key factors, or could presume them in the form of the questions. The plaintiff attorney, for example, could ask his surgical expert:

> Now, it's true that other doctors besides this one turn the fluoroscope on and off during this procedure, right?
>
> *Yes.*
>
> But it is your opinion, to a reasonable degree of medical certainty, that this is a much more dangerous approach to this procedure than needs to be taken, correct?
>
> *Yes.*
>
> Please tell us all why you think that.

And a description would follow. But, using presupposition, the lawyer could also approach the issue like this:

> Doctor, turning off the machine that allows you to see inside your patient's chest, just as you are inserting the sharpest instrument used in this procedure can cause several risks to patient safety, can it not?
>
> *Yes.*
>
> Can you list all the risks that not seeing where you are going can present for the doctor's patient, at the time?
>
> And what are all the possible consequences of those increased risks?
>
> Now doctor, you have done 2,000 of these placements, and the students you have taught have done ten times that many over the years, true?
>
> *Yes.*
>
> Just how many of those placements were done without being able to see where the doctor was going the whole time?
>
> *Not one.*

By directly asking the question, the act of turning off the light is reinforced as an option, a choice. And, in lay peoples' eyes, all other elements being equal, professionals always know more about their own choices than a juror or mediator does. But, by presuming the active element being chosen here is *seeing*, not being able to look, the story being built is free of many immediate concerns about medical propriety long enough to help decision makers focus on medical realities for the professional's patients. Note how the scope, viewpoint, and active party elements are reinforced through the phrasing with the witness, along with the driving analogy in "seeing where you are going," helping lay listeners relate better to the risks of not seeing. Now, when the expert is turned loose to discuss the horrible ramifications, the testimony is less likely to be simultaneously undercut by a listener more focused on a rule of the road than on the risks around the next, darkened corner.

In a similar vein, the defense attorney in the gas-inhalation story would likely never want to directly open up the question of the level of potential risk by the number of feet away the injured man happened to be from the deceased worker, much less whether he was in the line of sight of that man. The perceptual packaging those members of the focus group arrived at was not done by direct means, and therefore should not be invited in the case presentation by those means either. However, by using illustrative visuals depicting the broken sightline and the distance between the two men, as well as by spreading the lack of visual contact around among all eight of the workers that day in precursors to questions about when each man went up, who was doing what task, and so forth, the critical message can be consistently and effectively balanced in both channels, without being directly mentioned once.

When confronted with a story that rests, in part, on how important or effective science may be under the circumstances, presupposition can be invaluable in setting the perceived context for either a high or low value for science in the decision maker's minds. "The consistent results of this research have gone on for years and started exactly where, Dr. Jones?" invites one leaning, while "There are all sorts of surveys, studies and experiments listed in this expert report, Doctor, but I'd like to get a few important points straight with you first, such as what was left out of the measurements that went into the studies?" invites another.

In their book on NLP and trial practice,[23] Lucas and McCoy say it this way:

> The key here is where the listener's mind goes and what you want the listener to accept, understand, or believe without challenge or question . . . . In working with presuppositions . . . think of your proposition first, that is, what you want to say directly, and then put it in one of the presupposition forms.

Most of those forms, in one fashion or another, deal with juggling the old distinction between message context and message content. For example:

23. Lucas and McCoy, *supra*, n. 10, at 76–79.

Presupposing rule in context	➲	"Doctor, what rule or standard were you following when you discarded the previous note for one you put down after the fact?" (No such rule exists.)
Presupposing personal conduct in the content of the events	➲	"What did the doctor say when you called to inform her that you'd had that setback?" (No call was placed.)
Presupposing one factor, in content, overrides others in importance	➲	"From the hundreds of these steroid pills prescribed over this time, how far over the safe levels for such drugs in a patient's system was she forced to go?" (Discounting differences in drug brands, individual doses, metabolic rates, half life, periods without any drugs, etc.)
Presupposing that the context of time can become the content of harm	➲	"So for those twelve hours a week the first year, five hours a week the year after—624 hours or 26 full days—what were you most likely to have invested your time in, if it weren't for all this medical treatment?"
Presupposing the content of information is subordinate to the context of time	➲	"How many hours were the signs exactly as they should be, never off the middly of the safest zone of indicators?"[24]

When a witness challenges an effectively crafted and delivered presupposition, its effect for the decision maker can be multiplied many times over.

> Doctor, would you agree that among the top priorities for medical professionals, if not the number one priority, is patient safety?
>
> *No. I'm not sure I'd agree with that.*
>
> Really. Can you please list for us all right now how many other priorities you place above your own patients' safety?

Presuppositions invite everyone hearing them to assume facts not in evidence, and so can occasionally draw an objection. But, in truth, any question or statement relies on factual presuppositions to get any meaning across in the receivers' minds. All spoken messages, and visual ones, must be perceived, then referenced, then

---

24. *See also* Richard Bandler and John Grinder, *The Structure of Magic*, Vol. 1, Appendix B (Palo Alto, CA: Science and Behavior Books, 1975).

selected outside conscious reach to have any meaning, much less lead to judgments. The fact that an objection could be drawn should be no impediment to the careful planning for and use of this powerful, persuasive tool. For years, trial professionals presupposed there were only two variables they needed to keep track of in order to provide the best service to their clients: decision maker backgrounds and attorney choices in delivery. Presupposing a third variable exists in all the potential stories that a single case can germinate can prove extremely valuable to those trial professionals when crafting a case story presentation, even if it means there is so much more influencing the outcome to pay attention to and handle effectively. If the price of freedom is eternal vigilance, so, it appears, is the price of credibility.

8.12 2015 Supplement

With the exception of what the continuing research is advancing about what *mirroring* does for *rapport*, the most significant change in the approaches I advocate for managing the perceptions that drive any decision maker's story (re)construction focuses on managing images *with* them.

As I described in the Preface to this new edition, the lessons of almost ten years have refined a set of three tasks for the attorney tending to the fundamental job of developing and delivering a case as a story. She must be ready and able to manage three things with the decision makers she approaches: rapport with them, a story narrative with them, and the mental images they are invited to construct.

When it comes to the latter point, managing decision makers' mental images, there is one more hierarchy of three to incorporate in our delivery of your case as a story. There are three basic means of inviting decision makers to utilize imagery that will get results your clients would prefer.

Show them an image.

Evoke images for them.

Invite them to visualize.

Although I discussed the first two points in earlier chapter supplements (and their corresponding original chapters), I haven't yet delved into what knowing how to manage the decision maker's mental imagery can produce for your clients. Just as almost all nonverbal communication is seen (and is thus visual communication), most of the embodied narratives legal decision makers build to make sense of a client's case story are populated by images. And, since they are primarily mental images out of reach of conscious scrutiny, the influence you have on when and how they are envisioned can have a profound effect on the shape of the stories decision makers (re)construct.

You know now that anchors work best when the cue used to invite a particular conditioned response from decision makers is a phrase linked with an image. You also know that stories are most persuasive when they are consistently delivered in a sequence of frames that fill out a three step outline: context, conflict, resolution.

But, what exactly composes a frame?

Previously in Chapter Eight, I included a section on how effective demonstrative visuals can be when used to help decision makers reframe perceptions of key story factors. However, I didn't explain exactly what a frame is or how a decision maker can frame a case story, or how big a role images play in that process. Section 8.7.7, "Link/Anchor," included the following as one (of a about six) purposes served by proper visuals:

> Artfully presented images are far more effective than plain words in helping people form solid, reusable associations for impressions, perceptions, or ideas. Think of them as visual bells, prompting mental salivation—anchors.

Frames are what make anchors work. Frames are collections of our individually perceived experiences stored as references that give meaning to each *new* situation, event, thought, or action we experience. They provide the perceptual context with which we make sense of our world. And, anchors—images linked to or with phrases—invite sets of collected meaningful experience to come to the forefront from the mind's recesses. What comes to mind, your mind's eye, for instance if you envision someone shaking a fist in righteous indignation? Or, what comes to mind when you imagine someone you don't know well making an immediate, strong connection with you in a conversation at work? Or over coffee?

How about this one. What comes to your mind's eye when you are thinking of a paralyzed former ironworker isolated at home in his motorized wheelchair, waiting for his caretaker to arrive?

Embodied inner narratives constructed to process legal case stories are much more than perceptions of facts and law. The context they provide decision makers to work within is composed of frames taken from their own life experiences, both real and imagined. These frames form a vast collection that can be utilized with anchors to great persuasive effect. Because the perceptual territory of a frame is inextricably tied to visual perception, is it any wonder that the best tool to invite decision makers to use the frames you've developed for your case story is to offer them an image with a phrase to anchor each of those frames for themselves?

Consider the ironworker walking atop a girder. OSHA calls that eight inches of steel beneath his boots his "walking, working surface"—i.e., his elevated workstation. Most jurors have few experiences working high up atop a steel beam, but they all have experiences with heights, climbing, being lifted, falling, and *fearing* falling. So, what would be the best anchor to use to invite them to see—frame—the *risk* in a case where safety equipment was promised, but never delivered by the contractor employing this worker and all his colleagues, also working on elevated workstations? What about something that shows how that contractor not only *took away safety* but also *added hazard* in three distinct ways? Here is what that looked like for jurors at trial.

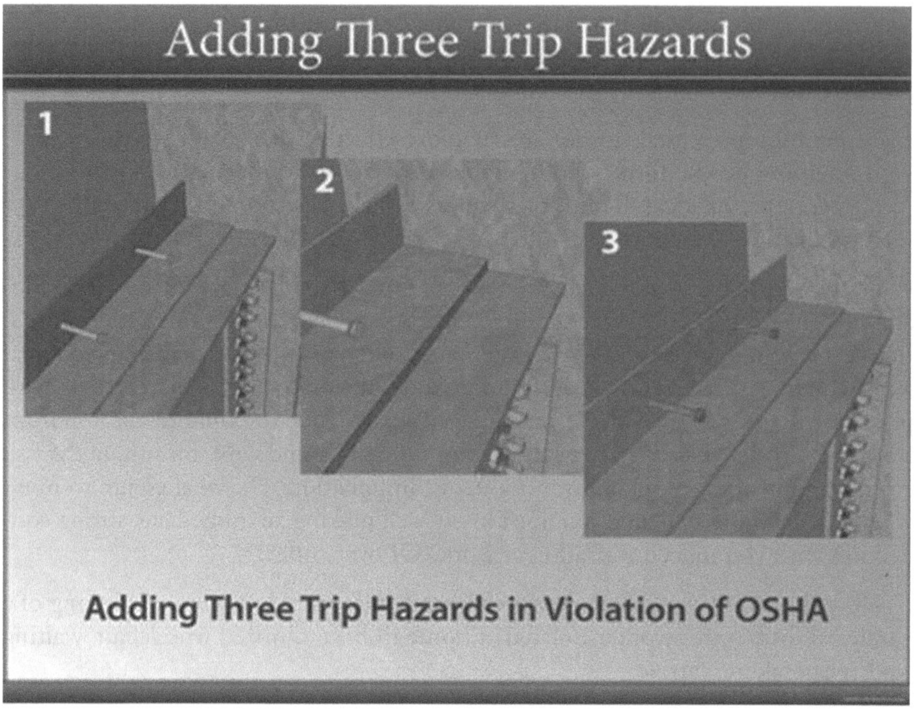

One of the contractor's bad acts deviating from the law was welding the studs (seen highlighted in red in window 3) while the steel was still on the ground. That flange, with those studs, is supposed to be welded in place by the ironworkers *after* it is lifted up to them to install, not *before* their "walking, working surface" arrives from below. The slide shows the flange with three separate *added hazards* (windows 1, 2, and 3, each hazard highlighted in red) that should not have been there at all; the raised edge, the uneven surface, and the studs are each recognized tripping hazards in their own right. Decision makers are being asked to "see" the hazards from a very particular perspective, though it is likely one they have never experienced in their own lives, or perhaps even imagined before seeing this visual. But, they have a lifetime of perceived experiences with which to "fill in" their own versions of the risk frame in this case story.

Once you have developed the seven to nine case story frames for your delivery, it's time to take a page from filmmaking and "storyboard" those frames. Illustrate each one with an image (or images), informed by the input from your focus group, to best evoke a particular frame—risk, rules, right way, deviant acts, and so on, that your particular story requires. For example, consider the image below (from the case referenced in Chapter Six, section 6.2, "Bridging and Blending") about a locally based retailer suing a national credit-card company for breach of contract in a venue known to be somewhat hostile to the retailer due to fallout for many local residents from the retailer's disruptive bankruptcy (around the same time as the contractual breach claimed, though not related to it at all).

You'll recall these focus group participants had added an element— competition—to the stories they were (re)building, though how competitive the marketplace was at the time did not directly address or affect the claims made. This was an example of the "if this, then that" analysis of focus group results, and in the case of this large retail company suing a credit card company, it invites an image that reflects two embodied reactions: *reliability* and *holding up your end* (of a deal). The consensus of the focus groups was that the plaintiff—even if bankrupt—was due consideration *if* "they did all they could to hold up their end" of the agreement. While the case had no claim that the credit company had proven unreliable, that was a central image in most stories being built and led to the following demonstrative visual suggesting just such an image for the decision makers to use in framing the first step—context—of their own stories.

In other words, the focus groups suggested the story be *less* about proving the specifics of the breach claims and *more* about the betrayal of the "mutual risk" both companies agreed to undertake as a team: that the retailer give its entire customer database to one of the first ever in-house branded subprime credit cards from the card company in exchange for a substantial, five-year promotion of those cards by the card company. Mutual risk for mutual reward. And, here is the *central image* of the story decision makers told us they wanted to see and hear, instead of the one we had been expecting to relate.[25]

As in the credit card case, often the *theme* and *central image* deserve a similar visual treatment to help invite decision makers to frame their private versions of the case story as you'd most like them to. Just as with anchors, you need to deliver images and phrases *together* that most likely invite decision makers to bring up the perceptions necessary for them to (re)build the most effective versions of your case story. Without strongly correlating images evoking perceptions and referencing evocative life experiences, your chance of hitting the right perceptual mark in the mind's eye of decision makers will be remote.

In the supplement to Chapter Five, I discussed the roles of the "right way" and "wrong way" story frames. The following images, from a different case, substantiate that your chosen images don't have to be complicated to get the job done well. In one trial,[26] Chicago trial attorney Brad Cosgrove presented a case in which a defendant doctor was negligent when it came to recognizing his patient's appendicitis. This kind of case is usually referred to by the anchor phrase, *failure to diagnose*, an unfortunate phrase that suggests rather weak imagery. The subjective frame of reference often associated with "failed to" is *human error*. Among students of legal decisions, that frame also is referred to as "*stuff just happens*" and almost always compels decision makers to render a defense verdict. The passive language (similar to the traffic wreck version *failure to yield*) tends to steer the mind's eye toward an image of a "blameless" sin of omission.

Here's what attorney Cosgrove did to avoid that trap in the framing of his case story delivery: "Rather than say this was a *failure to diagnose* appendicitis case, I got the doctor to admit [in deposition] that he was *thinking* appendicitis. Then it [became] a case about *correct* thinking but *wrong* actions. He *thinks* appendicitis but *does not act* like it is appendicitis." Although, at first glance, this tack appears to be giving the doctor some benefit of the doubt—after all, he correctly was thinking appendicitis—a closer look reveals that *framing* the danger, or risk portion, of the story as "correct thinking" about the possibility of appendicitis but then, *not acting*—i.e., doing nothing about it—invites decision makers to construct for themselves one of the most potent frames there is for a defendant's choices: *knowing wrongdoing*. The medical professional is seen as admitting he knows better than to do as he did.

---

25. *In re Kmart Corporation v. Capital One Bank.*, No. 03 C 8625, Bankruptcy No. 02 B02474 (N.D. Ill. Jan. 24, 2005).
26. *Stawarz v. Central Chicago Medical Clinic.*, No. 10L 10720 (Cook County, IL 2013).

The frame and its attendant mental images that are essential to help decision makers see the widest gap possible between what *should have* happened and what *was done* instead is the "right way" frame. In the domain of expert witnesses, the "right way" frame can be introduced as the answer to the question: "Under these circumstances, what would it have looked like if everything were done right according to the rules?" In this case of *knowing wrongdoing*, attorney Cosgrove used demonstrative visuals to help jurors see the gap between the right way and the wrong way. Whenever delivering "right way" procedures, standards, or precautions, always play it out to the "happy ending" where protection, health, or safety are achieved for persons facing risks common to the circumstances of the plaintiff. Ideally, that mirrors the experiences decision makers have associated with following the right rules in the face of certain risks in their own lives.

The demonstrative visuals Mr. Cosgrove produced at trial to help jurors condition themselves to see *knowing wrongdoing* by a doctor were simplicity itself:

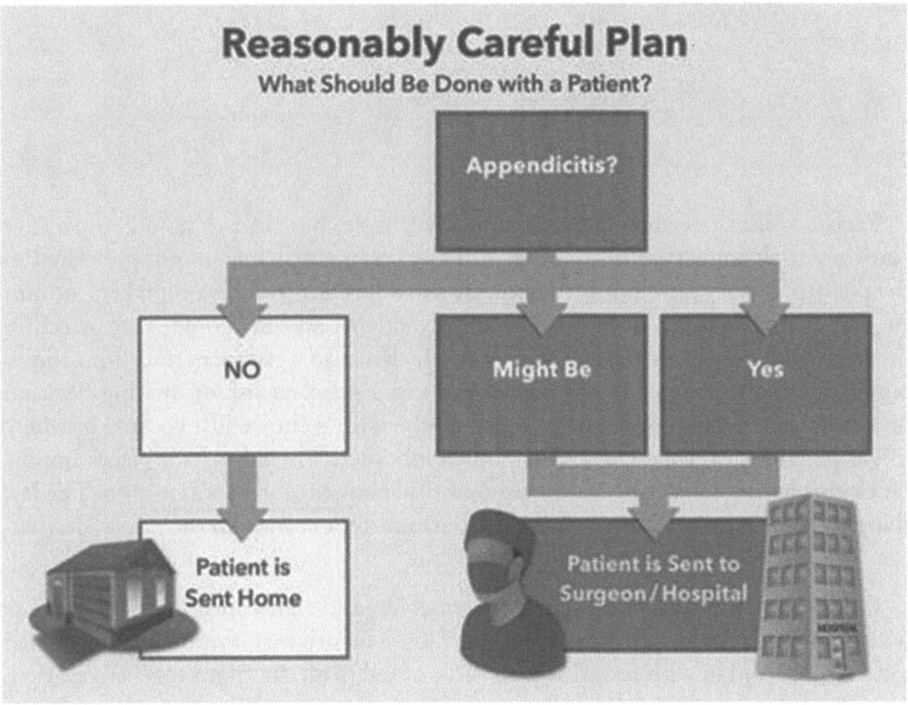

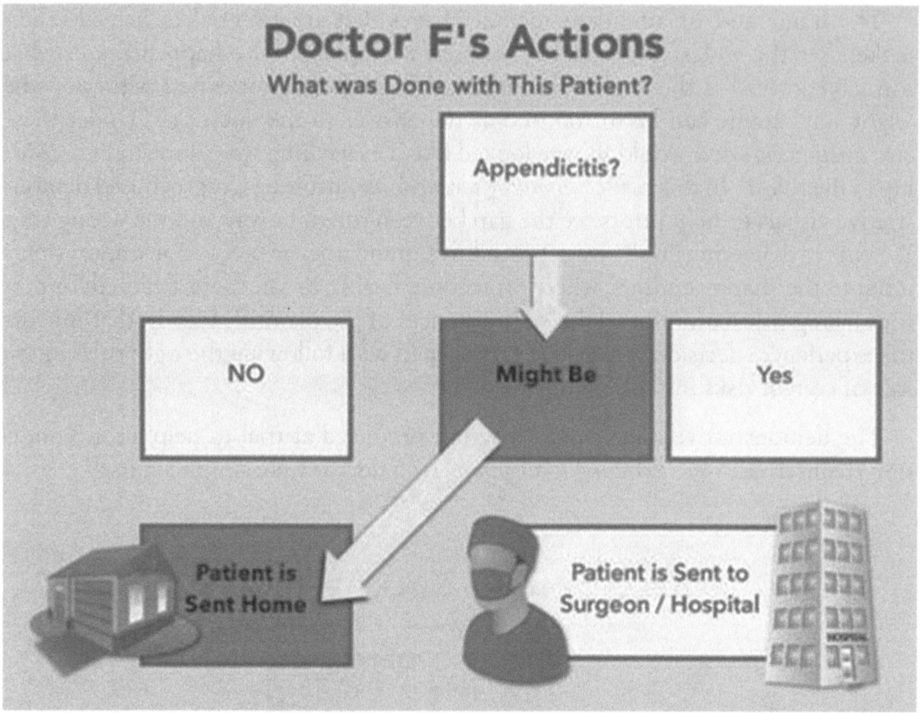

Each decision tree slide looks deceptively simple, but, in fact, as a comparative pair they took some careful thought to make certain that images not beneficial to the plaintiff's story were not inadvertently introduced into decision makers' minds. An earlier draft of the "right way" slide on the left had the "home" box placed in the upper left corner, instead of the lower left. Because westerners read from top to bottom and left to right, the former layout ran a needless risk of inviting decision makers to other-than-consciously "validate" the wrong choice just because of where it was positioned on the chart. Also, our "embodied" thread, which places important items higher up, could exacerbate that risk. Sequence is important too. The last thing to be read and retained will be the bottom right corner, so the safest "destination" for both boards is down and to the right.[27]

Cosgrove's demonstratives also show that color, and all the meanings we associate with a particular color (or colors), counts a lot. The original "wrong way" slide had some boxes filled in with the same green color used in all the "right way" boxes. Red, because of the negative and/or dangerous signal it indicates in the basic human narrative, was the obvious persuasive color choice for the "wrong way" box outlines and

27. There is a third basic function of our perceptual habits that make the "down and to the right" visual position so strong. For those aware of the sensory "semaphore" revealed by eye movements isolated and taught by the founders of the Neurolinguistic Programming communication model, note that is the spot our eyes drop down to when we are primarily experiencing *feelings*.

interiors. Additionally, making the arrows depicting the choices available in each decision tree different colors—and specifically very vibrant colors, i.e., bright yellow for the "wrong way," bright green for the "right way"—not only helps decision makers sort the right way from the wrong ways being shown to them, but also helps that much more to emphasize in their mind's eye, the defendant's fault of *knowingly* choosing to create injury where none ever need be in the first place.

Ultimately, though, the indisputable power of these visual demonstratives lies in the other-than-conscious *imagery* we connect with the alternative choice diagrams. Without those specific images evoking frames of reference and meaning, there is no real human narrative with which the decision maker can identify.

This type of *framing*, linked with demonstratives, can go a long way in producing a strong plaintiff case story delivery that even a three-year-old can grasp. I know this for a fact because trial attorney Cosgrove sent me a video of *his* three-year-old daughter pointing at the home and hospital images on the charts and chiding "that doctor" for sending the patient "home" instead of where he needed to be: "in the hospital." By framing the risk and right way parts of this medical neglect story as *knowing wrongdoing* instead of a *failure to diagnose*, Cosgrove was able to invite decision makers to build their own stories on a much firmer emotional basis. Because all legal decisions have an emotional basis, managing decision makers' perceptions—especially through mental images that steer people towards emotional reactions—is time and effort well invested.

Visually depicting the story frame of *harms and losses* can be a challenge even in the best of cases. In Chapter Eight, I discuss how Colorado attorney Larry Lee developed a visual technique for not only overcoming juror tendencies to minimize the value of time spent in treatments, doctor visits, rehab appointments, chiropractic treatments, and so on, but also to *increase* the perceived severity of such losses by depicting them as what I proposed as a "double loss."

Plaintiff injury cases considered to have just "minor" losses—i.e., those in which "catastrophic" injuries cannot be cited—still deserve some help in their delivery. The following calendar charts are a set of recent examples that proved extremely successful in helping decision makers disinclined by nature or outside influence, to treat the difficult points of such damages values seriously.[28]

The calendars visually represent the years following the plaintiff's car wreck and were shown to the jurors in this trial.[29] The final calendar shows the ongoing appointments—by this time, basically just maintenance therapy—right up to the day of trial.

---

28. Not only is this technique still alive, but so is attorney Larry Lee who introduced it to me. In Chapter Eight, I erroneously referred to him as the "late" Larry Lee.

29. *Dorado v. McGoig Concrete Co.*, Wayne County Circuit Court, Michigan (June 11, 2014).

The legend for each calendar includes a red square for surgeries, of which three appear in 2012 and another in 2013, and all are attributable directly to injuries caused by the defendant driver's negligence in the wreck. The first surgery's appearance a little over a year from the wreck, helped eliminate speculation about being "sue happy" and "quick, unnecessary surgeries" aimed at maximizing a recovery for a condition that was not "really serious." Conservative treatment was first exhausted before the needed surgeries were undertaken.

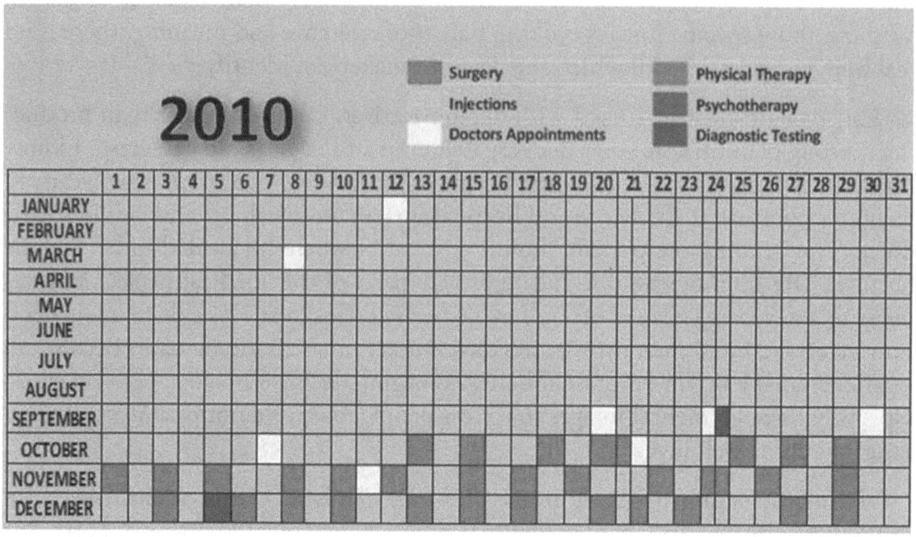

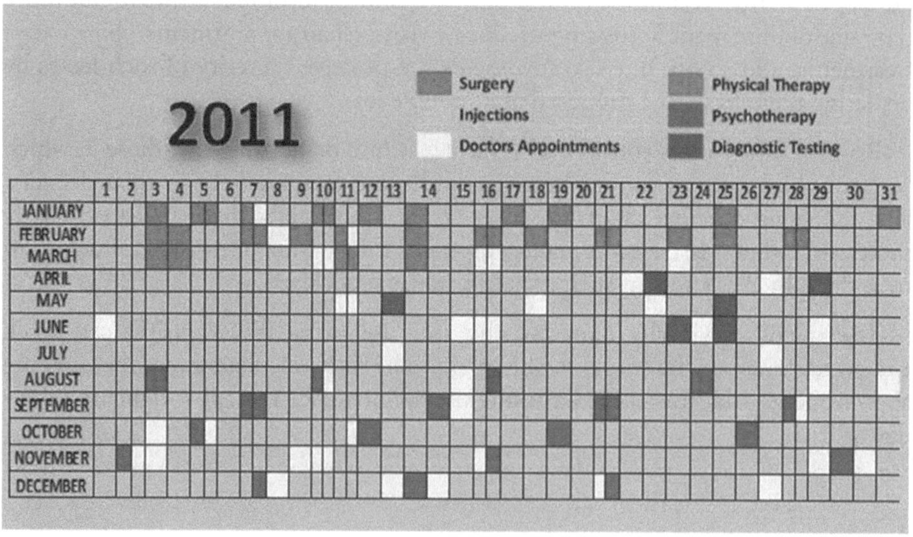

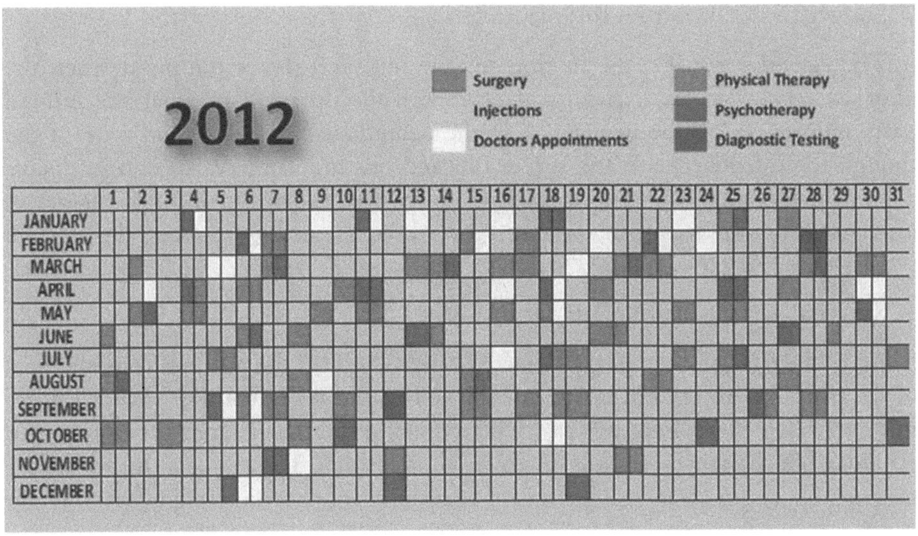

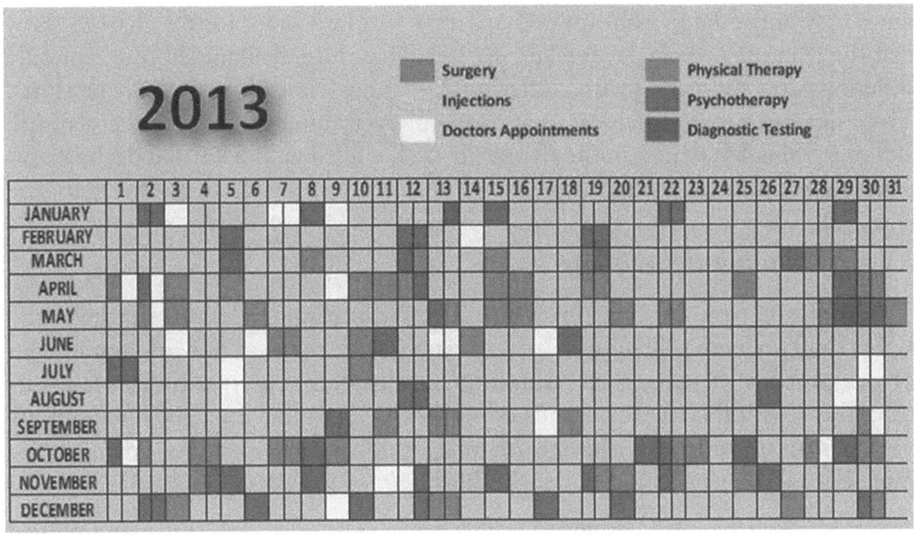

If these charts provide the images for decision makers to help build anchors for assessing damage values, then what phrases should the attorney link to these images to invite decision makers to build those anchors?

Renowned trial attorney, the late Mo Levine, whose idea that jurors should look for value in damage evidence, can be paraphrased as, "don't just show them what they *took* from him, show them what they *left him with*, too." Levine's understanding, coupled with the imagery of these charts, do the job of inviting decision makers to see a "double loss." In the First Edition of Chapter Eight, I wrote, "Time is not usually a commonly presumed element of harm, unless one can *see* it."

So, what was taken from this plaintiff?

The calendar visual(s) are in front of the jury and this is the point when the attorney relates family, friends, and coworker anecdotes about what the injured party enjoyed *before* the negligence of the defendant took all of that *away*. Even though the calendar has many spaces blocked out for "surgery, injections, doctor appointments, physical therapy, psychotherapy, and diagnostic testing," the spaces referenced should actually be the number of days *not* needing to access the medical system—i.e., very few.

So, what was the plaintiff left with?

All of the days on the calendar that are blocked off for the physical consequences of the plaintiff's injury not only represent where and when the old "before" activities have been eliminated, but also where previously unnecessary (not to mention everyday life changing) medical treatment and maintenance has been substituted.

A double loss.

Made even more real by a small "trick of the eye." Though some of these procedures may only take an hour (or perhaps less), it is important for the chart to show that the plaintiff's whole day is taken up with what the defendant left him, not only suffering with, but *dealing* with. Suffering doesn't take time off (even more of a loss). These demonstrative visuals act as anchors for everything taken from the plaintiff, and everything left to him in the aftermath—a life filled with pain, and dealing with pain, on a day-to-day basis.

8.12.1 Whither the Witness

Beyond the basic checklist for witnesses in your case—fully interviewing, reassuring, and preparing clients and lay witnesses (where they live or work, not in your office), properly prepping their testimony, getting decent expert witnesses, familiarizing them with the relevant details of your case, *and* presenting your five-minute focus group opening to them and inviting critiques and additions—there is one more critical element to add to the checklist: *witness sequence.*

Even a case story well developed in focus groups, carefully analyzed, and refined to create a strong and cogent plan for presentation, coordinated with well-executed and refined visuals, supporting exhibits and testimony culled and reorganized, and the attorney well rehearsed and confident can still come completely to naught.

How so?

No truly sufficient effort was made to correctly sequence the order of witnesses. Thus, the witnesses produced are rendered incapable of reinforcing and filling out the case story sequence because they do not appear in the order set up in voir dire, and then confirmed again by the story sequence delivered in opening statement.

I've heard all the excuses—especially expert availability—and I can tell you, there is *no* excuse for an attorney to actively undermine the jurors' (re)construction process of the case story just at the most critical point: when testimony begins. Just as story sequence has proven to be the best first step in prepping focus group presentations, and the best first step in analyzing and refining stories focus group members provide, so too is story sequence delivered by the first three or four witnesses the best way to be certain all that good work achieves the just results.

So, here is the "Rule of the *Witness* Road":

> If you are not committed to bringing witnesses early—at least the first three—who will "fill in" the case story sequence in the proper order of the frames of your case story, then there's no point in bothering with anything else.

It is that important. And, it is this simple:

- What witness can best address *and express* the risk for this story?
- What witness can best address *and express* the rules for this story?
- What witness can best address *and express* the right way for this story?

When I began working with plaintiff attorneys, back in the Pleistocene Era, a large part of my consulting work dealt with medical malpractice. I was regularly treated to florid recitations of how my attorney client had "eviscerated" the defendant doctor on the stand by jumping to call him as his first witness. As you might guess, I was never treated to the tales of when that brilliant tactic failed to produce for his or her unwitting client. After about four years of that (and I'd like to think no longer a nascent consultant), I started asking the question, "What did the doctor get to say after you sat down?"

Also, when I began working with plaintiff personal injury attorneys, I slowly learned that many worked from the same superstitious habits of mind that keep TV psychics, racetrack touts, cable TV stock tipsters, and any television network making a profit: they only counted the "hits" and completely forgot about the "misses" as soon as they happened.

I grew up in El Paso, Texas. In sports, we Texans can claim two big contributions: the 1966 Texas Western Miners (all-black starting five) against Adolph Rupp's Kentucky Wildcats (all-white starting five) in the NCAA championship, and golfer Lee Trevino. And it's Trevino who provides the stellar example of superstition superseding reason. In his best years, he was as likely to be in contention for a major tournament win as not, though he certainly won his share. If he was in the running and playing on Sunday, he could be counted on to sport a red shirt which he always referred to as "my money shirt." He lost more tournaments wearing his "money shirt" than he ever won. But, towards the end of his major career, in one of those

"Indian summer" stories sports is filled with, Mr. Trevino found himself leading in the U. S. Open one more time. Despite years of it getting him nowhere in countless failed efforts, on Sunday morning out comes the red "money" shirt one more time. As I recall, he won, but it is highly unlikely winning had anything to do with his shirt that Sunday.

So, here it is again, the Rule of the *Witness* Road:

> If you are not committed to bringing witnesses early—at least the first three—who will "fill in" the case story sequence in the proper order of the frames of your case story, then there's no point in bothering with anything else.

CHAPTER NINE

SOWING PREMIUM SEEDS: STORY DELIVERY

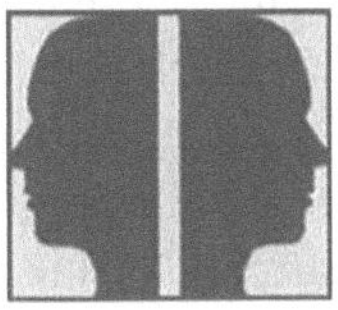

For every complicated problem there is a simple answer, and it's usually wrong.
—*H.L. Mencken*

9.1 Finished Products

The best-prepared plan doesn't achieve the best settlement outcome or win a case by itself. An effective presentation plan minimizes the introduction of landmines into the decision maker case stories being built, as it maximizes invitations to use the strongest story elements toward versions that can produce the preferred outcome. Given a chance, focus groups will suggest both how to plan the presentation of such a case and what that strongest story's elements probably are. But getting that case story from focus groups and learning from them how to best present it is just the start. Actually delivering the case story according to plan, inviting decision makers to use and reinforce all the story elements you want highlighted, minute to minute, without slipping and introducing riskier perceptions, positions, or points takes a sharp focus.

Many people find it easier to follow a plan once they've seen it done. In the interests of providing a few real-life examples of how presentation plans were developed and delivered, using the approach outlined in the preceding chapters, this chapter offers four examples.[1]

The first, a medical negligence case developed and delivered by the plaintiff attorney, presents a detailed review of the development and delivery process, from start to finish, and beyond. The remaining three examples—a defense of a first-degree murder charge, a defense of a design defect claim, and a plaintiff's professional misconduct claim—rely mostly on descriptions of process by the attorneys involved, with some added commentary. They tell their own stories about how well working on the case story functioned for them in each case.

1. All names have been changed with the exception of the footnoted case citations.

9.2 Case One: Surgical Neglect

9.2.1 *The Facts and Obvious Problems*

The attorney offered the following initial narrative description of the case story:[2]

> This is a gynecological malpractice case. Jackie was admitted to the hospital on July 5, 1994, under the care of Dr. Doolittle, for complaints of pelvic pain and right inguinal inclusion cysts. The doctor did a video-laser laparoscopy, which showed endometriosis in the cul de sac[3] and on the bowel. While removing a pocket of endometriosis in the cul de sac, the doctor [apparently] burned a hole in the bowel, not detected at the time of surgery. Jackie returned to the hospital the following day with post-operative pain complaints. Her doctor attributed this to an abdominal wall hematoma and not to a bowel injury. Two days later, she returned, and on July 8, was diagnosed with an "acute abdominal process." During the surgery [that] followed, a small, red, and inflamed hole was found on the lower side of her bowel. Studies done showed peritonitis involving the lower half of the abdomen, and a perforation of the sigmoid colon. A consulting doctor's impressions were of peritonitis and sepsis, both secondary to the sigmoid colon perforation. Jackie was discharged on July 20. On August 3, Jackie was seen by another doctor, who readmitted her to the hospital for elevated vital sign values.
>
> It was not till four years later, however, in February of 1998, that it was discovered she had severe adhesions of her Fallopian tubes and her ovaries. The right tube and ovary were so heavily encased they had to be removed. Her left tube and ovary were found severely adhered to the pelvic wall, an abnormal position for them. Plaintiff doctors—treating and expert—testify with a reasonable degree of medical certainty that the adhesions [were] formed at or near the time of the peritonitis. They go on to say the adhesions were the reason she had to have her tube and ovary removed.
>
> The defense position begins developing from the informed consent given by the patient, which acknowledged that a bowel perforation is a well-known complication for this surgery. The defense also includes facts that some surgery was indicated, the second surgery to repair the peritonitis was done quite well, the videotape of the operation itself

2. The case referenced in this article was tried in Jasper County District Court, Joplin, MO, in March 1999. The attorney for the plaintiff, whom I've worked with, was Ed Hershewe of the Hershewe Law Firm. The favorable jury verdict led to a settlement shortly thereafter.

3. An anatomical feature in the bowel.

> does not specifically show the bowel getting burned, and that there was another source of heat used in the operation—a cautery—which was used to stop a bleeder and may also have been the source of the perforation—again, a common complication.
>
> Additional features of the defense position included the prognosis the doctor gave Jackie prior to surgery, indicating about a five-year "clock" on her ability to get pregnant if her endometriosis stayed untreated (she was nineteen at the time), the doctor's successful experience with over 120 of these procedures, the patient's prior [gastrointestinal] problems, and a cyst discovered in her removed ovary, which could have affected her fertility regardless of the surgery and subsequent injury.

In the requested lists of strong and weak points for each side, additional strengths of the defense case mentioned were the plaintiff's tendency to act a bit whiny and the fact that some of her complaints (bloating, weight gain, pain, etc.) predated the first operation; her husband's fertility had never been tested; she failed to treat with any doctor in the intervening four years between her endometrial surgery and the operation on her adhesions; and she could likely still get pregnant through in vitro fertilization (IVF).

The plaintiffs could counter with the fact that the doctor chose not to use certain safety devices/precautions he had often used before, which would definitely have prevented the injury, and that there are big problems with IVF in her case, since carrying more than one fetus would not work due to her condition, and IVF greatly increases the chance of multiple births.

The plaintiff attorney had big concerns initially about the videotape of the procedure, which did not show the perforation being made; the many challenges to the damage case emerging from the four-year gap in time; and the indisputable fact that this kind of known complication can occur even when the highest degree of care is used during surgery.

Initial concerns regarding the presentation of this case story involved the fair number of hurdles and perceptual problems, presenting landmines often shared by many medical negligence case stories. These included:

- The patient signed the informed-consent form, which included the injury she sustained as a known complication of the surgery.
- Much of what happened in this operation, for good or ill, involved medical judgment.
- The story was rife with medical (and legal) terms of art and required substantial education of the jurors.

- The doctor had conducted over a hundred such procedures before, apparently with no major problems reported.
- There were potential alternative causes of both the injury (a benign effort to cauterize a bleeder) and the harm (cystic disease, which could affect her fertility regardless of her scarring).
- The plaintiff had prior physical problems in the same bodily territory, and she had a four-year gap in seeking any significant medical treatment. Her claim required the jurors to bridge that gap, finding an immediate cause for harms emerging four years later.
- The criminal mindset of most civil jurors prompts desire for proof of intent to harm before negligence can be found.
- Hindsight bias often works for plaintiffs and could here, as well, by driving the perceived importance of the neglected safety precautions. But it could also be turned against the plaintiff through speculation about the four-year time gap and all the possible "natural causes" of her fertility and other gastrointestinal problems, apart from this one, flawed operation and its quickly executed repair.
- The odd arrangement of some facts—particularly the time line—could increase the chances of jurors seeing the doctor as a victim of a legal system gone mad.
- A very popular attitude reframes many poor surgical outcomes as mere acts of God, the "complications happen" position.

In addition to all the standard hurdles presented, in any plaintiff's medical negligence case, by many juror preconceptions and predispositions—anti-litigation bias, pro-medical industry attitudes, authoritarian stances and such[4]—these particular predilections and possible perceptions of the client's case story seemed likely to prove problematic for this case at trial.

4. Anti-plaintiff bias in personal injury cases has been the subject of some long-term research efforts by board members of the former ATLA, Greg Cusimano and David Wenner. Their findings from nationwide focus groups are featured in their seminar, "Overcoming Juror Bias." References here are from a seminar in Atlanta, GA, March 15–18, 2001. Their material has also appeared in *Trial* (ATLA, Washington, D.C.). Authoritarianism is described, as it relates to higher conviction rates in criminal cases, in D. Narby, B. Cutler, and G. Moran, "A MetaAnalysis of the Association Between Authoritarianism and Jurors' Perceptions of Defendant Culpability," *Journal of Applied Psychology* 78 (1993): 169–172. *See also* Amy Pardieck, "Differ or Die: Prevailing in an Era of Rampant Anti-Plaintiff Bias," *News From the Mental Edge* (MetaSystems, Ltd., Summer 2004).

9.2.2 Focus Group Version of Events

Many of the anticipated challenges showed up in the single focus group[5] we were able to conduct, as did many potential solutions for their presentation at trial. Some specific lessons learned included various aspects of the case story:

Theme

Along the lines of a "prevention" theme, here is some of what members of one "jury" had to say in post-verdict discussion:

Jane:	Our primary issue was the negligence part. We couldn't come to an agreement of whether it would have happened or not had he used the backstop.
George1:	Our discussion—actually, I was one that was kind of set off from anybody else. I wasn't one way or another. I was kind of stuck down the middle. I felt like he should have used it, but I wasn't really swayed that if he had used it, it actually would have prevented this, that it would or wouldn't.
George2:	I believed that was something we could not prove, but as far as the scales are concerned, it would have—it tipped it more for the plaintiff's argument basically because—well, that's just something we could not prove or disprove. But, you know, if he did take the necessary precautions, that's something, you know, *if he did do everything necessary possible*, you know, at that time, scientifically through his methods and *he did everything that he knew how to do* to prevent something like that. We're not saying that it did cause, but, you know, but if he did, you know, if he did everything necessary to prevent it, then he would not necessarily be guilty of a malpractice issue.

5. Twenty-one participants heard four separate presentations by two attorneys: openings, two didactic evidence presentations, and closings. Participants were surveyed in writing twice, at the start and end, and debriefed as a group throughout the day. Three "juries" of seven deliberated without facilitation during the last hour of a 9:00 to 4:30 day.

The strong suit for the case was almost certainly the number of surgical standard violations the doctor perpetrated. They mostly involved the use of one of two recommended safety devices, each a form of "backstop" for the heat of the surgical laser. The experts and subsequent treating doctors also took issue with some of his technique during surgery done without the backstops. These actions were open to different characterizations. The defendant admitted to using the devices consistently in the past and offered "saving time" as his only reason for not applying them here, though the surgery wasn't under emergency circumstances. The technical problems all had to do with doing things too hard, too fast or too long. George2, and like-thinking focus group members, had taken a cumulative view of these many problems and, coupled with the definite safety provided by the backstops in the cause of the harm, had settled on multiple choices to forgo harm prevention as their proof of negligence. Of course, for neglect of prevention to make sense and be internally consistent, the cause of the harm had to be assumed in each of their stories, even if, as George2 points out, that cause link was not articulated among group members at the time.

The consultant's note to the attorney at the time, in the report of this part of the group's discussion, read:

> What George1 sought, according to his written forms and his taped discussion, was the direct link of the backstop preventing burning from either the cautery or the laser. He just missed the plaintiff's attorney saying it would, when that was said. Or perhaps he heard it and deleted that content, as very often happens when part of the story fails to fit the decision maker's story construct. This is why I'm wondering if putting too much of your presentation time into the exact mechanisms of how the different tools can burn things isn't a red herring, likely to help the defense. The two things they apparently really need to hear from you are that one leaves scars and the other leaves smoke, but that a backstop helps both. You may want to think about dumping the detailed visuals that compare the precise mechanisms of harm, and just make those points on cross-examination, using their stuff, if they bring it.

Negligence

The mechanism by which the injury apparently occurred has the doctor using a grabbing tool to pull pieces of tissue closer to the laser, which he then fires using a foot trigger. Experts indicate that, at one point or another, he grabs too much tissue and pulls some bowel up into the firing range, along with the endometrial tissue he's aiming at. All experts agree, watching the videotape of the procedure, he is moving very fast, burning far too large an area for the mild case this patient had, and is "too aggressive" in both grabbing and burning tasks. To the layperson's view of the videotape, these characterizations certainly *could* seem true, though many people also argued quite strongly that they had no standard for comparison to make that judgment. Apparently, a whole lot of surgery on videotape looks "aggressive" and painful to some observers.

This opened up a dangerous window typical of many personal injury cases, medical or otherwise: the view that an injury was "just a human accident" and not able to easily be foreseen or prevented at the time it happens. This position on the facts often leads directly to an "act of God/stuff just happens" theme in many juror case stories,[6] which in turn drives many defense verdicts. It seemed important to deliver a consistent perspective on the story the plaintiffs provide that does all that it can to avoid encouraging such positions on the facts. Here, for example, is a section of the report to the attorney, from one of the early, full group debriefs, including commentary in brackets.

Moderator:	The defense talked about that more than once, that on the videotape you see the action, but you don't see that other piece, the piece of the colon, actually show up. It doesn't show up on that video. Who heard that?
	[*Almost every hand is raised.*]
Moderator:	How many of you think that's significant?
	[*About half.*]
Moderator:	How so?
George3:	Well, if you don't see it and do not know it's there, how can you tell you're injuring it?
George2:	Yeah, it gives the impression . . . once the procedure's performed that it's actually happening. If you don't know about it, it gives the impression it's actually happening, even though you [the doctor] can't see it.
Jane2:	The way they explained the procedure was . . . it was a small, little incision. How could you see anything happen if it was a small, little incision, especially on a video? I mean, he knows what he's looking for, not us.

6. Eric Oliver, "Two Steps Forward: Structure, Function and Delivery of Case Themes," *News From The Mental Edge* (MetaSystems, Ltd., Winter 2000). *See also* J. Perdue, Sr. and J. Perdue, Jr., "Trial Themes: Winning Jurors' Minds and Hearts," *Trial* (April 1998): 35.

[This brings up a point I've pondered: should you reveal early in the story how big the area actually is? I'm inclined to say no, even if the defense tries to gain sympathy or distort his obligation by pointing out how small an area it actually is. The reasoning is that the videos and the demonstrative boards used here, which are these people's only real-life experiences of the scene, make it much, much bigger in their mind's eye, and that impression cannot easily be erased by conscious, verbal means—especially from a lawyer's argument. I'd caution you not to say anything about size at all. Avoid going overboard, for example, and saying things like, "There's plenty of room to see . . . ." Stay totally mute on the size front.]

Note that group perceptions of the injured spot being very small, hard to see, or completely unseen, can favor either side in the case. If the story is all about prevention and definitive safety with every recommended technique, then a doctor who "can't see it's there" has all the more reason to pursue protection of every unseen or barely seen body part. By the same token, if these injuries just happen sometimes, due to the easily obscured view of body parts close by, despite a doctor diligently doing his best, with a fully informed patient who chose to go forward in the face of those known challenges, then, in many jurors' eyes, she has agreed to accept a bad outcome as the risk of having surgery in the first place. Complications just happen.

When it came to perceptions of that part of this case story, it seemed prudent for plaintiff counsel to avoid doing or saying anything that could invite decision maker stories to tip in the direction of imagining how difficult protecting the patient and maintaining safety can be. Especially with something as otherwise innocuous as the size of the incision or of the surgical field, which would be dire considerations for lay people confronting the scene in their heads, but no big deal for an experienced surgeon familiar with that territory.

So, early on, as jurors were building their first views of how things looked in there, encouraging perceptions of tiny fields of obstructed views would certainly work directly against the plaintiff's aims, even if that message was passed unwittingly, by a lawyer simply "setting the visual scene" accurately—according to the medical facts he knows in his professional mindset—en route to describing the standard of care violations he intended to put forward. Very often, these seemingly preliminary and perfunctory parts of the presentation utterly undermine those that the attorney needs decision makers to use most and best. That is because persuasion has a nasty habit of happening every second, not just when the trial professional wishes it to work.

Scope in Time

Several aspects of time became significant as the group processed the two case stories. Initially, as often happens, the participants looked for a motive to explain why the doctor may have been negligent.[7] One of the most common presumptions turned out to have a basis in fact, with the doctor's admission that the safety devices had been foregone to save time.

Then participants learned of the hospital's policies for the booking and use of operating theaters. The institution recorded estimates of the time each surgeon said would be required to complete a series of procedures, and gave them a ten-minute cushion. After that, the surgeon would be required to "pay back" the hospital for the overtime, unless certain preapproved reasons could be cited for the delay. One period of discussion on this point, which had not stood out this much to us before the group, went like this:

Moderator:	That doesn't affect his professional judgment.
Jane3:	Sure it does.
Jane1:	Maybe he was running short on time by five minutes.
Jane3:	I even think you might lay this at the feet of the hospital.
George4:	That's what I'm thinking.
George1:	No, no. The hospital just provides a nursing service. The doctors are just affiliated with the hospital. That's where they practice at. The one thing the people all do at the hospital is follow the doctor's instructions, though, right? The hospital didn't put the constraints on the doctor.
Jane3:	It says right here. Hospital has a form, and the doctor has to justify to the hospital why he took longer.
George5:	It's scary to know there's a ten-minute window when it comes to your health.
Jane3:	I have a real response to this. We personally experienced where we lost our family doctor because he was not following their policy. So, you know, he lost a lot of patients—and he's a wonderful doctor.

7. I've described this desire to my attorney clients over the years as a "criminal mindset" held by civil jurors. People acting on it expect a higher standard of proof, singular fault, and proof of intent in civil cases, particularly those against doctors. *See also* Rick Fuentes, Robert Minick, and Galina Zeigarnik, "Using Storytelling Techniques to Craft a Persuasive Legal Story," DecisionQuest brochure (1997).

Six more people brought out similar stories about "good doctors" who got in trouble or lost positions from "taking too much" time, among other sins. Certainly, this issue was a big one for voir dire, but still dangerous for extended play in trial, since the hospital was not included in the suit. But a glancing inclusion of this factor in the plaintiff's presentation could take a common presumption about medical failures and make it a much more solid element of the plaintiff's case story in the minds of many of the actual jurors.

Also on the subject of time, as expected, the four-year time span became a big factor, though not exactly as we had anticipated. Instead of concentrating on the plaintiff's non-compliance or inattention to her health situation, and thus diminishing views of the negligence case, group participants focused their impressions of the four-year wait for the next surgical treatment almost exclusively on the harms. When considered in the light of the doctor's apparently fulfilled predictions about her chances for getting pregnant, as well as in the light of what many jurors knew about the process of IVF and all the possible causes or contributors to the patient's (apparent) lack of fertility, the four years seemed to make the plaintiff's biggest harm a long-distance call for many of these people. The long time span weakened the connection of the major harms discovered in 1998 to a cause back in 1994. It wasn't that the link didn't seem made for many people. Rather, that the *value* people were willing to place on that "delayed reaction" harm dropped significantly over those long years. If you added the anti-plaintiff associations still available for her noncompliance over the same span, this proved to be the major landmine we expected it might.

Communication

Market surveys have shown for years that poor communication, more than any other cited factor, is blamed for customers electing to leaving a business service provider. A similar pattern has been observed when people are asked what factor drove them to join those who actually file claims against professionals such as doctors—or lawyers. What is it about poor communication that makes it so memorable and compelling to those receiving it from a professional working for them? One answer may be that interpersonal communication sits on the edge of that interactive ground where doctor and patient still share equally in their respective levels of expertise. One need not go to medical school to know "good communication" when it is offered—or withheld. With a basis of trust built on interpersonal contact, patients (or legal clients) may well feel more comfortable with professional efforts beyond their experience. This is almost a universal, layperson's theme for judging "good doctors" as those who "treat me well," as well as giving me good treatment.

Because of this availability, especially in cases where medical judgment is a big factor, whether a claim about informed consent is included or not, discussion by the plaintiffs about the doctor's communication with the patient can often be very helpful. Since we know the signed consent form will be spotlighted by the defense, the importance of the conversation preceding its signing can be increased in juror's eyes by that emphasis, too, if the point has been raised for their consideration. As the topic of the doctor's informed-consent discussion came up during the focus group presentation, here is the note made for the attorney at that section of the report:

> This may be the strongest starting point for linking up the harms and damage with the descriptions of the negligent injury. Rather than starting with the [less accessible] surgical mechanics, perhaps decision maker thinking, priorities, and communication "standards" should come first, with the big comparison or contrast offered by the newest [treating doctor's] assessment of her being "healthy" beforehand and all that entailed, contrasted with what she is now. Not only does this accomplish the goal of linking up all the surgeries as nothing but the latest evidence of harm/damage, but it lessens the chance of the argument, which came out in deliberations, that the doc did just what he said he would—"It's about five years, and she's still hoping to get pregnant." It's a stronger way to play the hand: thought and communication failures first, then the five physical failures in his choices of action.
>
> One thing to seriously consider in this effort would be quickly establishing the communication failures (to inform of the full process and risks; cover all the alternatives; try drug treatment and other more conservative approaches first; eschew the five-year clock as leverage promoting the surgery; reveal his board certification status with this procedure; reveal his status with successful prior surgeries using the [safety devices]; offer an informed choice about the [devices]; explain the operating-room time constraints and where she would be coming in line that day) with the current [treating doctor] and your expert, then bringing the defendant up adversely to confirm the big points, with the demonstrative boards up staring him in the face the whole time, even if you don't question him on every single point they cover.

This tack put the choice of forgoing alternative, conservative treatments more into the foreground, which had both strong and weak points associated with it for the trial presentation. While the doctors for the plaintiff all agreed these treatments were valid choices, it didn't appear anyone was ready to say that choosing the most aggressive treatment first—this surgery—was malpractice in and of itself.

Standard of Care and Visual Anchors

Though it appeared our strongest evidence dealt with the three aspects of aggressive surgical technique, coupled with the refusal to use the two (safety devices), the focus group participants indicated that this was not a connection they could make with complete ease. The videotape seemed to play a significant role here, emphasizing for most who saw it the distance between the doctor's expertise and theirs, just as the mere fact of the size of the surgical and incision fields could do. This went more often to the doctor's credit, despite any visceral reactions to what they saw on that tape. The group members' sense of their lack of capacity to judge a doctor started with the appearance—or lack thereof—of the disease visible on the tissue in the video.

George6:	I don't know what a healthy one looks like. You know what I'm talking about? I didn't see nothing wrong in there. I didn't see any gross malformations. You know, I couldn't tell what was going on other than they was heating tissue.

This is a filling defect.[8] It came up in deliberations that there are two, as far as the standard of care goes. One, what "diseased versus healthy" looks like, and two, what "careful versus rushed" looks like. Either stills captured from the video or really good illustrations, taken from the video with very clear, graphically highlighted sections, will need to be produced. It's really what we discussed before about having your expert provide a compared-to-what image. Only it appears we need an extra one for the diseased tissue, too.

George6:	Why did he get down into that pocket—because I didn't see nothing wrong down there.
Jane2:	That's why he's the doctor.
George7:	We're not supposed to know.
Jane2:	Schooling and everything.
George6:	Well, you could tell the laser was doing lots of damage there. I mean you could see the damage and the smoke.
Jane4:	Very indiscriminate shooting. It didn't look precise and controlled.
George5:	Seemed to cover a pretty large area.
George4:	Well, I think I'd still personally like to see another video of it, *of the right way* of doing it.

8. "Many litigators believe that they can present the facts of a case clearly enough without having to tell a story. The problem with this is that if they do not use a story [and even if they do] to connect the facts, the jurors will make their own connections even where there are none." Rodney Jew, "Tell It to the Jury: The Role of Storytelling in Litigation," course materials, *Ultimate Trial Advocacy* Course, ATLA-NCA, Harvard Law School (March 23–28, 2002).

Jane2:	Of him doing it.
George4:	Because it looked to me like that claw, I mean, boy, it was getting with the program. I mean, you know, I don't know if the other way, the other way would go or not, you know?
George5:	Yank and burn.
Jane5:	I don't think the question is whether he did that part right or not. I think that's what that kind of surgery looks like. I think the question is—I think *any surgery we look at is going to look basically the same.* The question is did he go too far back and grab a piece of colon? That's what that looks like when you hit that with a laser. I don't think that's going to look any different.

Jane5's comments proved to be accurate. An exemplar videotape offered by one of the experts showed many differences. But it failed to pass the most basic test of whether a visual offered as a demonstrative aid to the jurors is worthwhile. It needed more explanation to be understood than it eliminated on its own.

The alternative, then, was a series of hard boards. For the same reasons that the full videotape was inadequate to the task, we quickly determined that video captures of several images demonstrating the various surgical problems wouldn't be productive either. And so, we settled on simple, graphic illustrations, which soon became known as the "Five Failures" (see Figures 14 through 17) boards.[9] The boards would be the central visual anchor for the entire case story—the central image. They offered several advantages over the videotape, an exemplary video, or still captures from either. First, they lasted as long as we wanted to display them. Second, they could be placed up in any order at separate times, as each failure in surgery was discussed. Third, they could accumulate over time, adding to the sense of avoidable errors and multiple instances of doctor negligence. And, fourth, they provided a memorable set of visual anchors, which jurors could use effectively to "inspect" any viewing of the full surgical tape. At their best, they can actually reframe the videotape, which both sides agreed in advance failed to show the burn happening, into visual evidence of repeated acts of negligence instead.

9. While a passive formulation such as "failure" doesn't usually meet the need of an active-voiced "sin of commission," this presentation plan provided an exception to the rule, because every failure depicted was a chosen act, and the alliteration was a big help to the verbal presentation and the need to anchor key points for the decision makers.

Learning that the point of view that we wanted decision makers to reference was actually that of the body parts as the doctor worked on them, suppressing the plaintiff's full humanity till harms and damages testimony and closings, we substituted the organs upon which the doctor was *acting* in his initial laser surgery. We had five failures to follow standards in that procedure. And we had five pictures of what that looked like. In truth, three of the simple graphic images depicting the surgical site were identical, but their captions described different sins in action. Participants reminded us that jurors had very little experience with surgery, especially from the viewpoint of the doctor or the open abdomen. The video taught them nothing, by itself. But, annotated by five individual boards with an image they could superimpose over the generally icky video scenes, it could be a big help. Each board had less than ten words on it, some as few as four or five. Each board heading was a key phrase—the name of one of the five failures, in plain English.

"THE FIVE FAILURES"

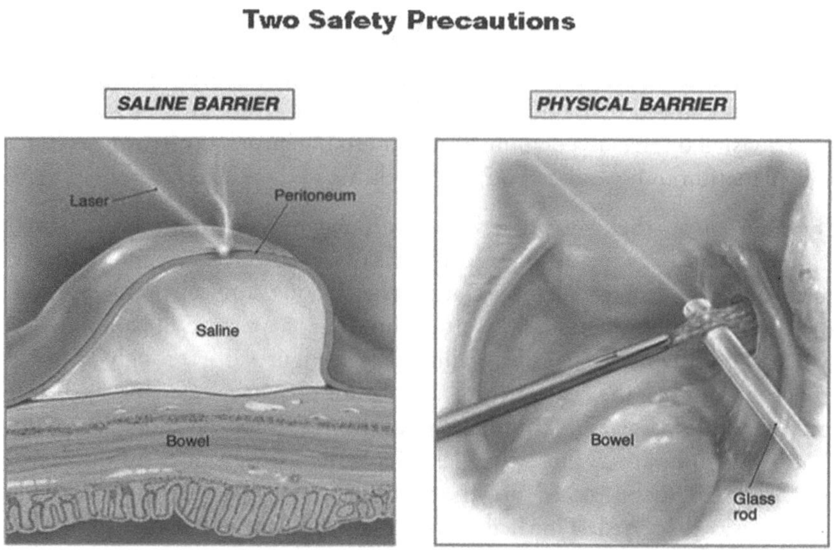

Figure 14

Grabbing and Tenting Bowel

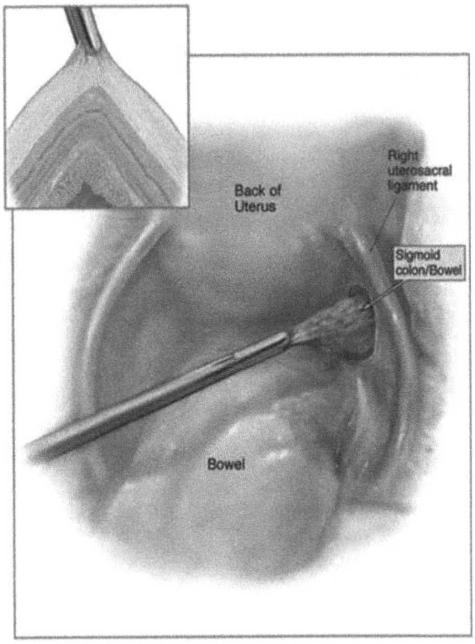

Figure 15

Treatment Too Hot and Too Long

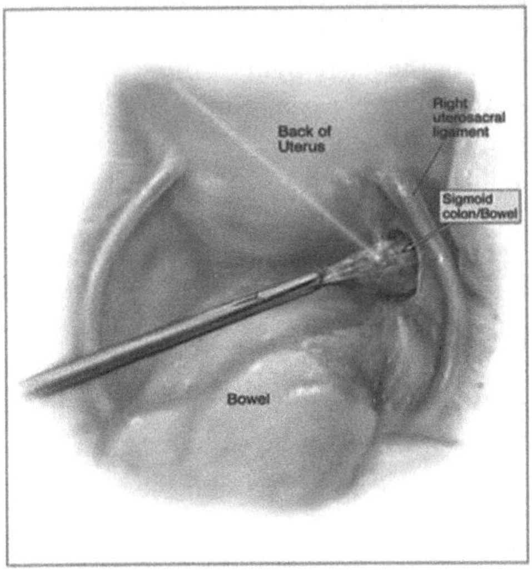

Figure 16

Sigmoid Colon not Identified

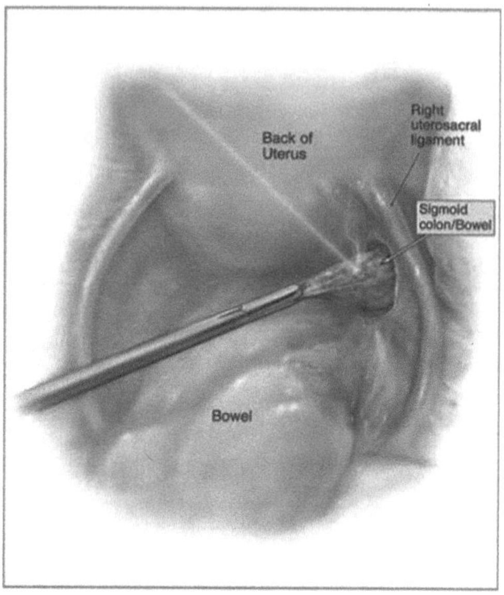

Figure 17

We offered a healthy view of the anatomy as a comparison, in electronic form, while the five failure anchors were produced on the large boards, each with an easel ready to hold it up in partial or full grouping. That enabled the doctor's choices to be referenced and reinforced, while the healthy compared-to-what image was switched to two different images of the likely sight of the scene of the surgical "crime" during the first and then the second "repair" surgeries. This left the cause of the harms, which came first in the story sequence, always present for comparison with the image of what should have been and the two images of what was—again, isolated from their actual four-year gap in real time—inviting that same perception to be imposed on the images in court. The illustration depicting the aftermath of the laser operation, requiring the "first repair surgery" and the image showing the situation requiring the "second repair surgery" were as similar in their presentation as possible, providing a visual cue to blend them, rather than separate them from one another. Naturally, they were displayed in exactly the same spot when either was shown.

9.2.3 Landmines

Anything—single facts, impressions, word choices, points of law, perceptions, prevailing biases, life experiences—anything that, all by itself, can distract a juror from a preferred leaning. The aim in compiling a landmine list from focus group input is not to develop a corresponding list of "answers," but rather to devise a plan for presenting the case story that avoids eliciting or reinforcing the largest number of these landmines, while reinforcing the positions we'd prefer. The list also provides a useful backdrop for planning voir dire and some witness examinations. In addition to many of the landmines proposed prior to the group above, some significant landmines cited in the report from this group included:

- Hindsight bias (if focused on the plaintiff during the four-year gap)
- Scope: the four years, perceptions of time overall
- The videotape
- Ineffective reinforcement of the standards violation
- Violations seen as too long past to drive damage positions
- Jurors isolate harms to the single event, rather than the damages initiated there
- Endometriosis was in "unexpected" spots when surgeon found it
- Plaintiff's history of physical problems in the abdomen and gastrointestinal tract
- Harms from the injury were not immediately apparent: "four years with no problems"
- Doctor reacted quickly to "fix" the bowel perforation
- Mild, Class I level of her disease overlooked or discounted
- Organs, such as the bowel, move around naturally during surgery
- Cysts versus adhesions
- "If laser vaporizes tissue, how could it cause adhesions?" Mechanism of injury unclearly presented
- Signed consent, talk with patient included a videotape instruction
- One hundred twenty-plus prior successes
- Plaintiff has since adopted a child
- "Complications happen" bias

9.2.4 *Planning and Planting*

By the end of the review of the focus group's input, several suggestions for the presentation of the case at trial had emerged. Some indicated that, in this case, the common-wisdom and "best practices" approaches to plaintiff presentations might need to be set aside in favor of getting this story across in a way most likely to serve our ultimate goal and play to the strengths of our specific case story as much as possible.

For example, though it may have seemed somewhat paradoxical at first, I suggested the attorney move to highlight the harms and damages very early in the case, while simultaneously working to dehumanize his client in the juror's eyes at that point. The American Association for Justice, among many others, recommends that in most personal injury cases these days, the safest and most effective tack in trial is to highlight the bad acts of the defendant first, rather than "leading with your chin" and describing the harms those acts produced first. Their suggestion is based on a solid foundation recognizing that there is a great deal of resistance today to injury claims and lawsuits in the public at large, as well as a great deal of suspicion of the legal system among jurors.[10] But the focus group had shown us how easily the four-year gap in our timeline could shrink the value of harms, even when they were accepted as being caused by the doctor's negligence. Starting with those harms, then *backtracking* to their negligent cause, seemed the best way to accomplish two goals in the presentation. First, it could help diminish the perceived significance of the four years, and second, it could help ease the trend of many jurors toward speculation and shifting the viewpoint of the story to that of the plaintiff instead of the defendant doctor.

In order to accomplish this point well for the majority of the panel, however, the tendency to scrutinize plaintiffs closely at the start of these trials and to attribute motives and speculate about activities not in evidence would have to be suppressed by the method we used. That is where the Five Failures boards and consistent use of certain viewpoint and language anchors became very useful. The plan for the case presentation indicated that, until well into the case, the plaintiff was to be represented only as the parts of her body involved in *both* the injury and the surgeries. This could work when it came time to re-humanize Jackie in part because the fertility problems and the loss of the chance to bear your own children had proved during the group to be extremely accessible injuries for the whole person with very little help.

This body-parts-only version of the plaintiff, leading with the harms then backing up to catch the cause and negligence proofs, had a couple of other advantages. First, it helped squeeze cause and negligence proofs into one perceptual box, along the lines discussed by George2 when he cited his one reason for not voting for the defense, even though he "couldn't prove" positively that the failure to use safety

10. Gregory S. Cusimano and David A. Wenner, "A Brief Look at Overcoming Juror Bias," *Trial* (June 2000): 45–54. The *National Law Journal*'s survey of juror attitudes, published in the November 2, 1998, issue, indicated that "suspicion" of the process was the prevailing attitude brought to courtrooms by jurors in all trials.

devices directly caused the burn not shown on the tape. By holding up the harms directly linked to the bad acts, then establishing just how many bad acts of both omission and commission occurred, in both communication and judgment, as well as in the physical acts in surgery, we helped jurors get to the "all he could do to protect patients and prevent harms" theme question in the most direct fashion. But, having started with the eventual harms at the beginning of the story, that conclusion on fault—which pretty much presupposes the cause proof—comes at the *end* of the string that begins with the damage done and its determined value.

Finally, and crucial for this case as it is for many, dehumanizing the plaintiff down to the involved body parts and starting with their damage, then reverting directly to their initial harm did as much as we could in court to keep the focus of the viewpoint for this story fixed where we needed it to be—on the doctor, his decisions, and his actions in reference to the open anatomy before him. Whenever the viewpoint shifted to the plaintiff as a whole person, on whatever subject and for whatever reason, the plaintiff's case suffered. At trial, we needed the perspective of the whole story for all the jurors possible to be maintained, as *consistently* as the attorneys were able to keep it, on the doctor.

The language tools we used for this were pretty simple. It is their consistent use, rather than their rhetorical flair, that makes them effective. The plaintiff's name was used very sparingly at the start, while the doctor's was used liberally, and always the same, with his title and last name. The harms were all discussed in the present tense, as were the subsequent discussions of the injurious acts and harmful choices that led to them. I suggested that whenever the lasting harms were discussed, universal quantifiers such as "all, every, complete, total, everything" be linked up with them. Naturally, the bridge back to the negligence part of the story could be made easier by the universal quantifier in our rhetorical question used for leverage and lifted directly from the group, *Did he really do everything he could?* The body part that took center stage in lieu of the plaintiff at the outset was "the bowel"—not "Jackie's bowel." Other terms included the endometriosis, the cul de sac, and the adhesions. The term *adhesions* was mixed frequently, and often delivered simultaneously, with the terms *scars* or *scar tissue*.

Though these scars developed from the exposure to bile and bowel products and the sepsis she went through, not the actual burning, many people seemed determined to develop ambiguity about this perceptual hurdle in the case. This ambiguity could be turned to the plaintiff's advantage by beginning with the harms and then backing up to the cause. Then the burden would shift to the defense to sort out any lingering misperceptions about the exact cause of adhesions on this uterus, and on these tubes and ovaries. We trusted that such clarifications by the defense would prove a distinction with no difference, as well as provide lots of reinforcement for the connection of the harms to the initial surgery, whatever the mechanisms of that connection.

The testimony had the surgeon and others referring to a "nick" in the bowel. This term was banished from the plaintiff's case. The substitute was "burn hole," which had the advantage of making the phrase an anchor for a sin of commission just by repeating it, as well as flattening the artificial distinction between cautery burns and laser burns, which had arisen as a bigger landmine than imagined during the focus group. Along with this shift, we settled on the consistent use of the terms "harm" and/or "damage" over "complications, infection, injury, problem, consequences" and other less definitive phrases, which so often creep in along with juror-distancing terms of art and the third-person positioning that permeates legal talk even before the medical scientists show up to add to the jargon fest.

One crucial linguistic device that, like all those listed above, would need to be consistently delivered by the attorneys in questions during testimony, not just in opening and closing argument, was the way we were packaging the multiple surgeries. This was one potential solution to offer decision makers for the time-scope problem. Again, with the aim of flattening the four-year gap to nothing in the jurors' minds, we settled on calling the initial event "Dr. Doolittle's Laser Operation," or just "the laser operation" or even "the operation." The "August '94 peritonitis and bowel operation" then became the "*first* repair surgery." Naturally, the "'98 adhesion removal and ovary excision" became forevermore the "*second* repair surgery." Nobody from our side of the room referred to them as anything else. Witnesses, aside from experts, do not typically need to be prepped in this kind of language selection, as they will almost always just adopt the terms used in the questions asked of them. And, as Doctor Kissinger reputedly once noted, "It has the added advantage of being true." Through these designations, all verbal references to ordinals that made the laser operation just the first in a string of difficult efforts that this "pre-damaged" patient required were eliminated.

Time as an overall factor in the case story had several persuasive features, as the group showed us. One we wanted to exploit was the "rushed" or "hurried" perception of the surgery, supported by the doctor's own testimony that he omitted the standard safety devices to save time. We selected a basic verbal anchor to carry the basic "dropped protection/prevention" theme: *shortcuts*. The other anchor phrase intended for the attorneys but not for the jurors was *coercion*. These two words were the reminders to all involved that there were two prongs, not one, of the negligence story about this doctor: poor communication and judgment—in that sequence—as well as harmful surgical acts, or the Five Failures (an anchor we *did* use with the jurors liberally). The theme I suggested then for the case reads today as *(Protection Sacrificed for) Shortcuts and Coercion*. Shortcuts has one other element that often proves helpful, and memorable, for listeners. It is a double entendre.

The facts lent themselves to a characterization of this surgery as unique in the doctor's prior experience, possibly helping to diminish the role his prior experiences might have. Doubling up with his poor choices and incomplete patient communication could do so even more. Because of the plaintiff's prior gastrointestinal troubles admitted to in deposition, it was fair to say that she had a more vulnerable bowel than the average bear, which was discovered along the way during the focus group processing. It was also in testimony and beyond dispute that the endometriosis had appeared to the doctor in an "unusual spot," the cul de sac, where he had not anticipated it. This set up a rule-of-three rhetorical device for the attorney, who was fond of the "running medical stop signs" metaphor, which came out like this toward the end of opening statement at trial:

> Instead, consider that, knowing Jackie had bowel trouble, that this bowel might be a bit more vulnerable to harm—consider what use Dr. Doolittle made of this knowledge. You'll learn from other doctors that this was one of three medical stop signs he ran through. The experts will tell you that there are three times Dr. Doolittle could have STOPPED, thought about, and considered his patient and prevented all the harm he caused. Number one—even before he began the procedure, he needed to STOP and think about the accepted standard he was taught and why he should follow the standard here. Number two—before he even fired his laser, he needed to STOP and identify this more vulnerable bowel, when he knew he could injure even a perfectly healthy one if he did not. Then, when he saw the endometriosis in the cul de sac, so close to the bowel, what he says is an "unusual" spot, he definitely needs to STOP and think, "What should I do here so I won't do any harm to the patient?"

9.2.5 Delivery and Receipt of the Story

So the final plan for the presentation of the case story at trial included these elements, among many others, summarized here in order of importance:

Theme: *(Protection Sacrificed for) Shortcuts and Coercion.*

Scope: Narrowed (elimination of the four-year gap). Narrow on people and numbers. Broad on bad acts and choices.

Point of view: The doctor.

Sequence:

1. Damage from failures to act or inform (shortcuts or coercion).
2. Standards broken—in thought and deed.
3. Refusal of responsibility for lasting harms.

    ➲ Visual anchors for both communication and the five surgical failures.

- ➲ Eliminating time as an important story element, from the rushed operation on, by reversing the sequence of the chronology and collapsing the gap in delivery.
- ➲ Dehumanizing the plaintiff, early on.
- ➲ Starting with the harms caused.
- ➲ Consistently reframing "complications" as foreseeable, preventable damage.
- ➲ Raising the doctor's communication duty to an equal status with his surgical one.
- ➲ Establishing two repair surgeries, made necessary by a single laser operation.

Voir Dire

In voir dire, we sequenced the subject topics—in the central section covering biases and "experience lessons" closest to the case story—in the order deemed most likely to mirror the receipt of that story as it would be delivered in opening statement shortly thereafter. We wanted to explore what people had learned about life experiences related to our story as closely as possible to the sequence in which that story was about to be presented. The attorney concentrated as much as possible on minimizing discussion of the specific case facts, and maximizing discussion of related personal experiences that would shortly be used to reference those facts. These topics, in order, included:

1. The business of medicine
2. Health/fertility/adoption (both gastrointestinal problems and fertility and all forms of reproductive health challenges)
3. Doctor communication and second opinions
4. Complications and risks
5. Videotaped operation
6. Informed consent
7. Prior medical problems/cysts/four years (briefly)

In opening statement, the jurors heard the following at the outset (taken from the attorney's notes):

> ***Surgery.*** When we start to slip under anesthesia, aren't the last thoughts about the trust placed in the person holding the knife? In July of 1994,

> Jackie went under anesthesia, and under Dr. Doolittle's laser, expecting to have her trust in him rewarded with better health. Instead, our evidence will reveal for you how *both* the things Dr. Doolittle chose to do, and the things he chose *not* to do with his laser in Jackie's womb, began a long line of harms—like hundreds of falling dominoes—that haven't let up yet: physical and emotional harms affecting her ordinary functions, her recreation, even her reproductive chances.
>
> By the time we hand this case over to you for your deliberation, *how* Dr. Doolittle set those harms in motion may be obvious to you, as well as how he easily could have prevented them. You will learn how he used the laser—far too *aggressively*, other doctors will tell you—and how he didn't do all he could to protect her, by taking *shortcuts on safety*. Finally, you will hear how the whole mess could have been prevented, because the surgery he picked was the wrong one—far too *radical* for her condition at the time. What he did do, he did badly. What he didn't do could have saved her from harm. And, ultimately, he need not have done this particular type of radical surgery at all!
>
> All that should be more than clear to you by the time you head back to deliberate. The facts you may find more alarming as you are rendering a fair judgment for Jackie, [are] how the doctor she trusted as she slipped from consciousness had *rushed* to his own judgment—in doing a radical operation he need not have done, in shortcutting on safety measures, and in aggressively firing the laser—despite running through no less than three medical STOP signs—any one of which could have told him to reconsider what he *did*, what he *didn't do*, and whether he needed to be doing it at all. You'll discover that, as she was lying on the table as the anesthesia began working, Dr. Doolittle had never told Jackie about a lot of the factors [that] could affect the judgment to operate on her—he kept a lot of those factors to himself. You'll learn he didn't fully inform his patient about the potentials for harm in what he was doing and how he was doing it. He kept a lot of things secret from the woman who woke up suffering all the harms those actions caused, who sits here suffering from them still today.
>
> There are three areas of ongoing harms resulting from what Dr. Doolittle did and what he didn't do: the bowel and abdominal area [*show visual*], the pelvic area [*show visual of female organs*], and her inability to have a baby now naturally.

What followed in the opening were five pages detailing the harms to the body parts involved, pretty much shifting the view toward that of the doctor examining and working with those parts, after starting with the harmful results of those acts.

After rendering a plaintiff's verdict and an award at twice the level of the final demand, five jurors were reached and agreed to posttrial interviews. Four of the five stuck strictly to the viewpoint of the doctor throughout their remarks, and the fifth had adopted the more general overview of medicine as the perspective through which she viewed the story. Themes in the stories they retold dealt with safety the most, then the physical procedures, and finally the profession of medicine.

On a landmine list including thirty-two identified items in perception, beliefs or factual/legal problems, these people volunteered discussion of only three: the plaintiff's ability to still work, the "complications happen" position, and her age at the time of the surgery. My posttrial, juror interview report to the lawyers read, in part:

> The first was clearly a major factor in deliberations, as it was mentioned prominently by one juror, and independently in passing by two others, and by implication only by a fourth of the five we reached. The second landmine—stuff happens—was attributed to only one juror in deliberations, the younger man, GJ, who apparently ended up coming back into the fold when he saw the (relatively) lower damage numbers and—according to two different people—actually ended up lobbying for a slightly higher award in the end. The last landmine, Jackie's age, was commented upon by only one juror, Mr. M. However, from the context of his comments, I believe it was a mitigating factor in the damages discussion.
>
> But in almost any situation where you face lots of trouble, three landmines standing out in juror's recalled stories out of thirty-two seems a decent percentage. And if you take a look at the major deletions: those factors that were either *presupposed* by jurors in their story constructs, or so far from conscious thought that they were *eliminated* from the conscious part of their judgment processes before anyone had a chance to run with them, it appears the story as delivered helped people steer clear of most of the landmines.
>
> ***Harm.*** We led with damages, and I know it pained you to do so. But compare the discussions and even rampant speculations of the three focus group "juries" about the nature, extent, cause, and effect of her harms with what these people revealed to us about the very same life experiences replayed to them in court. The notion, which apparently panned out, was to hold the strongest card—culpable negligence—for the second of the three we played in order. My sincere hope was that, based on the damage-first presentation, these people would simply *assume* not only that was she harmed in a way that was

ongoing, but the elimination of any picking of nits about the four-year gap and the doctor's responsibility compared to the patient's. That's where the anchors labeling the first and second repair surgeries, and that of "Dr. Doolittle's burn hole" came in. By all accounts, there was no dispute on her accumulated harms, but more than that, there was no dispute that those damages would almost surely result in another "corrective" surgery soon, for which, by most accounts, they willingly awarded damages early on. (One juror reframed "repair" surgery to "corrective" surgeries while adopting our anchor.)

The plaintiff. We were worried. With this presentation, we needn't have been apparently. By focusing on her body parts, and his actions on them, and the *ongoing* consequences from his point of view, you effectively did the impossible according to common, plaintiff attorney wisdom—you dehumanized your client into an award.

Stuff happens/Act of God. One guy, by all accounts, and he changed his mind.

Four-year gap with no doctor visits. Gone. Made no appearance by all accounts.

The doctor's history, the number of times he'd successfully done the procedure, and the need for good doctors in your town. Your mayor [a juror] raised this exact point, "We need doctors in Ourtown," in his abortive attempt to run away with your jury, very early on in the process. Not only was he rejected, and sent away to stand by the window with GJ till he rejoined the rest, but his actions and ideas were denigrated to me by his fellow jurors, and characterized as injecting his "personal problems where they didn't belong."

Plaintiff's lifestyle and character, along with medical judgment, apparently were non-factors in deliberations as well.

The focus group confirmed a lot of our early fears about how this plaintiff's story could be taken in ways that would distract jurors from a verdict on her behalf. And they also indicated that in order to avoid that outcome it might be necessary to defy common wisdom and begin with highlighting the harms, reducing her to a bowel and a uterus in the jurors' eyes, and first reverse, then eliminate, time as a factor from her story—while keeping it as a salient feature in the defendant doctor's. Then, all we had to do was line up our images and phrases in the most consistent way we could to keep those perceptual balls in the air. As the world-renowned juggling artists, the Flying Karamazov Brothers, are fond of saying: "And it's just that easy."

9.3 Case Two: First-Degree Murder

9.3.1 Dead to Rights

The defense attorney's letter[11] described the situation in clinical terms that didn't bode well:

> Our client is an alcoholic. The victim was fourteen years younger than he, and also an alcoholic. She was his fourth wife. They had a history of marital strife, including physical violence, destruction of property, arson and at least one time he shot at her. The night of the shooting, her blood alcohol was .22. He had been drinking heavily, too, but his level was not taken. She did not have a gun. The ballistics say he shot from four feet away. There are no witnesses. She was parked in front of their townhouse, and the front door was open, yet he claims she came around to the back door. He says he left by the front to drive away till things cooled off, and she never got in, yet her coat, purse and keys were photographed on the kitchen counter. Police report that he never claimed self-defense at the scene, that she had called telling him she was getting a gun and going to kill him, repeating that threat at the back door. Instead, police at the scene said he said, "I was fed up with her and I shot her."

More details followed. The situation the defendant found himself in was that he had shot his fourth wife with a handgun on one foggy and cold, dark night in front of their apartment, from a distance of as little as four feet. While she was reportedly yelling, she was unarmed. She had definitely been drinking, and he admitted he had, too. They were known in this small community for their mercurial, extremely hot and cold relationship, which escalated in tumult over its full thirteen years. He ran a large family business, and was pretty prominent in the area. She had made his acquaintance out of state, moved there to be with him, and had a history of problems with drinking, some drugs, and psychiatric misadventures. He made do with drinking a good deal, hanging out with his friends, carrying a pistol in his sport coat pocket, and having a volatile marriage. Extramarital problems were not a major force in their periodically loud and sometimes physical confrontations. He indeed had discharged a gun into her car once before, while she was driving the vehicle at him. Needless to say, furniture and knickknacks had flown in the past. His story of the unwitnessed event was that she'd called threatening him with a gun, woken him from a beer-aided sleep much later by banging on the back door, and confronted him a short while later out front with what he expected was that gun. She turned out to be unarmed.

---

11. The attorney in the matter was Jim Lees of Charleston, West Virginia. The case was *State of West Virginia v. William David Holliday*, tried in Raleigh County Circuit Court, beginning August 14, 1998.

Here, years later, is what the attorney recalled about his focus groups' input:

> They obviously thought he was guilty. They obviously felt that carrying the gun—just happening to have a gun in your pocket—wasn't a story they were going to buy. I remember they told me, which is what we later discussed planning the presentation, that the story becomes more believable the more people see the relationship as tumultuous. They were asked, "If you knew that such craziness had gone on in the past would you be more likely to believe this story or less likely?" And the answers were consistently "more likely." That this type of relationship was so foreign to most people who had more normal relationships made it really hard for them build a believable story from this man's perspective.

Comments from some of the group members backed this view up:

> *I bet a million dollars he was pissed off because she was cheating on him.*
>
> *Was she trying to provoke him?*
>
> *She was going to provoke something.*
>
> *A good case of domestic violence going both ways.*
>
> *She cut up his property but never done anything physical to him.*
>
> *I believe she threatened to kill him at least 50,000 times before.*
>
> *Pride is in the equation somehow. She was a status symbol (young girl, older man), if not to him then to his cronies.*
>
> *Were there other police incidents in their past?*
>
> *If she was really scared, why did she go out partying? And then, why go home?*

But it was the rest of the relationship questions that pointed in a much more hopeful direction—a direction in which jurors might be invited to construct a more productive vision of events. The first was the most telling:

> *He stayed with her all these years. Why?*
>
> *Why put up with this for thirteen years? He was an older man with a younger woman, and he held out hope?*
>
> *Does he still love her?*

The attorney continued:

> Based on the focus groups' input, views of the relationship became absolutely crucial. The more warped [from the norm] the relationship,

> the more believable his story became. The more normal the relationship was presumed to be, the less believable his story would be assumed.

And the relationship was *definitely not* what most would imagine as a normal one. In their first few years, words were thrown. Then objects. Then, she burned his house down and he took a shot at her while she allegedly tried to run him down in the driveway of their home. But what the casual observer couldn't know was that—according to friends, family and everyone in between—this was indisputably the most successful relationship either one of them had ever experienced. Ever. And they always made up. So one question the focus groups answered was about point of view, and how each party needed to be referenced. This applied especially to how the more negative information about the wife, which many trial professionals might see as strong leverage, had to be offered to its best effect.

The attorney remembered it this way:

> We learned that we couldn't talk badly about her until we had the jurors' permission to do so. And, we only got permission to do so by talking well about her first. One of the ultimate conclusions of this whole plan was that it could never be about either one of the parties isolated from the other. We couldn't have a story just about him, and we couldn't have a story just about her. It didn't work either way. We had to treat them as a unit, because we knew the focus groups were pointing us at the middle of the relationship, not either side of it.
>
> After we got that message, we were very careful in the voir dire, in opening, and in the direct examination of every witness. We pre-loaded everything with what a great person she was. She was nice, she was loving, she was this, she was that, she was great . . . until she was drunk, or got on the drugs and into her mental, chemical imbalance. There was nothing that said he had been unfaithful, but plenty that said she had. But, again, the focus groups said you couldn't go after that without earning the decision makers' permission first.

There were other concerns emerging from the groups about exactly how people viewed chronic drinking troubles. In voir dire, we asked about things such as AA membership, although it wasn't necessarily helpful to have drinking viewed as a disease. But they did need to know very well how it can screw up relationships.

Focus groups had revealed a slew of perceptual hurdles and other landmines for the case. From an initial list of thirteen of the most severe, the apparent top four were isolated to drugs and drink, troubled relationships, guns (possession and use), and the self-defense plea. Time considerations dictated sectioning off the top four from the longer list for primary attention during voir dire. An additional concern was that women, particularly younger women, seemed to have a good deal of trouble with the man, his demeanor, and his colorful turns of phrase. (This, tellingly, even included women who were working to defend him.)

9.3.2 Theme and Story Elements

The answer to the question of what this story was really all about appeared to be *chemistry*. As a double entendre, it covers both bases that seemed to most require covering. First, it offers the relationship—May-December, fire and ice, "What do they see in each other, and what keeps them together?" in the perceptual framework most likely to aid the defense position. This established the point of view or reference point for the successful defense case story: that is, the couple-as-unit, indistinguishable as individuals. That was essential, because two separate individuals can too easily assume the mantels of victim and assailant in the mind's eye of the decision makers.

The second side of the chemistry theme had to do with another big hurdle—chemicals themselves, and what happens after they are introduced into the mix of the relationship's primary, emotional chemistry. So, from one angle, this is all about the chemistry of inexplicably lasting relationships, and from the other, it's about the chemicals that, when periodically introduced into the partners' marriage, inevitably led to explosions of greater and greater intensity. Eventually, the full stories about her huge mood swings when she was drinking and taking drugs would need to emerge, as well as the fact of his habitual, daily drinking and what it could do to his judgment. But, again, the other side of their chemistry was evident even in this alcohol and drug abuse history. She had been in severe trouble with drugs shortly after he first met her, and once or twice since. He had worked to get her professional help, treatment for the influence of chemicals in her life, and consequently their lives. That was all part of the chemistry between them, too.

The chemistry theme not only dictated the viewpoint from which the story would best be retold, but it also made the most productive scope very clear for the stories we would invite jurors to construct. If the stories jurors reauthored were to carry both meanings of a theme such as chemistry, no single episode in the full thirteen years of the relationship could be allowed to stand out in isolation from all the others. Juror stories had to incorporate the full arc of the relationship, across its entire life, up to its sudden end. The broader the scope, the better.

The attorney described how the history of their volatile chemistry fit within the case story package the focus groups had pointed us toward:

> That was the theory; to show how, through their whole time together, they fought, they made up, they fought, they made up, they fought, they made up, they fought, they made up, they fought, they made up. The making-up part was good. But the fights kept escalating. The story we were going to take into court is that this is not a guy that wanted to get rid of her as the prosecution claimed. And the source of his not wanting to get rid of her was this chemistry. Despite all the times they fought, they always made up. We focused on some of the things they enjoyed together, like travel and cooking and such, to provide

mental images of the good chemistry side of their life together. At its heart and soul, we were able to paint a story of two people who thoroughly enjoyed each other and each other's company—at times.

Which was kind of the bulwark against the prosecution theory that he just wanted to be rid of her. And that served a two-fold purpose, I think. One is, it thwarted the prosecution theory or motive for the crime and then, second, by showing the good chemistry we were able to create a pretty good picture of this woman within this relationship. Which then set up the Jekyll and the Hyde, earning us permission to reveal less admirable parts of her character and her actions. First, we showed how she was in the good chemistry situation. That gave us the permission to say, "But when she drank or took drugs, here is what the bad chemistry was like."

That's what we worked out in our plan. The prosecution was going to dwell on how these people fought and hated each other and that he killed her, simply because he wanted to be rid of her, based mostly on his disputed statements at the scene. They held him out as thinking she was nothing but a pain in the ass. Our plan was to invite jurors to build a story around a total relationship, which, as we all know, has good parts and bad parts. If we showed the good parts of the relationship, we would begin to counter the prosecution's poorly supported conclusion that he just wanted to get rid of her. By the simple logic, and I do think it is logical, that if the chemistry had gotten so bad, that there was no good chemistry left and therefore the prosecution is right, he just wanted to get rid of her, why didn't he just divorce her? And the reality is, he didn't divorce her because he didn't want to get rid of her. And how did we know he didn't want rid of her? Because of all this good chemistry. There is still all this good chemistry. This answers the key question from the focus group: "Why would he stay with her—and she with him?"

9.3.3 **Sequence**

This *chemistry* theme also helped set the sequencing of the case presentation, from voir dire on. First, during voir dire, the attorney learned about people's experiences with volatile, inexplicably strong relationships, which seemed to last despite their obvious failings. Then, he explored the life experiences of the jury panelists surrounding drugs, drink, and prescription pharmaceutical use. The gun and self-defense issues trailed this establishment of the mental, double-edged sword of chemistry, with which the lawyer advanced into trial.

Once we settled on the theme, the major issues revealed by the focus groups almost automatically fell into their proper sequence for presentation. Clearly, the first hurdle, troubled relationships, was the biggest, and thus it was the first issue for voir dire, and on through the case. After all, how would it help us to know, after fifty minutes of inquiry, that several people didn't have knee-jerk responses about guns, if they had no life experiences with volatile, incomprehensibly connected couples? If they couldn't see the two lovers as one unit, and even marvel at the thirteen-year connection a bit, they simply weren't equipped perceptually to appreciate and build on the defendant's version of the stack of facts.

Drugs clearly followed relationships as the second prong of the reframe, so guns and self-defense had to bring up the rear. It was critically important that this sequence stay consistent in its delivery with each witness, from start to finish. For the lawyers, who already know the case stories in and out, a consistent sequence is optional. But for a group of jurors, who have never heard the client's story once, consistency in delivery can be critical. The three steps of this case story sequence, like every other element, were dictated by the double-edged relationship theme: they meet, they mix, they marry, they explode.

9.3.4 Theme Delivery

To get a theme across most effectively, there are three tacks: implicit, direct, or indirect. As suggested in earlier chapters, there is a lot to be said for simply implying the theme. The most common practice among trial professionals that emphasize themes in the retelling of case stories, is to directly and repeatedly invoke the theme phrase aloud. In this case, the attorney took the middle ground, using the term, but using it to reframe the two big hurdles jurors needed to cross perceptually. First, the chemistry of "kismet" (fate). Then, the more mundane chemistry of drugs and alcohol, and their volatile effect on the former, more sublime version. The true, implicit message—the biggest perceptual hurdle—was covered by this dual reframing. While the twin chemistries worked their inevitable sway, the couple could only be thought of as a single unit. One reason this theme worked well was that its various meanings were allowed to resonate with the experiences of the people in the box, and the stories of their own lives. They all knew people who were together because of chemistry, and others whose lives had been ruined by chemicals. They owned that compass. It was just our job to remind them it was there, and how it applied to this particular story.

Then, in the sequence that repeated and respected that order in their experiences, the story was replayed for them from the stand. Finally, the thesis—the reason why the leaning they hopefully had developed by then was the proper one—would help close the door on any lingering doubts about their decisions. As much as anything, especially bearing in mind the role that repetition is supposed to play in adult learning, consistency in the frequent deliveries of your theme can convey the greatest credibility for the jurors, even if the phrase you know as your theme never reaches their ears. In this case, of course, it did. Here is how it came out in opening statement:

Good morning. I want to begin this trial by going back to something that I discussed with you a little bit in the questioning process, and that is the concept of chemistry and relationships.

There is among human beings, and you all experience it I'm sure, chemistry in the relationships that you have with people. There is a reason why you love someone; there's a reason why you are attracted to someone; there's a reason why you fight with someone sometimes; there's a reason why we make up; there're reasons why we do things. To shortcut that, I guess I refer to it as the chemistry that develops between people. In this case you're going to hear a lot about the chemistry between David Holloway, our client, and Melinda Holloway, who is dead, and you're going to hear about good chemistry, [and] you're going to hear about bad chemistry.

The prosecution began by telling you [about] some of that bad chemistry. They mentioned drinking, they mentioned arsons and DUIs, and "bad tapes" and things like that.

But I want to begin with trying to outline for you what this evidence is going to show you and what we can learn together, as we go through it, about Melinda and David and the good chemistry. Because I don't think, quite frankly, [that] this case is going to make sense to anybody unless we learn together what brought these two people together and what, more importantly, kept them together. Because the logical question (. . . logic I'm not sure plays a whole lot in this . . .).

One of the logical questions you are going to have to form before this case progresses too long is: "Why the heck didn't these people get a divorce? What kept them together?"

[This invites jurors to approach this story from a similar mindset as the one advertised by those focus group participants that built the most productive versions of the story for themselves. He invites jurors to start out asking the very same questions the group participants ended up asking at the end.

Later on, introducing the second stage of the sequence, depicting how the bad chemistry escalated over time, note how the implied suggestion of these two people as an inseparable unit is reinforced and maintained by the use of the anchor for the chemistry theme.]

I guess the escalation point that I want to alert you to is that, like a relationship, you begin with insults being thrown in a relationship. You know, first you throw words and most people stop there. Well, this one, it didn't stop with throwing the words. The chemistry between these two people, when alcohol was at play, was insults being thrown,

> then ashtrays being thrown, then bottles being thrown, then cars being used, then guns. And it progressed, periodically broken by treatment, help, counseling, medications.

9.3.5 And Your Little Dog, Too

Like it or not, most case stories about murder are pretty well set when it comes to the primary, central mental image most decision makers will rely on in building their versions of the story. The fatal event itself tends to dominate the mental scenery, all other influences being equal. And that image of him holding and firing a gun into his unarmed wife threatened to undo a great deal of hard work packaging and delivering a story about two people tied together as a unit. The potential harm to the preferred story structure is obvious: if we need people looking at the two together, yet the central image most people will conjure has him as the assailant and her as the unarmed victim, the inseparable couple is now very likely to be seen as two distinct pieces, not one unit.

This case, as all do, went through some changes during trial. The defense had some help with a late ruling allowing in a videotape of the wife, taken after one of her DUI arrests. Here is how the attorney recalled the value of that imagery, offered to the decision makers, in proper sequence, to edit their own mental movies.

> She had been arrested for drunk driving. And there was a tape, taken at the police station, of her in police custody while she was drunk. She could be one mean lady. She was "m-f'ing" and kicking and scratching and trying to beat the crap out of these cops.
>
> That tape coming in was just huge. It showed prior consistent behavior with the behavior we were trying to invite the jurors to see the night of the murder. We needed to help people create the distinct image of her marching down that sidewalk toward him with her arms in the air. But it would have fallen flat if we hadn't plowed the ground ahead of time to show that incident as a very predictable part of their history. This is the way to paint the story, there was the good Melinda, and this tape shows the bad Melinda. And that night, we needed people to still see the good Melinda had never gone away, and David wanted to stay with her. He did not want to divorce her. David did not want to leave her, therefore David didn't want to kill her. He had no motive to kill her, because there was still this good Melinda.
>
> In that moment, it happened that she was bad Melinda. A mistake was made. And the mistake was he shot her to stop her because he thought she had a gun. And you remember he went over and over and over, how it was the one thought in his mind at the time: the key word for him was "stop."

The voir dire on the subject of the fourth major landmine, self-defensive actions and claims, actually had provided an opportunity to lay down a very constructive foundation for the videotaped images of the wife's bad chemistry at work, incorporated to balance out the image of the trigger being pulled in an attempt to stop that bad chemistry, that night. Here is how the attorney recalls that element of viewpoint—and active party—getting an early boost from within the venire panel.

> The voir dire stands out in my mind, probably because I've used one of the voir dire pieces in lectures. It turns out that it was the woman that ultimately requested to get off the jury during the middle of the trial who helped us out. We had phrased the question on self-defense as, "When do you think it would be OK to kill another human being?" And the first person I picked looked like kind of a leftover hippie from the '60s. His response was, "The only time to kill another human being is when you know for sure that person is going to kill you." And I went through this little litany, kind of a little in fun, a little not, "What if you knew for sure he wasn't going to kill you but he was going to cut off your arm?" The guy says, "No." "Well, what if you do arms and legs?" and I kept upping the ante and this guy kept saying, "No." And then I eventually got to that one young housewife and she used the famous line: "Listen, Mr. Lees, if you threaten me, you threaten my children, you threaten my dog, and I'm wasting you."
>
> "You threaten my dog, and I'm wasting you." And obviously she ended up on the jury and the other fellow didn't. There is a classic example of people's belief systems. How the hell do we know, or should we care, how they got to that position? Based on their appearance you'd never have known. But for some reason this guy's view of the world on the issue of self-defense is this, and her view of the issue of self-defense is totally different. But that is a real important thing for us to know in this case. 'Cause if you've got a lot of people like him on the jury, you're dead. If you get people thinking like her on the jury, you have a chance. So she gets on the jury and he doesn't. Then, ultimately, you can see that she was so troubled by the facts of the case, she came and requested to get off the jury in the middle of the trial, because it was so upsetting to her, but the judge refused.

The two-edged chemistry theme invited decision makers into an all-inclusive mindset about this story. The whole arc of the relationship, the full meaning of both sides of the chemistry and the effect of chemicals on it, the unseparated image of the pair, not two individuals, and the complete history of the escalation of the bad chemistry, despite the inevitable return to the good, was an all-or-nothing position. At the end of the case presentation, that position became the attorney's focus for one more, major landmine very likely to come up during deliberation:

> The last big issue for this case came out when we were preparing the closing. My gut told me that they were not going to convict him of first-degree murder, but that they were going to compromise. So the closing argument was predicated on an assumption that (a) they would not convict on first, and (b) they would want to compromise. It had to be all or nothing. Therefore, the entire closing argument was a closing argument that said, "Don't compromise."

In the actual closing, the message (in part) came out this way:

> I'll be honest with you. I've got to tell you what scares me to death more than anything, in looking at you all, is I can almost tell that when you go into that jury room, there's going to be somebody, I don't know which one of you, but there will be somebody on this jury, around that table, that will say, "But we can't just let him go unpunished because she didn't have a weapon. He shot her, and it turns out, in hindsight, she didn't have a gun. We just have to do something." That's my fear, because then what will happen is you'll start to talk about a compromise. And, to satisfy certain people on the jury, my fear is you will go to this involuntary manslaughter as a way to satisfy somebody who wants to see some punishment, and that's not right. And it's not the law. That is not right. And that is not the law . . . .
>
> I hope nobody believes this guy intended to kill this woman. The issue of self-defense, the fear, I believe I've proved to you beyond any reasonable doubt . . . what was in his mind . . . . But I don't want to see some of you abandon the rule of law because you feel that something like this needs, somehow, to be punished. If you think David Holloway will go unpunished, merely because you return a verdict of not guilty, then you haven't listened to this case and you don't know this guy.

And, given the all-or-nothing choice the entire story had consistently delivered to them up until the point when they retired to deliberate, they chose nothing.

9.4 Case Three: Negligent Delivery of Service (Electrical Utility)

9.4.1 Include Us Out

The attorney representing the power company[12] in what amounted to a professional "malpractice" suit wanted help with the development and delivery of the case story for court. The case had survived summary judgment and mediation, and was headed to

12. The lawyer in this matter was Mike Hutchinson, and the case was *CNA Insurance, subrogee of Mexican Stamping and Fabricating v. Detroit Edison Company*, in the Circuit Court for Monroe County, Michigan, in November 1998.

court despite some shortcomings, which, though very obvious to those involved on behalf of the defense, had not yet made themselves adequately apparent to anyone else.

There were three main characters in the story: the insurer of the burned-down business, who was doing the suing; the business owner and operators; and the target of the lawsuit, the electrical utility that provided the power into the now defunct building. Despite a couple of major landmines in the insurance company's case—such as the fact that they had never inspected the property before insuring it, the owner had never applied for or been granted a certificate of occupancy and thus was never subject to city or state inspections, and the two very most likely causes for the fire being documented neglect of the premises and deliberate arson—the defense attorney was understandably concerned that the case had somehow survived to the point of being on the courthouse steps. The insurance company's experts had a theory of the case that required that the rules of law regarding duty to protect actually be applied in reverse from the way they were written, making an *outside* utility responsible for the internal duties to safety and proper power usage *inside* an independent business. The theory held that the power company had, without notice, been delivering more power, in greater levels than the metal-stamping company in the building could handle, and that a disaster was inevitable.

What became very apparent quite quickly, on review of the material, was that the power company had been delivering the story in a way that built up, rather than excluded, its own role in what, based solely on the facts alone, was a very unlikely negligence situation. It was, in some ways, actually inviting its inclusion in decision maker case stories. As the attorney said, many years later:

> I think that most defense attorneys probably would have behaved like me, focusing on the stack of facts, if you will. For example, take the organization of the parties as we presented them. In the eventual opening statement, we could separate them and talk about their individual roles, and especially their compared duties. When you look at that opening statement, you see something very different from the mediation summary, which was delivered before the presentation plan was put in place.
>
> There is a natural, habitual order—you can call it a logical order if you want—but the trouble is, your logic changes depending on what the object is that you are trying to reach. If you look at the mediation summary [pre-planning], I first start talking about the power company itself. Why? Well you can say it's logical because they are the client. But it may not be logical if you want to win the case.
>
> In the opening statement, we still say, I represent the power company, of course, but the first thing we do is tie the insurer to the duty to protect the building. I now emphasized asking, What was the insurer's job? Not, who are all the parties involved and what are their backgrounds. And we had that visual anchor, the T shape I drew in the air.

> This is where that visual reinforcement comes in. It separates the parties by their applicable duties, left to right, and then it separates them further by their likeliest roles in causing any of the damage suffered, drawn from top to bottom in the air. Going in, from the start, we want to separate these duties and to separate them by party. And you've got to have a way of organizing that for the jurors. We did it visually, with the insurer and its duty positioned on the left side [from the jurors' perspective] of the cross bar of the T, the plant owner and operator located in the middle, and the power company on the far right end. Likewise, when we marked out the most to least likely roles played in *causing* the fire, we started the vertical line up at the top with the insurer, the plaintiff in the case, moved down through the owner and operator, and stuck the power company in at the very bottom of the upright of our invisible T. The power company always came last in each three party line. So you've provided three different file cabinets for jurors to use, in a way. First, to the right, straight up, and then over here, to my left (their right). So, anyway, that's like a huge difference that stands out. Before, when I had organized the facts first, I did it logically the way I would normally do it. The way that I saw it, as the advocate. But it wasn't the most effective way to win the case.

The original package and sequence of the story had still brought out all the relevant facts, just not as persuasively for the people building their own versions of the case story from which to draw judgments. The following is an outline of how the story was delivered in the mediation summary, which failed to convince.

1. The parties: first the power company, second the stamping plant, and last, the plaintiff insurer.
2. The owner of the stamping plant was revealed to have fired two different lawyers, messing up discovery and losing the right to claim losses as a result.
3. The insurer was revealed to have failed in its inspection and protection duty before the fire, and its inspection and preservation job afterward.
4. The building was described.
5. Background facts about delinquencies, failures, and outright violations by the stamping company were listed.
6. The chronology of the event was retold.
7. Liability: the first line in the liability section read, "There is no evidence that the power company was negligent, or that the power company's negligence caused this fire."

8. The "overfusing" neglect, ostensibly allowing excessive current into the building to arc and cause havoc, was brought out immediately after the denial of power company neglect.

9. Duty is discussed, and distributed among the parties, but always starting with the power company as the reference point in the description. Then, the same pattern is followed for describing fault, and cause roles. The power company is named or referred to twenty-five times over the three pages discussing duty, fault and cause. The insurer and stamping company combined for the same number of references, in the same space, in the defendant's mediation summary.

10. Comparative neglect and evidence of arson are brought out next.

11. Specifics on the active neglect and evidence of likely arson are detailed.

12. Damages are dismissed.

If ever there were an example of how the facts cannot speak for themselves, this document provides it. But a thoughtful review of the packaging and delivery of the power company's case story as represented in this outline can show how the facts were not being helped to speak up on the utility's behalf. How they were delivered clearly overrode what they had to say for themselves. The point of view for the story told in the summary was that of the defendant power company, quite strongly. The initial defense was a denial of neglect, followed immediately by a description of how that theory of neglect worked. The scope was uniformly broad, starting by describing the massive reach of the power company's daily and yearly jobs, and the vast numbers of people and actions involved over time within those many, many jobs. Despite long lists of failings by the plaintiff insurer and their insured stamping plant, the positioning of those complaints in the summary worked to package them as additional blaming of a "not only that, but also this" character.

The presumption of a role for the power company in this story, and thus a duty and the chance to fail to meet that duty, was implicitly left open from the start, and actually reinforced, therefore, throughout the delivery. The power company came first in the sequence overall, and first when any accusations were outlined. Pointed and plentiful examples of the abysmal performance of both insurer and their insured got a chance to be reframed by some listeners as a "Not us, *they* did it" bit of finger-pointing from the power company on center stage. This, despite the outrageous character of the multiple sins of both commission and omission by both other parties. The theme that could be extrapolated from the presentation could easily have been seen by some observers as something like, "Don't blame us, they did it." Rather than excluding itself from a story in which, by rights, it played no part, simply by the way the power company organized and delivered the facts, it was asking some decision makers to *include* it in their stories of the case.

9.4.2 *Visible Branches and Roots*

In an effort to invite itself out of the story in most decision makers' heads, the power company's attorney revised his approach to the story completely. The much simplified story offered in his opening statement relied on the two visual anchors he described, inviting judge and jurors to see the insurer first, at the left end of the horizontal line composed of three points, with the power company last, not first. And, once duty had been properly linked to party on the horizontal bar, the cause proofs were offered with the most to least likely distribution going down the line vertically this time, again from insurer through their insured, all the way to the bottom, where the power company resided—last again. This highly visual approach allowed for the early introduction of a neglected story element, that of active party, or active ingredient, accompanying the shift of viewpoint or reference point to that of responsible insurers and stamping plants. As the attorney later remarked:

> At first, we had talked about the building burning, but we changed it to "was burned down." We implied that we are now two or three steps down toward intent, or negligence bordering on it. That carelessness bordering on intent. If it's not outright arson. Basically steering people toward the driving force in the actions of the events of the case. At first, we left it open—that the building had burned. As if the building itself were the active party, and jurors can take your pick for causes. But when we say, the building "was burned down," there was some active party behind it. We've offered people one more lever to take advantage of the way we've visually set up the parties here. If you say the building was burned down, they are invited to ask: "By whom?" And you are offering them the person at the top of the vertical line of likely causal agents, then you are offering them a second person in the middle of that line on the way down. That is all long before they ever get to us as even a possible cause. So one element, the visual linking of parties to duties and likelihood of cause supports the other, of the most likely, the next likely and then the least likely active party.

The opening statement followed a different outline from the mediation summary:

1. Insurer tied to duty to protect the building

   —Laws, rules and regulations that dictate the duty

   —Every prudent method they could have used to accomplish their job

2. Insurer tied to the owner and operator of the plant

   —For whom they took the risk

   —Who he was and how he handled the business badly enough that he abdicated his right to gain from the suit

3. The owner's two most reasonable ways of causing the fire

—Documented, massive and illegal neglect

—Arson: listed many "unfortunate" and "coincidental" signs of the crime being planned and executed.

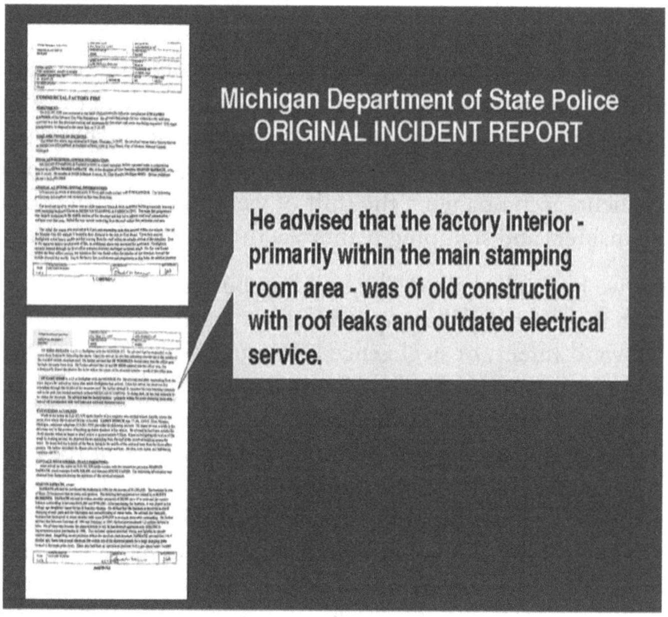

Figure 18

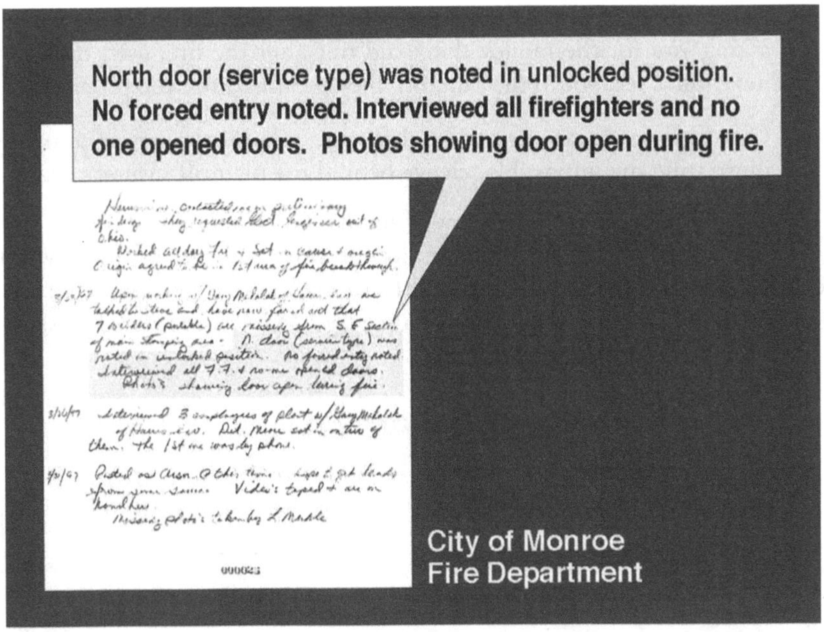

Figure 19

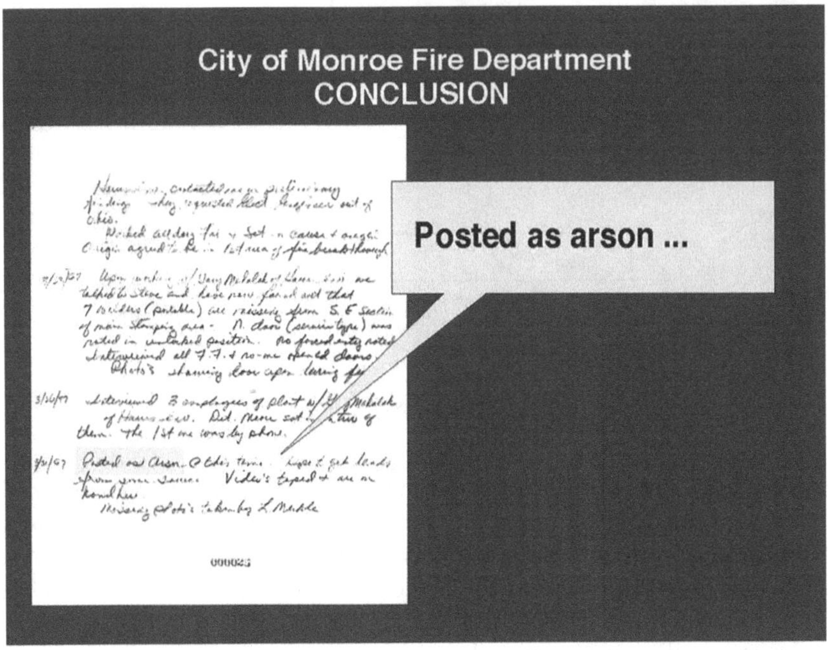

Figure 20

4. "The only party [that] could have fixed this problem is the one party now asking you for the money they paid out after the fire, even though they never once set foot in the building they promised to keep protected."

5. Cast final doubt on the potential for any role for the power company by illustrating the impossible science behind the plaintiff insurer's claim.

This presentation plan included a lot of visuals. The main one, of course, is invisible. The fundamental element in delivering the story and the surprisingly not-so-self-evident facts was the big turn-around from the way the story had been crafted before. We shifted, among other things, from a very detailed and verbal presentation to a very visually dependent presentation.

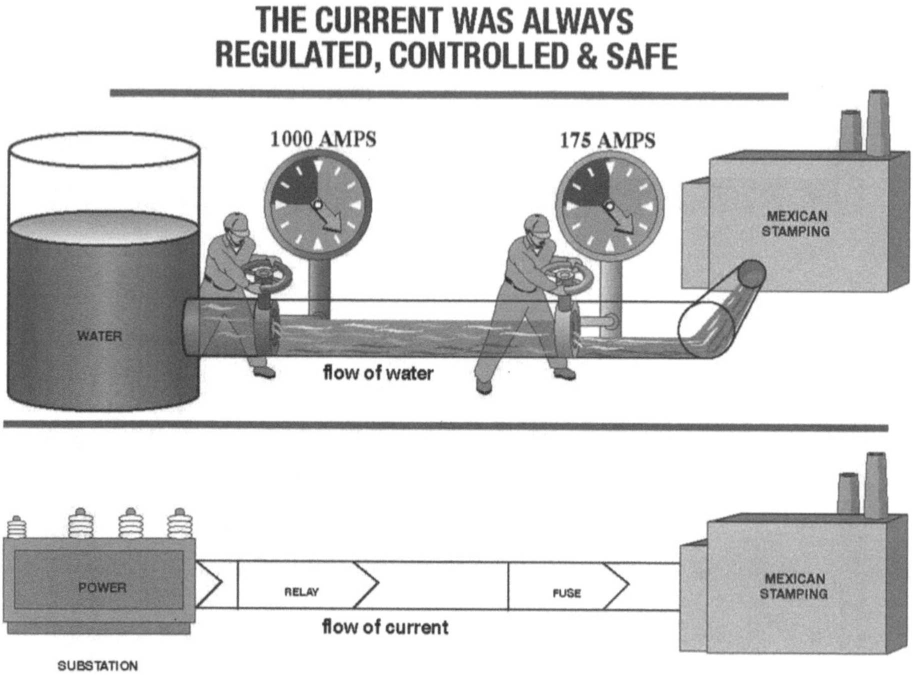

Figure 21

Inviting judge and jurors to see people in their designated positions, seeing where the action is, seeing who the major and therefore the minor players are, provides the setting and perceptual context for the story. That's where consistency really counts. If you lay out those basics about who is the major player, who is the minor player, where all the major actions are—and you are very consistent in that—you can be inconsistent in delivering individual details of how it all played out. But it never works in reverse.

If you are inconsistent in laying out the initial story, then you are doubly in trouble with any inconsistencies later on. That's why, in both civil and criminal cases, it's more important for the defense to come in with a consistent approach to the story, early in the case. And it usually falls down just as the defense gets up to cross-examine the first plaintiff's witness. They frequently dump their own story in favor of chipping away at the plaintiff's. Ultimately, they reinforce the perceptual frames the plaintiff's story put in, by taking them on at their level, rather than asking questions in cross-examination that reinforce their version of the story.

The attorney involved agreed, discussing how he would go about cross-examining the first plaintiff witness:

> Well, as I recall, he called some lineman, who was a particularly poor witness in deposition. And he wanted to establish something technical, like fusing on the pole. Something really technical. I'd use my visuals. It's the first witness, so the jurors and judge have got to remember a fair bit from my opening statement. So even if the guy knows little about it, I'd say, "You understand the insurer is the plaintiff in this case, right? Do you know what they did or what they didn't do in order to sell the policy of insurance that insured the stamping company?" He either said yes or no, but it doesn't matter. Then we go on to the owner and operator of the stamping plant, "Did you ever meet with him?"
>
> And the lineman does know stuff, as we move down the vertical line of the visual anchor from the most to least likely cause or contributor. "As a lineman, you've gone and inspected facilities after something has happened, and you go around and make repairs in facilities where something hasn't happened, where things are running smoothly, right?" "What do you see in terms of how the companies that are in charge of these places take care of them or not?" So he can actually address, first, what could they do to protect it? And, second, what could they do to maintain it? He can do that based on his own experience, and we turn their power-company employee witness into an opinion witness for our own case, just by asking him questions about our story, in our story sequence, about the active parties in our story.

Not only did the facts end up speaking rather more loudly at trial, once they had a story and a visual delivery to support and reinforce them for judge and jurors, but they apparently came across strongly enough, when it counted, to not only successfully invite a defense verdict, but to also induce the judge to charge all the defense costs off against the plaintiff insurance company as well.

9.5 Case Four: Professional Misconduct

9.5.1 Emerging Stories and Problems

This plaintiff's case story, concerning the professional misconduct of a general practitioner over the entire length of his career in a particular town, offers an example of how addressing several case story elements in creative ways can help turn around a very challenging matter.[13] It also provides a warning about how experience can shape expectations and action in less than productive ways. For instance, the way in which an attorney presents a case story may be shaped by how he or she is first introduced to the story by clients and discovery witnesses. The following is this lawyer's description of how the experiences of her clients became a part of her own life stories.

> The first woman who came to me showed up about a year and a half before the second one. She had bad experiences with the doctor over two or three months, covering several different visits. Her complaints involved inappropriate language and conduct, but not poor medical treatment also, as others did. She is among those patients of his who had an assaultive rectal exam that came just after she complained to him about something that he had done. It was not until much later, I think it might have only been right before the trial, that I realized how bad that exam was. It was really hard for her to talk about. She came to me with her husband, referred by a friend who had declined the case. They had made a complaint to the HMO, and they had met with the director. They also had made a complaint to the medical board. Both had happened about six months before we met. The HMO had told them, "We're sorry this happened. We've handled it."
>
> I remember the husband told me that as they left this guy's office, he had turned around to the director and said, "You need to do something about this guy because he is going to hurt other people." He was told, "We can't tell you what we've done, but we've handled it."
>
> Their complaint to the Medical Board was in writing. They submitted a few other things in writing, too. The board never interviewed her personally. She would call periodically and try to talk to the investigator to find out what was going on. They wrote her several letters, thanking her for notifying them, saying, "We are working on it." Then they got a letter telling them the matter was handled and closed. She did have one conversation with a woman investigator, who told her to get over it and get on with her life. That had not yet happened at the point we

13. The attorney in this case, as noted in the previous chapter, was Elizabeth Kuniholm. The matter was *Baker v. Evans*, Wake County Superior Court, Raleigh, NC, November 1999.

met, but she was in the middle of the Medical Board process and had been told the HMO was finished, and she was mad as hell. We talked, and I feel sure at that point that I did not fully understand the extent of the assaultive exam that she had. He had used several slang or swear words about her body parts, in addition to the physical misbehavior, and the punitive rectal exam following her criticizing him.

I felt I had to send her away. I told her to just follow through with the Medical Board. There really isn't anything you can do. He is going to deny it. Who knows how much a jury will value this conduct, or your harms. Your life will be made an open book, and you could be destroyed by the litigation in several ways. At the time, I told her a lawsuit was not the most useful thing and to just trust the Medical Board. So I turned them away, and that was that.

Then, about eighteen months later, another woman came to me with an independent complaint about the very same doctor. Similar, but slightly different. Her complaints involved an inappropriate breast exam that was not indicated for why she was in there. It's hard to describe, but he indulged [in] a "turning the dials" kind of thing. He was in front of her, grabbing both breasts, when her complaint was about a rash on her leg, which she got as an allergic reaction to medication. This was medication he had prescribed to her, as her boyfriend's doctor. The boyfriend had gotten bronchitis or flu, or something like that. He had said, "My girlfriend has this, too, can you give her a prescription, too?" And the doctor prescribed for her without meeting her.

During the assaultive exam, the boyfriend was in the room. The display was kind of like a challenge, "Look what I can do in front of your boyfriend." A little bit like that. So she came to me because she was so infuriated, partly because her boyfriend got mad at her for letting the doctor do it. By the time she came to me, I had been doing enough sexual abuse cases to know that if similar complaints are showing up more than once, then there is probably a pattern. These two events were about two and a half years apart. The statute of limitations was about to run [out] for the first woman to file a complaint, while the second woman's incident had just happened. I also knew enough that if these were the brackets, then there probably were a lot more in between and most likely a lot more before.

So I called the first woman back. And I said that I had gotten a complaint from another woman with the same doctor, and if she was interested in doing something, I would represent the two of them and bring a case against the doctor for them both. She agreed, and filled me in on how the rest of the Medical Board effort had played out. We filed against the doctor on behalf of both, and against the HMO as well for the first, alleging improper credentialing and supervision of him as one of their agents.

It was picked up by the local newspaper, in a series of articles, probably about six. We filed the case in July of 1995, and the articles continued to appear through about September. After the first article, we started getting calls. I got a total of approximately sixty-five calls. In all the sixty-five calls, the scenario was typical and went back to 1979, the year after he opened his practice. They included at least three people [that] had been molested in [the] current year of 1995. The other pattern apparent in those calls was that a number of people, eight to ten of the sixty-five, I think, had made complaints to the Medical Board and their insurance companies and virtually none got any definitive response. They got responses like, "There isn't anything that we can do about that." Insurers sometimes said, "You need to call the Medical Board about that, that's not our business." One woman I recall had several telephone conversations of many hours each with somebody at the Medical Board. The upshot of that effort was that they wanted her to go back and write down everything they had already heard from her! She asked them, "Isn't what I've told you good enough?" And they responded, "No, we need you to write it all down now," and she got discouraged and angry at that point. But, for all these women, there was virtually no response.

We ended up with individual stories almost like book ends. It was amazing. One of the '95 people was a woman [that] had an almost identical assaultive rectal exam as the first one I met. This woman has turned out to be a success story in the end. She was recently married, and is doing fabulously. She got one of the better settlements. She had a very serious complaint. But she was a person [that] had a very serious history of child sexual abuse by her father, and also involving her father giving her to other men, on top of physical abuse. She had never talked to anyone about it. Later, she'd had two horrible, violent marriages that produced three children. By the time she had come to us, she was kind of making it, she was back on her own, and trying to make it as a single mom, doing pretty well. She had ended up having a physical reaction to DayQuil, and had gone to this doctor because he was on the list from her insurance company. She remembered he had stuff all over his waiting room like the Ten Commandments, and other religious paraphernalia. Being a very religious person, she thought she had found a home. He pulled this history of sexual abuse out of her in the first visit, although she had never before talked to anyone about it. I will never forget her deposition. I wish I had her on video. I recall she was looking up to one side, and it was very much like she was in a dream: describing going into his office, seeing all the religious stuff, feeling very comforted, and his gentle manner as he pulled all this history out, and she cried and talked about it. Then she paused after relating all that, saying, "I thought to myself, this man really knows me. And he did, didn't he?" So, anyway, that was the background.

He told her, "You can be my patient, and I require a physical exam for everybody." So she came back for a major physical, and during the process, he got her lying on the table and did inappropriate fondling of her breasts, and then had her lie down and did a pelvic exam where I believe that he tried to digitally stimulate her. She got completely upset, began to cry, and didn't know what to do. And he said to her, "What's wrong?" real angrily. "What's wrong?" And she said something like, "I don't know, I don't understand. This whole exam is really upsetting me," something like that. He then does that same sort of assaultive rectal exam on her after her complaint to him, while she is still in the stirrups. She tries to get away from him by pulling her bottom up on the table, and he pulls her back down so he could continue to have access to her. She bled, and I think, though we were never able to offer this, that she had a lot of scar tissue in her rectum and anus.

She also had severe migraines, and he had her come into his office, where he'd put her in a dark room on some medicine, and he came in and touched her and fondled her. She ended up going into therapy and managed to get away from him. She had a lot of trouble after that. That all happened between January and April of '95. She then got away from him, but was really a wreck afterwards. Because, for her, it revived all her childhood sexual abuse; she was having flashbacks and she was having a hard time. She would get bills from his office, but she was putting them in a drawer without opening them.

When we sued him, his practice had been taken over by some California physician-management companies, and they fired him within a week of the suit filing. When he got fired, he sent a letter to all of his patients saying, "I've been accused of professional misconduct. It's not true, and I have decided to retire from the practice of medicine in order to defend myself against these allegations." When she got the letter, she was down visiting her brother at his store in the country. She got so confused about it, and there was a prosecutor from a neighboring county there, a friend of her brother's, and she said, being an innocent, almost out-of-it person, she asked this prosecutor, "What is professional misconduct?" The guy said, "What are you talking about?" So she showed him the letter, and he recognized, since he had been

> reading the newspaper, he recognized the doctor's name and told her to call me. She hadn't been reading the paper and had no idea.
>
> But those were the bookends of the clients. And, in essence, the complaints were all of a pattern, including inappropriate language, inappropriate conduct and some inappropriate medical treatments, as well as more than one patient with whom he also took a punitive route if they made any complaints.

This description reveals a number of potential landmines for any decision maker confronting this story, as well as a likely mindset of any attorney approaching the retelling of all these stories, and they can very easily work together against the plaintiffs' purposes. The likely mindset a trial professional could adopt, after hearing these stories face-to-face from the women directly involved, could very well be to try and let the facts speak for themselves. To relate the details of the patients' experiences with the doctor, one after the other, in chronological order, letting the litany of facts make the wrongdoing plain. But this mindset tempts professionals to overlook a very real difference in the life experiences of decision makers hearing and seeing a representation of these events from that of the patients, or even the attorney doing the retelling.

Consider just the time factor within the story element of scope. Note that this lawyer had a year-and-a-half between hearing the details of the first woman's experiences with the doctor and the second. In the meantime, she had increased her level of experience and developed professional expectations about sexual abuse and misconduct by professionals in ways almost no decision maker, including mediators, arbitrators, and judges, could match. The decision-making juror or judge experiences both women's stories almost simultaneously, in the moments they are retold.[14] That can lead to far different reactions than those of a trial professional holding the mindset that facts will always speak the same message, on their own, no matter how, when, where, or under what circumstances they are delivered. And since we tend to project our own mindsets onto those around us, trial professionals could easily succumb to the biasing aspect of their "talking facts" mindset, conducting their efforts to persuade by simply assuming the listeners *should* hear and accept the story as they themselves first received and reacted to it. This kills the chance to seriously consider

14. This inescapable feature of any attempt to review case stories at a later time, in a formal representation of the realities involved at the time, but not during the retelling, is a distorting factor all trial professionals would do well to keep always near the front of their minds. People can consciously distinguish between what happens to someone else in front of them today and what happened to that person a year or two before. But when it comes to the real-life experience of hearing, seeing, and experiencing the presentation of a case story, in many ways that count most to the persuasive effects of the retelling, it is necessary to realize that the observer listening has his own experience of the stories. And, no matter how broad the scope of the actual events, the decision maker is hearing, seeing—and responding—to these retold events as if they were happening all at once, in the moment of the retelling.

how a decision maker might learn a totally different message from facts that seem self-evidently damning to the professional retelling them.

Many people reading through just the two descriptions above may have experienced the kind of response the focus groups shortly demonstrated for this attorney: interrupting the flow of the facts from the women's experiences to ask questions and interject suspicions, primarily about the women themselves. Embedded in the descriptions, for example, is a landmine related to the case, which proved to be quite volatile: *most of the patients filing complaints went back to the doctor again, a couple for over a year*. Some of the women had histories of abuse and alleged mistreatment at the hands of other men, which, to many, seemed to speak more to a pattern of complaints than to any pattern of professional misconduct. Also, pay attention to the persuasive aspects of deletion. Nobody ever accused this man of simply climbing atop them and raping them, or any other scenario typically associated with sexual misconduct. The complaints were similar in the three areas of inappropriate *conduct, language, and treatment*, but they each had idiosyncratic differences in detail that could capture and fix a listener's attention very quickly.

The biggest landmine of all in the successful reauthoring of the plaintiffs' case stories also ended up depending on our talent to delete elements from our private stories. By succumbing to the mindset that tilts a professional to simply lay out the facts of each woman's encounters with the accused doctor, the point of view or reference point of listener stories is invited to shift to each woman in turn, away from the doctor. The scope of the tale is reduced drastically to just those experiences each woman relates, in turn. The sequence automatically draws all the attention to the complaining women, first and foremost. And so the very notion that a medical professional has a set of rules governing his conduct with all patients, particularly those of the opposite gender, is invited to disappear. And for many in the focus groups, that's just what all those professional standards did. The following is a list of additional landmines drawn from the presentation plan:

- Anti-litigation bias and its anti-plaintiff subset
- Anti-"whiner" bias (minimizing, distracting, displacing, or distorting)
- News coverage, especially as an impetus to join a lawsuit
- Time spans covering complaints, and also length of time in his practice
- Women's prior histories: sex, complaints, doctors, character, psychological history
- Return visits
- He said—she said
- No "real" assault ("talk isn't abuse")
- Full appreciation of how "humiliation can equal gratification"

- ➲ Perceived collusion/conspiracy (they just read it all, mutual coaching, greed, etc.)
- ➲ Focus on differences in accounts, especially pain versus pleasure
- ➲ Pro-medical, pro-doctor attitudes
- ➲ Perceived delay in complaints, trial
- ➲ Hindsight and attribution biases: "Why go to a male doctor if ever abused before?"
- ➲ Subjective "gross negligence" standard
- ➲ Sequence and number of plaintiff presentations
- ➲ Education job on standards, harms, and the nature of professional abuse

9.5.2 Focus Groups Grow Their Own Versions

Ultimately, three HMOs and six insurance or professional services companies were sued, along with the doctor and his own corporation. The local practices of physician groups had gone through several purchase processes in the early '90s, as had some of the managed-care providers administering these practice groups. This doctor and his group were one of the most desirable, fiscally, among those being considered for purchase. The many investigations of his conduct and the internal warnings he had received were a part of the due diligence process, which netted a one-year contract for him with the new owners and managed care directors, along with the purchase of the entities he played so large a role in. Around twenty complaints came to light during this purchase process, as well as some letters of reprimand and some efforts required of the doctor by his third-party providers. And after the business dealings were done, and all this information collected, two or three other plaintiffs in the suit experienced their contact with the doctor's approach to good care, allowing the knowledgeable oversight companies to be named as parties to the misconduct they knew went on before, and during, their business exchange, based in part on their knowledge that it was likely to go on. While the complaints had been found to lack merit, the doctor had been reprimanded, counseled, and allowed to self-refer to an impaired doctors' program, having had his style of patient treatment declared inappropriate, though this focused primarily on his propensity for hugging and kissing women patients outside the exam room.

From an initial group of nineteen plaintiffs, attrition of various kinds produced a solid group of fifteen. The judge consolidated the cases for discovery, and the defendants made a joint motion to bifurcate, as well as to hold separate trials for all defendants. The judge elected to try the first case with six plaintiffs, all but one of whom had coverage from the same HMO. Six women plaintiffs would try their cases against just the doctor and his corporation for compensatory damages, first, and pending that outcome and a consent agreement from the defendants, a different panel of jurors was to hear the claims against the corporate management defendants and the HMO, and claims for punitive damages against all defendants.

And so focus groups were convened by the attorney and a colleague; the following is what she recalls about that part of the story:

> Once the form of the trial was set, my attorney friend with a lot of focus group experience agreed to come and help me with these focus groups for the six. For the groups, we made summaries of each of the six people's complaints. In the last of three focus groups, one with all [women] participants,[15] we barely got through maybe half of the stories before people started interrupting to tell us how wrong the plaintiffs were. They were brutal in that last group. It was very traumatic. I really wondered how we could ever possibly win this case. The defense clearly had done their own groups with similar results, and were definitely declaring full speed ahead. So they were stunned by the eventual verdict.
>
> For our groups, we had put together a list of what each person's allegations were, and what the doctor's response was to each. And then we had put together some video of each one of the six from their depositions, as well as video taken from his deposition. We treated it very clinically and we just read the allegations. And what we verified in spades was what they call defensive attribution, or blaming the plaintiff. We verified that one in spades. We verified that if these ladies were going to make the complaint, they were going to be sharply scrutinized first.
>
> At the same time, right in the middle of this, I participated in a different set of focus groups, for a younger lawyer [testing] a case involving an adult male, who was retarded, who claimed he had been the victim of sexual harassment on the job. He had sued his employer over it. And what had happened with this guy was that the men in this company had started to harass him by saying that he was gay. They started by throwing things in the back of his truck, but it culminated in a gang rape in the bathroom of the company. I bring this up only because it was so much a repeat of our focus groups again. I remember the attorney standing in front of the group in a little horseshoe arrangement, with a black woman, close on his right as he stood there. He went through a narrative of what happened to the guy, and then we started talking about it. And this woman leans back in her chair, folds her arms and says, "Huh, I bet he *was* gay, he was probably getting off on it." And that's really sort of the response we got in that third focus

15. These groups followed more of a "concept" approach, and as such were much smaller than twenty-one participants.

group of ours: that the women were getting off on it. As far as the doctor, himself, they liked him—as did much of the jury in the eventual trial. That confirmed another problem with a lot of these cases. The perpetrator is often extremely likeable, that's part of it. My former partner used to say, "I never met a child molester I didn't like."

The big . . . giant focus group we had [for] the trial verified another huge landmine, that of most of the patients going back to him after their first incidents. When we put the groups together, I was focused on the idea of what it could do to people's responses to know that it happened over and over and over again. Because I thought that—even if participants had a reaction of initial disbelief—by the time you got through patient number six, people would get past that and they would be really mad. We hoped people would withhold their judgment long enough to let the impact accumulate. But it didn't really work that way at all. It accumulated, it just went exactly the other way.

What it did was it made them really motivated to explain why it was happening. Because the resistance to seeing a doctor be this way was really great. It was so high, that the group members became more intensely interested in trying to explain it away, the more they heard. What they did was try to figure out all the ways in which the behavior of the woman caused it all to happen. The story first became about the women, presuming he was OK, and then the trick was to explain all the complaints. So they looked to the women to do that. First, a "He said—she said" perception, and, giving the doctor the benefit of the doubt, they looked to explain why there were these complaints by scrutinizing the women.

In the third, all-women's group, one very strongly argued answer was from a woman who had been sexually abused herself. She thought there was a motivation to get something, trying to cash in. Then there were some reactions more like regret on the morning after. Like, "I really liked that but now I need to explain it to my husband, so I better make a complaint about it." Then there was something specific said about Jane, the sixteen-year-old plaintiff, who had been humiliated by both the positions he put her in for a simple physical exam for school sports, as well as his crude language, like "Does it bother you to have your titties hanging out like this?" They minimized it and they also had some explanation that she misinterpreted or she was . . . well, there was at least one was saying that she was making it up. Couldn't say why she would want to make it up, aside from some troubled teenager sort of thing. But there was a good deal of this thing that I saw in the other lawyer's group, there was some number of them saying that it was something that they had enjoyed and now were turning around trying to complain about it.

The defense's misinterpretation and misunderstanding theme had a lot of early traction in our groups. One of the things that we believed after the focus groups was that medically trained and experienced people could be risky—and this is why it was such a leap to leave the obstetrician's daughter on the jury, with both she and her husband also involved in medically related jobs. We discovered, and I think this is true, that the experience of being a healthcare provider and working in the healthcare system can make someone suspicious of patients; because patients misinterpret things, patients don't understand what is involved in medical exams and medical care. That, and the experiences with some patients who are crazy and are going to make stuff up anyway. So we thought [that] people can be inclined by close experience with the medical profession to build stories that look at the plaintiff's role first. I see this in my daughter, actually, who is an emergency room physician. If you're involved in any kind of healthcare that is on the front lines with the public, you see alcoholics, you see people that are just on the street, you see people who come in again and again. You see people who make things up, and who are just plain ignorant. You can get very cynical about patients, and suspect those [that] make complaints. Then there is also a process inside healthcare where patients that make complaints get labeled, and then they are never believed, based on the labels they get once they start making complaints.

We also seemed to confirm that women, in general, may be more inclined to generate stories that blamed these women plaintiffs for their circumstances. And not from just this case, but from a couple of other cases, too, it seemed that people with a history of their own abuse have the same, or higher, level of difficulty as medical people when it comes to these kinds of stories. We didn't purposely sort for them to be included in the groups, but we happened to get some from just the numbers who have [had such a history]. I had an experience in another case—not a sexual abuse case—where my plaintiff had a history of abuse and incest. Her daughter, now in her thirties, was probably still having an ongoing sexual relationship with the father, her ex-husband. That was a huge issue we had to learn about in jury selection. We had a jury questionnaire, and ended up having people answer whether they themselves or somebody that they were close to had either alleged or had alleged against them some sort of sexual abuse. The focus groups in the case against the doctor confirmed what I had learned in the previous case, that it's really rough for people with similar experiences in their backgrounds to write an accepting version of these case stories, unless they've developed some distance and perspective on their own incidents.

> There were two things that emerged from this previous case, when we found somebody that had a sexual abuse history. We took them in chambers and we talked to them about it. There were two people. One woman said that she would tend not to believe someone [that] had made an allegation of sexual abuse, yet I believed she herself was the victim she cited in answering the question. Keeping with the negative-explanation drive, she said something about the ability and intent to manipulate being just too high. She was struck right away. Another woman who had an abuse history was very much the opposite. She seemed very sensitive and open to such a complaint. But she was taken off by the other side. But my feeling about it was [that] the difference seemed to lie in how they have processed their own experience, not just having had it. The first one was still apparently in the throes of the whole experience, while the other had obviously dealt with it a lot. It may be dealing with [the] level of denial that's key. There was another person I recall from the third focus group, who had a background in social work or some sort of public social interaction with people. In spite of the fact that the third group was really brutal, I remember that person as being very sympathetic to the women, while the woman who had been sexually abused as a child was the one that was the hardest on everybody.

9.5.3 Following Suggestions

This particular case story, as it developed through the focus groups, provides an example of how testing for the stories likely to be reauthored, rather than for the right types of people to hear a predetermined story, can prove to be of real value. If you were simply sorting for types, then these concept-type groups essentially said that almost any woman, probably married, and still within childbearing years, would be absolute poison. That was not the case. All things being equal, women in general may not have been the pool from which to pick the best decision makers for this case. But, in the specific case, it was a woman, and one who had extensive family and work backgrounds in medicine—not sex abuse treatment—who did fit the bill. As the lawyer said, "My absolute best juror was that obstetrician's daughter." If you had decided to strike panelists based on those two definitely dangerous background characteristics, you might just pass off the one whose life experience makes him or her an expert, such as the daughter of the obstetrician, a doctor's daughter. Judging solely by typing, that makes her trebly dangerous.

Somebody coming off the street looking at this case story might say that a healthcare provider will give the benefit of the doubt to the colleague. That isn't necessarily so. Someone actually involved in the field has their own ideas on how standards need to be applied. But on the interpretive side, if they are looking at why the complaint would be filed and they are inclined to look at the women first, healthcare providers may well be more inclined to suspect and interpret badly the motives, the observations, the actions of complaining patients first. Because that is what they do. There is not a lot of mystery to it. People tend to do more of what they have already done, and they get what they rehearse, regardless of their intentions. We do as we've done. The problem is that if you just try to screen out by associations to healthcare work before investigating further, you can lose a friendly "expert" on your client's behalf. Many jurors will defer to anyone from that field when it comes to interpreting the rules.

Other topics for voir dire emerging in the Case Presentation Plan included:

- Sex problems. All forms: work policies, violations, complaints as "just talk"; genital explicitness versus moral, religious, and taste objections.
- Humiliation as gratification.
- Rules: "say" versus "do," standards of medicine versus your own. Burden-level of proof—"more likely" versus "sure" still viable in this situation?
- Awkwardness with suing doctors—or anybody.
- Is unwanted sexual approach still "about sex"? How? How not? (Let them build up to the actual standards—legal and professional.).
- Heard phrases "clinical detachment" or "professional distance"? How did they come about? Are they important? How, specifically?
- Relationships with doctors, teachers, attorneys, or nurses; experiences and attitudes.
- People who go back, or don't say no. What might prompt? Still give a fair hearing? How?
- Doctors: Higher standard versus greater benefit of doubt?
- What could keep a woman silent or prompt her to speak up?
- Mistaken perceptions versus women can always tell inappropriate advances (both sides).

The following is what the attorney had to say when it came to dropping a cause challenge to the obstetrician's daughter working in the medical field:

> She was one of the last jurors to be interviewed. The thing about her is how extremely thoughtful she was in how she gave her answers. The thing that really settled that feeling was when she was asked to describe her father. She said three things about him. She said . . . I believe she said that he was highly ethical, that he was kind, and that he was very respected in the community. He was obviously a hero to her. I imagined she could be really offended learning the things the other doctor had done.

But this all begged the question that must come first and be answered correctly if the jurors were to have any chance of reversing the focus groups' trends: *Who—and what—is this whole thing really all about?* If the answer in juror and judge stories began with "These women who . . . ," the writing was clearly on the wall. Several things had to be done to help invite decision makers to construct stories different than those we'd seen so far.

9.5.4 Theme

The Case Presentation Plan included the following theme:

> I think the theme that carries the greatest strength and the fewest risks would be something like *Professional Standards (versus Personal Ones).* The real comparison you want them to make, challenging the most destructive presumption that was unchallenged by these test groups, is between the high bar held up by the medical profession, and the low bar this guy held his behavior to, set by nothing more than his own preferences. It would seem that this case is more likely to go your way if it's about his personal preferences for setting his lower standards than if it's about subjective judgments on how badly he treated each particular woman.

9.5.5 Scope

The Case Presentation Plan also defined the following scope:

> The defense of this case favors the land of specifics, details, and differences. The plaintiff's part of the presentations that I've seen so far has also occupied that territory. As a result, each plaintiff got picked apart in her turn. That tendency will always be there on any panel you eventually address, but that's no reason why you can't present the case in such a way that the trend is diminished as much as possible.

What that eventually entailed was an effort to unify the disparate details of each woman's bad treatment by the doctor under some simple categories defining the nature of these acts, rather than their individual, distinct replaying. So, rather than focusing on each item of misbehavior as it was experienced by a plaintiff—never known as patients but only as plaintiffs in the jurors' experiences—the acts, incidences, and people receiving the doctor's conduct all had to be set aside in favor of three general categories for every choice he made to act, in whatever way, at whatever time, with whatever woman patient.

The three categories offered to invite decision makers to subsume the individual stories under the umbrella of physician misconduct were designed specifically to make it easy for people to package and recall what the case was about: the doctor's chosen standards for how he alone decided he needed to act, so at odds with those of his profession. We knew we were on the right track in that task when the judge, during final pretrial motions, adopted our three phrases as his way of keeping track of the claims, putting the doctor in the position of the active party, and reinforcing that role simply by adopting and repeating our three categories, first in a written opinion and, later on, with the potential jurors during voir dire.

The following is a pretrial outline of how the eventual jurors were invited to use the three categories to regroup and reframe the dozens of bad acts.

> We tell things to our doctors that we do not tell other people. We undress and allow our doctors to touch private parts of our bodies that only our intimate partners can touch. We do these things willingly because we trust that our doctor is there to help and to heal us. We open ourselves and our bodies willingly to our doctors because we trust that they will not abuse that trust, that they will not take advantage of our vulnerabilities, and that they will only try to heal us. We let our doctors do things to us that are uncomfortable and even painful, because they must, and we go back willingly because we believe it is for our own good.
>
> We are secure in this trust because we believe that the physical exam will not be sexual, because we believe that it is not seen by the doctor as sexual and because we believe that there is no danger that it will become sexual. The clinical boundary must always be there. Otherwise, it is not a medical exam, it is something else, and the doctor violates his oath to act only for the benefit of the patient, serving his own needs instead.
>
> This case will reveal a doctor choosing to erase that rigid boundary. We will see here a doctor choosing to use his medical license to gain entry to private spaces to violate and humiliate his patients, and to gratify himself. The evidence of his *conduct, language, and treatment* will reveal this. Whether he intended the harm is not important for deciding this case. The only question you will be asked to decide here is whether he did indeed cross those rigid boundaries set up by professional standards he was obligated to follow. These are the ways the evidence will show that he made examinations into violation, humiliation and gratification [*holds chart up*]:

CONDUCT	➲ Sexualized/painful examinations: pelvic/rectal/breast
	➲ Uninvited hugging and kissing
	➲ Bizarre positioning and unnecessary exposure
LANGUAGE	➲ Unprofessional comments, not clinical descriptions
	➲ Unnecessary sexual histories
TREATMENT	➲ Harmful/unnecessary prescriptions
	➲ Unnecessary sexual histories
	➲ Uninvited sexual "counseling"

The chart was handwritten onto a flip chart, and referred to as the key visual anchor throughout the case presentation, from this moment in opening, forward. Note that if you begin trying to categorize the acts he chose within these categories, the shift to the reference point or viewpoint of the professional is almost automatic, as is the imposition on this doctor of active party status, when it comes to the driving force of the actions in the story being built.

9.5.6 Sequence

That left the landmine areas dealing with the deleted standards and the defense's thematic territory of simple misunderstanding and misinterpretation. Here is where sequencing of the story offered the greatest value. The "let the facts speak" mindset leads any professional to a chronological recitation of the claimed wrongs, patient by patient, in a long, painful row. And while, eventually, the individual stories did indeed have to be related, the focus groups demonstrated beyond doubt that an early invitation to concentrate on the patients—many of whom chose to return again and again to the doctor—would most likely be fatal. The plan offered this set of remarks (among others):

> That means a three-step approach to those pesky details. First, a comparison of the general medical standards of conduct to those the doctor decided on his own are good enough for him. Second, a "quantitative" presentation of the story of the similar results of his choice by the numbers, rather than the names, dates, and places, with the warning he received from the authorities plugged in along the way. You can *move* toward specificity here by accumulating things like "positions" he put women in versus those positions the rest of the medical world

uses; clothing arrangement comparisons; gynecological exam differences; number of overall complaints—if allowed (averaging one every other month for four years), etc.

Visuals to help these comparisons of the *similarities and frequencies* of his habitual offenses and the *differences*—this guy versus the medical world—will help set up the final, specific complaints of the women. Then the chances are far better that they can be used to *confirm* leanings already established *before* their individual backgrounds and characters ever have a chance to come into question.

1. General medical conduct and treatment standards versus doctor's own preferences
2. Quantitative presentation of his *conduct, language,* and *treatment* violations, concentrating on similarities and frequency, including things like clothing, exam styles top and bottom, and the gymnastic positions he prefers
3. Individual descriptions of mistreatment, with as much harm and damage [as] you are allowed to include

Thus, in sequencing the story—along with the structuring of an invitation to redirect the scope of developing juror stories—a perceptual distinction (similarities and differences) became a tool capable of providing the building stories some real help.[16] By first working to unify the disparate details of the individual claims under the three large category headings, and focusing more attention on enumerating occurrences of the bad acts over time before elaborating much on their individual infliction, we could effectively invite jurors to reframe one of the biggest story landmines for us, by turning their focus from the detailed *content* of each complaint to the overall *context* of the defied medical professional standards under which the harms were all inflicted.

The first step in the sequence was designed both to establish that context, reaching all the way back to ancient Greece to do so, and then to cut this one doctor from that historical herd of more conscientious healers. How he chose his way over the right way. Then the story delivery could begin to shift toward the categories of sins committed, but still in the *context* of the professional rules, not the individual patient experiences. Finally, the last step of the plan allowed the individual recitations of his bad acts to be used more to *confirm* than to reveal what had been done so badly with each of the six plaintiffs selected for this case. This plan was almost undercut in the actual trial by what appeared, at first, to be a good break.

16. See discussion of metaprograms in section 3.10.6, "Sorting or Organizing Filters."

The judge had previously ruled that each plaintiff was to be allowed testimony from only one other witness, who had her own tale to tell about the doctor, to establish the pattern of his practice. Naturally, with so many potential plaintiffs out there whose time for filing a claim had run out, to say nothing of those still awaiting their day in court, there were more than the six this ruling allowed ready to speak out. Both defense attorneys made the blunder in their openings, no doubt partly driven by their focus on details over the big picture, to openly compare the number of total patients he had ever seen with the six represented in court. This opened the door for thirteen, rather than just six other women (which the judge's ruling had restricted the plaintiffs to), coming in for what one member of the trial team referred to as "the week of sex" in testimony. Because the defense minimized the numbers, the plaintiffs were now allowed to challenge those assertions. By reinforcement of time spent talking about it alone, this massive run of individual stories shook the foundation of the case story planned for this trial. Fortunately, it didn't break it.

The focus groups had begun to question motives, at least of the complaining patients, almost immediately during their sessions. Motive is always a part of every case story, in or out of trial, for every decision maker, in or out of the legal profession. But motives typically do not gain conscious attention until a sense of whether a rule has been broken or a line has been crossed is already achieved. By offering, but not asserting, the connection between humiliation and gratification, out front, as the three categories were put in place for jurors to start using as the judge already had, the efforts to shift theme, scope, point of view, and sequence toward a focus on the professional made that conclusion much more available, when the time came for motive to be inserted in each individual juror's case story.

But the problem of setting the unique context for the case story about this lone doctor would not be fully dealt with without resorting to the inclusion of the visual channel in our efforts. Despite much initial concern, we devised some demonstratives both to illustrate the aberrant nature of the conduct, language, and treatment at hand, and to isolate it at the very same time from anything in the jurors' prior experience. The bizarre posture the doctor forced the youngest plaintiff to adopt, bent over before him with her hospital gown falling over her head, with not only her breasts exposed but with her hands touching the floor, while he stared at her from behind for several minutes, seemed to be the most compelling image of all (see Figure 22). And it didn't even depict physical contact. But it was a great help in drawing people out of their own expectations and associations with doctor visits, into the whole new situation that this story required. This case story was consciously delivered from both a more general and a more visual approach than the focus groups were provided.

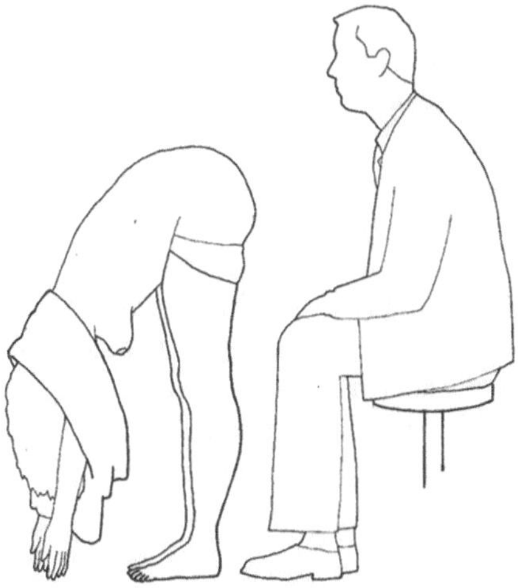

Figure 22

9.5.7 *Not Perfect, but Palatable*

The following are the remaining comments from the attorney about her recollection of the development and delivery of the case story, and what she learned about its reception by the panelists.

> There was one woman who slipped onto the panel by lying to me. After the trial, and after hearing all that evidence, she said, "Oh, I thought he was charming, I would go to him." In jury selection, she had lied about her own reaction to malpractice [on] her son, at birth. I believe that her son had been given a circumcision when she hadn't approved it. She had been pretty upset. But she told me in jury selection only that she had had a problem with a doctor, she said what it was, I think, but she said, "You know, it made me really upset, but I worked through it and it was OK." Later on in jury selection, she said she had had therapy, but having to do with her father's death, nothing about malpractice. The other jurors told me afterwards that, in fact, she had gone into therapy to deal with her anger at the doctor. She was apparently a big problem during deliberations, and they had spent time dealing with her for at least a day, because she was convinced all these women were weak and had bad motives just because they had brought a lawsuit at all. In comparison, it appears, she felt herself to be so strong, and unlike them, because she made the choice not to bring her own lawsuit.

The second set of topics in voir dire was the whole concept of being awkward about judging lawsuits against doctors. She lied to me about that. That turned out to be her big stumbling block. And they apparently spent a day or maybe two discussing her problem in deliberation, and her feelings on that very topic. She didn't want to agree to liability. The way everyone, including her, ended up agreeing to liability was because he had admitted enough bad acts for every single plaintiff, which he simply refused—in his deposition tape—to agree were wrong, that they were all able to agree that he had at least been negligent. The obstetrician's daughter set the ceiling on damages higher than we had asked, and the individual awards came in between half what we'd asked and the full amount for every plaintiff.

The consensus story we got from the jurors was much different than a bunch of "She said" stories about what "He did." Their stories were now all about him. I believe that there were some people on the jury who thought he was a really bad guy who did these things on purpose. But the consensus story, what led to the verdict, was that he was somebody that was misguided and did a whole lot of inappropriate things in his practice, and as a result of him doing those things, these people were hurt. I think that the consensus was this was kind of a stupid guy that didn't know how to do an exam right and didn't know that you weren't supposed to talk about certain things with people.

But the plaintiffs' motives continued to be an issue, because that was the defense against all of them. In closing, the arguments were made clearly that this was all about getting money. They also tried to say it was a conspiracy, a witch hunt, and that a lot of these people heard about it through the papers. One thing I'd done right preparing the case was that none of the women had ever talked to each other about what happened, and most hadn't read the news accounts. They had never talked to one another about what had happened. I had never told any of them what had happened to the other people. And they were not in the courtroom, so they didn't hear anybody's testimony. Even all the way through the verdict, they didn't know. And so there wasn't anything for the defense to work with except innuendo. So what the defense did was to focus on the plaintiffs' lawyer. They said, "Everybody has the same lawyer, and the exact same words were said by a lot of them about the things they claimed he did. Words that he supposedly used with them." They tried to imply that I had put all their words in their mouths. "Even though we can't prove any of them had talked to each other, we all know they talked to that plaintiff's lawyer."

I don't know exactly why, but the jurors trusted me. People say the more time you spend with a jury, the more likely they are to know who you are. You can't hide who you are. So if you're a lying so-and-so, they are going to know that by the end of the case. To me, that is why we won this case. Partly because of all that he admitted, on videotape, in deposition. And partly because the jurors put the story together the way we presented it: these are the rules, this is what he chose instead, and what happened as a result.

9.6 2015 Supplement

Since the original edition of *Facts Can't Speak for Themselves*, I have worked on many, many cases—all of which *can* speak for themselves as to the value of my concentrating as much on *how you say things* as on *what is said*—the relative effectiveness of indirect and direct suggestions has been revealed time and again. I couldn't help but notice one final deficit in the original publication, which I'm given the welcome chance to correct here.

Readers know I went to great lengths to imply, suggest, advise, and (even) implore that these research efforts and the resources invested in them have *equal* value for purposes of negotiation, arbitration and, especially, mediation as at trial. As my good friend and colleague Amy Pardieck[17] says: "Nine out of ten of your carefully crafted cases will never see one juror."

So, when I reviewed the First Edition and got to the "practical examples" section at the end—a criminal trial example, and three civil trial examples, one defense and two plaintiff—I realized there was no mediation example.

In the last couple of years, I've been concentrating a significant part of my efforts helping trial attorneys apply all these techniques—with or without the aid of focus groups—to the development and delivery of strong plaintiff case stories for mediation. One attorney I've worked with has developed a string of successful mediations that have one criteria: the ultimate outcome must be *double* what the client would have settled for—and indeed, his most recent mediation got his client *six times* that number.

So, what's the "Rule of the *Mediation* Road"?

> Do not agree to any mediation unless you can make a thorough and fair presentation of your client's case story (yes, the real story), complete with visual support, for at least twenty minutes.

If there is no presentation, there should be no mediation.

To make this point and to try to fill the case specific gaps left in the First Edition, I offer you the full text of an article, reproduced in full, below, Ms. Pardieck and I wrote about our separate experiences helping plaintiff attorneys maximize outcomes in mediation instead of continuing to treat them as an added cost only (at worst) or a stacked deck in a feeble settlement (at best).[18]

---

17. Amy Pardieck of Perceptual Litigation, LLC, is an experienced trial consultant and has worked with attorneys nationwide.

18. This article first appeared in my newsletter, *News From the Mental Edge* (Fall 2012), available at www.eric-oliver.com.

9.6.1 Settling for More: Raising the Value of Mediation

My wife says I can't drink no more—Well, I sure ain't gonna drink no less!
—*Seigel Schwall Blues Band*

Mediation—to mediate—is generally defined as an effort to resolve differences by *working with* (italics are ours) conflicting parties, or to act as an intermediary or a guiding link between parties. To these definitions we propose adding one more: mediation is a singular opportunity to increase your client's advantage overall—including a favorable trial outcome if an immediate settlement is not reached. Mediation can be an additional step in the process of dispute resolution, *not* an "also ran" alternative. If your efforts at mediation bring a successful outcome—thereby precluding the expense of a trial—then, in the "traditional" sense, you've won before even starting. However, if your mediation does not result in immediate resolution, the efforts you have put into its preparation and delivery will in no way be wasted; in fact, they will have already put you far ahead of the opposition in later settlement talks or if and when you do get to a trial.

Mediation as Opportunity

Whether official or unofficial, mandated by a judge or voluntary, mediation is always an opportunity to advance your client's positions in multiple ways that are not readily apparent during the mediation process itself, but which can make a huge difference in the eventual resolution of their case. Just because you don't win an immediate settlement does not mean it had no value; you can still "win" in many ways as a result of the mediation process—*if* you approach it well.

We've noted over the years a range of attitudes toward the mediation process among trial lawyers—from the enthusiastic, to the openly hostile, to the all too commonly resigned "here we go again." The latter predisposition is particularly troublesome as it provides a handy excuse to forgo any kind of *serious* preparation which, unfortunately, will only result in leaving many of the advantages you could have gained from mediation still on the table when you leave. Not only can your case be undermined, it very likely also will be badly *damaged* if your inclination is just to "show up"—regardless of how long the mediation lasts—without more than a bare minimum of effort having been put into preparing for the process. You will have passed up a golden opportunity to improve your client's position even in the event that you *don't* achieve a favorable settlement on the spot.

By choosing to use mediation as a *strategy* capable of producing multiple advantages for you and your client—rather than considering it some kind of dead end—you can immediately raise your expectations for what could come from the mediation as high as you are willing to put effort into the process. How to fulfill those expectations is what this article is aimed to help you achieve.

Mediation Decisions and Their Makers

According to Marc Galanter in *The Vanishing Trial: An Examination of Trials and Related Matters in Federal and State Courts*,[19] the ABA estimates that fewer than two percent of federal cases filed, and fewer than sixteen percent of state court cases filed, actually go to trial. While a portion of these cases are dismissed, "settlement" is the primary outcome for the rest of them. Yet many attorneys still question the value of investing much time, energy, or resources in mediation. A few common (and misperceived) objections include mediations with no resolution are a waste of resources, they are like fishing expeditions, i.e, a delaying tactic used by the opposition or a deliberate attempt on their part to "smoke out" your case or just plain wear you down. Yet, experience tells us that if you put in *little to no effort* preparing for a mediation, you will almost always guarantee *no return* from such an opportunity, thereby also guaranteeing a self-fulfilling (and erroneous) prophecy. Whether the mediation is mandated or voluntary, a "garbage in" approach will usually produce a "garbage out" result—*against* your client's interests *and* at your client's expense. As long as you are going to be there, we suggest you come prepared in order to get the full value from the opportunity *and* from your client's investment.

Interestingly, a view of mediation as increasingly *significant* to the process of garnering favorable settlements has emerged alongside the more familiar "here we go again" position. Jeffrey Sterns suggests in his article *Is Negotiation Outside Mediation Pre-Historic?*[20] that a reliance on independent negotiation, i.e., private negotiation between attorneys on behalf of their clients, has faded due to the proliferation of mediation as the preferred settlement method. Stern offers a list of factors he sees that have helped to raise the perceived value of the mediation process for many lawyers. Two of these factors are the "Floor-Ceiling" scenario and the "Projected Weakness" perception issue.

In the Floor-Ceiling scenario, Stern suggests opposing parties have come to expect, and rely on, mediation as the first *serious* effort towards resolution of any case in litigation. Therefore, any independent negotiation is viewed as too risky because either precipitously raising the floor *or* setting the ceiling lowers the possibility of success. Framed that way, negotiating *outside* mediation not only is becoming a lost art, but is also a risk you don't want to run.

"Peacemakers" may be blessed, but in the contentious arena of trial law the person willing to make the first move toward reconciliation is likely to be viewed as a loser rather than a saint. Stern also points out that mediation brings parties to the first step all at the same time, therefore avoiding the threat of "Projected Weakness." However, there is still a potential pitfall in waiting until the start of mediation to begin serious thinking about resolving a case. Many trial lawyers are familiar with

19. American Bar Association, 2004.
20. A 2006 article, cited by American Society of Trial Consultants member Ed Schwartz.

the harried feeling that comes from trying to prepare an adequate opening statement on a Sunday evening before a Monday morning court date. Just like an opening prepared too late, waiting too long to properly prepare your mediation positions and delivery will almost surely hurt the eventual resolution of your client's case by conceding ground you cannot regain.

Whether you are of the mindset that tends to deny the value of mediation or believe that it is a method of default, one thing is certain: settlement outcomes, like verdicts, are *not* preordained. When it comes to the *value* of settlements in mediation, just like the *value* of jury verdicts, the case story delivered by the strongest presentation has the most power to prevail. It is the decision makers' perceptions of the facts that drive decisions, and in *every* venue it is the persuasively presented stories that drive perceptions.

In our experience, many accomplished and successful trial lawyers—who have confirmed through their own experience the value of systematic planning for the delivery of a case story in order to lay a foundation for trial presentation planning, including taking advantage of focus group research—still retain an unfortunate blind spot regarding the value of investing the same kind of effort and resources when preparing for mediation. Yet, they all know that upwards of ninety-five percent of their client case stories will never be seen or heard by jurors. Instead, they will be decided by judges sitting behind a bench, at an arbitration hearing, or by the opposing parties in conjunction with their lawyers at mediation. In far too many attorneys' minds, the hard-won insights from focus groups or independent case presentation planning is considered strictly for use with a group of jurors at trial. When it comes to using the same carefully planned material to influence the decision makers that, nine times out of ten they *actually will be* trying to influence and/or persuade, attorneys give little to no thought to the advantages that will most certainly be lost as a consequence of not planning, not preparing for and not delivering, their client's case story at mediation with the same caliber of effort as for a jury trial.

The real danger in acting from the mindset that requires full effort only when preparing to persuade jurors is revealed by what happens when the decision makers in mediation are deprived of the results of that level of preparation. Now, *neither* jurors *nor* legal professionals are supposed to be the final arbiters in mediation—the parties themselves are, with the aid of their attorneys—but for many lawyers treating "the parties themselves" as "decision makers" is a difficult departure from the "juror-centric" decision maker image most likely in the front of their minds. And those omnipresent jurors can dominate far too much of an attorney's mental landscape when planning a persuasive mediation presentation. However, there's a bit of a twist here: mediation decisions are *not* strictly in the hands of "the parties themselves," they are also in the hands of the third party in the mix, the *mediator*.

Rehearsing for Success

By the very nature of litigation, trial attorneys tend to *rehearse* a mental and perceptual bias toward *outcome* and away from *process*. But, far more often than not, those habits, especially the ones that distort perceptions of the persuasive landscape at hand, will achieve *only* what is rehearsed, regardless of the best intentions. By concentrating too much on the *outcome* of mediation, an attorney may be led by habit to miss the advantages to be gained from focused efforts to influence the ongoing decision making process. In mediation, the embodiment of this process is the *mediator* who, for all intents and purposes, is a third advocate influencing the case, though not as a representative of the interests of a client, but as an advocate in the interests of gaining a settlement. The ongoing decision making process of the mediator will be a major determinant of just how much advantage can be gained during mediation especially when—or regardless of whether—you do *not* settle on the spot.

How so?

When it comes to *process*, no matter what "format" or "template" a particular mediator chooses to work from, nobody is immune to effective persuasion—nobody. Regardless of their years of experience, their years of training, their professional acumen, or their particular approach to acting as a "guiding link between parties," mediators are driven by the same decision making rules as the rest of us. The only difference during the mediation process is that the mediator is the one who can have the major impact on its eventual outcome. Like a television producer, a film director, or an editor of a newspaper, the mediator is the one making the choices of which way to go next at every step of the process. And the choices that ultimately count the most toward influencing everyone's perceptions during the *process* of mediation are the choices made, at any given moment, to emphasize, exclude, question, isolate, incorporate, reframe, or empower one part of a case story in relation to all the rest. However, despite the fact that it is the mediator who chooses which parts of the story are selected for focused attention, and which aren't, the attorneys present can strongly influence those choices—and their impact on everyone involved—through and, far beyond, the process of the mediation itself. The raw material of reality is perception and one secret to success is not to focus only on which parts of the story have been chosen for attention, but also on how—and *when*—they are described, envisioned, and *perceived* during the mediation process, i.e., on how they are *delivered*.

How does one create a strong mediation presentation? The answer is simple: preparation, preparation, preparation. By preparing the case as if mediation were as important as a trial,[21] an attorney not only increases negotiating power but *also*

21. Since, in nine out of ten times, it is.

completes vital groundwork for taking full advantage of any further steps in the resolution process in the event that an immediate settlement is not reached.

Wherever decisions are made, and regardless of who makes them, effective presentations always translate into significantly more favorable settlements. While it is true that there can be significant upfront costs associated with developing a strong case presentation, these costs are dwarfed by the potential for a favorable settlement amount *or,* when mediation doesn't produce an immediate resolution, the potential valuable advantages to be gained for the next step in the case. However, just as with trial, preparation for mediation should be just one part of the strategy. The client's case *story* must still be strongly *delivered* to the decision makers, directly or indirectly, depending on the style of mediation being used. A presentation delivered poorly can literally wipe out the entire value of the rest of your case preparation.

Nobody is immune to the effects of interpersonal communication, regardless of whether the communication is delivered positively or negatively. Since perception of the facts—rather than some arbitrary "objective" version of them—rules the legal judgment process, including during mediation, then whoever is better able to manage the decision makers' perceptions of the facts in competing case stories will be the one more likely to reap the benefits of those efforts from *all* decision makers present, including the opposing party, who naturally will be resisting the process. However, it is the mediator trying to bridge gaps between opposing parties who will be most affected by *the way* the material is being discussed, omitted, put off, exaggerated in importance, or framed in helpful or unproductive ways.

Clotaire Rapaille, author of *The Culture Code,*[22] is a world-renowned market researcher who specializes in the factors that drive selling and buying behavior. He is also the man who popularized the term "reptilian brain." When asked what set him apart from the massive marketing departments of the many Fortune 500 corporations who had hired him, he famously said: "They listen to what people *say.* I don't." Trial attorneys who have experience with well-run focus groups and effective post-trial juror interviewing know very well how dangerous it is just to take decision makers at their word when it comes to what they *say* is the most important piece of evidence, the most probative issue in the case, or the one thing that made them side for, or against, the plaintiff or the defense.

Professional legal decision makers—judges, arbitrators, and mediators—have little inherent interest in the concerns of a particular party's conflict, and even the most extensive efforts an attorney might put into preparing and developing a case won't change that view. Influence happens during communication, but how compelling that influence is, and whether it will work favorably or not, depends

---

22. Clotaire Rapaille, *The Culture Code: An Ingenious Way To Understand Why People Around the World Live and Buy as They Do* (San Francisco, CA: Jossey-Bass, 2010).

almost entirely on how efforts to persuade are *received*, not on a show of conviction by the communicator, nor certainly on any inherent "probative" value of its content. It is always the decision makers' *perceptions* of the facts in the story that determine the level of influence on their leanings during the process. So, practicing the most effective means of managing perceptions in mediation is as important as it is in trial.

The brilliant author and student of the mind and brain, Daniel Kahneman, describes a mental habit of one of the fundamental thinking systems in the brain with the acronym WYSIATI: "What you see is all there is." When a lawyer who knows better acts as if all that matters is whatever the opposing counsel or party *says* about their responses to his presentation of his case story or his arguments about it, to paraphrase Kahneman, they act as if "What they say is all there is." This is a dangerous fallacy that long-standing habit drives too many lawyers to accept without a second thought in focus groups, in voir dire, and in mediation, to the detriment of client interests.

When it comes to mediation, the influence of the mediator on the perceptions of either side's position can be profound, especially as they are likely to say one thing and do another in the overriding interest of achieving a resolution. It can be harmful to just take the mediator's word for what they *think* is, or is not, influencing them. The truth is, they don't know. Nobody knows. That's why Rapaille wisely doesn't listen to conscious, after the fact, interpretations of the influence someone's persuasive efforts are having—or not. When it comes to their legal decisions, when asked "why?" people either will lie, or occasionally tell the truth, i.e., "I really don't know."

We all often assume a much greater degree of conscious control over our mental processes than really exists. After all, if the opposing parties, their lawyers, and the "independent" mediator all possess total conscious control over all their reactions to any efforts to persuade them, no influence could ever occur. What could lead them to allow themselves to be influenced if they were capable of completely stopping it from the start? In the context of mediation, reasonable minds *will* disagree, right up until they perceive no other alternative to agreeing. What would cause them to accommodate any conflicting interests, if they had the power to stay completely immune to the influence of any other position simply by willing it to be so?[23]

But of course, that's not the way it works. Influence and persuasion are not only possible, they are inevitable. The question, then, at the start of each and every mediation should be, "Are you ready to deliver the goods, or not?" The presentation of a client's case story can go a long way in engaging professional decision makers,

23. Attributing the influence you have had on *their* thinking to a third party like the judge or a group of jurors party ("Well, you may fool a couple jurors into thinking . . . ."), as if they—not the attorney—could be persuaded or "fooled" by your efforts is proof positive of that influence existing for that lawyer at that time. Otherwise, how would they know to worry about the same response in a third party at all?

opposing counsel, and their clients—and most often will, when approached properly and delivered well. That delivery must be designed, developed, and presented with an eye to influencing the parts of each decision maker's mind that do more than the parts that only speculate out loud about what's actually going on between their ears and behind their eyes, once you sit back down.

Investing in Success

So, how can you "win" in mediation—even when you don't settle immediately—using a strong, well-prepared presentation? A strong presentation automatically shifts the perceived settlement value your way in the mind of the opposition no matter what they *say* out loud. Just perceiving the extent of effort preparing such a presentation requires starts raising the bar. The persuasive impact of an effective presentation is not lost on the side that has to imagine—*during your delivery*—having to prepare a similarly persuasive counter. Development of their case story, along with the investment of time and resources necessary to counter your delivery, suddenly become part of their calculation. You've raised the bar on the perceived "cost" of pressing forward.

The confidence and cohesiveness of the "team" on the other side can be shaken by your mounting a smooth, professional presentation, especially when you bring along a fully integrated set of visual aids and introduce them seamlessly as you proceed. Having to try and match your level of persuasive delivery, with little to no preparation of their own beyond the usual "Sunday night opening" effort, can turn the other side away from questioning *you* to questioning *themselves*. And, when you do this, don't discount the favorable impact on the mediator during the rest of the process. You've raised the bar on perceived effort by your opponents to try their case.

Your own overall performance in bench conferences, motions hearings, discovery (written and in deposition), subsequent settlement discussions (if needed), subsequent case presentations including practice in front of a "serious "audience" like a focus group, and at trial, will all be enhanced by the work you've already invested. You can get focus group level input from the mediator, from the opposition "team," and from your own people as well. How well you are prepared to do so will determine just how much added value you will gain from your participation in mediation, regardless of whether a settlement is immediately forthcoming or not. You've raised the bar on your own persuasive case story development *and* delivery.

A focus group prior to your mediation can offer a test scenario for defining the most persuasive story line and for determining how to present evidence that is the most powerful, while also showing the way to reframe weak case story points into strengths. Assuming that the group reactions are positive, attorneys can use the results of a focus group—if it is conducted properly—to cast doubt on an opponent's predictions of likely victory. However, that is the least of the potential benefits of weaving focus group material into your mediation presentations. A focus group can reveal how decision makers might go about assessing the potential value of the case. While there is no guarantee that the results of pretrial research will mirror an actual jury verdict, it will still produce valuable information when analyzing case *values* for mediation. You *also* can get focus group level input from the mediator, from the clients you are opposing, as well as from your own people and from the opposition "team" too.

You can use the mediation presentation itself as a finely targeted *focus group* presentation in at least three ways.[24]

1. You also can use the mediator as, literally, a one-person focus group during your presentation. The mediator's reactions to your story delivery—spoken, unspoken, and, especially, implied—can reveal the positions of any of the other legal *professionals* who will possibly hear and see your work when, and if, you move beyond the mediation phase. In mediation, unlike in trial, the mediator not only must talk to you about their impressions of your story *as you deliver it,* but also must take immediate positions on it in order to *move the process along.* Therefore, taking into account which of your frames stick, which of your language choices are adopted, repeated, reframed or rejected, which of your mental or demonstrative images are referenced directly (or indirectly) in the mediator's input following your presentation, is all *very* valuable "grist for your mill." You've raised the bar on *the edge* you can achieve with the professionals involved, including the current mediator, in the future resolution of your client's case.

2. During the same mediation session, you also can consider the opposition "team" as focus group participants during your presentation. Their spoken, unspoken, and implied reactions to your story delivery (and whether they want to or not, they *won't* be able to keep themselves from reacting) not only can offer valuable feedback about *potential* reactions from future decision makers, but also can identify the areas the other side perceives, for themselves, as strong points—or weak points—and especially, which parts of your story delivery come across as unpleasant surprises or wounds. This kind of feedback is invaluable. Because if it comes from an unfriendly decision maker's perspective, it not only helps you refine future work on your presentation plan, but also helps you target your planning for cross exams and discovery. Now, you've raised the bar on *the strength* of the next stage of your delivery.[25]

---

24. If you are facing a mediator who does not agree to making presentations, you will want to rethink your choice of mediator.

25. While you do want to approach mediation with an "all guns blazing" position, what you learn from reactions to your delivery and subsequent efforts in case development must be used to adapt, change, and refine the package for your next presentation: at trial. It ought not to be just a longer version of the same presentation.

3. You can use your *own* reactions to your mediation presentation, along with those of your team members, as a kind of focus group as well. Just by noting the delimitative responses from yourself and your team while making your presentation in a critical—if not openly hostile—environment can help reveal which parts of your story delivery work well, work somewhat well, or fall flat. Finally, you've raised the bar on *the quality* of your own delivery.

Remember, when you dive in and use mediation as a focus group, the unedited, spontaneous responses from all present can include some of the most valuable feedback possible about a case story and its presentation. Nobody is immune to the effects of anchoring, or responses conditioned in the moment. And, nobody can fully hide the effect when they experience it, though many try to deny doing so afterward. Fortunately, these denials take place *after* you have already used the opportunity, "in the moment," to observe and record the actual reactions.

In most mediation sessions, direct exchanges between representatives of the parties, or the parties themselves, are not allowed. However, in mediations when exchanges are allowed, using the process as an opportunity to "conduct" a focus group can be done very directly. And, compared with the cost of a full-scale focus group, the cost of using mediation in this way is, practically speaking, no cost at all.

At a mediation when direct exchanges are allowed, follow the basic steps of a well-run focus group. Ask the right questions, ask even more of the right follow-up questions, and listen. This task requires a fundamental shift from presenting and arguing to listening and following up. This may sound simple enough but, for most attorneys learning to do so won't happen overnight. It is very similar to the difference between doing ninety percent of the listening in voir dire instead of ninety percent of the talking. If you are a ninety percent listener in voir dire, that is who you want to be in this type of mediation. If you are a ninety percent talker in voir dire, chances are you will adopt a similar posture in mediation, in which case, you want to rethink your strategy in both situations.

Effective questions to ask are similar to effective questions asked in voir dire. First, identify the topics of concern, and then ask, "How so?" or "Tell me more." For example, when advocating for the plaintiff in a car wreck case, and the defense attempts to minimize damages due to a pre-existing injury, you might ask, "How, specifically, could a ten-year-old injury affect the one this wreck caused today?" And, no matter what the defense says, your response should be, "Tell me more," "Tell me more," "Tell me more." Or, in a mediation in which you are the defense attorney and the plaintiff is claiming the warnings were inadequate, your questions should be, "How so specifically?" *And* . . . "Tell me more," "Tell me more," "Tell me more."

For example, in the case of a complex breach of contract going to mediation, there were seventy-two depositions, a room full of documents, and a daunting number of thorny side issues. Factually and legally, there appeared to be a solid basis for each side's interpretation of the contract, the only difference being whether eight million dollars belonged to the plaintiff or to the defendant. When both sides stand on relatively equal footing as in this case example, the advantage usually will go to the defense. The plaintiff had to do *something* to gain an edge.

What did they do? They identified nine main topics, key story *frames*, and all relevant facts, exhibits, and testimony were assigned to one of those frames, thereby giving particular *meaning within each story frame* to those facts, exhibits, and testimony. Selected highlights from the depositions and documents were chosen to illustrate each frame. The plaintiff streamlined the information into a twenty-minute PowerPoint presentation using nine (one for each frame) professionally designed demonstratives, five deposition excerpts, and eleven exhibits with call-out text boxes holding testimony excerpts. The frames: hierarchy, property, standards, commercial versus private commitments, breaking commitments, timelines, alternatives, costs, and consequences, all referred to the *human* elements the contract defined, i.e., people, places, property, rules, reliability, time, numbers, and harms.

It came down to which side's interpretation of the contract was going to rule when it was time for each side to make their presentation. The defense typically began by running down a chronological rendition of events, using dated exhibits to move through their timeline. They did not address the specific *frames* the plaintiff's had previously set up; rather they focused only on documents ("The evidence will show"). Their emphasis was on "words and dates on paper," thereby distancing themselves from any "real world" elements of the human narrative—people, places, property, rules, reliability, time, numbers, and harms.

After their presentations, each side retired to separate rooms and the mediator began shuttling between them. Then, the "focus group" began. Both sides relied on the mediator to ask and answer questions; the plaintiff to plumb the opposition—nine times.

> **Question 1**: "How does the defense refute our slide about the *hierarchy*?" (The hierarchy in this story simply showed which companies held control over which others and over which subsidiaries.) Power and control are key factors when it comes to perceptions of who may be seen as ultimately responsible. Framed that way, the mediator sees the common sense in the question and delivers it to the defense. The mediator had not previously received an answer and so went back with the question and returned with a simple answer: "They don't refute the facts on the slide, but they see no relevance."

> **Question 1a**: The plaintiff asked their *other* focus group "participant," the mediator: "What do you make of their answer?" His response: "The defense refuses to acknowledge the relevance because that weakens their position." The defense apparently had lost some credibility in the mediator's eyes.

Question 2: "How will you determine whose definition of property is correct?" The mediator responded with his own professional (and likely personal) criteria for defining property. This was very helpful as it was different from *either* the plaintiff's or the defense's criteria. Now, adjustments could be made by either side based on input from this de facto "focus group" to align more closely with the decision maker's view.

Question 3: "How will you decide whether the industry standards are the measuring stick for the defendant's conduct or—as the defendants are proposing—that industry standards are irrelevant; that the only thing that matters is a 'black and white' interpretation of the contract language?" Again, the mediator, acting in a participatory role, is likely to reveal positions of his "fellow participants" when offering his responses.

Question 4: "When you think about your own experiences with professional and/or private commitments, how would you prefer that contracts be interpreted? More like the defense version or more like the plaintiff version?" This question led the mediator to consider instead, how *jurors* would most likely evaluate the case. The mediator predicted that jurors would most likely interpret the contract the way they would want their own contract interpreted were they in the plaintiff's shoes—an assessment the defense, in its turn in the "rotation," said it refused to believe. This prompted an exchange between the two sides (though the mediator reserved his opinion during the exchange) of plaintiff and defense conducting a *formal* joint focus group—an unexpected turn in *any* mediation—in order to see for themselves which side jurors would more likely identify with in the case. A joint focus group was professionally conducted (at a later date), and it did indeed confirm the mediator's original predictions—and the case settled. Although the joint focus group could have gone the other way and contradicted the mediator's prediction, the plaintiff assumed that the worst-case scenario would be that they would go to trial, so *why not* do a focus group on the chance that the defense would "see the light." (This same mediator now occasionally recommends conducting joint focus groups when cases become stalled in mediation and the obstacle seems to be a debate over how jurors might react to certain key aspects of the case.)

Although the formal focus group was conducted at a later date, the following questions outline the rest of the ways the plaintiff made use of mediation as a de facto focus group. We leave it to you to consider how the potential responses to these framing questions could help strengthen the case story structure and eventual delivery to decision makers, in or out of mediation. Remember, these questions are posed to the mediator who is shuttling his negotiation efforts between the parties in separate rooms, thereby becoming an active participant in questions *and* responses.

Question 5: "Do you see 'broken commitments,' and if so, how?"

Question 6: "Does it make a difference to you if we revise our timeline of events to be more consistent with the defense's chronological approach, or is it more persuasive to you as is?" Asking a mediator to "rule" on the *persuasive*, not the supposedly *probative* effect, of a visual presentation tool in the case story delivery turns the attention to process and individual reactions, and away from a focus on just numbers and outcomes, which generally lie outside the human narrative.

Question 7: "Do we reinforce the defense by ruling out all their alternative interpretations, or do we need to address each one?" Again, learning how any kind of decision-making professional sees the story's strengths or weaknesses is a great help going forward.

Question 8: "How can we improve the credibility of our cost calculation?" This is where the plaintiff's case was most vulnerable because the plaintiff's expert already had changed the calculations in his report twice. The first time after the defense had pointed out an error and, the second time when a loss claim had been dropped. So, feedback from the mediator on this point was especially important to the plaintiff lawyers because they had considered settling for less *just because* of this perceived credibility weakness.

Question 9: "How can we bolster the consequences of the harms to the plaintiff without our efforts coming across as ploys for sympathy?" Asking, in essence, for coaching tips on presentation of the damages case form an active decision maker in real time.

Feedback from the mediator on each of the nine frames was invaluable to the plaintiff. They had been able to educate the mediator on their case story by going through the slides and asking the questions, and then were able to incorporate the mediator's feedback into revisions in their presentation for the joint focus group. The defense had been expecting the plaintiff to give the same presentation at the focus group as they had at mediation and were caught completely off guard. The more input sought after and received, the more your story delivery can evolve.

Even if a formal "no exchanges" presentation is insisted on at the start of the mediation there are still opportunities to engage in some form of debriefing, if only by carefully observing what's happening on the other side of the table. Or, if the other side is sequestered in another room, you can press the mediator into service for your cause by sending them back to the opposition with specific follow-up questions—though be sure to insist on a couple of follow-ups after your initial questions of "How so?" "What else?" and "Tell me more." These kinds of questions will most likely get substantive answers if you are clear, concise, and indicate that you are committed to the process. After all, if the other side refuses to answer your simple questions, *they* start to appear less and less like participants "in good faith."

In another example of a mediation where presentations took place but direct exchange between the parties was not permitted, the participants themselves proved to be highly valuable as a "focus group."

A medical neglect claim centered on a post-surgical follow-up, i.e., getting the patient seen, as having been delayed until it was far too late to do any good. There were three medical professional defendants seated along one side of the conference table as the plaintiff attorney had his paralegal set up a portable screen at the far end. From all indications from the mediator, this was a little unusual. Recognizing this, the plaintiff lawyer framed his departure from the expected routine by saying: "I've never really done this kind of thing before. But (eyeing the opposition counsel and the mediator in turn) because I really think there is a serious chance for settling this case here today, I'm just going to lay our cards right out on the table."

He proceeded to deliver an abbreviated version of the current opening for the trial, *with* demonstrative aids and excerpts of primarily *defense* witness statements displayed next to pictures of their faces—the very same faces sitting across the table. He only cut things short as he arrived at the details of the damages because several interesting and valuable responses were forthcoming.

This presentation produced definite input from the other professional "focus group" participant, the mediator. This mediator (who was also an attorney, which is often the case) had a long history of working with medical neglect cases, usually on the side of the doctors and the hospitals involved. The lawyer representing the plaintiff in the room had actually worked against him in a few prior cases representing injured patients of those same hospitals and doctors. He had noted a strong attitude this mediator had expressed consistently over that time: he typically placed a low—or even no—value on future medical procedures claimed as necessary by an injured plaintiff.

This case presentation dealt with just such a claimed harm and, in fact, it was a major feature of harms being claimed. Remarkably, in the first private discussion with him after the presentations, the mediator indicated he had already informed the defense that—contrary to his long-standing habit—he was viewing this "future" harm as one of the most *compelling* features of the plaintiff's case. His validation confirmed the power of the language choices, demonstrative aids, and sequencing of the delivery of that part of the plaintiff's case.

In particular, a slide had been produced that showed the interior anatomy of the plaintiff's affected limb. This anatomic illustration was reproduced across the chart nine times, in two horizontal rows. Each very red, mostly muscle-focused image was labeled with a date and a name for the procedure that had been tried in order to help relieve the plaintiff's pain and restore the function of his arm. The first eight images had the international "NO" symbol of a red circle with a diagonal slash through it superimposed over them. But the last one had a big question mark with the name of the procedure below: "Amputation." The doctors treating the plaintiff had agreed that the best chance for relief of pain or possibly even a slightly improved level of function was replacing his flesh-and-blood arm with plastic and metal.

In later trial testimony, each operation on this plaintiff would be exhaustively examined from every aspect of advisability and effectiveness. But, on this chart, the line of anatomical images leading, finally, to amputation invited viewers to build a chain of inevitability in their own minds about the need for, or *value* of, the last surgery. While the mediator never directly referenced the slide itself, his reactions and comments certainly did.

During the plaintiff presentation, the medical defendants at the table each revealed (because they were each unsuccessful at concealing) which parts of the story being delivered they strongly agreed with (to the point of smugly crossing arms and nodding vigorously) and, which points they strongly disagreed with (self-righteous snorts and eye rolling) and perhaps most importantly, which points they were most fearful of, or reluctant about (and were overwhelmed by a need to check their Blackberrys). With no words at all, they helped the plaintiff attorney refine his presentation strategy, sharpen his cross-examinations, identify the need for further discovery, and hone his case story for an eventual trial.

One defendant, a religious man by reliable accounts, raised his hands and pressed his palms together during one section of the case story. The topic was this medical professional's obligation to confirm any dangerous condition simply by *seeing* his patient, or at least, having some other medical professional take a look. Reading a bit of unspoken remorse in the defendant's unthinking gesture, the plaintiff attorney retooled his cross of the doctor for trial suggesting (but not directly declaring) *remorse* as an appropriate response to the defendant's repeated refusals to look at his own patient. When the time came for that stage of cross in trial, the doctor cried on the stand, which the jurors apparently took as a significant reaction because they subsequently assigned that doctor the lion's share of fault.

In another mediation concerning a car wreck case, the mediator started out by saying: "After reviewing both sides' written statements, we have to discuss the facts before we get to the numbers, because both sides are miles apart in terms of what this case is really all about. The defense statement does not address the plaintiff's position and vice versa." This mediator actually *requested* presentations from both sides to address specific topics in the case. For example, the effect of speed on impact and injury, an MRI that doesn't show brain injury, the effect of the natural aging process on injury, and other alternative causes of the claimed harms. Because they were not pivotal to the plaintiff's story, these topics had all been downplayed in their written mediation statement and, naturally, they *were* the core of the defense story. The plaintiff took the gist of the mediator's request to be "show me how you would reframe these defenses so I know how to negotiate each point."

The plaintiff took advantage of the opportunity to arm the mediator with their best story including consistent visual aids to back up the key points. In this way, the mediator and all those in the room had a compelling context within which to perceive and understand the specific topics. Perception being reality, managing both words and images significantly boosts influence during the process. The visuals showed that it was the *angle* of impact, more than the speed, that caused the injury; that the timeline, not an MRI (MRIs don't image this kind of injury) linked the injury to the impact; and that the path to estimating influence of the aging process on the injury was based on the post-impact history. All of these facts rendered any alternative causes of harm null and void.

As the presentation reframing each defense proceeded, the mediator visibly nodded in rhythmic confirmation with the pace of the plaintiff's oral delivery. The defendants visibly tensed during the presentation, confirming the areas where they felt most vulnerable. The content had been structured well in writing but it was the actual presentation that gave life to the story and how it would be perceived, gave negotiation tools to the mediator, and confirmed the defendant's weaknesses. Relying on a written statement alone could never have achieved this level of persuasion. After successful completion of the mediation, the mediator—who teaches CLEs on mediation—asked permission to use the plaintiff's visual presentation as an example in upcoming seminars.

Rehearsing for Failure

What if the other side opposes presentations in a mediation claiming they are beyond being influenced about their position on their case? Regardless of what posture they assume, what they are really saying is that they know that if they watch your presentation, there's a chance they could be influenced by you as to how *they* value the case and thus subsequently affect their chances in negotiating successfully for their side. This is what makes doing a presentation an *essential* part of a successful mediation process. The fact that during effective presentations influence really *does* happen is usually what drives the other side to try to *prevent* you from presenting. When the other side insists on no presentations, on no consideration of what the case is about, or even on no consideration of the value of the case, that is all the more reason that you should *insist* on delivering one. Doing so is essential to persuading your opponent to move from their self-protected tunnel vision toward *receiving* the different perspectives you have presented.

The same holds true for influencing a mediator. Mediators are capable of reacting much like all those judges you know who oppose voir dire conducted by attorneys—not only because of the judge's inherent bias, but because they have been forced to sit through so many badly managed voir dire examinations run by attorneys. Many mediators have the same knee-jerk negative reaction to the suggestion of attorney presentations simply because they've had to sit through so many *bad* ones, e.g., the plaintiff in a personal injury case just pushing "play" on their day-in-the-life video of their catastrophically injured client.

Often, the resistance to presentations is couched as being beneath the dignity of the participants ("We don't need to sit through a dog and pony show"). This response to the use of presentations suggests that all the professionals present are somehow immune to their effects. But, in fact, the opposite is true. Even if they may have been immune to poorly delivered presentations ("dog and pony shows") in the past, mediators and attorneys are just as susceptible to being strongly influenced by a presentation delivered well—however unwilling they may be to admit or, even recognize, that fact. Regardless of background or education we all make these decisions in the same way: we *reconstruct* the case story through *our own* filters based on *our own* perceptions of both the facts and the law and, on how the story has been delivered to us. The following is an excerpt from correspondence from opposing counsel prior to mediation:

> We are agreeable to mediating with plaintiffs prior to May 10 but do not think formal mediation is necessary. We do not believe it would be productive to have a neutral party tell us what our case is about or how it should be valued; *we understand what the case is about and how it should be valued.* Unfortunately, we do not believe that your clients have that same understanding.

Even if the other side's position is not expressed as crassly as in the above excerpt, the sentiment often can be undeniably present. If there is to be no presentation, then the risk for opposing counsel of actually being persuaded is eliminated, allowing them to sink deeper into their entrenched—and conveniently untested—position. Contrary to the spirit of our adversarial system, trying to avoid or run from potentially being influenced by fighting a presentation while, at the same time, loudly declaring "they've got nothing" starts to sound very much like someone who, as Shakespeare wrote, "doth protest too much."

These days, a large number of mediators choose to identify their style or approach as being aligned with one of two opposing poles: "facilitative" or "evaluative." These terms have been adopted to identify a mediator prone either to encourage *negotiation* or, to act like mediation is simply an arena for *arbitration.* The methods of approach differ in that a "facilitating" mediator asks more questions of each side, and an "evaluating" mediator makes more declarations to each side. With a mediator of the first type, the parties are *asked* "What *can* happen?" With a mediator of the second type, the parties are *told* what *will* happen.

When it comes to persuasion and influence, there are at least two immutable, though somewhat confounding, truths. The first is that, for all of us, *perception is reality.* But, the second is that, also for all of us, *things are not always what they seem.* It would *seem,* for example, that the more controlled, declarative, and "evaluative" mediator would be likely to oppose formal presentations. And though that is accurate, perversely, the more controlled, declarative, and evaluative the situation, the more susceptible to influence the mediator and all the participants are from even a minimally well-developed presentation—simply *because* the opportunities for influence to occur are so sharply curtailed in that environment. Just *one* potent, well-delivered reframe, can have a hugely disproportionate effect on an "evaluative" mediator than five so-so reframes offered to a "facilitative" mediator.

And, let's not forget their *own* reluctance most lawyers feel about preparing for and delivering a strong, well-crafted (including strong visual support), well-rehearsed mediation presentation. Unfortunately, there are usually just too many other things calling for attention on an attorney's plate, that mediation—the perennial "also-ran" of dispute resolution competition—tends to get pushed to "the bottom rung of the ladder." That means, just in terms of the odds, that nine times out of ten, his client's interests are sitting on that bottom rung too.

Avoiding making reasonable efforts to resolve a case at mediation isn't the only mistake attorneys risk making when they discount the value of mediation. Imagine for a moment, the way all parties involved in a *perfunctory* approach to mediation act—and interact. They walk in and immediately agree that any formal presentations are certainly beneath the "professional" (safely untested) level of discourse they want, i.e., the level that leaves their precious preconceptions unchallenged. As a result, *neither* attorney is tasked to present anything at all, much less a compelling story. The opposing sides are not required to consider anyone else's story or, much less any value put forward. Without presentations in the mediation process, strong movement from either side on differing perceptions of facts, events, applicable law or values of harms is suppressed.

In this kind of mediation environment, the mediator, whether of the "evaluating" school or the "facilitating," having a simple set of guidelines, all in neat black and white numbers, supplemented by unreliable juror verdict averages—everyone is more likely to be pushed farther apart on the way to either a poor resolution, or none at all. It would be difficult to construct a format more likely to discourage rapport while also avoiding useful grounds for serious discussion. Many decision-making professionals tend to think of such stripped-down, dollar-focused mediation sessions as more in line with a "real world" approach to case valuation and the resolution process. In fact, this approach is a severely impoverished reflection of the "real world," more so than most of these decision makers (attorneys, adjustors, etc.) would ever willingly admit—or even be able to recognize.

When an attorney simply throws down a number and continues to stand on that number instead of engaging, there is little to none of her client's *actual* ("real world") case story under consideration, i.e., the story behind the facts of the case. Nor is it being delivered with the best efforts of the professional advocate the client hired. As a consequence, the case story remains undelivered and *unheard* by the opposing parties and their representatives. The "reality" has been relinquished to the self-serving presumptions of the other side who "already know what this is about and what it's worth.

Instead of offering the other side the broadest opening for appreciating and understanding the many aspects of your positions, a narrative devoid of its human elements will only invite a flat wall of resistance, not the give-and-take of engagement or compromise. This is true more often than not because, regardless of what parts of the story actually manage to surface, their delivery will not be *within* the best case story context that could have been developed. With no compelling story to engage the decision makers on the opposing side, there is no emotional basis, no level of engagement (as with that of a well delivered story) from which their decisions *could* arise. There is nothing "on the table" that requires them to detach from their *own* preconceived presumptions about the case, its legitimacy or value. What's worse, without an opportunity to deliver a compelling case story, any strong challenge to what the other side sees as the accurate and reasonable value of the case has no perceptual foundation. Additionally, in their eyes, any visceral reactions on your part to strong—though unjustified—resistance on their part, will drive a wedge in any rapport with them (if there even *is* any at this point) serving only to make matters worse, not better when trying to move forward. This kind of mediation scenario makes for stubborn bargaining, which, in turn, encourages "chest bumping" over respect.

Without *both* sides presenting even a simple sketch of their case story, the brain's ability to decide and resolve that case story is handicapped. All cases are established, maintained, and eventually resolved in the minds of decision makers as human, face-to-face narratives, regardless of the legal claims being disputed. The reconstruction of every legal case story as an "embodied narrative" (that's what the framing and decision making experts call it) is the reality most legal training (and practice) does not take into account.

Legal decision-making research has recognized, since the early 1970s, that the "translation" of each case by each decision maker into their own *private case story* is an essential step in producing legal judgments. The perceived reality of any legal decision maker comes from constructing their own private *embodied narrative* of a case story. Nobody is immune to this inner narrative process. Nobody can avoid it. Nobody is above it. Accommodating this basic fact of legal life and adjusting your persuasive efforts to take advantage of it is what we are promoting here. Refusals to attend and consider presentations during the mediation process and continuing to stand on numbers alone, is nothing more than assuming, without question, that the case will be resolved through "chest bumping."

And even when cases *are* resolved in mediation this way, the "chest bump" approach leads to one of only two possible types of settlement outcomes:

1. A comprehensive and worthwhile resolution will be undermined by the "aftertaste" produced by unnecessary disengagement and antagonism.

2. An inadequate, unreasonable, and even unfair settlement will be recorded.

The chest-bumping approach to mediation which actively—sometimes aggressively—opposes using presentations, or even discussing, a case story, is analogous to how the current healthcare industry's priorities seem to be misaligned. Their approach to healing primarily puts patients and their families last. People familiar with modern medical business know that a hospital is set up, first and foremost, in the interests of its private ownership entity. Next comes its allegiance to healthcare providers, i.e., the insurance folks who refer to money paid out for patient medical care as their "loss." Next on the list, the institution's administrative needs and wants; after that come the requirements and requests of the hands-on healthcare workers. The very last priority of our current medical care system are the needs, concerns, and wishes of patients and their families.

Showing up for a mediation and opting only to go through the motions, still committed to standing on a particular number, almost *guarantees* that neither side will ever seriously challenge their *own* views—views that are by nature self-serving—of what "we know about the value of the case." Choosing not to prepare or deliver a presentation is choosing not to allow your client's position to be revealed to its best advantage in order to ensure the most favorable outcome possible. Cases get resolved either way, but the numbers only, "chest-bump" approach will never leave a lawyer with a sense of certainty that all was actually done that could have been done to gain the most advantageous resolution for his client.

Interestingly, the justification often cited for sticking with the numbers first, and numbers only, approach are the jury verdicts "in these kinds of cases" published in verdict research. Believing that juror responses to a particular case presentation on a particular day can be accurately and reliably quantified and predicted ranks among the worst examples of the misuse of legal research data. Just because this data is so commonly used "don't make it so." It's a fictional endorsement of its value in resolving individual matters. The truth is, jurors can be and often are the least predictable and most challenging element in the whole legal decision making system—by design they are the ultimate "wild cards."

Setting the Stage for Mediation

There is another way to think about the process of mediation as you approach it in each case. The potential advantages especially accrue for plaintiff attorneys who choose to rethink old attitudes. Imagine rethinking the approach to mediation from a viewpoint of, "I'll try and get this case settled . . . maybe," to a viewpoint of "I wonder just how many gains we can make, whether or not we resolve this case today."

Would you choose to do some, no, or lots of preparation? Would you hold out for an oral presentation or make no presentation at all? If you choose an oral presentation, would you prepare and present visual demonstratives with it or not? How would you seek out a mediator? How much thought would you give to location and facilities and their possible influence on the proceedings? How would the list of participants be set up? Would you choose to send your presentation materials out ahead of time? How would you decide whether to do so or not? How would you determine how much time to invest? How would you determine the most worthwhile goals for the process? What would be included in your presentation, e.g., focus group video excerpts, PowerPoint programs, witness video clips, etc. How often would you rehearse your presentation, and who would have critical input on your performance?

These are just some of the variables that can affect the relative value of resolution in mediation, either in terms of a settlement on the spot and/or gains in other areas beyond immediate resolution. In order to give you, your client, and her case story the best shot at the best outcome, you can—and should—determine beforehand all the relevant needs and potentials of your mediation presentation and negotiation.

And speaking of the case story, it really helps if you have one. Focus groups, well run and conducted before mediation, can also reveal the best *frames* and *anchors* that will put your case across *as a story* instead of just as a "case." Compare in your mind the difference between an opening statement that is a dry inventory of facts, i.e., "the evidence will show," and an opening statement that is a compelling human narrative that engages one and all—girded by the facts. In any conflict, there are many factors to investigate and many threads to develop in order to craft the strongest story package for the facts—and for the law. Likewise, there are many resources to draw on for a more comprehensive review of them all.[26]

The following are four essential factors to developing and delivering a strong case story package for the mediation process:

1. **Point of View**. A strong case story needs a central character that remains central throughout. For example, the American Association for Justice, through its senior members and researchers Greg Cusimano and David Wenner, have long recommended that, as a default position for plaintiff personal injury cases, case stories are stronger and achieve better results when delivered with the *defendant* "on stage" as the central character through whom the rest of the characters are presented *and* perceived. A singular point of view helps to quickly invite decision makers to build their own private stories of each case, reliably sorting out the main and minor *characters*, as well as the main and minor *actions* undertaken by those characters, and with one consistent player at the center.

---

26. Oliver, supra, n. 6. *See also* Jim Perdue, *Winning With Stories: Using the Narrative to Persuade in Trials, Speeches & Lectures*, State Bar of Texas, Houston, TX (2006); and Ball, David, *Theater Tips and Strategies for Jury Trials* (Louisville, CO: National Institute for Trial Advocacy, 2003) for a start.

2. **Active Ingredient**. What is the primary force driving the events of the story? This is similar to asking, what is the "motive" driving the choices and actions of the "characters" in the story. Once efforts to develop a story *as a story* have revealed the strongest motive, the work is only half done because the driving force behind choices and events is best delivered to the other side *indirectly*. A lawyer simply standing up in front of decision makers and accusing the other side of, say, being "greedy," is a lawyer satisfied with only "bumping chests" with the other side. Although it takes some work to devise the strongest, yet indirect way to get the active ingredient of a case across to the other side, experience will show that it is worth the effort.

3. **Language and Images**. These help to build the *anchors* of your story that decision makers can condition themselves to employ. An effective delivery of a case story relies on carefully thought out and carefully presented language, i.e., a vocabulary list or "glossary" of the story is essential to creating a string of mental images, a "storyboard" of your story's key "chapters." As anchor points, the mutually supportive phrases and images provide the cues for the story each *individual* listener builds from your presentation.

4. **Story Sequence**. Presenting a story in a sequence, designed (and preferably already tested in focus groups) to invite decision makers to build the most engaging and memorable narrative they can, may be the most influential factor of all. Keep in mind that sequence is not always about chronology. Think about starting a medical neglect story at the point of injury, then jumping back to the original medical circumstances and covering the risks, the proper procedures and what the outcome is when the rules are followed and procedures are done correctly, thus delivering the patient from the hazards risked under those circumstances. Imagine the difference between the internal narratives decision makers would build from listening to that kind of sequence as opposed to listening to a more chronological sequence in which the patient gets sick or hurt, seeks help from medical care professionals and, despite their many persistent and heroic efforts on the patient's behalf, despite all the care, something goes wrong (medical professionals are "only human" after all). Where you start, and the steps you follow through to the end of the story—delivered consistently in every recitation of the story—can be quite persuasive for decision makers in, or out, of court.

No matter how you choose to develop the sequence of your case story, or which factors you choose to use in that process, when you walk into mediation you want to be ready to deliver *that* story and reference *that* story, and revive *that* story at each stage of the process for the mediator *and* for the parties who will ultimately decide the matter. Doing so ensures that all the other benefits of the efforts you've put into the mediation process will continue to accrue.

Getting Points Seen

Put the argument into a concrete shape, into an image,
some hard phrase, round and solid as a ball,
which they can see, and handle,
and carry home with them, and the cause is half won.
—*Ralph Waldo Emerson*

A visual story is a powerful story. It uses visual aids to invite decision makers to create their own mental imagery linked to your key word and image anchor points and, is consistently presented in the best possible story sequence. These kinds of *anchor effects* can be successfully achieved by way of a carefully delivered sequence of words or phrases, tied to select well-crafted images, thereby managing and guiding the perceptions of decision makers along the path you would like their private case stories to follow. Facts and law do not decide cases, *perception* of facts and law do. Imagine for a moment, walking into your next mediation with a powerful case story, fully supported by well-considered and well-prepared visuals, ready to catch your opponent—and perhaps the mediator too—a bit off guard. Preparing for mediation with a *storyboard* of key visual images to invite *anchoring effects* for the key phrases in the delivery of your case story, is a long way from being resigned to the self-defeating "here we go again" approach.

Consider the format of your written mediation statements. Many attorneys follow a mediation statement format that has been predefined by their firm for use in every case, even when the sequence or topics may not be persuasive for, or even relevant to, the case at hand. For example, the typical topic sequence for the plaintiff is: Introduction, Liability, Personal Life and Activities, Injuries and Treatment, Damages, and Conclusion. Knowing that the most persuasive story is the one which will suggest the most productive topics and sequence to use, avoid encouraging construction of case stories you don't want embedded in the decision makers' minds. The written part of your preparation is an opportunity to engage the mediator on a higher level by also including visual support to illustrate the case story. Embedding visual anchors in a written narrative that is sent to the mediator and/or other side ahead of time can help you start the process on a completely different footing. By "embedding" we mean using small, full-color versions of your storyboard visual aids within the text at the proper points, not indexed and tabbed on the back end. Your written presentation with its supporting visuals can capture the readers' attention before mediation even begins.

We live in the age of "screens"—television, desktop, laptop, iPad, cell phone—and they all predispose us to being moved by *potent* visuals. As well, since we live in such a visually saturated media culture, decision makers likely could feel distinctly deprived if they aren't provided images to help them turn a phrase into an *anchor*. So, knowing how powerful the visual image is in our culture, what would keep you from preparing and showing images you most want to be used by decision makers?

Preparing to deliver—both to show and to tell—a powerful case story is crucial. Not only must the delivery of the case story's strengths be as persuasive as possible, the story must also be presented in such a way as to most effectively undermine the other side's story strengths and to undermine, if not negate, their rebuttals. And in the legal arena, there is no other presentation device or technique so consistently underappreciated, underutilized, or undervalued than the tool of the visual demonstrative aid, i.e., "putting the argument into a concrete shape." Most lawyers tend to think of demonstrative aids as first, a *cost* to them and their clients, and second, as typically linked only to trials. As a result, attorneys generally do not commit the time, energy, and resources necessary to create strong visual aids until the case has moved to the trial phase. But, by then, they've often squandered the time they could have had to do the important job of influencing decision makers' visual perceptions.

Recently, the plaintiff's bar has become very interested in the human capacity for self-conditioning. Conditioned responses are also the result of what frequently turns up in CLE events and journal articles under the heading "Anchoring Effects." The most common anchors under discussion are numbers used to condition damage amounts for decision makers and how smaller order numbers, often linked to "hard" damages can needlessly serve to drive down non-economic numbers.[27] *Anchors* are conditioned responses to certain cues, so for example, a low cost number shown early in evidence for a "hard" number, let's say the high four-figure cost of a funeral can become associated with a response by the decision maker (who is other than consciously using that number as a "ceiling" to use when considering values of all the harms) for how low the *overall* damage picture should be. Perceived that way, additional amounts will tend to "look better" to that person when they are smaller and reduced, not larger or expanded.

The cues that we all use to condition our responses have two basic parts. The first is typically a *word* or a *phrase* from the "vocabulary" of a particular story; the second is a *mental image* also linked to that story. A properly delivered *mental image* accompanying a set phrase, encourages the decision maker to "stick" the anchor in their *own* mind for their response. *Mental imagery* is the part most attorneys have not been trained to value, never mind use, to their client's best advantage. However, the properly delivered mental image and phrase encourages the decision maker to stick the anchor in their mind as if projected there on an internal "screen."

27. Most plaintiff attorneys look for substantial "hard" or economic damages to lead their discussion of harms and loss values under the mistaken impression they will be used as the lawyers wish they will be used: as a floor, not a ceiling. Anchors rarely work that way, unless you help them.

If a plaintiff's attorney drops the phrase "hard working family" into their story delivery without providing visual cues tied to that phrase, they are less able to manage what mental images—if any—may come up in a decision maker's mind. Some decision makers will be cued, as was intended, to bring up certain responses; others will be cued to do the opposite. Instead of conditioning a response of high value to the phrase and images about well-being among that family, the response elicited could be that of suspicion of lawyers trying to make verbal appeals to sympathy during legal proceedings. Though both responses can be elicited by conditioning, neither response is automatic. With carefully delivered cues in a case story, influencing *perceptions* can influence *associations*. Doubling your potential impact by tying words to images in your delivery just makes good sense.

The good news is that almost anyone will accept the "invitation" to link the anchored phrases and images in their heads *as long as* they are delivered well within the overall context of the case *as a story*. Managing mental images takes a bit more thought, preparation, and skill than just asking the spouse of the injured party to give you a copy of the last family portrait to blow up for viewing during mediation, or than pushing "play" on a DVD settlement brochure. If the combined phrase and image are going to serve as a constructive anchor point in the case story, there is some artfulness required when trying to find—and deliver—the images that will have the most persuasive effect on decision makers' responses to the phrase "close, hard-working family."

Vivid visual demonstratives of different areas of life enjoyed by the "close, hard-working family," before the events leading to the lawsuit, can help when sequenced carefully throughout your presentation. The image of family members gathered "closely" and engaged in highly valued, "traditional" activities, even just hinted at with visual aids—photos or snippets of family "home movies"—and depicted as a storyboard of several events over time, is a fine start to introducing *mental imagery* into your presentation. But keep in mind, the response you are looking for, the link you want your decision makers to make, is a sense of the *loss* of that aspect of well-being; of its having been *taken away* or *removed* by the acts of the defendant. For example, showing one member of the family as literally "missing" from the "before" images of "family well-being," by leaving an empty silhouette, or showing an insert of how, or where, that person has been—perhaps permanently—separated from, or relegated to a position outside of the family whole, invites the desired responses you had intended decision makers to associate with the imagery. Think then, if they are also hearing—while the imagery is in front of them—something like, "You can still hear the voices, and the sounds of [the event, activity] just around the corner, as the sun slowly heads toward the horizon. But, sadly, the strongest voice, the loudest laugh, has been taken away, because the person with that voice can be found, virtually imprisoned indoors every day, unwillingly absent from their spot in the family; instead dealing with the treatment, the physical therapy, or the debilitating effects of medication, while trying to manage the immobilizing pain the defendant's actions left him with after . . . ."

A growing trend in the field of mediation preparation has been the use of professionally created video presentations. Whether from depositions, witness interviews, "day in the life" clips, or choice statements from focus group participants, video can be a powerful medium to use when delivering a client's story. This is the ideal opportunity to get feedback on your witnesses "straight from the horse's mouth." The mediator, opposing counsel, and their client are usually very forthcoming with critiques of a witness's credibility, demeanor, contribution, and overall effectiveness. However, when it comes to presenting witnesses on video in mediation (or focus groups), less really *is* more. From your chosen witness's performance, carefully select only the very best (or worst) parts for a presentation of no more than five minutes overall. You will be surprised by the wealth of impressions and responses to brief, but targeted, displays like this, even from experts testifying on very complex subjects.

During mediation, showing short video excerpts from the group process and discussions of a focus group already conducted for the case can create leverage with opposing counsel and a mediator, both of whom otherwise would only have the jury verdict averages in "similar" cases to rely on. While focus group results are not predictive of trial verdicts, they are a strong part of litigation research that can offset the results of jury verdict reports—reports that are often inaccurate predictors of future individual case results. Also, showing video clips of focus group participant discussions at mediation is often more persuasive than presenting the numeric results the focus group produced. The mediator and opposing party can judge the participants' credibility and engagement for themselves as they hear individual versions of the case story (they thought they knew all about) reframed by "real life" decision makers.

These videos can also be interlaced with PowerPoint images, thereby creating powerful multi-modal presentations. Again, imagine how the negotiation dynamic will shift when one side enters the room with a polished and well-organized presentation of their story, while the other side has only a legal pad with several "killer" facts written on it. Using videos and visuals also demonstrates a commitment to the most effective delivery of your client's case that cannot be ignored.

What Can Happen?

Many attorneys fear "giving their case away" at mediation; they see mediation as only arming the opposition for trial. Let's look at the odds. If you are going to play the cards you have, there is an eighty-four percent chance that the opportunity to do so will be in mediation *first*. And, if you don't play your cards in mediation, you will likely never get an opportunity to play them *at all*, thus forfeiting the opportunity to reap their potential benefits. Second, mediation offers an opportunity to learn where you stand with your best story delivery *to date.* As pointed out earlier, the lessons available from using mediation as a focus group enable you to improve your story presentation, to better strengthen your position in the event of an actual trial. Lastly, if you *don't* show and tell the whole story at mediation, the feedback you get will be unreliable. Remember, decisions are based on the sum of the whole, not on isolated parts. You need to provide the mediator and the other side with your *whole* story, in its most current form, in order for them *to provide you* with any feedback of real *value.*[28]

One caveat here. If you do end up at trial, you never want to go with precisely the same story presentation you used in mediation. Always revise your story frames, edit your storyboard demonstratives, and perhaps alter your story sequence in order to raise your story presentation to the next level. There is never just one way to tell the story and never just one demonstrative aid to illustrate the facts about a single case. If the other side is smart, they will do the same.

The cost of litigation is often steep. But, so is the cost of the outcome of a poorly managed settlement. When plaintiffs settle cases prior to trial—as most do—the attorney needs to be able to provide their clients with the reassurance that all that reasonably could be done *has* been done to assure that a proper value was reached in the resolution of their case. More and more plaintiff attorneys are discovering what a key role a proper presentation in mediation plays in achieving that end.

Consider these comments from a team of two attorneys who had been dealing with lengthy litigation in a particular variety of insurance bad faith cases regarding the many post-sale coverage products offered to car buyers. They made the choice to invest the time and resources to craft the best possible mediation presentation. Here's what they said afterward:

> After spending seven and a half years in litigation, which included two appeals, significant motion practice and literally thousands of documents, [we were able to] organize, sequence, and present the evidence in a way that made it speak volumes for our cause. I am absolutely convinced that our opposing counsels were blown away by our presentation . . . . After seven and a half years without a single meaningful offer, we were successful resolving our case just two days after [our presentation].

And:

> We got our case simplified to the point it could be presented in just a few, simple slides. After cross-examining the opposing parties' insur-

28. This principle applies to focus group work as well. "Piecemeal" research gets broken results.

> ance expert using [our presentation] sequencing, and when the other side saw our demonstrative aids . . . we were able to settle the case.

The two attorneys had utilized the story sequence they had carefully crafted for mediation as a story line to follow in their cross-exam of the other side's expert, all while referencing visual aids to help in conditioning decision maker's responses. They were able to consistently turn *the other side's* best witness into a witness consistently supporting perceptions of the plaintiff's side. A couple of days later, the demonstrative aids they had created to serve as visual anchors for the key phrases in their story line *erased* over seven years of stiff opposition to basically *any* resolution of that case, never mind a worthwhile one!

It can be challenging adding new techniques to your presentation repertoire, like story sequencing, anchoring, and reframing, but waiting for trial to try all of it for the first time can be suicidal. When it comes to developing new skills in persuasion, the experience of delivering the story *as a story*, even in written form, is invaluable. For example, preparing a presentation for mediation in a medical neglect case, plaintiff's counsel was having a hard time delivering one part of the story sequence while keeping the viewpoint of his story locked on the defendant doctor. The solution he employed was to "create" another set of characters—by carefully presenting the *proper* choices and actions in the case story context as they *should* have been executed under the circumstances of the defendant's negligent acts at the time by *reasonable medical professionals* acting according to proper standards.

The key persuasive task was to establish and reinforce the anchor—through a mental image—of a hypothetical *reasonable surgeon* who did things the right way *before* introducing the negligent choices and acts of the defendant. Part of the value of this tack in story sequencing is not only to create the sharpest contrast possible between the *right* way and the *wrong* way of doing things by a professional, but also to help decision makers focus on the story from the point of view of the professional (the doctor) and *not* the patient. And definitely *not* from the point of view of an injured patient with yet *another* of those notorious personal injury lawsuits. After a successful resolution, the attorney took the written part of his presentation around to several individuals in order to test his efforts at sequencing the defendant and hypothetical *reasonable surgeons.* Here's what he had to say:

> I polled everyone I let read the submission. Without exception, everyone's comments were only about [defendant doctor] and what he did/did not do when asked what their initial impressions and thoughts were about the case. Nothing about [plaintiff] until I brought her up, and then the comments were that she should get everything she asked for. It was almost as if the point were assumed.
>
> Interestingly, a couple of people even commented that it was clear how the "good surgeons" do this particular procedure. I couldn't believe it

> when I heard it. They were talking about the hypothetical surgeon like s/he was a real person that I had identified by name.[29] I know these techniques work even better when done verbally, but this was a good first step . . . . I had time to stop and think about what I was trying to do since I was writing it.

In the case of a workplace brain injury caused by severe neglect of safety training and oversight by a residential home construction company run by a charity, the plaintiff attorney had been laughed out of the office and off the phone several times by the team representing the well-known charity and its insurers. Much like those lawyers who wrote how well ". . . *we understand what the case is about and how it should be valued*," the attorneys on the other side had been "spared" any truly persuasive experiences that might compete with their position and, further, that might well take root in the minds of decision makers. That is, until they got to the plaintiff attorney's mediation presentation.

There, they discovered a story line that was sequenced in a unique way, where the verbal and visual aid anchors of the key story points were delivered according to what they—the defense—had indicated they look at as *their* stronger points, finishing, naturally with their oft repeated point: "Nobody is going to award a huge verdict against this charity, especially in the town where it's based!" The plaintiff's case story sequence began with the least of the defense's "strong points," reframing each with a demonstrative aid and a word or phrase to help decision makers anchor, or condition, themselves to that point inside the overall story narrative.

The final anchor was a series of demonstrative aids, all with headings (in red typeface) with the key phrase: "What kind of 'charity' does/says/withholds/keeps/does not . . . ?" Within eight hours and with the help of that brand new perspective on the case—the case that the other side had insisted it "understood so well"—the value of settlement had risen so far above the small number it had been stagnant at for years that the plaintiff's attorney told her client it was a settlement value they simply could not refuse.

Because so few cases get to trial, getting experience practicing more persuasive influence skills in your delivery can be a real challenge. Many attorneys will prepare a presentation for a focus group, but don't realize that preparing and presenting for mediation offers an invaluable addition to getting that practice in without waiting for trials. Not only is the aim of adding persuasive presentations to your mediations "settling for more, not less," adding them almost *always* ensures that more, not less, *will be* the outcome.

---

29. Actually, the hypothetical surgeon *was* identified by name—"reasonable surgeons"—and by the mental images marshaled to reinforce that perception. Anchoring effects work.

Afterword

These are my principles, and if you don't like them . . . well, I have others.
—Groucho Marx

Appendix One

Function Follows Forms

The following are some examples of some basic survey forms that can be used during focus groups to track private impressions near the start, near the end, and even afterwards. Every one can be expanded for help with the particular needs of the case story you are presenting, but be careful about the temptation to tell people what you want by way of the questions you ask, in lieu of finding out what they really have to offer.

The second confidentiality form is for use with the professionals working a focus group (court reporters, video, hotel, and research facility people) as well as any other observers that may be watching the event.

Confidentiality Agreement and Release

In participating in this focus group today, I understand that issues under discussion can include actual cases being prepared for trial. Names of litigants, attorneys, and other information about the case(s) may be revealed to me.

By signing below, I agree to hold all such information completely confidential until such time as I am made aware that the case has been legally resolved.

I also understand that videotaping of the group may be used for educational purposes and/or preparation of a case, and I agree to the use of that tape for those purposes only.

______________________________________ Name (please print)

______________________________________ Signature

______________________________________ Address

______________________________________ City, state, zip

______________________________________ Daytime phone

Confidentiality Agreement and Release

In providing professional services for, or observing focus group projects involving [company], I understand that material used in each such project can include actual cases being prepared for trial. Names of litigants, attorneys, and other information about the case(s) and consulting methods may be revealed to me and employees of ____________________ working on these projects.

By signing below, I, and all employees and/or agents of ____________________, agree to hold all such information completely confidential until such time as I am made personally aware that any such case has been legally resolved. And I agree to refrain from adopting or using such methods observed, which may be particular to services provided by [company], without first obtaining written permission to use them.

I also understand that videotaping of any groups observed by employees and/or agents of ____________________ may be used for educational purposes and/or preparation of a case, and agree to the use of that tape for those purposes only.

____ Name (please print)

____ Signature

____ Address

____ City, state, zip

____ Daytime phone

Name: ____________________________

Post-Opening Questions

It is almost certain that your leanings, your understandings, and eventual conclusions will change as you hear more. But, going by just what you've heard so far—and knowing your view can change a lot later—please answer the following six questions with your <u>first and strongest</u> impressions.

1. What brought about this lawsuit? ____________________________

2. Around what person, group, or organization does this case seem to revolve?

Who next, after that? ____________________________

3. What will you expect to hear from the plaintiff's side? ____________________________

4. What will you expect to hear from the defense? ________________

____
____
____
____
____
____
____

5. About what one thing (you can only pick one) are you most curious to learn more facts? ________________

____
____
____
____
____
____

6. How will knowing that help you? ________________

____
____
____
____
____
____
____
____

Post-Closing Surveys

In a couple lines, as if telling your best friend, describe what this case is really all about. ______________________________

____

____

____

____

____

If you were the attorney defending [XX], doing the best job you possibly could, what would you be sure the jury understood? ______________________________

____

____

____

____

____

____

____

____

____

If you were the plaintiff's lawyer, what would you be sure you got across to the jury? ______________________________

____

____

____

____

____

____

____

____

____

____

For the attorneys who presented the case to you today, please comment honestly on how each of the following parts of their presentation came across to you. Use complete sentences, please.

DEFENSE COUNSEL:

Eyes, gestures, and voice quality: ______________________________

Overall presentation: ______________________________

PLAINTIFFS' COUNSEL:

Eyes, gestures and voice quality: ______________________________

Overall presentation: ____

____

____

____

____

____

____

____

Just before deliberating, do you tend to favor the plaintiff or the defense side?

____

____

____

How did you come to that position? ______________________________

____

____

____

____

____

____

____

____

____

____

____

For you to change your mind, what will have to be shown to you? __________

____

____

____

____

____

____

____

____

____

____

____

If you could have more information on only one topic in the case before you, what would you most want it to be about? ______________________

Name: ______________________

Post-Verdict Survey

Almost all deliberations demand compromising on some points. Often those compromises are made without even stating them aloud, just to get an agreement. Now that you have finished, take a moment and please answer these questions as if you were the sole person, completely in charge of the decision in this case.

1. If it were just up to you and nobody else, how different—or similar—would your personal verdict be?

Similar in these ways: ______________________

Different in these ways: ______________________

2. Which points in the case do you and your group agree were strong or important? ________________________

3. To which points do you think they failed to give enough attention? ________

4. If it were you, would you bring this lawsuit to court? Yes ____ No ____

If **yes**, please explain: ________________________

If **no**, please explain: ________________________

Appendix Two

Glossary

Active Ingredient

The driving force behind the events in a **case story**.

Active Party

The driving agent behind the events in a **case story**; often, but not always, the **point of view** of a **case story**.

Anchors

A phrase connected with an image (actual or imagined) that conditions or cues a reaction, such as an emotional response or a **frame of reference** from the individual decision maker's life experience.

Case Story

The case developed to be delivered *as a story* is different—and more than—just the legal elements collected to prove—or disprove—a claim. All stories follow a three-step narrative: **Context, Conflict, Resolution**.

Case Story Construction

The **case story** a decision maker develops is best seen as "construction project." Each decision maker (re)builds his own version of the **case story** being presented to him by an attorney; that private version of the **case story** is the one from which he will realize a judgment.

Case Story Sequence

To *deliver* a case *as a story*, **context**, **conflict**, and **resolution** need to be filled out with basic story **frames** (key topics), up to three per step. Frames cover the details of the circumstances, the rules or laws that apply to those circumstances, the way things would look when handled properly, what actually happened, what that did (or did not) cause, and what are the consequences (if any) that decision makers need to be concerned with in order to realize a judgment. The **sequence** of story **frames** must be defined within the three-step narrative not only during *development* of the **case story** but also for *delivery* of the **case story**. The **sequence** of story **frames** dictates every part of delivery, including voir dire (where allowed), opening statement, and who the first four to five witnesses will be as they must be the witnesses best able to deliver the story—in sequence.

Context, Conflict, Resolution

Context—what the circumstances are; who the characters are

Conflict—actions and what they cause to happen to the characters under the circumstances

Resolution—in the legal arena, there are two parts to this step: 1) defining what happens to the characters as a result of the actions under the circumstances and 2) answering the question, "What do we want decision makers to do about that?"

Demonstrative Visual(s)

Illustrations, photos, graphs, or any type of visual tool (alone or in combination) reflecting a key topic or factor through imagery in the **case story** being presented. *Each* **frame** in a **case story sequence** needs a **demonstrative visual** to serve (in conjunction with a word or phrase) as an **anchor** for that **frame** in decision makers' minds. Displaying **demonstrative visuals** in the proper **case story sequence** helps to anchor and reinforce that sequence for decision makers. For the most persuasive effect during delivery, **demonstrative visuals** should always come first, *then* testimony and document exhibits to *support* what the **demonstrative visuals** have evoked in decision makers' minds.

Follow-Up Questions

A key factor in developing valuable information with focus group participants, during voir dire and with witnesses, is the use of short, *non-leading* **follow-up questions** that actually invite individuals to *expand* their answers by filling them in from their own experiential **frame of reference** on that topic. The formula I suggest are two or three **follow-up questions** after each initial answer on each important topic. For example, "How so?", "What else?", and "Please, say some more."

Frames, Framing, Frame of Reference

Frames—the basic building blocks, or key topics, of the **case story sequence**

Framing—the overall structuring of the **case story**

Frame of Reference—is cued or evoked in a decision maker by **anchors** that reinforce her collection of life experiences as sorted by similar content or meaning, i.e., attitudes toward work, sympathetic reactions, protective responses, sense of "fair play," biases, authoritarian or "underdog" attitudes, political or moral beliefs, etc.

Generalization, Deletion, Distortion

These are the three fundamental cognitive filters affecting our conscious appreciation of the kinds of perceptions from which a **case story** is (re)built by decision makers. Their effects on focus group participants' story building can be tracked and later used to improve a **case story** presentation's persuasive effect.

Generalization— "What do all reasonable physicians do under these circumstances?"

Deletion— "Once he's in the next hospital, little can be done to stop the advanced disease process." (invites deletion of first hospitalization)

Distortion— "Almost all patients with this kind of injury recover and return to work within six months and have no future problems." (invites distortion of conditions of patients who do not recover in this way)

"Empathic Resonance"

See **rapport**, below.

Juror Job

During voir dire, the "job frame" applied to potential jurors, and reinforced with the seated jurors during trial, can provide multiple persuasive benefits. For example, most people want to do "their job" as well as it can be done and are typically not intimidated by working at a challenging new one, such as juror.

Landmine

Any factor, large or small, perceptual, factual, or legal, that could distract a decision maker from (re)building a preferred version of the **case story**.

Mirroring

An either automatic or deliberate matching of postures, gestures, movements, voice tones or volumes, rate of speech, and other behavioral expressions; the physical, behavioral pathway that produces **rapport**.

Organizing Filters

The basic elements which define a story's **scope** for an individual (re)authoring that story, i.e., person(s), place(s), time, action(s), or data and information; sometimes referred to as sorting filters.

Other-than-Conscious

The majority of mental functioning that takes place outside of conscious awareness of that functioning. As such, it can be said that story (re)construction by the decision maker and his eventual judgment reflects decisions that are more "realized" than they are "made" in the traditional sense.

Point of View

The person, character, organization, or entity in the **case story** that depicts for decision makers who (or what) occupies "center stage," i.e., who (or what) is the story primarily about. Often, but not always, the **active ingredient** of a **case story**.

Presuppositional Questions

Questions that assume a fact, a condition, or situation exists without directly expressing it. These kinds of questions are very useful for focus group participants, potential jurors during voir dire, and witnesses. For example, often it is valuable to ask a question that presupposes *an answer* without presupposing the *right answer.* "Who here has some thoughts about that?" presumes there are thoughts to share. "Who thinks that is the most important thing about this?" pushes the "right" answer. "Does anyone have any thoughts about that?" presumes the whole answer can be just a simple "Yes" or "No."

Rapport

The sense of "connection" that fosters interest, and even altruism, between human beings. In its most intense form, it creates what is known as "**empathic resonance**," and you can't get there without **mirroring**, first.

Scope

The perceived reach of a story—narrow or broad—in terms of numbers, people, actions, time, or places. A narrow story scope would be reflected by something like a "split-second decision." A broad story scope would be reflected by something like "a dozen designers working over a number of years."

Sensory Preferences

Of the five sensory systems—gustatory, olfactory, visual, auditory, and kinesthetic—three of them are the fundamental building blocks through which we perceive our inner realities: visual, auditory, and kinesthetic. Perceptions of facts decide cases, and the basic material that those perceptions are constructed from are images, words, and feelings. Each need to be addressed congruently during the delivery of a **case story**.

Theme

Each **case story** should have only one **theme** in its presentation. When asked, "What is this really all about?" regarding a **case story**, if the decision maker's answer encompasses the emotional, moral, and rational basis for the story, it is a statement of that person's **theme** for that **case story**. The attorney's job is not to repeat a theme phrase over and over, for example, "this case is about putting process over people," but rather to deliver the **anchors** and **frames** that make up his client's best **case story sequence** well enough to evoke similar, though usually not identical, answers to the question, "What is this really all about?" from every decision maker involved.

Appendix Three

Theory in Practice
Sample Opening Statements

While Planning Other Things

Here are three more examples of how attorneys rose to the challenge of introducing their case stories to focus groups inside the five-to-seven-minute time constraint. In each, the attorneys' targets are given for the elements of their particular story to be presented and tested with the group. Then, the text of their presentations appears and, appended to the end of each opening, there is an analysis made at the time of how well they hit those targets. As you read each opening, take some time to do your own assessment of how well the intended elements are being communicated. Then, compare your findings with those appearing at the end of each statement.

Make every effort to put yourself in the position of a participant, struggling to make sense of the two stories being introduced, just after you've heard the introduction in Chapter Four. Avoid planning what you would do or say differently. On the first pass through, simply concentrate on the scope of the story you are learning about, who the major and minor characters are, what the major and minor actions are, in what order they are introduced, and roughly what it is all about from your non-professional vantage. Review the text again for its story structure, and then compare your notes with both the targets being aimed at and the observations in the analyses done at the time.

Case One

Plaintiff—Suggested Story Elements

Scope	Generally narrow on Place and Time, but broader on Acts, Numbers (especially responsibilities of reasonable owners)
Point of View	Responsible Work-Site Owner
Sequence	1. Premises owner, work-site safety rejections. 2. Should have done versus what they actually did. 3. Injury, consequent harms, permanent damages.
Theme	*Rejected Responsibility for Worker Safety*

OPENING STATEMENT

Mr. Harris:

In August of 1999, a healthy young man went to work at the Real Steel Company. He arrived for work at the appointed time, just before four a.m. By 6:30 a.m., he was at General Hospital, where he was being treated for severe carbon monoxide poisoning. How this gentleman got to General Hospital and who let him down in those two hours is what this case is all about. Ladies and gentlemen, my name is Michael Harris, and I represent that man. His name is Andy Taylor.

Now Andy Taylor was thirty-five years old when this incident occurred. And although the physicians at General Hospital were able to save his life, he's going to be a mental cripple for the rest of his life because of carbon monoxide poisoning. At the time that this happened, he was a boilermaker, and now he can barely carry on a conversation.

One of the things we're going to learn in this case, one of the first things, is there is absolutely no question that the carbon monoxide that injured Andy was produced by the Real Steel Company. We're going to learn that the Real Steel Company owns the entire plant; they own the foundry; they own all the buildings; they own the mill, and they own and control all the equipment on this site. They know all about making steel, they know and control the production and they operate and control what we call—what they call the Baumco Tower. This diagram that we see up here, it's been up here for the whole time, this shows this exhaust apparatus where the accident occurred. Mr. Taylor was standing up here on what they call the Secondary Venturi platform when he was overcome by the carbon monoxide.

Now why is Real Steel Company responsible for Andy's injury? Well, it breaks down to three reasons, and they have to do with, number one, the nature of the danger that he was exposed to. It has to do with what a reasonable work-site owner would do under the circumstances. And it has to do with what Real actually did in this case, OK. So three things.

What's the nature of the danger? Well, we're going to learn in this case that carbon monoxide is colorless, it's odorless, it's tasteless and it's deadly in just seconds. And what do you do if you're a responsible work-site owner with a colorless and odorless, tasteless and deadly-in-seconds gas?

Well, we know what a responsible work-site owner would do. A responsible work-site owner would have walked Andy through the work site at the Secondary Venturi platform. They would have trained him what to look for. They would have warned him about carbon monoxide. They would have issued him a small, inexpensive personal carbon monoxide detector that would alert him to the fact that the levels of carbon monoxide in the area were increasing. They would have supplied him with a supervisor [that] was familiar with the area and familiar with the risks. They would have established emergency procedures in case something went wrong. They would have established a communication system so that people could be contacted in case something did happen.

Now, what Real [Steel] did instead, we're going to learn in this case, they abandoned Andy. Instead of doing what a responsible work-site owner would do, they sent him to the Baumco Tower where there was a cloud of carbon monoxide gas that killed his coworker, [who] was standing just a few feet from him, and seriously injured Andy. We're going to learn also in this case that Real Steel Company never performed any sort of test at the work site that morning. We're going to learn they didn't do an explosion test; we're going to hear that they didn't test for carbon monoxide, and the results of their failures, two workers, two outside contract workers like Andy, one's dead, one's injured, and that's out of five people that were there that day.

In fact, we're going to learn that Real [Steel] had issued a work permit allowing Andy and his crew to come on to the premises and get up onto the Baumco Tower. And this permit was issued actually the day before. And when Andy got there with the crew at four a.m., they made him wait till about 4:20 before he could go to the work site. And we don't know exactly what Real Steel Company was doing in that twenty minutes, but we do know they weren't testing the site like they should have been. This permit was signed by two separate Real Steel employees. [The] permit fails to say anything about the dangers that are well-known to Real Steel, including the presence of carbon monoxide. And it doesn't even mention anything about transferring the risk of carbon monoxide to contract workers like Andy. Doesn't have anything on it at all about [a] hazard communication plan or emergency procedures in case there is carbon monoxide. All right.

So what happened to Andy when he got to his work site? He was overcome by this colorless, odorless, tasteless and deadly-in-seconds gas. At first he was a little tired, then he noticed his friend was lying on the grating next to him. He couldn't revive him, and by that time the carbon monoxide had done its work on Andy. He lost consciousness, and that's the last thing he remembers until he was being revived down below and being taken to General Hospital. Now, we're going to learn that what happens is . . . hemoglobin is the thing in your blood that carries oxygen to the brain and keeps you alive, keeps you thinking, keeps your brain alive. And when you inhale carbon monoxide, it gets onto the hemoglobin and won't let any oxygen attach. So if you breathe enough carbon monoxide, there's not enough room left for oxygen to get onto that blood and get up into your brain. And if you don't have enough oxygen, brain cells die. And if enough die, you become unconscious. And if more die, if you lose enough brain cells, even if you're revived, even if you wake up, you'll never be the same. In Andy's case, he can no longer remember things like he could, like you or I can. He can no longer read like he could before the accident because the brain cells that you need to think and to reason are gone, they're dead. He's seriously and clinically depressed, suffers from anxiety, headaches. He's never going to be able to work again. In fact, his sisters have been appointed by the probate court as his guardians because he can't manage his own affairs anymore.

So what are we going to do here today, we're going to present this case to you in just a few moments and show you the actual evidence, and then we're going to ask you to render an award against Real Steel Company to compensate Andy for these injuries that he suffered as a result of Real Steel. Thank you very much.

Story Elements as Delivered

Scope	Place and Time—narrow. Acts and People—broader (numbers of responsibilities, risks)
Point of View	Hazardous Property Owner
Sequence	1. Owner—nature of the risks present. 2. Protections denied. 3. Injury and consequences.
Theme	*Abandoned Worker Safety*

DEFENSE—Suggested Story Elements

Scope	Broaden Time frame, numbers of jobs, Acts and prior visits, the routine and repeated nature of this work. Also link and maintain a larger scope view of the subcontractor managers, supervisors, and all coworkers
Point of View	The Subcontractor and Union Pros (avoid "workers" wherever possible)
Sequence	1. Known hazards and reasonable safety provisions. 2. Reasonable precautions versus unreasonable acts and expectations. 3. Hurting, but not physically injured.
Theme	*Leaving Safety Behind*

OPENING STATEMENT

Mr. Fife:

Good morning. My name is Bill Fife, and I represent Real Steel Company in this claim brought by the plaintiff, Andy Taylor. As counsel has indicated, Real Steel Company is a manufacturer of steel. That is what they do. When they manufacture steel and they use this equipment, this Baumco Tower, it is used to exhaust certain gases that are created when the blast furnace occurs when they're making the iron-ore process. This equipment wears out regularly. It is known. Now, what Real Steel does is it hires professionally trained companies, professional companies such as Metro Industrial Corporation, where the plaintiff worked. And this company has job duties to maintain, repair and fix this equipment and similar equipment at Real Steel Company. In fact, they have contracts. And you'll learn during the course of this case that they have certain contractual obligations when they come on and they do this work. They enter into an agreement with Real Steel Company.

Now there are many other professional companies that come onto Real Steel and do work. Metro is one of them. And what makes them professional is that they have skilled journeymen tradesmen that take years of training to learn how to do this work. They just don't take people off the street and find them lining up at a bus stop and say come on in and get up here and do this skilled work in this area and use this equipment, the welding equipment and the various equipment that a boiler-maker would use, such as a trade that the plaintiff was in. These union journeymen have done this work for ten, fifteen, some of them twenty to thirty years. The plaintiff has been doing this for fifteen years. He's a skilled journeyman. He holds a journeyman's card. These are called skilled tradesmen for a reason, because there is a skill that they have and they learn. And one of the skills that they have is that they know about the hazards of repairing the Real Steel equipment.

They know because they come out here regularly to repair this equipment. They're there on a regular basis. They come out and they do this type of repair approximately every six months, along with other repair work that they do regularly at Real Steel Company. Metro Industrial Company is at Real Steel Company so often, almost daily, that they have their own work trailer permanently on-site at Real Steel Company. They are there every day.

When I say that they know about the hazards that these trained skilled journeymen have, they know that the carbon monoxide is a common by-product in the steelmaking process. They know that because they're there regularly. They know before they can do their job that this area has to be purged; there's certain work that Real Steel does prior to them showing up, because this is a scheduled repair that they do. The wear and tear that occurred in this particular case is that holes develop throughout this equipment, throughout the steel equipment. The job, the very essence of the job [for which] the plaintiff and Metro Industrial [were] there was to fill these holes up. They know, as Plaintiff counsel points out, that carbon monoxide is colorless and it's odorless, and they know that because they know they're required to wear protection devices. And these are called CO monitors, carbon monoxide monitors. Again, the day of this incident was a routine maintenance, planned repair work.

The day before this incident Metro Industrial and their skilled trades journeymen went up and did a pre-inspection to see what kind of work; how much are we going to have to do there; what kind of equipment they're going to have to bring up; how much metal will we have to bring up to do the repair on the holes that were created during the steel-making process in this equipment. And when they came up the day before, they came up—other employees, not the plaintiff, but other employees of Metro Industrial—and they had their CO monitors. They knew to wear their CO monitors because that's what they agreed to do in the agreement with Real Steel for this work that they were performing. They agreed to perform it in a safe manner. Again, this is a job that is done regularly.

When they come up on the day of the incident—and, by the way, let me point this out as well. They have what is called a toolbox talk with the employees of the vendor, the other people that come on, because again Real Steel makes steel. They bring in other companies to do other things for them. They don't maintain all this equipment, they make steel; they hire other companies to do this work. They had a toolbox talk the day before with the Metro people. One of the things is protect yourself, carry and know how to use a CO monitor.

The day of this incident they came on [at] approximately four a.m., as counsel said, and they're waiting around. Real Steel supervisors said—gave them two warnings to the Metro Industrial supervisors: We are still purging, which will make the area safer, and then we will do a test for you. And they also advised them, don't go—don't go up and start yet. And yet, for some unknown reason, Metro Industrial took their crew and a Metro Industrial leader takes the crew up and they go up to this level where the incident occurred involving the plaintiff and the other individual, and they come up without their CO monitors. Which if they had the CO monitors, we wouldn't be here today.

Now they know from their experience, because of their skill and training, that the CO, the carbon monoxide can be a cloud, it can be in and out, it can come and go. They don't know where it is. They know that sometimes pockets of CO will last for eight to ten hours after the shutdown. That's why they have the monitors. That's why they have the toolbox talk. That's why we have the contract. When they get up there, the Metro leader senses that there may be CO in the area. And what does he do? Does he say, let's bring the crew down? He leaves the crew up there; he goes down to get the monitors. By the time he gets back up, the crew has been affected by the CO, this known product that's going to be part of the steelmaking process every time you make steel, this known product has affected the plaintiff in this case.

What do they do? As soon as that happens, as soon as they find out, they put an emergency plan into action, they get immediate medical attention to Mr. Taylor, he's taken down off the platform and he's taken by emergency ambulance to General Hospital, and there he is treated with the best care in the world that you can have. He's put into an oxygen chamber, called a hyperbaric chamber, that forces oxygen into the body. And his blood is taken, blood readings are determined. And what we know, what will be undisputed from the evidence from the General Hospital evidence, is that the carbon monoxide exposure to Mr. Taylor was, in fact, fairly low. And we know that because of the sophisticated testing that General Hospital can do and did in this case. They know by drawing the blood . . . they can determine how much oxygen is in there and how much carbon monoxide, and by scientifically reliable data that has been developed for years because of studies on carbon monoxide poisoning, how much carbon monoxide Mr. Taylor really had. And what really Mr. Taylor had was an exposure to carbon monoxide that would be similar to someone that is not a smoker going into a very, very heavily smoked room and staying in there for an extended period of time. It's not fatal, it is not enough to cause permanent damage. This is scientifically proven, and the General Hospital records will support that without contradiction.

What happens is that he will have headaches and he will have nausea, just like if somebody who's a nonsmoker sits in a room full of cigarette smoke or cigar smoke for an extended period of time. You're not accustomed to that, you're going to have nausea, you're going to have headaches. He is discharged from the hospital within twenty-four hours of this incident; sent home. He doesn't feel well, of course he's upset, his coworker, who was much closer to a heavier concentration of CO, passed away from it. But there was not enough exposure to cause any permanent damage to the plaintiff, and that will be supported by the General [Hospital] records and . . . treating doctors and by an expert witness that is an expert in carbon monoxide poisoning.

Three weeks after this, after the incident, the plaintiff is ordered or told to return to General Hospital for further check-up and care. Instead he goes to a lawyer-referred doctor and starts a series of treatments there, and here we are today. We know scientifically that there is not enough exposure to carbon monoxide to support the kind of damage that the plaintiff is claiming. We also know that Real Steel did not do anything wrong in this case. They hired a professional company, skilled tradesmen, skilled journeymen. At the end of this case, I will ask that you return a verdict of no cause for action, that means no money for the plaintiff. Real Steel did not do anything wrong in this case. Thank you.

Story Elements as Delivered

Scope	Broad on Time, Places (historical), Actions, and Numbers
Point of View	Subcontractor and Skilled Workers
Sequence	1. Subcontractor role, history both outside and in this plant. Repair routine.
	2. Day before, day of—two warnings, yet abandoned own employees.
	3. Objective tests establish levels of harm. Emotional pattern.
Theme	*Known Danger, Ignored Protections and Warnings*

Case Two

Plaintiff—Suggested Story Elements

Scope	Broad in almost every area to keep perspective out of the single incident
Point of View	Generic, Caring Doctor
Sequence	1. Policies for providing for patient safety. Conditions linked to deprivation of facilities and expertise. Standards violations as cause versus known smoking risks.
	2. Vivid depiction of and proscription against discharge in active labor. "But for" position on risks out of reach, causes here, pros criticizing amateur's technique.
	3. Injuries, harms and punitive frames.
Theme	*Out of Sight, Out of Mind*

OPENING STATEMENT

Mr. Vincent:

Good morning. My name is Stan Vincent. And I'm here for the plaintiff. In this case the plaintiff is a four-year-old little girl by the name of Mary Shelley. This case is all about her. That's the whole reason we're here . . . to talk about her problems that she has from her birth. She was born on December 20th, 1996. She was scheduled to be born on January 14th, 1997. She was premature.

This case is about her and about the problems that she has. It's really about two problems she had right at the time of her birth. And the problems are that her brain didn't get enough oxygen and it didn't get enough sugar. Those are the two central themes of this case. Her brain didn't get enough oxygen. She didn't get enough sugar.

Now the story starts about 6:00 in the morning on December 20th, 1996, when her mother goes to Franklin Hospital. She goes to the hospital. She tells the nurse there "my water's broken; I think I'm in labor." They keep her there at the hospital. They figure out that her contractions are coming about three minutes apart. While she's there, she's examined by a doctor, the defendant doctor in this case, by the name of Dr. Garcia. He's one of the defendants, and Franklin Hospital is one of the defendants. He comes by to see her twice. She's there about four hours, and he sees her twice during that time. Each time he sees her, he does a digital exam. A digital exam is an exam where he sticks his finger in her vagina, probably two fingers, to see if she's dilated, to see how far the pregnancy is coming along and whether or not she's in labor. OK. The exam shows that she's two centimeters dilated and that she's ninety percent effaced. She's moving toward labor. This baby is moving toward coming into the world.

While she's . . . in the hospital she's put on a fetal heart monitor strip. That's a piece of equipment that's used to monitor the health of the baby. It also records the strength and duration of the contractions. Well, this strip showed that the baby was healthy, doing fine, and the contractions are coming about every three minutes. Now, four hours after she comes into the hospital Mary's mother is sent home. She's sent home despite the fact that she's two centimeters dilated, that she's ninety percent effaced, that she's having contractions about two to three minutes apart now. That's right. When she's sent home, her contractions are closer together than when she came in. They're coming more frequently and they're coming regularly. But she's told to go home.

And that's where Mary's troubles began. That's where this case starts. Mary's mother is sent home from the hospital at about 10:10 in the morning. Now, Mary—her mother lives about thirty minutes away from the hospital. They get her home, she starts to get in a bath when she gets home. And as soon as she steps into the bath, she has a labor pain. She gets out. She yells to her mother in the other room, "This baby's coming now."

They immediately call 911. And Mary is born on the bathroom floor of her mother's house. For the first five minutes of this baby's life, she's on the floor with her mother in the bathroom. And there's no medical personnel there at all. And that's where these problems started. Because if there were medical personnel there, her brain wouldn't have been deprived of this oxygen and this sugar. She wouldn't have had the problems that she has that you'll hear about. Now the reason she didn't have medical personnel there is because she was at the hospital and they told her to go home.

Well, should the doctor have sent her home, should the nurses have let her go home, should the hospital have let her be discharged? I'm here to tell you the answer to all those questions is no, they shouldn't have sent her home. Now, what should they have done? What could they have done to prevent these things? That's the question. I said I'd tell you what they didn't do. What should they have done? Well, they should have followed their own policies. They have rules and regulations that say this is what we do. In this case, here's what it is.

The rules and regulations are, you know, if a woman's in active labor, you can't send her home. Not only is that the hospital rule, it's a federal regulation. It's a law. You can't send her home if she's in active labor. If the baby's premature, like Mary was, and it's not her due date yet, if it's premature, the woman's water's broken, you can't send her home. It's in the policies, it's in the rules, it's a law. They didn't follow that. Well, we know they didn't follow those because of what eventually happened. But they thought that her water wasn't broken. They told her you're having false labor, your water's not broken, go home.

They didn't know whether or not her water was broken. They just guessed. The digital exam, it's not enough. All the experts you're going to hear today say it's not enough to determine whether or not the water's broken.

There are four tests. There are four simple tests that tell when the water's broken. None of these tests were done. I'm going to run through them real quickly. One's a pelvic exam. The pelvic exam is not the same as the digital exam. In the pelvic exam, the woman gets on a table. It uses a speculum. It's a metal instrument. I understand the exam is much more uncomfortable for the woman. But it's an in-depth exam, and there's no question if the water's broken or not broken. The other tests are even simpler than that. One is the nitrazine paper. It's a paper they use to put some of the fluid that's coming out of the woman on the paper. The paper will react if there's amniotic fluid. If it's amniotic fluid, you know the water's broken. If it's not, you know the water hasn't broken. The other test is a ferning test. It's basically the same thing except they take some of that fluid, they put it on a slide and they look at it under a microscope. OK. Again, no question whether or not the water's broken. The last one is an ultrasound, just like almost every woman has during pregnancy. You put an ultrasound on, you can see if their water volume has decreased and whether or not the water's broken. Four simple tests, all available there at the hospital, all routinely given to determine if the water's broken. None of them were given in this case. They sent this woman home not knowing whether or not her water was broken.

All the experts you're going to hear from the plaintiff's side will say, oh, her water was broken. She was in active labor. They broke the law. They didn't follow their procedures. They caused these problems.

The other important thing that you need to know about this is the history of the mother. In this case this was not her first delivery. That's one of the reasons she knew her water was broken. She'd had a child before. The child she had before is named Tyler. That's Mary's older brother. Tyler is fine. But he was also born at home. He was born at home because she went to the hospital, they told her she wasn't in labor, they told her that her water wasn't broken, sent her home. And then she had what's called a precipitous delivery. It's a very quick, very, very fast delivery. It doesn't last very long. OK. Now, in his case it turns out that her water hadn't been broken. Her water broke the moment she had the baby very quickly. Now, Tyler was born fine. But that's because the paramedic was there right when he was born. The ambulance got there faster than they did in this case. But the important thing is the precipitous delivery. The first baby that comes precipitously; that is, very fast, you don't know about. You can't predict it.

The second baby that comes that way, you do, 'cause if you've had one precipitous birth, chances are your next child's going to be precipitous. Another good reason the hospital, the nurses, should not have sent this [woman] home.

The only other thing I need to tell you here in the opening is what are Mary's problems. Mary's problems are what's called global development disorder. And I'm not going to go into the specifics here. But I want to tell you [that] global development simply means it affects all the areas of her life. She has psychological, physical, behavioral, and emotional problems. All the experts you're going to hear from today say that this is because she was denied what—the oxygen and the sugar to her brain at and around the time of her birth. They're going to say that all these things are related. She can't walk correctly. She can't talk correctly. She's partially deaf in one ear. She can't hear particularly well when she does hear. She doesn't react to her environment the way other people do. She's going to be frustrated. She's going to be behind. She's going to be developmentally disabled and slow the rest of her life. And the reason for that is because four simple tests weren't done, because her mother was sent home in violation of the rules, the regulations, and the law. And that's the reason we're here today.

Story Elements as Delivered

Scope	People—narrow. Acts (especially tests), Numbers (on standards), Time, and Place—all broader

Point of View	Baby (medical people referenced through the baby)
Sequence	1. O_2/sugar deprivation. Water break, four-hour hospitalization, with two physical exams, and monitor, no labs.
	2. Contractions quicker, discharged home. Precipitous birth before = warning. Brother had pros present, no harms.
	3. Policies and standards re: discharge in labor, or after water breaks. Four tests. Global development disorder.
Theme	*Precipitous Discharge, Prevention Withheld*

DEFENSE—SUGGESTED STORY ELEMENTS

Scope:	Narrow in almost all factors, focused almost exclusively on Mom and her choices before and during the birth
Point of View	This Careless Mom
Sequence	1. Alternate causes: genetics, cord problem, and smoking. Reason to doubt conditions she had, her early good progress.
	2. Lack of actual labor linked to all policies and procedures followed. Mom's neglect—times told to quit, (any) noncompliance in prenatal, asking to go home, voluntary aspects of prior home birth, failure to return. "Can't tie them down to treat."
	3. Blaming staff for things they never got a chance to do—or even know. Overburdened professionals.
Theme	*A Mother Should Know*

OPENING STATEMENT

Mr. Harrison:

Good morning. My name's Earl Harrison, and I represent Dr. Garcia and Franklin Hospital. As you've heard, Mary is the daughter of Martina. And she was born on December 20th, 1996. Like most children in the world, she was born at home. Granted, that's not the way it happens here in the United States. But it does happen. On December 20th, 1996, what happened is Martina went to Franklin Hospital in the early morning hours. Her due date was January 14th, 1997. So her due date really wasn't for another three weeks or so.

The doctor and the nurses admitted her to the hospital. And when they admitted her to the hospital, they took a history from her. And when they did that, they hooked her up—they gave her a bed and they hooked her up to a monitor. And the monitor was a fetal heart monitor that monitored the baby's heart rate. Now, why is that important? Because it tells you how well the baby is doing. When a baby gets under stress in utero, you can't see that. But the first sign of stress usually goes up in the heart. The same way with adults. So they were monitoring the baby's heart rate. And they did that over the course of the observation period that morning. The baby's heart was beating well. And it beat well the entire time that it was being monitored.

During the course of the observations from about 6:00 in the morning till 10:10 when the mom was discharged, the mother had minimal contractions. And what that means is although she had contractions, they were not sufficient contractions to move the baby down the birth canal. What happens is the contraction starts out—and anybody that's been pregnant knows this better than I do. But it starts out, and the contractions are what moves the child's head down the pelvic inlet and out the birth canal. So remember, the baby was not ready to be delivered. The due date was the 14th. The mom really wasn't having contractions consistent with a labor pattern to bring the baby down the birth canal. In addition to that, the mom was dilated two centimeters, [whereas] ten centimeters is fully dilated. So for four hours the mom was still—at four hours of observation the mother was still two centimeters dilated. And she was effaced. But there had been no change in the progress of the dilatation . . . of the cervical dilatation or opening.

Martina had mentioned to the nurse that she thought her water had broken. And the nurse put that down. But what happened over the course of the four hours is this was what they call a short-term observation, STO. It was an admission to the hospital, because they were uncertain as to whether this was true labor or false labor because the due date was three weeks away. So what the nurses did was . . . in addition to monitoring the baby, monitoring the contraction activity, and doing exams, they also observed her fluid, because with contraction activity if you have ruptured your membrane, you're going to be leaking out fluid. That just happens. And they'll be changing the pads. Anybody that's had a baby knows that they change those pads constantly because they get fluids on them. Well, in this case, from the time the mom was in to when she was sent home, she'd been examined many times and they were observing it. But they really hadn't noticed any fluid coming out. So after being examined—and I have the record. I think she was examined one, two, three, four, five, six times over the course of four hours. And when I say "examined," that's where they really come in and do an exam of the mom and look at her. They were looking at the fetal heart monitor strip more often than that because the nurse is right there. But actual physical examinations to see how she's doing, there hadn't been much progress in the child.

The doctor made a diagnosis of Braxton Hicks contractions, which is false labor. And he gave the mother instructions to go home and to come back when the contractions were closer together and of sufficient quality to—where they really hurt and to come back to the hospital, so that they were more intense in their quality. So the mom went home. And she lived in Ourtown. And she drove back home. When she got home, she had what was called a precipitous birth. That is a birth that came after about four contractions that came quickly. And there was nothing in the record of how you can diagnose this. There's no way you can diagnose a precipitous birth. So this birth—as you know, the baby coming out in just four pushes is unreal. So this baby came in a matter of minutes when they got home. And the baby was born at 11:19. As a matter of fact, the baby was born so quick that when they called the ambulance, which got there in five or six minutes, the baby had already been born. So this was not a very long labor.

The baby was taken back to the hospital, and the mom was taken back. And the baby had some diagnosis of polycythemia. But the baby had no symptoms in the newborn period. In other [words], there was feeding, it wasn't vomiting, it had no fever, no infection. It was breathing on its own. It was taking oral intakes after three days. This baby was doing all the things you want babies to do. It had good urine output. It had good bowel movements. The baby was for all intents and purposes—except for some evidence of polycythemia, the baby was a healthy baby and went home. About sixteen months after the baby was born, the mother started noticing problems with the child. Up to that time, the child had been seen by a lot of doctors. But no one had ever diagnosed any problems with the baby, especially any mental problems with the baby. And no doctor up to the time that the mom and her lawyers filed the case had ever diagnosed any problems related to the birth of the child, directly related to the birth of the child.

As you hear the evidence portion, we intend to establish that there was no breach of the standard of care in the medical practice, that they followed the hospital policies and procedures, that they followed good medical practice, and there was no way to anticipate a precipitous birth in this case, such a rapid delivery, because remember, the due dates were three weeks away. The doctor didn't want to deliver the baby early. It's better to keep the baby in and deliver it in and around the due dates.

There is no dispute that the baby has problems. But the problems are not because of an out-of-the-hospital delivery. Some of the factors you're going to hear about, [which] may have contributed to the baby's developmental delays, are that the mother smoked. And the mother smoked during the pregnancy, even though being warned about that. And I know a lot of people smoke. And a lot of people think, well, they hear the statistics and they see the package of cigarettes that say pregnant mothers be warned, don't smoke, 'cause it can cause fetal injury, it can cause low birth weight, and it can cause prematurity. But everybody thinks that that ain't going to happen to their child. And it doesn't in a lot of instances. Sometimes smoking is linked to polycythemia. It's linked to other problems. The mother has one other child that has asthma. And she's been told to smoke—not smoke around that child. But there's still smoking that goes on in the home. As you listen to the experts in this case, they're going to tell you the biggest risk is smoking. And smoking is a personal lifestyle, like drinking. We make no judgment about whether it's good or bad. The issue is what did the smoking cause. And the doctors have all admitted that they had informed the mom that she should quit smoking during the pregnancy, at least for the baby's sake. So that is one issue. In addition, there is an issue of other things that came up. But we're going to hear about those in the later part of the presentation. Thank you very much.

Story Elements as Delivered

Scope	People, Place and Time—narrow Acts and Numbers—broader
Point of View	Mother

Sequence

1. Not due, not in labor. History, monitor and six exams. Baby fine. Minimal contractions, two cm (versus ten) dilation, no effective progress and no fluid seen.

2. Instructed mother. False labor diagnosed. No way to diagnose the birth in four contractions, ambulance couldn't even get there.

3. Alternative causes. Baby OK at start. All signs, input and output normal. Sixteen months before first complaints, but no doctor diagnoses any birth problems before lawsuit. Smoking causes polycythemia.

Theme

Good Medical Practice versus Smoking and Leaving

CASE THREE

PLAINTIFF—SUGGESTED STORY ELEMENTS

Scope	People, Acts, and Place—narrow (to avoid prior wreck and injuries, and others on the road)
	Time—broaden into the future, but not the past
Point of View	Bath Shoppe's Driver (focus more on driver as agent, less as person)
Sequence	1. Fault without question. Stack fault facts and link to cause.
	2. Personal responsibility—for choices and judgments behind the wheel. Minimize trucker and any prior conditions.
	3. Permanent harms.
Theme	*Just Consequences*

OPENING STATEMENT

Mr. Harvey:

Responsibility and accountability, that's what this case is all about. Responsibility to obey the law and accountability of those [that] break the law. What we're going to learn in this case is that the defendants broke the law and they caused a collision, and as a result of that collision a person was very, very seriously injured.

Good morning, ladies and gentlemen, my name is Michael Harvey and I represent Donna Brazos. Donna Brazos is thirty-four years old and she has two children, two preschool children. She married her high school sweetheart and has been married to him for the last eleven years. He's a Martin County policeman. For the ten years before this collision caused by the defendants, Donna was employed by a doctor's office. She was the office manager for this particular group and she worked five days a week, about six hours a day. And June 2nd, 1999, started out like any other day for Donna. She went to work at the usual time; she got to work; she worked the regular day and she left at the usual time, 2:24 p.m. That's when she left every day. And she took the same route home that she would take every day, and I think some of you may be familiar with the route that she took. She went south on Grand Avenue until she got to Mason just at the southern end of the Martin Mall. There she made a right-hand turn and started driving down the side. I think you're all familiar with the road there, thirty-five-miles-an-hour speed limit.

She's driving down the road when a red Cavalier shoots out from the Martin Mall right directly in front of her. No warning, no time. She didn't have time to turn the wheel. She didn't have time to put on the brakes. All she could do was grab the wheel hard and flinch and the accident happened. Her car was rated as totaled by her insurance company. In fact, I've got a picture of it. This is her car or what's left of it at the junkyard. You can't see that? Let me turn it. I'll hold it up. That's her car in the junkyard.

Now, just so that we understand how this particular accident happened, I've put together a diagram.

I want you to take a look at that now, if you can. This will show Mason, Grand Avenue would be on this side, she's coming south on Grand Avenue. Donna gets to Mason, she makes a right-hand turn and she goes down Mason. As she's driving down Mason, you recall at the Martin Mall there are several of these driveways that come onto Mason. The one I'm talking about is the one toward—it's the last one that would be to the west side of the mall.

Now, in this particular diagram, if you all take a look at it, you'll see there's a label here for a truck. Now, this diagram is going to be used both by the defendant and the plaintiff. This truck I don't believe is here, but we put it here so that you could see . . . when the defendant [attorney] gets up and he wants to say there's a truck there, you know where he says it was, OK. Over here we see the defendant, her name is Hilton, and behind her is a witness and over here is another witness in cars waiting to come out.

So Donna . . . just to review this, Donna makes a right-hand turn, she drives down Mason at the speed limit, and as she gets up to this driveway, Hilton pulls out in front of her. In this case we're going to learn that Hilton was employed by the Bath Shoppe. You recall there's a store in the mall there, the Bath Shoppe. Hilton was either in a hurry to take some merchandise from that particular store . . . and was on her way to make a delivery. But we're going to learn that when she pulled out in front of Donna, she did three things. The driver for Bath Shoppe pulled out blind into the roadway.

All right. When she pulled out, we will learn in this case, she didn't see any traffic coming from the east going west. She never saw Donna's white car—Donna's car that we just showed you. All right. The second thing that Bath Shoppe driver did when she pulled out onto the road was that she broke the law. We're going to learn in this case—remember we're talking about responsibility to obey the law and accountability for those that break it. We're going to learn that the law provides that whenever a driver is about to pull out from a driveway onto a road, they have to do certain things. And I'll bet you we all know what that is. You have to make sure that you can pull out safely before you enter the main street. And the law tells us that the driver must stop and, here's the magic words, yield the right of way to vehicles approaching on the road. We're going to learn that the Bath Shoppe driver didn't do that in this case and that's what caused the accident. Now, the third thing that the Bath Shoppe driver did when she pulled out blindly into traffic and breaking the law was to cause this collision.

Now, what are the consequences of that collision? Well, we're going to learn that the impact caused by the defendants was so severe that, although Donna was belted in her car and although the air bags deployed, she was momentarily knocked unconscious. By the time the emergency personnel arrived at the scene, it was clear that she was going to have to be taken to a hospital, and not just to the emergency room, but that she was going to be an inpatient. And, in fact, the emergency personnel took her to St. Francis Hospital, and she was an inpatient there for three days. And we're going to learn that the injury that the defendants caused in this case required her to stay in the hospital three days, and when she was discharged on the fourth day, she had to come back on the fifth day for additional testing because she was having additional pain.

While in the hospital she was examined, as you would expect, by a number of physicians. And we're going to learn that those physicians treated her for three things, three injuries that the defendants caused. They treated her for a herniated disc in her neck; they treated her for nerve trauma to her right shoulder; and the third thing that the defendants caused was a brain injury. Now, the consequences of the collision don't stop there. We're going to learn in this case that she had to seek follow-up care after the hospital discharge from seven different doctors of different specialties. One was a surgeon and he had to operate on her right shoulder. Fortunately her shoulder is doing better today and she's able to move it pretty well, although she's not back [to] playing tennis.

More important to this case and to your decision is that she suffered a traumatic brain injury. You will learn in this case that the traumatic brain injury has prevented her from ever going back to work at any time up to today, and probably she won't be able to go back to work in the same job ever. That's because, as a result of the collision caused by the defendants, she can no longer remember as she could before the accident. If she starts reading a book, she'll forget what it's about after she reads a few pages. So it's become frustrating, she can't read a book. We're going to learn that she can't take care of her children the way she could before the collision caused by the defendants. She needs attendant care. Somebody has to be with her, even today, eight hours a day while she's at home to make sure she doesn't do something that would be dangerous to herself or to her family. Leave something on the stove that might start a fire because she forgets. She'll walk into a room and forget why she's there. So these things that we take for granted every day, she's now missing. And understandably, this has resulted in her suffering from a very severe bout of depression. All right. So what's [the] case about? It's about responsibility and accountability. Responsibility to obey the law and accountability for those [that] break the law and cause collisions like this. Thank you very much.

Story Elements as Delivered

Scope	People, Place, Act—narrow Numbers and Time—broader, re: future harms
Point of View	Defendant's Driver
Sequence	1. Details of wreck with defendant's driver as active party. 2. Three active sins: pulled out blind, broke the law, caused collision. 3. Consequences of collision. Force intensity, three immediate harms: disk, shoulder nerve, TBI.
Theme	*Responsibility and Accountability*

DEFENSE—SUGGESTED STORY ELEMENTS

Scope	Acts, Places, Numbers, People and Time all broader, more diverse and diffuse
Point of View	The Jurors/Third Person. (case first, not the story)
Sequence	1. Four choices for fault. Defendant always no higher than three on the list by choices, cops' input, etc. 2. Four choices for cause. Three different objective measures at scene and hospital all say no head injury or consciousness loss. 3. If, then—bunch up the alternate possibilities for her condition against the objective proofs of just the healed shoulder injury. Minimize fault and cause in review, assign value only to shoulder emerging from accident.
Theme	*Claims versus Proofs*

OPENING STATEMENT

Mr. Batson:

Good morning. My name is Brad Batson, and I represent the Bath Shoppe, which is the employer of Ms. Hilton, who was the, well, we saw, she was the driver [that] was stopped at the stop sign and was pulling out of the mall. [The] Bath Shoppe is a company you may be familiar with, they sell bath and personal care products at small retail stores mostly in malls, and you may have seen them in your local mall.

This is the beginning of the case and at the start we've heard plaintiff counsel tell us what the plaintiff is claiming. Now let's jump all the way to the end of the case. At the very end, before you go into the jury room, the judge is going to give you instructions and you're going to get a verdict form. And one of the last things the judge is going to instruct you is regarding the burden of proof that the plaintiff has in order to prove [her] case. And as you listen to the evidence in this case, keep in mind that your job will include answering these questions on the verdict form at the end of the trial, and you'll need to answer, was the plaintiff injured? Was the defendant negligent? And was the defendant's negligence a proximate cause of the plaintiff's injuries. And each of those questions, if you're to answer in favor of the plaintiff, you must answer on a preponderance of the evidence, that it's more likely than not that the plaintiff has proven on each of these things. But you may well find that the answers lead to the conclusion that this was just an accident. That no individual stands out as being more wrong or more at fault than anyone else so that it requires a finding of one individual's fault. And you may well find that, in doing your job and making your determination, that you're doing absolutely the best job that you can do as a juror if you determine that no one was at fault at all.

Now, this case illustrates something that most experienced drivers on the road are familiar with, the concept of teamwork. That all the drivers on the road are members of a team, and when that teamwork breaks down, accidents will happen. In this case, our team consists of the truck driver, Plaintiff Brazos, who's somewhere on the road going westbound, Defendant Britney Hilton, witness Kent and witness Olsen. This team needs to do their job on the road for this accident not to happen. In this case, when the truck driver signaled Ms. Hilton to go out left, and you're going to hear testimony in that regard, she followed his direction and was blindsided by Plaintiff Brazos. But before we get into everything on the accident and the issue of fault, again, the first thing that you're to consider is whether or not the plaintiff was injured. Plaintiff Brazos must prove not only the existence of her injuries, but the extent of her injuries. Now, she claims that her injuries are substantial. That they've seriously impaired the quality of her life. We are going to discover that, fortunately, her injuries are much less serious than she claimed. We are going to learn that she does not have a closed-head injury.

You know, sometimes a diagnosis in a closed-head injury has been, well, it's been compared to like looking for the wind. You can't see the wind, you can't see a closed-head injury, but you can see evidence of both. For instance, somebody standing there and their hair is blowing backwards, you can look out the window and see their hair blowing backwards, you say it's a windy day, the wind's blowing your hair, you know the wind exists. Likewise, to see inside someone's head to see if they've had a trauma that's caused a closed-head injury, we look for evidence of a head trauma, getting hit in the head. We look for loss of consciousness. We look for post-traumatic amnesia. That's amnesia that's from the point of the accident forward till now, not backwards in time, but from the point of the accident forward. From the point that it happened. We look for positive medical tests such as MRIs,

CAT scans, other positive mental tests that will show something is wrong. And we're also going to look for abnormal neuropsychological tests, and this has to do with answering batteries of questions and interviews with psychologists. In this case, although Plaintiff Brazos complains of a gale-force injury, you will see very little evidence of any closed-head injury at all.

We are also going to learn that she has made a complete and full recovery from her right shoulder injury. We are going to learn that she did not have any other significant injuries from this accident. We are going to learn that some of her other complaints, in particular her neck complaint, when she's talking about a bulging disc at C-5, C-6, that that problem existed prior to this accident and that she had an accident three years before this, that she received a year and a half of treatment for this. You are also going to learn that Plaintiff Brazos did not go to her usual doctors to get treatment for this accident. Instead of going back to the doctor that's been treating her for a year and a half at the other hospital, instead of going to her usual OB/GYN, instead of going to the—she works at a dental office. Instead of going to the medical professionals in her office to get a referral, she got a referral from I think it was her husband's cousin who referred her to a doctor, who then . . . either that doctor or the plaintiff's counsel referred her to a bunch of doctors [that] are regularly testifying on behalf of plaintiffs in courtrooms like this.

Now, next after the issue of injury, the plaintiff must prove that Defendant Hilton was negligent and that it was her fault rather than the truck driver's fault, the fault of the other drivers or the fault of nobody in particular.

On this issue we're going to hear evidence about how the accident happened from all of these people on the team, these drivers. We're going to hear that on June 2nd, 1999, Britney Hilton was working as a management trainee at the Martin Mall Bath Shoppe. Her manager asked her to transfer some baby merchandise from that store to another store. She drove a red Cavalier through the parking lot, she came up to the stop sign, she stopped, she put on her left turn indicator. She looked left, she looked right, she looked left, she looked left and she sees a truck blocking her view of westbound traffic on Mason. She can't—the truck driver appears that he's waiting for her to exit, you know, he makes a wide right turn and can't get into the driveway until she comes out, so she starts inching out trying to see past the truck to her left. And she looks and the truck driver's waving her on, going (indicating), giving her the signal. She assumes the traffic is all clear and she proceeds to pull past the front of the truck when Plaintiff Brazos—the right front of Plaintiff Brazos' car hits the left front of Defendant Hilton's car. They collide like that, they slide across to the south side of Mason and stop there. We're going to hear that witness Kent stops right behind her car. She can't back up to let the truck in and witness Olsen is even farther back. Witness Kent sees that truck, too. He didn't see the truck driver waving, but he saw how she was blocked.

We're going to hear that Plaintiff Brazos comes down here every day and is familiar that traffic is exiting here, and we're going to see that just like Hilton's view was blocked, Plaintiff Brazos' view was blocked also, creating a blind driveway that she didn't slow down for and increase her assured clear distance ahead of her, you know, make the stopping distance less. As you are listening to the accident evidence, please ask yourselves, you know, would most reasonable drivers, those who are trying to follow the rules of the road, have followed the truck driver's signal on that day, believed it was all clear and proceeded with their left turn? Ask yourselves that as you're listening to the evidence regarding the accident.

And finally, Plaintiff must prove beyond preponderance of the evidence that if Defendant Hilton was negligent, that that negligence was a proximate cause of the injuries alleged by Plaintiff Brazos. And they must prove that of all the factors that contributed here, that it was not the truck driver's fault, not the fault of the other drivers, not the fault of [anybody] at all, not the fault of some accident that happened on another day, but it was the defendant's fault that caused the injury to the plaintiff. That they were the natural consequence of the negligence of the defendant. Now we will learn in this case that not every violation of law equals negligent fault.

One of the important legal concepts that the judge is going to instruct you on at the end of the trial is the concept of proximate cause, which requires that negligent conduct must have been a cause of the plaintiff's injury. In other words, if the defendant did something wrong, such as breaking the law, but that conduct did not naturally result in the plaintiff's injury, then the defendant is not legally responsible. Here's an example. Suppose Britney Hilton forgot to renew her driver's license on her birthday. Now, she'd be driving illegally on the road. But since that driving violation, having a suspended license for failure to renew, was not the cause of the accident, was not the cause of the injuries to the plaintiff, the law doesn't care in this courtroom whether or not her license was suspended or not. Even if it's happening—even if that violation of law is happening at the exact moment of this accident, the law [is] going to ignore that as a proximate cause.

To conclude my opening remarks, Plaintiff Brazos has made a number of claims, but before you can decide those claims in favor, you must determine beyond a preponderance of the evidence that the injuries exist and the extent of the injuries. You must determine that Ms. Hilton was at fault rather than the truck driver, the other drivers, or nobody at all. And you must determine that the negligence of the defendant was the proximate cause of the injuries, other than anyone else who's involved on this roadway or nobody at all or from an accident that happened on another day. Now, at the end of the trial when the proofs are concluded, we're going to ask you to determine that, among all the people on the roadway that day, that the case has not been proven for the negligence of Defendant Hilton. We're going to ask you to find that Defendant Hilton was not responsible for the claimed injuries that the plaintiff asserted. Thank you.

Story Elements as Delivered

Scope	People, Acts, Numbers and Place—broad overall, limits on injuries. Time—very narrow
Point of View	Jurors/Third Person
Sequence	1. Juror jobs. Verdict rules on fault and proximate cause, plus burden standards. Many hands in the events. Blame—shift and spread, while diminishing nature of sins.
	2. Circumstantial signs of any head injury. Objective testing, objective indicators. Limit harms.
	3. Comparative fault spread to all available hands. Laws against everyone. No cause scenario after returning to fault finding.
Theme	*Accidents Happen (sometimes with no fault at all)*

APPENDIX FOUR

SMALL GROUP STANDARDS AND GUIDELINES

Excerpted from the Code of Professional Standards of the American Society of Trial Consultants

(For the full code, see ASTCWeb.org)

Practice Area C—SMALL GROUP RESEARCH [SGR]

For the purpose of these Professional Standards and Practice Guidelines, the following definition of Small Group Research (SGR) applies: Trial consultants use SGR to study individuals' beliefs, attitudes, opinions and behavior relevant to issues in litigation. SGR is characterized by participant interaction in a group setting. SGR can be used, for example, to help clients evaluate evidence, assess arguments, develop themes, and inform case strategy. Examples of possible SGR design components include but are not limited to arguments from opposing parties, questionnaire data collection, individual and group verdict decisions, and facilitated or non-facilitated participant group discussion about case-related issues. The specific form of SGR a trial consultant chooses to implement is based in part, but not limited to, the trial consultant's experience and expertise, the research questions the SGR project is designed to address, and the research methodology used to answer the research questions. Trial consultants recognize that SGR can take many different forms. The ASTC does not endorse one form of SGR methodology over another.

SMALL GROUP RESEARCH: PROFESSIONAL STANDARDS

I. Appropriate Applications of SGR

A. Trial consultants shall recommend and employ small group research in those instances when, in their professional judgment, such research is well suited to the research problem at hand.

B. Trial consultants shall not knowingly convey to the client that results of SGR be accorded greater confidence than the research design and findings warrant.

II. Duty to Clients

A. Except with the permission of the client, trial consultants shall not disclose, and shall use their best efforts to prevent disclosure, concerning: a) the fact that SGR was conducted or b) results associated with an SGR project.

B. Trial consultants shall use best efforts to prevent the identity of the SGR client(s) from being disclosed unless and until the client(s) clearly indicate(s) they wish to be so identified to research participants.

III. Duty to Participants

A. Trial consultants shall inform SGR participants that their participation is voluntary.

B. Trial consultants shall treat SGR participants with respect and consideration at all times.

C. Trial consultants shall obtain written permission from participants when they may be observed and recording devices may be used or when their recorded image may be used for educational, marketing or for purposes other than the original research project.

D. Trial consultants shall use their best efforts to protect the anonymity of research participants.

IV. Methodology

A. When reporting SGR results, trial consultants shall present the results accurately and draw inferences and make interpretations consistent with the research findings.

SMALL GROUP RESEARCH: PRACTICE GUIDELINES

I. Appropriate Applications of SGR

A. Advise clients about the appropriate applications and strengths of SGR, such as assistance with case presentation planning.

B. Inform clients about the limitations of using SGR to predict litigation outcomes.

C. When appropriate, before conducting SGR, inform the client(s) of the purpose, estimated costs and appropriate uses of proposed SGR.

D. Recognize that there are a variety of ways to design and implement SGR, and explore with clients the approach that best meets the client(s)' needs.

E. When appropriate, advise client about the limitations of using SGR to design criteria for exercising challenges.

II. Duty to Clients

A. Obtain written agreement from SGR participants to maintain the confidentiality of any case specific information as a condition of participation.

B. Examples of measures that may be implemented to maintain client confidentiality include, but are not limited to:

1. Requiring recruiters, research facilities and other outside vendors to sign confidentiality agreements;
2. Using additional "decoy" names when recruiting to shield the identities of the litigants;
3. During the recruitment process, disqualifying participants with probable case-related connections;
4. Overseeing the recruiting process on a frequent basis;
5. Re-screening participants prior to the research exercise;
6. Requiring participants to present identification on-site to ensure participants' identities;

7. Using best efforts to avoid recruiting participants who could be called as prospective jurors in the case;

8. Limiting exposure to the nature and findings of the research by limiting the amount of case-related information and participant discussion to which vendors and non-client assignees are exposed.

C. In situations in which clients wish to disclose the SGR sponsor to SGR participants, discuss with the client(s) the pros and cons of revealing the sponsor(s)' identity.

D. Discuss with the client(s) the pros and cons of presenting witness testimony to SGR participants, including the potential risks of discoverability.

E. With the permission of the client, trial consultants may use SGR results which are presented in ways that protect the client, case and participant identities for marketing, education or other purposes.

III. Duty to Participants

A. Hold as confidential information that is likely to identify a participant with his or her responses, unless the participant requests or permits such disclosure.

B. Inform SGR participants if it is probable that they will be exposed to emotionally-sensitive material and explain that participants are free to withdraw their participation from the research if they feel uncomfortable.

C. When SGR participants have been deliberately misled, trial consultant conducts a final debriefing to mitigate potential harms, if the consultant believes any are likely.

D. Inform participants of the person(s) responsible for on-site supervision of the SGR research to whom they may address any questions or concerns.

E. Examples of ways that trial consultants may protect the confidentiality of SGR include, but are not limited to:

1. Inform SGR participants that if called to serve as a juror on a case involving the same parties or the same case facts as addressed in the SGR, the prospective juror should request a conference with the judge concerning his/her knowledge of the case, outside the presence of other prospective jurors. Remind participants

that while they should discuss their personal knowledge with the judge, they should not discuss their personal knowledge with other prospective jurors.

2. If SGR participant names are sought through legal discovery, to protect participant anonymity, suggest that the client(s) seek to use attorney work-product or other privileges to protect discoverability of the SGR participant names.

F. If SGR participant names are compelled by the Court, discuss the following options with the client(s):

1. The client(s) can ask the judge to compare the venire list with the list of SGR participant names *in camera.*

2. The client(s) can offer to compare the venire list to the SGR participant list and submit an affidavit regarding the presence or absence of research participants in the venire.

IV. Methodology

A. Communicate to the client the limitations associated with the research design implemented.

B. Communicate to the client the bases for research findings and recommendations.

C. Communicate to the client the best means of using the research findings following the research project.

D. Communicate to the client the research methodologies employed in the design, juror-participant recruitment[1], data analysis and reporting of research results.

1. Recruiters use various advertising and recruiting techniques that should be fully explored by the trial consultant.

INDEX

Q

R

S